Culture and Human Rights: The Wroclaw Commentaries

Edited by
Andreas Joh. Wiesand, Cologne
Kalliopi Chainoglou, Thessaloniki
Anna Śledzińska-Simon, Wroclaw

In collaboration with
Yvonne Donders, Amsterdam

DE GRUYTER

The ideas and opinions expressed, or the terminology used, in this publication are those of the authors of the individual articles. They do not necessarily represent the views of, and do not bind, the editors, the Scientific Committee, the City of Wroclaw or the Patrons of the Handbook. The same applies to institutions and organisations (such as e.g.: UNESCO; the Council of Europe; European Union bodies; national and local governments; universities; NGOs) the authors are affiliated with.

ISBN 978-3-11-044050-8
e-ISBN (PDF) 978-3-11-043225-1
e-ISBN (EPUB) 978-3-11-043236-7

Library of Congress Cataloging-in-Publication Data
A CIP catalog record for this book has been applied for at the Library of Congress.

Bibliographic information published by the Deutsche Nationalbibliothek
The Deutsche Nationalbibliothek lists this publication in the Deutsche Nationalbibliografie; detailed bibliographic data are available on the Internet at http://dnb.dnb.de.

Cover images: Rafal Cichawa/iStock/thinkstock and bpk Bildagentur
Typesetting: le-tex publishing services GmbH, Leipzig
Printing and binding: CPI books GmbH, Leck
♾ Printed on acid-free paper
Printed in Germany

www.degruyter.com / www.arcultmedia.de

Andreas Joh. Wiesand, Kalliopi Chainoglou, Anna Śledzińska-Simon
with Yvonne Donders (Eds.)
Culture and Human Rights: The Wroclaw Commentaries
De Gruyter Handbook

Acknowledgments

The editors and publishers of this handbook are grateful for the Patronage of these eminent personalities:
Gabriella Battaini-Dragoni, Deputy Secretary General of the Council of Europe
Gerhart Rudolf Baum, Human rights lawyer and former German Minister of the Interior (in charge of culture)
Rafał Dutkiewicz, Mayor of the City of Wroclaw
Farida Shaheed, UN Special Rapporteur in the field of cultural rights, 2009–2015

The editors and publishers would also like to acknowledge the material or professional support this publication and its preparation received from:

The City of Wroclaw

The European Union Initiative of "European Capitals of Culture"

The National Centre for Culture, Warsaw

The Council of Europe/ERICarts "Compendium of Cultural Policies and Trends in Europe"

The European Association of Cultural Researchers (ECURES)

Table of Contents

Part I: **Overview articles (Scientific Committee)**

Part II: **Keyword articles**

List of Abbreviations

Structural Elements in the Keyword Entries (Part II)

CASES:	The essence of European and international case-law
CONCL:	Conclusions and proposals for policies or future reforms
DEF:	Definitions or descriptions of issues at stake
INSTR:	Summaries of core messages of legal instruments
VIEWS:	Prevailing and important dissenting opinions in the literature.

In a few entries, these additional abbreviations were used:

HIST:	Historical overview of legal or political developments
INTRO:	Introductory remarks or positions of the author

Organisations, Unions, Courts and Bodies

AfComHPR	African Commission of Human and Peoples' Rights
AU	African Union
CAHMIN	(former) Committee for the Protection of National Minorities
CESCR	UN Committee on Economic, Social and Cultural Rights
CM	Committee of Ministers of the Council of Europe
CJEU	Court of Justice of the European Union
CoE	Council of Europe
ECHR	Convention for the Protection of Human Rights and Fundamental Freedoms (European Convention on Human Rights)
ECtHR	European Court of Human Rights
ECJ	European Court of Justice (later: CJEU)
EEC	(former) European Economic Community
ERICarts	European Institute for Comparative Cultural Research
EU	European Union
ECSR	European Committee on Social Rights
FIA	International Federation of Actors
FIM	International Federation of Musicians
FRA	European Union Agency for Fundamental Rights
HRC	UN Human Rights Council
HRCee	UN Human Rights Committee
IACtHR	Inter-American Court of Human Rights
ICC	International Criminal Court
ICCROM	International Centre for the Study of the Preservation and Restoration of Cultural Property
ICJ	International Court of Justice
ICOM	International Council of Museums
ICOMOS	International Council on Monuments and Sites

ILA	International Law Association
ILO	International Labour Organization
IUCN	International Union for Conservation of Nature and Natural Resources
OECD	Organisation for Economic Co-operation and Development
NATO	North Atlantic Treaty Organization
NGO	Non-governmental organisation
OAS	Organization of American States
OAU	Organisation of African Unity
OHCHR	Office of the UN High Commissioner for Human Rights
OSCE	Organization for Security and Co-operation in Europe (previously: CSCE)
UN	United Nations
UNESCO	UN Educational, Scientific and Cultural Organization
UNHCR	UN High Commissioner for Refugees
UNICEF	UN Children's Emergency Fund
UNIDROIT	International Institute for the Unification of Private Law
WHO	World Health Organization
WIPO	World Intellectual Property Organization
WTO	World Trade Organization

Treaties, Declarations and Covenants

2005 UNESCO Convention	Convention on the Protection and Promotion of the Diversity of Cultural Expressions
ACHPR	African Charter of Human and People's Rights
ACHR	American Convention of Human Rights
AfCRWC	African Charter on the Rights and Welfare of the Child
CEDAW	Convention on the Elimination of All Forms of Discrimination
CFR(EU)	Charter of Fundamental Rights of the European Union
CRC	Convention on the Rights of the Child
CRPD	Convention on the Rights of Persons with Disabilities
ECRML	European Charter for Regional or Minority Languages
FCNM	Framework Convention for the Protection of National Minorities
ICCPR	International Covenant on Civil and Political Rights
ICESCR	International Covenant on Economic, Social and Cultural Rights
(I)CERD	International Convention on the Elimination of All Forms of Racial Discrimination
ICH Convention	Convention for the Safeguarding of the Intangible Cultural Heritage
TEU	Treaty on European Union
TFEU	Treaty on the Functioning of the European Union
UDHR	Universal Declaration of Human Rights
UNDRIP	UN Declaration on the Rights of Indigenous Peoples

Preface I

The main duty of the Mayor of Wrocław – as probably of any Mayor around the world – is to help secure and, hopefully, improve the wellbeing of the city's inhabitants. This task has material as well as spiritual or intellectual dimensions.

As regards the latter, I recently attended an interesting lecture of Luigi Sacco in Brussels. Based on empirical studies, this Italian researcher claims that the feeling of satisfaction with life increases as the participation in cultural life grows. In our cultural environment, this includes taking part in cultural events, such as going to concerts or visiting theatre performances, both with a strong correlation to citizens' feeling of satisfaction with life – in other regions, different cultural practices or habits might come into play, and not all of them have necessarily the same effects. For example, an earlier German survey underlined a definite link between cultural participation and civic engagement, including the readiness to criticise conditions giving cause for concern.

While these and other motivations should already prompt us to give more attention to, and create better opportunities for our fellow citizens' participation in cultural life, the same must also be said as concerns the material dimensions of wellbeing.

In economic terms, a number of factors could be mentioned, such as the money circulating within a city or region as well as the number of available jobs, average wages, productivity and the quality of goods. Whatever parameter you choose with the aim to improve economic conditions or social growth, the importance of innovation will come into the picture.

Once again studies have clarified the strong links between culture and the climate for innovation or, to be more precise, the correlation between expenditure for culture and the level of innovation. Both in the 'old' European Union (EU-15) and in the now enlarged one (EU-28, or 27 after the Brexit), the volume of expenditure for culture remains strongly correlated with innovativeness: Where the expenditure is high, innovativeness grows, and where the spending is low, the chances for economic innovation also remain low. In this sense, spending on culture – with its direct or indirect effects on e.g. design and architecture or on a more informed consumer behaviour – could be seen as a specific form of investment into the future of a city, that will become profitable over time.

For culture to flourish in a central European meeting place like Wrocław, our manifold traditions as well as the imagination and innovative impulses of both citizens and artists or intellectuals must be of prime concern. This has been our policy since many years and we could highlight it again during 2016 with a great number of *European Capital of Culture* activities.

In case you are wondering: Why does he start his opening remarks to the *Wroclaw Commentaries* project and handbook with these thoughts? Indeed, it is my firm belief that we need to be constantly aware of the social and economic environment in which cultural life develops – or declines. And the same could actually be said about a 'Culture of Human Rights' which, as this book clearly demonstrates, is by no means static; rather it can, and needs to be, shaped and further developed.

As regards laws and policies, important inputs to further debates and actual reforms can be expected from the new Handbook; they will surely reach far beyond the city's limits. I'm proud that the first initiatives our city and the National Centre for Culture have taken in 2013 resulted in a publication and interactive web platform that will further spread the name of Wrocław across Europe and the world. The editorial team of ARCult Media led by Professor Andreas Wiesand, the Scientific Committee led by Professor Yvonne Donders, and the many contributing experts can be congratulated for realising this critical compendium of culture-related human rights instruments and case-law, for the first time in history.

In a sense, the *Wroclaw Commentaries* also delineate the status of what we have originally called a 'right to culture'. My interpretation of such a universal human right is that it should enable free individual intellectual and spiritual growth as well as shaping interpersonal relations leading to innovation, social cohesion and welfare, facilitated through mutual respect. Does this right still need to be achieved? Is it already, at least partly, being guaranteed? Or is this just a 'European problem' as the notion is not sufficiently reflected in either the European Convention on Human Rights or in the EU Charter of Fundamental Rights? From what I have learned about the content of the handbook, all of these viewpoints could be seen as co-existing, at present, depending also on the degree to which provisions in current legal instruments are respected and implemented.

However, compared with other rights of access and individual or collective guarantees that we have become accustomed to, at least in the Western world, such as rights to education or social and health protection, there seems to be still some way to go until a right to culture has turned into reality.

Let me close with two remarks directed to opponents of the notion of a right to culture:

First, trivial critics of this proposal raise the argument that there can also be crime-filled cultural expressions. That's why you should not be using the general notion of a 'right to culture' without specifying the forms or nature of what needs to be protected – and what not. These critics do not understand how language works, on a subconscious level. For example, when we refer to the right to education, we mean good, solid education, not failed efforts. Again, when we speak of a right to culture we are, of course, referring not to harmful cultural practices. Therefore, this simple notion needs no strengthening with any additional descriptions.

Secondly, when we speak of a 'right to culture' we refer to the ambitious goal of complementing one of the European 'constitutions', the European Convention on Human Rights. That goal is certainly bold, possibly even far-fetched. There is no way of knowing whether and when it can be fulfilled. However, quite often the thrill of the chase is already more important than the final catch.

The dialogue on how to best secure or improve culture-related human rights is important in its own right. And, as can be seen in the *Wroclaw Commentaries*, it has already brought many a good thing.

Rafał Dutkiewicz
Mayor of Wrocław

Preface II

Cultural rights are increasingly taking their rightful place in the international human rights' arena. The Council of Europe's European Court of Human Rights has been largely instrumental in improving the standing of cultural rights through its dynamic interpretation of the different Articles of the European Convention on Human Rights, gradually recognising substantive rights which may fall under the notion of 'cultural rights' in a broad sense, and establishing key principles for future development.

The publication *Culture and Human Rights: The Wroclaw Commentaries* aims to bring together these references to cultural rights as an integral part of human rights, in an easy-to-digest and unique resource. As such, and through its comparisons with other international treaties and related case-law, it contains a vast treasure of concise topical articles and detailed keyword sources, offering insight into the key role which culture plays in human development and in keeping human rights alive. Perspectives offered by this Handbook may not be shared by every reader. Whilst the values of democracy and human rights, and the legal and institutional systems which protect them, are products of culture, they also protect culture itself: culture as seen in a broader sense, including the arts, creativity, heritage and aspects of identity formation and belonging, as well as all related economic, social and educational impacts.

Culture and cultural co-operation have played a major role in bringing Europeans closer together, through increased dialogue since the creation of the Council of Europe in 1949 and once more after the fall of the Berlin wall in 1989. Today, Europe is facing serious challenges in light of globalisation, interdependency, mobility, migration and the difficulties linked to managing diversity. Some say the European project is in danger and Europe is in need of a new narrative. This is why it is even more pertinent in the current context to understand the richness of legal and political frameworks for culture and human rights, and their evolving nature, to keep up with societal changes. This richness is reflected in the case law of the Council of Europe's European Court of Human Rights.

The Council of Europe's legal protection system further includes the work of the Commissioner of Human Rights, the Committee of Ministers, advisory bodies like the 'Venice Commission' and parliamentary control mechanisms, as well as activities of the Conference of International Non-Governmental Organisations. Collectively, this is a well-tuned and forceful tool kit, allowing for fact-finding, monitoring, guidance and standard-setting.

I wholeheartedly invite you to use this rich commentary collection and take the opportunity to congratulate the authors and editors on their outstanding achievement.

Gabriella Battaini-Dragoni
Deputy Secretary General of the Council of Europe

Introduction

"Above all it should be noted that we frequently view the same things from a range of perspectives, and that the same events can often generate the most different ideas"
Georg Adam Forster: *A Voyage round the World in His Britannic Majesty's Sloop Resolution, Commanded by Capt. James Cook, during the Years, 1772, 3, 4, and 5*, London 1777

"The more we share, the more we have"
Mohamed Mounir, Egyptian singer, author and actor at the "Salam Ramadan" event, Philharmonic Hall of Cologne, 13 and 14 October, 2007

"ALL THAT IS BANNED IS DESIRED"
Motto of the World Conference on Artistic Freedom of Expression, held on 25 and 26 October 2012 in Oslo, organised by the *Fritt Ord* Foundation and *Freemuse*

"Identities Are Changeable"
Title of the 2014 CD of Puerto-Rican Saxophonist Miguel Zenón

1. Background

The idea for the *Wroclaw Commentaries* emerged from two conferences on 'The Right to Culture as a Human Right' held in Wroclaw (Spring 2013) and Warsaw (Autumn 2013), both co-organised by the City of Wroclaw and the National Centre for Culture (Warsaw). These meetings brought together experts from Poland, as well as from the Council of Europe/ERICarts *Compendium of Cultural Policies and Trends in Europe* and the European Association of Cultural Researchers (ECURES). On both occasions, the participants discussed the desirability and possibility of adopting an Additional Protocol on the right to culture to the *European Convention on Human Rights (ECHR, 1950)*, the most important human rights instrument of the Council of Europe. *Inter alia*, they studied the 'demand that all citizens be given the opportunity to participate in cultural and artistic life' and 'that public authorities be charged with specific duties with regard to guaranteeing such participation', thus going beyond the present situation with its merely 'declaratory' statements (*The Right to Culture as a Human Right – A Call for Action*, Position Paper, Warsaw/Wroclaw, 2014).

Trying to understand the absence of a provision on the right to culture or cultural participation in the ECHR, some speakers found that, on the one hand, a consensus over the precise content of such a right – that could hold public authorities responsible for its breach – would be difficult to determine. On the other hand, they noted that the 'right of everyone to participate in cultural life' already exists in international legal instruments such as the *Universal Declaration of Human Rights* of 1948 (Article 27) and the UN *International Covenant on Economic, Social and Cultural Rights* (ICESCR, Article 15), but has not been spared from doubts about its justiciability, i.e. the opportunity for individuals to invoke this right before courts and semi-judicial bodies. At the same time, they expressed the belief that culture, both in a narrower and broader sense, needs to be protected as a human right. They also shared concerns over a growing number of incidents, both in Europe and worldwide, violating cultural rights that 'could erode the universal nature of fundamental rights and freedoms that have their basis in human dignity', considering particularly 'freedom of artistic expression' to be 'a cornerstone of liberal democracy' (ibid.).

As these conferences became a new starting point for further debates about the role of culture in human rights law, their organisers must be congratulated for this initiative. Yet, these events revealed the difficulty of translating basic human needs into the language of rights and triggered a number of questions, including, but not limited to:

- Would a 'right to culture' be a new right or is it perhaps an element of the, already recognised, 'right to participate in cultural life'?
- What is the relationship between a 'right to culture' and the notion of 'cultural rights'?
- Is the 'right to culture' a right of access and/or a freedom?

Clearly, each of these views of culture-related rights denote a different aspect of human activity regarding culture, while focusing on the individual or collective dimension, the active or passive role of the rights holder, and a different nature of correlated obligations of duty bearers (the state or other actors). Today we can already conclude that one should probably focus less on a particular 'right to culture' and more on how diverse culture-related human rights and the existing legal instruments could be better understood and effectively enforced, as well as on what human rights standards are still missing or could be considered underdeveloped (e.g. as regards the digital world).

During the past decades, efforts to rectify the lack of clauses related directly to culture in the ECHR had actually been made within the Council of Europe (CoE). For various reasons that will be explained later in the Handbook, these efforts did not result in a 'Cultural Protocol' to the ECHR. Still, in January 2012, the Parliamentary Assembly of the CoE, in its Recommendation 1990 on 'The right of everyone to take part in cultural life', considered this right as 'pivotal to the system of human rights'.

Moves towards a more explicit recognition of cultural human rights in European and international standard setting instruments have also been promoted by academic and civil society initiatives, such as the *Fribourg Declaration on Cultural Rights* (2007). 14 years earlier, a CIRCLE Conference on *Human Rights and Cultural Policies in a Changing Europe* in Helsinki had already proposed 7 essentials for the implementation of the right to participate in cultural life.

Moreover, in 2009 two important developments took place in the UN system: the mandate of a UN Special Rapporteur in the field of cultural rights was agreed by the Human Rights Council and the UN Committee on Economic, Social and Cultural Rights adopted a *General Comment on the Right to Take Part in Cultural Life*. Obviously, the times when culture-related human rights had to be considered 'neglected or underestimated' (Symonides, 1998) have gone, even though they are still not always respected or fully implemented. In fact, it can be argued that we experience a growing 'culturalization' of human rights (Lenzerini, 2013), backed up by international legal instruments, as well as relevant case-law.

However, there remained a definite need to clarify, in greater detail, the relationship and interaction between culture and human rights and, following the 2013 Warsaw conference, one of the later editors of this Handbook proposed a research and stock-taking exercise: The best experts should be asked to identify, and then comment on, the most important culture-related issues, having regard to both already existing rights and jurisprudence in European and international human rights law as well as to remaining deficits. Given the city's previous engagement in this matter, the programme and preparatory work of Wroclaw for its term as the *European Capital of Culture 2016* has been identified as an ideal context for conducting this project, which resulted in what are now the *Wroclaw Commentaries*.

2. The Relationship between Culture and Human Rights

The main purpose of the *Wroclaw Commentaries* is to fill a gap in the existing literature on the relationship between culture and human rights. Yet, like in any research-based work on 'cultural' issues, the editors of this volume had to take a position on the meaning of this term. At the outset of the project it appeared that law, and specifically international human rights treaties, seem to avoid a precise definition of culture. Therefore, it was necessary for the editors, the members of the Scientific Committee, and to some extent also for the authors of this Handbook, to first adopt a common approach to 'culture' in order to analyse its relationship with human rights.

It seems that all humans know what culture is or at least have an intuition how to distinguish culture from nature. Yet, already this distinction may be disputable since the concept of nature can also be understood as a cultural concept (Junker, 1999). Moreover, nature, including landscapes or the underwater world, may fall under the definition of cultural heritage, regardless of whether it has actually been shaped by human activity or natural forces. Notably, the word 'culture' originates from the Latin *cultura* and *colere*, which denotes processes of cultivation, originally used with regard to agricultural development efforts influencing natural growth. In analogy, what culture and human rights share is the preservation of human values and the achievements of humanity, and the orientation to human growth.

However, the meaning of 'culture' appears to be culture-dependent, for many 'cultures' have their own, distinctive understanding of cultural achievements or processes and, of course, their specific languages to express these differences (Blake, 2015). Moreover, their understanding often relates to intangible cultural heritage or some particular aspects of living and interacting together, such as food traditions and dining manners, clothing, family structures, conversation habits and the use of body language, the way of constructing houses or the use of building materials, etc. Taking into account the cultural differences in the approach to culture, the risk had to be avoided that a definition of culture will settle with a Eurocentric view or restrict the definition of culture to such domains like fine arts, film, literature, music or theatre (which are, nevertheless, important parts of it).

Consequently, this Handbook takes an open-ended approach to culture and tries not to prioritise either 'high culture' or the modes and symbols of daily life. Instead, it tries to assess the relationship between culture and human rights from the position of culture as a basic need of all individuals which includes, but is not restricted to, the canons of artistic creation and encompasses tradition and innovation, conservation and modification, doctrinal purity as well as hybridity and experimentation. While the editors recognise that an institutional approach to culture is often dominating current discussions, the *Wroclaw Commentaries* do not subscribe to the notion of a 'core culture'.

In other words, the editors of this Handbook want to emphasise that human rights are indivisible and apply to everyone alike, independent of his or her profession. If artists and intellectuals, writers and journalists, publishers and Internet bloggers are more frequently involved in disputes about culture and fundamental rights or their status is even taken as an 'indicator' of the freedom enjoyed in a particular society, this has less to do with an accentuated role attributed to them in European and international human rights law. It rather has to do with their stronger presence in public life and related 'communicative action' (Habermas, 1984), often paired with individualistic mindsets, with more independent ways of thinking off the beaten track or with their disposition towards passion and compassion. To name just one example: Well-known artists like Hans Haacke, Walid Raad or Ashok Sukumaran are among the organisers of the *Gulf Labor Artist Coalition* (http://gulflabor.org/), raising awareness about the poor living and working conditions of migrant workers involved in the construction of the Guggenheim Abu Dhabi, the Louvre Abu Dhabi and other arts and education facilities in the Gulf region.

Most importantly, the approach to culture adopted in this volume is inclusive in terms of subjects, contents and forms. The inclusive approach to culture implies that any particular category of persons may not by definition be excluded from active or passive participation in culture (Laaksonen 2010). Moreover, this approach aims to promote equal access to culture of persons belonging to minorities or other vulnerable groups, facilitating their cultural activity and recognising their 'culture(s)'. For this reason, one of the focal points in this Handbook is the analysis of social and socio-cultural groups such as children, youth, older persons, indigenous peoples, national minorities, migrants, refugees, persons with disabilities, women, LGBT, and their culture-related rights or right-claims. Yet, while including these categories of subjects in the broad concept of culture, the Handbook does not predetermine which culture-related rights need to be protected. Rather it recognises these categories of persons as potential authors or participants in culture.

For the same reason, the *Wroclaw Commentaries* do not exclude any particular content or forms from the definition of culture. For example, we recognise the relevance of 'social media', blasphemy, defamation, obscenity, trolling or 'shitstorms', or even hate crimes for current and future debates about culture and human rights. While the Handbook, in its overall approach, does not establish which specific content or forms deserve legal protection, it aims to pose questions for law and policy-makers about implications of laws and policies which do not take the cultural aspects of such activity into account.

Last but not least, the Handbook recognises the role of new technologies and, particularly, digital media for cultural development, while being aware of the challenges they bring for the protection of traditional authors' rights/copyright, and for the status of artists, journalists and publishers or other media producers. However, this example should remind us that while human rights law underlines basic values, sets standards for law making and other actions of public authorities and provides tools to settle severe conflicts, it is as such not the proper instrument to solve concrete professional issues or problems of specific groups of the population. Indeed, the latter require effective and transparent policies, be it in the arts and media, in social security and cohesion, in education, or in many other domains reflected on in the contributions of the authors of this Handbook.

The *Wroclaw Commentaries* take an open and inclusive approach to the relationship between culture and human rights. There seem to be at least three understandings of this relationship:

First, culture can be considered as an *area of human activity*, which falls in the scope of human rights protection. In this regard, it is put on the same plane as education or sports – even if, in a broader understanding, they could also be considered to be part of 'culture'. And yet, like health or social security, culture requires an active role of the public authorities with regard to providing institutions, infrastructure, and funding. At the same time, culture and particularly the arts and media denote an area of freedom, which needs to be protected against unjustified interference of the state and third parties. While the social dimension of culture necessitates state regulation, the personal aspects of culture imply freedom from state intervention. In this meaning, the relationship between culture and human rights refers to the norms and relevance of legal and policy instruments in the area of culture.

Second, the relationship between culture and human rights could suggest that, generally, the *interpretation of human rights is culture-dependent*. This approach follows the universalism and cultural relativism debate which gains significance in times of ideological crusades led by states, religious authorities and political groupings trying to dictate their particular interpretation of human rights standards and norms. Recognising the importance of cultural pluralism, there is increasing consensus among states, legal practitioners and scholars that the, necessary, universal application of human rights does not imply their uniform implementation, leaving room for what has been called a 'localisation' of human rights (De Feyter, 2006) that takes specific historical, cultural, social and economic conditions into account.

Third, the relationship between culture and human rights could be explained in terms of a *culture of human rights*, which denotes a legal culture based on human rights. This approach follows the main tenet of democracies which not only recognise the fundamental value of rights, but also accept that rights set the limits for state actions, and establish a set of obligations such as the duty to respect, protect, and fulfil human rights. Clearly, human rights, and in particular, human right instruments entail a specific language, which is used by monitoring bodies, including international human rights courts or committees, as well as National Human Rights Institutes, human rights defenders, NGOs, and human rights activists. Moreover, there are human rights discourses, 'dialogues' between courts, and other channels of human rights communication like strategic litigation, social campaigns, street protests, etc. All these activities produce 'artefacts' of a culture of human rights. To the most important ones among these artefacts count judicial decisions which, similar to pieces of art, are subject to interpretations of legal experts, as well as to commentaries in other than legal fora.

The *Wroclaw Commentaries* do not favour any of these approaches, but try to elaborate on all of them and show the interaction between them. Therefore, the Handbook emphasises the multiple dimensions of the relationship between culture and human rights, rather than endorsing cultural relativism. It also aims to advocate openness rather than dogmatism; and increase freedom rather than restraint. Last but not least, the *Wroclaw Commentaries* provide many examples demonstrating the interrelatedness and interdependence of human rights, rather than their hierarchy. In any case, they should not be read as a promotion of a particular worldview or interpretation. Instead the intention of the editors and members of the Scientific Committee was to summarise the state of art in the protection of culture-related human rights and to discuss its future challenges and developments.

3. Aims, structure and methodology of the *Wroclaw Commentaries*

The importance of culture for individuals and communities, and its presence in all aspects of human lives, providing an essential part of individual and collective identities, is no longer underscored in legal research. As well, questions of how to better understand the relationship between culture and human rights are broadly discussed among legal experts, while efforts to 'translate' culture into law and policy making – including international processes such as development, conflict prevention and conflict resolution – receive growing attention among politicians, arts and media professionals and civil society organisations. Yet, while the dialectic relationship between culture and human rights is appreciated among specialists, it often remains neglected in practice.

There is still limited understanding and knowledge about how to source culture within human rights law; how to guarantee the universality, the interdependence, and the indivisibility of human rights while acknowledging that a variety of cultural issues come into play in relation to their scope of protection; and how to assure that culture does not become an excuse for the denial of fundamental human rights, either individual or collective, at national, regional and international levels.

The international community has come a long way since the adoption of the UDHR. Since 1948, international human rights law has greatly expanded and domestic legal orders have accordingly been largely influenced by the transformative impact of international human rights standards. At the same time, this transformative potential has been limited in practice due to political tendencies, unavailability of public policy space, economic crises or cultural and religious barriers. Within this setting, the intersection between culture and human rights has not only invited debates over their boundaries regarding their scope and enforcement, but has clashed with issues of state sovereignty and political legitimacy, policy priorities and institutions, judicial proprietary and resource allocation.

However, the current political practice to address global challenges, for example the refugee crisis, with short-term solutions that do not capture the complexity of the issues and lack sustainability is not without danger, because it tends towards diminishing diversity instead of promoting it. Indeed, if this trend would continue, it could one day put the whole European project of 'unity in diversity' into question. In that context, the editors do not wish to be considered naïve: They are well aware of the time and efforts it takes to transform human rights principles into sustainable policies and practices. They also know about the difficulties to open up narrow mindsets or to give clear answers to vague fears. In fact, we could even consider and debate the controversial thought of anthropologist Claude Lévy-Strauss (in his last work *Le regard éloigné*, 1983) that, in order to sustain cultural diversity and creativity, it can be perfectly legitimate 'to feel little drawn to other's values' as long as such a 'relative incommunicability' is not taken as a pretext for 'oppression or destruction'. In that regard, human rights instruments can be seen as an important, if not the main, barrier against all kinds of abuses of power, be they of a political or a commercial nature, as well as – to be further developed – tools to safeguard the culture(s) and dynamic identity of Europe.

Against this background, the *Wroclaw Commentaries* intend to serve as a basic guide to culture-related issues (in the wider sense) and their significance in the domain of human rights. The aim of the Handbook has been to provide, on the one hand, a user-friendly tool for the daily needs of policy- or law-makers at various juridical, administrative or political levels and, on the other hand, an introductory reference for other stakeholders working, researching or teaching in the field of culture and related domains.

The Handbook addresses – in 7 comprehensive overviews and over 120 keyword-entries – legal questions, as well as political consequences related to safeguarding human rights and cultural diversity, including freedom of, or access to, the arts, heritage and (old/new) media, questions of religious and language rights, the protection of minorities and other vulnerable groups, and further pertinent issues. Specialists from Europe and around the world define issues at stake (in the alphabetic entries abbreviated as DEF), summarise or comment core messages of legal instruments (INSTR), the essence of case-law (CASES) as well as prevailing and important dissenting opinions in the literature (VIEWS), ending with conclusions and/or proposals for future reforms (CONCL). Literature references for further reading are included.

The title of the handbook: "Wroclaw Commentaries" reflects that it differs from a dictionary or a more neutral encyclopaedia. The authors of the commentaries were asked to not only outline the issues at stake, but to reflect upon them and put them in perspective. The plural term 'Commentaries' also implies that in this handbook different authors have written on related subjects and issues whereby different interpretations and opinions are possible – and sometimes necessary, depending on the issue at stake (visible, for example, in entries dealing with intellectual property/copyright issues). Clearly, the *Wroclaw Commentaries* involve the work of specialised authors who are both experienced in their field and able to discuss their topic with an open mind. In order to assist readers in their uptake of the keyword entries, the editors ensured that the authors follow a certain technical order of argumentation and referencing, but they were not asked to abandon their individual writing style or sacrifice their approach to a specific subject. The resulting diversity of viewpoints and expressions has been more than welcome and is by all means intentional: It should stimulate needed debates and should be considered the strength of 'cultural worldviews' in times of globalisation.

In terms of methodology, preparatory research, including a comprehensive annotated collection of bibliographical resources, a selection of topical case-law and a first concept for the Handbook, had been carried out by ARCult Media experts in 2014 and discussed with the Mayor of Wroclaw and his team. This concept could best be sketched with two principles:

Thematically: A legal handbook on culture-related issues in the domain of human rights that is open to other relevant disciplines;

Geographically: A primarily European approach that is open to the world and, particularly, to global issues affecting all of us.

The editors and the Scientific Committee agreed on adopting a vertical and horizontal structure for the Wroclaw Commentaries. To set out the horizontal structure, a preliminary research was carried out based on the available international and European case-law (mainly coming from the European Court of Human Rights and other European judicial mechanisms) as well relevant provisions in the international human rights instruments. This research resulted in identifying the overview subject areas upon which the long, medium and short-sized keywords would then be selected.

With regard to the number of cases in particular areas, e.g. freedom of expression, the recent recognition of the human rights dimension of certain issues such as cultural heritage, or the vulnerability of social/socio-cultural groups, seven overview areas were identified and dealt with by the members of the Scientific Committee in their overview articles in the first part of the Handbook:

- Culture and Human Rights: Concepts, Instruments and Institutions (Andrzej Jakubowski);
- Freedom of Expression in the Arts and Media (Annamari Laaksonen);
- Cultural Diversity and Cultural Identity (Yvonne Donders);

- Access to Culture, Media and Information in the Digital Age (Paul de Hert);
- Rights and Protection of Social/Socio-cultural groups (Federico Lenzerini);
- Freedom of Religion or Belief (Heiner Bielefeldt);
- Cultural Heritage in the Human Rights System (Janet Blake).

During eight meetings between editors and, since 2015, members of the Scientific Committee in Wroclaw and other places, about 150 relevant culture-related keywords were identified, the great majority of which led to articles that can now be found in the Handbook. The keywords had been categorised into long, medium or short-sized keyword-entries and some 'brief references' based on their legal value in the context of culture and human rights as recognised by jurists, scholars and practitioners in the field and on the availability of standard-setting instruments and relevant case law. A few keywords that lacked substantial case law background were nevertheless included in the *Wroclaw Commentaries* as it was agreed that their political, economic or social relevance could help to clarify legal issues at stake. Finally, certain entries were added based on their topicality and relevance to European societies as reflected in academic fora, conferences, international research projects and the media. Nevertheless, the relevance of the content of the *Wroclaw Commentaries* for global culture-related issues and particularly for those faced by European societies – which definitely includes learning from international experiences! – remained a criterion for the inclusion of all new entries. This concept and main issues dealt with in the Handbook were first publicly presented and discussed at a research forum held November 2015 in connection with the 14th Council of Europe/ERICarts *Compendium* Experts' Assembly in Wroclaw.

Most of the keyword entries of the Wroclaw Commentaries review the relationship between culture, human rights, governmental policies and measures, practices or societal attitudes. The Handbook intends to develop a normative and interpretive context of the legal framework on culture and human rights, thus bridging the gaps between dispersed, partly unspecific, references to 'culture' (in the wider sense) in the human rights literature, in legal instruments or in court cases. While the Handbook deals with its subjects mostly from a legal point of view, multidisciplinary elements are also part of the methodological approach, particularly as regards definitions and conclusions. The book aims to shed light on disputed points regarding the current normative framework of human rights protection (*de lege lata*) as well as to raise some crucial points for future law- and policy-making in the area of culture (*de lege ferenda*).

As the original starting point for the Handbook has been the perceived absence of a 'right to culture' in the ECHR, the editors found that assessing existing legal sources as well as the case law of the ECtHR and the Court of Justice of the European Union or quasi-judicial or expert bodies within the Council of Europe such as the European Committee of Social Rights should play an important role in the preparation of articles. However, the authors were also asked to look beyond the European jurisprudence and include messages from the UN treaty bodies and international courts and tribunals, e.g. American or African human rights courts as well as national courts where appropriate.

While the majority of invited authors come from the European continent, this structure has been frequently amended following discussions with the Scientific Committee: A number of non-European authors were invited to contribute on keywords which are of interest to the broader international community. In all cases, the editors and reviewers of the Handbook aimed at securing accurate and fair texts. However, still remaining factual errors brought to their attention will be corrected as soon as possible, e.g. in the next edition of the Handbook and/or on the related web site.

The editors value the *Wroclaw Commentaries* as an ongoing research process which, due to its originality, will continue evolving. The team set up by ARCult Media has developed a website that will serve as an interactive platform building on the scaffolding created for it by the *Wroclaw Commentaries* – many of the specialists involved in the Handbook already agreed to contribute to this information and debate space (www.culture-rights.net). In addition, the Internet platform offers some exclusive content related to the Handbook, such as abstracts prepared by the authors for their keyword entries.

Both the editors and the members of the Scientific Committee are aware of the fact that this stock-taking of existing culture-related human rights instruments and jurisprudence and, in particular, the choice of issues that led to the Handbook's keywords are by no means exhaustive: As could be expected in a domain as multi-faceted as 'culture', some issues are missing in the *Wroclaw Commentaries*, so there is clearly room for extensions in future editions and online. For example, the "Burkini" controversy in France (Summer 2016) could not be reflected upon in this volume. Moreover, a handbook with relatively concise entries cannot, and does not intend to, replace the relevant literature, documentary evidence and numerous advocacy initiatives in the field. The many references provided in this publication and in the related website should, nevertheless, invite the readers to using the *Wroclaw Commentaries* as a starting point for further inquiry, scientific research, political or civil initiatives and policy design.

The editors and the chair of the Scientific Committee wish to thank the City of Wroclaw, in particular its Mayor Rafał Dutkiewicz and his support team managed by Jan Wais, for making the *Wroclaw Commentaries* possible. They are grateful to the other Patrons of this Handbook: Gabriella Battaini-Dragoni (Council of Europe), Gerhart Rudolf Baum (Human Rights lawyer, Cologne/Berlin) and Farida Shaheed (former UN Special Rapporteur in the field of cultural rights) for their encouragement of a complex project that had to start from scratch. They are deeply indebted to the authors of the Handbook articles for their valuable contributions, often delivered at short notice, and to the members of the Scientific Committee for their conceptual advice and their engagement in the reviewing process. Special thanks go also to supporting organisations and networks and to the very cooperative specialists at De Gruyter publishing house, Berlin. Last but not least, the undersigned would like to congratulate the project team set up by ARCult Media, especially the editorial assistant during the final project phase, Hans Fischer-Kerrane, and the Web developer Jörg Torkler.

Amsterdam / Cologne / Thessaloniki / Wroclaw, August 2016

The Editors:
Andreas Joh. Wiesand
Kalliopi Chainoglou
Anna Śledzińska-Simon

The Chair of the Scientific Committee:
Yvonne Donders

REFERENCES:

Blake, Janet: *International Cultural Heritage Law*, Oxford: Oxford University Press (2015).
Council of Europe/ERICarts: *Compendium of Cultural Policies and Trends in Europe*, Strasbourg/Bonn (www.culturalpolicies.net – accessed 08/2016).
De Feyter, Koen: *Localizing Human Rights*, Discussion Paper 2006.2, Institute of Development Policy and Management, University of Antwerp (2006).
Donders, Yvonne: "The International Covenant on Economic, Social and Cultural Rights: Accessibility and the Right to Information", in: Tarlach McGonagle and Yvonne Donders (eds.): *The United Nations and Freedom of Expression and Information, Critical Perspectives*, Cambridge University Press (2015).
Fisher, Rod / CIRCLE (eds.): *Human Rights and Cultural Policies in a Changing Europe: The Right to Participate in Cultural Life*, Report of the European Round Table Held in Helsinki, 30 April–2 May 1993. Organised by CIRCLE and the International Movement of Rights and Humanity in co-operation with the Council of Europe; Helsinki: Arts Council of Finland (1994).
Habermas, Jürgen: *The Theory of Communicative Action*. Boston: Beacon Press (1984).
Jakubowski, Andrzej: *Cultural Rights as Collective Rights. An International Law Perspective*, Brill (2016).
Laaksonen, Annamarie: *Making* culture *accessible* – Access, *participation and* cultural *provision in the context of* cultural *rights in Europe*. Strasbourg: Council of Europe (2010).
Lenzerini, Federico: *The Culturalization of Human Rights Law*, Oxford: Oxford University Press (2014).
Lévi-Strauss, Claude: *The View from Afar*, New York: Basic Books (1985)
Junker, Kirk W.: "Reading nature through culture in Plato and Aristotle's works on Law", *Phronimon – Journal of the South African Society for Greek Philosophy and the Humanities* Vol. 7 Iss. 1 (1999).
Symonides, Janusz: "Cultural rights: A neglected category of human rights", *International Social Science Journal*, Issue 158 (1998).

Part I: **Overview articles (Scientific Committee)**

Culture and Human Rights: Concepts, Instruments and Institutions

Andrzej Jakubowski, Warsaw

Culture and Legal Regulation

Culture and cultural rights have always been uneasy subjects for the law and its practice. Legal instruments usually refer to culture in the singular, restricting its working notion to determined areas of people's life. In fact, most of the existing legal frameworks in matters of culture, both on national and international levels, though relating to the variety of cultural manifestations and distinct societal contexts, are generally the product of the West, and Western traditions in managing and administrating the spheres of art and culture. Unsurprisingly, legal instruments and institutions in the cultural domain are predominantly characterised by a top-down approach, within a given operating mandate. Even though legal scholarship has gradually tended towards the concept of cultural law, encompassing '(t)he core themes of linguistic and other cultural rights, cultural identity and differentiation, cultural heritage, traditional knowledge, sports, and religion' being 'of fundamental importance to people around the world' (Nafziger, Kirkwood Paterson, Dundes Runteln: 2010; intro), culture is still operated by the law within methodologically differentiated areas of legal regulation. Indeed, cultural law is profoundly fragmented and comparted into specialised almost 'self-contained' regimes, often marked by the lack of harmony between various norm-systems and institutions.

At the national level, legal regulation in cultural matters has traditionally referred to freedom of conscience, belief and expression (including the protection of the moral and material interests resulting from any scientific, literary or artistic production). In this guise, cultural rights have essentially been associated with freedom of art and creativity seen as rights and entitlements enjoyed by individual persons. On the other hand, national legislation has set out for the rules for the protection and management of spiritual, artistic and historical heritage. Thus, the latter area has related to state or more generally broader community interests, whereas the former has referred to the protection and enforcement of rights and interests of individuals. With time, cultural law and policy have greatly expanded, covering various areas of social life, including minority rights. Moreover, a number of references to culture, cultural heritage and cultural guarantees have also been introduced to national constitutional regulations. Yet the proliferation of legal instruments in cultural rights has been only partially developed within the realm of administrative and judicial institutions. Thus the recognition and enjoyment of cultural rights of entitlements of individuals and groups is usually subject to institutional systems and practices characterised by horizontal, unequal relations of power and cultural hegemony between rights holders and law-enforcement authorities.

At the international level, the legal regulation of cultural matters mirrors the traditional nature of international law made by states and for states. In other words, international law has long perceived cultural issues as an exclusive domain of states and their vital, pragmatic interests, including their joint action undertaken in the name of their collective cultural interests (particularly, the 1972 *Convention concerning the Protection of World Natural and Cultural Heritage*). Accordingly, international legislation in cultural matters mostly refers to the protection of *human creativity* and the protection and preservation of →cultural heritage. These conceptual and methodological limitations have resulted in detaching cultural legislation from the realm of international human rights, originally focused primarily on the advancement and implementation of civil and political guarantees.

Culture Rights as International Human Rights

International human rights law does not offer a formal definition of 'culture' or 'cultural rights'. Only few binding international human rights instruments address the protection of cultural elements of human existence, thus making the catalogue of cultural rights and their conceptualisation as international human rights a contested issue (see Francioni and Scheinin, 2008; Jakubowski, 2016). Although certain human rights which are cultural in nature, such as the protection of literary and artistic works, or religious and linguistic rights of →national and ethnic minorities had been enshrined in international law instruments at least since the late nineteenth century, the link between culture and human rights became universally addressed for the first time within the United Nations system. The →Universal Declaration of Human Rights (UDHR) recognises several human rights guarantees as having a direct connection with culture (freedom of thought, speech, right to education). It also enshrines the rights explicitly referring to culture: the right to freely participate in the cultural life of the community, and to enjoy the arts and to share in scientific advancement and its benefits (Article 27(1)). Yet the fierce debate over the exclusion of group rights and minority rights in relation to culture from the text of the UDHR, and the simultaneous failure of broadening the legal notion of →genocide, beyond its biological dimension in the text of the *Convention on the Prevention and Punishment of the Crime of Genocide*, cast a shadow on the entire international cultural rights' debate (Stamatopoulou, 2007: 11–35). In fact, the UN system tied minority rights, including their cultural rights within the broader human rights regime, for the sake of the protection of states' internal stability and their internal cultural policies. Accordingly, the two fundamental, universal human rights treaties, the →International Covenant on Economic, Social and Cultural Rights (ICESCR) and the *International Covenant on Civil and Political Rights* (ICCPR) were driven by the individualist approach to cultural rights (see →Rights and Protection of Social/Socio-cultural Groups). Moreover, both of them are rather enigmatic in determining which protected human rights guarantees are to be considered cultural ones. Significantly, the ICESCR, though including cultural rights in the title, does not make clear which of its provisions belong to the category of cultural rights.

Indeed, this deficit of culture in the UN human rights treaties essentially arises from the inherent nature of cultural rights which may belong to individuals *and* collectivity, e.g. specific communities, thus transcending the individualistic framework of human rights regimes, as well as traditionally exclusive, state-oriented notions of culture and cultural heritage in international legal relations. This is also the case of regional human regimes established after WW II: the *American Convention on Human Rights* (San José, 1969 (ACHR)) and the →European Convention of Human Rights and Fundamental Freedoms (Rome, 1950 (ECHR)). Although the →Inter-American system of human rights does address certain cultural rights (in particular see the 1988 *Protocol of San Salvador on Economic, Social and Cultural Rights*), the ACHR hardly pays attention to such guarantees as substantive rights. Similarly, the ECHR and its protocols, enforcing basic rights set out in the UDHR, does not provide for any explicit cultural guarantees. Moreover, the individual nature and scope of the rights protected by the ECHR seems to preclude their interpretation in a collective dimension.

Important developments in this regard occurred at the time of decolonisation. In particular, the *International Convention on the Elimination of All Forms of Racial Discrimination* (New York, 1965) enshrines the principle of non-discrimination in relation to the access and participation in cultural life and activities, while the *African Charter on Human and Peoples' Rights* (Banjul, 1988) contains several cultural rights and provides for collective (→Peoples' Rights), including the right to cultural development and →cultural identity (Article 22). A separate regime has emerged in respect of indigenous peoples, treated as distinctive groups due to their differing historical circumstances, linked to colonialism and foreign domination. Moreover, the representatives of indigenous communities have claimed that their suppression did not cease with the emancipation of former colonies. The first efforts to accommodate the rights of these groups were undertaken by the International Labour Organization (ILO) and led to the adoption of the *Indigenous and Tribal Populations Convention* (No. 107, 1957) applicable to members of tribal or semi-tribal populations in independent countries. The Convention *inter alia* required states parties to respect the cultural differences of such communities and to promote their cultural development. In 1989, the ILO revised the 1957 treaty. The new adopted instrument (No. 169) acknowledged the collective rights of →Indigenous Peoples to preserve and develop their own cultural identity. Yet the most extensive explicit catalogue of cultural rights is enshrined in a recent UN instrument: the 2007 UN *Declaration on the Rights of Indigenous Peoples* (UNDRIP), which states *inter alia* that indigenous peoples have 'the right to practice and revitalize their cultural traditions and customs', including 'the right to maintain, protect and develop the past, present and future manifestations of their cultures, such as archaeological and historical sites, artefacts, designs, ceremonies, technologies and visual and performing arts and literature' (Article 11(1)). The UNDRIP also places upon states positive commitments to 'take effective measures to recognize and protect the exercise of these rights' (Article 31(2)), and to 'provide redress through effective mechanisms' of their cultural claims arising from the past injustices (Article 11(2)). Notwithstanding the non-binding nature of this instrument, it is claimed that many of its provisions correspond to rules of customary international law (*ILA Resolution No. 5/12*).

The end of the Cold War, followed by territorial and political transformations in East-Central Europe reopened the question of minority protection. The fulfilment of minority standards formed one of the requirements of the conditional recognition of new states. After 1989, this question became part of the broader human and cultural criteria established by the →European Union (at that time still 'European Communities'). Importantly, the 1989 *Vienna Concluding Document* issued by the Conference on Security and Co-operation in Europe (cf. →OSCE – Organization for Security and Co-operation in Europe). According to this document, the participating states 'will ensure that persons belonging to national minorities or regional cultures on their territories can maintain and develop their own culture in all its aspects, including language, literature and religion; and that they can preserve their cultural and historical monuments and objects'. Moreover, the ethnic conflicts in the territory of the former Yugoslavia also accelerated work on the universal and European instruments for the protection of minorities: the UN 1992 *Declaration on the Rights of Persons Belonging to National or Ethnic, Religious and Linguistic Minorities*, and the 1995 →Framework Convention for the Protection of National Minorities, adopted by the CoE member states. Both instruments often mention 'culture' as one of the fundamental spheres of minority protection. Importantly, the latter instrument obliges its state parties to undertake 'to preserve the essential elements of their identity, namely their religion, language, traditions and cultural heritage' (Article 5(1)). Yet, it does not treat such cultural minority rights as 'truly' enforceable rights. Moreover, the adoption of this treaty stopped the initial works on an additional →cultural protocol to the ECHR, undertaken within the mandate of the CoE Ad Hoc →Committee for the Protection of National Minorities (CAHMIN). The decision not to extend the competences of the →European Court of Human Rights (ECtHR) in the field of individual cultural rights was driven by both the legal difficulties in defining such rights as substantive rights, whose protection would impose specific positive obligations on states (Thornberry, Martín Estébanez, 2004; 204–206).

Indeed, international human rights treaties focusing on substantive rights may seem impertinent for the protection of cultural rights in their complexity. Arguably, with very few exceptions, they do not devote the necessary attention to cultural rights, which in turn do not enjoy the same level of protection enjoyed by civil and political rights. Even if some of them directly refer to rights to culture, they do not entail concrete positive obligations on state parties and their organs, but rather certain political commitments in respect of the legitimate cultural expectations of the right holders. Moreover, the controversies surrounding the recognition of collectiveness and international collective standing in relation to cultural rights, beyond states, may undermine their fitting within international human rights instruments. The existence of collective rights is also often challenged by the traditional liberal approach to human rights, which perceives them as individual rights. Accordingly, it is often claimed that collective cultural rights cannot be 'truly' accepted as human rights since they are group-differentiated rather than universal to all people just by virtue of being human (Nimni, 2008), involving potential clashes between them and fundamental human rights.

International Cultural Law and Human Rights

Fragmentation, Compartmentalisation and Expertisation of International Cultural Law
As already addressed, international cultural legislation has long been detached from the realm of human rights, leaving 'culture' and 'cultural heritage' as the exclusive domain of states. In particular, the international cultural heritage law originally consisted in recognition of the right of every state to identify, physically control, and protect its tangible cultural heritage against irreparable loss in the event of armed conflict (1954 *Hague Convention for the Protection of Cultural Property in the Event of Armed Conflict*) and its unlawful removal from a state's territory during both war and peacetime (1970 UNESCO *Convention on the Means of Prohibiting and Preventing the Illicit Import, Export and Transfer of Ownership of Cultural Property*). This state-oriented perspective of international cultural heritage legislation, aimed at preserving national heritage against 'external' threats to its integrity, has been gradually broadened, and today encompasses a vast range of cultural manifestations and interests attached to them.

The expansion of multiple regimes relating to cultural matters has also led to their compartmentalisation according to the different types of cultural human activities, within their tangible and intangible dimensions. Moreover, various aspects of cultural domain are regulated under distinct instruments and fall under the competences of numerous authorities and monitoring bodies, undermining the global cultural governance. This often makes 'meaningful communication' between them (and other actors and stakeholders involved) as well as 'solution-oriented thinking' very difficult (Burri, 2012: 579). Another feature of international cultural law is its alleged 'expertisation'. In fact, cultural issues are handled on the international level by institutions of different (universal and regional) origin and composition. Most importantly, cultural matters are managed by →UNESCO and its associated bodies and agencies dealing with specific topics and areas of governance. All of them use 'impartial' expert knowledge aimed at translating cultural concepts into law and policy constructions. The recourse to 'external' expertise is also designed to smooth out conflicts and social differences (Lixinski, 2013: 432). On the other hand, cultural experts and professionals strive to expand their self-created professional legitimacy and importance. This may lead to a lack of communication and harmony amongst cultural regimes under UNESCO. It may also contribute to unequal power/knowledge relations between the interests of experts and those of individual and collective rights holders, thus undermining the effective enforcement of international cultural instruments and their objectives (Smith, 2006).

Arguably, these shortcomings of international cultural law also characterise regional legal and institutional systems. In particular, numerous initiatives of the →Council of Europe (CoE) provide a very broad legal framework for cultural and heritage policies. Culture entered on the agenda of the CoE with the *European Cultural Convention* (Paris, 1954), which created a legal platform for cultural cooperation between the CoE member states with the objective to safeguard and develop European culture and promote national contributions to Europe's common cultural heritage. However, CoE's cultural treaties essentially aim at standard-setting in matters of culture and cultural heritage within distinct specific areas of national policies. In fact, only one CoE treaty, the 2005 *Framework Convention on the Value of Cultural Heritage for Society* (Faro Convention), currently with a rather low rate of ratifications (17 of 47 of member states of this organisation have ratified it), fosters the broader concept of culture, addressing the questions as to why and for whom the heritage is transmitted, and employing an expanded and interdisciplinary concept of cultural heritage, the core of which are rooted in peoples and human values. Furthermore, none of CoE cultural instruments provides for a proper monitoring system, leaving the implementation of their standards to states' discretion. This is also the case with the →European Union (EU), the most integrated regional regime, based on an autonomous legal system, characterised by supranational and intergovernmental decision-making. Culture and cultural rights belong to the EU common action, though harmonisation of the laws and regulations of the member states in cultural matters is excluded. Accordingly, in the cultural dimension of European integration, the EU institutions adopt non-binding legal acts with the objective to co-ordinate, support and supplement the action of the member states, respecting national, regional and linguistic diversity. Thus, the level of the EU's involvement in cultural issues is limited by the nature of competences in this area, and in practice, by the defence of states' national cultural autonomies and identities.

Human Dimension of International Cultural Law

The methodological boundaries between cultural international law and human rights are gradually being broken. In fact, the link between various cultural law regimes and the international protection of human rights has recently been strengthened. It is observed that the emergence of a new international conscience, stemming from the awareness that culture, cultural heritage and →cultural diversity represent holistic concepts inherently connected with the identity of peoples as well as with all human rights in their individual and collective dimensions (Borelli, Lenzerini, 2012; also Vrdoljak, 2013; Blake, 2011). This process has occurred within various layers of international law, leading to a gradual re-interpretation of existing human rights guarantees in view of cultural rights and entailments. Importantly, the 2005 *Convention on the Protection and Promotion of the Diversity of Cultural Expressions* recognises cultural diversity as the common concern of humanity, and reaffirms its importance for the full realisation of human rights and fundamental freedoms. Similarly, the 2003 *Convention for the Safeguarding of the Intangible Cultural Heritage* links its protective regime with the 'existing international human rights instruments, as well as with the requirements of mutual respect among communities, groups and individuals, and of sustainable development' (Article 2). Perhaps the most ambitious conceptualisation of culture, cultural heritage and human rights is offered by the CoE *Faro Convention.* It is founded on the idea that knowledge and use of cultural heritage form part of rights vested in everyone, alone or collectively, to participate in cultural life as defined by the UDHR and guaranteed by the ICESCR. Culture and cultural heritage are presented as resources for human development, for the enhancement of cultural diversity, and for the promotion of intercultural dialogue. Within this framework, the Faro Convention sets out positive obligations upon the parties which are *inter alia* required: to protect cultural heritage situated under their respective jurisdictions, regardless of its origin; to promote cultural diversity; and to establish processes for conciliation to deal equitably with situations where contradictory values are placed on the same cultural heritage by different communities.

Considering these developments within various culture-oriented treaties, it appears that nowadays international cultural human rights legislation has expanded beyond the realm of human rights instruments. This makes the legal basis for cultural rights legislation one of the most diverse and complex area of international law with all the uncertainties that it may entail.

International Human Rights Institutions and the Enforcement of Cultural Rights

In the light of the above-addressed observations, the question arises as to how and to what extent the observation and promotion of cultural human rights are approached and enforced in the practice of international institutions.

Monitoring and Adjudicating International Human Rights Bodies

Within the system of the UN human rights institutions, the Committee on Economic, Social and Cultural Rights (CESCR) may appear to be the most important one as it supervises the operation of the ICESCR – the fundamental, universal human rights treaty directly referring to cultural rights. It considers the five-yearly reports submitted by state parties on their compliance of the ICESCR obligations. Moreover, since 2013, pursuant the provisions of *2008 Optional Protocol*, the CESCR can hear complaints brought by individuals, groups and representative organisations. However, to date the most significant activity of the CESCR in respect of cultural rights relates to its general comments. Its memorable General Comment No. 21 (2009) on the right of everyone to take part in cultural life, the CESCR stated that '(c)ultural rights protect the rights for each person, individually and in community with others, as well as groups of people, to develop and express their humanity, their world view and the meanings they give to their existence and their development through, inter alia, values, beliefs, convictions, languages, knowledge and the arts, institutions and ways of life. They may also be considered as protecting access to cultural heritage and resources that allow such identification and development processes to take place.' In this, it gave effect to the evolving conceptualisation of cultural rights addressed by epistemological communities and most significantly elaborated in the 2007 *Fribourg Declaration on Cultural Rights*. Moreover, the CESR concretised a set of positive international and national obligations arising from Article 15(1)(a) of the treaty and defined the parameters of assessing the compliance with their requirements.

Some important developments as to the recognition and enforcement of cultural rights have also been observed in the practice of the Human Rights Committee (HRCee) relating to the rights of persons belonging to ethnic, religious or linguistic minorities to enjoy their own culture, to profess and practise their own religion, or to use their own language, in community with the other members of their group (Article 27). In its General Comment No. 23 (1994), the HRCee fostered a very broad concept of culture which may manifest itself in various forms, 'including a particular way of life associated with the use of land resources, especially in the case of indigenous peoples. That right may include such traditional activities as fishing or hunting and the right to live in reserves protected by law.' Importantly, the HRCee underlined that '(t)he enjoyment of those rights may require positive legal measures of protection and measures to ensure the effective participation of members of minority communities in decisions which affect them'. Although, the HRCee does not have competence to hear collective complaints, it has already pronounced several times on the role of culture, perceiving it as essential for the functioning of a minority [e.g. LÄNSMAN ET AL, 2005; KITOK, 1988; LUBICON LAKE BAND, 1990]. Moreover, it addressed its anthropological evolving notion and understanding within a given factual and societal context [LÄNSMAN ET AL, 1994].

Certain trends towards a broader recognition of cultural rights are also to be found in the practice of other UN human rights treaty bodies (see Lenzerini, 2014), yet perhaps the most significant role in international standard-setting in the area of cultural rights within the UN system has been played by the Human Rights Council (HRC). In a series of resolutions, the HRC has recognised cultural rights as crucial for human well-being, both individually and collectively. Moreover, in 2009 it set up a special procedure on cultural rights, establishing a mandate of an independent expert and since 2012 of a special rapporteur in the field of cultural rights. Farida Shaheed, the first mandate holder (2009–2015), published ten thematic reports dealing with various aspects of the operationalisation of cultural rights in their individual and collective dimensions, and offering recommendations on further implementation of such rights. Among others, the 2013 report dealt with the right to artistic freedom and creativity (UN HRC, 2013), enhancing its role for individual experience and development and joint (collective) social practices. The tasks of the HRC in this regard are continued by Karima Bennoune, the current special rapporteur, with particular focus on a human rights approach to the intentional destruction of cultural heritage. In their reports, the special rapporteurs have adopted a holistic approach to cultural rights, referring to culture in the plural, perceiving the enjoyment of culture as part of basic human rights.

The practice of regional human rights institutions has also shown some important developments in relation to the implementation of cultural rights, though their founding treaties do not, or only marginally refer to such rights. In fact, only the African Commission on Human and Peoples' Rights (AfComHPR) and African Court of Human and Peoples' Rights operate within a treaty system which explicitly guaranties cultural rights, in their complex individual and collective aspects. Yet the practice of these

African human rights bodies in relation to culture is still rather limited, most importantly [CENTRE FOR MINORITY RIGHTS…, 2010] concerning the pastoral way of life). It has even been claimed that the AfComHPR has concentrated its efforts mainly on civil and political rights to the detriment of economic, social and cultural rights (Agbakwa, 2002: 194). As regard the Inter-American and European human rights regimes, the deficiency of their founding treaties in relation to cultural rights has progressively been addressed by the evolutionary approach followed by regional human rights monitoring bodies. Significantly, the Inter-American Court of Human Rights (IACtHR) has interpreted the right to property, under Article 21 ACHR, recognising certain cultural rights of indigenous peoples and local traditional communities, especially in relation to land [see MAYAGNA (SUMO) AWAS TINGI, 2001; MOIWANA COMMUNITY, 2005; YAKYE AXA INDIGENOUS COMMUNITY, 2005; and SAWHOYAMAXA INDIGENOUS COMMUNITY, 2006], and to their cultural identity [KICHWA INDIGENOUS PEOPLE OF SARAYAKU, 2012].

In turn, the ECtHR through a dynamic interpretation of various provisions of the ECHR has recognised a catalogue of substantive rights in relation to culture. The provisions most often invoked in relation to cultural rights are Article 8 (the right to respect for private and family life), Article 9 (freedom of thought, conscience and religion) and Article 10 (freedom of expression) of the Convention, as well as Article 2 of *Protocol No. 1 to the ECHR* (Paris, 1952), concerning the right to education. Accordingly, the ECtHR has identified several substantive rights that can be labelled as cultural rights or rights with a cultural content. Importantly, it has made implicit references to the right to cultural identity of persons, and their associations, belonging to national, cultural, linguistic or ethnic minorities, recognising their right to maintain their minority identity and to lead one's private and family life in accordance with their traditions and culture [e.g. CHA'ARE SHALOM VE TSEDEK, 2000; CHAPMAN, 2001; CYPRUS v. TURKEY, 2001; MUÑOZ DÍAZ, 2009; CIUBOTURU, 2010; AHMET ARSLAN AND OTHERS, 2010]. As pointed out in a research report of the ECtHR (2011), the Court has also recognised: the right of access to culture; linguistic rights; the right to education; the right to seek historical truth, using culture as a positive argument in order to strengthen the implementation of specific rights recognised in the ECHR and additional Protocols. Moreover, the ECtHR has adopted a certain relativist notion of culture balancing its distinct, though parallel, conceptualisations within the CoE system: the value a common heritage of Europe, diversity and autonomy of national cultural and individual cultural rights, in particular the freedom of expression [AKDAŞ, 2010]. Thus, in some cases the ECtHR has used the cultural argument to limit the enforcement of individual rights in favour of the legitimate interest of the wider society. In fact, it has usually accepted *a priori* the existence of a general community interest in protection of, and access to, cultural heritage as a legitimate aim of state interference into property rights, albeit without exploring the very nature of interest [e.g. SCEA FERME DE FRESNOY, 2005; RUSPOLI MORENES, 2011]. In some other cases, the ECtHR has recalled wider, universal cultural interests [BEYELER, 2000] and values enshrined in the CoE cultural law instruments [DEBELIANOVI, 2007]. On the other hand, the vast practice of the ECtHR relates to freedom of speech, including →artists' freedom of expression, seen as fundamental for both the individual and collective human development in a democratic, pluralist society. In fact, the complexity and extensiveness of the ECtHR case-law in this regard evidences the significance of the freedom of expression for Europe and European civil society (also manifested in the work of various NGOs struggling for the protection and enhancement for individual freedom of expression in the arts and media).

This dynamic practice of the regional human rights monitoring bodies in relation to culture is sometimes labelled as 'culturalisation of human rights' (Lenzerini, 2014). This is understood as the attempt to advance the effectiveness of human rights standards by interpreting them within a given cultural and societal context. In such a guise, culture is addressed in a pluralistic manner, enabling and smoothing conflicts between various rights within their individualistic and collective cultural dimensions.

Non-human Rights International Institutions and the Right to Be Protected from Cultural Destruction

Alongside the developments which occurred at the level of human rights bodies, the recognition and implementation of cultural rights have been strengthened by the practices of other international institutions. Undoubtedly, the renewed attention paid to →cultural genocide is the most significant area in which the issue of culture has been addressed. The right of a community to be protected from cultural destruction has been subject to judicial examination at national and international levels. The fundamental role is played by the jurisprudence of the International Criminal Tribunal for the Former Yugoslavia (ICTY). In particular, in [PROSECUTOR, 2004], the ICTY, while analysing the prerequisites of the crime of genocide, found that the deliberate destruction of a group does not have to be caused only by physical destruction, but also 'through purposeful eradication of its culture and identity resulting in the eventual extinction of the group as an entity distinct from the remainder of the community'. In further cases, the ICTY equated the destruction of cultural heritage to a crime against humanity (persecution), due to the existence of a discriminatory intent (i.e. the intention to destroy the group to which the relevant heritage belongs). Therefore, the deliberate destruction of religious and cultural heritage belonging to members of a group can be treated as the evidence of intent to destroy the group. The reasoning of the ICTY has been followed by other criminal tribunals, including the Extraordinary Chambers in the Courts of Cambodia (ECCC) [Case 002, 2010], and more recently by the International Criminal Court (ICC). In fact, on 24 March 2016 the ICC Pre-Trial Chamber I confirmed the charges against Ahmad Al Faqi Al Mahdi, accused of war crimes allegedly committed in 2012, in Timbuktu (Mali), through intentionally directing attacks against buildings dedicated to religion and/or historical monuments. Significantly, the Prosecutor's argumentation in relation to the gravity of charges greatly invokes the human rights dimension of the crime: violation of cultural rights of the local community, including religious rights, aimed at the annihilation of this group. Finally, the cultural dimension of cultural genocide was approached by the International Court of Justice (ICJ). In [BOSNIA AND HERZEGOVINA, 2007] and [CROATIA, 2015], the ICJ transposed the *aquis* of the ICTY relating to the cultural dimension of genocide to the realm of state responsibility. Accordingly, the ICJ held that attacks on cultural and religious property during an armed conflict constitute a violation of international law. Furthermore, such acts may be considered as evidence of a genocidal intent aimed at the extinction of a group.

(Im)Pertinence of International Human Rights Instruments and Institutions in the Realm of Culture and Cultural Rights

The core of the criticism relating to the operationalisation of cultural rights within the international human rights systems refers to the virtual absence of cultural guarantees within the texts of the most important human rights treaties, undermining their implementation and enforcement as substantive laws. Moreover, it has been rightfully pointed out that most of the existing international human rights complaining mechanisms do not offer unhindered access to justice in cultural matters, leaving cultural rights standards and their interpretation in the realm of exclusive competence of national jurisdictions. It is also true that the very nature of the international legal system (inter-state foundations of law-making, limited competences of monitoring and adjudicating bodies, low degree of participation of rights holders in decision-making and their absence or scarce representation in international institutions) favours or even promotes the interests of states, including their cultural policies, at the expense of individuals, NGOs and societal collectivities. Thus, due to the little presence of culture and cultural rights in the texts of international human rights treaties, the vagueness of international obligations provided by them, and the conceptual problems with the notion of cultural rights, such rights have often been defined as most neglected human rights in respect of their scope, legal content, and enforceability (Symonides, 1998; Meyer-Bisch, 1993).

This critical, pessimistic vision cannot, however, be fully sustained. The cultural determinations of human existence are increasingly recognised as crucial for the promotion and full implementation of all human rights and safeguarding of human dignity. As already highlighted, these developments have occurred on the level of international treaty law within originally distinct or separate areas of legal regulations. Indeed, a number of cultural law instruments have linked their implementation with the observance of human rights and freedoms, enhancing the role of the human dimension in implementing cultural and cultural heritage policies. On the other hand, the recent instruments designed to protect collective rights extensively linked their observance with explicit cultural guarantees. As regards the practice of international human rights institutions, it has been evidenced that many of them perceive the existing human rights regulations as living, constantly evolving organisms. This has led to a systematic re-interpretation of existing human rights guarantees which would encompass certain cultural rights, including those relating to cultural heritage. Moreover, cultural dimensions of human rights existence have also been addressed in the practice of other, non-human rights international institutions, such as the ICJ (see Polymenopoulou, 2014).

The above summarised developments at the level of international instruments and institutions give rise to a number of questions as to the future of practical operationalisation of culture and cultural rights within the system of international law. Arguably, the major concern refers to the access to international justice and a wider participation of cultural rights' holders in international decision-making. To date, these two fundamental aspects are still underdeveloped, calling for more concrete solutions which would facilitate a better governance of cultural matters, reconciliation of cultural and social conflicts, and the continuous development of all humankind.

REFERENCES:

Agbakwa, Shedrack C.: "Reclaiming Humanity: Economic, Social and Cultural Rights as the Cornerstone of African Human Rights" 5 *Yale Human Rights & Development Law Journal* (2002) 177.

Blake, Janet: "Taking a Human Rights Approach to Cultural Heritage Protection" 4 *Heritage & Society* (2011) 199.

Burri, Mira: "The International Law of Culture: Prospects and Challenges" 19 *International Journal Cultural Property* (2012) 579.

Donders, Yvonne: *Towards a Right to Cultural Identity?*, Antwerp: Intersentia (2002).

Francioni, Francesco and Scheinin, Martin (eds.): *Cultural Human Rights*, Leiden–Boston: Nijhoff (2008).

Human Rights Council: *Reports of the independent expert in the field of cultural rights*, available at www.ohchr.org (accessed 05/2016).

Jakubowski, Andrzej (ed.): *Collective Cultural Rights – An International Law Perspective*, Leiden–Boston: Brill (2016).

Lenzerini, Federico: *The Culturalization of Human Rights Law*, Oxford: Oxford University Press (2014).

Lixinski, Lucas: "International Cultural Heritage Regimes, International Law, and the Politics of Expertise" 20 *International Journal of Cultural Property* (2013) 407.

Meyer-Bisch, Patrice: "Les droit culturels, forment-ils unde categorie specifique de droits de l'homme?", in Partice Meyer-Bisch (ed.): *Les droits culturels, une categorie sous-developpee de droits de l'homme, Actes de VIIIe Colleque interdiciplinaire sur les droits de l'homme*, Fribourg: Editions Universitaires Fribourg (1993).

Nafziger, James A. R., Kirkwood Paterson, Robert and Dundes Renteln, Alison (eds.): *Cultural Law: International, Comparative and Indigenous*, New York: Cambridge University Press (2010).

Niec, Halina (ed.): *Cultural Rights and Wrongs*, Paris: UNESCO Publishing (1998).

Nimni, Ephraim: "Collective Dimensions of the Right to take Part in Cultural Life" UN Doc. E/C.12/40/17 (9 May 2008).

Polymenopoulou, Eleni: "Cultural Rights in the Case-Law of the International Court of Justice" 27 *Leiden Journal of International Law* (2014) 447.

Riedel, Eibe, Giacca, Gilles, Golay, Christophe (eds.): *Economic, Social, and Cultural Rights: Contemporary Issues and Challenges*, Oxford: Oxford University Press (2014).

Smith, Laurajane: *Uses of Heritage*, New York: Routledge (2006).

Stamatopoulou, Elsa: *Cultural Rights in International Law: Article 27 of the Universal Declaration of Human Rights and Beyond*, Leiden–Boston: Nijhoff (2007).

Symonides, Janusz: "Cultural Rights: A Neglected Category of Human Rights" 50(158) *International Social Science Journal* (1998) 559.

Thornberry, Patrick and Martín Estébanez, María Amor: *Minority Rights in Europe. A Review of the Work and Standards of the Council of Europe*, Strasbourg: Council of Europe Publishing (2004).

UN HRC: *The Right to Artistic Freedom*, UN Doc. A/HRC/23/34 (2013).
Vrdoljak, Ana Filipa (ed.): *The Cultural Dimension of Human Rights*, Oxford: Oxford University Press (2013).
AHMET ARSLAN AND OTHERS v. TURKEY (ECtHR 23/02/2010, No. 27138/04).
AKDAŞ v. TURKEY (ECtHR 16/02/2010, No. 41056/04).
APPLICATION OF THE CONVENTION ON THE PREVENTION AND PUNISHMENT OF THE CRIME OF GENOCIDE (CROATIA v. SERBIA) (ICJ 03/02/2015).
BEYELER v. ITALY (ECtHR 05/01/2000, No. 33202/96).
CASE CONCERNING APPLICATION OF THE CONVENTION ON THE PREVENTION AND PUNISHMENT OF THE CRIME OF GENOCIDE (BOSNIA AND HERZEGOVINA v. SERBIA AND MONTENEGRO) (ICJ 26/02/2007), ICJ Reports 2007, 43).
CENTRE FOR MINORITY RIGHTS DEVELOPMENT AND MINORITY RIGHTS GROUP (ON BEHALF OF ENDOROIS WELFARE COUNCIL) v. KENYA (AfComHPR 04/02/2010, 276/03).
CHA'ARE SHALOM VE TSEDEK v. FRANCE (ECtHR 27/06/2000, No. 27417/95).
CHAPMAN v. THE UNITED KINGDOM (ECtHR 18/01/2001, No. 27238/95).
CIUBOTURU v. MOLDOVA (ECtHR 27/04/2010, No. 27138/04).
CYPRUS v. TURKEY (ECtHR 10/05/2001, No. 25781/94).
DEBELIANOVI v. BULGARIA (ECtHR 13/11/2007, No. 61951/00).
KHIEU SAMPHAN AND NUON CHEA (ECCC 15/09/2010, Case 002) http://www.eccc.gov.kh/en/case/topic/2 (accessed 06/2016).
KICHWA INDIGENOUS PEOPLE OF SARAYAKU v. ECUADOR (IACtHR 27/06/2012, Ser. C, No. 245).
KITOK v. SWEDEN (HRCee 10/08/1988, 197/1985).
LÄNSMAN ET AL. v. FINLAND (HRCee 17/03/2005, 1023/2001).
LÄNSMAN ET AL. v. FINLAND (HRCee 26/10/1994, 511/1992).
LUBICON LAKE BAND (BERNARD OMINAYAK) v. CANADA (HRCee 26/03/1990, 167/1984).
MAYAGNA (SUMO) AWAS TINGI v. NICARAGUA (IACtHR 31/08/2001, Ser. C, No. 79).
MOIWANA COMMUNITY v. SURINAME (IACtHR 15/06/2005, Ser. C, No. 124).
MUÑOZ DÍAZ v. SPAIN (ECtHR 08/12/2009, No. 49151/07).
PROSECUTOR v. AHMAD AL FAQI AL MAHDI (ICC 02/05/2016, 01/12–01/15 – Pres-01/16 Decision constituting Trial Chambers).
PROSECUTOR v. KORDIĆ AND ČERKEZ (ICTY 26/02/2001, No. IT-95-14/2-T).
PROSECUTOR v. RADISLAV KRSTIĆ (ICTY 19/04/2004, No. IT-98-33-A).
RUSPOLI MORENES v. SPAIN (ECtHR 28/06/2011, No. 28979/07).
SAWHOYAMAXA INDIGENOUS COMMUNITY v. PARAGUAY (IACtHR 25/03/2006, Ser. C, No. 146).
SCEA FERME DE FRESNOY v. FRANCE (ECtHR 01/12/2005, No. 61093/00).
YAKYE AXA INDIGENOUS COMMUNITY v. PARAGUAY (IACtHR 17/06/2005, Ser. C, No. 125).
www.achpr.org (accessed 05/2016).
www.corteidh.or.cr/index.php/en (accessed 05/2016).
www.echr.coe.int/Pages/home.aspx?p=home (accessed 05/2016).
www.icty.org (accessed 05/2016).
www.ila-hq.org/en/committees/index.cfm/cid/1024 (accessed 05/2016).
www.ohchr.org/EN/Issues/CulturalRights/Pages/SRCulturalRightsIndex.aspx (accessed 05/2016).

Freedom of Expression in the Arts and Media

Annamari Laaksonen, Sydney

Freedom of Expression in Peril – Lessons from History

Human beings differ from other species for their capacity of spoken and written expression. A distinctive feature of the human nature is the urge to express feelings and ideas, including in artistic forms. The word 'freedom' derives from the Old-English word *freodom*, but is also found in other old languages, e.g. as *fridom* (Old Frisian), *vrijdom* (Dutch) or *vridom* (German); it signifies power of self-determination; state of free will; emancipation from slavery. Its meaning related to civil liberty dates from late 14th century. The equivalent word 'liberty' meaning free choice, also dates to 14th century (Old French) and derives from the Latin word *libertas*, signifying a free man (derived from the adjective *Liber, libera, liberum* meaning free, independent). The term 'expression' has again Latin roots: The noun *expressio* derives from *expressus* and *expressa* meaning tangible and vivid, related to the noun *exprimere*, meaning 'pressing out'. Since the early 17th century, expression has been considered as 'an action or creation that expresses feelings'.

As strong as the desire to express and communicate opinions, ideas and artistic or intellectual creations has been throughout history, as strong has been the will to control these expressions. In ancient Greece, epic poet Homer supported free expression as did playwright Euripides (480–406 BC) several centuries later. However, others such as the lawmaker Solon (638–558 BC), who set the ground for democracy and the economic and political development of Athens, banned speaking against the dead and the living, especially if the latter held a public office. The trial of Socrates, sentenced to drink poison in 339 BC for his 'corruption of youth and his acknowledgement of unorthodox divinities' is probably the most famous case of state →censorship in ancient times. The lasting legacy of the rule of Pericles, the most prominent and influential Greek statesman was freedom of speech as the 'defining distinction between Athens and Sparta'.

Before the Enlightenment, censorship has been widely practiced by governments and the church. In particular, the Catholic Church acted rigidly and harshly in opposing ideas perceived as subversive and heretical (quite similar to some authorities today which are guided either by →fundamentalism in their interpretation of religious laws or by the opposite: implacable →secularism). Following the invention and quick dissemination of the printing press in the mid-15th century, the church reacted with the introduction of the famous *Index Librorum Prohibitorium*. This first Index of prohibited books was ordered by Pope Paul IV in 1559 and subsequently published again 20 times before being abolished in 1966. In 1633, Galileo Galilei was hauled before the Inquisition because of confirming Copernicus' theory on the earth revolving around the sun. Other victims of the Inquisition were Joan of Arc (1421) and Thomas More (1535). Outside

Europe, the burning of the Maya Codices in the 16th century meant the loss of important cultural heritage and →literary expressions.

The licensing act of 1643 (*Ordinance for the Regulating of Printing*) introduced by the Parliament of England instituted a pre-publication censorship – a reaction to the rapid growth of newspapers and other printed media. In 1644, John Milton wrote 'Areopagitica', a pamphlet against licensing and censorship. Milton's pamphlet is considered among the most quoted and influential defences of the freedom of expression. In his speech, Milton referred to Euripides and the ancient struggle for freedom of expression, and spoke of the liberty of conscience, knowledge and speech: *'Give me the liberty to know, to utter, and to argue freely according to conscience, above all liberties.'* In 1689, the licensing act was overruled.

In the 17th and 18th century Europe, freedom of expression was reinforced in political and philosophical thinking as a measure of liberal progress. Freedom of expression, rights, liberties and dignity became consolidated in individualist thought, albeit with a marked political character. Sweden was the first country to officially abolish censorship and to guarantee freedom of the →press in 1766, followed by Denmark–Norway in 1770. After Milton, authors such as Jefferson, Bentham, Tocqueville, Mill, Kant and Voltaire defended freedom of expression. That influence poured into doctrinal statements of the time, which are some of the first declarations of human rights: the *Virginia Declaration of Rights* of 1776 and the *Declaration of the Rights of Man and Citizen* of 1789, a fundamental document of the French Revolution that includes freedom of speech. Mill's *On Liberty* published in 1859 is a classic defence of the freedom of expression. However, it took until 1960 that Penguin Books won the right to publish *Lady Chatterley's Lover* by D. H. Lawrence in the UK (previously banned because of its alleged →pornographic content).

The First Amendment of the US Constitution (one of the ten amendments that constitute the Bill of Rights), adopted in 1791, guarantees five freedoms: religion, speech, press, petition and assembly. It established one of the highest standards of freedom of expression in any constitution, but did not prevent e.g. the banning of the *Adventures of Huckleberry Finn* by several public libraries (1885).

The rise of totalitarianism in the 20th century had a profound impact on all freedoms and, particularly, on freedom of expression. In the Soviet Union, Stalin institutionalised censorship imposed by Bolsheviks by establishing a state censorship body, which hit not only political →dissidents but also many writers, intellectuals and →artists. For example, in 1962, Aleksandr Solzhenitsyn was sent to exile for the publication of *One Day in the Life of Ivan Denisovich.*

Inspired by Joseph Goebbels, Hitler's minister for propaganda, students organised a massive book burning in 1933 to destroy books of Jewish and other authors considered ideologically not in line with the Nazi ideology and, therefore, 'un-German' – despite the fact that most of these authors were of German origin.

Freedom of Expression in Human Rights Instruments and Case-law

The United Nations General Assembly adopted, in its first session held in 1946, *Resolution 59(I)* which stated that 'Freedom of information is a fundamental human right and ... the touchstone of all the freedoms to which the United Nations is consecrated.' Since freedom of expression is inherent in freedom of information, this general opinion can be seen as paving the way towards future international legal and political action.

Firstly, in 1948, the →*Universal Declaration of Human Rights* (UDHR) with its Article 19, which is still today considered to be the 'preeminent international claim for freedom of expression' (Democracy Web). This article reads as follows: *'Everyone has the right to freedom of opinion and expression; this right includes the right to hold opinions without interference and to seek, receive and impart information and ideas through any media and regardless of frontiers.'*, The subsequent *International Covenant on Civil and Political Rights* (ICCPR, 1966) guarantees freedom of expression in its Article 19(1) in the same words but ends that sentence with some further specifications, namely: *'... either orally, in writing or in print, in the form of art, or through any other media of his choice.'* With respect to this article, the *General Comment 34*, issued in 2011 and replacing General Comment 10 on Freedom on Opinion, emphasises that 'freedom of expression and opinion are the foundation stone for a free and democratic society and a necessary condition for the promotion and protection of human rights.' This Comment addresses in detail issues of freedom of opinion and expression, media issues, the right of access to information and other questions.

Article 19(2) ICCPR also permits restrictions (expressly or implicitly) on grounds such as national security; public order; public health; morals; and the protection of the reputation, rights and freedoms of others. In that context, it is important to underline that these restrictions to the right can only be imposed subject to specific conditions. In particular, they a) must be provided by law, and b) necessary to achieve their intended goals. According to the UN Human Rights Committee, these 'restrictions must be applied only for those purposes for which they are prescribed and must be directly related to the specific need on which they are predicated' (*General Comment No. 34*, 2011). The laws upon which the restrictions can be placed must be formally recognised by lawmakers and do not permit 'vague' interpretations. In addition, Article 20 of the Covenant states that any propaganda for war or any advocacy of national, racial or religious hatred that constitutes incitement to discrimination, hostility or violence is (to be) prohibited by law – clearly another provision that is still not respected everywhere in the world.

It is significant that, even among professional circles in the arts and media, Article 19(1) ICCPR is more often taken as a reference for freedom of artistic expression than its counterpart in Article 15(3) of the →*International Covenant on Economic, Social and Cultural Rights* (ICESCR, 1966), which promises that states 'undertake to respect the freedom indispensable for scientific research and creative activity'. This may have been caused by the fact that 'freedom of expression' is not explicitly mentioned in the text of this treaty. In addition, it may be due to the formula used in this clause, which calls for the 'respect' of freedom on the part of states or governments, but does not address, like in the wording of the ICCPR, 'everyone' directly, including artists, →journalists and other cultural or media professionals, with a guarantee for their right to freedom of expression. On the other hand, in its much more prominent Article 15(1)(a) the ICESCR stipulates 'the right to of everyone to take part in cultural life'. This clause should not only be understood as a guarantee of access to the arts (which is also recognised in Article 27 UDHR), but correspondingly as a right to be active, alone or in community with others, in culturally diverse societies. With regard to freedom of expression it is, therefore, important to consider the potential relationship of both ICESCR provisions as a means to foster the development of civil societies that are aware of their cultural roots and, at the same time, open towards new experiences and willing to improve their →intercultural competence.

Among other UN treaties and declarations dealing with freedom of expression, the *Convention on the Protection and Promotion of the Diversity of Cultural Expressions* of UNESCO (2005) is an important document since it stresses, in the first of its Guiding Principles, that 'cultural diversity can be protected and promoted only if human rights and fundamental freedoms, such as freedom of expression, information and communication, as well as the ability of individuals to choose cultural expressions, are guaranteed' (Article 2(1)).

The *Convention on the Rights of the Child* (CRC, 1989) recognises the right to freedom of expression and information in the same terms as ICCPR Article 19. As with other rights of →children spelled out in greater detail in the treaty, this provision should be read with Article 5, which reminds states to 'respect the responsibilities, rights and duties of parents or, where applicable, the members of the extended family or community as provided for by local custom, legal guardians or other persons legally responsible for the child', thus including larger groups or communities in the task of safeguarding these rights. Article 17 CRC recognises access to information and material from a diversity of national and international sources. The provision calls on states to encourage access to 'information and material of social and cultural benefit' through mass media, children's literature and international cooperation.

The *Convention on the Rights of Persons with Disabilities* (CRPD, 2006) intends to move from viewing persons with →disabilities as 'objects' towards seeing them as 'subjects with rights, who are capable of claiming those rights and making decisions for their lives based on their free and informed consent as well as being active members of society' (UN Division for Social Policy and Development). The rights to freedom of expression and information of people with disabilities are recognised in Article 21 CRPD. The Convention specifies some of the measures needed and makes clear that positive measures and not only non-interference are required to ensure the enjoyment of these rights, including e.g. 'facilitating the use of sign languages, Braille, augmentative and alternative communication, and all other accessible means, modes and formats of communication of their choice.'

On the European level, the →*European Convention for the Protection of Human Rights and Fundamental Freedoms* (ECHR, 1953) underlines, in its Article 10(1), the right of everyone to freedom of expression: *'This right shall include freedom to hold opinions and to receive and impart information and ideas without interference by public authority and regardless of frontiers'*..., but it does *'not prevent States from requiring the licensing of broadcasting, television or cinema enterprises.'* The ECHR, in Article 10(2), sees this right connected with 'duties and responsibilities' and mentions, similar to the ICCPR, but in even greater detail, a number limitations that could affects its exercise, including: *'formalities, conditions, restrictions or penalties as are prescribed by law and are necessary in a democratic society, in the interests of national security, territorial integrity or public safety, for the prevention of disorder or crime, for the protection of health or morals, for the protection of the reputation or the rights of others, for preventing the disclosure of information received in confidence, or for maintaining the authority and impartiality of the judiciary.'*

However, as freedom of expression is a fundamental right, the laws or regulations limiting it must be truly necessary and the aims need to be legitimate. The →European Court of Human Rights (ECtHR), implementing in its case-law its 'principle of evolutive or *dynamic interpretation*' (Greer, 2000), underlined, as early as 1976: that *'Freedom of expression constitutes one of the essential foundations of [a democratic] society, one of the basic conditions for its progress and for the development of every man ... it is applicable not only to 'information' or 'ideas' that are favourably received or regarded as inoffensive or as a matter of indifference, but also to those that offend, shock or disturb the State or any sector of the population.'* [HANDYSIDE, 1976]. In this context, the ECtHR called for 'pluralism, tolerance and broadmindedness', which are indispensable for a 'democratic society' and, clearly, also a lifeline for the arts and media.

Cases before the ECtHR addressing issues of freedom of expression are numerous. For example, the Court [in VEREINIGUNG BILDENDER KÜNSTLER, 2007] recognised that the prohibition by domestic courts of exhibiting a painting depicting a politician of the Austrian Freedom Party in an unfavourable manner was 'disproportionate to the aim it pursued and therefore not necessary in a democratic society within the meaning of Article 10 § 2 of the Convention', also reminding the national authorities that satire 'naturally aims to provoke and agitate', so any restrictions should be carefully examined. In [THE SUNDAY TIMES, 1979], the court accepted that there was a violation to freedom of expression when in 1972 the newspaper prepared to publish an article about the investigation of the origins of the 'thalidomide children' case in which a British drug company had manufactured and distributed a drug containing an ingredient known as thalidomide. The Attorney-General had applied for an injunction restraining publication of the article on the 'grounds that it would constitute contempt of court'. The restriction was lifted in 1976. In [THE OBSERVER and GUARDIAN, 1991], the Court recognised a violation of freedom of expression in the case of two newspapers publishing short articles about details of a publication called *Spycatcher* that describes unlawful activities of the British Security Service. The government succeeded in obtaining an injunction preventing further publication until proceedings relating to a breach of confidence had been concluded. The ECtHR stated that although the injunction was lawful, as it was in the interest of national security, once the book had been published, there was insufficient reason for continuing the publication ban. On the other hand, the Court also held that limitations to artistic freedom of expression may be legitimate on grounds similar to those applied to other forms of expression, such as offending religious feelings [OTTO-PREMINGER-INSTITUT, 1994] or the protection of morals [MÜLLER AND OTHERS, 1988].

Freedom of expression is also protected by the →*Charter of Fundamental Rights* of the →European Union, covering culture with regard to freedom of speech (Article 11) and artistic freedom (Article 13). The →Court of Justice of the EU has linked, in its case-law, freedom of expression with the maintenance of media pluralism [UNITED PAN-EUROPE COMMUNICATIONS BELGIUM SA, 2007], underlining its importance as one of the fundamental rights guaranteed by the Community legal order.

A Permanent Challenge: Freedom of artistic creation and of the media

Artistic freedom and freedom of expression are indispensable for arts practice. In this respect, non-binding standard-setting instruments such as the UNESCO *Recommendation concerning the status of the artists* (1980) have so far proved to be of limited effect. The 2013 Report of the (then) Special Rapporteur in the field of cultural rights, Farida Shaheed, entitled: *The right to freedom of artistic expression and creativity*, recognises that censorship still has a profound, negative impact on arts practice in many parts of the world. The report also builds links between freedom of →cultural expressions and other human rights including freedom of →assembly and association, →authors' rights and leisure. 53 UN member states reaffirmed the right to creative and artistic expression at the meeting of the Human Rights Council in its 30th session of 18 September 2015.

Even if censorship in the strict, institutional sense may have loosened or became obsolete due to the global success of the Internet and →social media, governments maintain, or even newly introduce, certain restrictions regarding freedom of expression, now based on legislative acts aiming to address national security, criminal acts or →obscenity and →blasphemy. As regards the latter, the *fatwa* against Salman Rushdie, issued by Ayatollah Khomeini (Iran) over the alleged 'blasphemous' content of his novel, *The Satanic Verses*, gained particular attention. While this fatwa was lifted in 1998, the global uproar caused by controversial →caricatures such as the so-called Muhammad cartoons published in a Danish newspaper in 2005, the massive prosecutions of →press editors and bloggers on doubtful grounds of →defamation of state authorities (e.g. in Turkey) and the worst-case scenario of terror attacks against the French magazine *Charlie Hebdo* in 2015 demonstrated, how topical such issues still are – and how even the life of journalists, artists and other creative professionals can be endangered, if they don't resort to conformance or self-censorship. Similar threats can also affect media →producers, independent as well as →public broadcasting stations, publishing houses or representatives of museums and other heritage institutions.

In 2015, the *Freemuse* annual report recorded censorship and threats on artistic freedom in over 70 countries. These include 469 cases of censorship and attacks on artists. According to this report, musicians and creators in the field of music are particularly in danger of being harassed or persecuted, probably due to the popularity their work can gain via diverse media channels or at stage events, especially in the younger generations.

Freedom of expression can also be compromised by state or commercial surveillance practices that undermine →privacy, by measures of →Internet content suppression or by security laws. For example, the 2006 (counter-) *Terrorism Law* in the United Kingdom criminalises any publication or public statement that is considered to 'encourage acts of terrorism, including statements that glorify specific terrorist acts, even if the individual of group making the statement did not actually intend to encourage terrorism'. In this law, terrorism is defined to include 'any political, religious, racial or ideological case designed to influence the government of any country or international organisation or to intimate any member of the public anywhere in the world.' In 2014, Russia issued a law to block 'extremist' websites that could be interpreted to encourage mass riots or publishing harmful content to the public.

In contrast, some countries try to progress towards more artistic and media freedom by introducing new legislation – or promoting the absence of control mechanisms. An example of the latest modifications of existing measures is France where, on 25 May 2016, the Senate approved a law related to freedom of creation, architecture and heritage (modified in its 10th lecture by the National Assembly). Iceland, followed by Estonia, has the fewest barriers to Internet freedom, according to a recent study of *Freedom House*, ranking countries based on obstacles to access, limits on content and violations of user rights.

Without doubt, civil society, with watchful NGOs, arts councils at arm's length from governments as well as transparent professional associations in the domains of the arts and the media have proven to be the best advocates for freedom of expression and cultural diversity. However, we should not neglect the difficulties this entails in times of economic globalisation that sometimes tends towards a standardisation of media content; the new rise of autocratic forms of leadership in a number of countries; populist reactions against increasing migration; as well as extremism and widespread terrorist attacks.

Therefore, the guarantees provided by international or regional human rights instruments and national constitutions; the complaints procedures offered by the respective courts or treaty bodies; the monitoring of new developments conducted by regional intergovernmental organisations such as the →Council of Europe (with regard to human rights compliance, cultural policies and heritage protection) or →OSCE (with regard to media freedom) as well as the reports of Special Rapporteurs in the UN system should be seen as more than last resorts, since their standards can serve as strong blockades once freedom of expression and information is at risk. In addition, a number of UN human rights treaties – including *inter alia* ICCPR, CESCR, CRC and CRPD – receive and consider individual complaints or communications from civil society, submitted, like in the case of CESCR, 'by or on behalf of individuals or groups of individuals,

...claiming to be victims of a violation of any of the economic, social and cultural rights set forth in the Covenant' by state authorities in a country that is a party to the treaty (UN General Assembly Resolution A/RES/63/117, 2008). If such opportunities would be used more frequently by civil society stakeholders, the development of a *human rights culture* could definitely progress, including as regards freedom of expression in the arts and media.

REFERENCES:

Farrington, Julia: *Beyond belief. Theatre, freedom of expression and public order – a case study*, Index on Censorship, 2011.

Freedom House: *Freedom of the Press 2016*, Annual Report, Washington, available at www.freedomhouse.org (accessed 07/2016).

Freemuse: *Art Under Threat. Freemuse Annual Statistics on Censorship and Attacks on Artistic Freedom in 2015*, available at http://artsfreedom.org/ (accessed 07/2016).

Greer, Steven: The Margin of Appreciation: Interpretation and Discretioon under the European Convention on Human Rights, Human rights files No. 17, Strasbourg: Council of Europe Publishing (2000).

ICNL – International Center for Not-for-Profit Law: *Global Trends in NGO Law*: "The Right to Freedom of Expression: Restrictions on a Foundational Right", Vol. 6, 1 (2015). Available at http://www.icnl.org/research/trends/trends6-1.pdf (accessed 07/2016).

Milton, John: "Areopagitica", in *Early Censorship in England*, Bridwell Library (2000).

Puddphatt, Andrew: *Freedom of Expression, the Essentials of Human Rights*, Hodder Arnold (2005).

Smith, David and Torres, Luc: "Timeline: a history of free speech", *The Guardian*. 5. 2. 2006.

UN Human Rights Committee: *General Comment No. 34 – Article 19 Freedom of opinion and expression*, CCPR/C/GC/34 (2011).

UN Human Rights Council / Special Rapporteur in the field of cultural rights, Farida Shaheed: *The right to freedom of artistic expression and creativity*, Geneva, A/HRC/23/34 (2013).

Van Mill, David: "Freedom of Speech", *Stanford Encyclopedia of Philosophy* (2014).

HANDYSIDE v. UNITED KINGDOM (ECtHR 07/12/1976, 5493/72).

MÜLLER and OTHERS v. SWITZERLAND (ECtHR 24/5/1988, 10737/84).

OTTO-PREMINGER-INSTITUT v. AUSTRIA (ECtHR 20/9/94, 13470/87).

R v. PENGUIN BOOKS (UK, 02/11/1960).

THE OBSERVER and GUARDIAN v. UNITED KINGDOM (ECtHR 26/11/1991, 13585/88).

THE SUNDAY TIMES v. UNITED KINGDOM (ECtHR 26/04/1979, 6538/74).

UNITED PAN-EUROPE COMMUNICATIONS BELGIUM SA AND OTHERS v. BELGIAN STATE (CJEU 13/12/2007, C-250/06).

VEREINIGUNG BILDENDER KÜNSTLER v. AUSTRIA (ECtHR 25/1/2007, 68354/01).

Cultural Diversity and Cultural Identity in Human Rights

Yvonne Donders, Amsterdam

The Concept of Culture

Culture is a concept of which the dynamics and complexity do not easily translate into legal (human rights) norms. It is not an inactive notion, but something that can develop and change over time. Cultures are not static, but dynamic; they are not end products, but processes, without well-defined boundaries and influenced by internal and external interactions. The concept of culture can refer to many things, varying from cultural products, such as arts and literature, to the cultural process or culture as a way of life. Culture has an objective dimension reflected in visible characteristics such as language, religion, or customs, and a subjective dimension reflected in shared attitudes, ways of thinking, feeling and acting. In addition, cultures have both an individual and a collective dimension. Cultures are developed and shaped by communities. Individuals identify with several cultural communities – ethnicity, nationality, family, religion, etc. – and in that way shape their personal cultural identity (Donders, 2010, p. 15).

Culture is considered to be important for both individuals as well as communities, as an important aspect of their identity, existence and dignity. Or, to put it in the words of the World Commission on Culture and Development: 'culture shapes all our thinking, imagining and behaviour. It is the transmission of behaviour as well as a dynamic source for change, creativity, freedom and the awakening of innovative opportunities. For groups and societies, culture is energy, inspiration and empowerment.' (World Commission, 1995, p. 11)

At the same time, culture is not an abstract or neutral concept: it is shaped by its instrumentalisation, in which negotiation, contestation and power structures play a role. Culture is not necessarily an intrinsically dignified concept. It may be a mechanism for exclusion and control. Culture may harm people or be oppressive to them and hinder their personal development. Some harmful aspects of culture reflected in cultural practices are very questionable from a human rights perspective (Donders, 2010, p. 15–16).

The broadness, complexity and sensitivity of the concept of culture have been the crucial challenges in the transformation of this concept into legal human rights norms. An important question in this respect is *who* decides to what extent cultural diversity should be promoted and which cultural aspects should be protected? As cultures are not static but dynamic, which interpretation of a certain cultural practice or activity, should be accepted? The creation and evaluation of cultural laws and policies requires a multi-stakeholder process, involving not only state actors but ensuring also proper representation and participation of cultural communities and individuals.

Cultural Diversity and Cultural Pluralism

Cultural diversity is defined in Article 2 of the *UNESCO 2005 Convention* as 'the manifold ways in which the cultures of groups and societies find expression. These expressions are passed on within and among groups and societies. Cultural diversity is made manifest not only through the varied ways in which the cultural heritage of humanity is expressed, augmented and transmitted through the variety of cultural expressions, but also through diverse modes of artistic creation, production, dissemination, distribution and enjoyment, whatever the means and technologies used.' It is worth noting that states have chosen to include and define cultural diversity in an international instrument that has primarily an economic feature, not a human rights one (Donders 2015). It does not give rights to individuals and communities, but is intended to 'reaffirm the sovereign rights of states to maintain, adopt and implement policies and measures that they deem appropriate for the protection and promotion of the diversity of cultural expressions on their territory' (Article 1h).

Cultural diversity describes the factual situation of existing cultural differences. It is an umbrella notion that might cover different levels: *between* individual states, regions, communities and individuals, but also *within* states, regions and communities.

Cultural diversity should be distinguished from the related notion of cultural pluralism. The difference and the connection between cultural diversity and cultural pluralism are explained in the *Universal Declaration on Cultural Diversity*. Article 2 states that 'cultural pluralism gives policy expression to the reality of cultural diversity'. In other words, cultural diversity, also termed 'plurality', reflects a factual situation. Cultural pluralism refers to the way cultural diversity is appreciated and translated into laws and policies. The term 'pluralism' is also used to describe differences in legal systems and procedures, or in institutional structures between and within states. Cultural pluralism implies that cultural diversity is considered to be a desirable and socially and politically beneficial condition (Donders, 2012, p. 9).

The →ECtHR has systematically maintained that pluralism is crucial for democratic societies. It has stated that 'the existence of minorities and different cultures in a country is a historical fact that a democratic society has to tolerate and even protect and support according to the principles of international law' [SIDIROPOULOS, 1998, paras. 41 and 44). It has furthermore stated that the state should not oppose possible tension between different communities by eliminating pluralism, but should ensure that different communities tolerate each other [SERIF, 1999, paras. 39, 45 and 50).

Pluralism implies that individuals and communities are given the opportunity to maintain their specific →cultural identity, provided that it is consistent with the laws, policies and values of the wider society. Consequently, although cultural diversity is the term mainly used in relation to human rights, what is often meant is cultural pluralism.

Cultural Diversity within Universalism

Human rights and cultural diversity have been discussed extensively in the context of the →universalism and cultural relativism debate. Moving beyond the traditional deadlock between these two extremes, the idea has taken hold that respect for cultural diversity can very well be consistent with the notion of the universality of human rights. Cultural relativism, in the sense of asking for respect for cultural diversity, not of challenging the legitimacy of international human rights norms as such, and universalism do not have to mutually exclude each other.

Firstly, formal universalism, or the universality of the subjects of human rights, does not present problems. The idea that human rights should be universally enjoyed – by all persons on the basis of equality – is not very controversial. No one will argue that some people in the world do not have any human rights at all. International human rights instruments clearly endorse this universal approach. The UDHR, for example, not only refers to universalism in its title, but also states in Article 1 that 'all human beings are born free and equal in dignity and rights.' The UDHR as well as the international human rights treaties speak of 'everyone', 'all persons' or 'no one', affirming that *all* human beings have these rights and freedoms, no matter where they were born or to which community they belong.

The universal value and application of human rights does, however, not necessarily imply the *uniform implementation* of these rights. In other words, while human rights apply universally to everyone on the basis of their human dignity, the implementation of these rights does not have to be uniform. The ECtHR has adopted this approach by stating that, while the purpose of the ECHR was to lay down international standards, 'this does not mean that absolute uniformity is required' [SUNDAY TIMES, 1991, para. 61]. Scholars have called this 'the universalisation of human rights' (Advisory Commission, 2008), the 'relative universality of human rights' (Donnelly, 2007), 'inclusive universality' (Brems, 2004) or the 'culturalization of human rights' (Lenzerini, 2014); the main idea being that while human rights apply universally, they do not have to be implemented in a uniform way. Human rights promotion and protection imply respect for and advancement of cultural diversity and cultural identities.

Cultural Diversity within Equality

Respect for cultural diversity has always been part of the human rights discourse. However, in developing international human rights law, states at first mainly emphasised the principle of →*equality*. Equality *between* them as sovereign states and equality as the basis for the enjoyment of rights by different individuals and communities *within* states. Although diversity was recognised as a fact, it was maintained that human rights should first and foremost promote and protect equality. This emphasis on equality formed the starting point for the UDHR (Donders, 2002, p. 163–166).

During the drafting processes of the various human rights treaties adopted afterwards, cultural diversity was increasingly emphasised as a value to be respected and promoted. This was broadly done in two ways: by developing the equality concept, acknowledging that it also implies the right to be different, and by adopting specific rights promoting and protecting cultural diversity.

Firstly, it was recognised that respect for cultural differences can be fully in line with the principle of equality. Having equal rights is not the same as being treated equally. Indeed, equality and non-discrimination not only imply that equal situations should be treated equally, but also that unequal situations should be treated unequally. International treaty bodies have maintained that 'the enjoyment of rights and freedoms on an equal footing...does not mean identical treatment in every instance' (HRCee, General Comment 18, 1989, para. 8; [THLIMMENOS, 2000, para. 44]; [D.H. AND OTHERS, 2006, para. 44]). Legal doctrine distinguishes in this regard between 'differentiation', 'distinction' and 'discrimination'. Differentiation is difference in treatment that is lawful; distinction is a neutral term which is used when it has not yet been determined whether difference in treatment is lawful or not; and discrimination is difference in treatment that is arbitrary and unlawful (Bossuyt, 2002, para. 91). Consequently, only treatment that results in discrimination is prohibited. Difference in treatment is allowed as long as the criteria for differentiation are reasonable and objective and serve a legitimate aim.

Difference in treatment may also involve affirmative or positive action to remedy historical injustices, social discrimination or to create diversity and proportional group representation (HRCee, General Comment 18, 1989, para. 10). This also follows from Article 1(4) of the *International Convention on the Elimination of Racial Discrimination*, in which it is stated that 'special measures taken for the sole purpose of securing adequate advancement of certain racial or ethnic groups or individuals requiring such protection as may be necessary in order to ensure such groups or individuals equal enjoyment or exercise of human rights and fundamental freedoms shall not be deemed racial discrimination, provided, however, that such measures do not, as a consequence, lead to the maintenance of separate rights for different racial groups and that they shall not be continued after the objectives for which they were taken have been achieved.'

Cultural Diversity and Cultural Rights

Apart from respect for diversity within the equality principle, many international human rights instruments include rights that specifically promote and protect cultural diversity. These rights are broadly classified as 'cultural rights'. Cultural rights are human rights that directly promote and protect cultural interests of individuals and communities and that are meant to advance their capacity to preserve, develop and change their cultural identity. While cultural rights may have particular interest and relevance for certain communities, such as minorities and indigenous peoples, and special regimes including cultural rights for these communities have been established, cultural rights as human rights are in principle for all. As such they truly echo the importance of cultural pluralism in international human rights law. They are rights protecting and promoting cultural objects as well as cultural subjects, including communities and individuals. Cultural rights accordingly represent the indivisibility and interrelationship of all human rights and they are individual as well as collective rights (Donders, 2012, p. 15).

But which rights are cultural rights? Although cultural rights are mentioned in the title of the ICESCR, the text of this treaty does not make clear which provisions in the treaty belong to the category of cultural rights. In fact, none of the international legal instruments provides a definition of 'cultural rights'. Consequently, different lists could be compiled of international legal provisions that could be labelled 'cultural rights'. Such provisions can be found in human rights instruments, but also for instance in international instruments on cultural heritage. The link between cultural heritage and human rights is increasingly recognised, for instance in the *UNESCO Convention for the Safeguarding of the Intangible Cultural Heritage* (2003). Here we focus on cultural rights in international human rights instruments.

Firstly, cultural rights include international human rights provisions that explicitly refer to 'culture'. Examples are the right of everyone to participate in cultural life (Article 27 UDHR and Article 15(1)(a) ICESCR) and the right of members of minorities to enjoy their own culture, practise their own religion and speak their own language (Article 27 ICCPR). Explicit cultural rights can also be found in various instruments on the rights of minorities and indigenous peoples. Secondly, cultural rights include those human rights provisions that have a direct link with culture. It might be defensible to claim that almost every human right can be linked to culture. However, the rights with the most obvious link are the right to self-determination, the rights to freedom of religion, freedom of expression, freedom of association, and the right to education. The ECtHR has, for instance, recognised that artistic or →literary expressions such as novels, poems and paintings fall within the scope of freedom of expression [MÜLLER AND OTHERS, 1988; VEREINIGUNG BILDENER KÜNSTLER, 2007; ULUSOY, 2007; KAR AND OTHERS, 2007; EKIN ASSOCIATION, 2001; AKDAS, 2010] and that the right to freedom of association also protects cultural organisations [SIDIROPOULOS AND OTHERS, 1998; STANKOV AND THE UNITED MACEDONIAN ORGANISATION ILINDEN, 2001; GORZELIK AND OTHERS, 2001].

Apart from human rights explicitly or directly related to culture, it appears that many human rights have a strong *cultural dimension*. Although some human rights may at first glance have no direct link with culture, most of them have important cultural implications. The right to health, for instance, may have important cultural connotations as far as certain treatments, the use of certain (traditional) medicines or the availability of male and female doctors is concerned. Culture also plays a decisive role in sexual and reproductive health, in which information and education are crucial. The Committee on Economic, Social and Cultural Rights has recognised in its General Comment 14 that the right to health includes that 'all health facilities, goods and services must be... culturally appropriate, i.e., respectful of the culture of individuals, minorities, peoples and communities.' Another example is the right to adequate →food. The preparation and consumption of food have a clear cultural connotation. The importance of the cultural dimension of food is also shown by the fact that several food traditions, such as French cuisine, the Mediterranean diet, and the traditional Mexican kitchen, have been recognised as intangible cultural heritage under the *UNESCO Convention*. The

Committee on Economic, Social and Cultural Rights has stated in its General Comment 12 that guarantees concerning the right to food should be culturally appropriate and acceptable.

Many civil and political rights also have a cultural dimension. For instance, the right to a fair trial includes the right to be informed of the charges in a language that one can understand, as well as the right to free assistance of an interpreter if a person cannot understand or speak the language used in court and such translation needs to be adequate. Specific ways of living related to culture, such as living in a caravan, which is the traditional way of living of →Roma or gypsies, may fall within the scope of the right to respect for private life and home [BUCKLEY, 1996; CHAPMAN, 2001; WINTERSTEIN, 2014). In respecting and protecting these rights, states have to actively find ways to accommodate cultural diversity, while at the same time balancing the different interests of individuals, communities and society at large. It is crucial that states make such processes transparent and inclusive, by informing and closely involving the affected individuals and communities.

Cultural Diversity and the Margin of Appreciation

States are allowed and are sometimes required to take national, cultural circumstances into account when they implement international human rights law, to accommodate cultural diversity *between* states, but also to balance different cultural interests *within* states. However, giving states unlimited freedom to interpret and implement international human rights law in totally different ways, would undermine the universal character and application of the norms and would lead to unacceptable differences in rights protection for different individuals and communities. Therefore, the states' discretion in implementing international human rights law is supervised by national and international bodies that have various mechanisms at their disposal and use various techniques to define the boundaries within which international human rights law should be implemented. One example is the doctrine of the margin of appreciation.

The →margin of appreciation or margin of discretion refers to the room for manoeuvre national authorities have in fulfilling their obligations under international human rights law. It is most developed in the European context by the ECtHR. The Court expressed this position for the first time in the [HANDYSIDE, 1976] case, arguing that there is no uniform European conception of morals and that the view on this in states parties varies and may change. Therefore, the Court found that 'state authorities are in principle in a better position than the international judge to give an opinion on the exact content of these requirements as well as on the necessity of a restriction' [HANDYSIDE, 1976, para. 49). The ECtHR should only intervene if it clearly finds that the state party has failed in that effort.

Some see the margin of appreciation doctrine as a danger to the universality of the norms (Benvenisti, 1998–1999). Others (Sweeney, 2005; Donders, 2012) consider the margin of appreciation as a valuable means for international supervisory bodies to allow states to diversify in the implementation of international human rights. This should, as is also emphasised by the bodies themselves, always go hand in hand with international supervision, to make sure that national implementation and supervision meet minimum standards. Also, the supervisory bodies should ensure that the use of the margin of appreciation does not merely protect majority interests in a state (Benvenisti 1998–1999, Brems, 2010).

Cultural Diversity and Harmful Cultural Practices

While international human rights law promotes and protects cultural diversity, it cannot serve as an excuse to justify harmful (cultural) practices that are in conflict with or limit the enjoyment of human rights. Cultural practices are very diverse, which makes it impossible to make general, abstract statements about their acceptability in relation to human rights. However, it should be emphasised that respect for cultural diversity cannot be a justification for systematic denial of human rights (Donders, 2010, p. 31; Donders, 2012, p. 23). This was also clearly laid down in the *Universal Declaration on Cultural Diversity* (Article 4) and the *UNESCO 2005 Convention* (Article 2(1)): no one may invoke cultural diversity in order to infringe upon human rights as guaranteed by the UDHR and by international law, or to limit the scope thereof.

It should however be noted that harmful cultural practices are often formally prohibited by national laws. Even so, they may be practised, and sometimes even condoned by states. This shows that law alone cannot solve all issues and cannot by itself change cultural practices. Changes in cultural practices are most successful if they arise within the cultural community itself and are not imposed from outside, by law or by the state. This does of course not relieve states from the responsibility to find ways to promote such changes, in close cooperation with cultural communities.

Several human rights treaties emphasise the role of the state in eradicating harmful cultural practices. The *Convention on the Elimination of All Forms of Discrimination Against Women* (CEDAW), for example, states in Article 5 that 'States Parties shall take all appropriate measures: (a) To modify the social and cultural patterns of conduct of men and women, with a view to achieving the elimination of prejudices and customary and all other practices which are based on the idea of the inferiority or the superiority of either of the sexes or on stereotyped roles for men and women.' The *Convention on the Rights of the Child* (CRC) contains in Article 24(3) that 'States Parties shall take all effective and appropriate measures with a view to abolishing traditional practices prejudicial to the health of children.'

Several →UN Treaty Bodies with monitoring tasks have also emphasised the role of the state in eradicating cultural practices that are against human rights. The HRCee has listed a number of harmful cultural practices as violations of human rights, including female infanticide, widow burning and dowry killings as violations of the right to life; forced abortion, forced sterilisation and forced genital mutilation as violations of the right not to be subjected to inhumane and degrading treatment; and forced male guardianship as a violation of the freedom of movement (HRCee, General Comment 28, 2000, para. 5). The treaty bodies on the rights of women and children have adopted a joint recommendation on harmful practices, in which they list FGM, child and forced marriages, polygamy and honour crimes as such. This recommendation also reiterates that the adoption of laws prohibiting harmful cultural practices may be necessary, but that it is not the only nor always most effective way to get rid of them: gathering data and prevention via education and awareness-raising are also important (CEDAW and CRC, 2014).

Cultural Diversity and Cultural Identity Define Humanity

Various international instruments confirm that cultural diversity is a defining characteristic of humanity that fosters human capacities and is essential to the full realisation of human rights. They confirm the importance of cultural diversity as a value to be promoted and protected and endorse the link between cultural diversity and human rights.

Human rights provide a moral and legal framework for promoting and preserving not only the diversity *between* cultures, but also the diversity *within* cultures. The universal human rights system offers many entry points to accommodate and promote cultural diversity. While applying universally, human rights norms include the necessary flexibility to be receptive to and to promote cultural pluralism, among and within states, communities and individuals.

Individuals and communities can use international human rights law to develop and maintain cultures and promote and protect their cultural identities. At the same time, cultural rights cannot be enjoyed unlimitedly and cannot be invoked or interpreted in such a way as to justify the denial or violation of other human rights or the exclusion of certain categories of persons, such as women, from the enjoyment of human rights.

Human rights and cultural diversity may have a mutually beneficial relationship, but this does not mean that, as in all relationships, there will be no complexities or (unexpected) issues that will continue to demand respect, flexibility and adaptability of one and/or the other. While states play a crucial role in this regard and should, indeed, secure conditions, or help to maintain infrastructures, that enable the →participation of everyone in a multifaceted cultural life, there cannot be merely top-down approaches. Cultures are determined and developed by individuals and communities, who should always be involved and consulted in cultural laws and policy processes, thereby making these laws and policies more human rights proof.

REFERENCES:

Advisory Council on International Affairs: *Universality of Human Rights. Principles, Practice and Prospects*, Advice No. 63, The Hague, November 2008.

Benvenisti, Eyal: "Margin of Appreciation, Consensus and Universal Standards", 31 *NYU Journal of International Law and Politics* (1998) 843.

Bossuyt, Marc: *Prevention of Discrimination – The Concept and Practice of Affirmative Action*, 17 June 2002, UN Doc. E/CN.4/Sub. 2/2002/21.

Brems, Eva: "Reconciling Universality and Diversity in International Human Rights: A Theoretical and Methodological Framework and Its Application in the Context of Islam", 5(3) *Human Rights Review* (2004) 5.

Committee on Economic, Social and Cultural Rights, General Comment No. 12, The Right to Adequate Food (Article 11), 12 May 1999.
Committee on Economic, Social and Cultural Rights, General Comment No. 14, The Right to the Highest Attainable Standard of Health (Article 12), UN Doc, E/C.12/2000/4, UN Doc. E/C.12/1999/5, 11 August 2000.
Committee on the Elimination of Discrimination against Women and Committee on the Rights of the Child, Joint general comment No. 18/general recommendation No. 31 on harmful practices, UN Doc. CEDAW/C/GC/31-CRC/C/GC/18, 14 November 2014.
Donders, Yvonne: *Towards a Right to Cultural Identity?*, Antwerp: Intersentia (2002).
Donders, Yvonne: "Do Cultural Diversity and Human Rights make a Good Match?", *International Social Science Journal 199*, UNESCO Blackwell Publishing (2010).
Donders, Yvonne (Inaugural Lecture): "Human Rights: Eye for Cultural Diversity", University of Amsterdam, 29 June 2012.
Donders, Yvonne: "Cultural Rights and the UNESCO Convention: More than Meets the Eye?", in: Christiaan De Beukelaer, Miikka Pyykkönen and J. P. Singh (eds.): *Globalization, Culture and Development – The UNESCO Convention on Cultural Diversity*, Palgrave MacMillian, (2015) 117.
Donnelly, Jack: "The Relative Universality of Human Rights", 29 *Human Rights Quarterly* (2007) 281.
Donoho, Douglas Lee: "Relativism Versus Universalism in Human Rights: The Search for Meaningful Standards", 27 *Stanford Journal on International Law* (1990) 345.
Francioni, Francesco and Scheinin, Martin (eds.): *Cultural Human Rights*, Leiden: Martinus Nijhoff Publishers (2008).
Human Rights Committee, General Comment No. 18, Non-Discrimination, UN Doc. CCPR/C/21/Rev.1/Add.4, 10 November 1989.
Human Rights Committee, General Comment No. 28, Equality of Rights Between Men and Women (Article 3), UN Doc. CCPR/C/21/Rev.1/Add. 10, 29 March 2000.
Kinley, David: "Bendable Rules: The Development Implications of Human Rights Pluralism", in: Tamanaha, Brian, Sage, Caroline and Woolcock, Michael (eds.): *Legal Pluralism and Development – Scholars and Practitioners in Dialogue*, Cambridge: CUP (2012) 50.
Lenzerini, Federico: *The Culturalization of Human Rights Law*, Oxford: OUP (2014).
Petersen, Niels: "International Law, Cultural Diversity and Democratic Rule: Beyond the Divide Between Universalism and Relativism", 1 *Asian Journal of International Law* (2011) 149.
Preis, Ann-Belinda S: "Human Rights as Cultural Practice: An Anthropological Critique", 18(2) *Human Rights Quarterly* (1996) 286.
Richieri Hanania, Lilian (ed.): *Cultural Diversity in International Law – The Effectiveness of the UNESCO Convention on the Protection and Promotion of the Diversity of Cultural Expressions*, Abingdon: Routledge (2014).
Sajo, Andras (ed.): *Human Rights with Modesty: the Problem of Universalism*, Koninklijke Brill (2004).
Sweeney, J.A.: "Margins of Appreciation: Cultural Relativity and the European Court of Human Rights in the Post-Cold War Era", 54 *ICLQ* (2005) 459.
Varennes, Fernand de: "The Fallacies in the "Universalism versus Cultural Relativism" Debate in Human Rights Law", 1 *Asia Pacific Journal on Human Rights and the Law* (2006) 67.
Vrdoljak, Ana (ed.): *The Cultural Dimension of Human Rights*, Florence and Oxford: OUP (2013).
World Commission on Culture and Development, *Our Creative Diversity*, Paris: UNESCO Publishing (1995).
AKDAS v. TURKEY (ECtHR 16/02/2010, 41056/04).
BUCKLEY v. THE UNITED KINGDOM (ECtHR 25/09/1996, 20348/92).
CHAPMAN v. THE UNITED KINGDOM (ECtHR 18/01/2001, 27238/95).
D.H. AND OTHERS v. THE CZECH REPUBLIC (ECtHR 07/02/2006, 57325/00).
EKIN ASSOCIATION v. FRANCE (ECtHR 17/07/2001, 39288/98).
GORZELIK AND OTHERS v. POLAND (ECtHR 20/12/2001, 44158/98).

HANDYSIDE v. THE UNITED KINGDOM (ECtHR 12/12/1976, 5493/72).
MÜLLER AND OTHERS v. SWITZERLAND (ECtHR 24/05/1988).
KAR AND OTHERS v. TURKRY (ECtHR 03/05/2007, 58756/00).
SIDIROPOULOS AND OTHERS v. GREECE (ECtHR 10/07/1998, 26695/95).
STANKOV AND THE UNITED MACEDONIAN ORGANISATION ILINDEN v. BULGARIA (ECtHR 02/10/2001, 29221/95).
THLIMMENOS v. GREECE (ECtHR 06/04/2000, 34369/97).
ULUSOY AND OTHERS v. TURKEY (ECtHR 03/05/2007, 34797/03).
VEREINIGUNG BILDENDER KÜNSTLER v. AUSTRIA (ECtHR 25/01/2007, 68354/01).
WINTERSTEIN AND OTHERS v. FRANCE (ECtHR 17/10/2013, 27013/07).

Access to Culture, Media, Information in the Digital Age

Paul de Hert, Brussels

The Meaning of 'Access' in the Human Rights Context

The relationship between 'access' and human rights is strained and in constant need of careful balancing. Conceivably, one's access limits the unhindered enjoyment of another's basic right. For example, while one has the right to real estate property, another's access (right of way) rights restrict such enjoyment. Patent rights, after all, only last for twenty years. Or, while one has the right of expression, (lawful) quoting limits the original thinkers' ideas. Or, one's right to research is, as all academics know too well by now, limited by the public's access rights to such research results. In other words, while human rights are at their core 'inward' looking, specifically designed to protect individuality, the act of 'access' performs essentially a social function: By definition access means participation into something that does not belong to the participant. Whether this participation ought to be encouraged or discouraged, granted or prohibited, and under which terms and conditions each time, this is exactly where the tension between the notion of access and human rights lies.

Of course, there is another category of human rights, the so-called positive or social human rights, where access resides in fact at the core of the right itself. In this case access constitutes the actual right, for example one's right to access education. Access to such public, non-proprietary goods poses no serious challenges. However, when access is requested to man-made, and owned, goods, such as the Internet, culture, science, or information, then the above conflict is raised once again: One's right to access is another's limitation of the right to fully enjoy a good he or she has created or lawfully owns.

An act of balance, as is so often the case in the field of human rights, is therefore needed in order to regulate this inherent tension. This balance needs to carefully assess and establish when access is transformed into intrusion or when the social good takes precedence over private interests. Even in cases that may appear at first sight harmless or in any event neutral and well-intentioned, for example access to culture, the need for identification of the contrasting interests remains: Although everybody would readily confess that public access to culture can only be good both for society and for creators, who self-evidently wish their work to be accessed, and used, by third parties, still questions may be raised as to, for example, the permitted acts of access (permitted reproductions) according to the perspective of the artist, his or her followers or, even, society. Or, doubts could be raised as to whether access to information, regardless whether personal or factual, needs to be unrestricted. Or, whether access to the Internet, where private companies pay the bills necessary for it to function properly, should be treated on an egalitarian basis (equal access to all) or on a meritocratic basis (whoever pays more gets better bandwidth). Given the inseparable connection between these questions and technological developments as well as modern lifestyle, this topic is practically inexhaustible. The brief analysis that follows will only attempt to identify some tensions falling within this field and, in this way, to demonstrate the complexity hiding behind such otherwise worthy causes and pursuits as access to culture, media and information.

Digitisation of Information; a Challenge for Human Rights, but Maybe the Solution Lies Therein

Particularly with regard to culture, information and the media, the qualitative change that occurred over the past few decades and transformed the notion of access refers to the digitisation of information. Works of art, cultural goods, artefacts, entire collections, rather than remaining idle in their place of origin or storage, have been reproduced electronically in an intangible yet accessible format. Inherent physical restrictions were thus raised: While for the past three thousand years of known human history individuals had to travel in order to access information or cultural goods, during the past thirty years this can be done from the comfort of their homes. The profound effect of digitisation on the notion of access hardly needs to be explained. Where the term was used in the past in order to describe at best local visiting rights of the few, after the digitisation of information the same right was granted to the masses. While the actual physical goods do maintain their value, and are the coveted acquisitions of museums and collectors across the globe, the term access is no longer used to describe the rights of visits to a museum, an archaeological site or a concert. Instead, today it is commonly used to describe the right of individuals to enjoy an electronic reproduction of a cultural good or other product of the human intellect whenever and in any way they please.

In addition to the above qualitative change, an equally important quantitative change was brought forward through the advent of the Internet. Digitised reproductions of cultural goods or other information would do little good to humanity if they had to be exchanged in the real world, by way of physical exchanges of the magnetic means upon which they are recorded. The Internet afforded to individuals and organisations the option to freely and immediately broadcast information to the whole of the world regardless of their place of residence. In this way already digitised information broke their local boundaries and were made available to anyone, anywhere on the globe. Moreover, the Internet dealt the final blow to the traditional distribution channels of these few categories of cultural goods (namely, books and music) that were *prima facie* unaffected by the digitisation of information described above. Individuals, although they actually never needed to travel in order to purchase a book or a music recording, are no longer dependent on the exhaustible resources and storage capacity of their local shopkeepers. Electronic commerce applications enable direct access, and immediate download, from any place in the world, crushing in this way any last trace of control publishers and other rights holders hoped to maintain over intellectual property goods.

The above two developments led to the well-known extreme of Internet piracy, namely the unlawful reproduction and mass sharing over the Internet of protected, proprietary material. At times these unlawful practices were attempted to be justified on the basis of such notions as public access. While an argument that would otherwise merit some analysis, the volume of these unlawful reproductions was such that established case law by now regards them as infringing the rights of rights holders and therefore prohibited. In the meantime, however, entire well-established industries, such as the music industry, were brought to their knees, presumably never to return to their former glory. The film industry these days faces more or less the same predicament. The only thing that keeps the traditional publishing (book) industry protected, for the time being at least, is that individuals are not accustomed to reading on screen. Technology has changed the way humans access and use culture and information; their right to access has exponentially grown to threaten the very reason of its existence, culture itself.

Internet Access (and Content Suppression)

The term 'Internet access' in the human rights context has a twofold meaning: access to the Internet and, once online, access to content on the Internet. With regard to the former, while several countries across the globe have introduced a (social, under the distinctions made above) basic right to access the Internet in their constitutions, still the right cannot yet be considered established. A number of reasons make this development unlikely. To begin with, the exact content of such a right may create confusion: what is actually meant by 'access to the Internet'? Does it include a state of the art Internet broadband connection for all? Or would even a dial-up connection availability suffice? Does it also include installing public Wi-Fi hotspots everywhere? And, in each case, at what price? Should all this be provided for free? For a reasonably low price? At market value? Even if these questions were resolved, still the basic question would remain to whom exactly is this right addressed. Is it addressed to the state that needs to take all necessary measures? This could be a potentially tricky question, given that the Internet market is primarily a private market and state intervention would border on competition distortion. Or, could this right be addressed to private parties (Internet providers) as well, enabling for instance employees to ask their employers for Internet access in their workplace regardless whether necessary while executing their work? This however would mean that a state's constitution awards rights, and places obligations, upon and between private parties, a legal theory ('Drittwirkung' theory) still not undisputed among legal scholars. Finally, some confusion may even exist as regard its beneficiaries: While it is clear that individuals will be its primary intended recipients, would that be a right also addressed to legal persons (corporations, non-governmental organisations, associations, foundations, etc.) as well? Or even, could telecommunications companies potentially profit from it, asking the state to make the necessary investments, and procure relevant public works, so as for this right to be effected? In view of the above confusion, while a worthy cause and well-discussed case, it is unlikely that the right of individuals to be provided with access to the Internet will be firmly established as a basic human right any time soon.

On the other hand, once online Internet users may (or may not) have a right to access Internet content. In this case the term Internet content denotes digital content published over the Internet. Such digital content usually includes software (all webpages and Internet services essentially constitute computer programs), text, pictures, music and video. It therefore remains to be seen whether in this case there exists a right of Internet users to access such content, and, if yes, under what terms and conditions.

Despite its origins and rhetoric, the Internet is a proprietary medium. Notwithstanding 'cable' technicalities (that however will be briefly examined below, under net neutrality) the Internet is essentially run, and belongs to, digital content providers. These can be anything from huge Internet social networks providers or search engine providers, to humble, simple users that upload a few webpages about themselves or about any specific topic over the Internet. In addition, one ought not forget that any single webpage or Internet site are essentially computer programs. Taken together, all these Internet publishers are the rights holders over the Internet. Do users have a right to access their content? Or are the publishers free to enjoy their proprietary rights unhindered, imposing any rules they please upon access to their content?

The simple reply to this question is that rights holders of property (proprietary) rights over the Internet enjoy more or less the same rights as these of the natural world: unhindered enjoyment of their (intellectual) property, except from some restrictions placed upon it in order to serve the, perceived, public good. Consequently, if seen from the users' perspective, a right of access to Internet content outside the license terms of rights holders exists only in these few cases where the law expressly grants it. In particular, access to Internet content is provided to Internet users by means of an 'end user license agreement'. This agreement is usually incorporated into the respective websites' terms and conditions. It regulates the manner under which any Internet user may access and use content (including the computer program itself) found on any specific Internet site. Any user action exceeding this limits is to be considered unlawful.

While the general rule is that an Internet user's right to access Internet content does not exist outside the borders of the respective license agreements, there are cases where the laws applicable each time grant to individuals a right to access regardless of the same license stipulations – or, for the same purposes, the rights holders' will. These are the cases, for instance, of limited reproductions or reproductions for educational purposes in the EU *sui generis* database right context; Or, access to the source code of computer programs for interoperability purposes, in the computer programs EU directive context. Under the same category of access rights would probably fall special notions in the copyright doctrine like 'fair use' or 'private copy'. In the same context, the recent right to data portability in the EU *General Data Protection Regulation* (in its Article 20) is aimed at providing to individuals (Internet users) with access to their profile information over Internet social networks in an accessible and machine-readable format in order for it to be transferable to other similar platforms. While the above are all cases of a right to access by Internet users, if seen from the reverse point of view, they constitute the only ones available, in the sense that whatever is not prescribed by law is not allowed (as regulated by the terms of the license imposed by the rights holders).

Internet content suppression turns the focus of the right to access Internet content to another realm, that of national security or criminal law. The Internet has become a potent medium of communication, directly affecting the lives of hundreds of millions of its users that use it daily for anything from entertainment to information or work. In this context, national governments across the globe frequently feel tempted, or obliged, to intervene on content made available on it. The purposes of such intervention may vary considerably to include anything from national security to prohibiting access to illegal content or even combatting Internet piracy. The means to accomplish an Internet content suppression effect could involve both legislative and technical measures. However, because such practices ultimately impede the possibility to access, receive or impart information and thus impose restrictions on an individual's right to freedom of expression, they need to be carefully balanced, the principle of proportionality (a necessary measure within a democratic society) being a useful tool to this end.

Net Neutrality

While the net neutrality discussion may sound technical and outside the borders of a human rights approach on culture, media and information, because it is intrinsically connected to the (right to) access the Internet, it is believed that brief mention ought to be made to it within the limits of this analysis. In short, the debate on net neutrality develops upon the telecommunications providers' complaint that, while it is them that provide and pay for the necessary infrastructure upon which the Internet runs (essentially, cable installation and operation), they are not compensated for their services; instead, it is Internet companies (the providers referred to above) that make the profit out of the Internet without paying anything for its necessary infrastructure. The debate culminates into the request by the complainants (the telecommunications companies) to be compensated for their services. Their preferred model is that of 'bandwidth prioritisation', meaning that they would be allowed to charge differently by users or content or application or protocol etc. Therefore, net neutrality denotes exactly the opposite, the undertaking by governments and providers that all Internet traffic be treated equally. Its counter-arguments range from basic human rights' line of thinking (there can be no scalable approach to a human right or, even in the case that such a status is not acknowledged to Internet access, a necessary instrument for the exercise of other human rights) to the important concerns raised by any other alternative (namely, that a scalable approach raises the question who chooses which content is made available to which individuals).

Regardless of the merits of each side's arguments, from a human rights point of view net neutrality is instrumental to individuals' access to culture, media and information. Keeping in mind that the Internet constitutes today the preferred, if not necessary, medium of dissemination of all relevant information, unhindered, unprejudiced access to it is imperative in order to warrant to individuals open passage to such information.

On the other hand, this does not necessarily mean that access to the Internet itself should be provided on an egalitarian assumption or in a non-scalable manner. While a worthy cause, equal access rights to all is conditional upon the, mostly private, actors involved in making it possible. Space for price differentiations may or may not be advisable, depending on each society's circumstances and particularities.

Within the EU the right to net neutrality (or, as per its own terms, the '*open Internet*') today is firmly established. Special legal provisions (Regulation 2120/2015), that came into effect on 30 April 2016, not only warrant to individuals access to the Internet content and services of their choice but also provide them with an enforceable right to this end. The EU approach to this matter is that no blocking or throttling of online content, applications and services is allowed within the EU. All traffic has to be treated equally, meaning without any paid prioritisation of traffic in the Internet access service. Exemptions to this rule are limited (three exhaustive cases: compliance with legal obligations; integrity of the network; congestion management in exceptional and temporary situations) and users are free to use their favourite apps no matter the offer to which they subscribe. Consequently, the discussion at least for the foreseeable future within the EU is decidedly closed, in favour of open, egalitarian access to the Internet, and the information it holds, to everybody.

Access to Information

The right to access information occupies a distinct sub-category within the above analysis on the strained relationship between the notion of access and human rights, because in this case 'information' is not necessarily to be perceived as proprietary. Although it is to be expected that information has been created by somebody, and that somebody owns it, variations to this basic model may be found in practice: for example, the ownership link may be weak by definition, for instance when the creator of information is the state, or ownership rights may have expired or may have been diminished by choice of their own holder. Each one of the above instances, in other words any relaxation in information's ownership regime, leaves space for development of an individual's right to access such information. Indeed, the discussion around a right to access information mostly evolves around the right to access governmental information (cultural information obviously constituting a subset of such information), that is usually effectuated through a relevant 'freedom of information act' that is ultimately connected with a 'right to know'.

From its part, the term 'information' itself may denote anything from simple, mundane data to highly sophisticated data usable only by experts. In addition, it may be made available in a variety of formats (electronic or paper constituting the basic distinction), whose usability may differ substantially and may ultimately affect gravelly the exercise of the right to access it. Finally, as outlined above, their proprietary status may differ, allowing certain (for example, household) but prohibiting other (for example, business) uses. This is why when talking of a right to access information special attention should be given to the particular circumstances accompanying it. Such modalities could also include a positive obligation of the state to provide information, including addressees such as vulnerable groups with reading or language problems.

Keeping the above distinctions in mind, the individual's right to access information is firmly established by now in the list of basic, fundamental human rights. As highlighted in the keyword analysis that follows, apart of course from Article 19 of the UDHR, the UN *Convention on Access to Information, Public Participation in Decision-making and Access to Justice in Environmental Matters* (Aarhus Convention) can be seen as the most powerful international legal regime concerning access to governmental information for everyone. It covers notably governmental information on 'cultural sites', which are defined in Article 1 of the UNESCO *World Heritage Convention*, 1972, and could indeed be a model for legal instruments covering freedom of information in other domains, such as culture and media. In Europe, the ECtHR has found that Article 10 of the ECHR, that broadly follows the wording of Article 19 of the UDHR, constitutes a principle right of access to governmental information for journalists, as well as researchers, and for non-governmental organisations. With regard to EU institutions, Article 15 TFEU secures a right of access to official documents for everyone in the framework of a general 'concept of openness'.

The benefits of providing efficient means and opportunities to individuals to exercise this right are substantial: among them democratic participation and understanding, redress of past harms, improved decision-making processes as well as protecting other fundamental human rights are listed. Cultural information, depending on its ownership status, may be found at the epicenter of such an individual right to access it. Individual participation in cultural life, as analysed in the relevant keyword analysis that follows, is dependent upon its access to information. If access is prohibited or disproportionately burdened, then culture becomes irrelevant to these individuals who may not profit from all related information.

REFERENCES:

Banisar, Davis: "The Right to Information in the Age of Information", in Jørgensen, Rikke Frank (ed.): *Human Rights in the Global Information Society*, Cambridge: MIT Press (2006).

Cheng HK; Bandyopadhyay, Subhajyoti and Guo, Hong: "The debate on net neutrality: A policy perspective", 22(1) *Information systems research* (2011) 60.

Currie, David P.: "Positive and Negative Constitutional Rights", 53(3)*University of Chicago Law Review* (1986).

Donnelly, Jack: *Universal Human Rights in Theory and Practice*, 3rd edn., Ithaca: Cornell University Press (2013).

Engle, Eric: "Third Party Effect of Fundamental Rights (Drittwirkung)", 5(2) *Hanse Law Review* (2009 (available at www.ssrn.com accessed 06/2016).

Frau-Meigs, Divina: *Assessing the impact of digitisation on access to culture and creation, aggregation and curation of content*, Moscow: Council of Europe background paper, Governance of Culture (2013).

McDonagh, Maeve: "The Right to Information in International Human Rights Law", 13(1) *Human Rights Law Review* (2013).

Papakonstantinou, Vagelis and de Hert, Paul:, *Legal Challenges Posed by Online Aggregation of Museum Content: The Cases Of Europeana and the Google Art Project*, SCRIPTed, Volume 9, Issue 3 (December 2012).

Tully Stephen: "A Human Right to Access the Internet? Problems and Prospects", 14(2) *Human Rights Law Review* (2014).

Van Dijk, Pieter and Van Hoof, G.J.H.: *Theory and Practice of the European Convention on Human Rights*, The Hague: Kluwer Law International (1998).

Wu, Tim: "Network Neutrality, Broadband Discrimination", 2 *Journal on telecommunications and high technology law* (2003).

MGM STUDIOS, INC v. GROKSTER LTD. (United States Supreme Court, 545 U.S. 913 (2005).

Rights and Protection of Social/Socio-cultural Groups

Federico Lenzerini, Siena

Rights of Social/Socio-cultural Groups: A Huge Challenge for International Human Rights Law

Article 2 of the UDHR proclaims that *all* human beings are entitled to human rights – including economic, social and cultural rights – 'without distinction of any kind, such as race, colour, sex, language, religion, political or other opinion, national or social origin, property, birth or other status'. Indeed, a very well-established principle of international human rights law prohibits any →Discrimination based on whatever status, as confirmed by the main pertinent international treaties, including the ICCPR, (Articles 2, 4 and 26), the ICESCR (Article 2(2)), the ECHR (Article 14), the *American Convention on Human Rights* (ACHR, Article 1), as well as the *African Charter on Human and Peoples' Rights* (ACHPR, Article 2). By effect of this principle, Social/Socio-cultural Groups are fully entitled to the same measure of enjoyment of human rights as all other members of the human society, including those belonging to the cultural majority living in a given society. In the real world, however, members of such groups, as well as the groups as such – intended as collectivities – are frequently victim of discriminatory practices, social exclusion and marginalisation, as well as attempts of homogenisation within the broader society. People who are 'different' have always been approached with suspicion and discriminatory attitude by the majority, for a plethora of reasons, but mainly due to fear of diversity. As stated by Thomas Szasz, 'the plague of mankind is the fear and rejection of diversity (...) The belief that there is only one right way to live, only one right way to regulate religious, political, sexual, medical affairs is the root cause of the greatest threat to man'. Furthermore, it may be asserted that the requirement of '*mono-cultural* or homogeneous nationhood' is inherent in the Westphalian conception of 'state' (Okafor 2000, p. 73); this characteristic of modern nation-states obviously discourages the flow of minority or non-conformist cultural models. This reality is further exacerbated by what has been defined as 'the single voice organising principle of international relations' (Franck 1995, p. 481), on account of which the interests of Social/Socio-cultural Groups not corresponding to the majority of a state population are only very rarely represented in international fora.

In some instances, states even try to deny the existence of minority Social/Socio-cultural Groups. For example, in ratifying the ICCPR in 1980, the government of France made a declaration regarding Article 27 of the Covenant – which establishes the right of members of ethnic, religious or linguistic minorities to enjoy their own culture, to profess and practise their own religion, or to use their own language – which reads as follows: '(i)n the light of article 2 of the Constitution of the French Republic, the French Government declares that article 27 is not applicable so far as the Republic is concerned'. An identical declaration was made by France in 1990 when ratifying the 1989 *Convention on the Rights of the Child*, with respect to its Article 30 (having a content very similar to that of Article 27 ICCPR). These declarations were grounded on the assumption that, since the French Constitution prohibits any distinction between citizens based on origin, race or religion, no minorities would exist in France (Donders 2010, p. 26), while in effect more than five million people permanently living in France and its overseas territories belong to ethnic minorities, mainly of North African, Sub-Saharan and Turkish origin (see 'France's crisis of national identity', *Independent*, 25 November 2009). Similarly, when voting for the adoption of the *United Nations Declaration on the Rights of Indigenous Peoples* (UNDRIP) in 2007, before the General Assembly, some Asian countries declared that, while they were in favour of the UNDRIP in principle, the Declaration would not be applicable to them, on the basis of the misleading stance that no indigenous peoples exist in their territories (see ILA, 2010)).

Another common approach concerning minority Social/Socio-cultural Groups consists, as previously noted, in the attempt of homogenising them within the dominant society. Such an approach was epitomised by the 1957 ILO *Convention (No. 107) concerning the Protection and Integration of Indigenous and Other Tribal and Semi-Tribal Populations in Independent Countries*, which, having the purpose of assuring the progressive integration of the populations concerned into their respective national communities (see seventh recital of the Preamble), pursued their assimilation within the dominant society and, *a fortiori*, the extinction of their own distinctive cultural identity (see →Genocide (Cultural G.)). Fortunately, such an approach was later reversed by adopting the 1989 ILO *Convention (No. 169) concerning Indigenous and Tribal Peoples in Independent Countries* and the UNDRIP in 2007. This notwithstanding, states, in various parts of the world, still continue to pursue policies of marginalisation and attempted assimilation of →Indigenous peoples.

Virtually all Social/Socio-cultural Groups – especially vulnerable and disadvantaged groups – are the target, in certain parts of the globe, of practices which are discriminatory or, at the very least, at odds with internationally recognised human rights standards. The list of examples is endless. For instance, 'in many African societies, children are considered to be a 'gift of ancestors and God'. It is the responsibility of every member of the society to nurture them and ensure their well-being. This nurturing, however, is not devoid of what other societies would regard as mistreatment. Beginning from childhood, for example, some societies cut off the small finger of the child while others perform facial scarification as rites of incorporation to the broader society or for curative reasons. The notions of child abuse depend upon a culturally validated definition of what constitutes 'abuse', and the ensemble of everyday activities and ideologies of a particular ethnic group or class tend to vary in the way that they perceive child abuse' (Guma and Henda 2004, p. 98).

As previously emphasised, in many cases harmful practices against Social/Socio-cultural Groups are triggered by a common sense of fear for what is 'different'. This happens, for example, with respect to albino people, especially in Sub-Saharan Africa. In Tanzania, in particular, where the scale of albinism is higher than in any other part of the world, ranging at a rate of one in every 1,429 births (Cruz-Inigo, Ladizinski and Sethi 2011, p. 79), there are a number of common myths and misconceptions regarding albinism, including the beliefs that parts of albino bodies are a necessary ingredient for witchdoctor potions, that albinos and their mothers are possessed by evil spirits, that the devil stole the original child and replaced it with an albino, that albinism is contagious and spread through touching, as well as that albinos are housed by ghosts of European colonists (ibid., p. 80). Albino people are therefore the target of frequent killings and attacks, including mutilations, violence, rape and attempted abductions. In the last few years alone 166 killings and 273 attacks have been reported in 25 African countries, although the actual number of killings and attacks is most likely much higher as many cases are never reported or documented (see "Reported Attacks of Persons with Albinism", 2016). Most of the killings are perpetrated 'with a view to using (the victims') body parts for ritual purposes' (see UN Human Rights Council, Preliminary study on the situation of human rights of persons living with albinism, UN Doc. A/HRC/AC/13/CRP.1, 30 July 2014, para. 10), on account of 'beliefs and myths, heavily influenced by superstition (…) (which) are centuries old and are present in cultural attitudes and practices around the world' (see Human Rights Council, Persons with albinism, UN Doc. A/HRC/24/57, 12 September 2013, para. 15). Cases of human sacrifices of albino children accused of witchcraft are also reported (see UNICEF, 2010).

In other cases, harmful practices perpetrated to the detriment of Social/Socio-cultural Groups are the effect of cultural traditions which, although formally prohibited by domestic law, continue to be very common among local populations, especially in rural areas. For instance, honour killing is a traditional practice which originated over 2,000 years ago and continues to be carried out in many areas, especially Muslim countries or countries where significant enclaves of Muslim people live, since, although it predates Islam, it is perceived as a sort of religious dictate. Women 'are killed brutally by brothers, fathers, uncles, husbands or other male and even female relatives on the grounds that their actual or perceived behaviour has undermined the authority of men and tarnished the family honour. Such behaviour could be illicit relationships, extra marital affairs, speaking to unrelated men, desiring to choose one's spouse or marrying a man of one's choice, refusal to accept a forced marriage, divorcing an abusive husband, loss of virginity or bringing shame on the family by being raped, all actions which threaten men's control of women's behaviour and sexuality. Despite the availability of legal measures to punish these acts of violence, killers are rarely punished and may, in fact, be treated by the community as heroes who have defended the honour of their families, while women are denied their right to life' (ESCAP, Gender and Development Discussion Paper Series No. 21, p. 22). Other unfortunate examples of harmful practices supposedly grounded on religion include female genital mutilation – which is known to be practiced in at least 25 countries in Africa, in some Asian countries (particularly Indonesia, Malaysia and Yemen), in addition to some European states and Australia among immigrant communities (Office of the High Commissioner of Human Rights, Fact Sheet No. 23, p. 4) – and the Devadasi system, still common in

South India. The latter is a practice consisting in dedicating a woman to a deity through a ritual marriage. The term 'devadasi' literally means 'slave of God', as the women concerned devote their entire life in the service of the god and the temple (see Gupta 2013, p. 1). While the devadasis originally enjoyed a privileged position granting them religious and economic benefits, as well as social honour, the practice gradually evolved into forced prostitution and sex work in favour of the priest administering the temple and the other men of the community (Ibid., p. 2; Anti-Slavery International 2007, p. 2).

These examples – which represent just a drop in the ocean of existing cultural practices harmful for Social/Socio-cultural Groups – show how the protection of such groups should be a primary concern for international human rights law. Conversely, it is important to emphasise that, due to their cultural specificity and social vulnerability, those groups have special cultural and social needs which must be adequately addressed in the context of the implementation and enforcement of human rights standards (see Lenzerini 2014). Therefore, while the members of Social/Socio-cultural Groups are of course entitled to the full enjoyment of all categories of human rights and freedoms as recognised by international law – to the same extent of any other human being – cultural rights play in their respect a fundamental role. In fact, effective enjoyment of cultural rights represents an essential condition for preserving their existence as distinct groups, for perpetuating their own distinctive cultural identity, as well as, *a fortiori*, for ensuring in their favour the realisation of all other human rights.

Main Answers and Trends Developed by the International Community in Most Recent Decades

In the context of human rights law, Social/Socio-cultural Groups trigger three main problematics. First, since these groups are the main bearers of cultural diversity – which, according to Article 1 of the 2001 *UNESCO Universal Declaration on Cultural Diversity*, 'is as necessary for humankind as biodiversity is for nature' – and have special cultural needs, human rights standards must be 'adapted' to the extent possible so as to cover such needs. Additionally, and more in general, they are entitled to the enjoyment of cultural rights, as generally recognised by international law. Secondly, members of Social/Socio-cultural Groups need to be protected from harmful cultural practices which, while in some cases are perpetrated by people from outside the Social/Socio-cultural Group, in other circumstances directly emanate from the same social or cultural group of which they are part. Last but not least, another priority of the international community should be that of protecting these groups against marginalisation and social exclusion. In the last few decades, international law has positively evolved to effectively address these problematics.

As regards the first point, the evolution of international human rights law towards the recognition and enforcement of *collective rights* (→ Peoples' rights) is of particular significance. This has happened not only through *directly recognising* such rights in human rights instruments (as made in particular by Articles 19–24 ACHPR), but also, most notably, in an *indirect manner*, through an evolutionary and extensive interpretation of rules originally construed to protect individual rights (see Lenzerini 2016). This practice is today widespread among human rights monitoring bodies and many pertinent examples could be used. For instance, in interpreting Article 27 ICCPR, the Human Rights Committee has affirmed that, '(a)lthough the rights protected under Article 27 are individual rights, they depend in turn on the ability of the minority group to maintain its culture, language or religion. Accordingly, positive measures by states may also be necessary to protect the identity of a minority (...) (t)he protection of these rights is directed to ensure the survival and continued development of the cultural, religious and social identity of the minorities concerned' (see General Comment No. 23, 1994, paras. 6.2 and 9). Similarly, the Inter-American Court of Human Rights (IACtHR) has interpreted Article 21 ACHR – concerning the right of everyone to the use and enjoyment of his property – as covering the traditional collective possession by indigenous peoples of their ancestral lands and resources located therein (see, among the many pertinent judgments, [CASE OF THE MAYAGNA (SUMO) AWAS TINGI COMMUNITY v. NICARAGUA, 2001; CASE OF THE YAKYE AXA INDIGENOUS COMMUNITY v. PARAGUAY, 2005; CASE OF THE XÁKMOK KÁSEK INDIGENOUS COMMUNITY v. PARAGUAY, 2010]).

Evolutionary interpretation also represents the tool through which human rights monitoring bodies adapt existing standards to the cultural needs of Social/Socio-cultural Groups, 'filling' them with a content adequate to make the enjoyment of rights effective under the perspective of the individuals and communities concerned (see Lenzerini 2014). A formidable example of this approach is again offered by the practice of the IACtHR. In particular, in a case concerning a massacre perpetrated by the army of Suriname in the N'djuka Maroon village of Moiwana in 1986, the Court found that the fact of depriving the surviving members of the community of the possibility to honor and bury the remains of their loved ones in accordance with fundamental norms of N'djuka culture amounted to a violation of the right to humane treatment contemplated by Article 5 ACHR. This finding was reached through attributing value to the cultural perceptions of the community concerned as an element worth protecting. In fact, the situation created by the government of Suriname gave rise to one of the greatest sources of culturally-determined suffering for the Moiwana community members, because, '(i)f the various death rituals are not performed according to N'djuka tradition, it is considered a profound moral transgression, which will not only anger the spirit of the individual who died, but also may offend other ancestors of the community (...) This leads to a number of 'spiritually-caused illnesses' that become manifest as actual physical maladies and can potentially affect the entire natural lineage' [CASE OF THE MOIWANA COMMUNITY v. SURINAME, 2005, para. 99].

Regarding the related aspect of recognition of cultural rights, members of Social/Socio-cultural Groups are obviously entitled to the full enjoyment of cultural rights as generally recognised by international rules and instruments in force, including Articles 22 and 27(1) UDHR, Article 27 ICCPR, Article 15 ICESCR, Article 26 ACHR, Article 14 of the 1988 *Additional Protocol to the American Convention on Human Rights in the Area of Economic, Social and Cultural Rights*, Articles 17(2) and 22

ACHPR. In addition, specific provisions on cultural rights exist concerning individual Social/Socio-cultural Groups. For instance, Article 13(c) of the 1979 *Convention on the Elimination of All Forms of Discrimination Against Women* (CEDAW) provides for the right of all women, on a basis of equality with men, 'to participate in recreational activities, sports and all aspects of cultural life'. More generally, Article 5 of the 1994 *Inter-American Convention on the Prevention, Punishment and Eradication of Violence Against Women* establishes that every woman is entitled to the 'free and full exercise of her', *inter alia*, cultural rights, also recognising that 'violence against women prevents and nullifies the exercise of these rights'. As regards children, the 1989 *Convention on the Rights of the Child* (CRC) deals with cultural rights at Articles 4, 29 (establishing that child education shall be directed to, *inter alia*, the development of the child's own cultural identity), 30 and 31 (providing for the right of the child to participate fully in cultural and artistic life). Similar provisions are included in Articles 11(2)(c) and 12 of the 1990 *African Charter on the Rights and Welfare of the Child*. Also with respect to children, the Human Rights Committee has held that, '(i)n the cultural field, every possible measure should be taken to foster the development of their personality and to provide them with a level of education that will enable them to enjoy the rights recognised in the Covenant, particularly the right to freedom of opinion and expression' (see General Comment No. 17, 1989, para. 3). A wide variety of collective rights is also contemplated by the 2006 *African Youth Charter* (see →Youth), ranging from the right of young people belonging to ethnic, religious and linguistic marginalised groups or youth of indigenous origin 'to enjoy their own culture, freely practice their own religion or to use their own language in community with other members of their group' (Article 2(3)), to the obligations of states parties to ensure that the education of young people is directed to the preservation and strengthening of positive African morals, traditional values and cultures and the development of national and African identity and pride (Article 13(3)), as well as to promote and protect the morals and traditional values recognised by the community (Article 20). Cultural rights are also provided for by the 1990 *International Convention on the Protection of the Rights of All Migrant Workers and Members of Their Families* (Articles 17, 31, 40, 43, 45) and by the 2007 *Convention on the Rights of Persons with Disabilities* (Articles 4(2) and 30). The latter are also the object of specific cultural-rights-related provisions included in the 1999 *European Social Charter (Revised)* – which, at Article 15(3), establishes that their full social integration and participation in the life of the community must be promoted, 'in particular through measures (...) aiming to (...) enabl(e) access to transport, housing, cultural activities and leisure' – and in the African Charter on the Rights and Welfare of the Child, whose Article 13(2) affirms the right of children who are mentally or physically disabled to have effective access to training, preparation for employment and recreation opportunities in a manner conducive to allow their fullest possible cultural development (see →Disabilities (Persons with D.)). As for →Older persons, they are entitled by Article 23 of the European Social Charter (Revised) to social protection, implying, among other things, the right to play an active part in social and cultural life.

Equivalent rules are established by Article 25 of the 2000 *Charter of Fundamental Rights of the European Union* and Article 21 of the 2015 *Inter-American Convention on Protecting the Human Rights of Older Persons*. Special attention is dedicated to the aspect of cultural rights by international instruments concerning minorities and indigenous peoples. With respect to the former, Article 27 ICCPR and Article 30 CRC contemplate the right of members of ethnic, religious or linguistic minorities to enjoy their own culture, to profess and practise their own religion, or to use their own language, in general terms and for children respectively. The same right is provided for by Article 2 of the 1992 UN *Declaration on the Rights of Persons Belonging to National or Ethnic, Religious and Linguistic Minorities*, also recognising their right to participate effectively in cultural, religious, social, economic and public life; other relevant provisions of the Declaration are Article 1, promoting the identity of such minorities, and Article 4, establishing the duty of states to take measures 'to create favourable conditions to enable persons belonging to minorities to express their characteristics and to develop their culture, language, religion, traditions and customs', as well as to learn their mother tongue or to have instruction in their mother tongue. Similarly, the 1995 Council of Europe's *Framework Convention for the Protection of National Minorities*, at Article 5, requires states parties to 'promote the conditions necessary for persons belonging to national minorities to maintain and develop their culture, and to preserve the essential elements of their identity, namely their religion, language, traditions and cultural heritage', while Article 15 establishes that the 'conditions necessary for the effective participation of persons belonging to national minorities in cultural, social and economic life and in public affairs' must be created (see →National Minorities). As far as indigenous peoples are concerned, the provisions of Article 27 ICCPR and Article 30 CRC also extend to them, although under international law minorities and indigenous peoples are two well-distinguished entities; the applicability of Article 27 ICCPR to indigenous peoples has been established by the uniform practice of the Human Rights Committee (see, e.g., General Comment No. 23, paras. 3.2 and 7), while the text of Article 30 CRC explicitly refers to 'persons of indigenous origin' in addition to minority members. Obviously, since cultural rights attain special importance for indigenous peoples, international legal instruments specifically devoted to them make extensive reference to such rights. This is the case of Articles 2, 4, 5, 7, 10, and 13 (the latter recognising the inextricable connection between cultural identity and indigenous peoples' traditional lands) of the 1989 ILO *Convention (No. 169) concerning Indigenous and Tribal Peoples in Independent Countries*, as well as of several provisions of the UNDRIP, particularly Articles 5, 8, 11, 12, 14, 15, 16, 24, 26, 31, 36.

With regards to the issue of protection of members of Social/Socio-cultural Groups from harmful cultural practices, the urgency of developing adequate action in this respect is emphasised by many human rights instruments and monitoring bodies. Starting with the UDHR, its Article 25 generally affirms the right of everyone to security 'in the event of unemployment, sickness, disability, widowhood, old age', as well as that motherhood and childhood are entitled to special care and assistance. The Committee on Economic, Social and Cultural Rights has found that states have the duty to protect women and children from harmful traditional cultural practices affecting their health (see General Comment No. 14 (2000), paras. 21 and 22), as well as to 'to prevent third parties from coercing women to undergo traditional practices, e.g. →Female Genital Mutilation; and to take measures to protect all vulnerable or marginalised groups of society, in particular women, children, adolescents and older persons' (ibid., para. 35). Failure 'to discourage the continued observance of harmful traditional medical or cultural practices' constitutes a violation of the right to the highest attainable standard of health provided for by Article 12 ICESCR (ibid., para. 51). The Committee has also held that cultural diversity cannot be invoked 'to infringe upon human rights guaranteed by international law, nor to limit their scope' (see General Comment No. 21 (2009), para. 18), and that applying limitations to the right of everyone to take part in cultural life established by Article 15(1)(a) ICESCR 'may be necessary in certain circumstances, in particular in the case of negative practices, including those attributed to customs and traditions, that infringe upon other human rights' (ibid., para. 19). When a state party to the ICESCR fails 'to take steps to combat practices harmful to the well-being of a person or group of persons (...) including those attributed to customs and traditions, such as female genital mutilation and allegations of the practice of witchcraft', a breach of Article 15(1)(a) occurs. The prohibition of harmful traditional cultural practices is also established by all main conventions concerning women and children, including Article 5(a) CEDAW, Article 6 of the Inter-American Convention on the Prevention, Punishment and Eradication of Violence Against Women, Articles 2(2) and 5 of the 2003 *Protocol of the African Charter on Human and Peoples' Rights on the Rights of Women in Africa* (all of them requiring states parties to take all appropriate measures to modify the social and cultural patterns based on the idea of the inferiority or the superiority of either of the sexes, or on stereotyped roles for women and men), Articles 12 and 42 of the 2011 *Council of Europe Convention on preventing and combating violence against women and domestic violence* (the latter prohibiting that 'in criminal proceedings initiated following the commission of any of the acts of violence covered by the scope of this Convention, culture, custom, religion, tradition or so-called 'honour' shall not be regarded as justification for such acts'), Article 24(3) CRC and Articles 1(3) and 21 of the *African Charter on the Rights and Welfare of the Child* (the latter making explicit reference to female genital mutilations and circumcision). Harmful traditional practices are also prohibited by Article 39(2)(d) of the 2004 *Arab Charter on Human Rights* and Articles 20(1)(a) and 25 of the *African Youth Charter*. The Committee on the Rights of the Child, in its General Comment of 2009 on indigenous children, stated that 'cultural practices (...) under no circumstances may be justified if deemed prejudicial to the child's dignity, health and development. Should harmful practices be present, *inter alia* early marriages and female genital mutilation, the state party should work together with indigenous communities to ensure their eradication' (para. 22). The Committee on the Elimination of Racial Discrimination has taken the position that harmful traditional practices, including caste discrimination, caste-based or religious-based prostitution, female genital mutilation or marriage customs, amount to racial discrimination (see UN Doc. E/C.12/40/15, 9 May 2008, paras. 18–19). Also of significance, the European Court of Human Rights has affirmed that '(i)t is not in dispute that subjecting a child or adult to F(emale)G(enital)M(utilation) would amount to ill-(inhuman or degrading) treatment contrary to Article 3' ECHR (see Decision as to the Admissibility of Application no. 43408/08 by ENITAN PAMELA IZEVBEKHAI AND OTHERS AGAINST IRELAND, 17 May 2011, para. 73). Finally, as regards particular categories of Social/Socio-cultural Groups, the obligation to prevent and suppress harmful cultural practices is provided for, *inter alia*, by Article 8 of the 2007 *Convention on the Rights of Persons with Disabilities* and Article 4 of the UN *Declaration on the Rights of Persons Belonging to National or Ethnic, Religious and Linguistic Minorities*.

The third main problem relating to Social/Socio-cultural Groups consists of ensuring special protection for these groups against marginalisation and social exclusion. This applies in particular to *disadvantaged* and *vulnerable groups*. Under a broad perspective, *all* Social/Socio-cultural Groups considered in this section are either disadvantaged and/or vulnerable. In fact, just to mention a few examples, women (see →Gender equality), →Children, →Migrants, →Refugees, victims of human trafficking, →Indigenous Peoples, →Older Persons and →LGBT are actually disadvantaged and/or vulnerable groups within the society, for a number of reasons which include poverty, inherent fragility or poor health conditions, insufficient 'political' representativeness in the society's decision-making, intolerance or persistence of social and cultural patterns resulting in their discrimination. As seen, the Committee on Economic, Social and Cultural Rights has recommended that states 'take measures to protect all vulnerable or marginalised groups of society, in particular women, children, adolescents and older persons' (see General Comment No. 14 (2000), para. 35). At the same time, it is true that, also *within* the groups just mentioned there are some persons who are particularly disadvantaged or vulnerable. The fact that both perspectives are valid is demonstrated by the definition of 'vulnerable groups' provided by the European Quality Assurance in Vocational Education and Training (EQAVET), according to which they are '(g)roups that experience a higher risk of poverty and social exclusion than the general population. Ethnic minorities, migrants, disabled people, the homeless, those struggling with substance abuse, isolated elderly people and children all often face difficulties that can lead to further social exclusion, such as low levels of education and unemployment or underemployment'. Indeed, while, for instance, older persons may be considered as a whole a vulnerable group, 'isolated elderly people' are a particularly vulnerable category within a generally vulnerable group. Similarly, for example, ill or disabled children may be considered the most vulnerable of the vulnerable, who are children generally speaking. The same can be said with regard to pregnant women *vis-à-vis* to women in general. The situation of these groups is addressed by international human rights law taking into account both perspectives, depending on the circumstances, and, particularly, on what is concretely necessary to protect the relevant groups from marginalisation and social exclusion. In general, as emphasised by the Committee on the Elimination of Racial Discrimination, vulnerable (and disadvantaged) groups must be protected against discrimination through 'alleviating and remedying disparities in the enjoyment of human rights (...) (which) include but are not confined to persistent or structural disparities and *de facto* inequalities resulting from the circumstances of history that continue to deny to vulnerable groups and individuals the advantages essential for the full development of the human personality' (see General Recommendation No. 32 (2009), para. 22). Many human rights instruments include specific provisions concerning disadvantaged and vulnerable people. For instance, Article 30 of the *European Social Charter (Revised)* provides for the right to protection against poverty and social exclusion, referring in particular to persons, and their families, who live, or risk living in a situation of social exclusion or poverty. With respect to women, CEDAW includes specific provisions concerning, *inter alia*, rural women (Article 14) and women in status of pregnancy or maternity (Articles 11 and 12). Even more advanced, the *Protocol of the African Charter on Human and Peoples' Rights on the Rights of Women in Africa* requires states parties to adopt special measures for the protection of women in armed conflicts (Article 11), widows (Article 20), elderly women (Article 22), women with disabilities (Article 23) and women in distress (Article 24). Concerning children, the CRC addresses with *ad hoc* provisions children temporarily or permanently deprived of their family environment (Article 20), adopted children (Article 21), refugee children (Article 22), mentally or physically disabled children (Article 23), children belonging to minorities or indigenous peoples (Article 30), children deprived of their liberty (Article 37), children victim of armed conflict (Article 38), children victim of neglect, exploitation, abuse or ill-treatment (Article 39). Similarly, the *African Charter on the Rights and Welfare of the Child* provides for the obligation to adopt special measures in favour of, *inter alia*, handicapped children (Article 13), children victim of armed conflicts (Article 22), refugee children (Article 23), adopted children (Article 24), children separated from parents (Article 25), children of imprisoned mothers (Article 30). Also, the *African Youth Charter* stipulates the right of young people belonging to ethnic, religious and linguistic marginalised groups or youth of indigenous origin 'to enjoy their own culture, freely practice their own religion or to use their own language in community with other members of their group' (Article 2(3)). As regards migrants, Article 17 of the *International Convention on the Protection of the Rights of All Migrant Workers and Members of Their Families* devotes special attention to such workers and members of their families who are deprived of their liberty, to be treated with humanity and with respect for the inherent dignity of the human person and for their cultural identity, while the 2000 *Protocol to Prevent, Suppress and Punish Trafficking in Persons Especially Women and Children*, supplementing the *United Nations Convention against Transnational Organized Crime*, at Article 6, contemplates a detailed series of measures to be applied for ensuring assistance to and protection of victims of trafficking in persons. Last but not least, the 2007 *Convention on the Rights of Persons with Disabilities* is to be mentioned, as an instrument dealing in its entirety with a disadvantaged and vulnerable group.

The Way Forward: Policy Issues and Recommendations

The existence of such a huge amount of instruments and provisions concerning Social/Socio-cultural Groups is an encouraging sign of the positive evolution of international law towards their effective protection. However, having rules written on paper alone is not enough, if these rules are not effectively implemented and enforced in the real world. Generally speaking, effective implementation is the most important part of human rights protection, but also the most problematic one. With respect to Social/Socio-cultural Groups, it is an ongoing but rather slow process, which is progressing but needs continuous fuel and especially a cultural change within the civil society. This change should be aimed at establishing a sympathetic social and 'environmental' background which may allow the promotion of the effective integration of such groups in the society at large, and eliminate bad attitudes and discrimination against them. Indeed, discrimination suffered by Social/Socio-cultural Groups and their members translates into a plethora of different negative attitudes and harmful practices which may only be effectively and stably removed through developing a culture of appreciation for diversity, tolerance and mutual understanding among different communities and groups (see Lenzerini 2007). As stressed by the Committee on the Elimination of Racial Discrimination in 2012 in its Concluding observations concerning Israel, 'in addressing issues that affect various vulnerable population groups, the State party [has to make] it quite clear, in its discourse and its action, that it has the political will to promote understanding, tolerance and friendship between individuals irrespective of their origin' (see Un Doc. CERD/C/ISR/CO/14-16, para. 23). Similarly, Article 6 of the *Framework Convention for the Protection of National Minorities* emphasises the need to 'encourage a spirit of tolerance and intercultural dialogue and take effective measures to promote mutual respect and understanding and co-operation among all persons living on their territory, irrespective of those persons' ethnic, cultural, linguistic or religious identity, in particular in the fields of education, culture and the media'. Therefore, in addition to further strengthening the normative apparatus concerning human rights of Social/Socio-cultural Groups, it is especially important to promote a cultural change within all the world's societies, leading people to perceive the positive value of the diversity embodied in the distinctive identity of those groups, so as to allow them to be fully integrated within the society in relation to all aspects of their life, including full enjoyment of cultural and other human rights.

REFERENCES:

Anti-Slavery International: "Ritual slavery practices in India – Devadasi, Jogini and Mathamma", (July 2007) (available at www.antislavery.org accessed 4/2016).

Bisaz, Corsin: *The Concept of Group Rights in International Law*, Leiden–Boston: Nijhoff (2012).

Cruz-Inigo, Andres E., Ladizinski, Barry and Sethi, Aisha: "Albinism in Africa: Stigma, Slaughter and Awareness Campaigns", 29 *Dermatol Clin* (2011) 79.

De La Vega, Connie, Zeleke, Kokeb and Wilch, Esther: "The Promotion of Economic, Social and Cultural Rights of Vulnerable Groups in Africa pursuant to Treaty Obligations: CRC, CEDAW, CERD, & CRPD", 14 *Washington University Global Studies Law Review* (2015) 213.

Donders, Yvonne: "Do Cultural Diversity and Human Rights make a Good Match?", 61 *International Social Science Journal* (2010) 15.

Economic and Social Commission for Asia and the Pacific (ESCAP): "Harmful Traditional Practices in Three Countries of South Asia: culture, human rights and violence against women", Gender and Development Discussion Paper Series No. 21 (available at www.unescapsdd.org accessed 4/2016).

Franck, Thomas M.: *Fairness in International Law and Institutions*, Oxford: Clarendon Press (1995).

Guma, Mthobeli and Henda, Nomvo: "The Socio-cultural Context of Child Abuse: A Betrayal of Trust", in Linda Richter, Andrew Dawes and Craig-Higson Smith (eds.): *Sexual abuse of young children in southern Africa*, Cape Town: HSRC Press (2004).

Gupta, Ishita: "Perceptions of Prostitution: The Devadasi System in India", (30 April 2013) (available at www.academia.edu accessed 4/2016).

ILA Committee on the Rights of Indigenous Peoples: "The Hague Conference (2010) Report", (2010) (available at www.ila-hq.org accessed 05/2016).

Ippolito, Francesca and Iglesias Sánchez, Sara: (eds.), *Protecting Vulnerable Groups. The European Human Rights Framework*, Oxford: Hart Publishing (2015).

Lenzerini, Federico: "Fostering Tolerance and Mutual Understanding among Peoples", in Abdulqawi Yusuf (ed.): *Standard-setting in UNESCO, volume I: normative action in education, science and culture, essays in commemoration of the Sixtieth Anniversary of UNESCO*, Paris/Leiden: Nijhoff (2007).

Lenzerini, Federico: *The Culturalization of Human Rights Law*, Oxford: Oxford University Press (2014).

Lenzerini, Federico: "The Safeguarding of Collective Cultural Rights through the Evolutionary Interpretation of Human Rights Treaties and Their Translation into Principles of Customary International Law", in Andrzej Jakubowski (ed.): *Cultural Rights as Collective Rights: An International Law Perspective*, Leiden: Brill (2016) forthcoming.

Lichfield, John: "France's Crisis of Identity", *The Independent* (25 November 2009) (available at www.independent.co.uk accessed 05/2016).

Okafor, Obiora Chinedu: *Re-Defining Legitimate Statehood. International Law and State Fragmentation in Africa*, The Hague: Kluwer Law International (2000).

UN, Office of the High Commissioner of Human Rights, "Fact Sheet No. 23, Harmful Traditional Practices Affecting the Health of Women and Children", (available at www.ohchr.org accessed 4/2016).

Under the Same Sun, "Reported Attacks of Persons with Albinism (PWA) – 1 Page Summary", (17 February 2016), (available at www.underthesamesun.com accessed 04/2016).

UNICEF, "Children Accused of Witchcraft: An anthropological study of contemporary practices in Africa", 2010 (available at www.unicef.org accessed 4/2016).

Freedom of Religion or Belief

Heiner Bielefeldt, Erlangen

The Human Rights Approach to Handling Religious Diversity

Safeguarding everyone's right to freedom of religion or belief is not the only conceivable way of shaping peaceful coexistence in religiously diverse societies. One historical alternative was the search for a theological or philosophical common denominator seemingly running through all major religions or denominations. The idea promoted by Nicolaus Cusanus shortly after the fall of Constantinople that 'within the variety of rites, there is only *one* religion' (*religio una in rituum varietate*), foreshadowed the various attempts undertaken by philosophers of the European Enlightenment to establish a 'natural religion', which they thought should prevail over any remaining denominational differences. In the words of Immanuel Kant, 'the concept of a divine will, determined merely according to purely moral laws, allows us to think of only *one* religion which is purely moral, just as *only one* God'. Another traditional way of coming to terms with religious pluralism was the politics of limited tolerance. It can be traced back to ancient empires, like the Persian Empire or the Roman Empire, which as a matter of prudence accommodated the deities and rituals of subjected peoples. A politics of limited tolerance furthermore characterised the way in which the Ottoman Empire treated religious minorities, while unequivocally upholding the hegemony of Islam. After a century of traumatising confessional wars in the wake of the Protestant Reformation, the 1648 Westphalian Peace and other early modern European Peace Conferences likewise established regimes of limited tolerance, which conceded minorities certain spaces under the hegemony of Catholicism or Protestantism, respectively. This way of handling diversity prevailed for a long time. The *Act of Tolerance* issued in 1781 by Emperor Joseph II, still upheld the Catholic monopoly of public worship while permitting the followers of other religions or denominations to practice their faith in private.

The right to freedom of thought, conscience, religion or belief (henceforth in short: freedom of religion or belief) is frequently mistaken as a modern version of the two attitudes just sketched out. However, it differs conceptually from both of them. Rather than searching for a common religious or philosophical denominator, freedom of religion or belief does not intend to turn existing differences into a mere 'variety of rites', to cite Cusanus. Instead, it appreciates religious and belief-related diversity as an expression of human freedom. Accordingly, freedom of religion or belief aims at empowering human beings to freely find their own ways within the vast area of religious (or non-religious) convictions, conscientious positions, community-based practices, religious socialisation processes etc. Far from making the world ideologically uniform, freedom of religion or belief brings to the fore the existing and emerging diversity of religions and beliefs, provided they are freely expressed by human beings who are the holders of this human right. Moreover, in contrast to the politics of tolerance, freedom of religion or belief does not start from a hegemonic confessional viewpoint. While the politics of tolerance typically granted minorities certain rights under the auspices of a predominant religion, freedom of religion or belief represents a universal right to which everyone can lay claim to on the *basis of equality* and non-discrimination. And instead of entitling the government to define those minorities who would benefit from religious tolerance, the starting point is the religious and belief-related *self-understandings* of human beings – and indeed all of them – which the state is supposed first of all to respect.

Freedom of religion or belief follows the logic of the human rights approach generally, which has been summed up succinctly in Article 1, first sentence, of the 1948 *Universal Declaration of Human Rights* (UDHR): 'All human beings are born free and equal in dignity and rights.' It is in this spirit that the right to freedom of religion or belief has been enshrined in Article 18 of the UDHR, Article 18 of the *International Covenant on Civil and Political Rights* (ICCPR) and other international human rights instruments. The wording of Article 9 of the 1950 *European Convention on Human Rights* (ECHR) shows a striking similarity to Article 18 of the UDHR, after which it was largely modeled.

However, the actual policies of handling diversity in many countries across the globe continue to reflect traditional or newly-established religious hegemonies. Even at the level of constitutional and legal norms, the rights conceded in that field are sometimes limited to predefined lists of religious options. While in some states only the followers of the monotheistic religions of revelation receive full legal recognition, other states refer to concepts like 'known religions', 'normal religious practices' or 'traditional religions', 'national religions', with the typical result that members of less known, new, 'foreign' or alternative communities face exclusion or discrimination. The realities in quite a number of countries – including within the Council of Europe – thus remain conceptually close to ideas of a limited tolerance rather than fully endorsing freedom of religion or belief as a human right. In order not to dilute the human rights approach in handling religious diversity, it is all the more important to stick to a clear understanding of freedom of religion, which enjoys the status of a universal right held by all human beings.

Beyond Essentialism and Nominalism: Defining the Scope of Application

Freedom of religion or belief takes the self-definition of human beings as its starting point, thereby exceeding any 'lists' of religious options predefined by the state. This naturally opens up a broad range of views and practices for which people may claim recognition under freedom of religion or belief. Indeed, the UN Human Rights Committee in charge of monitoring the implementation of the ICCPR argued for a wide application of freedom of religion or belief. In its *General Comment No. 22* (1993), the Committee pointed out: 'Article 18 protects theistic, non-theistic and atheistic beliefs, as well as the right not to profess any religion or belief. The terms 'belief' and 'religion' are to be broadly construed.' Likewise, the ECtHR has gone in its jurisdiction way beyond the sphere of 'classical religions' (whatever that may mean) by *inter alia* accepting claims of pacifists or vegetarians as falling under the remit of Article 9 of the ECHR.

Not surprisingly, such a wide application has given rise to concerns that it might, in the long run lead to an increasing trivialisation of freedom of religion or belief. In opinion polls carried out in the UK some people have named 'Star Wars' as their "religion", and there are rumours that some coffee shops in the Netherlands would like to rename themselves as 'religious communities' in order to sell drugs under the auspices of a liturgical practice. Be that as it may, we certainly face the challenge to avoid a trivialising inflation of demands without slipping back to predefined lists of legitimate religious options. The question is, how to define a plausible way between nominalism and essentialism in the understanding of freedom of religion or belief. In [CAMPBELL & COSANS, 1982] the ECtHR coined a helpful formula, which has provided guidance in subsequent cases. In order for a person's view to fall within the ambit of Article 9 ECHR, the Court states, that the view must display 'a certain level of cogency, seriousness, cohesion and importance'. While the criteria of cogency, seriousness and importance imply an existential urge rooted in a profound personal conviction, the element of cohesion requires that the respective position has an impact on a person's identity in a somewhat coherent manner. Thus, the Court makes it clear that not any position which someone just happens to have today can claim the status of a religion or belief. At the same time, the four criteria remain purely formal and thus open for a broad variety of convictions and practices, religious or otherwise.

Dimensions of Freedom and Criteria for Limitations

Freedom of religion or belief is a multifaceted right. People have the freedom to search for an ultimate meaning in life and to come to most different (or no) results in such endeavours; to communicate convictions, beliefs or doubts openly; to insist on not being publicly exposed in their religious identity without explicit consent; to live in accordance with the tenets and norms of their faiths; to hold worship alone or together with others; to grow up and remain within a faith communities or to abandon their inherited belief; to develop appropriate infrastructures needed for the development of their communities; to defend old or create new religious organisations; to engage in religious charity activities; to manifest religious or belief-orientations visibly, including by obeying particular dress codes; to promote religious convictions publicly and invite others to join; to educate their children in conformity with their own religious or moral convictions and to organise community schools for this purpose, and many other activities. Freedom of religion or belief thus exceeds the sphere of personal faith and spirituality by also covering public manifestations and infrastructural aspects of religious life. Moreover, no one can be free to do something unless he or she is also free not to do it. That is why freedom of religion or belief also covers freedom *not* to profess a religion or belief, *not* to attend worship or just *not* to care about religious or philosophical issues etc.

The ECtHR has generally confirmed such a multifaceted, open understanding of Article 9. For instance, in the famous judgment on [KOKKINAKIS, 1993], which marks the beginning of its jurisdiction on freedom of religion or belief, the Court clarified that Article 9 also covers non-coercive missionary activities undertaken by a Jehovah's Witness. In [EWIDA AND OTHERS, 2013], the Court decided in favour of a woman who insisted on wearing a visible cross around her neck also in her work place. The judgment in [JABÓBSKI, 2010] recognised the claims of a prisoner who, due to his convictions, wished to receive vegetarian food, and with the judgment in [BAYATAN, 2011], the Court accepted a claim of conscientious objection to military service, etc. While at the beginning mainly focusing on rights of individuals, the Court subsequently broadened its jurisdiction on Article 9 by including claims of communities [see e.g. METROPOLITAN CHURCH OF BESSARABIA AND OTHERS, 2001].

It is a truism that freedom cannot be completely unlimited. However, the general need for some limitations can easily become a pretext for imposing far-reaching, arbitrary and discriminatory restrictions. The question of where to draw limits and how to prevent the frequent abuse of limitation clauses is one of the most sensitive issues in human rights law. Due to the specific status of freedom of religion or belief as an inalienable right, the onus of proof always falls on those who argue on behalf of limitations, not on those who wish to exercise their freedom. In other words, the relationship between freedom and its limitations must remain a relationship between rule and exception. In case of doubt the rule prevails, and exceptions always require an extra burden of argumentation concerning both empirical evidence and normative reasoning. Moreover, for limitations to be justifiable, they must be legally prescribed and they must be 'necessary in a democratic society in the interest of public safety, for the protection of public order, health or morals or for the protection of the rights and freedoms of others' (Article 9(2) of the ECHR). The formula 'necessary in a democratic society' demands that limitations remain within the realm of proportionality, which *inter alia* means they must be confined to the minimum degree of interference needed to pursue one of the listed legitimate goals. Finally, the inner nucleus of a person's faith or conscientious position cannot be exposed to any justifiable limitations.

When dealing with the issue of limitations, the ECtHR has granted states a certain 'margin of appreciation'. Whereas that concept generally makes sense given the role of the Court as a supervising body for a broad number of states, the margin of appreciation has often been particularly wide in cases involving freedom of religion or belief, for instance in relation to headscarf issues [see LEYLA SAHIN, 2005]. By conceding a wide margin of appreciation, the Court wishes to acknowledge the existing variety of legal traditions within the Council of Europe concerning the handling of religious diversity. Critics have objected that the Court has factually surrendered its supervision on the reasonable application of limitations clauses and in particular of the proportionality test. Such criticism has also come to the fore in some dissenting votes [see e.g. SAS, 2014].

Equality and Non-discrimination

The preamble of the UDHR links the 'inherent dignity' of all human beings to 'their *equal* and inalienable rights' thus highlighting the specific status of the principle of equality for the understanding of human rights. Indeed, the idea that human beings should have certain fundamental rights *just because they are humans* necessarily implies equality of all in those rights. Equality therefore is one of the defining principles of the human rights approach in general.

In practical terms, equality chiefly means non-discrimination. All major human rights documents contain provisions for non-discrimination. Article 2 of the UDHR, Article 2 of the ICCPR, Article 14 of the ECHR and many other human rights instruments *inter alia* list 'religion' as one of the explicitly prohibited grounds of discrimination. In a number of cases, the ECtHR has based its judgments on Articles 9 and 14 of the ECHR seen in conjunction, thereby explicitly linking freedom of religion or belief to the principle non-discrimination [see e.g. RELIGIONSGEMEINSCHAFT DER ZEUGEN JEHOVAHS, 2008].

The non-discriminatory implementation of freedom of religion or belief in all areas of society presents a complex task. First, it implies a consistent policy of non-discrimination within state institutions, e.g. by ensuring accessibility of public positions regardless of religious or belief-related orientations. Furthermore, the state should combat discriminatory practices within society at large by issuing comprehensive anti-discrimination laws and policies. Finally, the state should also tackle the root causes of societal discrimination by promoting a general climate of societal openness, providing fair information about different religious or belief traditions as part of the school curriculum, facilitating encounters of people from different denominations and encouraging interreligious communication.

Between State Religion and Secularity

Not only at the global level, but also within Europe very different regimes of regulating the relationship between states and religious communities exist. While France epitomises the idea of a strict separation between state and religion, Greece or Denmark are examples of states which in their constitutions recognise the special status of one traditional church. Already at the legal level, the existing systems display a broad range of possibilities. Political realities are even more diverse. The formally 'secular' nature of their constitution does not prevent many states, such as Russia or Turkey, from cherishing very close ties with the predominant religions in their countries, which results in discrimination against members of other religious communities.

Freedom of religion or belief does not prescribe one particular model of regulation the relationship between state and religion. Different societies may follow different ways and find different solutions in this regard, provided they honour their human rights obligations. As already mentioned, the ECtHR has conceded a wide margin of appreciation in this regard. This does not mean, however, that freedom of religion or belief would remain entirely 'neutral' *vis-à-vis* the various existing systems. Under international as well as European human rights law, the state functions as the formal guarantor of human rights for everyone under its jurisdiction. With regard to freedom of religion or belief this requires that the state provide an open space within which religious or belief-related diversity can unfold freely, safely and without discrimination. This certainly presents a challenge to countries in which certain religions and state institutions are closely interwoven, in particular countries with an official religion or state religion. It seems difficult to conceive an application of the concept of state religion that in practice does not have adverse effects on religious minorities – unless the state religion is just a historical 'formality' without any real impact on state and society.

The obvious alternative to a system of state religion seems to be the 'secular state'. However, it is well known that notion of the secularity can have very different meanings, which is a source of much confusion. The same is true for the term '*laicité*'. On the one hand, the secularity of the state can represent a formal commitment to accommodate religious pluralism in fairness to all. On the other hand, the term secularity can also become a proxy for non-commitment of the state in this area. On top of that, it can even describe restrictive policies of pushing religion into a mere private sphere, which would be at variance with freedom of religion or belief as entrenched in international and European human rights law.

From a systematic point of view, it seems plausible to assume that the state, in order to be able to guarantee the right to freedom of religion or belief for everyone without discrimination, should not identify itself with any particular religion or belief, including doctrinal secularism. A policy of deliberate non-identification of the state with any religion or belief does not necessarily require a clear-cut separation between state and religious communities, which strictly speaking would be illusionary. Rather, it implies creating an open and inclusive institutional framework that gives breathing space to the existing and emerging religious diversity. It furthermore requires a self-critical attitude in order to discover and remove possible biases, which could even be hidden underneath *prima facie* 'neutral' norms. In order to make it clear that such deliberate non-identification, despite the seemingly negative formulation, has a positive significance one may further qualify it as *'respectful non-identification'*. After all, it is out of respect for everyone's freedom of religion or belief that the state is supposed to exercise and institutionalise such self-restraint.

Intersection With Other Human Rights (The Example of Freedom of Expression)

As pointed out in the beginning, freedom of religion or belief follows the same logic as other human rights. It shows a particular closeness with freedom of expression. Although in practice issues brought forward under those two rights can at times collide, freedom of religion or belief and freedom of expression ultimately reinforce each other mutually. It is all the more surprising that the relationship between these two rights has sometimes been described as antagonistic. While freedom of expression seems to represent a classical liberal right that protects all sorts of free speech, artistic experimentation, public criticism and non-violent provocation, religious freedom has at times been construed as a less liberal counter-right, as it were, in that it allegedly aims at putting limits to an 'overly extensive' expressive freedom. This perceived antagonism often rests on the false assumption that freedom of religion or belief abstractly promotes 'the cause of religion', whatever it is. As a human right, however, freedom of religion or belief empowers human beings, rather than protecting religions in themselves.

Some judgments of the ECtHR have contributed to the described antagonistic misperception. A much discussed example is the case [OTTO-PREMINGER-INSTITUT, 1994]. The Austrian administration had confiscated a film deemed offensive to the feelings of Christians, since it placed central persons of the Christian tradition in a pornographic context. In its judgment the Strasbourg Court did not see a violation of the complainant's freedom of expression. The Court held that the issue 'involves weighing up the conflicting interests of the exercise of two fundamental freedoms guaranteed under the Convention, namely the right of the applicant association to impart to the public controversial views (...), on the one hand, and the right of other persons to proper respect for their freedom of thought, conscience and religion, on the other hand'. In a dissenting vote three of the judges sitting in that chamber argued that the assumed antagonism between freedom of religion or belief and freedom of expression did not exist. The Convention does not, in terms, guarantee a right to protection of religious feelings. More particularly, such a right cannot be derived from the right to freedom of religion, which in effect includes a right to express views critical of the religious opinions of others.

Similar debates have taken place in the United Nations, sometimes leading to emotional controversies. Over the years, the UN Human Rights Committee as well as the UN Special Rapporteur on freedom of religion or belief have consistently emphasised the positive interrelatedness of freedom of religion or belief with freedom of expression. At the peak of the controversy around the Danish Mohammed cartoons, Asma Jahangir, UN Special Rapporteur on freedom of religion or belief from 2004 to 2010, pointed out that there can be no right of a person or group to be free from criticism or even ridicule. Postulating such a right could lead to the end of a free society based on open public discourse. Jahangir clarified that blasphemy laws do not only restrict freedom of expression; they typically also threaten religious minorities and dissidents. She thus took a position similar to the minority vote in the Otto-Preminger case. At the same time, she clarified that no general antagonism exists between freedom of expression and freedom of religion or belief, which as human rights closely belong together.

REFERENCES:

Ahdar, Rex J./Leigh, Ian: *Religious Freedom in the Liberal State*, Oxford: OUP (2nd edn. 2013).

Bielefeldt, Heiner/Ghanea, Nazila/Wiener, Michael: *Freedom of Religion or Belief. An International Law Commentary*, Oxford: OUP (2016).

Evans, Malcolm *D: Religious Liberty and International Law in Europe*, Cambridge: CUP (1997).

Ferrari, Silvio/Benzo, Andrea (eds.): *Between Cultural Diversity and Common Heritage*, Ashgate (2014).

Foblets, Marie-Claire et al (eds.): *Belief, Law and Politics: What Future for a Secular Europe?* Ashgate (2014).
Glendon, Mary Ann/Zacher, Hans F. (eds.): *Universal Rights in a World of Diversity: The Case of Religious Freedom*, Pontifical Academy of Social Sciences (2012).
Lindholm, Tore/Durham, W. Cole Jr./Tahzib-Lie Bahia (eds.): *Facilitating Freedom of Religion or Belief: A Deskbook*, Leiden: Nijhogg (2004).
Taylor, Paul M.: *Freedom of Religion: UN and European Human Rights Law and Practice*, Cambridge: CUP (2005).
BAYATYAN v. ARMENIA (ECtHR 07/07/2011, 23459/03).
CAMPBELL and COSANS v. UK (ECtHR 25/02/1982, 7511/76 and 7743/76).
EWEIDA and others v. UK (ECtHR 15/01/2013, 48320/10 etc.).
JAKOBSKI v. POLAND (ECtHR 07/10/2010, 18429/06).
KOKKINAKIS v. GREECE (ECtHR 25/05/1993, 14307/88).
LEYLA SAHIN v. TURKEY (ECtHR 10/11/2005, 44774/98).
METROPOLITAN CHURCH OF BESSARABIA and others v. MOLDOVA (ECtHR 13/12/2001, 45701/99).
OTTO-PREMINGER-INSTITUT v. Austria (ECtHR 20/09/1994, 13470/87).
RELIGIONSGEMEINSCHAFT DER ZEUGEN JEHOVAS v. AUSTRIA (ECtHR 31/07/2008, 40825/98).
SAS v. FRANCE (ECtHR 01/07/2014, 43835/11).

Cultural Heritage in the Human Rights System

Janet Blake, Tehran

The human rights value of cultural heritage

In international law, the related ideas of 'cultural property' and 'cultural heritage' have gathered an accumulated mass of meaning over the years, beginning with a focus on monuments, sites and movable cultural property (important on the national level, *inter alia*, for cultural, historic, archaeological, scientific, ethnographic and aesthetic reasons) situated on land or underwater. Later, in the early 1970s, the notion of 'world heritage' was developed, comprising cultural and natural sites (and →cultural landscapes) of a 'universal significance' to humankind and whose global importance merited international cooperation for their protection. At the same time, there was a strong push from countries newly-independent from colonial domination to assert claims to restitution of cultural property (some of which was of a monumental nature) as a national right. However, this focus on both the 'heritage of humanity' and 'national patrimony' contained within it some degree of contradiction with the specific significance that heritage holds for the cultural community that creates, maintains and transmits it and the local community that enjoys it. As a consequence, a greater focus has been placed on the →intangible cultural heritage since the late 1990s. In addition, particularly within the European context, cultural heritage is now being viewed as a cultural, social and economic resource of communities.

In Section 3 below, more detail is provided on some of the developments at the international policy level that have informed our understanding of cultural heritage and, in particular, the broadening out of the notion that occurred during the 1980s and 1990s to include, for example, not only material culture of a monumental or nationally valuable kind, but to include also vernacular and even quite mundane cultural elements as well as non-material aspects of heritage such as oral expressions, performance arts, rituals, social practices, belief and knowledge systems etc. From this author's point of view, it is important to recognise that, as much as all cultural heritage represents a human rights value (as set out below), it is in its intangible dimension and manifestations that the importance of the human dimension is clearest: intangible cultural heritage is a living heritage whose very existence is dependent on the human context (individuals, groups, communities and the wider society). Hence, safeguarding this heritage cannot easily be divorced from human rights and, in particular, the economic, social and cultural rights of its bearers and practitioners.

→Cultural identity, whether operating at an individual or group/community level, is an essential component of →human dignity and cultural heritage, as a whole, plays a central role in the construction of both personal and group identities. Since the protection of human dignity is a fundamental basis for human rights, safeguarding cultural heritage should be regarded as an essential part of protecting human rights. The human right to cultural identity encompasses the right of individuals to choose, alone or in community with others, their cultural identities (most of us have more than one) and self-identification, the right to choose one's own cultural identity or identities, is essential for protecting individuals' rights. The right to a cultural identity includes the right not to have an alien culture imposed on one, the right to positive discrimination in favour of minorities to participate in the cultural life of the wider community and the right of each cultural group to preserve, develop and maintain its own specific culture. Innumerable attempts made to strip people of their human dignity during periods of colonial domination or →armed conflict frequently involve attacks on their cultural heritage, clearly demonstrating the importance of cultural heritage as a marker of individual (and often collective, group) identity.

Cultural identity issues are notoriously complex, and it is not uncommon for the right of a specific community or people to a special relationship with their cultural heritage to conflict with the right of others to access and enjoy it as a local or national cultural heritage or even a cultural heritage of mankind: The Aboriginal rock art at Kakadu National park in Australia (listed as a World heritage Site under the 1972 *World Heritage Convention*) is regarded as having a universal significance for humankind In view of its richness and traditional character (dating back thousands of years), while it also represents a heritage of immense and special significance for the Aboriginal communities of that area, whose unique identity it symbolises. Partly in response to such cases, the *Convention on Safeguarding of Intangible Cultural Heritage* (UNESCO, 2003) places the right of communities to identify, safeguard and manage their own cultural heritage at its centre, thus recognising both an important cultural right and the procedural human rights principle of participation. The idea of a national identity based on ethnic or cultural factors has also, in too many cases, led to territorial expansionism and armed conflict (both internal and external) and, in its most extreme form, ethnocide. Denial of the right of access to sacred sites and the damaging impact that such exclusion has on the excluded religious community and its individual members is also relevant here. As the *'Hague' Convention on the Protection of Cultural Property in the Event of Armed Conflict* (UNESCO, 1954) notes in its Preamble, 'cultural heritage is an important component of the cultural identity of communities, groups and individuals, and of social cohesion...(and)...its intentional destruction may have adverse consequences on human dignity and human rights'.

Since cultural heritage is extremely diverse in all its forms and manifestations, its protection contributes significantly to the goal of preserving global cultural diversity. Indeed, two of UNESCO's cultural heritage Conventions (the 2003 Convention and the 2005 *Convention on the Protection and Promotion of Cultural Expressions*) grew directly out of the *Universal Declaration on Cultural Diversity* (UNESCO, 2001). This instrument characterises cultural diversity as a heritage of humankind whose preservation for present and future generations is an ethical imperative. With regard to the relationship between cultural diversity and human rights, Article 4 of the 2001 Declaration is unequivocal, stating that '(t)he defence of cultural diversity is an ethical imperative, inseparable from respect for human dignity. It implies a commitment to human rights and fundamental freedoms, in particular the rights of persons belonging to minorities and those of indigenous peoples'. Moreover, cultural diversity is also now recognised as a key vector in ensuring sustainable development and this requires a holistic approach to the safeguarding of cultural heritage, tangible and intangible. The Preamble to the 2003 Convention makes this clear in its second recital, as follows: 'Considering the importance of the intangible cultural heritage as a mainspring of cultural diversity and a guarantee of sustainable development, as underscored in... the UNESCO Universal Declaration on Cultural Diversity of 2001'.

Main approaches/answers currently found in this field

Cultural heritage received its first formal endorsement as a proper subject for human rights in the Report of the UN Independent Expert in the field of cultural rights adopted in 2011; this Report examined the right of access to and enjoyment of cultural heritage and considered both the scope and content of this right and the types of measure required for states to fulfil their obligations to support, protect and promote it. It stated unequivocally that, as reflected in international law and practice, 'the need to preserve/safeguard cultural heritage is a human rights issue', particularly because of its 'significance for individuals and communities and their identity and development processes' (at paragraph 1). The enjoyment of and access to cultural heritage is understood to be an element of the human right to participate in cultural life. This right was first formally expressed in Article 22 of the →Universal Declaration on Human Rights (UN, 1948) which sets out the right of everyone to 'participate freely in the cultural life of the community', to enjoy the benefits of scientific progress and to the moral and material benefits of their individual creativity. This article also makes explicit the linkage between the right of each individual to enjoy their cultural rights with their human dignity. It was then given binding status in Article 15 of the →International Covenant on Economic, Social and Cultural Rights (UN, 1966) in somewhat modified terms as the 'right to take part in cultural life' ('take part' being regarded as synonymous with 'participate' here) along with the right to benefit from science and its applications and to associated moral and economic (→intellectual property) rights. The right to participate in cultural life includes, then, a general duty on the states parties with regard to the various cultural heritages within the state and, as noted in paragraph 3 of Article 15, support for 'the conservation, development and full diffusion of ... (the) culture' of all citizens of the country.

General Comment no. 21 of the Committee on Economic, Social and Cultural Rights (CESCR), notes that this right includes the obligation on governments to adopt '...specific measures aimed at achieving respect for the right of everyone, individually or in association with others or within a community or group... to have access to their own cultural and linguistic heritage and to that of others'. In addition, this right is interpreted as one of individuals and communities to access and enjoy cultural heritages that are of significance to them, whether their own (with priority access), local, national or event universal/global. The General Comment further notes that the rights of access to and enjoyment of cultural heritage are inter-dependent and include, *inter alia*, to know, understand, enter, visit, make use of, maintain, exchange and develop cultural heritage, as well as to benefit from the cultural heritage and creations of others, without political, religious, economic or physical obstacles. Access and enjoyment also implies community participation in the identification, interpretation and development of cultural heritage, as well as the design and implementation of preservation/safeguarding policies and programmes, as is supported by the UNESCO's 2003 Convention.

The model of access initially developed for the right to education with the five elements of availability, accessibility, acceptability, adaptability and appropriateness has been applied to cultural heritage in the General Comment. This notion of access involves: physical access to cultural heritage; access through digital technologies; economically affordable access; the right to seek, receive and impart information on cultural heritage; and access to decision making and monitoring procedures, including administrative and judicial procedures and remedies. At the same time, there are different levels of this right as accorded to individuals and communities with priority given to those with the closest connection to the heritage as follows, ranging from source communities who are the bearers of a specific cultural heritage, who keep it alive and safeguard it, to local individuals and communities who regard the cultural heritage as an integral part of the life of the wider community (but who are not necessarily directly involved in it), scientists, artists and the general public.

In addition to this right, of course, the principle of non-discrimination interacts with the right to enjoy and access cultural heritage, with special attention paid to minorities and other disadvantaged groups in society. The special status rights of members of ethnic, religious and linguistic minorities to practice their culture and traditions are supported by Article 27 of the *ICCPR*. This places an obligation on states not to interfere with the enjoyment by such minorities of 'their own culture'. This includes ensuring access to their cultural heritage and not preventing them from creating, practising, enacting and transmitting their cultural heritage and traditions. Effectively, this places the obligation on all states to abstain from policies or actions that would result in the destruction, damage, alteration or desecration of cultural objects or spaces important for maintaining minority cultural heritage as well as preventing the risk of destruction or damage to such heritage, including by third parties. The *Declaration on the Rights of Ethnic, Religious and Linguistic Minorities* (1992) provides further clarification of the content of the rights of minorities under Article 27. At Article 4(2), it requires states to "take measures to create favourable conditions to enable persons belonging to minorities to express their characteristics and to develop their culture, language, religion, traditions and customs ....' This would, of course, include the protection of the cultural heritage of such groups. In addition, international Conventions against discrimination on grounds of sex and race and setting out the rights of migrant workers and persons with disabilities also include provisions relevant to cultural heritage. Diasporas and →migrants represent two rather challenging groups of cultural minorities since they generally share a cultural identity with a national (or other) community residing in another state. This raises questions as to how far their state of origin may intervene to protect and safeguard their cultural heritage. Migration has been a fact of human civilization for millennia, but more recent migrations in response to economic, environmental and security pressures raise fundamental questions concerning what is both local and national heritage, who identifies it and who 'owns' it. This is important for any discussion of human rights related to cultural heritage, in particular what the relative roles of the host state and state of origin may be.

A further significant group that enjoys special rights with regard to heritage are →indigenous peoples. Given the historical experience of dispossession of their land and heritage experienced by indigenous peoples, the international community increasingly accepts that special rights to off-set generations of discrimination are justified (Anaya, 1996). Such special treatment extends to their heritage, sacred places, secret knowledge and human remains etc. and includes restoring their cultural heritage to them, ensuring their access to it and respecting associated customary laws and practices. Indigenous understandings of heritage do not correspond closely with the definitions of 'cultural heritage' commonly used in international law since it includes such elements as human remains, natural landscape features, plant and animal species and other natural resources. As a consequence, the protection of indigenous heritage cannot be treated separately from their claims to rights over ancestral lands, control over natural resources and internal, if not external) self-determination. Hence, Article 31 of the *Declaration on the Rights of Indigenous Peoples* – UNDRIP (UN, 2007) endorses the right of →indigenous peoples to 'maintain, control, protect and develop their cultural heritage, traditional knowledge and traditional cultural expressions, as well as the manifestations of their sciences, technologies and cultures, including human and genetic resources, seeds, medicines, knowledge of the properties of fauna and flora…'. Article 11 of UNDRIP makes direct reference to their rights with regard to heritage, stating that: '(they) have the right to practise and revitalize their cultural traditions and customs. This includes the right to maintain, protect and develop the past, present and future manifestations of their cultures, such as →archaeological and historical sites, artefacts, designs, ceremonies, technologies and visual and performing arts and literature'. An important disconnect exists, however, between classical human rights approaches based on minority rights from the rights claimed by indigenous peoples: The former are based on protecting rights of individual members of minorities while indigenous peoples stake claims to a collective identity that has to be supported by collective rights.

Many civil and political rights are also implicated in the protection and safeguarding of cultural heritage. Other (non-cultural) human rights are also relevant to cultural heritage in general and without which it would be extremely difficult, if not impossible, to realise the rights of individuals and communities with regard to their cultural heritage. For example, freedom of expression (Article 19(2) of the ICCPR) is a fundamental right that is essential for the creation, enactment, maintenance, enjoyment and transmission of cultural heritage, especially true for minority and indigenous heritage. Other relevant rights include: the rights of freedom of religion and association, expressed in Articles 18 and 22 of the ICCPR; the right to education as set out in Article 13 of the ICESCR; the right of parents to choose the kind of education given to their children found in Article 13(3) of the ICESCR and Article 29(1)(c) of the *Convention on the Rights of the Child* (UN, 1989) (CRC). The protection afforded to this right in the CRC requires '... respect for the child's parents, his or her own cultural identity, language and values' balanced in a manner of interest here with 'the national values of the country in which the child is living, the country from which he or she may originate, and for civilizations different from his or her own'. Moreover, the right to cultural development, with regard to cultural heritage, can be understood as the right of the members of a cultural group to preserve, develop and maintain their own specific culture and cultural heritage (including myths, traditions and symbolic culture) and to have this identity respected by the State and others. The *African Charter on Human and Peoples' Rights* (AU, 1981) is the sole binding (regional) instrument so far that directly expresses human rights in relation to cultural heritage, referring as it does to the right to preserve and develop a culture, at Article 22(1), and the right of equal enjoyment of the common heritage of mankind at Article 22(1).

The move in recent years towards a more human rights-based approach to cultural heritage protection in which cultural communities are placed at, or nearer to, the centre (as that taken by the 2003 Convention) is, in part, an attempt to respond to this human rights dimension of heritage. Under the 2003 Convention, heritage is viewed as comprising a value whose safeguarding is of common concern to the international community while its primary significance to the community is respected. This allows for the notion of ownership to be decoupled from that of the need to safeguard and it leaves a space for the immediate cultural community to be directly involved in its identification, inventorying and safeguarding as a whole. Increasingly, cultural heritage is viewed as a social, cultural and economic resource of individuals and the communities they live in, contributing to the development of the capabilities needed for achieving full human development. For example, the *'Faro' Convention* of the Council of Europe (2005) defines cultural heritage as 'a group of resources inherited from the past'.

In addition to this, newer approaches towards cultural heritage also operate in tandem with the move towards accepting the collective character of cultural rights or, at the least, as rights of individuals exercised as part of a group or community. As the UN Independent Expert on cultural rights has noted, 'the existence of collective cultural rights is a reality in international human rights law today'. Indeed, according to logic, cultural rights must protect the interests of the community in order for the individual to protect his or her own rights; hence, a purely individual conception of human rights cannot respond adequately to those (many) societies in which individual identity and dignity are intertwined with membership of the community. However, this does not resolve a potential clash between accepting a collective character for cultural rights and forms of cultural relativism that can lead to harming individuals' human rights. Here, a subtle and sophisticated approach is required that can allow for some recognition of important local specificities in cultures and systems and the need to implement universal human rights standards appropriately, while protecting the core *substance* of the right.

The international policy dimensions

Important developments in international cultural and development policy areas since the 1970s have had a direct impact on human rights related to cultural heritage. Up until then, →development was generally conceived as exclusively related to economic growth; as a corollary, traditional culture and/or heritage was viewed as a break on development. During the 1970s, Africa and Latin America developed the 'endogenous development' approach in which local and ethnic cultures (and languages) were given greater value, culture was substituted for the economy in the development model and traditional ways of life were emphasised. Further to this, the *Declaration of the World Conference on Cultural Policies* for the first time articulated a view of 'culture"' as a broad notion encompassing ways of life, social organisation and value/belief systems as well as material culture; it also, importantly, linked this with the idea of cultural identity.

Important new international development occurred during the late 1980s and early- to mid-1990s, with the introduction of the social development, sustainable development and human development approaches. The value of local and indigenous cultures and their heritage within the wider society and as a resource for its overall development was also becoming better understood at this time. The adoption of the *'Rio' Declaration* of UNCED in 1992 in which sustainable development was first given universal international endorsement marked a turning point, with its 'third pillar' constituting socio-cultural factors and the central roles given to participatory approaches and to indigenous and local communities. It is important to recognise that each of these development approaches contained strong human rights aspects – beyond the solidarity human right to development itself – emphasising, as they did, human capacities (supported by rights) and social justice.

The publication of the Report of the World Commission on Culture and Development in 1996 was particularly significant since it clearly stated not only the constitutive role of culture in development, but also the important place of cultural heritage in this. Another key document in this area was the *Action Plan on Cultural Policies for Development* (UNESCO, 1998) which recognised as its first Principle that, '(s)ustainable development and the flourishing of culture are interdependent' which then lead to the formulation of its first Objective as: 'To make →cultural policy one of the key components of development strategy'. Specifically targeted towards cultural heritage, Objective 3 calls on member states to '(r)einforce policy and practice to safeguard and enhance the cultural heritage, tangible and intangible, moveable and immovable, and to promote cultural industries'; this approach includes revising the traditional conception of heritage to include 'all natural and cultural elements, tangible or intangible, which are inherited or newly created. Through these elements social groups recognize their identity and commit themselves to pass it on to future generations in a better and enriched form'. Hence, the connection is made explicitly here between heritage as a holistic concept, the imperative to safeguard it for future generations and the role of heritage in the formation of *group* identity. The outcome document of the United Nations Conference on Sustainable Development (Rio+20) held in 2012 made direct reference to culture, emphasising that the three dimensions of sustainable development, namely the economic, socio-cultural and environmental dimensions, should all be given importance in UN programming for sustainability. However, it contains only a few, rather modest, references to the role of culture for sustainable development. UNESCO has therefore been working to place culture firmly within the international development agenda, its *Hangzhou Declaration: Placing Culture at the Heart of Sustainable Development Policies* (UNESCO, 2013) calling for a specific international development Goal focused on culture being included in the post-2015 UN development agenda, 'based on heritage, diversity, creativity and the transmission of knowledge'.

In the field of cultural rights, so often viewed as the poor relation of the human rights canon, belated attention was being paid from the mid-1990s to the mid-2000s to developing these human rights and better understanding their scope and content. From 1993, ECOSOC began its work on developing a draft *Declaration on indigenous rights*, although it took until 2007 for the UN General Assembly to adopt the UN Declaration on this subject. In tandem with this process, UNESCO was working alongside experts such as the University of Fribourg to codify cultural rights. This work culminated in the adoption of the (unofficial) *Fribourg Declaration on Cultural Rights* in 2007 that states in its Preamble that, 'respect for diversity and cultural rights is a crucial factor in the legitimacy and consistency of sustainable development based upon the indivisibility of human rights'. A further important policy context is the development of →intellectual property protection for 'traditional knowledge' and 'traditional cultural expressions' that began, in its most recent efforts, with the establishment of the intergovernmental committee on genetic resources, traditional knowledge and folklore within WIPO in 2000. This work continues and two draft provisions (on these two areas) were adopted in 2014.

Exploring eventual trends during the last decades

Beyond the human rights field set out above, important developments have occurred in both international environmental and cultural heritage law. In the former, this has mainly been with regard to the protection of traditional ecological knowledge, and has been most clearly expressed in Article 8(j) of the *UN Convention on Biological Diversity* (1992) that calls upon the Parties to '(r)espect, preserve and maintain knowledge, innovation and practices of indigenous and local communities embodying traditional lifestyles relevant for the conservation and sustained use of biological diversity and promote their wider application with the approval and involvement of the holders of such knowledge, innovations and practices…'. In addition, the *Convention on Combating Desertification* (UN, 1994) places a high importance on the knowledge and practices of local communities and their participation in national programming and the *Treaty on Plant Genetic Resources for Food and Agriculture* (FAO, 2001) stresses the need to protect farmers' rights, such as in the use of seeds. International conservation treaties also commonly contain exceptions to prohibitions on capturing or killing protected species for indigenous peoples employing traditional methods of hunting, as in the *Agreement on Conservation of Polar Bears* (1973 at Article III.1) and the *North Pacific Fur Seal Interim Convention* (1957 at Article VII).

The human rights dimension has been present in cultural heritage treaties since the early treaty-making in the 1950s, although this has become much more explicit in more recent treaties. UNESCO's 2003 Convention refers in the first paragraph of its Preamble to the main human rights instruments and, specifically, to the 1948 UDHR and the two Covenants of 1966. Importantly, the definition it gives of intangible cultural heritage (Article 2(1)) is as a heritage that provides 'communities and groups and, in some cases, individuals' with 'a sense of identity and continuity.' If we look at particular human rights in turn, it is also possible to identify specific contributions that cultural heritage treaties make to their protection and promotion. The *Convention on the illicit movement of cultural property* (UNESCO, 1970), for example, notes the importance of cultural property as a vehicle through which 'peoples may gain consciousness of their own dignity'. This treaty also seeks to protect the right of a people to its own artistic, historical and cultural wealth. At the same time, since the retention of cultural objects is necessary to the →participation in cultural life, the 1970 Convention also contributes to the enjoyment of this right. Furthermore, the whole range of cultural heritage treaties can be seen as supporting cultural diversity, although it is the two most recent UNESCO cultural heritage treaties (adopted in 2003 and 2005) which grew directly out of the *Universal Declaration on Cultural Diversity* (2001) that make this connection most explicitly. For example, the *Representative List of the Intangible Heritage of Humanity* of the 2003 Convention underscores the idea that the inscribed elements are chosen as *representative* of different genres of ICH that the List is testimony to the *diversity of this heritage*.

The right to education is fundamental to supporting cultural rights and many of the heritage Conventions, especially more recent treaties concluded after 2000, include provisions relating to public education, capacity-building and awareness-raising. Since non-formal means of education where the target group is often a minority cultural community, this can involve mother-tongue language education as well as a culturally-appropriate educational methodology. Public education is also directly connected with the ability of individuals and communities to participate in heritage protection. In UNESCO's 2003 Convention, ICH is defined in relation to the cultural communities and practitioners that produce and enact it and, as such, their participation (expressly required under Articles 2(1), 11(b), 12 and 15) is central to the Convention. Intellectual property protection also forms part of human rights with regard to heritage and, since it protects '(cultural) expressions that result from the creativity of individuals, groups and society and have a cultural content', the *Convention on Diversity of Cultural Expressions*

(UNESCO, 2005) notes in its Preamble the importance of intellectual property rights to sustaining those involved in cultural creativity (at paragraph 16). The intellectual property aspects are also viewed as important in safeguarding ICH.

The notion of a 'common heritage of mankind' is expressed in the Preamble to the 1954 *Hague Convention* which notes that 'damage to cultural property belonging to any people whatever means damage to the cultural heritage of mankind'. The approach of the *World Heritage Convention* (UNESCO, 1972) is predicated on the notion that some heritage has an 'outstanding universal value' that goes beyond national heritage. Of course, the concept of a global heritage contains a potential conflict with the special significance the heritage has for a community (or nation) and the 2003 Convention seeks to balance the 'common interest of humanity' in this heritage with the primary place of communities in identifying and safeguarding it. This notion also contains within it some sense of a collective interest in protection as well as the idea, present in all cultural heritage, of an obligation towards future generations: these two characteristics of heritage protection treaties mirror important elements of the solidarity human rights (such as the right to development or peace). At the same time, the value of cultural diversity and of specific and local cultures is increasingly recognised: hence, the principle of equal dignity of and respect for all cultures is expressed in the 2005 Convention (Preamble at Principle 3).

Given the 'soft law' character of much international cultural heritage law and the high degree to which states have reserved their sovereign jurisdiction in the treaties, human rights can offer an effective strategy for communities and individuals to safeguard their cultural heritage. Furthermore, the disjunction that can occur between cultural heritage and the concerned community as a result of the pressures of modernity and globalisation is an important human rights issue. It requires empowerment of communities and not limiting heritage protection to technical issues of safeguarding, but responding also to the role cultural heritage plays in society and people's lives. This has been most clearly recognised by the *Faro Convention* (Council of Europe, 2005) which defines cultural heritage as: '(A) group of resources inherited from the past which people identify, independently of ownership, as a reflection and expression of their constantly evolving values, beliefs, knowledge and traditions' and which takes a human rights approach to heritage safeguarding. UNESCO's 2003 Convention also makes explicit reference in the first paragraph of its Preamble to the main human rights instruments, especially to the 1948 UDHR and the 1966 Covenants, thus placing it firmly within a human rights framework.

REFERENCES:

Committee on Economic, Social and Cultural Rights: "General Comment no. 21 on The right of everyone to take part in cultural life (art. 15, para. 1 (a)" UN Doc. E/C.12/GC/21 (21 December 2009).

Donders, Yvonne: "The legal framework of the right to take part in cultural life" in Yvonne Donders and Vladimir Volodin (eds.): *Human Rights in Education, Science and Culture – Legal developments and Challenges*, Paris: UNESCO Publishing (2007).

Forrest, Craig: *International Law and the Protection of Cultural Heritage*, London and New York: Routledge (2010).

Francioni, Francesco and Martin Scheinin: *Cultural Human Rights*, The Hague: Martinus Nijhoff (2008).

Graham, Brian and Peter Howard: *The Ashgate Research Companion to Heritage and Identity*, Aldershot, UK: Ashgate Publishing (2008).

Human Rights Council: *Report of the independent expert in the field of cultural rights, Farida Shaheed*, UN Doc. A/HRC/14/36 (22 March 2010).

Human Rights Council: *Report of the independent expert in the field of cultural rights, Farida Shaheed*, UN Doc. A/HR/C/17/38 (21 March 2011).

Lenzerini, Federico: The Culturalization of Human Rights Law, Oxford: OUP (2014).

Lenzerini, Federico and Ana Filipa Vrdoljak (eds.): *International Law and Common Goods—Normative Perspectives on Human Rights, Culture and Nature*, Oxford: Hart Publishing (2014).

Logan, William S.: “Closing Pandora’s Box: Human Rights Conundrums in Cultural Heritage Protection” in Hilaine Silverman and D. Fairchild Ruggles (eds.): *Cultural Heritage and Human Rights*, Springer Science, Business and Media (2007).

Niec, Halina (ed.): *Cultural Rights and Wrongs*, Paris: UNESCO (1998).

Silverman, Helaine and D. Fairchild Ruggle (eds.): *Cultural Heritage and Human Rights*, Springer Science and Business Media, LLC (2007).

Tomasevski, Katarina: “Report of the UN Special Rapporteur on the Right to Education” UN Doc. E/CN.4/1999/49 (1999).

Vrdoljak, Ana Filipa: *The Cultural Dimension of Human Rights* Oxford: OUP (2013).

Vrdoljak, Ana Filipa: ‘Human Rights and Cultural Heritage in International Law’ in Federico Lenzerini and Ana Filipa Vrdoljak (eds.): *International Law and Common Goods—Normative Perspectives on Human Rights, Culture and Nature*, Oxford: Hart Publishing (2014).

Part II: **Keyword articles**

Access Control Technologies
(Digital Rights Management)

DEF: Access in the digital context, and controls over it, concerns digital content – within the meaning of 'works' as per the → Intellectual Property (copyright) system and including also content in databases protected under the *sui generis* right, excluding therefore the physical world, software *per se* and hardware. Consequently, this entry is about controlling access to such digital content. According to the Internet Security Glossary, 'access' means 'the ability and means to communicate with or otherwise interact with a system to use system resources either to handle information or to gain knowledge of the information the system contains', and 'access control' means 'a process by which use of system resources is regulated according to a security policy and is permitted only by authorised entities (users, programs, processes, or other systems) according to that policy'. While the technical parts of access controls (identification and authentication, identity management, technical measures) are of no interest here, Digital Rights Management (DRM) is a term that may be used interchangeably with Access Control Technologies for the purposes of this entry, both denoting technologies that are used to restrict the use of digital content.

INSTR: Digital content is protected by (copyright) law and a right to access it without the rights holder's permission (meaning reimbursement) is only permitted in rare cases and under exceptional circumstances (for instance, academic or library purposes or system interoperability). Access Control Technologies effectuate this system through technical means. In a way they constitute a 'by design' system or a rights holder-imposed system architecture or, even further, an application of the 'code is law' ideas into the Intellectual Property (IP) rights realm. As such, they ought to be perceived in principle as lawful (see Article 11 of the *WIPO Copyright Treaty*, introduced in the EU by the EU *Copyright Directive*, on Technical Protection Measures). Nevertheless, the fact remains that they are designed and implemented by rights holders without any state or other ratification as to the rules they force upon users. In fact, DRM technologies have been accused of enforcing unlawful business practices by technical means (see, for instance the Apple and SONY BMG class action lawsuits). Among others, DRM implementations have drawn criticism on the basis that they rarely adhere to the pro-user basic IP law principles of 'fair use' (in the USA) or 'private copy' (in the EU), as well as to the IP doctrine of the first sale (they attempt to regulate the sale of 'used' IP). Accordingly, the CJEU has ruled that 'those measures must be suitable for achieving (their) objective and must not go beyond what is necessary for this purpose'.

CONCL: Access Control Technologies, while useful in enforcing IP rights in an on-line environment of mass unlawful downloading of proprietary digital content, are prone to unlawful implementations, because they are designed and implemented by rights holders alone. Users and the public are generally suspicious of their 'false neutrality', because they constitute enforced measures they cannot escape or negotiate. Stricter regulation and monitoring is imperative in order to achieve a balance of protecting both rights holders' and lawful users' rights and interests, according to the principle of proportionality, as prescribed by the CJEU.

REFERENCES:

Brousseau, Eric; Marzouki, Meryem and Meadel, Cécile (eds.): *Governance, Regulation and Powers on the Internet*, Cambridge: Cambridge University Press (2012).

Stamatoudi, Irini (ed.): *Copyright Enforcement and the Internet*, Alphen aan Den Rijn: Kluwer Law International (2010).

NINTENDO v. PC BOX (CJEU 23/01/2014, C-355/12).

Paul de Hert and Vagelis Papakonstantinou

Administration
(Public Cultural A.)

DEF: Public cultural administration refers to all structures and behaviour affecting the fields of culture with the aim of planning, organising, directing, coordinating, and controlling government operations. Adopting another common definition of administration, it is the formation and implementation of public policy in these fields. The providers of public cultural administration are central addressees of culture-related human rights, insofar as the latter limit their power.

INSTR: In a narrow sense, as reflected e.g. in Article 4(6) of the 2005 *UNESCO Convention*, actions of cultural administrations are mainly 'those policies and measures relating to culture (...) that are either focused on culture as such or are designed to have a direct effect on cultural expressions'. In this sense, public cultural administration is mostly focused on public management and funding of cultural institutions and projects – and in a number of countries, of course, on censorship. Such functions are often related to the domains of organisational units of national, regional or local →governments, which are explicitly responsible for 'cultural affairs' (e.g. a ministry or department).

In a wider sense, the term also covers policies and measures, which focus on other tasks, but have more or less direct, often unforeseen, effects on cultural life. In fact, the efficacy of cultural human rights is frequently more endangered by those 'non-cultural' policies and measures (e.g. action of public authorities in fields like taxation, labour laws, public space, venues or building regulations). In such contexts, cultural →values can be found in strong competition with various other norms and interests, many of them with more influential lobbies.

As regards legal approaches beyond typical cultural legislation in the narrow sense (e.g. for heritage protection or legislation concerning →libraries), so called mainstreaming or cross-cutting clauses were established to boost interdisciplinary administrative thinking. This was considered of particular importance in fields without a strong lobby tradition, e.g. environment, gender equality or culture (see the, not yet fully explored, 'cultural awareness clause' in Article 167(4) TFEU). Manifold culture-related soft norms in national and subnational constitutions (e.g. in Estonia (Preamble), Greece (Article 24), Lithuania (Article 42), Hungary (Article P), Italy (Article 9); Bavaria (Article 3, 140), Catalonia (Article 22), Lower Austria (Article 4(5)), Vaud (Article 53)) could potentially work in a similar way. Methodologically, especially in the view of the OECD, →Impact Assessment (IA) has proved to be an ideal-typical instrument to manage the variety of factors and interests (including public participation) in policy making. However, as IA pertains only to measures with a special importance and needs time, it does not help to restrain restrictions of cultural freedoms in the daily administrative practice, especially at the local and regional level.

CONCL: For 'culture' to flourish, the education and attitudes of administrative staff members are essential. In case these are ignorant, an effective implementation of cultural human rights depends on the capabilities and, often enough, good will of a judicial system, which has to regard administrative discretion, with its staff, which is not necessarily open for every sort of 'culture', and its costs, which mostly impede judicial review. →Intercultural competence as a developing key competence of civil servants in a globalising world could turn out to be an important strategy to generally increase administrative cultural awareness.

REFERENCES:

Laaksonen, Annamari: *Making culture accessible*, Strasbourg: Council of Europe Publishing (2010).

Norman-Major, Kristen A./Gooden, Susan T. (eds.): *Cultural Competency for Public Administrators*, Armonk, London: M. E. Sharpe (2012).

Psychogiopoulou, Evangelia: *The Integration of Cultural Considerations in EU Law and Policies*, Leiden, Boston: Nijhoff (2008).

Jörg Michael Schindler

Affirmative Action

DEF: Affirmative action (hereafter AA) is one of the most controversial and disputed aspects of equal protection. It rests on the notion of substantive equality and equal (enjoyment of) rights which complements the notion of formal equality and equal treatment in the realisation of the principle of →equality. Whereas formal equality requires that like are treated alike, substantive equality takes difference (race, national or ethnic origin, gender, disability, social status, etc.) into consideration and mandates unequal treatment with a view to achieve equality of opportunities or equality of results. AA means that a special or preferential treatment is provided to individuals due to their particular characteristics or minority status. It is based on the conviction that a formal legal or programmatic approach is not sufficient to achieve *de facto* equality which implies a redistribution of resources, an improved participation (e.g. in arts activities) or a balanced representation in various institutions and structures of power.

INSTR: AA is a legal term used in countries like the US, South Africa, Canada or Brazil. In India the system of quota-based policies facilitating promotion in education and employment of certain social classes (based on caste, gender, religion or other status) is called 'reservation'. In Canada and South Africa the term 'employment equity' was coined to avoid negative connotations with AA. In France and the UK AA is called positive or reverse →discrimination which may be misleading because in some situations the failure to provide special or preferential treatment constitutes unlawful discrimination.

In comparison, international instruments use the notion of 'positive measures' or 'temporary special measures' to denote a special or preferential treatment (Article 1(4) ICERD, Article 4 CEDAW, Article 5(4) CRPD, Article 7(2) ECRML). This corresponds to 'positive action' used in the EU law (Article 23 CFR, Article 157(4) TFUE, Article 3 of the Directive 2006/54/EC (Recast Directive), Article 6 of the Directive 2004/113/EC (Gender Goods and Services Directive); Article 5 of the Directive 2010/43/EC (Race Equality Directive) and Article 7 of the Directive 2000/78/EC (Framework Employment Directive). EU member states apply a variety of positive actions with regard to gender, race, national and ethnic origin, disability and age in the area of education, access to goods and services, employment, civil service and elections (Equinet 2014).

Positive action as a term is broader in scope than the privileged treatment as it also covers apparently neutral policies ('purposefully inclusionary measures' known also as 'indirect affirmative action') aimed to address structural problems of underrepresentation and outreach measures aimed to remedy the lack of equal opportunities through targeted promotion of vacancies and recruitment, training and professional orientation (Fredman, 2013:237). Positive actions may also involve monitoring and redefinition of merits (McCrudden, 1986). However, some authors also define AA so broadly as to include indirect affirmative action, outreach measures and direct affirmative action (Sabbagh, 2011). This approach is now frequently found in European →cultural policies.

Under international human rights law states have the obligation to adopt special measures with regard to some protected categories of individuals. Such measures may have a temporary or permanent character. Article 2(2) CERD requires that states take special and concrete measures 'when the circumstances so warrant (...) in the social, economic, cultural and other fields (...) to ensure the adequate development and protection of certain racial groups or individuals belonging to them, for the purpose of guaranteeing them the full and equal enjoyment of human rights and fundamental freedoms. These measures shall in no case entail as a consequence the maintenance of unequal or separate rights for different racial groups after the objectives for which they were taken have been achieved.' In contrast, the obligation to protect ethnic, religious or linguistic minorities stipulated in Article 27 ICCPR implies permanent facilitation of minority culture or language (HRC, General Comment No. 23 (1994)). Such understanding of equal rights implying a different treatment has been well-established under international law (PJIJ, Minority Schools in Albania, Advisory Opinion (1935)).

Although UN legal instruments promote the human rights approach, AA is also advanced in conflict prevention and management strategies at international level. On the one hand, AA could be used as a transitional justice mechanism, in particular in distribution of political offices and civil service (i.e. in South Africa, Sudan, Rwanda or Bosnia and Herzegovina). In post-conflict societies the goal of AA is to prevent social tensions and ultimately to include members belonging to a particular racial, national or ethnic group to decision-making and positions of power. In literature concerning responses to genocide and mass atrocities AA is presented as a collective remedy to victims for violation of their rights. According to Siri Gloppen '(i)nequality created by past repression is best addressed through social reform and affirmative action programs, rather than through individual compensation to victims.' (Gloppen, 2005:39).

On the other hand, using AA in the post-conflict context may reinforce racial or ethnic segregation and discrimination. For some authors special measures 'fail to accomplish social solidarity necessary to remediate future risks' (Kielsgard, 2015:222). In Europe many countries provide permanent advantages to minority groups through election rules regarding reserved seats, proportional representation, minority lists, exceptions to threshold requirements or the use of minority language. In some countries such minority-conscious arrangements are safeguarded in constitutions or international peace treaties (i.e. the Constitution of Bosnia and Hercegovina or the Doha Peace Agreement, 2011, paras. 19–21).

According to the CEDAW Committee, special temporary measures have a collective and compensatory character. Unlike permanent special measures (used in case of pregnancy or maternity), they are temporary (introduced for a particular period of time) and apply to all areas of life. They may take the form of 'outreach or support programs; allocation and/or reallocation of resources; preferential treatment; targeted recruitment, hiring and promotion; numerical goals connected with time frames; and quota systems' (General Recommendation (CEDAW) No. 25 on temporary special measures, 2004, para. 22). The Committee considers special temporary measures mandatory when accelerating *de facto* gender equality is necessary and appropriate.

In recent years gender quotas have become increasingly popular as the most effective mechanism changing the gender imbalance and the character of gender representation (Franceschet, Krook & Piscopo 2012). Gender quotas are mostly used in candidate selections for elections and corporate boards. In France and Italy, the adoption of electoral gender parity and quota laws necessitated constitutional amendments. Prior to these amendments, laws could not promote equal access of women to elective offices and posts as well as to professional and social positions. Also the EU recognized the need to promote gender equality by means of quota laws. Following the EU Strategy for equality between men and women (2010–2015), the European Commission proposed the introduction of gender quotas in companies listed on stock exchanges as a temporary measure improving the gender balance among non-executive directors (Women on Boards Directive). Under this proposal, which is still pending, member states would have to implement a 40% gender quota in corporate boards provided that priority given to equally qualified female candidates over male candidates was not automatic and unconditional but includes a 'saving clause' which warrants the possibility of granting an exception in favour of male candidates.

CASES: At national level, AA is legal either as mandatory or voluntary plans. Under the US Civil Rights Act 1964 private, voluntary affirmative action aimed at eliminating traditional patterns of racial segregation does not amount to discrimination. However, in the USA any classifications based on race are always suspect and need to pass a strict scrutiny test [BAKKE, 1978]. Hence, race could be taken into account only as one of the factors in individual assessments of candidates provided that the AA policy is narrowly tailored and that other racially neutral policies were not sufficient to attain the aim of racial diversity. According to the most recent decision of the Supreme Court, the Equal Protection Clause neither prohibits nor mandates AA [SCHUETTE, 2014]. In consequence, AA may be banned by state constitutions.

In the EU, positive action in employment is permissible provided that it passes the proportionality test. To date, the CJEU has decided only cases concerning gender-based positive measures. It found that women may be given priority in employment when there are fewer women than men in a particular sector of employment or post, only if they are equally qualified (in terms of their suitability, competence and professional performance) and there are no specific reasons that tilt the balance in favour of a male candidate [MARSCHALL, 1997]. Such reasons may not be indirectly discriminatory (i.e. refer to the 'breadwinner' status or company seniority). As well, the ECtHR has accepted that Article 14 does not prevent states from taking special measures in order to 'correct factual inequalities' [STEC, 2006].

In sum, AA varies across countries with regard to (1) groups of beneficiaries; (2) policies it introduces; (3) legal norms from which it derives (constitutional, statutory, administrative laws or voluntary rules); (4) domains of implementation; (5) the ultimate goals; and (6) the degree to which it targets the beneficiaries (Sabbagh, 2011:110). For example, in France the law is blind to racial, national and ethnic minorities, but permits allocation of resources to economically and socially disadvantaged areas whereby national or ethnic origin becomes only a secondary consideration. In the USA and EU affirmative/positive action is lawful as long as it does not result in segregation, absolute and unconditional preference for the privileged group or absolute bar to other groups.

VIEWS: The moral justification of AA is less certain than it is legality. Arguments used to justify AA have different strengths in different contexts and jurisdictions. Decisions in which courts upheld AA policies often refer to the history of oppression (segregation) and the need to compensate (remedy) for the past. Other dominant justifications rely on theories of justice which emphasise a particular function of this principle (i.e. restorative justice, distributive justice, compensatory justice), as well as transformative equality, social inclusion and democratic participation (i.e. Rosenfeld, 1993, Hepple, 2013). Today the most popular argument is based on the proven imbalance in representation and the need to ensure greater diversity. For example, in Northern Ireland AA is mandatory only in case a fair participation of religious groups (Protestants and Catholics) does not exist or is not likely to exist, while each employer has the duty to systematically monitor and review this situation. In the USA, courts gradually rejected justifications based on the reparation rationale and banned rigid forms of AA programs. The US Supreme Court also held that the decision as to whether to adopt AA and whom to cover by its scope should be in the hands of legislators rather than judges.

Although AA plans may invite other groups claiming access to similar benefits, it is hard to imagine schemes designed to promote sexual minorities, whereas persons with →disabilities may benefit both from AA and individualised measures (reasonable adjustments/accommodation). Opponents of AA programs argue that they reinforce biases and stigmatisation of the entire group and discourage individual beneficiaries from striving to maximise their capabilities. As a matter of fact, AA programs often result in discrimination complaints filed by those who are not covered by their scope. In consequence, social costs of AA may be significant. Yet, AA policies are usually expanded to other groups (i.e. economically disadvantaged members of the majority) and give priority to individuals from underprivileged groups only if they are equally qualified. Hence, the principle of meritocracy is compromised only in case AA policy does not require equal qualifications (i.e. the Employment Equity Act in South Africa (No. 55 of 1998, Sections 20(3) and (5)), which offers preferential treatment to non-whites who lack necessary qualifications provided that a candidate has the capacity to acquire such qualifications in a reasonable time.

CONCL: While there is a broad consensus regarding the principle of equal treatment and non-discrimination, the sentiment against AA proves to be persistent. Although the use of numerical standards to attain the objective of *de facto* equality may be more effective than equal treatment, quotas and inflexible targets are controversial due to their visibility, especially as they are intended to eliminate 'invisible' forms of discrimination. Many opponents of AA claim that constitutions and laws should remain blind to particular differences ('colour', gender, caste, etc.). Yet, AA takes differences into consideration in order to initiate a structural/institutional, social and cultural change (including free or reduced admissions to cultural services).

AA as a collective remedial mechanism may be problematic from the perspective of intersectional studies because it essentialises group characteristics and requires →community identification which prompts self-identification as members of a particular, often backward group. The intersectional approach also reveals the dilemma of improving the representation of women that may run against the goal of improving the representation of minorities (Lépinard 2013). AA may also lead to assimilation and adoption by members of the underprivileged or minority group of the social roles of the dominant group. However, there is a great potential that AA not only fulfils its remedial function, but also creates a specific culture – the culture of diversity within institutions and organisations.

REFERENCES:

Equinet: Positive Action Measures. The Experience of Equality Bodies, Brussels (2014).

Franceschet, Susan; Krook, Mona Lena and Piscopo, Jennifer, *The Impact of Gender Quotas*, Oxford: Oxford University Press (2012).

Fredman, Sandra: *Discrimination Law*. 2nd edn., Oxford: Oxford University Press (2013).

Gloppen, Siri: "Roads to Reconciliation: A Conceptual Framework" in: Skaar, Elin; Gloppen, Siri and Suhrke, Astri (eds.), *Roads to Reconciliation*, Lanham: Lexington Books (2005).

Hepple, Bob: "Transformative Equality: The Role Of Democratic Participation" in: *Facing development: the North–South Challenge to Transnational Labour Law*, LLRN Barcelona (2013).

HRC, General Comment No. 23, Article 27 ICCPR (1994), U.N. Doc. HRI/GEN/1/Rev.1 (1994), 38.

Kielsgard, Marc: *Responding to Modern Genocide: At the Confluence of Law and Politics*, Oxford: Routledge (2015).

Lépinard, Éléonore: "For Women Only? Gender Quotas and Intersectionality in France" 9 *Politics and Gender* (2013) 276.

McCrudden, Christoph: "Rethinking Positive Action", 15 *Industrial Law Journal* (1986) 219.

PJIC, Minority Schools in Albania, Advisory Opinion, 1935 P.C.I.J. (ser. A/B) No. 64 (Apr. 6).

Rosenfeld, Michel: *Affirmative Action and Justice, A Philosophical and Constitutional Inquiry*, New Haven: Yale University Press (1993).

Sabbagh, Daniel: "Affirmative Action: The US Experience in a Comparative Perspective", 140 *Dedalus, the Journal of the American Academy of Arts & Sciences* (2011) 109.

UN Committee on Elimination of All Forms of Discrimination Against Women (CEDAW): *General Recommendation No. 25 on Article 4 paragraph 1 of the CEDAW – Temporary Special Measures* (2004).

Venice Commission: *Report On Electoral Rules And Affirmative Action For National Minorities' Participation In Decision-Making Process In European Countries*, 15 March 2005, CDL-AD(2005)009.

MARSCHALL v. LAND NORDRHEIN-WESTFALEN (CJEU 11/11/1997, Case C-409/95).

REGENTS OF THE UNIVERSITY OF CALIFORNIA v. BAKKE, 438 U.S. 265 (1978).

SCHUETTE v. COALITION TO DEFEND AFFIRMATIVE ACTION, 572 U.S. (2014).

STEC and OTHERS v. UNITED KINGDOM (ECtHR 12/04/2006, 65731/01).

www.culturalpolicies.net (accessed 06/2014).

Anna Śledzińska-Simon

African Human Rights System

On 25 May 1963 the Organisation of African Unity (OAU) was established, with the main objective to rid the African continent of apartheid and colonisation. In 2002 the OAU was replaced by the African Union (AU), which today associates 54 member states. Under the auspices of the AU, an African human rights system was created. This regional human rights system is based on the *African Charter on Human and Peoples' Rights* (Banjul or African Charter). The system is composed of two entities: the African Commission on Human and Peoples' Rights (the Commission) and the African Court on Human and Peoples' Rights (the Court). The Commission was established under the African Charter and is the premier African human rights body. Its responsibilities are monitoring and promoting compliance with the African Charter. States as well as individuals can bring complaints to the Commission alleging violations of the African Charter by states parties. Furthermore, every two years, each state party is required to submit a report on its efforts to comply with the African Charter. In addition, the Commission can appoint special rapporteurs and working groups to deal with thematic human rights issues, can conduct on-site visits and can adopt resolutions on human rights issues. To complement the work of the Commission, the Court was established by a Protocol on the Establishment of an African Court of Human and Peoples' Rights. The Court has conciliatory, contentious and advisory jurisdiction under this Protocol. States parties, the Commission and African intergovernmental organisations have automatic access to the Court. The access for non-governmental organisations and individuals depends upon whether the concerning state has accepted the jurisdiction of the Court to hear relevant applications.

The African Charter contains several cultural rights, such as the right to take part in the cultural life of the community and the right to education (both in Article 17) as well as freedom of religion (Article 8). The African Charter also contains collective rights (→peoples' rights), for instance the right of all peoples to their economic, social and cultural development, with due regard to their freedom and identity (Article 22). According to the African Charter individuals also have duties, including the duty to "preserve and strengthen positive African cultural values in his relations with other members of the society, in the spirit of tolerance, dialogue and consultation" (Article 29). The African Commission has dealt with several cases concerning (indigenous) peoples and their cultural rights. Landmark cases are those of the Ogoni people against Nigeria and Endorois against Kenya.

REFERENCES:

Evans, Malcolm and Murray, Rachel (eds.): *The African Charter on Human and Peoples' Rights: The System in Practice 1986–2006*, Cambridge: Cambridge University Press (2008).

Heyns, Christof and Killander, Magnus: 'Africa', in Moeckli, Daniel, Shah, Sangeeta and Sivakumaran, Sandesh (eds.): *International Human Rights Law* (Oxford University Press 2014).

Killander, Magnus: 'African Human Rights Law in Theory and Practice' in Joseph, Sarah and McBeth, Adam (eds.): *Research Handbook on International Human Rights Law*, Cheltenham: Edward Elgar (2010).

Kufuor, Kofi Oteng: *The African Human Rights System: Origin and Evolution*, New York: Palgrave Macmillan (2010).

Ssenyonjo, Manisuli: (ed.), *The African Regional Human Rights System*, Leiden: Martinus Nijhoff publishers (2012).

Viljoen, Frans: *International Human Rights Law in Africa*, Oxford: Oxford University Press (2nd edn.) (2012).

CENTRE FOR MINORITY RIGHTS DEVELOPMENT KENYA AND MINORITY RIGHTS GROUP INTERNATIONAL ON BEHALF OF ENDOROIS WELFARE COUNCIL v. KENYA (African Commission on Human and Peoples' Rights, Communication 276/2003, 2009).

THE SOCIAL AND ECONOMIC RIGHTS ACTION CENTER AND THE CENTER FOR ECONOMIC AND SOCIAL RIGHTS v. NIGERIA (African Commission on Human and Peoples' Rights Communication 155/96, 2001).

Yvonne Donders

Alliance of Civilizations

HIST: The Alliance of Civilizations (UNAOC) was established in 2005, at the initiative of former UN Secretary General Kofi Annan and, at the outset, co-sponsored by the governments of Spain and Turkey. A High-Level Group of Experts was formed to explore the causes of polarisation between societies and cultures today. Their Report identified four priority areas for action: *Education, Youth, Migration, Media* and proposed practical recommendations that led to the establishment of the UNAOC. Later, the High Representative of the UNAOC added *sports, music and entertainment* and 'other forms of collective expressions of human values' to the priority areas to be addressed.

INSTR: In 2009, the UN General Assembly expressed its support for the Alliance and acknowledged it as a platform. Today, the UNAOC collaborates in its activities with other UN agencies such as UNESCO or the FAO, and has also signed agreements with regional organisations like the OAS and the African Union. In addition, a global network of partners, including states, civil society groups, foundations, and private companies supports the activities of the Alliance, focusing on improving cross-cultural relations between diverse nations and communities, fostering inter-religious dialogue and regional conflict-prevention and promoting social cohesion as well as 'culturally sensitive' development policies. For example, in 2011, the UNAOC launched, together with UNESCO, a public relations campaign entitled 'Do one thing for diversity and inclusion'. Developed to enhance the profile of World Diversity Day, it was carried out in collaboration with private sector partners, including Dell, Pfizer, Deloitte, Intuit, Johnson and Johnson, and Sodexo. In 2014, the League of Arab States adopted the Unified Arab Strategy for Dialogue of Civilizations.

REFERENCES:

UN General Assembly: "The Alliance of Civilizations", Resolution of 22 December 2009, A/RES/64/14.

http://www.unaoc.org (accessed 06/2016).

Andreas Joh. Wiesand

Archaeological Heritage

DEF: Archaeological heritage comprises of all traces of human existence having a cultural, historical or archaeological character, especially places relating to manifestations of human activity, abandoned structures, and remains of all kinds of human activity (including subterranean and →underwater sites), together with all the portable cultural materials associated with them (for complete definitions see *ICOMOS Charter for the Protection and Management of the Archaeological Heritage*, 1990 and UNESCO 2001 *Convention on the Protection of the Underwater Cultural Heritage*, Article 1(1)).

Installations still in use are mostly excluded from the definition of archaeological heritage, for example installations that are located at the seabed but are still in use, as provided for by the 2001 Convention, Article 1(1). In some cases a certain age is also required (ibid).

Archaeological heritage faces many challenges. It is threatened by commercial exploitation and pillage (both especially relevant for underwater cultural heritage), as well as by environmental, technical, social and economic challenges. Industrial activities threaten to accidentally destroy numerous sites, while in the context of →armed conflict and/or occupation, or of treasure-hunting, archaeological heritage is intentionally destroyed, a practice which targets especially very important sites.

INSTR: The core purpose of legal instruments: securing professional standards for the protection of the archaeological heritage, as well as efforts to prevent looting, vandalism or the destruction of sites, e.g. during armed conflicts or by commercial exploitation, have long been major concerns of international bodies.

Instruments for achieving this include *inter alia* the UNESCO 1954 *Hague Convention for the Protection of Cultural Property in the Event of Armed Conflict* and its *1999 Second Protocol* (in particular, Article 9), the UNESCO 1956 *Recommendation on International Principles Applicable to Archaeological Excavations*, the UNESCO 1972 *World Heritage Convention*, as well as the UNESCO 2001 *Convention on the Protection of the Underwater Cultural Heritage*. Other regulations are found in the Council of Europe *Recommendation on the Underwater Cultural Heritage* (No. 848, 1979) and in *Recommendation Concerning the Protection and Enhancement of the Archaeological Heritage in the Context of Town and Country Planning Operations* (No. R(89)5, 1989) as well as in the *European Convention on the Protection of Archaeological Heritage* (Revised) of 1992 (Valetta Convention).

In general, all these legal instruments aim at increasing the protection and conservation of archaeological sites. Through their corresponding guidelines, they suggest actions against commercial exploitation, pillage, and accidental industrial destruction or intentional destruction in the event of armed conflict and/or occupation. They also call for the application of scientific methods in archaeological research and the prevention of illegal or unscientific excavations.

CASES: By providing legal interpretations, courts assist in indirectly creating guidelines on how matters endangering or destructing archaeological heritage are to be viewed by the law and also what sanctions are generally imposed. As it appears, questions of ownership and of appropriate jurisdiction are common issues in legal proceedings, see for instance a case in the USA [ODYSSEY MARINE EXPLORATION, INC., 2012] concerning the question of who owned the cargo of the Spanish *Nuestra Señora de las Mercedes* wreck and who held jurisdiction over the site. Also questions of damage caused by unscientific interventions are presented to courts, as for instance in the case of the French *Palavas-Les-Flots* shipwrecks in 2015. In this case, a group of persons were sentenced to up to four years in prison by the Court of Montpellier (France), for damage deliberately caused to archaeological sites and the pillage of Gallo–Roman, Etruscan and modern archaeological artefacts.

As seen above, there is existing case-law regarding pillaging or commercial exploitation of archaeological sites on land or under water. Until recently, no significant case-law for destruction of archaeological sites during armed conflict constituted sufficient precedent. In that regard, a case at the International Criminal Court [THE PROSECUTOR, 2016] changed the situation. The confirmation of charges hearing took place on 1 March 2016 before Pre-Trial Chamber I of the ICC. The charges against Ahmad Al Faqi Al Mahdi – which he conceded – consisted in directing attacks against a number of shrines, monuments and mosques in Timbuktu. In this regard, the Prosecutor submitted to the Pre-Trial Chamber on 15 January 2016 her written submissions gathering factual and legal elements to support the accusations. On 27 September 2016, the ICC ruled that the acts of Mr. Al Mahdi were indeed war crimes as defined by Article 8(2)(e)(iv) of the *Rome Statute*.

The timing of this proceeding is critical, due to the recent trend of rampant deliberate destruction of cultural heritage that constitutes damage to the cultural heritage of all of humankind, notably in Iraq and Syria.

VIEWS: Significant is the case of the Islamic Republic of Iran against the Barakat Galleries [GOVERNMENT ..., 2007], whereby the issue of ownership and right to possession was raised, when addressing the question of returning antiquities (illegally excavated) to the state. In particular, Barakat Galleries (based in London) had purchased antiquities from France, Germany and Switzerland under laws which allegedly had given it good title to them. Eventually, the Court of Appeal (UK) found that Iran's rights were 'so extensive and exclusive that they should be regarded as giving ownership'. Yet, for this conclusion to be reached, years of lengthy and expensive litigation passed. The initial ruling of the High Court dismissed Iran's claim due to lack of proof of ownership.

It therefore becomes obvious that in disputes over movable property and particularly antiquities, issues of ownership and rights to possession create great controversy, especially when national legislation is either unclear or different from other legislation. Despite international acceptance of the desirability of protection of national heritage, national legislation should always be clear in matters of ownership, right to possession and protection of archaeological heritage to avoid lengthy litigation.

CONCL: The conservation, protection and management of archaeological heritage is essential for safeguarding the collective legacy of humankind and contributing to the sustainable development of society. Culture, including archaeological heritage, is a key element of the United Nations 2030 Development Agenda. To this effect, an improved cooperation between national and local authorities, managers, researchers and other experts, as well as the development of adapted national and regional policies, remain crucial goals.

REFERENCES:

Cameron, Christina and Rössler, Mechtild: *Many voices, one vision: the early years of the World Heritage Convention*, Ashgate Publishing Limited (2013).

Francioni, Francesco and Lenzerini, Federico (eds.): *The 1972 World Heritage Convention: A Commentary*, Oxford Commentaries on International Law, Oxford: OUP (2008).

Klesmith, Elizabeth A.: "Nigeria and Mali: The Case for Repatriation and Protection of Cultural Heritage in Post-Colonial Africa", *Notre Dame Journal of International & Comparative Law*: Vol. 4: Iss. 1, Article 1 (2014).

Korka, Elena (ed.): *The Protection of Archaeological Heritage in Times of Economic Crisis*, Newcastle: Cambridge Scholars Publishing (2015).

O'Keefe, Patrick J.: "The European Convention on the Protection of the Archaeological Heritage" 67(255) *Antiquity* (1993) 406.

O'Keefe, Patrick J. and Prott, Lyndel V. (eds.): *Cultural Heritage Conventions and other Instruments. A compendium with Commentaries*, Builth Wells: Institute of Art and Law (2011).

Pickard, Robert: *European Cultural Heritage: Intergovernmental Co-operation: Collected Texts*, Volume 1, Strasbourg: Council of Europe Publishing (2005).

Scovazzi, Tullio: "The Law of the Sea Convention and Underwater Cultural Heritage", in David

Freestone (ed.) *The 1982 Law of the Sea Convention at 30: successes, challenges and new agendas*, Leiden: Nijhoff (2013).
BEYELER v. ITALY (ECtHR 05/01/2000, 33202/96).
GOVERNMENT OF THE ISLAMIC REPUBLIC OF IRAN v. THE BARAKAT GALLERIES LIMITED (EWCA Civ 1374, 21/12/2007, WL 4368237).
KOZACIOĞLU v. TURKEY(ECtHR [GC] 19/02/2009, 2334/03).
ODYSSEY MARINE EXPLORATION, INC. v. UNIDENTIFIED SHIPWRECKED VESSEL (11th Cir. 2011, 657 F.3d 1159, *cert. denied*, 132 S. Ct. 2379).
POTOMSKA AND POTOMSKI v. POLAND (ECtHR 29/03/2011, 33494/05).
SEA HUNT, INC. v. UNIDENTIFIED, SHIPWRECKED VESSEL OR VESSELS (4th Cir. 2000, 221 F.3d 634, *aff'g in part & rev'g in part* 47 F. Supp. 2d 678, E.D. Va. 1999).
THE PROSECUTOR v. AHMAD AL FAQI AL MAHDI (Confirmation of charges Press Release and Pre-Trial Information Sheet, www.icc-cpi.int, accessed 1/2016).

Jan Hladík/Ulrike Guérin/Arturo Rey da Silva/ Gloria Lee/Irene Drakou/Khalid Ermilate

Architectural Heritage

DEF: Heritage – Latin: *patrimonium* – is the process of a ceaseless reinterpretation of the past in which the key roles are played by our memory and our choice. It must be pointed out here that although a monument belongs to the past, heritage serves contemporary purposes and heritage concerns not only the material objects of culture, but also our memory and identity. Not everything is heritage, but anything can become heritage. Therefore, the *meaning* of tangible heritage and, more specifically, of the built and architectural heritage is the crucial issue.

INSTR/CASES: Cultural heritage reflects both the society's attitude to the world of values and the dynamic processes of creating and reinterpreting heritage. Heritage belongs to all of us and the access to it is inherent in the basic human right to participate in cultural life, as defined in the *Universal Declaration of Human Rights*. The social and human dimension of heritage and 'the need to put people and human values at the centre of an enlarged and cross-disciplinary concept of cultural heritage' is clearly underlined in the Council of Europe *Framework Convention on the Value of Cultural Heritage for Society* ('Faro Convention', 2005).

Architectural heritage as a specific form of 'social capital' needs effective protection. Related systems and regulations for the protection of monuments can be seen as a significant criterion for the efficiency of a modem state under the rule of law. However, this protection system cannot be separated from a wider context – including not only cultural patronage of the state, but also principles of spatial policy, of social heritage education and, finally, systemic issues.

Heritage regulations are a domain reserved for the state, but some states also willingly appropriate architectural heritage for the needs of their own ideology. In Europe, a contemporary standard for state policies towards the protection of architectural heritage may be boiled down to a few principles. The first principle places an equation mark between the terms: culture goods and cultural heritage, leading to the term 'our common heritage'. This should exclude the danger of a selective protection of monuments following ideological or political criteria and include, for example, the heritage of national minorities or religious communities as our joint responsibility. A second fundamental issue is the necessity to maintain a conservation service and its apolitical character. The third one concerns the mechanism of financing the protection of heritage. The basis of an effective protection of monuments in a democratic state is the principle of a limited ownership right, reflecting a general social interest. The limitation of ownership must not, however, infringe its essence. Thus the state creates a system of assistance compensating additional responsibilities of the owners of monuments. In a Grand Chamber judgment [KOZACIOĞLU, 2009], the ECtHR has underlined that the failure to consider specific architectural or historical characteristics of a listed building when assessing the compensation for an expropriation can be a violation of Article 1 of Protocol No. 1 to the ECHR, since it may impose an excessive and disproportionate burden on applicants. On the other hand, the Court also reiterated 'that legitimate objectives of 'public interest' may call for less than reimbursement of the full market value of the expropriated property.'

CONCL: Architectural heritage today takes various dimensions: local, regional, national and – finally – universal. An effective protection of the cultural heritage is possible only once its diversity is accepted. Since heritage belongs to all of us, it is not the domain of a narrow group of experts.

Its value is determined by the users. Thus one of the fundamental questions related to cultural heritage is a question of its ownership and also a question of who creates, interprets, protects and manages heritage. A separate category today is the heritage of those disinherited and the heritage without heirs, the 'product' of the 20th century tragedies: the Holocaust and ethnic cleansings. Wroclaw – the largest city in Europe and in the world in which, as a result of WWII, the population was exchanged by one hundred per cent – is a very good example of this phenomenon. After 1945 Wroclaw became a polygon for conservation works consisting of the reconstruction of the destroyed city and a true laboratory of heritage understood as memory and identity: For the first Polish settlers, the ruins of the German Breslau meant the heritage of the enemy! For the next decades, the attitudes of subsequent generations of Wroclaw citizens to their small homeland evolved from the heritage of a neighbour to domesticating the heritage and noticing its universal values. The example of Wroclaw lets us better understand the strength and the importance of intangible heritage, our memory and identity as well as the dynamics of heritage as a process.

REFERENCES:

Compendium of basic texts of the Council of Europe in the field of cultural heritage, Strasbourg 1998.

Howard, Peter: *Heritage: Management, Interpretation, Identity*, London–New York: Leicester University Press (2003).

Second International Congress of Architects and Technicians of Historical Monuments: *The Venice Charter* (1964).

UNESCO Convention Concerning the Protection of the World Cultural and Natural Heritage, Paris (1972).

KOZACIOĞLU v. TURKEY (ECtHR 19/02/2009, 2334/03).

Jacek Purchla

Armed Conflict
(Cultural Property Protection in A. C.)

DEF: Access to, and interpretation of, an individual's or group's tangible cultural property (sites, buildings, objects etc.) and intangible cultural heritage (stories, songs, dances etc.) is a fundamental human right (UDHR 1948) (Stone, 2011). Cultural property is however frequently damaged during armed conflict and cultural heritage lost through loss of life and displacement. Most international humanitarian law (IHL) focuses on the protection of cultural property during conflict, rather than the protection of cultural heritage – as the latter is carried by individuals and noncombatants are protected under the 1949 *Geneva Conventions*. Recently work has addressed how to mitigate such damage during conflict.

INSTR: Avoidable damage to cultural property during conflict goes against customary international law and is specifically prohibited under the 1954 *Hague Convention on the Protection of Cultural Property in the Event of Armed Conflict* and its two Protocols of 1954 and 1999 (see Gerstenblith, 2009); the 1977 Additional Protocol I to the *Geneva Conventions* (Articles 53 and 85[4] [d]); and in the 1998 *Rome Statute of the International Criminal Court* (Articles 8(2)(b)(ix) and 8(2)(e)(iv)). IHL also stresses that occupying forces should not withdraw until there are competent authorities to whom governance can be handed over. No-one implies that cultural property protection (CPP) in times of armed conflict is easy (e.g. Bevan 2006) but the responsibility of belligerents to plan to protect cultural property, under IHL is unequivocal. Since the failure of the US/UK led coalition that invaded Iraq in 2003, Western militaries have begun to take CPP more seriously. The academic heritage community has also begun to accept its responsibilities to support their armed forces in the identification of cultural property and in helping to train those in uniform to be alert to their responsibilities for CPP. A '4 Tier Approach' (Stone 2013) has been developed to act as a framework for this collaboration.

CASES: The protection of cultural property was explicitly mentioned in the Agreement on the Status of UNIFIL in Lebanon (REF) and in the UN MINUSMA deployment in Mali. As yet there have been no prosecutions under the Hague Convention. The UN International Criminal Tribunal for the former Yugoslavia (ICTY) has been the primary contemporary international court to address charges relating to the destruction of cultural property. Pavle Strugar and Miodrag Jokić were sentenced to 7.5 and 7 years imprisonment respectively for the shelling, not justified by military necessity, of the World Heritage site of Dubrovnik. The ICTY prosecution of Dusko Tadiç was the first that found the prohibition on attacking cultural property also applied to non-international armed conflicts and the ICTY prosecution against Dario Kardić and Mario Čerkez clarified further individual liability for cultural property destruction (Tusiray 2015). In 2015, the Niger authorities surrendered Ahmad Al Faqi Al Mahdi to the International Criminal Court (ICC) pursuant to an ICC arrest warrant charging him with war crimes in connection to the destruction of cultural property in Mali in 2012 (Tusiray, 2015).

VIEWS: Not all heritage professionals accept that they have a responsibility to assist the military in CPP. Critics suggest that any liaison with the military is wrong as it provides an academic legitimacy to war. Discussing in particular the 2003 invasion of Iraq, some of them focus on the appalling human tragedy of conflict and suggest that it 'challenges seriously our (archaeologists) very ethical foundations and exposes the ethical crisis at the heart of the discipline' (Hamilakis, 2003, 108). Bernbeck (2008), following the concepts of 'neutrality' and 'impartiality', two of the seven principles of the Red Cross (ICRC 1996), extends this argument by suggesting that archaeologists (and others) are carrying out 'structural violence' against the civilian populations caught up in the conflict, and also suggests that the drift of the armed forces into humanitarian work, previously the reserve of NGOs, causes confusion and puts NGO staff at considerable risk. Key to Bernbeck's views is that humanitarian work should be carried out by impartial and neutral agencies thus by definition ruling out any military activity in such areas.

CONCL: While CPP has not been the subject of much legal success there is now a general agreement within the cultural heritage community that they need to engage with CPP. While much focus has been on the protection of museums and archaeological sites, colleagues working in both public and private libraries and archives are also increasingly engaging with such activity under the 'Blue Shield', an organisation originally set up under the *2nd Protocol to the Hague Convention.* Given that many of the actors and requirements are the same, the Blue Shield has expanded its remit to include CPP following environmental disaster. UNESCO, with Blue Shield, is preparing generic training material for the military based on the '4 Tier Approach' and addressing the seven reasons that cultural property gets destroyed during conflict (Stone, 2016). The military has also begun to take its responsibilities more seriously and proactively protected archaeological sites identified before conflict by the Blue Shield (NATO, 2012). More armed forces are including CPP as part of training; NATO is currently discussing the development of an organisation-wide CPP Doctrine; and the NATO affiliated CIMIC Centre of Excellence has just published *Cultural Property Protection Makes Sense* (Foliant 2015).

REFERENCES:

Bernbeck, Reinhard: "Structural Violence in Archaeology", *Archaeologies* 4(3), 390(2008a).

Bernbeck, Reinhard: "Who Has, and Who Should Have Power over the Past and its Remains?", Lecture at *Culture Wars: Heritage and Armed Conflict in the 21st Century*, Centre for Research in the Arts, Social Sciences & Humanities, University of Cambridge, December 2008 (2008b).

Bevan, Robert: *The Destruction of Memory: Architecture at War*, London: Reaktion Books (2006).

Foliant, Yvette: *Cultural Property Protection Makes Sense*, The Hague: Civil–Military Cooperation Centre of Excellence – CCOE (2015).

Gerstenblith, Patty: "Archaeology in the Context of War: Legal Frameworks for Protecting Cultural Heritage during Armed Conflict", *Archaeologies* 5 (1) 18–31 (2009).

Hamilakis, Yannis: "Iraq, Stewardship and 'the Record': An Ethical Crisis for Archaeology", *Public Archaeology* 3(2), 104 (2003).

NATO: *Cultural Property Protection in the Operational Planning Process*, Fact Sheet, Lisbon: Joint Analysis and Lessons Learned Centre (2012).
Stone, Peter G.: "A four-tier approach to the protection of cultural property in the event of armed conflict", *Antiquity*, 87(335), 166–177 (2013).
Stone, Peter G.: "The challenge of protecting heritage in times of armed conflict", *Museums International* 265–268, 40–54 (2016).
Tusiray, Timur: "The International Criminal Court Takes on Attacks on Cultural Heritage, But is it Enough?" (2015), (available at www.itsartlaw.com (accessed 1/2016).
Blue Shield International, www.ancbs.org (accessed 1/2016).
Excellence – CCOE (2015), www.cimic-coe.org/ (accessed 1/2016).
International Criminal Tribunal for the former Yugoslavia (ICTY): www.icty.org (accessed 1/2016).

Peter Stone

Artists' Freedom of Expression

DEF: Freedom of expression in the arts involves the right of artists to express beliefs and ideas in any artistic or creative form, free from private or public restriction. This right is closely linked to other human rights, including the right to take part in cultural life and freedom of expression, but requires distinctive treatment, not least because of artists' resort to fiction and exploration of the imaginary (UN Special Rapporteur in the field of cultural rights, 2013). Restrictions on freedom of artistic expression may take the form of explicit or implicit →censorship, as well as limited opportunities for the production or distribution of certain works, authors or aesthetics.

INSTR: Artists' freedom of expression is explicitly recognised in Article 15(3) of ICESCR, which establishes that states '...undertake to respect the freedom indispensable for... creative activity'. Strong links exist with other human rights, most notably including freedom of expression – as stressed by article 19(2) of ICCPR, which indicates that '(freedom) of expression... shall include freedom to seek, receive and impart information and ideas of all kinds... either orally, in writing or in print, in the form of art, or through any other media...'. The UN Special Rapporteur on Cultural Rights has also identified connections with other rights, including freedom of opinion and conscience and the right to leisure, among others (UN Special Rapporteur in the field of cultural rights, 2013). Freedom of expression in the arts may also be seen as a core part of the broader notion of 'participation in cultural life' (UN Committee on ESC Rights, 2009, para 15(a)). The connection with other rights, particularly freedom of expression, has enabled the ECtHR to underline the importance of artistic expression in the context of the ECHR (Council of Europe), even though the latter does not refer explicitly to this nor to other cultural rights [ECtHR, 2011]. Other relevant international standards include UNESCO's 1980 *Recommendation concerning the Status of the Artist*.

CASES: By relating the right to artistic expression to freedom of expression, the ECtHR has emphasised that the former contributes to the exchange of information and ideas which is essential in a democratic society [MÜLLER and OTHERS, 1988]. Additional nuances stressing the specific nature of artistic expression have been introduced, including the recognition that satire 'naturally aims to provoke and agitate' and, accordingly, restrictions in this field should be examined with particular care [VEREINIGUNG BILDENDER KÜNSTLER, 2007]; as well as, interestingly, the fact that some artistic expressions, such as poetry or novels, appeal to a narrow public and thus tend to have limited social impact [KARATAŞ, 1994; ALINAK, 2005]. However, the Court has also recognised that limitations to freedom of expression in the arts may be applied, on grounds similar to those that apply to other forms of expression, including offending religious feelings [OTTO-PREMINGER-INSTITUT, 1994] and the protection of morals [MÜLLER AND OTHERS, 1988]. The Court has also argued that, when fiction works introduce non-fictional characters, such as political figures, respect for others' reputation and rights should be considered, in a way not dissimilar to other forms of expression [LINDON, OTCHAKOVSKY-LAURENS AND JULY, 2007].

VIEWS: Overt violations of freedom of artistic expression are relatively rare in Europe nowadays, although some high-profile cases exist (e.g. the imprisonment of members of Russian punk band Pussy Riot). However, more subtle restrictions can be found in the form of social, political or economic pressure, self-censorship or limited production or distribution opportunities for certain works or authors. Examples include the pressure from fellow community members experienced by some artists, including those with a migrant background, when addressing religion (e.g. the cancelled presentation of the play *Behzti* in Birmingham, 2004) or because of their choice of a professional career in the arts (as in the case of Norwegian singer Deeyah), as well as the cancellation of installations seen to contain implicitly racist elements (e.g. Brett Bailey's show *Exhibit B*, 2014 – see also Denselow, 2013; Polivtseva, 2015). Instances of corporate →censorship, e.g. legal or financial pressure, or the threat thereof, towards artists who publicly denounce private companies, have also been described (Denselow, 2013). European civil society groups and, to a lesser extent, public institutions have increasingly paid attention to freedom of artistic expression in other world regions – including the European Parliament's inclusion of artists as human rights defenders in its Human Rights Reports (Cuny and Polácek, 2012).

CONCL: Freedom of expression in the arts stands as a cornerstone for the exercise of cultural rights and the development of a sustainable cultural sector. Its fulfilment can be enhanced through the adoption of enabling measures in cultural policy and other fields, such as the promotion of →arts education, enabling →children, young people and adults to interpret and critique cultural contents in a more positive way than that embodied by censorship or restriction (UN Special Rapporteur in the field of cultural rights, 2013). Attention should also be paid to the existence of bureaucratic procedures or selection criteria in public or private support schemes which may in practice prevent or limit the production or distribution of certain forms of artistic expression, when these may amount to covert censorship (see examples in countries outside Europe in Polivtseva, 2015). Local, national and international policies in this area could take inspiration from, or support, the increasing work done by civil society organisations, acting in a 'watchdog' and awareness-raising role (e.g. Freemuse; freeDimensional; Index on Censorship; Observatoire de la liberté de creation; Article 19; Arts Rights Justice) or providing shelter to writers and artists at risk (e.g. the International Cities of Refuge Network – ICORN or some Writers in Exile schemes that work closely with PEN International and its national chapters).

REFERENCES:

Cuny, Laurence and Polácek, Richard: *Arts and Human Rights*, Brussels: Access to Culture Platform (2012).

Denselow, Robin (rapporteur): *All that is Banned is Desired. World Conference on Artistic Freedom of Expression*, Copenhagen: Freemuse (2013).

European Court of Human Rights: *Cultural rights in the case-law of the European Court of Human Rights*, Strasbourg: Council of Europe (2011).

Polivtseva, Elena (rapporteur): *The Cultural Sector: megaphoning free expression*, Brussels: IETM (2015), available at: www.ietm.org.

UN Committee on Economic, Social and Cultural Rights: *Right of everyone to take part in cultural life (art. 15, para. 1 (a), of the International Covenant on Economic, Social and Cultural Rights)*, Geneva: Economic and Social Council (2009), E/C.12/GC/21.

UN Special Rapporteur in the field of cultural rights. *The right to freedom of artistic expression and creativity*, Geneva: Human Rights Council (2013), A/HRC/23/34.

UNESCO: *Recommendation concerning the Status of the Artist*. Paris: UNESCO (1980).

ALINAK v. TURKEY (ECtHR 29/3/2005, 40287/98).

KARATAŞ v. TURKEY (ECtHR 8/7/1999, 23168/94).

LINDON, OTCHAKOVSKY-LAURENS and JULY v. FRANCE (ECtHR 22/10/07, 21279/02 and 36448/02).

MÜLLER and OTHERS v. SWITZERLAND (ECtHR 24/5/1988, 10737/84).

OTTO-PREMINGER-INSTITUT v. AUSTRIA (ECtHR 20/9/94, 13470/87).

VEREINIGUNG BILDENDER KÜNSTLER v. AUSTRIA (ECtHR 25/1/2007, 68354/01).

Jordi Baltà Portolés

Arts Education

DEF: Arts education relates to all learning environments defined by the European Commission (2000) and UNESCO (2009): formal, non-formal, informal learning. However, due to more or less far-reaching concepts of 'arts' and 'culture', a binding definition of the term is difficult to reach – for example, in some European countries 'cultural education' is a more commonly used expression. Expert discussions are caught between a very narrow understanding of arts education, focusing mainly on the fine arts, music, literature, etc., and a very broad perception of the term, whose challenges could be seen in the fact that it can, potentially, reach out to many customs, manifestations and societal processes. At the individual level, a sensible usage of cultural tools in terms of translation and expression of individual experience, communication with society, and developing self-identity is frequently emphasised. At the social level, the focus is often on handling traditions, cultural diversity, identity and creativity. Mediating the 'arts' is closely connected with fostering reception, production and reflection or positioning. The concept of 'learning through the arts', including the development of different learning contexts by means of arts education, is another option.

INSTR: In policy contexts, arts education is strongly connected with cultural expressions and participation. It contributes meaningfully to implementing human rights such as 'the right freely to participate in the cultural life of the community, to enjoy the arts ...' (Article 27, UDHR). This 'right to culture' is also spelled out in the ICESCR (Article 15) or in the UN *Convention on the Rights of the Child* (Articles 13, 29 and 31). Another reference source for arts education is the UNESCO *Convention on the Protection and Promotion of the Diversity of Cultural Expressions* (Articles 10 and 11), which calls on states, together with civil society, to 'encourage and promote... the diversity of cultural expressions, inter alia, through educational and greater public awareness programmes'. Similar provisions do not yet exist in Europe, even if case law has extended the guarantee of freedom of expression (Article 10, ECHR) to manifestations in the arts and media.

As regards national policies and infrastructures for arts education and its promotion in formal and non-formal contexts, conditions vary a lot between countries worldwide. At the second UNESCO World Conference on Arts Education 2010, the *Seoul Agenda* was adopted, which formulated development goals like ensuring accessibility to qualitative arts education for all and using its principles to cope with today's social and cultural challenges.

CONCL: Empirical studies have demonstrated that arts education, especially in its non-formal and informal varieties, is key to the realisation of cultural participation (Keuchel/Larue, 2012). This underlines that providing arts institutions and related services alone will not be sufficient to implement a 'right to culture'. What's needed are also provisions that enable and foster access to arts education for all demographic and social groups.

REFERENCES:

International Yearbook for Research in Arts Education, Vol. 1–4, Münster/New York: Waxmann (2013–2016).

Keuchel, Susanne and Larue, Dominic: *Das 2. Jugend-KulturBarometer*, Cologne: ARCult Media (2012).

UNESCO Institute for Lifelong Learning: *Global Report on Adult Learning and Education*, Hamburg: UIL (2009).

Susanne Keuchel

Asian Values

DEF: The expression 'Asian Values' (AV), often synonymous with 'Confucian values,' became a powerful rhetorical tool in the 1990s, when it started to be used by prominent East Asian leaders – in particular the Former Senior Minister of Singapore, Lee Kuan Yew, and the former Prime Minister of Malaysia, Mahathir Mohamad – to define a system of values proper to Asia, also with a view on the 'Asian economic miracle'. These values, broadly speaking, place economic development first and foremost above everything else, support collectivity and harmony rather than individual and personal freedom, and reaffirm the principles of sovereignty and non-interference. On the grounds of the relativity of values, AV have been set in opposition to what was perceived, at the end of the Cold War, when the Soviet alternative had lost much of its power, as a hegemonic process of universalisation of 'Western values' in the form of universal human rights instruments and democratic forms of government.

INSTR: Although many Asian leaders used the rhetoric of 'Asian Values' and a working group for an Association for Southeast Asian Nations (ASEAN) human rights mechanism was created in 1995, there still exists no Asian charter of rights in which such values are codified. The political movement promoting AV reached its peak in the *Bangkok Declaration* of 1993, which was adopted by Asian states in preparation for the World Conference on Human Rights held in Vienna in the same year. Through this declaration, the Asian states, while accepting the principle of human rights, reaffirmed the cultural, historical and religious specificities of Asian nations, and supported the principle of sovereignty and non-interference. Despite previous disagreements over which human rights could be considered truly universal since the proclamation of the →Universal Declaration of Human Rights (UDHR) in 1948, the *Vienna Declaration* of 1993 reaffirmed that all human rights are universal, indivisible, interdependent and interrelated. At the same time, the Vienna Declaration recognised 'the significance of national and regional peculiarities and various historical, cultural and religious backgrounds.'

CASES: An analysis of the various Asian constitutions shows that they share some distinctive elements: the prevalence of collective rights over individual rights, the emphasis on rights guaranteed by the law and limitations or suspension of rights in the name of general interests. Moreover, Asian constitutions put special emphasis on national sovereignty and economic development. However, these similarities do not give a definite answer to what is meant by the label 'Asian Values'. There are no court rulings that refer explicitly to AV. This is due partly to the lack of Asian human rights instruments and monitoring mechanisms like a regional court or similar bodies. Despite the absence of cases that directly mention AV, international courts are, nevertheless, inclined to take into account cultural specificities in the implementation of human rights (as explained under →Universalism and Cultural Relativism). This flexibility is also reflected in the doctrine of the →margin of appreciation developed by the ECtHR. Although human rights monitoring, led by the UN and supported by NGOs, continues to track human rights abuses in the Asian–Pacific region according to common standards, the particular social and cultural context of Asian countries is usually taken into account in this process.

VIEWS: The promotion of AV by political leaders has prompted a lively debate. One of the major points of critique has been the impossibility of defining Asia univocally, because of its complexity and its variety of economic, political, legal and religious traditions: As there is not a monolithic Asia, there cannot be a monolithic and static set of 'Asian Values'. Critics also argue that it is misleading to set Asian and Western values into opposition to each other. Since supposedly AV such as family responsibilities and kinship can be found to differing degrees in all cultures, the same is true for alleged 'Western Values.' For instance, studies dismissed the perception that Confucianism would not support the idea of individual human personalities as well as of human rights and democracy. Human rights have their roots in many cultures and it is risky to essentialise any civilisation, whether 'Asian' or 'Western', and its corresponding set of values. Within a particular culture and civilisation, contestation is not uncommon, as people have different aspirations. Thus some political leaders have argued that the debate on AV is not so much about cultural values and cultural diversity, but rather about political power and structures: Political leaders promote the values that fit with their agenda.

CONCL: The 'Asian Values' debate experienced a setback after the Asian crisis in 1997. Today the strongest advocate for them is China. China's economic prosperity allegedly linked to its alternative 'Asian model,' – which values more a central authoritarian government over pluralism, social harmony over dissent, economic development over civil and political liberties –, seems to question universalism of human rights. While acknowledging the important fact that Asia is as such not a homogenous geographical or political area, conceptually and historically, we could today take the ASEAN +3 countries (China, Japan, Korea) as a reference. However, the cultural or traditional communalities that might characterise the area of ASEAN+3 are difficult to render into law, and the similarities in the understanding of human rights found in Asian countries' constitutions is not necessarily the result of the existence of a set of AV. These constitutions are constantly changing and evolving. This transformation, rather than being the result of AV, reflects the different cycles of constitutional development. The relativism promoted by AV seems to go against the aspirations of the UDHR 1948, which was to promote universal and indivisible human rights, so as to avoid people being treated as subhuman. The history of how the UDHR has been developed actually highlights the complexity of cross-cultural dialogue about fundamental rights and reaffirms the need to find a balance between universal rights and their implementation in local cultural and traditional environments. This task, reflected in inter alia the doctrine of the → 'margin of appreciation', remains very much alive today.

REFERENCES:

Blondel, Jean: *Political Cultures in Asia and Europe: Citizens, States and Societal Values*, London: Routledge (2006).

De Bary, William Theodore: *Asian Values and Human Rights: A Confucian Communitarian Perspective*, Cambridge, Mass: Harvard University Press, (1998).

De Varennes, Fernand (ed.): *Asia–Pacific Human Rights Documents and Resources, vol. 2*, The Hague: Martinus Nijhoff Publisher (2000).

Groppi, Tania (ed.): *Asian Constitutionalism in Transition: A Comparative Perspective*, Milan: Giuffrè (2008).

Jacobsen, Michael and Brun, Ole (eds.): *Human Rights and Asian Values. Contesting National Identities and Cultural Representations in Asia*, London: Curzon Press (2000).

Pye, Lucian W.: "Asian Values: From Dynamos to Dominoes?" in Lawrence E. Harrison and Samuel P. Huntington (eds.): *Culture Matters, How Values Shape Human Progress*, New York: Basic Books (2000), 244.

Sen, Amartya: "Human Rights and Asian Values", *The Sixteenth Morgenthau Memorial Lecture on Ethics and Foreign Policy*, Carnegie Council on Ethics and Foreign Affairs (1997) (available at: www.carnegiecouncil.org/ accessed 2/2016).

Tan, Hsien-Li: *The ASEAN Intergovernmental Commission on Human Rights: Institutionalising Human Rights in Southeast Asia*, Cambridge: Cambridge University Press (2011).

Yee, S: "The Role of Law in the Formation of Regional Perspectives in Human Rights and Regional Systems for the Protection of Human Rights: The European and Asian Models as Illustrations", in *Singapore Yearbook of International Law and Contributors* (2004).

Maria Adele Carrai

Assembly and Association

(Freedom of)

DEF: This right enables people to form or join associations, e.g. political parties, trade unions, or in the context of national and ethnic minorities, associations for cultural, religious, socio-economic and other purposes. It also covers assemblies, including for peaceful protests. It is not an absolute right and may be subject to restrictions. Further, it is essentially a negative right (the State must refrain from action that interferes with this right), but the State may also have a positive obligation to ensure the effective enjoyment of this right. In practice, this right is often read in connection with the freedoms of thought, conscience and religion and expression.

INSTR: Under Article 11, ECHR, all have a right to join or form an association or to assemble with others peacefully. The right is not absolute and can be restricted, as long as restrictions are according to the law and necessary in a democratic society. No explicit mention is made of culture in this Article, but the ECtHR case law has developed in this direction.

The *Framework Convention for the Protection of National Minorities* (FCPNM, 1995) is more specific and in a cultural context provides that national minorities have the right to freedom of peaceful assembly and association. Its preamble presupposes the right, giving it greater context by stating that a democracy should respect the ethnic, cultural, linguistic and religious identity of national minorities, and also create appropriate conditions for them to express, preserve and develop this identity.

The HRC, in its *Resolution 15/21* (Sept. 2010), has recognised the importance of association for enabling individuals to “engage in literary and artistic pursuits”. In *Resolutions 21/162 and 24/53* it has reiterated the key role of new information and communication technologies in enabling and facilitating association, which could be relevant for culture in connection with →digital media/ arts and freedom of expression.

CASES: In [SIDIROPOULOS AND OTHERS, 1998], the ECtHR held that the right was not limited to associations of a political nature, despite Article 11§1 only expressly referring to trade unions. More specifically, associations for preserving minority consciousness were not caught by the limitations in Article 11§2, as they were not a threat to democratic society. In particular, the *Document of the Copenhagen Meeting of the Conference on the Human Dimension* of the CSCE and the *Charter of Paris for a New Europe* – both signed by Greece – allowed the applicants to form associations to protect their cultural and spiritual heritage.

Creative arts were more concretely referred to in [GORZELIK, 2004]. Here the ECtHR stressed that in addition to political parties, other associations were important for pluralism which depended, among others, on respect for artistic and literary ideas.

The right was delimited in [SCHIMANEK v. AUSTRIA, 2000], where the ECtHR emphasised that it did not extend to associations formed for purposes incompatible with democracy and human rights. As an example, in [REFAH PARTISI AND OTHERS, 2001], the Court found the dissolution of the Refah Party by the Turkish authorities did not violate Article 11 as the party’s principles could undermine democracy.

Finally, the UN Special Rapporteur in the field of cultural rights (2013) has recalled that the right of assembly and association is also a right for artists to enjoy in a political context, enabling them to form and join trade unions.

VIEWS: While the [REFAH PARTISI, 2001] case essentially dealt with the right to assemble of a political party, it also concerns this right in relation to a group of people with a set of cultural values which were seen as a threat to secularism and the democratic values of the Council of Europe. A minority of judges stressed, among others, that democratic debate required a diverse range of political views, including even those that may be considered incompatible with current State principles and structures.

CONCL: The freedom to join with others is essentially a political right, and most of the case law concerns a political context: i.e. attempts of people to assemble, e.g. in peaceful protest, or form an association, e.g. a trade union.

However, this freedom is strongly connected to the freedoms in Articles 9 (thought, conscience and religion) and 10 ECHR (expression, including artistic expression as per the case law). It is therefore an important freedom for arts and culture, and should be facilitated in a cultural context wherever possible. In its case law, the ECtHR has stated that the freedom extends to associations for protecting the dynamics of cultural traditions, ethnic and cultural identities, religious beliefs, artistic, literary and socio-economic ideas and concepts.

Despite the lack of case law for creative culture, it is nonetheless hard to imagine that the right would not apply to an association formed to promote creativity if ever a public authority refused to register, or decided to dissolve, an association of this type.

More case law in the arts field may be forthcoming with the recent recognition by the HRC of the important role of new information technologies for freedom of association, in connection with the freedoms of expression, thought, conscience and religion, as well as the rise of hate speech groups on the internet. Policy should look at augmenting digital access and fostering responsible Internet practice.

REFERENCES:

Boyle, Kevin: "Human Rights, Religion and Democracy: the Refah Party Case", *Essex Human Rights Review* (2004).

Council of Europe, Committee of experts on cross-border flow of Internet traffic and Internet freedom (MSI-INT): *Draft report on freedom of assembly and association on the Internet*, MSI-INT (2014)08 rev 2, 11 May 2015.

Council of Europe, Research Division: *Cultural rights in the case-law of the European Court of Human Rights*, Strasbourg (2011).

Equality and Human Rights Commission: "Article 11: Freedom of assembly and association", in *Human Rights Review 2012*, London (2012).

GORZELIK AND OTHERS v. POLAND (ECtHR 17/02/2004, 44158/98).

REFAH PARTISI (THE WELFARE PARTY) AND OTHERS v. TURKEY (ECtHR 31/07/2001, 41340/98, 41342/98, 41343/98 and 41344/98.

SIDIROPOULOS AND OTHERS v. GREECE, (ECtHR 10/07/1998, 57/1997/841/1047).

www.article19.org (accessed 01/2016).

Siobhan Montgomery

Authors' Rights / Copyright

(in a Human Rights Context)

DEF/INSTR: Internationally, the material and moral interests of authors regarding the protection of their scientific, literary or artistic works have been defined as particular Human Rights (UDHR, Article 27(2); ICESCR, Article 15(1)(c)) and, especially in Europe, as intellectual property (UDHR, Article 17; Protocol no. 1, ECHR, Article 1; ECtHR [ASHBY, 2013]; CFR Article 17(2)). These rights, however, are part of a set of other rights and freedoms, such as freedom of expression (UDHR, Article 19; ECHR, Article 10); the right to education, to culture, to the benefit of scientific progress (UDHR, Articles 26 and 27; ICESCR, Articles 13 and 15; CFR, Articles 13 and 14); the right to privacy and to the protection of personal data (ECHR, Article 8; CFR, Articles 7 and 8); or the freedom to conduct a business (CFR, Article 16).

In the twentieth century, the international and European (TRIPS; WIPO treaties; EU directives) as well as some of the national legal frameworks with regard to literary and artistic property became excessive:

(1) poorly defined criteria relating to protection led to an *almost unlimited expansion of protected subject-matter* (including e.g. instructions, forms of candies, tourist routes, sports events, etc.);
(2) *new rights* (resale right, private copying, reprography, rental, lending, fair remuneration);
(3) *protection of computer tools* (software);
(4) *exclusive rights protecting investments* (neighbouring rights of phonogram and video producers, of broadcasting organisations, *sui generis* right of database producers, of newspaper publishers);
(5) *extension of copyright* (to 70 years *post mortem auctoris) and neighbouring rights* (to 70 years from the first act of exploitation), creating in the 20th century a real 'black hole' in the exploitation and archiving of works;
(6) *legal protection of locking systems*, also blocking the application of exceptions and restrictions and the utilisation of the public domain;
(7) *introduction of enhanced penalties* (criminal and civil, such as suspension of access to the Internet in France).

However, the proliferation of exclusive rights and rights to remuneration only marginally assists authors and artists ('Authors' rights help only a tiny minority of artists to survive', Pierre Langlais 2015) and, instead, mainly benefits the holders of exploitation rights to creative works and →intangible cultural heritage (editors, music industry, collective management companies, Internet and broadcast platforms, etc.).

CASES: When several fundamental rights are in conflict, the high courts of justice tend towards ensuring a fair balance between them. For example:

a) In support of copyright:

- A restriction on the freedom of speech and information must be interpreted strictly, and must be based on 'a pressing social need'

and 'be proportionate to the legitimate aim pursued'. A restriction may be justified by an act of infringement against fashion designer's copyright, as the latter is also a fundamental right under intellectual property [ASHBY, 2013].
- The freedom of information and the freedom of enterprise can't be opposed to the injunction of blocking a website that infringes copyright [UPC TELEKABEL, 2014].

b) In support of the freedom of expression and information, the right to →privacy and the freedom of enterprise:
- Access to the Internet is a fundamental right (FR Const. Ct, 2009);
- An unrestricted injunction to install a filtering system on all electronic communications to identify the circulation of works in electronic format (peer to peer) infringes fundamental rights [SCARLET, 2011]; similarly for online social networks [SABAM, 2012];
- Linking and framing is not considered to be an act of communication to the public if the work is already freely available on another Internet site [SVENSSON, 2014; BESTWATER, 2014].

VIEWS: In the last decades, the ownership of intangible assets based on the assumption that →intellectual property is *per se* useful to the common good (Convention establishing the WIPO, Article 3) since it protects against competition and stimulates innovation and creativity in a post-industrial, high added value market, has increasingly been met with criticism. In order to justify this assumption, *individual creativity* is substituted by *economic investment*: rewarding the latter forms the basis for the European Commission's recent development policy for the digital single market.

Some question this utilitarian justification of what is considered to be an excessive and useless appropriation: no serious study appears to demonstrate that intellectual property protection would be more effective than the free market and common law in stimulating creativity and its dissemination. Consequently, a now frequent view is that the public domain should be expanded by reducing the terms of protection and avoiding technological or contractual locking.

Others consider that the system of intellectual and artistic property has developed to the detriment of other fundamental rights such as the right to personal and social development based on the freedom of human creativity, expression and information as well as to the right to participate in cultural life and science. In this view, a new balance must not only allow access to works and scientific knowledge but should indeed facilitate informal training and research, the aggregation of digital modules, data mining, etc. as well as the creative, derived, interpretation of works, contrary to some court rulings on 'moral rights' [e.g. Paris Court of Appeal, BERNANOS v. TCHERNIAKOV, 2015]. Similar concerns regarding freedom of artistic expression vs. copyright have already been positively taken up in a recent case on music sampling [German Federal Const. Court, 1 BvR 1585/13, 2016].

CONCL: The global, digital civilisation of the twenty first century puts the right to literary and artistic property into a new societal perspective. Basing the latter on *fundamental rights* (spelled out in the UDHR) and the *general interest* should result in an improved balance between the right to ownership, authors' moral and material interests, and the right to participate in cultural life and scientific knowledge. In the words of Farida Shaheed, Special Rapporteur in the field of cultural rights of the UN HRC, 2014: '*Both cultural participation and protection of authorship are human rights principles designed to work in tandem.*' This 'pressing social need' has already spontaneously materialised through the voluntary establishment of non-appropriable public domain tools using existing law (General Public Licence, Creative Commons Licences; Open Access; Wikipedia; etc.). However, more *structural reforms* are required (e.g. the *Adelphi Charter* 2005, Royal Society for the Encouragement of Arts, Manufactures and Commerce, UK; *Copyright for Creativity – A Declaration for Europe*, 2010). They relate to the nature of intellectual property rights (temporary privilege granted by the state to benefit the general interest); improved criteria for access to protection; transparency to identify the protected objects; a reduced term of protection; an obligation to enable normal exploitation under penalty of loss of rights; legal licences rather than exclusive rights; the simplification of legislation and the protection of the public domain. In addition, the exercise of an artistic activity should be facilitated by guaranteeing authors and artists the freedom of creation and recreation, an appropriate income, especially by means of a more effective regulation of their contracts, a clear and better →status of artists in terms of social, fiscal and other rights, as well as through appropriate information.

REFERENCES:

Buydens, Mireille: *La Propriété intellectuelle – Evolution historique et philosophique*, Bruxelles: Bruylant (2012).

Commission européenne: *Vers des règles européennes du droit d'auteur adaptée à l'ère numérique*, Communiqué de presse, Bruxelles, 9 décembre 2015.

Council of Europe: *Copyright and Human Rights*, Report prepared by the Group of Specialists on Human Rights in the Information Society (MS-S_IS), Directorate General of Human Rights and Legal Affairs, Strasbourg, June 2009, H/inf (2009).

Hugenholtz, P. Bernt: "Copyright and Freedom of Expression in Europe", in Cooper Dreyfuss, R., Leenheer Zimmerman, D., First, H. (eds.): *Expanding the Boundaries of Intellectual Property, Innovation Policy for the Knowledge Society*, Oxford: Oxford University Press (2001).

Jones, Susan: "Artists low income and status are international issues", *The Guardian*, 01/12/2015.

Langlais, Pierre-Carl: "Le droit d'auteur ne fait vivre qu'une infime minorité d'artistes", 08/04/2015 rue89.nouvelobs.com (accessed 06/16).

Reda, Julia: Rapport sur la mise en oeuvre de la directive 2001/29/CE "Droit d'auteur et Société de l'information", Parl. Eur. 2014–2019, 15. 1. 2015, P.E.546.580v02-00.

Shaheed, Farida: *Copyright policy and the right to science and culture*, Report of the special Rapporteur in the field of cultural rights, U.N., Human rights Council, A/HRC/28/57, 2014.12.24.

Volat, Gwendoline: "Auteurs du livre affiliés à l'Agessa: dégradation des perspectives de revenus au fil des générations", *Culture chiffres* 2/2016 (n° 2).

ASHBY DONALD AND OTHERS v. FRANCE (ECtHR, 10/01/2013, 36769/08).

SCARLET v. SABAM (CJEU 14/11/2011, C-70/10).

SVENSSON AND OTHERS v. RETRIEVER SVERIGE AB (CJEU 13/02/2014, C-466/12).

UPC TELEKABEL WIEN v. CONSTANTIN FILM VERLEIH / WEGA FILMPRODUKTION (CJEU 24/03/2014, C314/12).

Suzanne Capiau

Belief

(Freedom of Conscience and Religious B.)

DEF: A belief is a form of conviction or a set of values concerning reality or the spiritual or philosophical premises informing human conduct. They can include deistic, atheistic or non-theistic convictions and worldviews. Belief is protected in international law of human rights similarly to religion and the difference between the two is often fluid and uncertain. The threshold of what views constitute a protected form of belief remains frequently disputed and is subject to case by case determination. The important characteristics of seriousness, importance and cohesion have been, however, established as the minimum threshold for recognition of a protected 'belief'.

INSTR: Freedom of belief is protected together with freedom of religion in numerous international legal documents, such as Article 18 of the UDHR, Article 18 of ICCPR, Article 9 of the ECHR and Article 10 of the *Charter of Fundamental Rights of the EU*. Other regional conventions such as the *American Convention on Human Rights* and *African Charter on Human and People's Rights* also include provisions on freedom of conscience. Provisions securing freedom of conscience (including religion and belief) typically secure freedom to manifest one's belief in worship, teaching and observance and change one's belief.

Freedom of conscience is not an absolute right and can be limited by law. Article 9(2) of the ECHR allows for limitations that *'are prescribed by law and are necessary in a democratic society in the interests of public safety, for the protection of public order, health or morals, or for the protection of the rights and freedoms of others'*. Additionally, Article 2 of Protocol 1 to the ECHR guarantees parents the right to education of their children in conformity with their religious and philosophical convictions. The jurisprudence of the court has dealt with the relationship between beliefs and 'philosophical convictions'.

CASES: The key problems in the case law on freedom of belief are the threshold of protected belief, the question whether any belief is protected by the ECHR and the relationship between protected beliefs and philosophical convictions. Jurisprudence regarding Article 2 of Protocol 1 has considered these issues in [X,Y AND Z, 1997] where the ECtHR held that the threshold of protection is reserved for beliefs with a certain level of cogency, seriousness, cohesion and importance.

In [CAMPBELL AND COSANS, 1982] the ECtHR added that in ordinary meaning the word 'convictions', taken on its own, is not synonymous with the words 'opinions' and 'ideas', it is more akin to the term 'beliefs' and denotes the views that attain a certain level of cogency, seriousness, cohesion and importance. When combined with an adjective 'philosophical', the expression 'philosophical convictions' denotes beliefs worthy of respect in a 'democratic society'. The freedom is applicable to both minority and majority beliefs. The ECtHR has argued in [BAYATYAN, 2011] that 'respect on the part of the State towards the beliefs of a minority religious group (...) by providing them with the opportunity to serve society as dictated by their conscience might (...) ensure cohesive and stable pluralism and promote religious harmony and tolerance in society'. In a case regarding the parental rights of access that had been denied by regional authorities because of a father's alleged 'irrational worldview', the Court considered this to be 'no reasonable relationship of proportionality' [VOJNITY, 2013].

VIEWS: The possibility of too low a threshold that would embrace beliefs not meeting the ECtHR's threshold of seriousness and the possibility of protecting fictional religious movements has attracted diverse responses. Some see the low threshold as advantageous for removing administrative discretion in protecting beliefs (Martinez-Tórron, 2001). In practice, however, some of the newly emerging beliefs – like the 'Church of the Flying Spaghetti Monster' that applied in vain for registration in Poland – are often considered as 'parody religions' (Laycock, 2013) and therefore refused protection. As well, beliefs that are commonly considered controversial often have difficulties in acquiring legal protection. The 'Church of Scientology' and cases concerning its registration before national courts and the ECtHR illustrate the problematic of protecting all beliefs equally [see e.g. CHURCH OF SCIENTOLOGY MOSCOW AND OTHERS, 2007; CHURCH OF SCIENTOLOGY v. SWEDEN, 1979; SCIENTOLOGY KIRCHE DEUTSCHLAND, 1997]. Some critics insist that concerns about fictional beliefs may result in unjustified classification which reinforces traditional image of a legitimate belief (Taira, 2010, Gozdecka, 2016), thus limiting the effective exercise of religious pluralism that would also include beliefs about religions.

CONCL: Belief and its protection in human rights law is crucial for the existence of a religiously plural society. As underlined by the ECtHR: 'freedom of thought, conscience and religion is one of the foundations of a "democratic society" within the meaning of the Convention. It is, in its religious dimension, one of the most vital elements that go to make up the identity of believers and their conception of life, but it is also a precious asset for atheists, agnostics, sceptics and the unconcerned. The pluralism indissociable from a democratic society, which has been dearly won over the centuries, depends on it.' [KOKKINAKIS, 1993, para. 31]. The problems of threshold between religion and belief and between belief and nonbelief illustrate more general dilemma concerning the essence of the protection of the freedom of thought granted in international law of human rights. The contentious issues concern the scope of protection and the distinction between those elements of freedom enshrined in Article 9 that can and cannot be limited. While similar elements are contested when it comes to the protection of recognised religions, the fluid and more open-ended nature of belief renders the boundaries of the freedom even harder to determine.

REFERENCES:

Gozdecka, Dorota Anna: *Rights, Religious Pluralism and the Recognition of Difference: Off the Scales of Justice*, Abingdon: Routledge (2016).

Laycock, Joseph P: "Laughing Matters: 'Parody Religions' and the Command to Compare." 42(3) *Bulletin for the Study of Religion* (2013).

Martinez-Tórron Javier: "Freedom of religion in the case law of the Spanish Constitutional Court", *Brigham Young University Law Review* (2001).

Minister Administracji i Cyfryzacji, Decyzja Odmowna (Refusal), 25 February 2013, available at: www.klps.pl/pliki/decyzja.pdf. (accessed 07/2016).

Taira, Teemu: "Religion as a Discursive Technique: The Politics of Classifying Wicca." 25(3) *Journal of Contemporary Religion* (2010).

BAYATYAN v. ARMENIA (ECtHR 07/07/2011, 23459/03).

CAMPBELL AND COSANS v. THE UK (ECtHR 25/03/1982, 7511/76).

CHURCH OF SCIENTOLOGY v. SWEDEN (ECtHR 05/05/1979, 7805/77).

CHURCH OF SCIENTOLOGY MOSCOW AND OTHERS v. RUSSIA (ECtHR 05/04/2007, 18147/02).

KOKKINAKIS v. GREECE (ECtHR 25/05/1993, 14307/88).

SCIENTOLOGY KIRCHE DEUTSCHLAND v. GERMANY (ECtHR 07/04/1997, 34614/96).

VOJNITY v. HUNGARY (ECtHR 12/02/2013, 29617/07).

X, Y AND Z v. THE UK (ECtHR 22/04/1997, 21830/93).

Dorota Gozdecka

Blasphemy

DEF: Blasphemy is an act of showing contempt or disregard for deity or sacred objects, in particular religious symbols. It can be committed in any form which conveys a defamatory message, verbal or non-verbal. There is no single legal definition of blasphemy in Europe. In non-legal contexts, it is commonly interpreted as any attack on religion or religious convictions. However, blasphemy should be distinguished from such legal concepts as religious insults (insult to religious feelings, insult based on belonging to a particular religion), religious discrimination, or incitement to hatred on grounds of religious affiliation or convictions (Report, 2008, 8–10).

INSTR: Insulting or disrespectful behaviour towards holy persons or sacred objects is usually condemned by religious communities whose beliefs are being affected, and for a long time it was also a criminal offence in many parts of the world. Even today some states preserve anti-blasphemy laws, with the intention of protecting believers from facing messages about their religion which they consider shocking or disturbing. However, prosecution of blasphemy, while protecting religious freedom, may at the same time seriously affect the free exercise of freedom of expression.

In Europe, blasphemy is a criminal offence in a minority of the states and it is rarely prosecuted. The severity of punishment varies from one legal system to another, not exceeding six months of imprisonment in most cases (with a notable exception of Greece, incurring a penalty of up to two years for malicious blasphemy).

International conventions on human rights, which mention certain aspects of religious freedom deserving legal protection, do not address explicitly the issue of blasphemous speech. The introduction of blasphemy as a criminal offence into domestic legal systems is not required by the ECHR or by the →*Charter of Fundamental Rights of the European Union*.

CASES: The issue of blasphemy has been rarely addressed by the ECtHR. It seems that its essential findings in that matter may need to be revised, as the social reality of Europe has changed considerably since those findings were made.

According to the ECtHR, it may be necessary in certain democratic societies to sanction, or even prevent improper attacks on objects of religious veneration, as long as the measures involved are proportionate to the legitimate aim pursued [OTTO-PREMINGER-INSTITUTE, 1994, § 49]. This being so, blasphemy as such is not required to be a criminal offence, since there is a wide range of measures aimed at safeguarding religious freedom against such attacks.

At the same time, the ECtHR has so far not been willing to find anti-blasphemy laws incompatible with the ECHR. The reason for this reluctance is the lack of sufficient common ground in the legal and social orders of the European states to conclude that preserving anti-blasphemy laws is, in itself, unnecessary in a democratic society [WINGROVE, 1996, § 57].

In a more recent recommendation, the Parliamentary Assembly of Council of Europe stated that 'blasphemy, as an insult to a religion, should not be deemed a criminal offence. A distinction should be made between matters relating to moral conscience and those relating to what is lawful, and between matters which belong to the public domain and those which belong to the private sphere' (Rec 1805 (2007)). The Venice Commission shared that view (Report, 2008, 63).

VIEWS: The cautiousness of the ECtHR with regard to anti-blasphemy legislation has received some criticism in the legal discourse. The judges who expressed disagreement with the majority opinion in [OTTO-PREMINGER-INSTITUTE, 1994] reiterated that freedom of expression was an essential feature of a democratic society, and that it was applicable not only to ideas that are favourably received by the authorities or the population, but particularly to those that shock, offend or disturb other people. They noted that having accepted the above observation, it would be hardly understandable to guarantee this freedom only as long as it is used in accordance with common religious convictions. The dissenting judges also questioned the majority's view that the legal protection should depend on whether a particular statement may contribute to any form of public debate. In their opinion, such a decision should not be left to the authorities [OTTO-PREMINGER-INSTITUT, 1994, joint dissenting opinion of judges Palm, Pekkanen, Makarczyk, § 3].

Blasphemy as a legal term may be seen as vague and lacking the precision required by modern criminal law standards. Moreover, it confronts the domestic courts with the necessity of analysing theological issues in order to determine if a challenged statement could be seen as an insult to holy persons. Finally, anti-blasphemy legislation is criticised for its predominantly Christian orientation (Uitz, 2007, 160).

CONCL: Blasphemy tends to cause an outrage to believing people. Statements and images which may be considered gratuitously offensive or defamatory to religion effectively obstruct intercultural communication. As a consequence, they impede mutual understanding and dialogue between people belonging to different religious traditions, while such a dialogue is essential in any pluralistic society.

However, anti-blasphemy legislation should not be seen as an adequate remedy. Instead of striking a fair balance between freedom of expression and freedom of religion, such laws run the risk of suppressing the public debate and imposing disproportionate restriction on free speech, thus proving to be a serious threat to liberal democracy. It appears that free art performance can be particularly affected by such laws.

It should be noted that in several domestic legal systems an overlap between anti-blasphemy laws, religious insult provisions and hate speech provisions was identified. Moreover, specific legislation aimed at combatting blasphemy may have a chilling effect, encouraging self-censorship of →artists and →journalists (Framework, 2015, 85).

It seems that the necessity of anti-blasphemy laws should be seriously reconsidered, and the recent approach of the Council of Europe bodies suggests that preserving such provisions in the domestic legal systems may at some point in future be found incompatible with the ECHR.

REFERENCES:

Dacey, Austin: *The Future of Blasphemy: Speaking of the Sacred in an Age of Human Rights*, London: Bloomsbury (2012).

European Commission for Democracy Through Law (Venice Commission): *Report on the relationship between freedom of expression and freedom of religion: The issue of regulation and prosecution of blasphemy, religious insult and incitement to religious hatred*, Venice, 17–18 October 2008, CDL-AD (2008)026.

European Parliament, Directorate-General for Internal Policies: *The European legal framework on hate speech, blasphemy and its interaction with freedom of expression*, Brussels (2015).

Leveleux-Teixeira, Corinne: Entre droit et religion: le blasphème, du péché de la langue au crime sans victime, *Revue de l'histoire des religions* 2011, No. 4, 587.

Martínez-Torrón, Javier, Cañamares Arribas, Santiago (eds.): *Tensiones entre libertad de expresión y libertad religiosa*, Valencia: Tirant lo Blanch (2014).

Parliamentary Assembly of Council of Europe: Recommendation 1805 (2007) on blasphemy, religious insults and hate speech against persons on grounds of their religion.

Uitz, Renáta: *Freedom of religion in European constitutional and international case law*, Council of Europe Publishing (2007).

OTTO-PREMINGER-INSTITUTE v. AUSTRIA (ECtHR 20/09/1994, 13470/87).

WINGROVE v. UNITED KINGDOM (ECtHR 25/11/1996, 17419/90).

Wojciech Brzozowski

Caricatures / Cartoons

DEF: Now mostly used synonymously, the terms caricature (from Lat. *carrus* > Ital. *caricare*, to overload or surcharge, and hence to exaggerate) and cartoon (Lat. *charta* > Ital. *carta, cartone*, carton or cardboard) denote the satirical and hyperbolical representation of persons or societal and political issues by graphic means. Viewed through a cultural lens, the rights related to caricatures *as* culture have been most prominent. Caricatures can be considered a means for individuals, groups and communities 'to build their world view representing their encounter with the external forces affecting their lives' (cf. CESCR, General Comment no. 21, 2009). Offering, in the words of Sigmund Freud, a means to unmask disingenuous grandeur and to disparage the powerful, caricatures have been an important element in Western political discourse since at least the 18th century (Fuchs, 1921; Langemeyer, 1984). Cartoonists such as James Gillray, Honoré Daumier, Thomas Nast, David Low or, more recently, Kevin Kallaugher have provided poignant commentary on current affairs; satirical periodicals such as *Simplicissimus, Punch, La Caricature*, or *Charlie Hébdo* have a long tradition as well.

More recently, however, caricatures have also been perceived as a *threat* to culture, namely in the context of lampooning faiths and religious figures. Both aspects – caricatures as an important means of criticism and as an attack on religion – have been at evidence in the so-called Mohammed cartoons controversy that originated in a series of drawings published in a Danish newspaper in 2005.

INSTR: As an expressive medium, caricatures are protected by international and regional provisions on freedom of speech; on the national level, they may enjoy – often congruent – constitutional protection as works of art (e.g. in Article 5(3) of the German *Grundgesetz*). Article 19 ICCPR, which safeguards the right to 'impart information and ideas of all kinds in the form of art, or through any other media', and Article 10 ECHR, which protects 'information and ideas', also cover caricatures, as does the pertinent provision in the *American Convention on Human Rights* (Article 13(1)). The differing wordings in other regional instruments, however, already indicate varying scopes of protected expressions, possibly hinting at cultural differences as well: Article 9(2) ACHPR protects the right to express one's opinions 'within the law'; according to the *Cairo Declaration*, 'everyone shall have the right to express his opinion freely in such manner as would not be contrary to the principles of the Shari'ah' (Article 22(a)), and the revised *Arab Charter on Human Rights* requires 'conformity with the fundamental values of society' (Article 32(2)). Nor is speech unlimited under the ICCPR or the ECHR: As any other form of expression, caricatures may be restricted if they infringe, *inter alia*, upon the rights and reputations of others. Incendiary or racist caricatures are not protected either: In the case of the ECHR they may be considered incompatible with the provisions of the Convention (Article 17), and Article 20 ICCPR obliges state parties to prohibit by law any advocacy of national, racial or religious hatred that constitutes incitement to discrimination, hostility or violence. This provision was also invoked when, in the wake of the Danish cartoons, members of the Organisation of Islamic Co-operation (OIC) intensified their efforts to introduce new international norms prohibiting 'defamation of religions'.

CASES: Since caricatures have generally been subsumed under provisions of free speech, the criteria developed by courts for limiting speech are also applicable, particularly with regard to defamation. Under the ECtHR's categorisation, caricatures will likely constitute value judgments rather than factual statements; therefore, they may not require proof but can still be prosecuted if excessive [PALOMO SÁNCHEZ, 2011]. There is very limited scope, however, for restrictions if a caricature is political in nature or expresses views on questions of public interest [FÉRET, 2007]. The ECtHR acknowledges that caricatures rely on satirical elements, and that satire is 'a form of artistic expression and social commentary and, by its inherent features of exaggeration and distortion of reality, naturally aims to provoke and agitate.' As a consequence, the Court examines 'with particular care' interference with an artist's right to such expression [VEREINIGUNG BILDENDER KÜNSTLER, 2007; ERKANLI 2002; LEROY 2008]. Humour, however, does not justify racism or incitement [M'BALA M'BALA, 2015], and it may also be counterbalanced by the protection of morals. On several occasions, the ECtHR has deemed the protection of religious feelings a legitimate aim [e.g. OTTO-PREMINGER-INSTITUT, 1994]. Yet the ECtHR has not assessed the Danish cartoons on the merits [BEN EL MAHI, 2006], nor has any other international body [cf. SAID AHMAD, 2008]. In proceedings before Western national courts, these caricatures have been protected as legitimate speech on politically relevant matters [DET ISLAMISKE TROSSAMFUND (2), 2008; VAL, 2008]. In Jordan and Yemen, however, editors who republished the cartoons were found guilty under (religiously inspired) provisions prohibiting defaming the Prophet.

VIEWS: The assessment of the Danish cartoons differed not only in the courts according to jurisdiction. There were also significant differences in their political and scholarly appraisal. When first published in 2005, the drawings were mostly criticised by politicians as unnecessarily divisive and offensive. When violent attacks on publishers and cartoonists ensued, however, more emphasis was put on the cartoons as exercise of free speech; after the attacks on the French satirical Charlie Hébdo in January 2015, the right to criticise religion was elevated to a central tenet of public debate.

In the literature, those critical of the cartoons highlighted the multicultural aspects of the controversy and saw it as evidence of increasing 'Islamophobia' and of lacking acceptance for religious minorities (Sutcliffe 2007; Cram 2009; Doebbler 2009). It was also pointed out that previous case law (especially of the ECtHR) did not rule out regulation of religiously offensive speech or of a discriminatory nature (Cerone 2008; Kahn 2011).

Particularly in the context of efforts to restrict 'defamation' of religion, however, most authors have underlined the important role that caricatures play in public discourse; recourse to religious norms was considered unsuitable in a liberal democracy; the conceptual and procedural difficulties when protecting religions from insult would also be considerable (Boyle, 2006; Post, 2007; Bielefeldt, 2012).

CONCL: Caricatures can be considered a (regional) cultural practice that is entitled to protection, within the legal framework and the limits established for other forms of expression. This protection extends to satirical attacks on religious tenets, which have been an early and continuing feature of caricature, as illustrated by the third-century Alexamenos graffito in Rome or the anti-Papal and anti-Lutheran drawings of the Reformation and Counter-Reformation. The controversy over the Danish cartoons has shown, however, that there are stark cultural differences with regard to what may be the subject of criticism and ridicule, particularly with regard to religion.

Yet the OIC's attempts to establish 'defamation of religion' as a new limitation on the international level of expression in general and satire in particular have failed. On the contrary, the debate over defamation has led to a clarification – and fortification – of the protection that caricatures and other potentially offensive means of expression enjoy within the political and societal discourse, regardless of potential offence to religions (cf. Venice Commission, 2010; CCPR, General Comment No. 34 (2011)). Still, the cartoon controversy has shown that while protection for cultural rights may well be universal (CESCR, General Comment no. 21 (2009)), in many instances the objects of such rights clearly are not. The converse legal reactions to the cartoons indicate some significant differences in legal culture(s). Where religion continues to provide the main rationale for a legal order, religious precepts on blasphemy, sacrilege and even apostasy may require the prohibition of certain caricatures. In a secularised legal order, on the other hand, religion may be an object of protection, yet it does no longer determine the substance of commands and prohibitions (Langer, 2013). Under a human rights approach, the religious sensitivities of the faithful may well be safeguarded; a religious creed or its prophets, on the other hand, are not protected.

REFERENCES:

Bielefeldt, Heiner: "Freedom of Religion or Belief: A Human Right under Pressure", 1 *Oxford J. Law & Rel.* (2012).

Boyle, Kevin: "The Danish Cartoons", 24 *Neth. Q. Hum. Rts.* (2006).

Cerone, John: "Inappropriate Renderings: The Danger of Reductionist Resolutions", 33 *Brook. J. Int'l L.* (2008).

Cram, Ian: "The Danish Cartoons, Offensive Expression, and Democratic Legitimacy", in I. Hare & J. Weinstein (eds.): *Extreme Speech and Democracy*, Oxford: Oxford University Press (2009).

Doebbler, Curtis F. J.: "Danish Cartoons: Freedom of Speech versus Freedom of Religion?", in S. Yee & J.-Y. Morin (eds.): *Multiculturalism and International Law*, Leiden: Marinus Nijhoff (2009).

Fuchs, Eduard: *Die Karikatur der europäischen Völker*, 2 Parts, 4th ed., Munich: Langen (1921).

Kahn, Robert A.: "A Margin of Appreciation for Muslims: Viewing the Defamation of Religions Debate through Otto-Preminger-Institut v. Austria", 5 *Charleston Law Review* (2011).

Langemeyer, Gerhard et al. (eds.): *Bild als Waffe: Mittel und Motive der Karikatur in fünf Jahrhunderten*, Munich: Prestel (1984).

Langer, Lorenz: *Religious Offence and Human Rights: The Implications of Defamation of Religions*, Cambridge: Cambridge University Press (2014).

Post, Robert C.: "Religion and Freedom of Speech: Portraits of Muhammad", 14 *Constellations* (2007).

Sutcliffe, Adam: "Power and the Politics of Prejudice", in M. Bunzl (ed.): *Anti-Semitism and Islamophobia*, Chicago: Prickly Paradigm Press (2007).

Venice Commission: *Blasphemy, Insult and Hatred: Finding Answers in a Democratic Society*, Strasbourg: Council of Europe Publishing (2010).

BEN EL MAHI & OTHERS v. DENMARK (ECtHR 11/12/2006, 5853/06).

DET ISLAMISKE TROSSAMFUND I DANMARK v. JYLLANDSPOSTEN (2) (Vestre Landsret (High Court), 19/6/2008, U.2008.2302.V).

ERKANLI v. TURKEY (Admissibility) (ECtHR 25/6/2002, 37721/97).

FÉRET v. BELGIUM (ECtHR 16/7/2009, 15615/07).

LEROY v. FRANCE (ECtHR 2/10/2008, 36109/03).

M'BALA M'BALA v. FRANCE (ECtHR, 10/11/2015, 25239/13).

OTTO-PREMINGER-INSTITUT v. AUSTRIA (ECtHR 20/9/1994, 13470/87).

PALOMO SÁNCHEZ AND OTHERS v. SPAIN (ECtHR 12/9/2011, 28955/06, 28957/06, 28959/06, 28964/06).

SAID AHMAD & ASMAA ABDOL-HAMID v. DENMARK (CCPR, 18/4/2008, UN Doc. CCPR/C/92/D/1487/2006).

VAL & ET AL. v. UNION DES ORGANISATIONS ISLAMIQUES DE FRANCE (Cour d'appel, Paris, 12/3/2008, no. 07/02873).

VEREINIGUNG BILDENDER KÜNSTLER v. AUSTRIA (ECtHR 25/1/2007, 68354/01).

Lorenz Langer

Censorship

DEF/HIST: Basically, we could distinguish between *ex-ante* censorship (or 'prior restraint'), i.e. the suppression of free expressions, including artistic or media content, before their creation, presentation or publication, and *ex-post* measures executed to prevent their exposure to a wider public. However, in the digital age such distinctions tend to become obsolete, especially due to the simultaneity of producing and distributing information and other content on the Internet. More sense, especially in legal and policy terms, could make a differentiation between direct (via a mandated institution, e.g. of the state) or indirect censorship, the latter often related to 'self-censorship'.

In China, Greece and other ancient societies, 'censorship was considered a legitimate instrument for regulating the moral and political life of the population' (Newth, 2010) – a goal that survived, in some countries, the ages until the 21st century. The actual term dates back about 2500 years when in Rome the office of a *censor* was established for the first time. Most prominent, and often rigidly enforced, has been the *Index Librorum Prohibitorum*, introduced by the Catholic Church in 1559 and abolished as late as 1966. This 'Index' intended to ban books considered to be heretical or morally / ideologically dangerous and has become a synonym for traditional forms of censorship. Similar practices have been, and partly still are, used by other religious denominations or political systems, particularly against intellectual →dissidents.

The focus of censorship today has generally shifted from books or →literary expressions to more popular media and cultural manifestations such as images (e.g. →caricatures), computer games and other →digital media, music and films. In addition, the current means of controlling content are far more sophisticated than in the past, ranging from corporate interventions such as →Internet content suppression to different forms of state surveillance, which endanger →privacy and thus motivate self-censorship, often in an act of self-defence. Private companies increasingly employ their own mechanisms of content supervision, including in the controversial form of →access control technologies, implemented in digital media to shield →intellectual property.

INSTR: According to the Council of Europe/ ERICarts 'Compendium' monitoring system, several European states abolished their previous forms and institutions for censorship during the past decades (e.g. Armenia; Croatia; Georgia; the Netherlands; Russia; Sweden and the UK, the latter as regards theatre scripts). However, free speech and artistic or media freedom can still be confronted with legal or practical limitations in these and many other countries. For example, Article 5 of the German Constitution (*Grundgesetz*) guarantees freedom of expression and information and specifically mentions the arts, science, research, teaching, the press, broadcasting and films. While Article 5(1) officially rules out censorship, the following Article 5(2) stipulates that 'these rights shall find their limits in the provisions of general laws, in provisions for the protection of young persons, and in the right to personal honour.' In principle, such potentially far-reaching exemption clauses are compatible with major instruments protecting human rights like the →ECHR or the ICCPR, the latter enabling, in Article 19(3), limitations of freedom of expression that 'are provided by law and are necessary (a) to protect the rights or reputations of others; (b) to protect national security or public order, or public health or morals'.

Even in Europe, for example in Malta, national regulations leading to direct or indirect forms of censorship created problems for →artists and arts institutions. While they are sometimes justified with the above limitations, the UN Human Rights Committee (ICCPR) underlined that 'the mere fact that an idea is disliked or thought to be incorrect does not justify its censorship.' (ECP / IFACCA / Creative Scotland, 2013). In addition, regulations have to: (a) 'meet standards of clarity and precision so that people can foresee the consequences of their actions'; (b) 'be a legitimate aim... For example, a desire to shield a government from criticism can never justify limitations on free speech'; and (c) 'Any limitation of the right to freedom of expression must be truly necessary.' (ibid)

Currently, controversial issues regarding state interventions concern incitement to (e.g. racial) hatred and 'defamation of religion'. The former appears to be settled already with Article 20 ICCPR – which calls for the legal prohibition of 'any advocacy of national, racial or religious hatred that constitutes incitement to discrimination, hostility or violence' – as well as through related case law [e.g. ROSS, 2000]. As regards religion, it has been pointed out that 'human rights law protects individuals and groups, not belief systems. You cannot defame a religion. In fact, it should be possible to scrutinise, openly debate, and even harshly criticise belief systems, opinions, and institutions, including religious ones' when exercising one's right to freedom of expression (Pillay, 2013).

Regulations aiming to protect children/youth from offensive content exist in nearly all countries worldwide, sometimes with a spill-over effect to adults. In contrast with measures trying to control or suppress political views or religious beliefs, this task can also be achieved with some success through mandatory industry standards such as consumer age ratings replacing former state control mechanisms. An example is the *Pan European Game Information (PEGI)* content rating system that has been developed by the Interactive Software Federation of Europe (ISFE) and is supported by the European Commission. With regard to such classification procedures, the UN Special Rapporteur in the field of cultural rights (2013) calls on states to ensure (a) the independence of classification bodies; (b) the participation of evaluators from the arts field; (c) transparent terms of reference, rules of procedure and activities; and (d) effective appeal mechanisms.

CASES: Until now, the ECtHR did not deal directly, i.e. under that term, with censorship issues in the cultural domain, even if the expression has been occasionally used in matters regarding media freedom [e.g. SALIYEV, 2010]. Nevertheless, claims against censorship can be assessed in the light of the court's consistent call for a spirit of openness and tolerance in democratic societies, especially if →public broadcasting and other public media or institutions are involved, for which the ECtHR has demanded legal and practical guarantees for a 'pluralistic' service [cf. WOJTAS-KALETA, 2009]. In the case of the assassinated Turkish–Armenian journalist Hrant Dink, the court recapitulated its opinion about states' obligations to guarantee freedom of expression and ruled that Turkey had failed to 'create a favourable environment for participation in public debate by all persons concerned, enabling them to express their opinions and ideas without fear' [DINK v. TURKEY, 2010]. In certain cases, the state could also be obliged to protect the right to freedom of expression 'against interference by private persons' or companies [PALOMO SÁNCHEZ AND OTHERS v. SPAIN, 2011]. However, according to the court [MELNYCHUK v. UKRAINE, 2010] this 'does not give private citizens or organisations an unfettered right of access to the media in order to put forward opinions', e.g. when insisting on the 'right of reply'.

Other issues related to claims of censorship concern the domain of →authors' rights. Within the Anglo–American doctrine of *copyright*, authors often feel at the mercy of commercial users of their works, especially if the latter fall under the category of 'work for hire'. In the continental European tradition of so-called 'moral rights', even the heirs and estates of deceased playwrights consider themselves entitled to suppress new artistic interpretations, like in the well-known case of Bertolt Brecht's inheritors, who consistently rejected stage directors and actors they consider inappropriate to represent the works of the author. If this understanding of the disclosure right would have been as 'eternal' as some of its protagonists are asserting – and could have been rigidly enforced – 'we would have lost Virgil's *Aeneid*, possibly Ovid's *Metharmophoses*, most of Kafka, all of Foucault's posthumous works, some of Philip Larkin, Sainte-Beuve, T.S. Eliot, Anatole France, George Sand... Emily Dickinson's poems would be known only in her family's heavily edited version.' (Baldwin 2014). Luckily, contemporary case law now tends towards underlining the need to find a balance between conflicting rights, often in favour of the freedom of new artistic expressions, e.g. in the case of a play of Heiner Müller who extensively quoted Bertolt Brecht [GERMANIA 3, 2000].

With regard to digital media, the UN Human Rights Council recently (2016) reaffirmed its position that human rights people enjoy offline are also protected online. In this context, the HRC denounced measures to prevent or disrupt access to the Internet or specific platforms, while recognising the importance of access to information and online privacy for the realisation of the right to freedom of expression and to hold opinions without interference. In a similar spirit but with regard to the demands of a copyright licensing society for the installation of an Internet content filtering system, the CJEU [in SCARLET, 2011] ruled that such practices 'would involve a systematic analysis of all content and the collection and identification of users' IP addresses', which 'could potentially undermine freedom of information since that system might not distinguish adequately between unlawful content and lawful content.'

VIEWS: According to the Special Rapporteur of the UN Human Rights Council in the field of cultural rights, Farida Shaheed (2013), 'artists should be able to explore the darker side of humanity, and to represent crimes or what some may consider as 'immorality', without being accused of promoting these.' Rather than excluding 'controversial works' from public display because of 'unprepared audiences', she pleads for an enhancement of →arts education, which she sees as 'a strong and efficient alternative to censorship.'

While the literature deals with censorship mostly in the context of balancing different rights at stake, e.g. freedom of expression vs. →defamation and safeguarding the reputation of persons or companies, a number of international NGOs (e.g. *Article 19*) as well as advocacy and professional organisations on regional or national levels (e.g. *Culture-Action-Europe* or *IETM*) turned this issue into a key element of their campaigns for free arts and media. In this context, annual lists of violations of artistic freedom are published (e.g. by *Freemuse*), which suggest an on-going practice of censorship, especially in Asia and in the Arab countries.

However, Mette Newth (2010) reminds us that when criticising censorship and other human rights abuses in different parts of the world, Western activists 'should not forget the dark history of censorship in Europe and its colonized countries', including 'the cruel suppression of indigenous cultures, languages and non-written literature for which Europeans also are responsible'. In addition, she insists that we should not fail to look at our own abuses of human rights: 'The lack of criticism in the UN of European censorship – for example the systematic purging of libraries in Southern France by *Front National* – gives perpetrating governments such as China or Burma a welcome opportunity to accuse Western countries of one-sided criticism' and will not 'create or improve a climate of open-minded dialogue'. Indeed, we should not hesitate to underline that, according to different world indexes, state surveillance of the Internet is probably as pervasive in the USA as in Russia and that a number of NGOs committed to defending human rights are currently facing difficult times not only in Egypt or India, but also in Israel or Hungary.

CONCL: It is highly significant for our topic that this contribution, scheduled to be written by an author in an Asian country, had to be reassigned last minute to one of the editors. Conditions for the free exercise of human rights vary greatly around the globe which, in this particular case, could have endangered the future professional life of the expert had he insisted in delivering the article like originally planned. This shows, in a nutshell, that we still have a long way to go until the promises of freedom of expression and cultural diversity, enshrined in international legal instruments, can successfully stand the reality test. In fact, many states seem to use their →margin of appreciation to draw additional boundaries in the name of principles like 'social cohesion', security, national honour or the protection of religious feelings and morals. Some pressure groups in society as well as media and companies or institutions in the cultural domain play their part in this development, be it for financial reasons or even political correctness. Precautionary self-censorship may become the norm instead of an exception – and open-minded artists will be the first victims of this trend.

REFERENCES:

Atkins, Robert and Mintcheva, Svetlana (eds.): *Censoring culture, Contemporary threats to free expression*, New York: The New Press (2006).

Baldwin, Peter: *The Copyright Wars. Three Centuries of Trans-Atlantic Battle*, Princeton: Princeton University Press (2014).

Council of Europe/ERICarts (eds.): *Compendium of Cultural Policies and Trends in Europe*, Strasbourg/Bonn (accessed 07/2016 via www.culturalpolicies.net).

ECP / IFACCA / Creative Scotland (eds.): *Introduction to Policy – Freedom of Expression*, Background Paper for the Edinburgh Symposium, 24 – 26 September 2013.

Korpe, Marie; Reitov, Ole and Cloonan, Martin: "Music censorship from Plato to the Present", in Brown, Steven and Volgsten, Ulrik (eds.): *Music and Manipulation. On the Social Uses and Social Control of Music*. New York/London: Berghahn Books (2006).

Newth, Mette: *The Long History of Censorship*, Oslo 2010 (accessed 07/2016 via www.beaconforfreedom.org/).

Pillay, Navanethem: *Freedom of Expression and incitement to hatred in the context of International Human Rights Law*, Lecture at the London School of Economics by the United Nations High Commissioner for Human Rights, Lon-

don, 15 February 2013 (accessed 07/2016 via www.ohchr.org).
Stoycheff, Elizabeth: "Under Surveillance: Examining Facebook's Spiral of Silence Effects in the Wake of NSA Internet Monitoring", *Journalism & Mass Communication Quarterly*, 1–16 (2016).
UN Human Rights Council: *Resolution on The promotion, protection and enjoyment of human rights on the Internet* (27/06/2016, A/HRC/32/L.20).
UN Special Rapporteur in the field of cultural rights: *The right to freedom of artistic expression and creativity*, Geneva: Human Rights Council (2013), A/HRC/23/34.
GERMANIA 3 (German Fed. Const. Court 1 29/06/2000, *BvR* 825/98).
ROSS v. CANADA (HRCee 18/10/2000, no. 736/1997).
SALIYEV v. RUSSIA (ECtHR 21/10/2010, 35016/03).
SCARLET EXTENDED SA v. SABAM (CJEU 24/11/2011, C-70/10).
WOJTAS-KALETA v. POLAND (ECtHR 16/07/2009, 20436/02).
Examples of websites of international NGOs engaged for freedom of expression and/or against censorship (all accessed 07/2016):
www.article19.org/
www.freedomhouse.org
freemuse.org/
globalfreedomofexpression.columbia.edu/
www.indexoncensorship.org
rsf.org/en

Andreas Joh. Wiesand

Charter of Fundamental Rights of the European Union (CFR)

INTRO: The CFR (the Charter) is a bill of rights binding the European Union and EU Member States acting within the scope of the EU law. Although the EU does not have a formal, written constitution, the Charter could be regarded as a part of substantive constitutional legal order. It was adopted by the European Convention on 7 December 2000 to make fundamental rights more visible to EU citizens and other persons living in the EU. Initially, there was no political consensus to make the Charter part of the EU treaty law. The Charter remained as a solemn declaration until 2009 when it entered into force. Although the planned *Treaty establishing the Constitution for Europe* incorporated the Charter in its provisions, it failed in the ratification process due to the negative outcome of national referenda in France and the Netherlands. Eventually, the *Treaty of Lisbon* recognised the rights, freedoms and principles set out in the Charter as a part of the treaty law (Article 6(1) TEU). Yet, this recognition is based on the existing division of competences between the EU and Member States. The Charter neither establishes new rights nor new competences of the EU. Rather the obligation to respect fundamental rights and freedoms sets the limits on the exercise of competences by the EU institutions with due regard to the principle of subsidiarity.

INSTR: In its Preamble, the Charter proclaims that the EU 'contributes to the preservation and to the development of these common values while respecting the diversity of the cultures and traditions of the peoples of Europe as well as the national identities of the Member States and the organization of their public authorities at national, regional and local levels.' The Charter contains guarantees of rights, freedoms and principles although the distinction between these categories is far from clear. It covers personal and political rights and freedoms enshrined in the ECHR and additional protocols; rights and freedoms of EU citizens; and other rights and principles recognised in the case-law of the CJEU. In its substantive part, it is divided in chapters corresponding to values underlying the Charter which are: dignity, freedom, equality, solidarity, justice and citizens' rights. Notably, cultural rights have only been affirmed in the context of the principle of cultural, religious and linguistic diversity (Article 22) and the right of elderly to participate in social and cultural life (Article 25). Although several rights in the Charter are defined in a progressive way, they are subject to national laws governing the exercise of these rights. Therefore, there is no possibility that the right to marry and the right to found a family (Article 9) will be interpreted contrary to national laws and traditions, in particular when national law defines a marriage as a union between a man and a woman. Likewise, Chapter IV of the Charter does not create justiciable social rights beyond rights already provided for in national law.

The scope, the interpretation, and the application of the Charter remained the subject of political and legal controversy, which led to the adoption of the Protocol (No 30) on the application of the Charter of Fundamental Rights of the European Union to Poland and to the United Kingdom (so-called British Protocol) and the Declaration concerning the Charter of Fundamental Rights of the European Union attached to the Treaty of Lisbon. Although the British Protocol was often presented as an opt-out, the CJEU confirmed that the Protocol does not exclude the applicability of the Charter in Poland or the United Kingdom. Hence, the value of the Protocol is merely explanatory with regard to Article 51 of the Charter. According to the CJEU, the Protocol 'does not intend to exempt the Republic of Poland or the United Kingdom from the obligation to comply with the provisions of the Charter or to prevent a court of one of those Member States from ensuring compliance with those provisions' [N.S., 2011, para. 120].

CASES: The application of the Charter to national law has been clarified in [ÅKERBERG FRANSSON, 2013]. The CJEU explained that the applicability of EU law entails the applicability of the Charter. Hence, national courts need to ensure compliance with rights guaranteed by the Charter in any case which falls within the scope of the EU law even if relevant national provisions were not adopted to implement EU law. Still, potential conflicts with regard to the application of the Charter are likely to arise in cases before national courts, in particular →Constitutional Courts, may decide to deny the application of EU acts in order to protect constitutional identity of member states (see i.e. Resolution of the Federal Constitutional Court of Germany, 2015). The core of this controversy lies with the question whether member states may apply a more far-reaching protection of fundamental rights in areas where EU law harmonises the protection standard [MELLONI, 2013]. Having regard to the principle of primacy, national law, including constitutional law, should not compromise EU law. Yet, it could be argued that the EU standard should take precedence only when the principles of primacy, unity or effectiveness of the EU law are at stake. As a result, even within the EU, in the area of application of EU law, there is some scope for diversity regarding values which member states consider essential for their constitutional identity. Still, the question whether national standards of protection may prevail ultimately falls under the jurisdiction of the CJEU. At least, it is the case as long as national courts remain in a dialogical relationship with the Luxembourg Court and the preliminary reference procedure to this aim.

CONCL: Notwithstanding the sensible relationship between the CJEU and constitutional courts defending constitutional identity of member states, the CJEU remains the ultimate judicial authority in charge of interpretation of the Charter. The CJEU also oversees whether EU acts and national laws implementing EU law comply with its provisions. Although Charter rights corresponding to rights guaranteed by the ECHR shall be accorded the interpretation established in ECtHR case-law, the EU may provide more extensive protection (Article 52(3)). Notwithstanding the evolutionary interpretation of Convention rights and freedoms, the ECHR contains only the minimum standard of protection. Although the interpretation of analogous rights set out in the Charter and the ECHR is often similar, the CJEU may develop its own standards in the view of the treaty objectives and values (i.e. in the areas concerning privacy, digital rights, positive measures). Until the EU accedes to the ECHR in pursuance of Article 6(2) TEU, the Charter will set out the framework of a system of human rights protection in the EU and the CJEU will remain the guardian of its autonomy. Following the [KADI, 2008] case saga, the same conclusion holds true with respect to international public law and the CJEU review of legal measures adopted by UN bodies binding upon the EU MS in the light of the Charter.

REFERENCES:

Morano-Foadi, Sonia, Lucy Vickers (eds.): *Fundamental Rights in the EU: A Matter for Two Courts*, Hart-Bloomsbury (2015).

Palmisano, Giuseppe (ed.): *Making the Charter of Fundamental Rights a Living Instrument*, Brill-Nijhoff (2014).

Peers, Steve, Hervey, Tamara, Kenner, Jeff, Ward,

Angela (eds.): *The EU Charter of Fundamental Rights: A Commentary*, Oxford: Hart Publishing (2014).
ÅKLAGAREN v. HANS ÅKERBERG FRANSSON (CJEU 7/05/2013, C-617/10).
R. v. OLG DÜSSELDORF (German Fed. Const. Court 15/12/2015, 2 BvR 2735/14).
KADI AND AL BARAKAAT INTERNATIONAL FOUNDATION v. COUNCIL AND COMMISSION. (CJEU 3/09/2008, C–402/05 P and C–415/05 P).
MELLONI v. MINISTERIO FISCAL (CJEU 2302.2013, C-399/11).
N. S. v. SECRETARY OF STATE FOR THE HOME DEPARTMENT and M. E. and OTHERS v. REFUGEE APPLICATIONS COMMISSIONER AND MINISTER FOR JUSTICE, EQUALITY AND LAW REFORM (CJEU 10/12/2010, joined cases C-411/10 and C-493/10).

Anna Śledzińska-Simon

Children

(Cultural Rights of Children)

DEF: A child is defined in the UN *Convention on the Rights of the Child* (CRC) as a person under the age of 18, unless national laws mandate an earlier age of majority (Article 1). International jurisprudence [THE STREET CHILDREN, 1999, para 188; BULACIO, 2003 para 133] tends to be in favour of the '18 years old' rule but the UN CRC Committee stresses that when states implement children's rights they must take into consideration the children's development and capacities.

INSTR: All human rights instruments, both universal and regional, apply equally to children and adolescents. The CRC guarantees, *inter alia*, a number of child-specific cultural rights for all children without discrimination of any kind, including immigration status or statelessness: right to religion (Article 14), right to rest and leisure, to engage in play and recreational activities appropriate to the age of the child and to participate freely in cultural life and the arts (Article 31); right to education and implementation of educational programmes that respect 'the national values of the country in which the child is living, the country from which he or she may originate, and for civilizations different from his or her own' (Articles 28 and 29); right of disabled children to physical, mental and cultural/spiritual development (Article 23). As minority/indigenous children are vulnerable to the denial of their cultural rights, the CRC provides for mass media to have particular regard to their linguistic needs (Article 17 (d)) and guarantees children's right to enjoy their own culture, language and religion (Article 30). The right in Article 30 for indigenous children is conceived as being both individual and collective and it 'may be closely associated with the use of traditional territory and the use of its resources' (CRC GC No 11, para 16). States are obliged to take special measures to enable minority, indigenous, migrant or disabled children to preserve and develop their culture and to have effectively access to cultural resources, infrastructures, activities and educational materials in accessible formats. Furthermore, while children are recognised as transmitters of cultural values and are entitled to their culture, states are obliged to protect them from practices perpetuated by culture and tradition (female genital mutilation, child and forced marriage, sex practices etc.) that are harmful to their health and development. Children's cultural rights are protected even during wartime (Articles 24 and 50 of 4th *Geneva Convention relative to the Protection of Civilian Persons in Time of War*, Article 78 (2) Protocol I to the Geneva Conventions).

In the European context, there are no child-specific provisions that protect children's cultural rights and they are dealt either within the broader context of socio-economic rights (i.e. Articles 7, 15, 17 and 30 ESCRev; Articles 14, 22, 26, 34 EU CFR), or under specific group rights (see Article 14 FCNM) or under specific provisions of the ECHR, (i.e. Articles 8, 9, 10, 14 ECHR, Article 2 of Protocol 1 to the ECHR (education)).

The African human rights system is the most vocal on the protection of children's cultural rights. The 1990 AfCRWC includes provisions on the right to education of the girls, gifted or disadvantaged and handicapped children (Articles 11(3)(e), 13), protection of children against apartheid (Article 26), the inclusion of 'Africa-specific' aims of education (Article 11(2), the right to leisure and participation in cultural life and the arts (Article 12) and a provision dealing expressly with protection against harmful social and cultural practices (Article 21). Girls' rights are further protected under the Protocol to the AfCHPR on the Rights of Women in Africa 2003 (Article 17 Right to Positive Cultural Context). Finally, the African Youth Charter 2006 contains provisions on the rights of persons between the age of 15 and 35 (Article 22 Leisure, Recreation, Sportive and Cultural Activities).

CASES: In the European context children's cultural rights have been largely unaddressed or underdeveloped. In a number of cases the ECtHR has held that states must take positive measures against wrongful placement of Romani children in special schools [e.g. in HORVATH 2013; ORSUS 2010]. The European Committee of Social Rights has found that educational practices regarding the placement of children with disabilities amounted to segregation and discrimination [AUTISM EUROPE 2003; MDAC 2010]. The ECtHR has also examined the issue of religious education and has held that education or teaching should be 'objective, critical and pluralistic' while ensuring respect for parents' religious and philosophical convictions [KJELDSEN 1976; FOLGERO 2007]. In two cases the ECtHR has found that Turkey had to reform religious education in schools because the subject taught was likely to raise a conflict of values in the children [MANSUR 2015; ZENGIN2008]. The ECtHR has held that the right to education does not guarantee the right to education in a particular language [LINGUISTIC CASE 1968]; however, the ECtHR has also found it difficult to dissociate language from education and the ethnic and cultural background of the children when they have received primary education in their mother-tongue [CYPRUS 2001, para 275–80]. Moreover, in a number of cases [see e.g. DOGRU; R. SINGH, 2009] which concerned the expulsion of pupils from French schools because of their wearing of religious garment and the alleged violation of the freedom of religion and the prohibition of discrimination, the ECtHR declared the claims of these applicants manifestly ill-founded on inadmissibility grounds. The same issue was addressed differently by the Human Rights Committee [SINGH HRCee, 2013] which held that the expulsion from school was neither necessary nor proportionate to the benefits achieved. International human rights judicial bodies often make reference to the CRC provisions when interpreting regional human rights instruments' provisions with regard to children's cultural rights and special measures of protection, i.e. minority or indigenous children' right to preserve their distinctive identity [see e.g. THE STREET CHILDREN, 1999, para 144; ADVISORY OPINION ON THE JURIDICAL CONDITION AND HUMAN RIGHTS OF THE CHILD, 2002, para 84]. The IACHR has held that Article 30 of the CRC 'establishes an additional and complementary obligation that gives content to Article 19 ACHR, and that consists of the obligation to promote and protect the right of indigenous children to enjoy their own culture, their own religion, and their own language' [XAKMOK KASEK, 2010 para 261; CHITAY-NECH, 2010, para 164–170]. The African Committee of Experts on the Rights and Welfare of the Child [ACERWC] has issued a decision on culture-related rights of Nubian children, i.e. non-discrimination, the right to name and nationality, the right to education and the highest attainable standard of health [IHRDA 2011].

VIEWS: Children's cultural rights are neglected in literature. To a certain extent this relates to the standing of cultural rights in the human rights spectrum (civil and political rights vs ESC rights) and the dominant paternalistic perceptions of children as passive objects of protection (Price Cohen 1991). The innovation of CRC in including all social, economic, cultural, civil and political rights in a single framework and affirming children's right to participate in all decisions affecting them has, on the one hand, provided room for children to be viewed as active bearers of rights and has, on the other hand, resulted in reading the CRC as a combination of protection, provision (states to provide access to services) and participation (i.e. children to act and participate in society and in decisions concerning them) rights (van Bueren 1995). However, there is still controversy as to the competence and capacity of children to exercise their rights independently and autonomously (Reynaert et al 2011, Verhellen 2015). This is reflected in the policies of some Arab and Asian countries too.

CONCL: Despite the overwhelming legal instruments and human rights monitoring and complaint mechanisms, violations of children's cultural rights remain either unreported or unaddressed. The UPR and the UN Special Rapporteurs (i.e. Special Rapporteur in the field of cultural rights, Special Rapporteur on the Rights of Persons with Disabilities, Special Rapporteur on the Right to Education, Special Rapporteur on the Rights of Indigenous Peoples, Special Rapporteur on Minority issues) are increasingly shedding light onto the existing legal, institutional, economic or cultural lacunae with regard to the poor recognition of children and adolescents' cultural rights, especially the rights contained in Article 31 CRC.

The situation of children's cultural rights has worsened during the past few years due to the financial crises and austerity measures that have led to severe cuts in public spending. To this end, the CRC Committee has affirmed states' minimum core obligations with regard to public spending to ensure the satisfaction of, at the very least, essential levels of cultural rights of boys and girls (CRC GC No. 19 para 37). The CRC Committee has also recognised the role and responsibilities of the private sector in the areas of recreation, cultural and artistic activities, as well as civil society organisations providing such services for children (CRC GC No. 17). In 2016, the UN Special Rapporteur in the field of cultural rights recognised the issue of the cultural rights of children and adolescents, both girls and boys, and education about the importance of cultural rights and cultural heritage as an urgent concern of high priority for her mandate.

REFERENCES:

Jancic Cvejic, Olga (ed.): *The rights* of the *child* in a *changing world: 25 years after* the *UN Convention* on the *Rights of the Child*, Cham: Springer (2016).

Liefaard, Ton and Jakob Egbert Doek (eds.): *Litigating the rights of the child: the UN Convention on the Rights of the Child in domestic and international jurisprudence*, Dordrecht: Springer (2015).

Price Cohen, Cynthia: "Jurisprudence on the Rights of the Child: Individual Rights Concept and their Significance of Social Scientists", 46 (1) *American Psychologist* (2005) 60.

Reynaert, Didier et al (eds.): *Kinderrechten: Springplank of struikelblok? Naar een kritische benadering van kinderrechten*, Intersentia: Antewrp (2011).

Van Bueren, Geraldine: *The International Law on the Rights of the Child*, The Hague: Kluwer (1995).

Verhellen, Eugeen: "The Convention on the Rights of the Child: Reflections from a historical, social policy and educational perspective" in Vandenhole Wouter et al: *Routledge International Handbook of Children's Rights Studies*, Oxon: Routledge (2015).

CEDAW: Joint General Recommendation/General Comment No. 31 and No. 18 CRC Committee on the Rights of the Child on Harmful Practices (2014).

CESCR: General Comment No. 21: The Right of Everyone to Take Part in Cultural Life (2009).

CRC: General Comment No. 11: Indigenous Children and their Rights under the Convention (2009).

CRC: General Comment No. 17: The Right of the Child to Rest, Leisure, Play, Recreational Activities, Cultural Life and the Arts (art. 31) (2013).

CRC: General Comment No. 19: Public Spending and the Rights of the Child (2015).

UN Committee on the Rights of the Child (CRC): General Comment No. 20: Implementation of the Rights of the Child during Adolescence (2016).

UN Human Rights Committee (CCPR): General Comment No. 17: The Rights of the Child (1989).

UN Human Rights Council: Report of the Special Rapporteur in the field of cultural rights, 3/2/2016, A/HRC/31/59.

ADVISORY OPINION ON THE JURIDICAL CONDITION AND HUMAN RIGHTS OF THE CHILD (IACtHR 28/8/2002, OC-17/02).

[AUTISM] INTERNATIONAL ASSOCIATION AUTISM-EUROPE v. FRANCE (European Committee of Social Rights 13/2002, 4/11/2003).

BULACIO v. ARGENTINA (IACtHR 18/9/2003, Series C No. 100).

CHITAY-NECH ET AL v. GUATEMALA (IACtHR 25/5/2010, Series C No. 212).

CYPRUS v. TURKEY (ECtHR 25781/94, 10/5/2001).

DOGRU v. FRANCE (ECtHR 4/3/2009, 27058/05).

FOLGERO AND OTHERS v. NORWAY (ECtHR 29/6/2007, 15472/02).

HASAN AND EYLEM ZENGIN v. TURKEY (ECtHR 9/1/2008, 1448/04).

HORVATH AND KISS v. HUNGARY (ECtHR 29/4/2013, 11146/11).
[IHRDA] INSTITUTE FOR HUMAN RIGHTS AND DEVELOPMENT IN AFRICA & OPEN SOCIETY JUSTICE INITIATIVE ON BEHALF OF CHILDREN OF NUBIAN DESCENT IN KENYA v. KENYA, (The African Committee of Experts on the Rights and Welfare of the Child, 02/2009, 22/3/2011).
KJELDSEN BUSK MADSEN AND PEDERSEN v. DENMARK (ECtHR 7/12/1976,5095/71; 5920/72; 5926/72).
[LINGUISTIC CASE] RELATING TO CERTAIN ASPECTS OF THE LAW ON THE USE OF LANGUAGES IN EDUCATION IN BELGIUM v. BELGIUM (ECtHR, 23/7/1968, 1474/62; 1677/62; 1691/62; 1769/63; 1994/63; 2126/64).
MANSUR YALCIN AND OTHERS v. TURKEY (ECtHR 16/2/2015, 21163/11).
MENTAL DISABILITY ADVOCACY CENTER v. BULGARIA (European Committee of Social Rights 3/6/2008, 41/2007).
ORSUS AND OTHERS v. CROATIA (ECtHR 16/3/2010, 15766/03).
R. SINGH v. FRANCE (ECtHR 30/6/2009, 27561/08).
SINGH v. FRANCE (Human Rights Committee 4/2/2013, 1852/2008, U.N. Doc. CCPR/C/106/D/1852/2008).
["THE STREET CHILDREN"] VILLAGRAN MORALES ET AL v. GUATEMALA (IACtHR 19/11/1999, 11, Series C No. 63).
XAKMOK KASEK INDIGENOUS COMMUNITY v. PARAGUAY (IACtHR 24/8/2010, Series C No. 214).
Note: Additional references can be found in an extended version of this article on http://www.culture-rights.net

Kalliopi Chainoglou

Churches
(European Ch. and Human Rights)

DEF: For the Christian Churches the idea of independent human rights was initially a challenge (Rivers 2007). Human rights were perceived as an anthropocentric rival ethics born out of the anticlerical (especially anti-Catholic) impulse of the Enlightenment and French Revolution. In particular, the human right of freedom of religion was perceived as a threat by traditional Churches inasmuch as it strengthened the status of minority religions [e.g. KOKKINAKIS v. GREECE, 1993]. Historically, Protestant Churches were more open to human rights than the Catholic Church, which accepted HR only in the 1965 Second Vatican Council (Glendon 2001), and the Orthodox Churches, which are still in the process of defining their position (Stoeckl 2014).

INSTR: Churches are challenged by provisions in the ECHR in the following way: article 9 (Freedom of Thought, Conscience and Religion) challenges the traditional majority status of Christian Churches in Europe inasmuch as it strengthens minority faiths; article 10 (Freedom of Expression) has an impact on Churches inasmuch as it guarantees a secular public sphere and the right to publicly criticise religions; article 11 (Freedom of Association and Assembly) also strengthens minority faiths and works against state-church relations that privilege the traditional majority confessions; article 14 (Prohibition of Discrimination) works both in favour of the Churches as well as to their detriment, inasmuch as it guarantees non-discrimination on religious grounds, but it also makes it more problematic for Churches themselves to discriminate against certain groups, for example women, the unmarried, or the non-religious. In addition, Article 2 of the First Protocol ('right of parents to ensure education and teaching in conformity with their own religious and philosophical convictions') includes challenges for Christian Churches. On the one hand, due to religious pluralisation in states where education still carries confessional remnants, and on the other hand, due to secularisation that pushes religion out of schools.

CASES: The ECtHR has given two principled responses in cases involving religious freedom and the status of Christian Churches in society. It has either shown judicial restraint, refraining from ruling into national models of religious governance, or it has tried to impose one model of religious freedom on individual member states. Over the first four decades of its existence, the ECtHR has shown strong judicial restraint, applying the margin of appreciation doctrine and affirming that the ECtHR was compatible with a variety of church-state relations [e.g. OTTO PREMINGER INSTITUT v. AUSTRIA 1994]. In the last two decades, by contrast, the ECtHR has increasingly promoted forms of institutional secularism. Reason for this inversion of tendency were the institutional reorganisation of the Court in the 1990s, the joining of new member-states from the former Eastern bloc, and increased litigation activism on the part of minority religious groups [e.g. KOKKINAKIS v. GREECE 1993] (Koenig 2015). The clash of these two tendencies was particularly apparent in the case [LAUTSI, 2011], in which the Court in its first judgment sought to impose a model of secular public sphere on Italy, but overturned the judgment in the appeal-case reverting to the margin of appreciation (Annicchino 2012).

VIEWS: European nation-states remain strongly embedded in a broader Christian culture and frequently models of religious governance are informed by historical favouritism vis-à-vis Christian Churches. At the same time contemporary European societies are increasingly challenged by religious pluralisation due to international migration, secularisation and new religious movements. This situation creates tensions in the governance of religion in many member states of the Council of Europe. Constitutional models of church-state relations in Europe range from strict state neutrality (e.g. France), to cooperation models (e.g. Austria, Belgium), to established churches (e.g. United Kingdom). The ECtHR does not directly interfere with these arrangements, but it indirectly regulates the permissible forms of relationship between religious institutions and the state by reference to religious freedom (Evans/Thomas 2006). Christian Churches have a vested self-interest in preserving traditional church-state relations. However, inasmuch as they are committed to HR as the guarantors of protection of religious freedom, Christian Churches can also become spokespersons for the faithful as such, including new religions (for example through ecumenical dialogue).

CONCL: In the juridical framing of religious freedom in front of the ECtHR, the traditional approach of balancing out an individual right, vis-à-vis the state and society as a whole, is being replaced by a confrontation of individual HR. Individual non-discrimination provisions are brought into direct confrontation, for example the prohibition of discrimination on grounds of sexuality and religion, as in the case where a marriage registrar claims the right to refuse to perform same-sex marriages on religious grounds [EWEIDA AND OTHERS, 2013]. It is to be expected that in this situation, the Christian Churches in Europe will be less and less able to rely on historically established privileges in church-state relations. As the ECtHR increasingly concentrates on guaranteeing the religious freedom of individual believers, and not the status of religious organisations, the Christian Churches are bound to become religious players among others even though they still represent the majority faith in many countries.

REFERENCES:

Annicchino, Pasquale: “Between the Margin of Appreciation and Neutrality: The Lautsi Case and the New Equilibria of the Protection of Freedom of Religion or Belief in Europe”, in Roberto Mazzola (ed.): *Diritto e Religione in Europa*. Bologna: Il Mulino (2012) 179.

Evans, Carolyn/Thomas, Christopher A.: “Church-State Relations in the European Court of Human Rights”, in *BYU Law Review* 699 (2006), 699.

Glendon, Mary Ann: *Catholicism and Human Rights*, University of Dayton: Marianist Award Lecture (2001).

Koenig, Matthias: “The Governance of Religious Diversity at the European Court of Human Rights”, in Jane Bolden and Will Kymlicka (eds.): *International Approaches to the Governance of Ethnic Diversity*, Oxford: Oxford University Press (2015).

Rivers, Julian: “The Church in an age of human rights”, *International Journal for the Study of the Christian Church*, 7:1 (2007), 3.

Stoeckl, Kristina: *The Russian Orthodox Church and Human Rights*, London: Routledge (2014).

EWEIDA AND OTHERS v. UK (ECtHR 15/01/2013, 48420/10, 59842/10, 51671/10 and 3651/10).

LAUTSI v. ITALY (ECtHR 18/03/2011, 30814/06).

Kristina Stoeckl

Circumcision

DEF: Male circumcision is defined as the surgical removal of all or part of the prepuce (foreskin) of the penis. The reasons for performing male circumcision are numerous and based on religious, cultural, social and medical motives. For example, circumcision is considered a required practice in the Islamic faith, and most branches of the Jewish faiths, but is also performed as a 'rite of passage' in other religions and cultures. Globally, approximately 30% of males are circumcised, of whom two thirds are Muslim (WHO, 2007). Circumcision performed on minors for non-therapeutic reasons has been legitimised by invoking freedom of religion and supposed medical benefits (e.g. reduced risk of HIV infection), even if studies relating to these benefits are highly controversial.

CASES/VIEWS: Male circumcision has recently become the subject of increased criticism in Europe (especially in Denmark, Germany, the Netherlands and Sweden). Debates intensified after the District Court of Cologne (Germany) ruled in 2012 that the circumcision of a four-year-old boy amounted to abuse, even though the surgery was medically performed competently and based on the consent of both parents. Central to this discussion is the right to religious freedom of parents that needs to be weighed against the right to physical integrity and self-determination of the child.

CONCL: Important is whether, and how much, harm is done to young boys when undergoing circumcision. For a long time, the prevailing view was that male circumcising was associated with little health risk. However, more research shows that it can have adverse effects on sexual, emotional, and psychological health (Boyle, 2002). As a consequence, stricter laws have been adopted in some EU countries regulating the circumcision of young boys (calling for example for sound medical supervision and anaesthesia). Although the CoE's Parliamentary Assembly included both →Female Genital Mutilation (FGM) and the 'circumcision of young boys for religious reasons' in the category of violation of the physical integrity of children (CoE, 2013), the practice has not been outlawed in Europe. It seems that – at least for now – the religious rights of the parents prevail.

REFERENCES:

Boyle, G.: 'Male Circumcision: Pain, Trauma and Psychosexual Sequelae', *Journal of Health Psychology*, (2002).

Council of Europe, Parliamentary Assembly Resolution 1952/2013: *Children's right to physical integrity* (2013).

World Health Organization, Department of Reproductive Health and Research and Joint United Nations Programme on HIV/AIDS (UNAIDS): *Male circumcision: Global trends and determinants of prevalence, safety and acceptability* (2007).

BESCHNEIDUNG (LG Köln/Cologne, Judgment of 7 May 2012, 151Ns169/11).

Annemarie Middelburg

Citizenship

DEF: There is no single definition of citizenship. The term has different meanings which were shaped in historical processes. Since Roman times, it can be understood as the basis for the enjoyment of different rights and/or as a formal, legal status of a person in a community to which different rights and obligations are attached (the latter understanding often referred to as nationality). The Greek *polis* developed an understanding of citizenship as active engagement in community life. Nowadays, citizenship is often understood as belonging to any given community with which a person identifies and where links of solidarity between people are developed. In this sense one can name different 'citizenships', such as 'ethnic citizenship', 'sexual citizenship', 'multicultural citizenship' or 'cultural citizenship' (Isin, Turner, 2002). In legal literature, citizenship is often understood as the legal bond between a person and a state to which different rights are attached and therefore synonymous to nationality.

INSTR: Legal acts in national as well as international contexts rarely define citizenship (nationality). The first convention that defines nationality is the *European Convention on Nationality* (ECN, 1997). According to ECN, nationality denotes the legal bond between a person and a state and does not indicate the person's ethnic origin (Article 2(a)). Before, different definitions appeared in judgments of international courts, e.g. in a case judged by the ICJ [NOTTEBOHM, 1955], where nationality was defined as 'legal bond having at its basis a social fact of attachment, a genuine connection of existence, interests and sentiments, together with the existence of reciprocal rights and duties'. This concept of so called 'effective nationality' has proved to be a useful concept in international law in deciding cases of positive conflicts of nationalities.

Citizenship was perceived for a long time as being exclusively within the domestic jurisdiction of the state. Such was the formulation of 1930 *Convention on certain questions relating to the conflict of nationality laws* (Article 1). The development of human rights instruments after World War II, however, resulted in nationality being perceived also as a human right. The right to a nationality was for the first time formulated in 1948 in the *Universal Declaration of Human Rights* (Article 15). The right of →children to nationality is formulated in the *Convention on the Rights of the Child* (Article 7). The right to a nationality is also part of the ECN (Article 4(a)). Moreover, there are many human rights instruments that restrict the competence of states in this domain, e.g. regulations adopted by states in this domain cannot be contrary to regulations of international law such as the principle of non-discrimination in enjoying nationality (Article 5 iii CRPD), the ban on arbitrary deprivation of nationality (Article 15(2) UDHR), and the obligation to avoid statelessness (Article 4b ECN).

Nationality does not have the same significance for an enjoyment of rights as in the past, where many rights were linked with this status. Shortly after World War II, H. Arendt wrote that nationality is 'a right to have rights' (Arendt, 1951). Today, nationality does not have such a fundamental meaning for a person due to universalization of human rights. For example, according to Article 15(1)(a) ICESCR, everyone has the right to take part in cultural life. This right applies to everyone including non-nationals, such as refugees, asylum-seekers, stateless persons, migrant workers and victims of international trafficking, regardless of legal status and documentation (CESCR, General comment No 20). In the national context, however, many rights are still restricted to nationals only (e.g. voting rights, protection from deportation, and the right to run for public office) and international conventions allow for such restrictions (e.g. Article 21 ICCPR).

The concept of citizenship of the →European Union was introduced in 1993 by the *Treaty of Maastricht*. According to the current EU Treaties '(e)very person holding the nationality of a Member State shall be a citizen of the Union. Citizenship of the Union shall be additional to and not replace national citizenship.' (Article 20(1) TFEU and Article 9 TEU). The citizenship of the Union adds an additional layer of rights to those linked with the status of a member state national. However, the enjoyment of the majority of these rights is dependent on how citizens exercise their rights of free movement throughout the Union.

CASES: For many years, nationality was seen as the exclusive competence of the state. Discretionary competence of states in nationality law is nowadays restricted by international human rights law [e.g. IACHR, YEAN AND BOSICO, 2005]. The ECtHR and ECHR do not recognise the right to a nationality of a particular state [KARASSEV, 1999]. However, the ECtHR issued rulings concerning a potential violation of Article 8 in the context of nationality. According to the Court, in certain circumstances the arbitrary refusal of nationality may constitute a violation of the right of private and family life guaranteed by Article 8 [SLIVENKO, 2003; KURIĆ, 2010]. To date, no judgment has found a violation of Article 8 in this context, which shows that the ECtHR provides states with a wide margin of appreciation in nationality matters. In addition, the ECtHR dealt with discriminatory provisions in nationality law [GENOVESE, 2011].

In the context of the UN system, the Human Rights Committee found that states cannot create arbitrary barriers in acquiring nationality [STEWART, 1996; CANEPA, 1997]. In the EU context, the CJEU stated that a withdrawal of member state nationality which could result in the loss of citizenship of the Union is subject to a proportionality analysis by the courts [JANKO ROTTMAN, 2010].

VIEWS: An interesting debate concerns the issue of devaluation of nationality (Soysal, 1994, Jacobson 1997). According to this argument, an erosion of nationality takes place because rights traditionally linked with citizenship are expanded onto foreigners. This process is linked with the development of human rights instruments and the creation of supra-national structures such as the EU. In this context, the traditional dichotomy 'national – foreigner' is undermined and we nowadays see rather a continuum of different statuses of an individual in a state. The term 'denizen' has been used to describe those foreigners whose status is very close to a citizen of a particular country (Hammar, 1990).

In recent times discussions have also been held on how far the issue of nationality is an exclusive domain of domestic jurisdiction, especially in the EU context following the CJEU's decision in the Rottman case (Shaw, 2016).

CONCL: Citizenship is a powerful concept. It encompasses the idea of belonging to any given community with which a person identifies and where links of solidarity between people are developed. This powerful message behind the concept was used when the idea of European Union citizenship became reality. As a legal institution, it is known in every modern state; it undergoes evolution linked mainly to the development of international human rights law.

REFERENCES:

Arendt, Hannah: *The Origins of Totalitarianism*, Berlin: Schocken Books (1951).

Committee on Economic, Social and Cultural Rights, General Comment No. 20, Non-Discrimination in Economic, Social and Cultural Rights (art. 2, para. 2) U.N. Doc. E/C.12/GC/20 (2009).

Hammar, Tomas: *Democracy and the Nation State*, Ashgate: Aldershot (1990).

Isin, Engin and Turner, Bryan: (ed.) *Handbook of Citizenship Studies* London: Sage (2002).

Jacobson, David: *Rights Across Borders. Immigration and the Decline of Citizenship*, London: The Johns Hopkins University Press (1997).

Shaw, Jo: "Has the European Court of Justice Challenged Member State Sovereignty in Nationality Law?: Concluding thoughts", Rottmann in context, (available at eudo-citizenship.eu accessed 04/2016).

Soysal, Yasemin: *Limits of Citizenship. Migrants and Postnational Membership in Europe*, Chicago: The University of Chicago Press (1994).

CANEPA v. CANADA (HRCee 3/04/1997, 558/1993).

GENOVESE v. MALTA (ECtHR 11/10/2011, 53124/09).

JANKO ROTTMAN v. FREISTAAT BAYERN (CJEU, 2/03/2010 r., C-135/08).

KARASSEV v. FINLAND (ECtHR 12/01/1999, 31414/96).

KURIĆ AND OTHERS v. SLOVENIA (ECtHR 13/07/2010, 26828/06).

NOTTEBOHM CASE [LIECHTENSTEIN v. GUATEMALA] (ICJ 06/04/1955, Rep 4, ICGJ 185).

SLIVENKO v. LATVIA (ECtHR 9/10/2003, 48321/99).

STEWART v. CANADA (HRCee 1/11/1996, 538/1993).

YEAN AND BOSICO v. DOMINICAN REPUBLIC (IACHR 8/09/2005 r., 12.189).

Dorota Pudzianowska

Clash of Civilisations

DEF: The term 'clash of civilisations' has entered the discourses of both international relations and cultural commentary, mainly but not exclusively in the West. It is based more on fantasy than empirical reality and, yet generates attitudes and positions that run diametrically counter to the spirit of both cultural rights and intercultural dialogue enshrined in the standard-setting instruments adopted by the organisations of the United Nations system and by regional bodies such as the Council of Europe. Indeed, the UN →'Alliance of Civilisations' is a deliberate and concerted effort to undo the ill-effects of the 'clash' paradigm.

The notion of a coming 'clash of civilisations' was elaborated over two decades ago by the Harvard political scientist Samuel P. Huntington, whose eponymous article and book (1993; 1996) argued that conflicts between cultures, of which 'civilisations' were the highest order expression, would be the key driver of international relations in the post-Cold War world, rather than economic competition or differences in political ideology, rendered obsolete by the triumph of so-called 'free market democracy'.

VIEWS: Despite its conceptual and methodological flimsiness – the author relied upon essentially anecdotal evidence for the sweeping overgeneralisations and reductionist reasoning that undergirds his monolithic concept of 'civilisation' (Anheier and Isar, 2007; Nederveen Pieterse, 2009) – the notion has acquired considerable purchase in the popular imagination. It has increasingly become a euphemism, once again mainly in the West, for a fear of Islam, perceived as monolithically anti-Western. In this guise it has provided much of the rationale for the US 'war on terror', yet since then it is also readily and regularly invoked by journalists and public intellectuals elsewhere, notably in the wake of terrorist acts by Islamist extremists (e.g., Bobb, 2015), despite the fact that such violence is driven more by clashes of interests, based on economic and political inequalities between 'haves' and 'have nots', rather than differences based on beliefs or 'culture'. In the wake of the November 2015 Paris terrorist attacks, the Egyptian–Belgian journalist Khalid Diab observed that 'although ISIL undoubtedly hates Christians and other non-Muslims with a passion and believes in just such a clash, buried amid its jihadist rhetoric of fighting the 'infidel' is a clear indication that the choice of Paris as a target was largely motivated by France's 'military assets' in Syria.' Diab thus added that 'ISIL's 'jihad' has been about territory politically, resources, economically, and, ideologically, its main enemy has been what it regards as errant Muslims who are worse than the 'infidel'...' Yet it is also true that both Osama bin Laden and the entourage of George W. Bush have used the 'clash of civilisations' paradigm to urge their followers on, the former arguing that people in the West really adhere to it – and are ready to become 'new crusaders'.

CONCL: Huntington advised the United States and other Western powers to draw closer together, maintain their strength, and, above all, recognise 'that Western intervention in the affairs of other civilisations is probably the single most dangerous source of instability and potential global conflict in a multi-civilisational world' (1996, p. 312). The implication is that the belief and value systems of 'the Rest' are simply incommensurable with those of 'Western Civilization': they are inherently conflict generating, and resistant to any form of dialogue or mutuality. Behind any 'cultural' difference lurks the spectre of conflict: the cultural dimensions of conflict on the one hand, and the conflict inducing dimensions of culture on the other. When the collective bearers of such difference are constructed as monolithic entities, or reduced to a single "culture" and set against each other in the process, it is difficult to realise the contemporary vision of cultural rights. The 'clash of civilisations' paradigm could be seen, then, as the contemporary equivalent of Kipling's line 'OH, East is East, and West is West, and never the twain shall meet, Till Earth and Sky stand presently at God's great Judgment Seat' but in a reading that disregards the next two lines of the poem, which anticipates today's ethos of intercultural dialogue: 'But there is neither East nor West, Border, Breed, nor Birth, When two strong men stand face to face, tho' they come from the ends of the earth!'

Ultimately, the 'clash of civilisations' is more often than not a self-fulfilling prophecy, one that, as G. John Ikenberry pointed out, is the equivalent of the 'security dilemma', in which misperceptions about the other create tensions and lead to conflict: 'Huntington wants the West to defensively guard against the coming clash, but to other powers like China and Japan the circling of the Western wagons will look like a declaration of a new Cold War' (Ikenberry *et al.*, 1997). In this sense, then, the paradigm negates and forecloses the positive vision of living together with difference upon which the cultural rights perspective is based.

REFERENCES:

Anheier, Helmut and Isar, Yudhishthir Raj (eds.): *Conflicts and Tensions. The Cultures and Globalization Series, 1*. London: SAGE Publications (2007).

Bobb, Dilip: "I, Tiresias. The clash that Huntington prophesied is upon us. Or is it?", in *Outlook*, 30 November 2015.

Diab, Khaled: "Isil and the illusion of a clash of civilizations", in *Al Jazeera*, 16 November 2015.

Huntington, Samuel P.: "The Clash of Civilizations?", in *Foreign Affairs*, Summer 1993.

Huntington, Samuel P.: *The Clash of Civilizations and the Remaking of World Order*. New York: Simon & Schuster (1996).

Ikenberry, G. John: "The West: Precious, not Unique: Civilizations Make for a Poor Paradigm Just Like the Rest", in *Foreign Affairs*, March/April 1997.
Nederveen Pieterse, Jan: *Globalization & Culture. Global Mélange*. Lanham, MD.: Rowman and Littlefield Publishers, Inc. (2009).
www.culturalrights.net.

Yudhishthir Raj Isar

Common Values
(C. V. of the European Union)

DEF: The European Union is founded on the values of freedom, equality and democracy, as well as respect for human rights, as laid down in the *Charter of Fundamental Rights of the EU* (in force since 2009). However, the sense of community that these 'common values' helped to create has come under severe strain in recent years. In the context of a spate of terrorist attacks, particularly the issues of migration and internal security, however tenuously they are related, have led politicians from populist but also mainstream parties to misuse the term in order to deliberately exclude communities whose roots or religion are deemed 'un-European'.

INSTR: The 'values...common to the Member States' described in the *Treaty on European Union* (Article 2), are 'respect for human dignity, freedom, democracy, equality, the rule of law and respect for human rights, including the rights of persons belonging to minorities.' The *Charter of Fundamental Rights* of the EU specifically mentions the term 'common values' in its preamble, which stresses that the 'preservation' and 'development' of these values should respect 'the diversity of the cultures and traditions of Europe as well as the national identities of the Member States...' The official motto of the EU is 'United in diversity', which expresses both respect for the many different peoples, languages and traditions it comprises and the fact that together these forge a greater whole.

CONCL: The fact that the term 'common values' is used so differently in public discourse and in the original concept behind EU legislation is of concern in itself, particularly as effective means are sought to prevent and combat radicalisation and extremism of various hues (minorities do not have a monopoly on extremist behaviour). However, this need not be a lasting phenomenon. It is vital to clarify that, whenever and in whatever context the phrase is used, common values can only be built on the basis of mutual respect, inclusion and the rule of law. This in turn is dependent not only on legislation, but also on ensuring well-resourced human rights education and civic awareness training for children and adults throughout the EU.

REFERENCES:

Consolidated versions of the Treaty on European Union and the Treaty on the Functioning of the European Union, (available at eur-lex.europa.eu accessed 04/2016).
Charter of Fundamental Rights of the European Union, (available at www.europarl.europa.eu accessed 04/2016).

Katya Andrusz

Community Identification
(Free Choice of Ethnic, Racial or National Identity)

DEF: Conceptualising ethnic, racial or national identity is a central issue in the social sciences. Whether there exists a free choice for self-identification and the eligibility for such a right under international law needs to be examined. Differing from other forms of identity, in particular gender or religion, the free choice of ethnic, racial or national identity as a free-standing right or principle is not secured in an explicit form under international law. On the surface level, the choice of identity, similarly to the freedom of thought or conscience, should not be restricted, as it is a mere intellectual and/or emotional (that is, non-legal or political) phenomenon. Seeing it as a practical matter, with implications of a legal, political and fiscal nature, the free choice of identity has two dimensions for state obligations: a positive and a negative one.

INSTR: According to the basic tenet of legal logic, if there was a proper right to free choice of identity allowing people to opt out from racial, ethnic or national (minority) communities, the very right necessarily would need to include the freedom to opt in either to the majority or to any chosen social group.

The negative aspect of the free choice of identity prohibits the state from creating an official, mandatory ethno-national identity (and classifications and registries) for individuals. Thus, people have an unconditional right to opt-out from any socio-legal construct that incorporates ethno-national classifications. This obligation (and people's right to formally assimilate or integrate into the majority) is reiterated in several international instruments and documents such as the Council of Europe's *Framework Convention for the Protection of National Minorities*, the 1992 UN *Declaration on the Rights of Persons Belonging to National or Ethnic, Religious and Linguistic Minorities*, the 1990 *Copenhagen Concluding Document on the Human Dimension* of the CSCE, the 2012 *Ljubljana Guidelines on Integration of Diverse Societies* of the OSCE, and the 2007 *United Nations Declaration on the Rights of Indigenous Peoples* (thus including even communities beyond strictly defined minorities).

The right to opt out is guaranteed by powerful data protection regulations. Due to the painful memories of the Holocaust, population transfers, and state-organised ethnic cleansing (all of which were built on easily accessible official registries containing data on ethno-national affiliation), the continental European legal framework establishes strict barriers to processing and collecting ethno-national data. Article 8 of the *European Data Protection Directive* (95/46/EC) creates a special category of sensitive data, and apart from a very narrow set of exceptions (set forth by law, having the explicit consent from the person in question, or anonymisation), prohibits the processing of data revealing racial or ethnic origin.

The 2007 UN *Principles and Recommendations for Population and Housing Censuses* also set forth that censuses should not require compulsory declaration of belonging to specific identities or groups, since nobody should be compelled to declare his or her belonging to a minority. International law also recognises the right to retain ethno-national identity in the sense that no one should be forced to assimilate into the majority.

The positive aspect of the free choice of identity encompasses the individual's right to join a group or community. In such an explicit form, the freedom to choose one's identity is rarely declared in legally binding documents.

CASES: International law suggests that states may actually set forth 'objective' membership criteria (for the national or ethnic minority communities) and implies that the state is authorised to either establish these criteria or adopt definitions provided by non-state agents like self-declared representatives of minority communities or other (academic or political) bodies fulfilling this task. The process of how the state comes to define the group or membership criteria, i.e. how individuals can choose to identify or declare affiliation, is a different issue, falling more or less within the competence of the domestic legislator. The European Court of Human Rights did not dispute the right of a government to require the existence of objective evidence of a claimed ethnicity [CIUBOTARU, 2010]. Similarly, the UN Human Rights Committee held that if the domestic legislation confines a minority right attached to the membership in a minority community, it should be objectively and reasonably justified [LOVELACE, 1981].

CONCL: The requirement of the active, affirmative involvement of the individual in group membership, accompanied by the prohibition of mandatory inclusion by the state, along with the prohibition of collecting sensitive data, thus, does not create an autonomous, *sui generis* right under international law for the free choice of identity, since it does not and cannot include the right (of choice) to opt in to any chosen group. The core of what exists entails the following:

(i) States cannot create mandatory ethno-racial or national classifications;

(ii) States cannot deny the right of individuals not to affiliate involuntarily with any given group – most of all for statistical and census-purposes;

(iii) States cannot forcefully assimilate individuals into the majority; and:
(iv) Insofar as individuals do not wish to make use of minority rights or preferential treatment, the state cannot make arbitrary ethno-racial classifications.

In addition, if individuals decide to seek affirmative action, preferential treatment or minority rights, under international law, states are indeed authorised to establish (objective) criteria for membership in the groups and the recognition of identification. In effect and practice, states are explicitly obliged to act if discrimination or hate/bias crimes are committed on grounds of a presumed or perceived identity or group membership. Also, under international law, while states cannot legally question an individuals' identification with the majority, there are no narrowly tailored litigable state obligations for the cultural and social integration and assimilation of persons belonging to minorities.

REFERENCES:

Barth, Frederik: *Ethnic Groups and Boundaries: The Social Organization of Culture Difference.* 1969, Reprint, Bergen/Oslo: Scandinavian University Press (1994).

Brubaker, Rogers, and Frederick Cooper: "Beyond 'Identity'" 29(1) *Theory and Society* (2000) 1.

Council of Europe: *Explanatory Report to the Council of Europe's Framework Convention for the Protection of National Minorities*, Strasbourg: CoE (1995).

Pap, Andras L.: "Is there a legal right to free choice of ethno-racial identity? Legal and political difficulties in defining minority communities and membership boundaries" 46(2) *Columbia Human Rights Law Review* (2015) 153.

CIUBOTARU v. MOLDOVA (ECtHR 27/04/2010, 27138/04).

LOVELACE v. CANADA (UN HRCee 30/07/1981, R/6/24).

Andras L. Pap

Constitutional Courts

DEF: The role of constitutional courts is determined by their power of constitutional review. In constitutional review, courts can invalidate statutes and other acts of public authority contrary to the constitution. The emergence of constitutional courts in post-war Europe was prompted by the horrors of war, as well as the failures and excesses of elected bodies (parliaments) which necessitated the establishment of institutional safeguards against a 'tyranny of the majority'. Today, the role of constitutional courts is additionally predicated on the need to provide protection of human rights, including rights of various minorities, beyond the politics of the day.

HIST: The power of the judiciary to invalidate laws contrary to the constitution was first proclaimed by the US Supreme Court [MARBURY, 1803]. Upon this decision, judicial reviews in the USA could be exercised by any court. Unlike such type of dispersed judicial review, in continental Europe constitutional review is concentrated in a specialised court or tribunal. This model was developed by Hans Kelsen and established for the first time in Austria in 1920, followed by Czechoslovakia (1920), Liechtenstein (1921) and Spain (1931). In both models of review – dispersed and concentrated, the role of a court is to ensure the supremacy of the constitution over other legal acts. In Europe, the Kelsenian model was not entirely followed and his warning against conferral of rights jurisdiction to constitutional courts had been politically ignored. The so-called 'new constitutionalism' in the post-war era was based on the strong belief that rights protection should be made an important part of the jurisdiction of constitutional courts (Shapiro 1998, 1999). The result has been that 'virtually no one writes a constitution without providing for rights protection and a mode of review.' (Stone Sweet, 2012)

INSTR: Today, constitutional review is part and parcel of any constitutional regime. Even in countries without a written constitution like Israel and the UK, supreme courts exercise the role of a constitutional court in cases concerning the protection of human rights. Still, there are important differences in the organisation of constitutional courts, the appointment of judges, jurisdiction, procedures and legal effects of their decisions (Venice Commission 2015). Moreover, conceptual differences exist between 'strong' and 'weak' types of constitutional review. In strong review countries, judges are not only 'negative legislators' but also play an active role in shaping legal standards by means of their dynamic interpretation, in particular in the area of human rights protection. In contrast, weak review countries permit courts to determine inconsistencies in legislation or disproportionate impacts on human rights, while leaving the content of rights to be determined by legislation (Waldron 2006).

VIEWS/CASES: According to Kelsen, the power of constitutional courts should be limited to declaring acts contrary to the constitution null and void. This approach excludes a positive determination of the scope of protection of constitutional rights which remains reserved for the legislature. Kelsen's views on the role of constitutional courts were founded on his understanding of the role of constitutions: to set up a framework for government.

Today, the debate about the role of constitutional courts and the character of constitutional review continues, as the legitimacy of their decisions is challenged by the counter-majoritarian argument implying that unelected judges should not overrule acts which reflect the will of the majority. Hence, constitutional courts need to establish their authority on the substantive notion of democracy, the respect for rule of law, and the protection of human rights. However, according to Aharon Barak (2008), their role is even broader: it is to bridge the gap between society and the law and to defend democracy.

In the era of global constitutionalism characterised by the plurality of legal orders, the role of constitutional courts is weakened by the authority of international tribunals. In this context courts not only compete for the power of the 'last word' but also engage in judicial dialogues. In Europe, the relationship between national constitutional courts, the CJEU, and the ECtHR is even more complex – on the one hand, it is based on the principle of mutual trust and recognition, on the other hand, it is a form of mutual control and oversight. Yet, without some degree of cooperation, courts risk marginalisation and the loss of influence. Notwithstanding the internal rivalry, constitutional courts, the CJEU, and the ECtHR co-shape European constitutional traditions and legal culture. Although there are important differences in constitutional systems of EU member states, the standards of protection of human rights in the EU are common, save exceptional cases in which a higher level of protection is granted to certain values or rights. These differences are permitted under the narrow exception of 'constitutional/national identity' [see e.g. OMEGA, 2004].

Given the above-mentioned challenges to the authority of constitutional courts, there is a gradual shift from the confrontational 'last word' approach, which overemphasises *who* has the final say, to *what* the limits of law are. In the latter approach, constitutional courts have the power of the 'first word,' which invites other parties, including other courts, to take positions and engage in a constructive dialogue. Especially in the EU, constitutional courts move away from their exclusive role of constitutional guardians and become involved actors of European constitutionalism, wielding persuasion rather than compulsion. Furthermore, proponents of political constitutionalism advocate shifting the authority of the 'last word' from courts to democratically elected bodies, while equipping them with the right to override judgements of constitutional courts, alongside judgments of international human rights courts (Bellamy 2007). Still, such solutions seem to be inadequate in new democracies where the ruling majorities have strong inclinations to remove any limitations of their power.

CONCL: In a democratic regime, a constitution is supposed to have a normative content as opposed to a mere declaratory (semantic) one. Therefore, a governing majority should be aware that there are constitutional limits to their democratic mandate and it is the province of the judiciary to set down these limits and enforce them in a judicious manner. For this very reason, the privileged stature of constitutional courts pits them against the political power. Yet, constitutional courts have their own constitutional promises to keep and respect the limits of their own institutional authority. Their existence reinforces the belief that democracy is not only about the electoral result, but also about fundamental values which last beyond next elections. Nevertheless, a mere existence of the constitutional court is not enough to provide effective safeguards against abuses of power or violations of fundamental rights. Equally important is the social legitimacy of their authority, as well as the normative framework which entails guarantees of their independence and undisturbed functioning.

REFERENCES:

Barak, Aharon: *The Judge in a Democracy*, Princeton: Princeton University Press (2008).

Bellamy, Richard: *Political Constitutionalism; A Republican Defence of the Constitutionality of Democracy*, Cambridge: Cambridge University Press (2007).

Peters, Anne: "Global constitutionalism" in: Gibbons, Michel et al (eds.), *The Encyclopaedia of Legal Thought*, Hoboken: Willey–Blackwell (2015).

Shapiro, Martin: "The European Court of Justice: of institutions and democracy", 32 *Israel Law Review* (1998) 1.

Shapiro, Martin: "The European Court of Justice" in: Craig, Paul, de Burca, Grainne (eds.): *The Evolution of EU law*, Oxford: OUP (1999).

Sweet Stone, Alec: "Constitutional Courts" in: Rosenfeld, Michel, Sajó András (eds.): *The Oxford Handbook of Comparative Constitutional Law*, Oxford: OUP (2012).

Venice Commission (Council of Europe): *Compilation of Venice Commission Opinions, Reports and Studies on Constitutional Justice*, CDL-PI (2015)002.

Waldron, Jeremy: "The Core Case against Judicial Review", 115 *Yale Law Journal* (2006) 1346.

MARBURY v. MADISON (1803, 5 U.S. 137).

OMEGA SPIELHALLEN- UND AUTOMATEN-AUFSTELLUNGS-GMBH v. OBERBÜRGERMEISTERIN DER BUNDESSTADT BONN (CJEU 14/10/2004, Case C-36/02).

Tomasz Tadeusz Koncewicz and Anna Śledzińska-Simon

Conversion

DEF: In the context of freedom of religion or belief, the term conversion covers two conceptually different but at the same time related dimensions: (1) changing *one's own* religion or belief and (2) inducing *others* to change their religious orientation, i.e. by way of missionary activities. 'Converts' are those who have adopted a new faith, thereby replacing their previous religion or belief by a new religious orientation. Members of the religion which the convert has abandoned often stigmatise that change as 'apostasy'. Communicative outreach activities aimed to convert others are sometimes criticized as 'proselytism'.

INSTR: Using the wording of Article 18 of the UDHR (1948), Article 9 of the ECHR entrenches the 'freedom to change' as a core element of freedom of religion or belief. While article 18 of the ICCPR does not repeat the highly disputed term 'change', it confirms everyone's freedom to 'have or to adopt a religion or belief of his choice', thus by implication clearly corroborating the right to change. This *forum-internum* dimension of freedom of religion or belief even enjoys unconditional protection and cannot be exposed to any justifiable limitations or restrictions for whatever reasons. Conversion in the second meaning of the word, i.e. inducing *others* to change their faith, falls within the broad range of 'manifestations' of religion or belief in 'worship, teaching, practice and observance', as also enshrined in Article 9 of the ECHR as well as the above-cited UN instruments. Unlike the freedom to change *one's own* religion or belief, inducing *others* to reconsider and change their faith is not beyond possible limitations. However, for limitations to be justifiable, they have to meet all the criteria set out in European and international human rights law, respectively. Non-coercive attempts of converting others thus are generally covered by freedom of religion or belief.

CASES: Internationally, no aspect of freedom of religion or belief has been more controversial than the two dimensions of conversion, as defined above. In a number of Islamic states 'apostasy' from Islam is considered a criminal offence, in a few countries possibly even leading to a death verdict. In many more states conversion can incur *de-facto* sanctions in family and inheritance laws, such as involuntary dissolution of marriage, loss of custody for children and denial of the right to inherit. In the face of ongoing human rights violations against converts in many parts of the world, UN forums and experts have repeatedly corroborated the right to change as an indispensable part of freedom of religion or belief and a test issue indicative of the understanding of that human right in general. While in Europe 'apostasy' laws no longer exist, a number of (mostly Eastern) European countries still prohibit 'proselytism', a term which typically does not receive a clear legal definition while obviously carrying quite negative connotations. Proselytism laws are aimed to protect the traditional religious landscape from unwanted missionary activities. The ECtHR had to deal with this issue in a number of cases. The [KOKKINAKIS, 1993] decision concerning non-coercive missionary activities of a Jehovah's Witness marks the very beginning of the Court's jurisdiction on freedom of religion or belief.

VIEWS: The issue of conversion continues to divide the international community, including (albeit confined to the aspect of proselytism) the member states of the Council of Europe. Controversies are also reflected in the academic literature on freedom of religion or belief. Critics have argued that by broadly including conversion, the right to freedom of religion or belief privileges those religious communities which actively recruit followers, while putting those communities in a disadvantaged position which do not engage in any missionary activities. Some critics go a step further by alleging that the prevailing view on freedom of religion or belief displays a 'Protestant' bias in the understanding of religion, which mainly focuses on individual believing while more or less ignoring collective religious practices or expectations of solidarity within the community. Yet others have contended that the term 'choice', as often employed in human rights language, indicates a shallow misconstruction of religion, which should not be treated in as a mere commodity in a marketplace of religious ideas and spiritual practices.

CONCL: Against a widespread misunderstanding, it should be noted that the right to freedom of religion or belief, as enshrined in international and European human rights instruments, does not protect religions or belief-systems in themselves. Instead, it aims to empower human beings, as individuals and in community with others. While having its specific scope of application, freedom of religion or belief thus follows the same logic as other rights to freedom, such as freedom of expression or freedom of assembly and association etc. The treatment of conversion has been, and continues to be, the litmus test for the understanding of freedom of religion or belief as a human right to be respected in all human beings, in recognition of their inherent human dignity. Without the option of changing one's religion or belief, decisions to remain within a certain religious community would by implication lack their qualification as manifestations of freedom. Moreover, rather than simply eroding communitarian loyalty, the right to change – in conjunction with the right to invite others to reconsider their orientation – may furthermore expose religious communities to a healthy competition.

REFERENCES:

Ahdar, Rex J. and Leigh, Ian: *Religious Freedom in the Liberal State*, Oxford: OUP (2nd edn. 2013).

Bielefeldt, Heiner, Ghanea, Nazila and Wiener, Michael: *Freedom of Religion or Belief. An International Law Commentary*, Oxford: OUP (2016).

Evans, Malcolm D: *Religious Liberty and International Law in Europe*, Cambridge: CUP (1997).

Ghanea, Nazila: "Apostasy and Freedom to Change Religion or Belief" in Lindholm, Tore, Durham, Jr., W. Cole and Tahzib-Lie, Bahia (ed.): *Facilitating Freedom of Religion or Belief: A Deskbook*, Leiden: Nijhogg (2004).

Sharma, Arvind: *Problematizing Religious Freedom*, New York: Springer (2011).

Taylor, Paul M: *Freedom of Religion: UN and European Human Rights Law and Practice*, Cambridge: CUP (2005).

KOKKINAKIS v. GREECE (ECtHR 25/05/1993, 14307/88).

LARISSIS and others v. GREECE (ECtHR 24/02/1998, 23372/94, 26377/94, 26378/94).

www.freedomofreligion.ohchr.org.

Heiner Bielefeldt

Council of Europe (CoE)

DEF/INTRO: The Council of Europe (CoE) is a regional intergovernmental organisation founded in 1949. It concentrates on promoting human rights, democracy and the rule of law in its member states and seeks to develop, throughout Europe, common and democratic principles based on the →*European Convention on Human Rights* and other instruments guaranteeing the protection of individuals. The CoE has 47 member states and is led and represented by the Secretary General. The main political components of the Council of Europe are the Committee of Ministers (CM), the organisation's decision-making body, and the Parliamentary Assembly (PACE) composed of 318 members representing national parliaments. The most visible institutions of the CoE in the field of human rights are the ECtHR, established pursuant to the ECHR, and the Commissioner for Human Rights. One of the key factors prompting the CoE activities and endeavours is the promotion of cultural rights through cultural cooperation and standard setting.

The main principle underlying CoE culture-related policies has been to develop the European cultural identity while at the same time protecting the distinctive features that are the source of the identity's richness. The right to take part in cultural life has been identified as 'pivotal to the system of human rights' (Recommendation 1990 of the PACE), so the cultural policies have as their aim the protection of both individual rights as well as collective rights in the field of culture. The idea of defining and protecting cultural rights has been developed through cultural cooperation coordinated by CoE expert bodies, in particular under the guidance of the Steering Committee for Culture, Heritage and Landscape (CDCPP) (under this head from 2012) which is responsible for activities of the CoE and its member states related to culture, heritage and landscape and for monitoring and evaluation of policies' implementation.

It also has to be underlined that the ECtHR, through its case-law, has significantly contributed to the definition of the scope of cultural rights protected in the framework of the ECHR realising in practice the principle of indivisibility of human rights.

Over the years, the CoE has further developed its basic idea that strengthening democracy, human rights and the rule of law implies promoting a relationship with culture. A range of CoE's activities clearly demonstrate that cultural activities and policies influence democratisation and sustainable development. The *dissemination and consolidation of a common constitutional European heritage*, playing a unique role for states in transition and generally in the process of democratisation, are ensured by the CoE advisory body on constitutional issues – the European Commission for Democracy through Law (Venice Commission).

INSTR: Basing on the fact that culture plays a unique part in forging a Europe of solidarity and shared standards especially in the field of human rights, numerous activities of the CoE concentrate on providing a legal framework for cultural and heritage policies. This activity started with the *European Cultural Convention* (Paris, 1954) whose purpose has been e.g. to safeguard European culture and promote national contributions to Europe's common cultural heritage. Later followed e.g. the *Convention on the Conservation of European Wildlife and Natural Habitats* (Bern, 1979), the *European Convention on Cinema Coproduction* (Strasbourg, 1982), the *European Convention on Offences relating to Cultural Property* (Delphi, 1985), the *Convention for the Protection of the Architectural Heritage of Europe* (Granada, 1985), the *Convention for the Protection of the Archaeological Heritage of Europe (revised)* (Valletta, 1992) and the *European Charter for Regional or Minority Languages* (Strasbourg, 1992).

Due to a number of political, economic and legal difficulties, the CM decided in 1996 to suspend the work of CAHMIN, one of its expert bodies which had been mandated with drafting a complementary ECHR Cultural Protocol, envisaged to include provisions guaranteeing individual rights. In 2000, the CoE confirmed its commitment to the protection of culture and heritage by adopting the *European Landscape Convention* (Florence, 2000). Next has been the *European Convention on Protection of the Audiovisual Heritage* (Strasbourg, 2001) which is the first binding international instrument introducing both a compulsory legal deposit of all moving-image productions as well as the accessibility of these collections for the public. Finally, the *Framework Convention on the Value of Cultural Heritage for Society* (Faro, 2005) is based on the idea that knowledge and use of heritage form part of the citizen's right to participate in cultural life as defined in the → Universal Declaration of Human Rights.

VIEWS: CoE's role as the key European organisation in the field of human rights is undisputed. However, it has not been spared from criticism alleging its lack of efficiency, its internal dispersion of activities and competencies as well as overlapping with other international organisations. Since 2009/2010, the CoE introduced certain long term reforms which pursue the following objectives:

- to revitalise the Council of Europe as a political flexible body and an innovative organisation; and
- to concentrate its work on fewer projects, selected according to the highest added value and comparative advantage (see, Council of Europe Reform: heading into the future Progress review report, 27/06/2011)

The process of undertaking reforms and increasing efficiency is ongoing. Only when the CoE succeeds in realising this goal will it remain a relevant actor on the European level.

It should be noted that the European system of protection of human rights created on the basis of the ECHR has also been subject to significant challenges in recent years, especially due to the enormous number of submitted applications. The first phase of its reform ended in 2004 with the adoption of Protocol no. 14 introducing significant changes to the ECtHR's internal process of dealing with applications. The next step is the fulfilment of goals identified by intergovernmental conferences on the future of the ECtHR (Interlaken, Izmir, Brighton, Brussels).

CONCL: The CoE has made many efforts to refocus culture as part of its function to protect human rights and foster democratic processes. Its cultural policies concentrate on:

- Standard setting activities;
- Organising events and introducing new initiatives, such as European Heritage Days, cultural routes and exhibitions;
- Developing information tools about policies and practical approaches for specialists, policy makers and the general public, e.g. HEREIN (European Heritage Network) and the Compendium of Cultural Policies and Trends in Europe;
- Managing projects to promote cooperation between member states in the cultural field, e.g. in the scope of intercultural dialogue or in programmes involving the training of specialists, administrative staff, heritage managers and policy makers, and setting up networks of cultural development agencies;
- Involvement in the audio-visual sector which it assists with setting standards as well as through financial support for film productions and distribution (Eurimages).

REFERENCES:

Bourquin, Jean-Fred: *Violence, Conflict and Intercultural Dialogue*, Strasbourg: CoE (2003).

Council of Europe: *Heritage and beyond*, Strasbourg: CoE (2009).

Council of Europe: Communication on the activities of the Committee of Ministers (September 1995 – January 1996), Statutory Report 1st Part of the 1996 Session of the Assembly (22–26 January 1996) CM(96)17 [Doc. 7460] and: *Council of Europe Reform: heading into the future*. Progress review report, 27/06/2011.

European Court of Human Rights: *Cultural rights in the case-law of the European Court of Human Rights*, report available at: www.echr.coe.int (Case-Law / Case Law Analysis / Research Reports – accessed 01/2016).

Laaksonen, Annamari: *Making Culture Accessible – Access, participation and cultural provision in the context of cultural rights in Europe*, Strasbourg: CoE (2010).

PACE Resolution 1689 (2009): The future of the Council of Europe in the light of its sixty years of experience.

Pickard, Rob (ed.): European Cultural Heritage: A review of policies and practice, Strasbourg: Council of Europe publishing (2002).

Council of Europe website: www.coe.int (accessed 01/2016).

Aleksandra Mężykowska

Court of Justice of the European Union (CJEU)

DEF: Originally founded 1952 under the *Treaty establishing the European Coal and Steel Community* and since the *Rome Treaties* commonly known as the European Court of Justice (ECJ), the Court of Justice of the European Union (CJEU) is now the main judicial authority of the → European Union and one of its seven principal organs. The CJEU's core function is to ensure that the law is observed in the interpretation and application of the EU Treaties. This function is performed through the following procedures: preliminary ruling, action against a member state, action for annulment, action for failure to act, action for damages.

INSTR: The CJEU is composed of three judicial bodies: The Court of Justice, the General Court, and the Civil Service Tribunal. The Court of Justice consists of 28 Judges (one from each EU Member State) and 11 Advocates Generals. Both the Judges and the Advocates General are appointed by common accord of the governments of the member states for terms of 6 years, after consultation of the special panel. The Judges and Advocates General chosen must be persons whose independence is beyond doubt and who possess qualification necessary for appointment to the highest judicial bodies in their respective countries, or are layers of recognised competence (Article 19 (2) TEU, Article 253 TFEU). The Advocates General assists the Court. The General Court (formerly the Court of the First Instance) was created in 1988 to support the Court of Justice. It includes at least one judge from each Member State. The Judges are appointed in the same procedure as the Judges of the Court of Justice. The Civil Service Tribunal, created in 2004 is the first specialised court established under Article 257 TEU. It is composed of 7 Judges appointed by the Council for a period of 6 years, following a call for applications and after taking the opinion of a committee established for that purpose.

With its main function: the interpretation and application of the treaties of the EU (Article 19 TEU), the CJEU constitutes the judicial authority of the EU. Together with national courts of the member states, it ensures, as an international court established under treaty law, the uniform and effective application and interpretation of the EU law. The role performed by the CJEU within the EU system of judicial protection is compared with the role of constitutional courts in national legal orders. The CJEU controls the legality of acts of the EU institutions as well as the observation of EU laws by the member states. The CJEU performs its function within the framework of jurisdiction conferred upon by treaties. It adjudicates within the following main procedures: action for failure to fulfil obligations (Articles 258 – 260 TFEU), action for annulment (Article 253 TFEU), action for failure to act (Article 265 TFEU), action for damages (Article 340 TFEU), preliminary ruling procedure (Article 267 TFEU), opinions on international agreements of the EU (Article 218 TFEU).

CASES: The CJEU has referred to culture as an element of EU policies in several decisions delivered in preliminary ruling procedure as well as actions against member states and actions for annulment. Case-law concerning the relationship between internal market and culture is of special practical importance. According to the jurisprudence of the Court, there is no doubt that cultural objects are goods in terms of the free movement of goods within the internal market [COMMISSION, 1968] and that cultural activity conducted by artists and cultural institutions (e.g. museums) constitutes part of the internal market of services or an element of free movement of establishment. As well, employees of cultural institutions are considered as workers within the internal labour market. According to the Court, some aspects of culture are also covered by the principle of respect of the national identities of the member states, which is strictly connected with respect for their cultural and linguistic diversity, as provided in Article 3(3) TEU and Article 22 CFREU. The protection of national languages as an essential element of cultural heritage has to be respected by EU law [MALGOŽATA RUNEVIČ-VARDYN AND VARDYN, 2011]. Culture is also recognised by the CJEU as a national value protected by the member states. The protection of national treasures possessing artistic, historic or archaeological value constitutes a legitimate aim for prohibitions or restrictions on imports, exports or goods in transit adopted by member states (Article 36 TFEU). According to the well-established case-law of the Court, cultural policy aims may constitute an overriding requirement relating to the general interest which can justify a restriction on the freedom to provide services [cf. COLLECTIEVE ANTENNEVOORZIENING GOUDA, 1991 and VERONICA OMROEP ORGANISATIE, 1993]. In addition, the *Charter of Fundamental Rights* of the EU covers culture with regard to freedom of speech (Article 11) and artistic freedom (Article 13). The CJEU noted [cf. UNITED PAN-EUROPE COMMUNICATIONS BELGIUM SA, 2007 and TV10 SA, 1994] that the maintenance of pluralism is connected with freedom of expression, as protected by Article 10 of *the European Convention on Human Rights and Fundamental Freedoms*, and constitutes one of the fundamental rights guaranteed by the Community legal order [TV10 SA, 1994].

CONCL: The CJEU, as the central judicial authority of the EU, performs its function of constitutional court of an autonomous legal system through reviews of the legality of the acts of the institutions of the European Union. It also oversees whether member states comply with obligations under the various Treaties, and cooperates with national courts by delivering authoritative interpretation of EU law. Since 1970, the Court adjudicates on cases concerning broadly understood 'culture' and cultural policy of member states *vis-à-vis* internal market freedoms. Thus, the Court, in cooperation with national courts, ensures a proper balance between interests of economic integration and the preservation of national cultural heritage.

REFERENCES:

Alter, Karen: *The European Court's Judicial Power*, Oxford: Oxford University Press (2009).

Bobek, Michal: "The Court of Justice of the European Union", *College of Europe Research Paper in Law* 02/2014.

Chalmers, Damian/Davies, Gareth/Monti, Giorgio: *European Union Law: Text and Materials*, in particular: "The Union Judicial Order", Cambridge: Cambridge University Press (2014).

De Witte, Bruno: "Market Integration and Cultural Diversity in EU Law", in Valentina Vadi & Bruno De Witte (eds.), *Culture and International Economic Law*, London–New York: Routledge (2015).

Iglesias Sânchez, Sara: "The Court and the Charter: the Impact of the Entry into Force of the Lisbon Treaty on the ECJ's Approach to Fundamental Rights" (2012) *49 CMLRev* 1565.

Psychogiopoulou, Evangelia: "The EU and Cultural Rights", in Ana Filipa Vrodljak (ed.), *The Cultural Dimension of Human Rights*, Oxford: Oxford University Press (2013).

Psychogiopoulou, Evangelia: The Integration of Cultural Consideration in EU Law and Policies, Leiden–Boston: Nijhoff (2008).

COMMISSION v. ITALY (ECJ 10/12/1968, 6/68).

MALGOŽATA RUNEVIČ-VARDYN AND ŁUKASZ PAWEŁ WARDYN v. VILNIAUS MIESTO SAVIVALDYBĖS ADMINISTRACIJA AND OTHERS (ECJ 12/05/2011, C-391/09).

STICHTING COLLECTIEVE ANTENNEVOORZIENING GOUDA AND OTHERS v. COMMISSARIAAT VOOR DE MEDIA (ECJ 25/07/1991, C-288/89).

TV10 SA v. COMMISSARIAAT VOOR DE MEDIA (05. 10. 1994, C-23/93).

UNITED PAN-EUROPE COMMUNICATIONS BELGIUM SA AND OTHERS v. BELGIAN STATE (13/12/2007, C-250/06).

VERENIGING VERONICA OMROEP ORGANISATIE v. COMMISSARIAAT VOOR DE MEDIA (ECJ 03/02/1993, C-148/91).

Official website of the CJEU: http://curia.europa.eu (accessed 03/2016).

Izabela Skomerska-Muchowska

Cultural Autonomy

DEF: Although there is no officially adopted legal definition of the notion of 'cultural autonomy' in international law, its historical concept refers to the establishment of self-governing minority cultural councils, which enjoy the status of self-ruled public law legal entities endowed with administrative functions and public powers to take binding decisions on minority cultural affairs (language, education etc.) and may levy taxes. Based on the personal principle of self-proclamation of its members, cultural councils exercise, as governmental institutions, jurisdiction over them, irrespective of their place of residence (non-territorial element). Their decisions cannot be overruled by the state authorities (autonomy element), unless they go beyond the scope of their competence (matters limited to issues of a minority culture).

INSTR: Cultural autonomy is argued to be a valuable vehicle for the protection of minorities' and indigenous peoples' cultural rights. However, there are no explicit references to it in international 'hard' law instruments relating to minorities. Only some weak provisions exist in very few 'soft' law texts on minorities, mainly the 1999 OSCE *Lund Recommendations* (paras. 17–18) and the 2008 Commentary on 'Effective Participation' (para. 135) of the Advisory Committee (ACFC) on the *Framework Convention for the Protection of National Minorities* (FCNM, 1995), which simply note respectively that 'non-territorial forms of governance'/'cultural autonomy arrangements' – especially in fields like education, culture, language rights or religion – are useful for the safeguarding of minority identity. Because of their general nature and vague wording, these statements certainly do not constitute a holistic approach to the issue. As regards indigenous peoples, ILO's legally binding *Indigenous and Tribal Peoples Convention* of 1989 makes no direct reference to the notion, though it emphasises, in a series of its stipulations (e.g. in Articless 6(1), 7(1) and 27(3)), the right to establish and develop their own institutions. Further, the non-legally binding 2007 UN *Declaration on the Rights of Indigenous Peoples* proclaims in Article 4, that these peoples have 'the right to autonomy or self-government' as well as the right to maintain their cultural institutions (Article 5) and control their educational systems (Article 12(1)). In both cases, however, the norms have a declaratory tone and are quite ambiguous regarding states' obligations.

CASES: Given the fact that neither the ECHR nor any other major international or regional human rights instrument refers explicitly to the right to cultural autonomy it comes as no surprise that there is no case law on the matter. In the present situation then, the ACFC is the body that could fruitfully contribute, through its mild, compromised opinions, to the elucidation of the normative content of cultural autonomy arrangements and to their proper implementation, at least to the member states of the FCNM that have introduced this model in their national legislation (e.g. Estonia, Hungary, Russia). Under this light, a first useful, though very general, observation regarding cultural autonomy that could serve as a working guideline for further elaboration is the one found in para. 136 of ACFC's Commentary on Effective Participation, namely that: 'the corresponding constitutional and legislative provisions should clearly specify the nature and scope of the autonomy system and the competencies of the autonomous bodies. In addition, their legal status, the relations between them and other relevant State institutions as well as the funding of the envisaged autonomy system, should be clarified in the respective legislation. It is important that persons belonging to national minorities be involved and that their views be duly taken into account when legislation on autonomy arrangements is being prepared or amended.'

VIEWS: Adherents of the cultural autonomy model argue that it could serve as an alternative to territorial autonomy, since the territoriality principle on which the latter is based is seen with suspicion by most governments as a first step on a slippery path leading to secession. In this context, they also assert that establishing non territorial cultural autonomy arrangements is the best way to avoid the phenomenon of creating 'minorities within minorities' that goes inevitably with territorial autonomy settlements. Further, they maintain that by de-territorialising the identities and demands of sub-state groups, cultural autonomy could reduce or prevent ethnic tensions between different cultural groups living in the same area. Finally, they suggest that cultural autonomy seems to be the most functional choice for small and dispersed groups that are not in a position, for obvious practical reasons, to seek territorial solutions. On the other hand, there are critical thoughts noting that there are examples where cultural autonomy has been used as a pretext for enforced segregation. Others observe that the assumption that all members of a group are equally committed to the protection of their culture is problematic, overseeing internal power conflicts and interest differences within the collectivity. As well, they point out that non territorial cultural autonomy challenges liberal conceptions of equality by granting rights only to certain cultural communities. Finally, they suggest that it may violate individual rights at the within-group level.

CONCL: In order to come to some conclusions regarding cultural autonomy's potential to prevent ethnic conflicts and safeguard cultural diversity, one should comparatively study the relative national legal frameworks. At first glance the situation seems rather disappointing. In some cases the regulations remained on paper and were never realised in practice (e.g. Latvia, Ukraine), while in others they did not function satisfactorily as the cultural autonomy bodies do not have clear legal status (e.g. Estonia) or enjoy a status similar to ordinary NGO's (e.g. Russia), with no real public functions and competencies. However, it is not the cultural autonomy model that is to blame for these failures, but the various tacit political motives behind its adoption in the specific spatial and temporal national context (the presentation of democratic credentials in the case of e.g. the Baltic States). Indeed, cultural autonomy arrangements, alone or in combination with some forms of territorial settlements, seem to produce positive results, though not without several flaws and shortcomings, for the protection of cultural rights of small and scattered minorities. The examples of Slovenia, Hungary and to a degree Serbia and Croatia are indicative in this direction. Thus, benevolence from the nation-states proves to be a crucial factor for the practical, even partial, success of the cultural autonomy model.

REFERENCES:

Eide, Asbjorn, Greni, Vibeke and Lundberg, Maria: "Cultural Autonomy: Concept, Content, History and Role in the World Order", in Suksi, Markku (ed.): *Autonomy: Applications and Implications*, Hague: Kluwer (1998).

Kymlicka, Will: "National Cultural Autonomy and International Minority Rights Norms", 6 *Ethnopolitics* (2007) 379.

Lagerspetz, Mikko: "Cultural Autonomy of National Minorities in Estonia: The Erosion of a Promise", 45 *Journal of Baltic Studies* (2014) 457.

Nimni, Ephraim: "National-Cultural Autonomy as an Alternative to Minority Territorial Nationalism", 6 *Ethnopolitics* (2007) 345.

Osipov, Alexander: "Non-Territorial Autonomy During and After Communism: In the Wrong or Right Place?", 12 *Journal on Ethnopolitics and Minority Issues in Europe* (2013) 7.

Smith, David: "Non-Territorial Autonomy and Political Community in Contemporary Central and Eastern Europe", 12 *Journal on Ethnopolitics and Minority Issues in Europe* (2013) 27.

Athanasios Yupsanis

Cultural Dimensions of Human Rights

INTRO: The clarification of cultural rights addresses one of the major gaps in the human rights protection system. Despite recent progress, the weak development of cultural rights and the massive attacks they still bear whenever they appear will require long and complex interpretation in history. Fact is that they concern the heart of the relationships between any person and cultural environments full of contradictions, the intimate experience each individual has with others, with objects, with traditions.

The relation between culture and modernity is sensitive, which is why cultural rights touch at the core of human relationships with politics, making us fear the worst deviations. For many, cultural rights go against the universality of human rights. In reality, they are at the cross-road between civil and social rights, in all the spaces where knowledge resources, or cultural resources, are essential, where freedoms have their roots. Cultural rights are only conceivable in democracy if they are firmly embedded in the system of human rights and share their universality. The development of cultural rights guarantees the interface between diversity and universality by securing the human rights' approach against four major risks – relativism, particularism, communitarianism and culturalism (Meyer-Bisch, 2011). In fact, cultural rights reside on all the frontiers, at the most intimate of human capacities, in this space of porosity where each of us can simultaneously be more dependent and more free. Cultural freedoms, rights and responsibilities consist in accessing, participating in and contributing to the cultural resources necessary to live and develop one's identity throughout one's life. *Central to the classical debate between 'formal' and 'effective' freedoms, there are freedoms 'educated' of their responsibilities.*

INSTR: Classically, cultural rights include the right to education (Article 26 of the UDHR, Article 13 and 14 of the ICESCR) and the right to take part in cultural life (Article 27 of the UDHR, Article 15 of the ICESCR and Article 27 of the ICCPR). The right to education and to life-long education represents the right to access and participate in the cultural resources necessary to one's existence. What is at stake in these two rights is the capacity to share a 'cultural life', understood as a series of activities related to cultural resources, and not merely to transmit a 'given' (Meyer-Bisch and Bidault, 2010, para 5.3). In the *Fribourg Declaration* on cultural rights, a civil society text elaborated in collaboration with numerous experts, we proposed a presentation with 6 substantive articles: the freedoms to exercise the cultural activities of one's choice (including linguistic, academic freedoms and creativity), the right to access heritage, to take part or not to take part in cultural communities, the rights to education, to information (education and information are inseparable), the right to take part in cultural policies (Fribourg Group, 2007; Meyer-Bisch and Bidault, 2010; CESCR, General comment 21, 2009).

The right to heritage beneficiated from further consecration through the Council of Europe, 'Recognizing the need to put people and human values at the centre of an enlarged and cross-disciplinary concept of cultural heritage', in the *Framework Convention on the Value of Cultural Heritage for Society* (Council of Europe, 2005, Article 4). The object of this Convention is to provide a common framework to existing technical instruments that define the right *of* heritage according to the different administrative categories, by proposing a transversal definition, and to centre this definition on human persons and on development. This human rights perspective on heritage has been taken forward by the UN Special Rapporteur in the field of cultural rights (2011 and 2016).

DEF: The various cultural rights cannot be reduced to a global «right to culture», as if «culture» could be understood as a unified whole. 'Cultural life' involves a variety of activities that imply many intertwined rights, freedoms and responsibilities.

The definition of culture used by UNESCO with only slight variations since 1982 has the unquestionable advantage of decompartmentalising the whole field of culture and, in doing so, of emptying it of its content, a 'right to culture' that would necessarily adopt a narrow understanding (the arts and heritage). But this definition is applied only to collectives (features 'that characterize a society or social group'). From a human rights perspective, a culture cannot be a frame that imposes itself upon an individual; it is only an environment comprising a wide variety of elements, often heterogeneous (A. Sen, UNDP, 2004).

A human rights based approach is required for such a wide definition to be operational, legitimate and realist. Human agency, each person's fundamental right to choose his or her own cultural references, individually or with others, and his or her capacity to extract some freedoms and creativity from the different conditions – natural and cultural –, have to be recognised as the rationale. Each person is then beneficiary and author of cultural resources. In the Declaration of Fribourg, the definition was made operational and concrete by centring it on the persons: *'The term 'culture' covers those values, beliefs, convictions, languages, knowledge and the arts, traditions, institutions and ways of life through which a person or a group expresses their humanity and the meaning they give to their existence and to their development'* (Fribourg Group, 2007, Article 2, al.1). This definition has been taken up and further developed in General Comment 21 of the CESCR (para 13).

The UNESCO Declaration and Convention have joined in this active interpretation by defining cultural goods as 'conveying identities, values and meanings'. This crosscutting approach to culture is both legitimate and operational because it is hermeneutic: what is cultural is understood as the work that enables the circulation of meanings across the different modes of life. In any milieu, a 'culture' is nothing more than a series of resources and knowledge from which people, individually or collectively, can draw and to which they also have the right, freedom and responsibility to contribute, for themselves and for others.

Generally speaking, *cultural rights are the rights and freedoms of a person to, individually or collectively, choose and express his or her identity and to access cultural references as the necessary resources needed for his or her process of identification, communication and creation* (Meyer-Bisch and Bidault, 2010, op.cit. p.17, pars 0.12 and 3.8; also Special Rapporteur in the field of cultural rights, 2010, para 9; 2012, paras 2 and 7; 2016, para 7). They allow each person, alone or in community with others, to freely live a rich cultural identity, to access and enjoy the necessary cultural works (knowledge possessed by people or entrusted into works and institutions) that will allow the development of the capacities to participate in cultural life in a unique and creative manner. They render the subject capable of drawing in the works as the indispensable resources of its development, expression and contribution. For example, the right to language is not just functional: it is the access to the capacity of conceptualisation, impression and expression, which gives access to all other capacities. In all cultural disciplines, a capacity of recognition and admiration is at stake, allowing the development of a freedom and a responsibility.

DISCUSSION: The actual promotion of cultural rights allows us to consider the origin of universality in each cultural environment, and therefore to respect the right of each person not only to adhere to the universality of rights, freedoms and responsibilities, but also to live and express this universality in the specificity of his or her own experience and environment. This has more evident implications for the definition of the right to self-determination, but can also be said of all other human rights, for which three main aspects need to be considered:

a) The cultural dimension of each human right: Each time the adjectives 'adequate' or 'appropriate' qualifies the object of a human right (adequate food, housing, health care, information,...) (CESCR, General Comment 4, 1992, para 8; General Comment 12, 1999, paras 7 and 15, General Comment 2003, para 11–12), the exercise of that right has to be legitimately appropriated by the subject. This is a major condition of the rights' effectiveness: the enjoyment of a right needs to be adapted to the conditions of the subject's specific environment. 'Appropriation' can be defined as the correspondence between the capacities of the subject and the resources available. Obviously, the appropriateness is also economic, sanitary, etc., but the cultural dimension of appropriateness requires respect and valorisation of the cultural freedoms and capacities of a person in his or her environment. It recognises each person's singularity in how they exercise their human rights.

b) The cultural interpretation of the content of other human rights: The cultural dimension also implies a culturally inclusive interpretation of each human right, one that recognises and verifies universality in the respect of singularity. This is not relativizing universality, it is bringing it into relation; it is adding to, and not diminishing, its value, it is an additional requirement. The cultural understanding of each human right contributes to a universality of human rights that is the opposite of standardisation.

This is particularly true of civil freedoms. Historically, the freedoms of opinion, expression, thought, conscience and religion and belief have been considered solely in formal terms, implying essentially negative obligations. Taking position on the content was avoided, understood as falling within private sphere and cultural specificities. The change of paradigm, formalised by the 2001 UNESCO *Declaration on cultural diversity*, consists in shifting our understanding of diversity from an obstacle or a limit to universality to the space where it has its roots. It forces us to reconsider more concretely the conditions for the exercise of 'intellectual' or civil freedoms. These freedoms all relate to knowledge and are built on them. So their content is cultural. What is a freedom of expression without knowledge and mastering of a language and its writings? What is a freedom of religion for someone who has only known a fundamentalist and discriminatory version of the religious tradition he or she refers to or tries to oppose? The analysis of the common content of these freedoms – the access to knowledge both specific to each content as well as susceptible to sharing – sheds light on their interdependence and on the shortcomings of formal analysis. The demonstration is furthermore obvious for the freedoms of research in the scientific field: their exercise cannot be reduced to non-impediment. Necessary training and fostering conditions have to be accessible.

One could say that cultural rights embody these freedoms.

The same can be said about the rights of persons before the law. A fair trail, that restores respect and appropriation of the law for the perpetrator has to fully take into consideration that person's capacities and environment, just as access to effective remedies for the victims and appropriate redress for society can only be achieved when considering the eminently cultural essence of the interpretation of the universality of the law. Finally, participation in a political community implies sharing its values, informed through permanent civic education and debate. The right to take part in cultural life is closely intertwined with the right to take part in political life, both needing appropriation of a series of common values, culturally constructed and discussed. Therefore, the cultural dimension is not just an improvement of the effectiveness: it touches directly on the substance of the right and contributes to a better understanding of the whole of the system.

c) The cultural construction of the grounds of discrimination: Finally, the issue of the cultural dimension is even more radical when one considers that the motives of discriminations are culturally constructed, and respecting the rights of the persons concerned requires the deconstruction of the motives of discrimination (Bouchard, Meyer-Bisch, 2016). If the rights of women are more frequently and severely violated than the rights of men, it is not only because of a natural vulnerability related in particular to maternity, but also because of the cultural construction of 'gender' relations that generally depreciates the role of women. The argument is also valid for the rights of the child: since the stages and limits of childhood, as well as the definition and division of responsibilities, are cultural constructions, the whole interpretation of the rights of the child depend on this construction. Similarly, the protection of older persons, migrants and detainees, indistinctly implies an interpretation of the value given to these distinctions that structure all societies and to the value given to the protection of the rights of these persons. In short, the conception – and therefore, the protection – of the rights of persons in disadvantaged situations is essentially a cultural question of major importance for the persons as well as the societies concerned. Whereas the principle of non-discrimination required until now a neutral approach, blind to cultural specificities, it needs to be interpreted today with the obligations related to the necessity to respect the cultural freedoms of each person and the values of knowledge without which the freedoms have no substance. What is emerging is a more demanding interpretation of the obligation to respect.

CONCL: The obligation to respect cannot be reduced to the duty of abstention from the state since, when violations are perpetrated, abstention becomes complicity. To respect does not only mean not to act, not to harm, but also to act in such a manner that one does not harm. Today, the obligation that should be at the forefront is the obligation to observe. It consists in 'listening' and 'observing' the victims and those witnessing violations, in the double meanings of this verb: to observe a situation and to observe the law. The first obligation of states is to ensure that systems of observation continuously exist and operate with the participation of all relevant stakeholders of the field concerned.

This principle applies to all human rights and cultural rights explicit their operations: democratic culture relies entirely on the practices of knowledge crossing. This means that each person has the right to participate in the crossing of knowledge. Each person also has the corresponding responsibility to contribute to it to the greatest extent of his or her capacities, in order to respond to the rights and freedoms of others.

REFERENCES:

Bidault, Mylène: *La protection internationale des droits culturels*, Bruxelles : Bruylant (2009).

CESCR: General Comments: No. 4 on the right to adequate housing (1992); No. 12 on the right to adequate food, (1999); No. 15 on the right to water (2003); No. 21 on the right of everyone to take part in cultural life (2009).

Council of Europe: *Framework Convention on the Value of Cultural Heritage for Society* (2005).

Council of Europe: *Heritage and beyond*, Strasbourg: Council of Europe Publishing (2009).

Fribourg Group: *Cultural rights: Fribourg Declaration* (2007) (available at www.unifr.ch/iiedh accessed 06/2016).

Knop, Karen: *Diversity and Self-Determination in International Law*, Cambridge: CUP (2008).
Meyer-Bisch, Patrice: "Les droits culturels ou le renforcement des capacités personnelles", in Bosset, Lamarche (ed.): *Droit de cité pour les droits économiques, sociaux et culturels : la Charte québécoise en chantier*, Montréal, Editions Yvon Blais (2011).
Meyer-Bisch, Patrice, Bidault, Mylène: *Déclarer les droits culturels. Commentaire de la Déclaration de Fribourg*, Zurich, Bruxelles: Schulthess, Bruylan (2010).
Meyer-Bisch, Patrice, Bouchard, Johanne: "Intersectionality and Interdependence of Human Rights: Same or Different?" *Equal Rights Review* (Special Focus: Intersectionality), Volume 16 (2016).
PNUD: *Rapport mondial sur le développement humain. La liberté culturelle dans un monde diversifié*, Paris: Economica (2004).
Special Rapporteur in the field of cultural rights: *Thematic reports*, in particular A/HRC/14/36 (2010), A/HRC/17/38 (2011), A/67/287 (2012), A/HRC/31/59 (2016).

Patrice Meyer-Bisch/Johanne Bouchard

Cultural Expressions
(and the 2005 UNESCO Convention)

DEF: According to Article 4(3) of the 2005 UNESCO *Convention on the protection and promotion of the diversity of cultural expressions* (hereafter the 2005 Convention), cultural expressions 'are those expressions that result from the creativity of individuals, groups and societies, and that have cultural content', the latter referring to 'the symbolic meaning, artistic dimension and cultural values that originate from or express cultural identities' (Article 4(2)). The notions of 'cultural expressions' and 'cultural content' are closely related to the concept of 'cultural activities, goods and services', referring 'to those activities, goods and services, which at the time they are considered as a specific attribute, use or purpose, embody or convey cultural expressions, irrespective of the commercial value they may have' (Article 4(4)). Some examples of cultural goods and services that convey cultural expressions are films, videos, books, magazines or songs, made on traditional but also digital support. The 2005 Convention does not define the 'diversity of cultural expressions', but only the notion of 'cultural diversity' which 'refers to the manifold ways in which the cultures of groups and societies find expression' (Article 4(1)).

INSTR: The 2005 Convention reaffirms the sovereign right of each state party 'to formulate and implement their cultural policies and to adopt measures to protect and promote the diversity of cultural expressions and to strengthen international cooperation to achieve the purposes of this Convention' (Articles 5, 6, 7, 8, 10, 12, 14–18). These commitments should be interpreted in the light of guiding principles, the first of which stating that 'cultural diversity can be protected and promoted only if human rights and fundamental freedoms, such as freedom of expression, information and communication, as well as the ability of individuals to choose cultural expressions, are guaranteed' (Article 2(1)). Moreover, 'the protection and promotion of the diversity of cultural expressions presuppose the recognition of equal dignity of and respect for all cultures' (Article 2(3)) and request an 'equitable access to a rich and diversified range of cultural expressions from all over the world' (Article 2(7)). In this regard, the Convention requires developed countries to 'facilitate cultural exchanges with developing countries by granting (...) preferential treatment to (their) artists and other cultural professionals and practitioners, as well as (their) cultural goods and services' (Article 16). Additionally, the promotion of 'objectives and principles' of the 2005 Convention in other international forums (Article 21) should result in the recognition of the specific nature of cultural goods and services in trade agreements, either by the exclusion of such goods and services from the scope of these treaties, or by the incorporation of cultural clauses that acknowledge their specificity.

CASES: In a case concerning television regulations requiring television operators to allocate a portion of their operating revenue to the funding of cinematographic films in one of the official languages of Spain [UTECA, 2009], the CJEU had to decide on a question submitted by the Spanish Supreme Court, related to the interpretation of some provisions in a European treaty and a European directive. The Court relied on the intrinsic link between language and culture, expressly referring to the UNESCO 2005 Convention, which states that 'linguistic diversity is a fundamental element of cultural diversity' and specified that the objective of promoting a language does not need to be accompanied by other cultural criteria in order for it to justify a restriction on one of the fundamental freedoms guaranteed by the EU Treaty. In numerous cases in the field of state aids, the European Commission recognised the very specific nature of the cultural sector, including e.g. films but also video games, by referring directly to the 2005 Convention (SA. 3413 2012/N; SA. 34030 2012/N; SA. 35227 2012/N; C 47/2006). On the international level, first steps towards an acknowledgment of the intangible dimension of cultural goods and services in →free trade disputes can be registered (WT/DS363/R).

VIEWS: During the negotiation of the 2005 Convention, tension arose between two groups of states: One group was in favour of a rather large scope of application of this instrument covering 'cultural diversity' in its broader sense, thus including intangible cultural heritage, cultural rights, culinary expressions, fashion design and even values and religious beliefs. The other states insisted on sticking to the terms of the negotiation mandate, which was limited to the 'diversity of cultural expressions' *stricto sensu* (Von Schorlemer, 2012). This narrow conception finally succeeded and, according to its Article 3, the Convention 'shall apply to the policies and measures adopted by the Parties related to the protection and promotion of the diversity of cultural expressions', these ones being conveyed by 'cultural activities, goods and services'. However, the Quadrennial periodic reports (QPR) presented by the parties since 2012 demonstrate that many of them continue to give interpretations of the term 'cultural expressions' that go beyond the scope of application of the 2005 Convention. Some refer to many cultural forms and manifestations of culture that are covered by other cultural instruments, for instance by the 2003 *Convention on the Safeguarding of the Intangible Cultural Heritage*. Some scholars also consider that food or culinary traditions, as well as handicraft, are cultural expressions falling into the scope of the 2005 Convention and, according to them, most useful for the protection of cultural diversity (Maffei, 2012).

CONCL: The 2005 Convention introduced the new concept of 'cultural expressions' in the language of diplomacy, i.e. in international legal vocabulary and that of cultural policies at all levels. References to the diversity of cultural expressions have multiplied in international legal instruments and national cultural governance systems. Ten years after the adoption of the 2005 Convention, an important number of policies and measures strengthening the value chain of creation, production, distribution/dissemination and access of cultural goods and services has been adopted and implemented, even though the needs and realities faced by many creators and producers of cultural expressions still have to be addressed (Obuljen, 2015). The 2005 Convention has also reinforced international cooperation in the cultural field (Van Graan, Sanan, 2015) and the parties have been promoting actively the objectives and principles of the 2005 Convention in other international forums. In this regard, some remarkable progress has been observed in trade agreements, especially those concluded by the EU, that frequently incorporate references to the diversity of cultural expressions. Such references have appeared in a 'cultural cooperation protocol' attached to some free trade agreements, recognising the dual nature of cultural goods and services and giving a preferential treatment to the other parties (Guèvremont, 2015). In addition, parties to the Convention reported an increasing number of policies, programs and strategies that integrate culture into sustainable development policies implemented in their own territories or in their international development assistance activities (UNESCO, 2015). Considering the fact that digital technologies enhance the interaction between cultures, but also represent a threat to some of them (Kulesz, 2014; Guevremont et al., 2013), the issue of identifying the best approaches to protect and promote the diversity of cultural expressions in the digital environment will certainly receive much broader attention from the 2005 Convention bodies in the years to come.

REFERENCES:

Guèvremont, Véronique et al.: *Implementation of the convention of the protection and promotion of the diversity of cultural expressions in the digital age: challenges, priority actions and recommendations*, Report presented to the Intergovernmental Committee of the Convention on the Protection and Promotion of the Diversity of Cultural Expressions, Seventh Ordinary Session, (2013).

Intergovernmental Committee for the Protection and Promotion of the Diversity of Cultural Expressions: *Strategic and action-oriented analytical summary of the quadrennial periodic reports*, CE/12/6.IGC/4, 10–14 December 2012.

Kulesz, Octavio: *UNESCO Convention on the Protection and Promotion of the Diversity of Cultural Expressions: Analysis of Parties' periodic reports and contemporary digital trends*, Intergovernmental Committee for the Protection and Promotion of the Diversity of Cultural Expressions, CE/14/8.IGC/INF.5, (2014).

Maffei, Maria Clara: "Culinary Traditions as Cultural Intangible Heritage and Expressions of Cultural Diversity", in Borelli, Silvia and Lenzerini, Federico (ed.) *Cultural Heritage, Cultural Rights, Cultural Diversity New Developments in International Law*, Leiden: Nijhoff (2012).

Richieri Hanania, Lilian (ed.): *The effectiveness of the UNESCO Convention on the Protection and Promotion of the Diversity of Cultural Expressions*, Oxford: Routledge (2014).

UNESCO: *Re/Shaping Cultural Policies*, 2005 Convention Global Report, UNESCO (2015).

Von Schorlemer, Sabine/Stoll, Peter-Tobias (eds.) *The UNESCO Convention on the Protection and Promotion of the Diversity of Cultural Expressions, Explanatory Notes*, Springer (2012).

China – Measures Affecting Trading Rights and Distribution Services for Certain Publications and Audiovisual Entertainment Products (2009), WT/ DS363/R (Panel Report).

UTECA – UNIÓN DE TELEVISIONES COMERCIALES ASOCIADAS v. ADMINISTRACIÓN GENERAL DEL ESTADO (CJEU 12/03/2009, C-222/07).

Véronique Guèvremont

Cultural Genocide

DEF: Cultural genocide refers to the destruction by the state or state organs of the culture of a community. Elements of cultural genocide could include unjustified restrictions and prohibitions of the use of native and regional languages, of the practice of religions, of cultural activities and expressions, as well as the destruction of cultural and educational institutions and cultural heritage (Donders, 2012). The Dalai Lama has called the situation in Tibet cultural genocide and the Canadian Truth and Reconciliation Commission concluded in 2015 that Canada's aboriginal policy 'can best be described as cultural genocide.' (Truth and Reconciliation Commission of Canada, *Honouring the truth, reconciling for the future*, p. 1)

INSTR: Although the original concept of genocide, as invented by Raphael Lemkin, also had a cultural dimension (Lemkin, 1944), the prohibition of cultural genocide is not explicitly incorporated in international law. The prohibition of 'ordinary' genocide is firmly established in the *Convention on the Prevention and Punishment of the Crime of Genocide* (1948). Moreover, the prohibition of genocide is recognised as a norm of *ius cogens* and as international customary law, which is binding upon all states. Cultural genocide does not fit in the common legal use of the word 'genocide' in the Genocide Convention, which presupposes the intent to physically destroy a certain group in whole or in part. Destroy is meant literally as the physical annihilation of people, which is why genocide is usually linked with violent conflict. The situations described as cultural genocide, such as that of the Tibetans in China or the indigenous peoples in the USA, Canada and Australia, have led to serious unrest and conflict, but they were not meant to systematically kill individuals or physically destroy the group. Instead, the aim was to forcibly assimilate these communities into mainstream society and culture (MacDonald and Hudson, 2012, p. 429). Cultural genocide was part of the draft Genocide Convention and the draft UN *Declaration on the Rights of Indigenous Peoples*, but it was not included (Donders, Short, 2010, p. 836). The remaining link is the prohibition of the forcible transfer of children (Article II(e)). This relates to culture, because the forced removal of children from their families might lead to imposing a distinct culture upon these children, which could lead to the disappearance of a community as a cultural unity (Donders, 2012; MacDonald and Hudson, 2012, p. 441; Mako, 2012, p. 177–179; Short, 2010, p. 844).

CASES: There is no international case law explicitly mentioning cultural genocide. The case law on genocide generally focuses on the intent to physically and biologically destroy a group. There are several cases before the International Criminal Tribunal for the Former Yugoslavia (ICTY) in which the Court confirmed the standpoint that attacking or destroying the cultural characteristics, property or symbols of a group does not fall under the definition of genocide. However, the Court also argued that the intentional destruction of cultural and religious institutions and monuments can lead to the triggering of the intent to destroy a group within the meaning of the Genocide Convention. Moreover, the destruction of cultural property with discriminatory intent against a cultural community can be prosecuted as a crime against humanity [ICTY cases: PROSECUTOR v. DARIO KORDIC AND MARIO CERKEZ, 2001; PROSECUTOR v. RADISLAV KRSTIC, 2001; PROSECUTOR v. VIDOJE BLAGOGEVIC AND RAGON JOKIC, 2005].

VIEWS: The prohibition of cultural genocide does not fall under the Genocide Convention, unless it fulfils the requirement of the intent to physically destroy. To make it an international norm would imply a different interpretation of genocide. The *Declaration on Rights of Indigenous Peoples* refers to the prohibition of 'any act of genocide', which could include cultural genocide (Mako, 2012, p. 188). Some argue to extend the concept of genocide to include 'the destruction of the social figuration' or cultural genocide, which does not necessarily imply mass killing (Short, 2010, p. 842–844). Bearing in mind that international legal instruments related to genocide and international crimes adopted after the Genocide Convention, such as the *Rome Statute on the ICC*, do not include a reference to cultural genocide, and the fact that Courts have not accepted such an interpretation, it seems to be that '... among international lawmakers this is a dead issue' (Schabas, 2000, 188). However, the main content of the norm of cultural genocide – not to destroy the culture of a community, including its language, religion, cultural heritage and institutions – can be found in several other international legal instruments, notably human rights treaties. International human rights instruments contain many rights in relation to culture, with special attention to vulnerable groups, such as minorities and indigenous peoples. The corresponding state obligations certainly include the prohibition to unlawfully and unjustifiably restrict or destroy cultures and cultural institutions. Cultural heritage is separately protected under heritage conventions, but also under international humanitarian law and international criminal law. According to these instruments, states are prohibited from damaging or destroying cultural heritage in time of conflict and to do the same, as well as to protect and promote it, in peace time. In short, existing international legal norms on genocide, cultural rights and cultural heritage taken together provide a legal prohibition of cultural genocide (Donders, 2012).

CONCL: Although Lemkin in his original conception of genocide included a cultural component, the Genocide Convention does not explicitly prohibit cultural genocide, apart from the prohibition of the forcible transfer of children. However, the normative content of cultural genocide – the destruction or suppression of cultures and the forceful assimilation of cultural communities into mainstream culture or society – is clearly forbidden in international law, in particular international human rights law, but also international humanitarian law and heritage conventions. Cultural genocide has been used as a label for situations where cultural rights violations have systematically taken place. In many parts of the world, cultures are limited or destroyed in very methodical but sometimes subtle ways. There may not be a violent conflict and people may not literally be attacked or killed, but their cultures are ridiculed, restricted, and eventually destroyed. By destroying cultures, the identities of cultural communities and thereby their existence inevitably dies as well.

REFERENCES:

Donders, Yvonne: "Old Cultures Never Die? Cultural Genocide in International Law", in I. Boerefijn et al (eds.), *Human Rights: Pre-Conflict, In Conflict, and Post-Conflict*, Mortsel: Intersentia (2012).

Lemkin, Raphael: *Axis Rule in Occupied Europe: Laws of Occupation – Analysis of Government – Proposals for Redress*, Washington DC: Carnegie Endowment for International Peace (1944).

MacDonald, David B.: "The Genocide Question and Indian Residential Schools in Canada." *Canadian journal of political science* 45(2) (2012) 427.

Mako, Shamiran: "Cultural Genocide and Key International Instruments: Framing the Indigenous Experience" *International journal on minority and group rights* 19.2 (2012) 175.

Morsink, Johannes: "Cultural Genocide, the Universal Declaration, and Minority Rights", 21 *Human Rights Quarterly* (1999) 1030.

Sautman, Barry: ""Cultural Genocide" and Tibet" *Texas international law journal* 38(2) (2003), pp. 173.

Schabas, William: *Genocide in International Law: The Crime of Crimes*, Cambridge: Cambridge University Press (2000).

Short, Damien: "Cultural genocide and indigenous peoples: a sociological approach." *The International Journal of Human Rights* 14(6) (2010) 833.

Truth and Reconciliation Commission of Canada, *Honouring the truth, reconciling for the future*: summary of the final report of the Truth and Reconciliation Commission of Canada (2015).

Vrdoljak, Ana F: *International Law, Museums, and the Return of Cultural Objects*, Cambridge: Cambridge University Press (2006).

Yvonne Donders

Cultural Identity

DEF: Cultural identity can be broadly described as the personification of culture. It is '...all those elements of culture through which individuals and groups define and express themselves and by which they wish to be recognised' (Council of Europe (CAHMIN), *Preliminary Draft Declaration of Cultural Rights*, 1995), or as '...the sum of all cultural references through which a person, alone or in community with others, defines or constitutes oneself, communicates and wishes to be recognised in one's dignity' (*Fribourg Declaration on Cultural Rights*, 2007). Cultural identities are dynamic and heterogeneous. They are not created within bounded areas, but within spaces of interaction. Elements of cultural identities are, for example, language, religion, heritage, education, arts and literature, but also traditions, customs and institutions. Cultural identity has an individual and a collective dimension. It is built by relationships with other individuals and with communities. It is important to individuals and communities, because it gives them a sense of belonging. The suppression or limitation of the development and expression of cultural identity can make people feel alienated, which seriously affects their human dignity. Accordingly, international processes such as decolonisation, globalisation and migration, where cultural identities have been suppressed or surpassed, have contributed to the increase in the awareness of cultural identity. This awareness has, in turn, led to the claim for the protection of cultural identity as a right.

INSTR: The concept of cultural identity is included in various international legal instruments, most of which concern minorities or →indigenous peoples (e.g. the UN *Declaration on Rights of Persons belonging to National or Ethnic, Religious and Linguistic Minorities*, the Council of Europe *Framework Convention on the Protection of National Minorities* and the UN *Declaration on the Rights of Indigenous Peoples*). Several UNESCO instruments also contain references to cultural identity (*Universal Declaration on Cultural Diversity* and the *Declaration on Race and Racial Prejudice*). There is however no 'right to cultural identity' legally established in international law. States do not seem to be willing to accept (legally binding) provisions on cultural identity, mainly because of the vagueness and the collective dimension of this concept. The instruments that include cultural identity mainly reflect soft law. Cultural identity is generally referred to not as a legal substantive right, but as a general value or principle that underlies other, more specific, human rights. Many legally binding human rights provisions, in particular cultural rights, play an important role in the protection of cultural identity. These rights include provisions that explicitly refer to culture, such as the right to participate in cultural life, the right to enjoy culture, language and religion for members of minorities, but also other rights that relate to cultural identity, such as the rights to freedom of expression, religion and association and the rights to respect for private life, home, education etc.

CASES: Although none of the international legal instruments contains an explicit right to cultural identity, there are many cases dealing with elements of cultural identity under different human rights provisions. The Human Rights Committee has, for instance, interpreted the concept of 'enjoyment of culture' in Article 27 ICCPR in a broad manner, including elements such as language and religion, but also economic activities related to land (e.g. *HRCee General Comment No. 23*). The ECtHR has referred to cultural identity directly or indirectly in cases concerning rights to freedom of expression, religion, association, and the rights to respect for private life and home. For instance, the ECtHR has argued that freedom of religion is a fundamental element of a person's cultural identity and emphasised that states should promote pluralism and ensure that religious communities tolerate each other [KOKKINAKIS, 2000; MANOUSSAKIS AND OTHERS, 1996; SERIF, 1999; THLIMMENOS, 2000; CHAÁRE SHALOM VE TSEDEK, 2000; LEYLA SAHIN, 2005]. The Court has also argued that cultural organisations set up to preserve and develop the minority culture and traditions are protected under the right to freedom of association [SIDIROPOULOS AND OTHERS, 1998; STANKOV AND THE UNITED MACEDONIAN ORGANISATION ILINDEN, 2001; GORZELIK AND OTHERS, 2001]. The Court has furthermore argued that the traditional way of life of a gypsy minority is protected under the right to respect for private life, family life and the home [CHAPMAN, 2001, CONNORS, 2004; WINTERSTEIN, 2013].

VIEWS: Behind the debate on a right to cultural identity lies a more general discussion on the possible ways of accommodating cultural differences in society. Policies of tolerance and multiculturalism have been developed to build a society in which different cultural communities can exist and are able and allowed to keep a distinct cultural identity against policies of assimilation. While cultural identity is appreciated as a value, its legal recognition remains in the form of soft law, having no legally binding force. Supporters of this right emphasise that the claim for a right to cultural identity originates from a situation of serious human rights violations and is necessary to protect and promote cultural identity as an important element of human dignity. Opponents point out that the existing human rights framework provides sufficient protection of cultural identity and that a right to cultural identity adds nothing to established human rights. Moreover, the concept of cultural identity is considered to be too vague to be transformed into a legal substantive right. Opponents also reject the possible collective subject of this right, because of the lack of a legal definition of the collective entity and the possible conflict between individual and collective rights. Another argument against a right to cultural identity is that this right could be interpreted as supporting questionable cultural activities. This links to the fact that a right to cultural identity, just as other human rights, cannot be enjoyed unlimitedly. Human rights can be limited by law for instance to protect the rights of others or general society, provided that these limitations are necessary and proportionate. A right to cultural identity as a legal norm in the form of hard law, which has legally binding force and could be invoked before a judge, is unlikely to be established at international level.

CONCL: The formulation of 'a right to cultural identity' is actually rather strange. The right to cultural identity implies the right to *have* or *be provided with* a cultural identity. This seems to be rather odd, since individuals and communities simply *have* a cultural identity, which cannot and should not be provided for by a state. Consequently, this right has been formulated in different ways. Some speak of the right to cultural *identification*. The Fribourg Declaration includes the right to choose and to have one's cultural identity respected. A better formulation would be the right to *freedom* of cultural identity. It seems that one of the central claims of a right to cultural identity is the right to decide *in freedom* to have, develop and preserve a cultural identity, as well as to change one's cultural identity. A right to freedom of cultural identity reflects the idea of cultural identity as a changeable process and of the importance of choice. Cultural identity does not have to be developed as a separate human right. Instead, as an important element of the dignity of human beings, it should be used as an underlying value for the development and implementation of human rights in cultural policies.

REFERENCES:

Council of Europe (CAHMIN): *Preliminary Draft Declaration on Cultural Rights*, CAHMIN(95)16 Appendix IV, May 1995.

Donders, Yvonne M.: *Towards a Right to Cultural Identity?*, School of Human Rights Research Series No. 15, Antwerp/Oxford/New York: Intersentia/Hart, 2002.

Francioni, Francesco and Scheinin, Martin(eds.): *Cultural Human Rights*, Leiden: Brill Publishers, 2008.

Human Rights Committee, General Comment No. 23, UN Doc. CCPR/C/21/Rev.1/Add.5, 26 April 1994.

Lenzerini, Frederico: *The Culturalization of Human Rights Law*, Oxford: OUP, 2014.

Vrdoljak, Ana (ed.): *The Cultural Dimension of Human Rights*, Collected Courses Volume, European University Institute, Florence: OUP, 2013.

BUCKLEY v. THE UNITED KINGDOM (ECtHR 25/9/1996 20348/92).

CHAPMAN v. THE UNITED KINGDOM (ECtHR 18/01/2001 27238/95).

CHAÁRE SHALOM VE TSEDEK v. FRANCE (ECtHR 27/6/2000 27417/95).

CONNORS v. THE UNITED KINGDOM (ECtHR 27/5/2004 66746/01).

GORZELIK AND OTHERS v. POLAND (ECtHR 20/12/2001 44158/98).

KITOK v. SWEDEN (Human Rights Committee, Comm. No. 170/1984 and 197/1985).

KOKKINAKIS v. GREECE (ECtHR 25/5/2000 14307/88).

LÄNSMAN v. FINLAND (Human Rights Committee, Comm. No. 671/1995).

LEYLA SAHIN v. TURKEY (ECtHR 10/11/2005 44774/98).

LOVELACE v. CANADA (Human Rights Committee, Comm. No. 24/1977).

MANOUSSAKIS AND OTHERS v. GREECE (ECtHR 26/9/1996 18748/91).

OMINAYAK v. CANADA (Human Rights Committee, Comm. No. 167/1984).

SERIF v. GREECE (ECtHR 14/12/1999 38178/97).

SIDIROPULOS AND OTHERS v. GREECE (ECtHR 10/7/1998 26695/95).

STANKOV AND THE UNITED MACEDONIAN ORGANSATION ILINDEN v. BULGARIA (ECtHR 2/10/2001 29221/95, 29225/95).

THIMMENOS v. GREECE (ECtHR 6/4/2000 34369/97).

WINTERSTEIN v. FRANCE (ECtHR 17/10/2013 27013/07).

Yvonne Donders

Cultural Institutions / Infrastructure

(Access to Culture / Public Financing of C. I.)

DEF: At a general level, 'cultural infrastructure' refers to the institutionalisation of culture. However, just as the term 'culture' is ambiguous and open to multiple interpretations, so is the notion of cultural infrastructure. From a public policy perspective, the term commonly refers to 'cultural institutions', i.e. organisational entities, foundations or establishments, providing cultural resources in the form of cultural activities, performances or services. Examples are museums, theatres, concert halls, libraries, sports stadiums (in some countries), cinemas, live performance institutions, and community cultural centres. What makes a cultural institution 'public' may depend on its legal status as public entity or the fact that its activities, performances or services are subsidised through public funding. By contrast, in an academic context, the term cultural infrastructure brings into focus what sociologists define as 'social institutions' and anthropologists as 'ways of life', i.e. social norms, conventions, and customs that organise and inform human relationships, with a special interest in their significance for the people who create, participate and maintain, or seek to change or revise them. Examples of these institutions are norms and practices related to dress, diet, worship, childrearing, social relations, etc.

INSTR: International human rights law entails no explicit recognition of the right to cultural infrastructure or state obligations to provide or finance related institutions. However, the claim that the institutionalisation of culture is indispensable to the actual enjoyment of cultural resources and also involves state obligations seems implicit in Article 15(2) ICESCR according to which: 'The steps to be taken by the States Parties to the present Covenant to achieve the full realization of this right shall include those necessary for the conservation, the development and the diffusion of science and culture'. The meaning of this provision is spelled out further in the CESCR's *General Comment no. 21* where the first principle mentioned is the availability of cultural goods and services, such as libraries and cinemas. Furthermore, according to the General Comment, states are required to take positive measures aimed at establishing and supporting public institutions and the *cultural infrastructure* necessary for the implementation of such policies; to grant assistance, financial or other, to artists, and other individuals and institutions engaged in scientific and creative activities; and to adopt measures to support minorities in their efforts to preserve their own cultures (para. 52). More recent human rights treaties establish more detailed provisions to this effect. For example, the *UN Convention on the Rights of the Child* (1989): 'States Parties shall respect and promote the right of the child to participate fully in cultural and artistic life and shall encourage the provision of appropriate and equal opportunities for cultural, artistic, recreational and leisure activity' (Article 31(2)). Also noteworthy is the *UN Convention on the Rights of Persons with Disabilities* (2006) which obliges states to take measures aimed at securing effective access to cultural institutions, including places for cultural performances or services, such as theatres, museums, cinemas, libraries and tourism services (Article 30). The UNESCO's *Convention on the Protection and Promotion of the Diversity of Cultural Expressions* (2005) is also of some relevance insofar as it provides the signatory states with 'a sovereign right to formulate and implement cultural policies' that include, in particular, measures aimed at providing public financial assistance and 'establishing and supporting public institutions' (Articles 5 and 6).

In the European context, attention should be given to the Council of Europe *Framework Convention on the Value of Cultural Heritage for Society* (Faro Convention, 2005), which goes beyond the right of access to promote the full participation of all parts of society in the valorisation, protection and dissemination of heritage, also urging states parties to 'promote cultural heritage protection as a central factor in the mutually supporting objective of sustainable development, cultural diversity and contemporary creativity' (Article 5(e)). Furthermore, *Recommendation 1990* (2012) of the Parliamentary Assembly of the Council of Europe on 'the right of everyone to take part in cultural life' affirms a conception of the state as a 'major cultural agent' which 'not only has a responsibility to ensure a wide supply of cultural services, through all its public institutions, but also acts as an initiator, promoter and regulator of synergies between public institutions and organisations in the non-profit and private sectors which contribute to the protection and promotion of cultural heritage, to artistic creative endeavour, and to public access to the full range of cultural and artistic resources' (para. 3).

Several European constitutions, e.g. in Italy, the Netherlands and Malta, Montenegro or Portugal, pronounce state obligations to provide conditions necessary for an actual enjoyment of culture (cf. Laaksonen, 2010; Council of Europe/ ERICarts, 2016). For example, the Greek constitution stipulates: 'Art and science, research and teaching shall be free and their development and promotion shall be an obligation of the State' (Article 16) and state authorities in Romania are obliged to guarantee that 'national culture is supported, arts are stimulated, cultural legacy is protected and preserved, contemporary creativity is developed and Romania's cultural and artistic values are promoted throughout the world' (Article 33(3)). In addition, constitutional provisions in several European countries mention the rights of national minorities or ethnic groups to develop their own cultures, and to establish and maintain their own cultural institutions (e.g. Article 34 of the Constitution of Slovakia).

CASES: Relevant rulings in this realm are mainly concerned with the adjudication of claims concerned with the maintenance of social institutions of minority cultures but without necessarily affirming state obligations to protect them. The ECtHR recasts these claims as those concerned with the limits of religious freedom, and has concluded that this freedom does not extend to the protection of, for example, the full-face Islamic veil in public spaces [e.g. S.A.S, 2014] or the construction of Minarets [OUARDIRI, 2011, and LIQUE DES MUSULMANS DE SUISSE, 2011]. As regards the protection of institutionalised forms of indigenous cultures, a more proactive judicial stance can be observed in Latin America, as illustrated in the case of [MAYAGNA (SUMO) AWAS TIGNI COMMUNITY, 2001].

The modest number of rulings can be explained in light of the fact that alleged violations of cultural rights have traditionally been regarded as 'not justiciable', although the entry into force of the Optional Protocol to the ICESCR on 5 May 2013 may produce a change in this regard. In addition, it must be recalled that a court like the ECtHR continues to lack jurisdiction over claims related to cultural rights in a narrow sense. While court rulings concerning the financing of specific cultural institutions such as museums or theatres are nearly absent, the German Federal Constitutional Court generally confirmed a mandate of the state – that considers itself as a 'cultural state' (*Kulturstaat*) – 'to preserve the freedom of the arts', including through public financing (decision of 5 March 1974, NJW 1974, p. 689). According to the court, this task should be interpreted as the 'responsibility to protect and support a free artistic life' and financial resources allocated to fulfil that goal should depend primarily on the 'economic power' of potential receivers of support, that is their ability or not to re-finance themselves through the market, notwithstanding their legal status (dismissing in this case the claim of phonographic producers to receive similar tax benefits like those enjoyed by book publishers).

VIEWS: What is required of states to more concretely fulfil the right of everyone to enjoy culture remains polemical, for example, whether they should promote the institutionalisation of 'high' or 'popular' or 'religious' cultures. According to the ECtHR [S.A.S, 2014] a balance must be struck between the rights of religious minorities to maintain their own cultural infrastructures with the 'rights and freedoms of others' and to open personal relationships which makes life together possible, with preference given to the latter. Meanwhile, human rights advocates tend to defend the rights of cultural minorities to maintain their own social institutions as an aspect of freedom of religion and expression, as long as no harm is done. Indeed, not all institutions are consistent with international human rights law, but can be directly harmful not least to women and children, such as female genital mutilation. As a result, feminist movements are inclined to stress the damaging role of culture-related arguments for human rights. To temper an altogether negative approach, the UN Special Rapporteur in the field of cultural rights proposes to 'shift the paradigm from one that views culture as an obstacle to women's rights to one that seeks to ensure equal enjoyment of cultural rights' in the belief that 'such an approach also constitutes an important tool for the realisation of all their human rights' (3 Feb. 2016, para. 28).

Recognising the present absence of concrete obligations of public authorities to guarantee access to culture, the Polish National Center for Culture and the City of Wroclaw started, in 2013, an initiative advocating a legal instrument binding all member states of the Council of Europe. Their main aim has been summarised as follows: 'We demand that all citizens be given the opportunity to participate in cultural and artistic life. We insist that public authorities be charged with specific duties with regard to guaranteeing such participation, as currently many cultural rights in Europe are merely declaratory in nature.'

CONCL: In spite of its recognition as a fundamental human right, state obligations to provide real support to institutionalised forms of culture are all too often ignored or neglected. Nevertheless, cultural institutions are usually eligible for some public funding and support. In this light, the claim about the legal obligation to take appropriate positive measures to give effect to this right seems fairly uncontroversial. However, as pointed out by the UN Special Rapporteur in the field of cultural rights, 'financial crises and austerity measures have led to severe cuts in public spending, resulting in unemployment among artists and the closure of cultural institutions' (3 Feb. 2016, para. 37). Such fluctuations point to the continued fragility of cultural rights and their lack of priority when in conflict with other public concerns. Another pressing issue is the need for adequate representation in cultural institutions of different parts of society, such as youth but also women and other vulnerable groups, including immigrants. The nationalistic legacy of seeking cultural homogeneity in the public sphere, currently boosted by racist, anti-Semitic and xenophobic elements in political discourses seriously undermines the prospects of guaranteeing the cultural infrastructures needed to secure the effective and meaningful enjoyment of cultural life for everybody.

REFERENCES:

There is no book or article concerned exclusively with cultural infrastructure and human rights. Considering that the literature is rather fragmented the following readings may be useful:

Almqvist, Jessica: *Human Rights, Culture and the Rule of Law*, Oxford: Hart Publishing (2005).

Council of Europe/ERICarts: *Compendium of Cultural Policies & Trends in Europe*, County profiles and comparative table "Cultural Access and Participation – Elements in European Constitutions" drafted by Olivier Göbel. http://www.culturalpolicies.net (accessed 04/2016).

Groni, Christian: "The right to take part in cultural life". Background paper. Day of general discussion. The right to take part in cultural life (article 15(1)(a) of the Covenant, E/C.12/40/3), (9 May 2008).

Laaksonen, Annamarie: *Making culture accessible: Access, participation and cultural provision in the context of cultural rights in Europe* Strasbourg: Council of Europe Publishing (2010).

National Centre for Culture and Wroclaw 2016 – European Capital of Culture: *The Right to Culture as a Human Right – a call for action.* Warsaw/Wroclaw (2015).

Report of the UN Special Rapporteur in the field of cultural rights, A/HRC/31/59, 3 February 2016.

Romainville, Céline: *Neuf essentiels pour comprendre les "droits culturels" et le droit de participer à la vie culturelle*. Bruxelles: Culture & Démocratie asbl, (2014).

MAYAGNA (SUMO) AWAS TIGNI COMMUNITY v. NICARAGUA (IACtHR 31/08/2001).

OUARDIRI v. SWITZERLAND (ECtHR 28/06/2011, 65840/09).

S.A.S v. FRANCE (ECtHR 01/07/2014, 43835/11).

Jessica Almqvist

Cultural Policy

DEF: Definitions of cultural policy have become common in the academic and policy field. The term may be broadly defined as 'the overall framework of public measures in the cultural field... taken by national governments and regional and local authorities, or their agencies' and requiring explicit goals and mechanisms for planning, implementation and evaluation (European Task Force on Culture and Development, 1997). The term is often used in plural, to express the wide range of actors implementing cultural policies in democratic societies (Martinell and Teixeira Coelho, 2015). Explicit connections between cultural policy and human rights are less frequent, as are legal cases in this area.

INSTR: Focusing on →cultural diversity, the *UNESCO 2005 Convention* stresses that states have 'the sovereign right to adopt measures and policies' in the field of culture (UNESCO, 2005, Article 2(2)). Previously, the 1982 World Conference on Cultural Policies established a link between states' measures in the field of culture and the right to take part in cultural life enshrined in the →Universal Declaration of Human Rights (UNESCO, 1982, para. 17). The cultural policy implications of this right have been examined by the UN Committee on Economic, Social and Cultural Rights (2009, para. 48): particularly as regards their obligation to *fulfil* that right states are required 'to take appropriate legislative, administrative, judicial, budgetary, promotional and other measures'. Policies should cover both the material aspects of culture and 'intangible cultural goods (such as language, knowledge and tradition)' (ibid, para. 70). The right involves paying particular attention to the conditions of disadvantaged groups and recognising 'the right to take part … in the definition, elaboration and implementation of policies and decisions' (ibid, para. 15(c)). This paves the way for participatory governance of culture and also involves that cultural (policy) aspects need to be taken into account when developing policies in fields other than culture (see e.g. EU, *Lisbon Treaty*, Article 167(4)).

CASES: As noted above, there is limited case law addressing cultural policy. However, developments such as the UNESCO 2005 Convention and its adoption by the EU and most European countries have reinforced the legal framework in this area. In this context, the ECJ has adopted judgments in a number of cases, mainly addressing the audiovisual and media field (→Broadcasting). Basic principles of these court rulings include the right of →governments to require public and private TV and radio operators to reserve quotas to →media content pursuing general interest aims 'such as the retention, pursuant to the cultural policy of that member state, of the pluralist character of the television programmes available in that territory' [UNITED PAN-EUROPE COMMUNICATIONS BELGIUM SA et al., 2007]; or to require TV operators to earmark part of their operating revenue for the pre-funding of European films and audiovisual contents, with additional measures adopted to support production in one of the official languages of the member state adopting those measures [UTECA, 2009].

VIEWS: While the need for governments to adopt cultural policies and measures has increasingly been accepted, their link with human rights is less visible. The *Fribourg Declaration on Cultural Rights* (2007, Article 9) calls public, private and civil actors to take initiatives that fully respect cultural rights as well as the cultural dimension of all human rights. UCLG has also established a link between cultural rights and the adoption of cultural policies at local level, stressing that 'local governments are on the front line in the defense and promotion of cultural rights as fundamental human rights' (UCLG, 2015). Increasingly, approaches to cultural policy have stressed the inevitability of a plural, complex governance of culture, including the involvement of a range of actors in appropriate negotiation and cooperation in policymaking processes and the exploration of synergies and tensions with economic, social, educational and other policy domains (Wiesand, 2013; Miralles, 2014). However, public funding cuts across many European countries in recent years have had a negative impact on cultural policies, including their ability to contribute to the fulfilment of basic rights, including access and participation in cultural life for all.

CONCL: Recent developments in the international legal framework, including the UNESCO 2005 Convention and contributions made by the UN Special Rapporteur on Cultural Rights, have reinforced the legal basis for the design and implementation of cultural policies. There is also an increasing acknowledgement that policies in this field are related to the exercise of human rights and the achievement of sustainable development. However, principles emerging from academic and professional sectors may not be sufficient at the policymaking level, particularly when confronted with broader policy objectives such as the reduction of public debt. Significant weaknesses include the limited availability of monitoring mechanisms addressing the impacts of cultural policies, including in terms of rights; and the limited understanding of how cultural policies can effectively guarantee the exercise of human rights. Nevertheless, several references to the connection between cultural policy and human rights have emerged in recent years, particularly at local and sub-state level.

REFERENCES:

European Task Force on Culture and Development: *In from the margins. A contribution to the debate on culture and development in Europe*, Strasbourg: Council of Europe (1997).

Fribourg Group: *Cultural Rights. Fribourg Declaration*, Fribourg: University of Fribourg (2007).

Martinell, Alfons and Teixeira Coelho: "Polítiques culturals: concepte, configuració i tendencies", educational material, course *Les polítiques culturals*, Barcelona and Girona: Universitat Oberta de Catalunya / Universitat de Girona (2015, revised edition).

Miralles, Eduard: "Transversalidad y gestión cultural", in Salvador Catalán Romero et al.:

Manual Atalaya: Apoyo a la Gestión Cultural, Cádiz: Universidad de Cádiz (2014).
Missling, Sven; and Scherer, Bernd M.: "Article 7: Measures to Promote Cultural Expressions", in Sabine von Schorlemer and Peter-Tobias Stoll (eds.): *The UNESCO Convention on the Protection and Promotion of the Diversity of Cultural Expressions. Explanatory Notes*, Berlin and Heidelberg: Springer (2012).
UCLG (United Cities and Local Governments): *Culture 21 Actions: Commitments on the role of culture in sustainable cities*. Barcelona: UCLG (2015).
UN Committee on Economic, Social and Cultural Rights: "Right of everyone to take part in cultural life", General Comment № 21, E/C.12/GC.21 (2009).
UNESCO: *Mexico City Declaration on Cultural Policies*, Paris: UNESCO (1982).
Wiesand, Andreas: *Finally: 'In from the Margins'?*, Keynote address, EU Presidency Conference "Ready for Tomorrow?", Vilnius (2013) (accessed 06/2016 via /www.academia.edu).
UNIÓN DE TELEVISIONES COMERCIALES ASOCIADAS (UTECA) v. SPAIN (ECJ 5/3/2009, C-222/07).
UNITED PAN-EUROPE COMMUNICATIONS BELGIUM SA et al. v. BELGIUM (ECJ 13/12/2007, C-250/06).

Jordi Baltà Portolés

Defamation

DEF: The term 'defamation' refers to the communication of a false statement which damages the reputation of a claimant. Defamation laws purport to protect claimants from false statements which cause harm to their reputation. Some jurisdictions distinguish between 'libel', referring to defamatory statements in written or some other permanent form, such as a broadcast, and 'slander', referring to spoken defamatory statements. Defamation laws can take the form of criminal or civil laws. Criminal defamation laws allow for defendants to be criminally prosecuted and punished with fines and/or imprisonment. Under civil defamation laws, a claimant may sue a defendant to recover pecuniary awards for the harm caused to their reputation. To avoid liability, defendants may be able to rely on defences such as 'the defence of truth' or 'justification', 'fair comment', 'public interest' and 'privilege'. A broad range of laws concerning defamation exist around the world. Many such laws protect 'honour' or 'feelings' in addition to or instead of reputation. Many laws on defamation protect particular individuals in society, symbols, ideas or entities from insult or disrespect. These include laws protecting the honour of public officials or authorities, laws on *desacato* and *lèse-majesté*, and laws prohibiting 'defamation of religions' or blasphemy.

INSTR/VIEWS: In 2011, the Human Rights Committee set out its authoritative interpretation of the compatibility of defamation laws with Article 19 of the ICCPR on freedom of opinion and expression. In *General Comment No 34*, the committee emphasised that in its view such laws: should not 'serve ... to stifle freedom of expression'; 'include such defences as the defence of truth and ... should not be applied with regard to those forms of expression that are not, of their nature, subject to verification'; avoid 'penalising or otherwise rendering unlawful untrue statements that have been published in error but without malice', especially in relation to comments about public figures; recognise public interest as a defence; avoid 'excessively punitive measures and penalties'; and 'place reasonable limits on the requirement for a defendant to reimburse the expenses of the successful party'. Regarding laws prohibiting 'defamation of religions', the committee stressed that blasphemy laws 'are incompatible with the Covenant, except in the specific circumstances envisaged in article 20, paragraph 2' on the prohibition of incitement. Significantly, the committee emphasised that 'imprisonment is never an appropriate penalty' for defamation and that the criminal law should only be applied 'in the most serious of cases', a position endorsed by the jurisprudence of the European, Inter-American and African Courts of Human Rights, and called on states to 'consider the decriminalisation of defamation'. Interestingly, successive Special Rapporteurs on the promotion and protection of the right to freedom of opinion and expression, together with similar intergovernmental mechanisms at the regional level, have taken an even firmer position against criminal defamation laws, having long argued for the repeal of all such laws. Such experts have also called for civil defamation laws to provide for proportionate financial awards, as well as non-pecuniary remedies, such as the issuance of an apology, correction or reply.

CASES: Some of the most significant court judgments around the world on defamation have resulted from public officials bringing complaints against the media. Notably, in [NEW YORK TIMES v. SULLIVAN, 1964], the US Supreme Court held that, under the First Amendment of the US Constitution, a public official may not recover damages in a defamation suit against a news outlet unless the official can prove with 'convincing clarity' that the outlet acted with 'actual malice' in publishing the information. The ECtHR has established that expression on matters of public interest, particularly concerning public officials, attracts heightened protection. Since the seminal decision of [LINGENS, 1986], the Court has held that the 'limits of acceptable criticism are ... wider as regards a politician as such than as regards a private individual' because 'the former inevitably and knowingly lays himself open to close scrutiny of his every word and deed by both journalists and the public at large, and must consequently display a greater degree of tolerance'. In that case, the Court also distinguished between facts, which 'can be demonstrated', and value-judgments or opinions, whose truth is 'not susceptible of proof'.

CONCL: Despite the standards developed by international and regional authorities, criminal laws and/or broadly-framed civil laws on defamation remain in existence in the overwhelming majority of states in the world. Even though there is a growing number of states that have repealed criminal defamation laws (such as Jamaica, Montenegro and South Africa), defamation remains a criminal offence in states with notoriously poor records on the protection of freedom of expression (such as China, Russia and Turkey), but also in many liberal democracies (such as Germany, Denmark and Spain). Non-governmental organisations – such as ARTICLE 19, Freedom House and International Press Institute – regularly argue that such laws present some of the most serious challenges to freedom of expression internationally because they exert a 'chilling effect' upon the media and also other members of society; such laws inhibit legitimate public debate and the free flow of information and ideas, which are essential in any democratic society. In recent years, new problematic trends involving civil defamation laws have emerged including: 'forum shopping' or 'libel tourism' to jurisdictions with no genuine, real and substantial connection to the parties; the practice of SLAPPs (strategic lawsuits against public participation), costly proceedings brought by corporations to silence criticism; the application of a 'multiple publication rule' (in contrast to a 'single publication rule') in some jurisdictions which consider each new publication of the same allegedly defamatory statement as a new cause of action; and the imposition of liability on Internet service providers for content produced by third parties. Such challenges require adjudicators and other decision-makers to adapt and apply established international human rights standards concerning defamation.

REFERENCES:

ARTICLE 19: *Revising Defining Defamation Principles: Background Paper* 2016 (available at www.article19.org accessed 05/2016).

Human Rights Committee: General Comment No 34, CCPR/C/GC/34, 12 September 2011.

Media Legal Defence Initiative and International Press Institute: *Freedom of Expression, Media Law and Defamation*, February 2015 (available at www.mediadefence.org accessed 05/2016).

Special Rapporteur on the protection and promotion of freedom of opinion and expression (www.ohchr.org accessed 05/2016).

Trionfi, Barbara; Ellis, Steven M and Griffen, Scott (eds.): *Out of Balance: Defamation Law in the EU and its effect on Press Freedom, A provisional overview for journalists, civil society and policymakers*, July 2014 (accessed 22. 05. 2016) (ipi.freemedia.at/ecpm/defamation-law-report.html accessed 05/2016).

LINGENS v. AUSTRIA (ECtHR 08/07/1986, 9815/82).

NEW YORK TIMES v. SULLIVAN, 376 US 254 (1964) (United States).

Sejal Parmar

Development
(Culture and D.)

DEF: The binomial 'culture and development' is understood nowadays in several different ways. Most commonly, as culture *for* development, or how cultural resources (in other words the 'cultural and creative industries') provide *content* for economic growth, through heritage tourism or the income and employment generated by the production, distribution and consumption of cultural goods and services. A related instrumental reading sees cultural expression as a source of social energy, engagement, inspiration and aspiration. A second understanding is of culture as *method* for development, as when different cultural forms are deployed to address developmental challenges, e.g. 'theatre for development'. A third is of culture *in* development, where culture provides a *context* that must be 'taken into account' if development is to be successful. Finally, under the most conceptually ambitious reading, culture, in the broad sense, is viewed as being *constitutive* of development. Only this last understanding, inspired by the 'human development' or capabilities approach, is directly articulated with the question of cultural rights, since in this view development must include the flourishing of a people's culture. Actually existing development, however, often does the reverse, as when, for example, entire populations are removed from their ancestral environments to make way for dams and highways, or when the socio-economic changes that accompany development reduce or eliminate cultural opportunities for minorities, the poor and other excluded sections of the population.

HIST: We must remember, of course, that in the development discourse of the 1950s, culture was in fact seen as an obstacle to 'economic growth': all the non-Western peoples were enjoined, explicitly or implicitly, to jettison attitudes and behaviours that were perceived to be 'backward' or retrogressive, in order to 'catch up' with the West. Development was a national project that meant modernisation, i.e. economic growth plus political and social modernisation along Western lines. It was only the massive decolonisation process of the 1960s across Africa that generated the about-face through which culture was transformed into a resource for the nation – and the 'national culture' in question was and remains state culture. So much so that today, nativists across the world increasingly claim that development is inherently a threat to cultural survival. This position is shared by sub-national groups, making the culture and development interface an arena of contestation and negotiation.

The 'culture and development' idea has evolved in and around UNESCO since the late 1960s. The first term for it was 'cultural development', taken over from the French notion of *développement culturel*, which UNESCO defined as 'a process of development or progress in the cultural life of a community, aimed at the attainment of cultural values and related to the general conditions of economic and social development' (UNESCO, 1981). Within this perspective was the idea that development itself needed to be revisited as a plural project, parsed in terms not just of an abstract idea of universal 'culture', but also and above all in terms of distinct ways of life, each with its own developmental path. Thus in the 1970s, 'cultural development' was succeeded by the 'cultural dimension of development'. Through a series of intergovernmental conferences in different world regions, the emphasis shifted from 'progress in the cultural life of the community' to the idea that culture – that is different cultures and cultural difference – must be made integral to the national development process: without the flourishing of its distinctive culture no nation could truly or authentically develop. Witness the celebrated definition adopted by the 1982 World Conference on Cultural Policies, where culture is '... the whole complex of spiritual, material, intellectual and emotional features that characterize a society or social group...' (UNESCO, 1982).

VIEWS: This expansive definition is a result of the considerable broadening of the notion that has occurred. Today, 'culture' is understood as both 'arts and heritage' and 'ways of life' (Williams, 1988) and the two understandings are often conflated. Thus 'protecting and promoting the diversity of cultural expressions' (to use the language of the eponymous 2005 Convention) is advocated, not primarily for the sake of those cultural expressions themselves, but because they embody the symbols of 'ways of life' that are seen to be threatened by globalisation (which often replaces 'development' as a leading term). This conflation leads to the confusion that Marshall Sahlins warned about, 'when culture in the humanistic sense is not distinguished from 'culture' in its anthropological senses, notably culture as the total and distinctive way of life of a people or society. From the latter point of view, it is meaningless to talk of 'the relation between culture and the economy', since the economy is part of a people's culture' (WCCD, 1996: 21). Such conflation has become a commonplace. Politicians and governments claim, rhetorically, to interpret culture in the so-called 'anthropological' sense (although none of their ministries or departments of culture deal with anything but the arts and heritage) just as do those who advocate for the place of culture in development.

These advocacy actors, whether they are national or international, adhere also to the 'sustainable development' discourse, under which the idea of 'sustainability' is deployed in ways that diverge considerably from the vision of the World Commission on Environment and Development of a process 'that meets the needs of the present without compromising the ability of future generations to meet their own needs' (WCED, 1987). Because the term 'sustainable' and its derivatives are so acceptable and malleable at the same time, they are easily yoked to the many-faceted and totalising process that is 'development', allowing many different actors to project different interests, hopes, and aspirations. The term has become a politically correct qualifier, often unthinkingly or ritually invoked and extended across a wide array of economic, social or political processes. Thus it can refer to the maintainability of a broad societal process such as socio-economic development. Or to whether this or that project has the capacity to endure. Or to the medium- or long-term financial viability of a project or institution. Or to the ways in which certain practices may be conducive to a better quality of life.

Indeed, in the run up to the adoption in late 2015 of the *Outcome Document* entitled 'Transforming Our World: the 2030 Agenda for Sustainable Development' by the United Nations General Assembly, a campaign led by a global alliance of cultural organisations, advocated for a greater presence of culture. The campaign's leaders, concerned that 'the Outcome Document falls short of a full understanding and affirmation of the importance of culture to sustainable development', issued a communiqué entitled 'The Future We Want Includes Culture' (2015), stressing 'the availability and accessibility of cultural infrastructure'. In other words, they foregrounded the instrumental contribution to development of the formally constituted arts and culture sector.

Such arguments have merit, to be sure, but they ignore the core issues of cultural rights. Yet abuses of cultural rights are at the heart of the dilemma. Tensions between and among ethnic and cultural communities, majorities and minorities, have arisen as development has transformed economic and social conditions. Through the politics of nation building, various contentions have arisen *inter alia* over rights to land, education, the use of language, political representation, freedom of religion, the preservation of ethnic identity, autonomy or self-determination (WCCD, 1996). The world's →Indigenous and tribal people in particular have suffered as the national development project has eroded their land and resource base and restricted the use of their languages, social and political institutions, traditions, art forms and religious practices – a form of internal colonialism if not ethnocide, sometimes due to systematic government policy but more often to the impersonal forces of GDP-led development. An observation made by an African leader many years ago is premonitory of Jürgen Habermas' (2010) thoughts on 'human dignity': as Alpha Oumar Konaré, then President of Mali, put it, 'the negation of the cultural specificities of any people is tantamount to the negation of its dignity' (in WCCD, 1996).

INSTR: The only international normative instrument that addresses this challenge is the 2007 United Nations *Declaration on the Rights of Indigenous Peoples*. Although it is a completely nonbinding text, the Declaration sets out the individual and collective rights of indigenous peoples, as regards their culture, identity, language, employment, health, education, etc. Article 23 gives them 'the right to determine and develop priorities and strategies for exercising their right to development... (stating that they) have the right to be actively involved in developing and determining health, housing and other economic and social programmes affecting them and, as far as possible, to administer such programmes through their own institutions.' Article 31 states that 'they have the right to maintain, control, protect and develop their cultural heritage, traditional knowledge and traditional cultural expressions, as well as the manifestations of their sciences, technologies and cultures, including human and genetic resources, seeds, medicines, knowledge of the properties of fauna and flora, oral traditions, literatures, designs, sports and traditional games and visual and performing arts. They also have the right to maintain, control, protect and develop their intellectual property over such cultural heritage, traditional knowledge, and traditional cultural expressions.'

There are few other meaningful references to cultural rights and development in international texts. The 1986 *United Nations Declaration on the Right to Development* states that 'the right to development is an inalienable human right by virtue of which every human person and all peoples are entitled to participate in, contribute to, and enjoy economic, social, cultural and political development, in which all human rights and fundamental freedoms are fully realized' (Article 1(1)). But it is hardly referred to or operationalised by 'culture and development' actors. The 2005 *Convention on the Protection and Promotion of the Diversity of Cultural Expressions* envisages 'Cooperation for Development' (Article 14) mainly as the strengthening of the cultural and creative industries in developing countries, despite references in the Preamble to cultural diversity as such or to 'situations where cultural expressions may be threatened by the possibility of extinction or serious impairment.'

CONCL: The international normative arsenal barely addresses the entanglement between development and the respect (or not) of cultural rights.

REFERENCES:

Habermas, Jürgen: "The Concept of Human Dignity and the Realistic Utopia of Human Rights". Lecture held at the International Congress *Human Rights Today: Foundations and Politics*, University of Frankfurt (2010).

UNESCO: *International thesaurus of cultural development*, Paris: UNESCO Publishing (1981).

Final Report of the World Conference on Cultural Policies (Document CLT/MD/1). Paris: UNESCO (1982).

United Nations: *Declaration on the Right to Development* (Document A/RES/41/128 (1986)).

United Nations: *Declaration on the Rights of Indigenous Peoples* (2008).

Williams, Raymond: *Keywords: A Vocabulary of Culture and Society*, London: Fontana (1988).

World Commission on Culture and Development: *Our Creative Diversity*. Paris: UNESCO Publishing (1996).

Yudhishthir Raj Isar

Digital Media

(Access to, and Freedom of, D. M.)

DEF: Digital media are any media that are encoded in a machine-readable format, which can be easily manipulated, distributed, and played by computers and transmitted over computer networks. Legal instruments and the related case law have barely succeeded in keeping pace with the digital revolution, in particular with its power to transcend national frontiers.

INSTR: The problems inherent in regulating digital media, particularly for human rights, means there is little in the way of law in this field, with softer instruments generally being preferred. The right to access the Internet, therefore, arises from provision existing prior to the digital age, and in particular the right to receive and impart information under Article 10, ECHR, on freedom of expression. Freedom of expression (FoE) is not absolute and can be restricted in certain ways, as long as these are according to the law and necessary in a democratic society.

Article 15(3) of ICESCR and Article 19(2) of ICCPR offer more explicit protection to artistic freedom respectively by requiring States Parties to 'respect the freedom indispensable for ... creative activity' and by specifying that FoE includes freedom to seek, receive and impart ... ideas of all kind 'in the form of art'. Article 2 of the 2005 UNESCO Convention focuses on cultural diversity which 'can only be protected and promoted if human rights such as freedom of expression, information and communication, as well as the ability ... to choose cultural expressions, are guaranteed'. More recently, the European Parliament, under the Digital Agenda, has adopted a set of rules for protecting net neutrality and ensuring access for all (2015). This means there can be no blocking or throttling of online content, applications and services.

CASES: Users are free to create, re-use and distribute content, including artistic content. According to the ECtHR, content can 'offend, shock and disturb', but not if it amounts to hate speech [LEROY v. FRANCE, 2008], or transgresses Convention values [NORWOOD v. UK, 2005], such as child pornography. FoE also includes the freedom to receive information which similarly extends to cultural expressions and entertainment: [KHURSHID MUSTAFA AND TARZIBACHI, 2008]. Duties and responsibilities may differ between Internet and traditional print [DELFI 2015], with platforms required to police content 'without delay' post publication to ensure compatibility with Human Rights standards. Excessive control of content, however, such that it substantially and arbitrarily affects the rights of Internet users, may violate Article 10 [AHMET YILDRIM, 2012]. This is less likely where content is restricted for copyright infringement [AKDENIZ, 2014], although a conviction here may nonetheless be seen as an interference with FoE. Similarly, a state restriction on commercial content is less likely to violate FoE than one on general interest content, even if it risks having a 'chilling effect' [ASHBY DONALD AND OTHERS, 2013]. The ECtHR has emphasized that control of State action must be effective [YILDRIM]. Blurred jurisdiction boundaries as a result of Internet's global nature means State action may now cross international borders [PERRIN v. UK, 2005].

VIEWS: The ECtHR case-law on digital media is growing, but as one issue is regulated, others appear. As a judge in Northern Ireland said, Facebook has 'created a monster it cannot control' (UK Human Rights Blog, 24 April 2013). In a recent case [DELFI, 2015], a minority of judges cautioned against holding news sites liable for readers' defamatory comments, exposing FoE to private-party censorship, as platforms may block content prior to publication to protect their liability, often with no court to deliberate on this censorship. According to the Parliamentary Assembly of the CoE, protection of authors' copyright has made further inroads on FoE through the policing of Internet creativity to protect against copyright infringement, upsetting significantly the balance between authors, investors and the general public. In its Recommendation 1906 (2010) it felt this imbalance would endanger the creative professions' survival, but also lead to the emergence of police states controlling all information exchanged by their citizens. Regulations pursuant to the EU's digital agenda, meanwhile, are feared by some to have caused a legal loop hole which could lead to a tiered Internet service. Some 'specialized services' will be allowed to use an Internet fast lane, which makes sense for devices that deserve priority, e.g. remote medical operations. The legal language may however allow large companies to pay for faster access and ISPs to speed up or slow down traffic depending on data sent, with the attendant effects on the creative outreach that digital media also facilitate.

CONCL: Through Digital media, a wide range of data is made available to a global population for a relatively small cost. Individuals can express their views and thoughts to others, with equal opportunities for communication. However, new ways to be creative leave many ordinary people guilty of copyright crimes of which they are unaware. Jurisdiction now crosses international borders, meaning an act legal in one country, can be prosecuted in another, undermining the principle that law must be clear. World-wide access to content limited pre-digitally to a much smaller audience may now cause cultural controversy. Not all Internet traffic is treated equally, and the Internet's development has given unprecedented power to a small number of companies from the US, with the attendant effects on European culture. The EC only adopted a set of rules aimed at protecting net neutrality and ensuring access for all in 2015. 8 EU countries, however, have warned against overregulation. Following [DELFI], private platforms may be over-policing comments boards, with the risk of free expression being governed by the private sector.

In resolving these issues, encouraging responsible Internet behaviour may be a better alternative to regulation, IT and social media experts' involvement is crucial to ensuring legal and policy decisions don't give rise to extra rights' problems and the international community may need to come to an agreement on jurisdiction issues to avoid incoherency.

REFERENCES:

Council of Europe: *Journalism at risk: Threats, challenges and perspectives*, Strasbourg: CoE (2005).

Directive 2000/31/EC of the European Parliament and of the Council of 8 June 2000 on certain legal aspects of information society services, in particular electronic commerce, in the Internal Market ('Directive on electronic commerce').

UN/Farida Shaheed: *The right to freedom of artistic expression and creativity*, Report of the Special Rapporteur in the field of cultural rights, 14/03/2013.

AHMET YILDRIM v. TURKEY (ECtHR 18/12/2012, 3111/10).

AKDENIZ v. TURKEY (ECtHR 11/03/2014, 20877/10).

ASHBY DONALD AND OTHERS v. FRANCE (ECtHR 10/01/ 2013, 36769/08.

DELFI v. ESTONIA (ECtHR 16/06/2015, 64569/09).

KHURSHID MUSTAFA AND TARZIBACHI v. SWEDEN (ECtHR 16/12/2008, 23883/06).

www.article19.org (accessed 01/2016).

www.coe.int/assembly.coe.int (accessed 01/2016).

ukhumanrightsblog.com (accessed 25/01/2016).

www.liberty-human-rights.org (accessed 01/2016).

Siobhan Montgomery

Disabilities

(Cultural Rights of Persons with D.)

DEF: The UN Convention on the Rights of Persons with Disabilities (CRPD) offers three dimensions to introduce cultural issues. The first is the right to culture, in its diverse expressions, that persons with disabilities enjoy and have access to. The second refers to the way in which persons with disabilities contribute to culture in society. The third is the culture developed by certain groups of persons with disabilities, generating a style of interaction and communication, as is the case of deaf persons.

INSTR: In the first dimension, the CRPD emphasises in Article 30(1), that states parties recognise the right of persons with disabilities to take part, on an equal basis, with others in cultural life, and shall take all appropriate measures to ensure access to cultural materials in accessible formats (e.g. TV programs, films, plays in theatres), to services such as museums, cinemas, libraries, theatres, and tourism services, and to monuments of national importance. This includes the obligation of states to take all appropriate measures, in accordance with international law, to ensure that laws protecting intellectual property rights do not constitute an unreasonable or discriminatory barrier to access to cultural materials for persons with disabilities.

The second dimension of the CRPD emphasises that states parties will take appropriate measures to enable persons with disabilities to have the opportunity to develop and utilise their creative, artistic and intellectual potential, not only for their own benefit, but also for the enrichment of society.

The third dimension notes that persons with disabilities shall be entitled, on an equal basis with others, to recognition and support of their specific cultural and linguistic identity, including sign languages and deaf culture. This is corroborated when the CRPD addresses the right to education and the right to freedom of expression, opinion and access to information.

CONCL: In order to mark the current trends, it is important to group together the jurisprudential path of the Treaty Body and monitoring of the Convention, in three lines of specific recommendations for states parties:

(a) Ratify and implement the *Treaty of Marrakech* as soon as possible, and to make the printed text accessible to blind and visually impaired persons;
(b) Ensure access for persons with disabilities to libraries, audio-visual materials, and radio and television broadcasting services. This

includes the accessibility in libraries for persons with cognitive or psychosocial disability, and deafblind persons;

(c) Ensure that policies and practices of tourism recognise the right to access and inclusion of persons with disabilities, and that the recommendations of the World Tourism Organisation for accessible tourism are disseminated, including among travel and tourism agencies.

REFERENCES:
www.ohchr.org/EN/HRBodies/CRPD (accessed 03/2016).

Maria Soledad Cisternas Reyes

Disability and Copyright

INSTR: In international copyright treaties, mention of disability is conspicuous by its absence: for instance, nothing related to this issue can be found in the *Berne Convention* (1886), in the *WIPO Copyright Treaty* (1996), or in the *Agreement on Trade Related Aspects of Intellectual Property Rights* (1994). Over 30 years ago, attempts commenced at international level to provide a mechanism that would result in meaningful ways in which the blind could access books through exceptions and limitations to copyright – a process that finally culminated in the *Marrakesh Treaty to Facilitate Access to Published Works by Visually Impaired Persons and Persons with Print Disabilities* which was finalised under the auspices of WIPO in 2013. The Marrakesh Treaty, as the name suggests, deals with access to works protected by copyright for the print disabled, and not with authorship of copyrighted works. Within the EU, the *Copyright Directives* do not mention disability – with the notable exception of the *InfoSoc Directive* (Directive 2001/29/EC), which exhorts member states to adopt necessary measures to facilitate access to works by persons suffering from a disability – once again the focus is on access and not authorship, and the measure has an unfortunate emphasis on the notion of 'suffering'. National copyright legislations vary in their treatment of disability; some, but by no means all, have provisions to enable those with disabilities to access works protected by copyright. The UK for instance has two exceptions: one which enables the person with a disability to make a copy of a lawfully obtained work in a format that helps to access the work (Copyright Designs and Patents Act 1988 – CDPA, s 31A); and a second which grants this right also to educational establishments and charity organisations (CDPA s 31B). Beyond that, copyright says nothing about disability.

CASES: So how then should copyright deal with authorship and disability? It would deal with it no differently to any other investigation as to whether a copyrighted work exists and, if it does, determining who the author is. Under copyright law in Europe, shaped by the Copyright Directives and interpreted by the EU Court of Justice (CJEU), a new, harmonised standard of originality is emerging which may have interesting repercussions for authorship and disability. The CJEU has stressed that the European scheme of protection for copyright protects works where the subject matter is original in the sense of being the author's own intellectual creation [INFOPAQ, 2008; BEZPEČNOSTNÍ, 2009]. What the work is called, in other words: whether it is a literary, dramatic, musical or artistic or any other kind is irrelevant, although it may be (in the UK at least) that a work would need to fall under the Berne Convention categories of literary or artistic works [SAS INSTITUTE, 2013]. The standard of originality for all types of work is the same: it has to be an intellectual creation [INFOPAQ, 2008; BEZPEČNOSTNÍ, 2009], (see also Rosati, 2011; Derclaye, 2010). To reach this level, the author should express her creative ability in an original manner by making free and creative choices and stamp her 'personal touch' on the work [PAINER, 2010]. Where choices are dictated by technical considerations, rules or constraints that leave no room for creative freedom, these criteria are not met [SAS INSTITUTE; 2013].

VIEWS: So how might this standard impact the relationship between copyright and disability? For many works, we would argue, not at all: seen through the lens of the law, the standard – creative ability, free and creative choices, personal touch – is one by which the creative input is judged, and one where the personal attributes of the author are irrelevant. Where originality sufficient for authorship may arise for authors with disabilities, but not for those without, is when works are developed where choices are dictated by technical considerations, rules or constraints that leave no room for creative freedom; in these circumstances no copyright would arise due to a lack of originality. In relation to performative works we have argued elsewhere that the creative input by an author with disabilities may be sufficient (Waelde, Whatley, Pavis 2014). In dance, for instance, a dancer with disabilities stamps her personal touch on a dance, including where interpreting the choreographer's instructions. While many may consider the choreographer to be the author of the dance, and the dancer follows her 'rules', this may not be the case for the disabled dancer as only she knows her body and how it will interpret choreographic instructions. We would argue that the same considerations may apply to tangible works: the law may well consider the input of the artist with disabilities to be creative even where ostensibly limited by technical considerations, rules and constraints.

CONCL: The rights of persons with disabilities have been an issue on policy-makers agendas for many years – a process that led to the international *Convention on the Rights of Persons with Disabilities* in 2006. Recognising copyright authorship of persons with disabilities is one small, but significant, way in which the Convention can be operationalised to empower and make a difference to individual lives.

REFERENCES:

Derclaye, Estelle: "Wonderful or Worrisome? The Impact of the ECJ Ruling in Infopaq on UK Copyright Law", 32(5) *EIPR* (2010) 248.

Directive 2001/29/EC of the European Parliament and of the Council of 22 May 2001 on the harmonisation of certain aspects of copyright and related rights in the information society, OJ L 167, 10.

Rosati, Elanora: "Originality in a work, or a work of originality: the effects of the Infopaq decision", 33(12) *EIPR* (2011) 746.

Waelde, Charlotte, Whatley, Sarah, and Pavis, Mathilde: "Let's Dance! But Who Owns It?", 36(4) *EIPR* (2014) 217.

BEZPEČNOSTNÍ SOFTWAROVÁ ASOCIACE v. MINISTERSTVO KULTURY (CJEU 22/12/2010, C - 393/09).

INFOPAQ INTERNATIONAL A/S v. DANSKE DAGBLADES FORENING (CJEU 16/07/2009, C-5/08).

PAINER v. STANDARD VERLAGS GMBH (CJEU 01/12/2011, C-145/10).

SAS INSTITUTE INC v. WORLD PROGRAMMING LIMITED (CJEU 02/05/2012, C-406/10).

SAS INSTITUTE INC v. WORLD PROGRAMMING LIMITED (EWHC 25/01/2013, 69 (Ch)).

Charlotte Waelde

Discrimination

DEF: Discrimination is a term with different connotations. In the legal sense to discriminate means to make unjustified distinctions based on personal characteristics which have negative consequences for the situation of persons discriminated against – i.e. in employment or access to goods or services. In the current human rights framework discrimination denotes different treatment of individuals on the basis of race, ethnic origin, gender, sexual orientation, religion or belief, disability, age or economic status which are commonly perceived as irrelevant in day-to-day social interactions. Using these grounds as justifications for different treatment is in principle prohibited unless there are objective reasons for drawing legal distinctions with regard to these characteristics.

INSTR: Discrimination is prohibited under international, regional (including European), as well as national laws. The prohibition of discrimination is also recognized as a fundamental principle of the European Union law. It is also a constitutive part of the human rights system of the Council of Europe. The prohibition of discrimination serves the realization of the principle of →equality which is rooted in international and European norms; constitutions and legal traditions of European states; as well as jurisprudence and legal doctrine. Non-discrimination is today not only an inherent element of human right law, but also a necessary instrument for their full implementation. It is a shared conviction that discrimination – including discrimination based on cultural grounds or discrimination in access to culture and cultural goods – significantly limits the chances of full and effective enjoyment of human rights. The legal standard of non-discrimination is evolving in result of the development of human rights treaty law, the migration of legal ideas and judicial dialogues. The European standard of protection against discrimination has been dynamically shaped by social and cultural changes, which constitute the context in which it operates.

CASES: The phenomenon of discrimination has been frequently dealt with by the ECtHR, the CJEU, national courts, as well as other competent bodies (e.g. UN expert bodies or national equality agencies). When assessing whether discrimination took place or not, courts, tribunals or other bodies need to ascertain whether individuals who were in a similar or comparable situation received a similar or comparable treatment. Yet, 'the enjoyment of rights and freedoms on an equal footing…does not mean identical treatment in every instance' (Human Rights Committee, 1989, para. 8).

The ECtHR established in its case-law that 'only differences in treatment based on an identifiable characteristic, or 'status', are capable of amounting to discrimination' and 'for an issue to arise under Article 14 there must be a difference in the treatment of persons in analogous, or relevantly similar, situations' [CARSON AND OTHERS v. UK, 2010]. The main factor determining the occurrence of discrimination is whether less favourable treatment grounded on the particular characteristic that is already protected under Article 14 ECHR or deserves to be protected by the Convention. Thus, in all discrimination cases the first step in the judicial analysis is to identify a person to whom the victim of discrimination can be compared. This test should lead to the conclusion whether a specific characteristic (ground of discrimination) was a motive of less favourable treatment. Still discrimination may also occur when a specific characteristic was not a direct motive of less favourable treatment. In such cases (indirect discrimination) the plaintiff needs to substantiate the fact of being adversely affected by an apparently neutral provision, policy or practice, while the defendant carries the burden of proving that such provision, policy or practice is objectively justified.

In the case-law of both European courts – the ECtHR and the CJEU – there is a noticeable trend towards a dynamic interpretation of anti-discrimination provisions and the expansion of the personal and material scope of protection of against discrimination. One of the most significant achievements of judicial interpretation has been the concept of 'discrimination by association' which refers to unequal treatment of persons who do not personally possess the protected characteristic but remain in association with persons belonging to the protected category – i.e. mothers taking care of children with disabilities [COLEMAN, 2008]. The dynamic interpretation of the Convention norms has also led to the development of anti-discrimination standards with regard to sexual orientation [E.B., 2008] or marital status [PETROV, 2008]. The ECtHR recognized that both categories deserve protection against discrimination even if the Convention does not explicitly cover them among the categories of protected grounds. This approach assures that anti-discrimination law is receptive to claims of various minority groups who seek legal remedies and social emancipation.

VIEWS: One of the most important issues in the discrimination discourse is the determination of the scope of anti-discrimination protection. Frequently, this debate leads to questions about the application of the →'margin of appreciation' doctrine or, on the contrary, about the limits of the dynamic and evolutionary interpretation of the ECHR. It also goes back to the question whether social and cultural changes taking place in Europe should have an impact on how the Convention is to be read and applied to the situation of individuals seeking protection. Another important theme in the legal discourse on combating discrimination concerns the notion of 'positive obligations' of the states and measures that should be employed not only in reaction to the manifestations of discrimination, but also with the view to promote equality as a fundamental value. This debate suggests a shift from the reactive to the proactive approach which seems to be necessary given the problem of structural discrimination. Hence, the core question is whether anti-discrimination laws effectively help to combat discrimination or perhaps the prohibition of discrimination needs to be complemented by the adoption of mandatory measures which aim to provide equal opportunities for all.

CONCL: The phenomenon of discrimination persists in Europe and other parts of the world and it has significant effects on the everyday-lives of millions of individuals. However, the current standard of anti-discrimination protection accepted at the European and national level allow for more and more effective responses. Recent achievements in this field result from progressive interpretation of the principle of non-discrimination, which expanded the category of protected grounds, as well as the creation of more detailed substantive and procedural norms and the institutional architecture. It is expected that these legal developments will bring about a change in the situation of individuals seeking justice and equality. The development of anti-discrimination laws might also bring a change in public perception on the importance of equality and non-discrimination.

REFERENCES:

Bell, Mark; Waddington, Lisa: "Reflecting on inequalities in European equality law", *European Law Review* (2003), Vol. 28.

Ellis, Evelyne (ed.): *EU Anti-Discrimination Law*, Oxford (2005).

Gerards, Janneke: "The Discrimination Grounds of Article 14 of the European Convention on Human Rights", *Human Rights Law Review* (2013), Vol. 13.

Handbook on European non-discrimination law, Luxembourg (2011).

Human Rights Committee, *General Comment No. 18, Non-Discrimination*, 10 November 1989.

Schiek, Dagmar; Waddington, Lisa; Bell, Mark (eds.): *Cases, Materials, and Text on National, Supranational and International Non-Discrimination Law*, Oxford–Portland (2007).

www.equalitylaw.eu (accessed 10/2015).

CARSON AND OTHERS v. UK (ECtHR 16/03/2010, 42184/05).

COLEMAN v. ATTRIDGE LAW (CJEU 17/07/2008, C-303/06).

E.B. v. FRANCE (ECtHR 22/01/2008, 43546/02).

PETROV v. Bulgaria (ECtHR 22/05/2008, 15197/02).

Krzysztof Śmiszek

Dissidents

(Culture of Dissent)

DEF: Originally a characterisation of religious dissenters, the term dissidents (D.) has more recently been used mainly for artists, intellectuals and activists of new social movements that openly disagree with governments or political and economic systems, expressing their views in artworks, hidden journals and books (*samizdat*), in public actions (e.g. *flash mob*), Internet blogs and campaigns, or in semi-public political debates (like the Polish *Flying University* 40 years ago).

Different types of D. can be distinguished, for example: *Political* (opposition against a ruling ideology, a political system, etc.); *nationalistic* or *ethnic* (calling for specific, e.g. cultural rights); *religious D.* (demanding religious freedom or conformity). Another way of looking at D. is to assess their respect or backing in larger parts of the population, which could result in the identification of *heroes* (serving as role models), *lonely voices* (isolated in countries without social movements, e.g. Belarus) or so-called *anti-patriots* (hated or excluded from society, e.g. some Indian students' movements). While opposition to a government, a ruling party or a whole political system may as such be risky enough, D. risk even more if they also oppose public opinion.

INSTR: Dissidence or civil disobedience gain importance when international guarantees of human and cultural rights, such as freedom of expression and information are not respected. In the past, and partly still today, certain topics or art forms could be subject to direct or indirect →censorship of state bodies or influential groups: Underground and alternative publications, musical editions etc. can disappear from (official) markets; films are barred in bunkers; books withdrawn from libraries; concerts blocked. Generally, defending the cause of dissidents can rely on international legal instruments such as the *ICCPR* (Article 19), or a number of regional instruments, including but not limited to the →ECHR (Article 10) or the EU →*Charter of Fundamental Rights* (Article 11).

However, these instruments are not always fully implemented or credibly monitored. For example, in some situations, dissidents come from a majority population, but are appalled with the treatment of minorities: caste, ethnic group or religious minority (Turkey, India, Albanians in the FYR of Macedonia...). Even in Europe, members of cultural and ethnic minorities often cannot count on collective rights related to their culture and heritage or use their language or script in the public realm (e.g. France has not ratified the *European Charter for Regional or Minority Languages*).

HIST/CASES: When creating a culture of dissent, numerous writers, artists, philosophers, historians, and other scientists have been, or still are, threatened, blacklisted, excluded from public life, if not put into jail. For example, trials against dissidents marked the history of the paranoid system of 'real socialism', often resulting in the alternative: forced labour in a Gulag or psychiatric treatment. For example, Alexandr Solzhenitsyn was sentenced an 8 year term in a labour camp, inter alia for 'anti-Soviet propaganda' (1945); Joseph Brodsky was found guilty of 'social parasitism': As non-employment was considered a subversive act against the state, the court ordered a psychiatric examination (1964–72); in Poland, Adam Michnik was sentenced to three years for 'acts of hooliganism' (1968); in former Yugoslavia, dissidents (e.g. Milovan Djilas; Mihajlo Mihajlov; Lazar Stojanović for his movie *The Plastic Jesus*) were convicted on grounds such as 'verbal offense' (§133 of the Criminal Law); debasing the 'reputation of a foreign state' (§175); or associating with 'subversive actions' (§136). In the absence of fair jurisprudence, dissidents often united and protested, despite all threats, through petitions, demanding from governments to respect human rights obligations (e.g. *Charter 77* in Czechoslovakia).

In democracies, dissident voices also gained importance, from time to time, e.g. in the USA during McCarthyism and later with student movements against racial discrimination, that were inspired or supported by church leaders and artists. A specific type of contemporary activists are →whistleblowers, who can turn into dissidents if their good intentions are answered with state repression, like in the case of Edward Snowden, who revealed a global surveillance program and was charged, in 2013, by the US Department of Justice of violating the 1917 Espionage Act and of stealing government property.

Two trends can be observed during the last 50 years: Increasingly, activists are turning from a more defensive stand for individual freedom towards calling for 'social justice', like most of today's dissidents in Africa, Arab countries, Asia, Latin America or Europe. The other trend is towards what could be called 'organised dissidence', as exemplified by e.g. *Green, Right to the City, Pro Asylum* or *Occupy* movements throughout the world and a growing number of interactive platforms on the Internet. Their focus is now often the governance of issues with a potential to hurt the whole of humanity (e.g. transnational economy and the banking system; global warming; investors' urbanism and speculation on housing; etc.) and they frequently include activist artists and intellectuals.

VIEWS: Political dissidents did not have the CSCE Helsinki accords foremost in mind when founding movements or protest actions like the *Charter 77*. They wanted to obtain more freedom and contribute to change of the political system. Their open petitions or 'underground activism' became a strong political movement only with *Solidarnošć* (Poland), with its first working class dissident leader Lech Wałęsa. After the political changes (1989), many dissident intellectuals and artists played an active role in democratic developments in Central-Eastern Europe, some even became presidents of their countries, like Václav Havel, Árpád Göncz and Dobrica Ćosić, other ministers in charge of culture or information like Anton Vrdoljak and Hrvoje Hitrec in Croatia or Nikolai Gubenko in the USSR.

Territorial or nationalistic dissidence throughout the world is linked to demands for minority rights or to liberation battles. Palestinian intellectuals in Israel, Tibetan priests and intellectuals in China, Okinawa artists in Japan, Tamil in Sri Lanka are often dreaming about independence and became an inspiration for political or even military battles (*intifada*) staged by their compatriots, thus frequently accused to be 'collaborators with terrorists'. In Europe several states were re-created (e.g. in the Baltic region), but Kosovo got partial international recognition for its independence via the imagination of a dissident national movement that, in 1997, took its military form.

Religious dissidence is mostly expressed in socialist states that officially proclaim atheism or in mono-faith countries. For example, emerging from the *qigong* movement (nationalistic revival of traditional Chinese medicine and knowledge), *Falun Gong* has been founded by Li Hongzhi and became popular in the 1990s, but is still banned today. Its 'civil disobedience' protest in April 1999 was seen as a challenge to the authority of the Communist Party, with the consequence of thousands of followers dead or in prison and some 100,000 sent to labour camps (Owenby 2008:15).

The strength and, at the same time, weakness of solidarity with or without support for dissidents can be seen in the fact that it usually involves mostly the intellectual community, which may somewhat limit the impact of e.g. giving the Nobel prize to Pasternak, Sakharov and Liu Xiaobo or the Berlin Film festival prizes to Makavejev, Žilnik and Iranian film directors.

CONCL: Still today, many regimes react with threats, torture and censorship against dissidents fighting for freedom of expression and association or political and economic change: They are imprisoned; sent to exile (or forced to 'inner exile'); deprived from their passports; fired from their jobs, etc. The same can be said with regard to the persecution of dissidents on religious grounds or for those belonging to other minorities. This calls for an improved, global monitoring of the implementation of relevant legal instruments (or an improved support for those platforms and NGOs already engaged in this field). We should not forget: 'Dissident speech, whenever it occurs, is both a test and a measure of the vitality of democracy' (Elrod, 2008).

REFERENCES:

Bolton, Jonathan: *Worlds of Dissent, Charter 77, the Plastic People of Universe and Czech culture under communism*, Cambridge Mass: Harvard University Press (2012).

De Cuir, Greg: *The Yugoslav Black Wave*, Belgrade: Film Center Serbia (2011).

Elrod, Jennifer: "Critical Inquiry: A Tool for Protecting the Dissident Professor's Academic Freedom", 96 *California Law Review* (2008) 1669–1691.

Falk, Barbara: *The Dilemmas of Dissidents in East-Central Europe; Citizen intellectuals and philosopher kings*, Budapest: CEU press (2003).

Glasius, Marlies: "Dissident writings as political theory on civil society and democracy", 38(2) *Review of International Studies* (2012) 343.

Judt, Tony: "The Dilemmas of Dissidence" 2(2) *East European Politics & Societies* (1988) 185–240.

Kott, Jan: "Polish Question", in: Rajčić, B. (ed.) *Polish question*, Belgrade: SIC (1985).

Milosz, Czeslaw: *The Captive Mind*, New York: Vintage International 1981 (1953).

Ownby, David: *Falun Gong and the Future of China*, Oxford: Oxford University Press (2008).

Renvick, Alan: "Anti-Political or just Anti-Communist? Varieties of Dissidents in East Central Europe and their implications for the development of political societies", 20(2) *East European Politics and Societies* (2006).

The VERSO Book of Dissent (from Spartacus to the Shoe-Thrower of Baghdad), preface by Tariq Ali, London: VERSO (2010).

Milena Dragićević Šešić

ECHR Cultural Protocol Debates / CAHMIN

DEF: In the process of implementing the *Vienna Declaration of the CoE Heads of State and Government* on 9 October 1993, an *ad hoc* Committee for the Protection of National Minorities (CAHMIN) was set up by the Committee of Ministers (CM). Its mandate was to draft a framework convention assuring the protection of national minorities and to start the work on drafting a protocol complementing the ECHR in the cultural field by provisions guaranteeing individual rights, in particular for persons belonging to national minorities.

INSTR/VIEWS: The first task of the CAHMIN resulted in the elaboration of the *Framework Convention for the Protection of National Minorities* (Strasbourg, 1995), whose parties undertake to promote effective equality of persons belonging to minorities in all areas of life, including culture, and to create conditions that facilitate the expression, preservation and further development of e.g. their culture, language and traditions.

In contrast, the process of drafting an additional protocol to the ECHR came up against a number of difficulties of a legal, political and economic nature. These difficulties concerned e.g. the problem of defining the concept of 'cultural field' mentioned in the CAHMIN terms of reference; the issue of identifying new individual rights which are fundamental and whose protection is both required and justiciable; and finally questions of defining the scope of positive obligations which could be incumbent upon states under the new protocol. Among the numerous proposals for rights to be included in the protocol, the following were discussed by the CAHMIN experts: respect for choice of one's cultural identity; the right to engage in cultural activities; the right to be treated as a member of a cultural community; the right to a name; the right to use the language of one's choice; the right to education; the right to cultural heritage; and the right of access to information.

CONCL: As a result of the failure to find widely acceptable solutions and taking into account the risks examined by the CAHMIN, the CoE CM (Ministers' Deputies) decided, in January 1996, to suspend the drafting of an additional protocol, but called for a continuation of reflections on the feasibility of further standard-setting activities in the cultural field. However, after the suspension of the CAHMIN's work and despite Recommendation 1990 of the Parliamentary Assembly of the CoE (January 2012) on 'The right of everyone to take part in cultural life', none of the expert bodies within the CoE has been called to continue the debate on drafting an additional protocol to the ECHR that would address cultural rights directly.

Still today there are proponents of the idea of giving a normative character to cultural rights in Europe. They underline that a 'right to culture' is not sufficiently perceived and realised by European states due to the lack of its direct inclusion into the catalogue of rights protected by the ECHR. Therefore, they demand rethinking of the legal content of the right to culture by defining obligations of entities obliged to its protection and securing the accessibility to culture for all Europeans (Project 'Right to Culture', conducted since 2013 in the wider context of Wrocław – European Capital of Culture 2016).

REFERENCES:

Council of Europe: CAHMIN debates and documents (accessed 07/2016 via www.coe.int/en/web/minorities/cahmin1).

Aleksandra Mężykowska

Equality

DEF: Equality is a principle found in most European constitutions and international human rights instruments. It evokes ideas of fairness, opportunity and justice. It often enjoys rhetorical support across the political spectrum, but differences surround its meaning and how it can be implemented in practice. A common distinction is between formal or substantive equality. Formal equality focuses on the consistent treatment of individuals irrespective of characteristics such as gender, ethnicity, etc. Substantive equality places greater emphasis on combating the inequalities experienced by certain groups in society, such as women, ethnic minorities, or people with disabilities. It accepts that achieving equality may entail unequal treatment in favour of the disadvantaged (Sen, 1995).

INSTR: European legislation has evolved from a simple prohibition of discrimination towards more complex responses to inequality. EU legislation on sex discrimination emerged in the 1970s, but over time a longer list of protected characteristics have been added to the law, such as racial or ethnic origin, religion or belief, disability, age, and sexual orientation. This has gone in parallel with a broader scope for the legislation, stretching beyond the labour market into areas like education, housing, and access to goods and services. The concept of discrimination now extends beyond less favourable treatment (direct discrimination), to include indirect discrimination (neutral measures having discriminatory effects) and harassment. In relation to disability, a failure to provide reasonable accommodation is now a form of discrimination according to the UN *Convention on the Rights of Persons with Disabilities* (CRPD, 2006). As well, the CRPD includes 'the right of persons with disabilities to take part on an equal basis with others in cultural life', Article 30). Law is still mainly focused on prohibiting discrimination, but there is a growth in measures that create duties to promote equality. These typically place organisations under an obligation to take steps to ensure equality for their staff and service-users.

CASES: The ECtHR has an extensive body of case-law on the right to non-discrimination under Article 14 of the ECHR. It holds that a difference of treatment is discriminatory within the meaning of Article 14 if it has no objective and reasonable justification. Over time, the Court has deepened its interpretation of what non-discrimination requires. Notably [in DH, 2006], it recognised that 'a difference in treatment may take the form of disproportionately prejudicial effects of a general policy or measure which, though couched in neutral terms, discriminates against a group'; this is the concept of indirect discrimination. It has also recognised that failing to accommodate difference can constitute a breach of the right to non-discrimination. This idea has been applied in relation to religious minorities [THLIMMENOS, 2000] and people with disabilities [GLOR, 2009]. In relation to certain characteristics, the Court holds that 'particularly weighty reasons' are needed to justify a difference of treatment. These characteristics include sex, sexual orientation, race or ethnicity, mental impairment, disability, HIV status [KIYUTIN, 2011].

VIEWS: There is a long-standing debate within equality law regarding the permissibility of positive action (also called affirmative action). In its most far-reaching form, this includes quotas; e.g. ensuring gender balance in company boards or in Parliamentary representation. In relation to employment, the CJEU has rejected laws that provide an 'absolute and unconditional' priority for the under-represented sex at the point of selection for a job [e.g. in KALANKE, 1995]. The debate exemplifies the question of the extent to which the law should pursue substantive equality.

More recent debates concern how the law responds to the intersection of characteristics such as gender and ethnicity. Critics have argued that equality law has tended to compartmentalise identities and that it fails to recognise that individuals often experience disadvantage due to a combination of characteristics (Crenshaw, 1998).

CONCL: Equality is firmly established as core component of fundamental rights and European social legislation. Yet advocates of equality often remain disappointed by the extent of progress in eliminating disadvantage. Even though EU gender equality legislation has existed for four decades, there is still frequent evidence of women being under-represented in senior management or receiving less pay than men. This poses the question of whether anti-discrimination legislation, with its typical emphasis on enforcement via individual complaint and litigation, is a sufficient mechanism to transform the socio-economic position of those groups who have historically experienced disadvantage.

The law has moved beyond the idea that equality simply means treating people in an identical fashion. In the area of disability, it is well-established that equality entails a duty to provide reasonable accommodation. An emerging challenge surrounds the extent to which a duty of accommodation should extend to other characteristics, such as religion (Alidadi, 2012). It is particularly difficult to resolve this question where conflicts may emerge between equality characteristics, such as religion and sexual orientation.

REFERENCES:

Alidadi, Katayoun: "Reasonable accommodations for religion and belief: adding value to art.9 ECHR and the EU's anti-discrimination approach in employment?", 37 *European Law Review* 693 (2012).

Crenshaw, Kimberlé, "Demarginalizing the intersection of race and sex: a black feminist critique of antidiscrimination doctrine, feminist theory, and antiracist politics", in Phillips, Anne (ed.): *Feminism and politics*, Oxford: OUP (1998).

Ellis, Evelyn and Watson, Philippa: *EU Anti-Discrimination Law*, 2nd edn., Oxford: OUP (2012).

Fredman, Sandra: *Discrimination Law*, Oxford: OUP (2011).

Hellman, Deborah and Moreau, Sophia (eds.): *Philosophical Foundations of Discrimination Law*, Oxford: OUP (2013).

Schiek, Dagmar, Waddington, Lisa and Bell, Mark (eds.): *Cases, materials and text on national, supranational and international non-discrimination law*, Oxford: Hart Publishing (2007).

Sen, Amartya: *Inequality Reexamined*, Oxford: OUP (1995).
DH AND OTHERS v. CZECH REPUBLIC (ECtHR 13/11/2007, 57325/00).
GLOR v. SWITZERLAND (ECtHR 30/04/2009, 13444/04).
KALANKE v. FREIE HANSESTADT BREMEN (CJEU 17/10/1995, C-450/93).
KIYUTIN v. RUSSIA (ECtHR 10/03/2011, 2700/10).
THLIMMENOS v. GREECE (ECtHR 06/04/2000, 34369/97).
http://www.equalitylaw.eu (accessed 02/2016).

Mark Bell

European Committee of Social Rights

The European Committee of Social Rights (ECSR) is the regional human rights body responsible for monitoring compliance by the states parties to provisions of the 1961 Charter, the 1988 Additional Protocol, and the 1996 *Revised European Social Charter*. Established as treaty body of the Council of Europe, the ECSR is composed of 15 independent members. It is designed to complement the European Court of Human Rights, which oversees the civil and political rights set out in the *European Convention on Human Rights*. The ECSR oversees compliance with economic and social rights, some of which are also important in cultural contexts. It operates through a collective complaints procedure and a state reporting system. The latter holds that states parties to the Charter need to submit a national report every year, indicating how they implement provisions of the Charter. The ECSR examines these reports and publishes conclusions on whether the situation in the states are in conformity with the Charter. If a country does not act in response to the decision of the ECSR to the effect that it does not comply with the Charter, the ECSR will also issue a recommendation to that particular country. Moreover, the ECSR is entitled to hear collective complaints. This means that trade unions or their international organisations can collectively file a complaint with the ECSR in relation to non-compliance with the Social Charter against states parties that have accepted this procedure.

REFERENCES:

Benelhocine, Carole: *The European Social Charter*, Council of Europe Publishing (2012).
Betten, Lammy: "European Social Charter", 6 *Neth. Q. Hum. Rts.* (1988) 69.
Churchill, Robin and Khaliq, Urfan: "The Collective Complaints System of the European Social Charter: an effective mechanism for ensuring compliance with economic and social rights?", 15(3) *European Journal of International Law* (2004) 417.
Greer, Steven: "Europe" in Moeckli, Daniel; Shah, Sangeeta; Sivakumaran, Sandesh (eds.): *International Human Rights Law*, Oxford: OUP (2014).
Harris, D. J.: "The European Social Charter", 13(3) *International and Comparative Law Quarterly* (1964) 1076.

Yvonne Donders

European Convention on Human Rights (ECHR)

DEF: The Convention for the Protection of Human Rights and Fundamental Freedoms (known as the European Convention on Human Rights, ECHR) was the first legally binding instrument to give effect to some of the civil and political rights stated in the →UDHR. The system of protection of human rights created on the basis of the ECHR proved efficient due to the existence of the →European Court of Human Rights (ECtHR) as a permanent judicial body supervising the fulfilment by member states of their obligations stemming from the ECHR, the applied methods of interpretation making the treaty a powerful living instrument for meeting new challenges and unique supervisory mechanism of the execution of the ECtHR rulings.

Although cultural rights are neither explicitly protected in the text of the ECHR, nor have they been explicitly recognised in ECtHR case-law, the ECtHR, through a dynamic interpretation of the ECHR, has demonstrated that the rights falling under the notion of '*cultural rights*' can be protected under the core civil rights.

The ECHR came into force in 1953. Adopted within the framework of the Council of

Europe, it was the first legally binding instrument to give effect to certain rights stated in the Universal Declaration of Human Rights. Since its adoption, the ECHR has been amended a number of times through protocols whose aim was to supplement it with additional rights and to improve and strengthen its control mechanism.

The importance of the ECHR has three main aspects. Firstly, it is the scope of the rights and freedoms it protects; the ECHR protects fundamental civil and political rights but through a dynamic interpretation of the different Articles of the ECHR, the ECtHR has gradually recognised substantive rights which may fall under the notion of economic, social and cultural rights. Secondly, the functioning of the ECtHR to which individual or state applications can be made directly alleging violations of rights and freedoms guaranteed by the ECHR. Thirdly, in the supervision by the Committee of Ministers of the CoE of the execution measures undertaken by states to comply with final rulings of the ECtHR.

INSTR/CASES: The ECtHR adjudicates in the field of cultural rights mostly invoking the following provisions of the ECHR: Article 8 (right to respect for private and family life), Article 9 (freedom of thought, conscience and religion) and Article 10 (freedom of expression) of the Convention, as well as Article 2 of Protocol No. 1 (right to education). Referring to those provisions the ECtHR has identified certain situations in which applicants can claim rights that can be perceived as constituting elements of the right to culture: right to artistic expression [OTTO-PREMINGER-INSTITUT, 1994], access to culture [AKDAS, 2010], cultural identity [CHAPMAN, 2001], linguistic rights [GŰZEL ERDAGŐZ, 2008; CASE RELATING TO CERTAIN ASPECTS OF THE LAWS ON THE USE OF LANGUAGES IN EDUCATION IN BELGIUM, 1968] (where however the ECtHR excluded the right to obtain education in the language of one's choice), right to education [CAMPBELL AND COSANS, 1982], right to cultural and natural heritage (although the ECtHR has so far not recognised the right to the protection of cultural and natural heritage as such, it has accepted that the protection of heritage can constitute a legitimate aim that may justify state interference with individual rights, especially with the right to property guaranteed under Article 1 of Protocol No. 1., [BEYELER, 1996], right to historical truth [CHAUVY AND OTHERS, 2004] and academic freedom [SORGUC, 2009].

VIEWS: While identifying certain rights which can be perceived as constituting elements of the right to culture, the ECtHR has not so far recognised it as such. Having as a basis for its case-law the ECHR, the ECtHR refers also to other international agreements relevant in the field of cultural rights. In particular, the ECHR relied on the CoE *Framework Convention on the Value of Cultural Heritage for Society* as a basis of its decision that the conservation of cultural heritage and its sustainable use have as their goal human development [SCEA FERME DE FRESNOV, 2005]. The ECtHR also used the *Framework Convention for the Protection of National Minorities* as evidence of an emerging international consensus recognising special needs of minorities and the member states' obligations to protect them in order to preserve cultural diversity [CHAPMAN, 2001]. It has also referred to the *European Cultural Convention* [LEYLA SAHIN, 2005].

An important contribution to the discussion about guarantees of cultural rights through the ECHR is an idea to draft proposals for an additional protocol to the ECHR designed to guarantee individual rights in the field of culture. The CoE entrusted the *ad hoc* Committee for the Protection of National Minorities (CAHMIN) with that task. The CAHMIN discussed related issues at its sessions in 1994 and 1995, in addition to drafting the *Framework Convention for the Protection of National Minorities* (1995). However, these →ECHR Cultural Protocol debates did not lead to widely acceptable solutions and the work of the CAHMIN on this subject was suspended.

It has to be underlined that new initiatives for the elaboration of a culture-related protocol to the ECHR might encounter difficulties for two main reasons: reluctance not only among CoE member states but also at the already overburdened ECtHR to further broaden the scope of protected rights due to the difficulties of defining individual cultural rights as substantive rights, whose protection would require states to fulfil certain well defined positive obligations.

CONCL: There are numerous factors which may explain the growing importance of cultural rights in the ECtHR case law. Apart from the constant broadening of the scope of the rights protected through the application of the idea that the ECHR is a 'living instrument' that must be interpreted in the light of present-day conditions rather than what the drafters thought back in 1950, many ECtHR decisions in this field are prompted by applications lodged by persons or entities belonging to national minorities, including cultural, linguistic or ethnic minorities. Another important aspect influencing the ECtHR jurisdiction in the field of cultural rights is the increasing cultural diversity of European societies which gives rise to issues of striking a fair balance between different rights guaranteed by the ECHR. Bearing in mind the scope of issues raised in the ECtHR case law, including cases concerning not only civil and political rights but also social and cultural rights, one may conclude that it realises in practical terms the idea of indivisibility of human rights.

Despite the proposals of drafting an additional protocol to the ECHR that will guarantee individual cultural rights, there are no prospects to realise it in the near future. Therefore, the ECtHR will have to face the challenge and adjudicate the incoming applications referring also to cultural rights on the basis of the current text of the ECHR.

REFERENCES:

Council of Europe website: www.coe.int (accessed 06/2016).

Cultural rights in the case-law of the European Court of Human Rights, (2011) report available at: www.echr.coe.int (accessed 1/2016).

Leach, Philip: *Taking a case to the European Court of Human Rights*, Oxford: OUP (2005).

Pickard, Rob (ed.): *European Cultural Heritage: A review of policies and practice*, Strasbourg: Council of Europe publishing (2002).

van Dijk, Pieter; van Hoof, Fried; van Rijn, Arjen, Zwaak, Leo (ed.): *Theory and practice of the European Convention on Human Rights*, Cambridge: Intersentia (2006).

AKDAS v. TURKEY (ECtHR 16/02/2010, 41056/04).

BEYELER v. ITALY (ECtHR 05/01/2000, 33202/96).

CAMPBELL AND COSANS v. THE UNITED KIDGDOM (ECtHR 25/02/1982, 7511/76).

CASE RELATING TO CERTAIN ASPECTS OF THE LAWS ON THE USE OF LANGUAGES IN EDUCATION IN BELGIUM (ECtHR 23/07/1968, 1474/62).

CHAPMAN v. UNITED KINGDOM (ECtHR 18/01/2001, 27238/95).

CHAUVY AND OTHERS v. FRANCE (ECtHR 29/06/2004, 64915/01).

GŰZEL ERDAGŐZ v. TURKEY (ECtHR 21/10/2008, 37483/02).

LEYLA SAHIN v. TURKEY (ECtHR 10/11/2005, 44774/98).

OTTO-PREMINGER-INSTITUT v. AUSTRIA (ECtHR 20/09/1994, 13470/87).

SCEA FERME DE FRESNOV v. FRANCE (ECtHR 01/12/2005, 61093/00).

SORGUC v. TURKEY (ECtHR 23/06/2009, 17089/03).

Aleksandra Mężykowska

The European Court of Human Rights (ECtHR)

DEF: The ECtHR is an international court set up in 1959. It handles individual and inter-state applications alleging violations of the civil and/or political rights set out in the →European Convention on Human Rights (ECHR) and the additional Protocols to this treaty. It has jurisdiction over 47 member states of the Council of Europe (CoE). The ECtHR is based in Strasbourg, France.

INSTR: The operation and organisation of the ECtHR is laid down in Section II of the ECHR. Each of the 47 member states of the Council of Europe has one judge in the court. A judge is elected for a nine-year term of office with no right of re-election. The judges are elected by the Parliamentary Assembly of the Council of Europe. Each member state nominates three candidates to run for one post. The Court may sit in a single judge formation, in committees of three judges, in Chambers of seven judges and in Grand Chamber composed of seventeen judges. The ECtHR may render a judgment on violation or non-violation of the rights and freedoms enshrined in the ECHR by a member state. The Court may also declare an application inadmissible or reject it by decision of one judge due to defects of form. The Court examines applications against a state party to the Convention (*ratione personae*) alleging a violation of a right guaranteed by the Convention (*rationae materiae*). Applications can be lodged by persons who are residents of or within the jurisdiction of one of the state parties to the Convention. An application must concern a violation of the Convention that occurred after the Convention had entered into force in the respondent state (*ratione temporis*) unless the violation is of a continuous nature. An application has to refer to a violation that occurred within the territorial jurisdiction of a member state or in a territory effectively controlled by a member state (*ratione loci*). Pursuant to Article 35 ECHR an application may only be lodged with the ECtHR when all domestic remedies have been exhausted. An application has to be filed within six months after a final decision of domestic authorities. The ECtHR shall not deal with any case that has already been handled under another international procedure. A victim to a violation is required to demonstrate that he or she has suffered a 'significant disadvantage' as a result of the state's violation of the Convention. The enforcement of the ECtHR judgements is supervised by the Committee of Ministers of the Council of Europe composed from representatives of the 47 member states. The member states are required to provide the Committee of Ministers with regular progress status reports with regard to the implementation of the Court's rulings. Recent years have seen the ECtHR subjected to widespread criticism, in particular centering on the protracted proceedings. With a high volume of applications filed with the Court (17,200 cases were brought in 2014) it takes several years to obtain a judgment. The majority of complaints come from Ukraine, Italy, the Russian Federation, Turkey and Romania.

The continuous problem with the enforcement of the ECtHR is the main challenge to its authority. Moldova, Russia and Ukraine are among the states, which due to political conditions have shown the greatest resistance to the implementation of the judgments of the ECtHR. Well-established democracies such as the United Kingdom also refuse to enforce certain judgments [e.g. HIRST, 2005]. The British government argues that the rulings of the Court interfere with its national policy.

CASES: The ECtHR has delivered more than 10,000 judgements since its foundation. The Court's rulings are based on the European Convention of Human Rights and the additional Protocols to the Convention. In [TYRER, 1978] the Court stated that the Convention was 'a living instrument' which must be interpreted in the light of present-day conditions. The Court thereby defined the principle of an evolutive (or dynamic) interpretation of the Convention and held that its case-law is to maintain the standards in the states parties to the ECHR. Over time the case-law began reflecting certain rights which were not directly laid down in the ECHR, e.g. the right to reputation [PFEIFER, 2007], the right to access to public information [SDRUZENI JIBOCESKE, 2006] or the right to a clean (healthy) environment [POWELL AND RAYNER, 1990]. These rulings are examples of the evolutive interpretation of the Convention adopted by the Court.

The Convention contains no direct provision on a right to *culture*. Nonetheless, many rights referred to in the ECtHR's judgements may fall under the notion of 'cultural rights'. Article 8 (right to respect for private and family life), Article 9 (freedom of thought conscience and religion), Article 10 (freedom of expression) and Article 2 of the First Protocol (right to education) are usually invoked in such rulings. The case-law on cultural rights began to expand as members of →national minorities were raising complaints against the barriers faced by them in maintaining their traditions in terms of culture, language and ethnicity [KHURSHID MUSTAFA, 2008]. Cultural rights comprise in particular: the right to artistic activities (*inter alia* [MULLER, 1988]), access to culture (*inter alia* [AKDAS, 2010]), right to cultural diversity (*inter alia* [CHAPMAN, 2001]), right to linguistic identity (*inter alia* [GUZEL ERDAGOZ, 2008]), right to education (*inter alia* [LEYLA SAHIN, 2005]), right to respect and protection of cultural and natural heritage (*inter alia* [BEYELER, 2000]), right to seek historical truth (*inter alia* [MONNAT, 2006]) or academic freedom (*inter alia* [SORGUC, 2009]).

CONCL: The Convention does not explicitly provide for the right to culture. The signatory states could only reach consensus on civil and political rights. Nonetheless, the ECtHR has through interpretation of the Convention recognised certain culture-related rights, among them the right to diversity, the right to →cultural identity and the right to linguistic identity. Therefore, individuals who stay or reside in the territory of a state party to the ECHR may lodge individual applications to the ECtHR if their cultural rights are violated. The state parties should treat the ECtHR's rulings as a guidance in adopting policies and enacting laws, in particular those relating to cultural rights. The popularity of the individual application made the ECtHR the victim of its own success. To increase the effectiveness of the judicial process, Protocol 14 to the Convention was adopted (13 May 2004) introducing a single judge decision on the admissibility process and the criterion of a significant disadvantage. On 16 May 2013, the Committee of the Ministers of the Council of Europe adopted Protocol 15 which reduces the time-limit for making an individual application from 6 to 4 months, removes the state's veto over the relinquishment of a case to the Grand Chamber and makes a reference to one of the interpretation principles established in the jurisprudence of the ECtHR – the doctrine of the →margin of appreciation. This is a doctrine which allows the Court to take into account the specific context of a state party to the Convention and grant national authorities discretion to tackle specific issues which do not yield to a uniform interpretation of the Convention. The Protocol will take effect when it is signed, accepted or ratified by each party to the Convention. On 2 October 2013, Protocol 16 to the Convention was adopted. The Protocol empowers the ECtHR to issue opinions at the request of national courts. To enter into force, the protocol must be signed by 10 member states. Additional protocols are limited to the modifications of procedures and do not extend to substantial rights. They make no reference to cultural rights either.

REFERENCES:

Borelli, Silvia: *Cultural Heritage, Cultural Rights, Cultural Diversity. New Developments in International Law*, Boston: Brill (2012) 3–29, 55–83.

Bychawska-Siniarska, Dominika and Bodnar, Adam: "Saving the Strasbourg Court", EUractiv.com, (30 January 2014).

European Court of Human Rights: *Cultural Rights in the Case-Law of the European Court of Human Rights*, Research Division Report, Strasbourg: Council of Europe (2011).

Føllesdal, Andreas; Karlsson Schaffer, Johan and Ulfstein, Geir: *The legitimacy of international human rights regimes: Legal, political and philosophical perspectives*, Cambridge: Cambridge University Press (2013).

Francioni, Francsco and Scheinin, Martin: *Cultural Human Rights*, Boston: Brill (2008) 171–186.

Harris, David; O'Boyle, Michael; Bates, Edward and Buckley, Carla: *Law of the European Convention on Human Rights*, Oxford: Oxford University Press (2014).

Keller, Helen; Fischer, Andreas; Kuhne, Daniela: "Debating the Future of the European Court of Human Rights after Interlaken Conference: Two Innovative proposals", 21(4) *European Journal of International Law* (2011) 1025.

Leach, Philip: *Taking a Case to the European Court of Human Rights*, Third Edition, Oxford: Oxford University Press (2011).

Rulka, Marcin: "Problem wykonywalności orzecznictwa strasburskiego na przykładzie wyroku w sprawie Hirst przeciwko Wielkiej Brytanii", 2 *Europejski Przegląd Sądowy*, (2015) 32–41.

AKDAS v. TURKEY (ECtHR 16/02/2010, 41056/04).

BEYELER v. ITALY (ECtHR 05/01/2000, 33202/96).

CHAPMAN v. THE UNITED KINGDOM (ECtHR 18/01/2001, 27238/95).

GUZEL ERDAGOZ v. TURKEY (ECtHR 21/10/2008, 37483/02).

HIRST v. THE UNITED KINGDOM (ECtHR 06/10/2005, 74025/01).

KHURSHID MUSTAFA AND TARZIBACHI v. SWEDEN (ECtHR 16/12/2008, 23883/06.

LEYLA SAHIN v. TURKEY (ECtHR 10/11/2005, 44474/98).

MONNAT v. SWITZERLAND (ECtHR 21/09/2006, 73604/01).

MULLER v. SWITZERLAND (ECtHR 24/05/1988, 10737/84).

PFEIFER v. AUSTRIA (ECtHR 15/11/2007, 12556/03).

POWELL AND RAYNER v. THE UNITED KINGDOM (ECtHR 21/02/1990, 9310/81).

SDRUZENI JIBOCKSE v. CZECH REPUBLIC (ECtHR 10/07/2006, 19101/03).

SORGUC v. TURKEY (ECtHR 23/06/2009, 17089/03).

TYRER v. THE UNITED KINGDOM (ECtHR 25/04/1978, 5856/72).
www.echr.coe.int / www.coe.int (accessed 07/2016).

Dominika Bychawska

European Union

DEF: The European Union (EU) is the political and economic association of 28 Member States in Europe. Established in 1993, the EU has enjoyed international legal personality since 2008. The EU's main objectives are to promote peace, →common values (respect for human dignity, liberty, democracy, equality, the rule of law and respect for human rights, including the rights of persons belonging to minorities) and the well-being of its peoples. The EU operates through a hybrid system of supranational and intergovernmental decision-making. In addition, 19 of its members are parties to the EURO monetary union. These features make the EU the most integrated international organisation worldwide. The EU also contributes to 'the flowering of the cultures' of its members, 'while respecting their national and regional diversity and at the same time bringing the common cultural heritage to the fore' (Article 167 TFEU). The EU co-ordinates, supports and supplements the actions of its member states in cultural matters, but does not attempt to harmonise the laws and regulations of itsmember states. However, the EU and its members must act and legislate consistently with the →*Charter of Fundamental Rights* of the European Union (CFREU), which enshrines certain cultural guarantees (such as freedom of speech and freedom of art). Moreover, the common action in other policy areas, including those where the EU enjoys exclusive or shared competences, often affect the realm of culture and cultural rights (e.g. free movement of goods and persons, intellectual property, customs, audiovisual industries, linguistic diversity).

INSTR: Until the adoption of the TEU in 1992, the European Communities focused predominantly on economic and political matters. Indeed, the *Treaty of Maastricht* introduced for the first time 'culture' as a part of the integration process and important element building the solidarity between the EU member states and their peoples in full respect for their history and traditions (Littoz-Monnet, 2013). Accordingly, the EU shall respect the 'rich cultural and linguistic diversity' of Europe and 'ensure that Europe's cultural heritage is safeguarded and enhanced' (Article 3(3) TEU). Article 6 TFEU defines the EU competences in the field of culture as supporting, coordinating or supplementing the actions of the member states, without thereby suspending their competence in this area, and without entailing harmonisation of member states' law. As determined by Article 167 TFEU, the Union 'shall contribute to the flowering of the cultures of the Member States, while respecting their national and regional diversity and at the same time bringing the common cultural heritage to the fore'. The EU's engagement relates to the following areas: 'improvement of the knowledge and dissemination of the culture and history of the European peoples'; 'conservation and safeguarding of cultural heritage of European significance'; 'non-commercial cultural exchanges'; and 'artistic and literary creation, including in the audiovisual sector'. The EU and its member states also commit themselves to 'foster cooperation with third countries and the competent international organizations in the sphere of culture', in particular the →Council of Europe. Moreover, the EU shall take cultural aspects into account in its action under others areas, particularly 'in order to respect and to promote the diversity of its cultures'. The action of the EU in the sphere of culture is thus focused on encouraging the cooperation between member states, protecting their cultural diversity and promoting the cultural dimension of European integration in relation with states, international organisations and NGOs. In this regard, the EU operates various programmes and agencies. It supports prizes for cultural heritage, architecture, literature and music which highlight Europe's artistic achievements. It promotes the mobility of artists and of collections in order to enhance the value and significance of cultural exchange between its member states and to facilitate the access to culture, creativity and cultural heritage. It also supports the programme of European Capitals of Culture. The EU's culture-related action is of special importance as it reflects one of the core features of the EU attitude to culture, i.e. the linkage between cultural and economic development and individual and collective well-being. The Programme is run, typically in 7-year intervals, by the Commission. The current programme is called 'Creative Europe' (2014–2020). Culture and cultural policy are also closely linked to the main policies of the EU such as the internal market. Therefore, the TFEU also refers to culture in other provisions *inter alia* in Article 36 (limitations in free movement of goods), Article 107 (state aid to promote culture and heritage conservation), Article 165 (respect for cultural and linguistic diversity in execution of competences in the field of education) and Article 207 (special procedure in case of international agreements concerning trade in cultural and audio-visual services, where these agreements risk prejudicing the Union's cultural and linguistic diversity). Moreover, the EU and its member states must act and legislate consistently with the CFREU, which provides for a catalogue of cultural guarantees, including freedom of speech (Article 11) and freedom of art (Article 13). The profound reform of the EU, introduced by the *Treaty of Lisbon* (2007) has not changed the EU competences in the areas of culture and cultural heritage. Yet the new legal and institutional framework, comprising a consolidated legal personality for the EU, deeper integration of member states, awaited accession of the EU to the ECHR as well as more efficient decision-making instruments and greater coordination and consistency in EU foreign policy, may bring new challenges to EU action in respect of cultural matters (Psychogiopoulou, 2008; Bátora & Mokre, 2011).

CASES/PRACTICES: The EU is founded on common values, to be shared and respected by all member states and their peoples: 'the cultural, religious and humanist inheritance of Europe, from which have developed the universal values of the inviolable and inalienable rights of the human person, freedom, democracy, equality and the rule of law' (Preamble, TEU). On the other hand, one of the crucial concepts of the European integration is that of →cultural diversity, respecting and emphasising cultural differences between its constituent parties (De Witte, 2006). Importantly, the EU and its members are parties to the 2005 *UNESCO Convention*. The EU does not aim towards cultural convergence, but perceives its common cultural identity as the product of interaction of various traditions. In this regard, the protection of national languages as an essential element of cultural heritage and cultural diversity is specially respected by the EU law and the →CJEU's jurisprudence [MALGOŽATA RUNEVIČ-VARDYN, 2011]. Such an approach is also reflected in the area of tangible cultural heritage. The EU fully respects internal legal solutions of the member states with regard to protective regulations and policies, as long as they do not constitute a form of arbitrary discrimination [COMMISSION, 2003] or a disguised restriction on trade between member states [COMMISSION, 1968]. To this end, it provides the uniformed common licence system for the export of cultural objects, protected under domestic legal regulations, beyond the EU customs area. As regards the circulation of cultural goods within the EU, a special regime for the return of national treasures unlawfully removed from the territory of a member state has been introduced. This is aimed at providing the mutual recognition of relevant national laws for the protection of cultural heritage and facilitating cross-border exchange of information on unlawfully removed cultural goods. The EU is also more concerned with international efforts to protect cultural heritage globally, including the fight against the movement of illicit cultural material. Another significant expanding area of the EU common action in the field of culture relates to cultural cooperation agreements, in particular in order to respect and to promote the diversity of its cultures, negotiated and signed within the realm of its external economic relations.

VIEWS: Though the EU is the most integrated of all regional organisations worldwide, the level of its engagement in cultural issues is limited by the nature of competences in this area. Thus, its (in)action is frequently criticised by NGOs for inconsistency or even lack of common strategies in respect of culture, cultural rights and cultural heritage (cf. e.g. Arts Rights Justice). On the other hand, the understanding and meaning of common cultural values, such as freedom, democracy, equality and the rule of law are sometimes questioned in political discourse. Moreover, the results of the 2016 United Kingdom's EU membership referendum, by the majority for a withdrawal of the

UK from the EU ('Brexit'), have revived calls for an institutional reform of the EU. The referendum's outcomes have also questioned the supranational organisational structure of the Union, enhancing the value and importance of the principle of national sovereignty in relation to internal politics, law-making and cultural autonomy, including the management of economic, social and cultural rights. The possible de-accession of the UK will be negotiated within the period of two years (Article 50 TEU) and may have a significant impact on the EU's political equilibrium, budget (comprising EU Cohesion funding) and cultural, scientific and educational sectors, both in the UK and EU member states (Exiting the EU, 2016).

CONCL: Since the establishment of the EU in 1993, culture has become a significant area of its common action. The EU co-ordinates, supports and supplements, but does not harmonise, policies and measures of its member states in cultural matters, including via its 'Structural Funds' (ERDF and ESF). Moreover, the EU institutions as well as its members must act and legislate consistently with the CFREU, which guarantees the observance of certain cultural rights. The EU approach to culture involves both commonality and diversity, thus making the 'European Cultural Space' a distinct phenomenon, profoundly shaped by the integration process, the diversity of European societies and regional human rights law, located *vis-à-vis* the plurality and variety of other cultures of the world. This justifies a more coordinated common action of the EU in respect of cultural and cultural heritage, both in its internal and external dimensions. However, the possible withdrawal of the United Kingdom may profoundly affect the EU's institutional structure, its legal system and cultural policies.

REFERENCES:

Bátora, Jozef, Mokre, Monika (eds.): *Culture and External Relations: Europe and Beyond*, London: Routledge (2011).

Craufurd Smith, Rachael (ed.): *Culture and European Union Law*, Oxford: Oxford University Press (2004).

De Witte, Bruno: "The Value of Cultural Diversity in European Union Law", in Hildegard Schneider and Peter Van den Bossche (eds.), *Protection of Cultural Diversity from a European and International Perspective*, Antwerp: Intersentia (2008).

De Witte, Bruno: "Market Integration and Cultural Diversity in EU Law", in Valentina Vadi & Bruno De Witte (eds.), *Culture and International Economic Law*, London–New York: Routledge (2015).

Littoz-Monnet, Annabelle: *Union and Culture. Between Economic Regulation and European Cultural Policy*, Manchester and New York: Manchester University Press (2013).

Psychogiopoulou, Evangelia: *The Integration of Cultural Considerations in European Union Law and Policies*, Leiden–Boston: Nijhoff (2008).

Psychogiopoulou, Evangelia: "The EU and Cultural Rights", in Ana Filipa Vrdoljak (ed.), *The Cultural Dimension of Human Rights*, Oxford: Oxford University Press (2013).

COMMISSION v. ITALY (ECJ 10/12/1968, 7/68).

COMMISSION v. ITALY (ECJ 16/01/2003, C-388/01).

MALGOŽATA RUNEVIČ-VARDYN AND ŁUKASZ PAWEŁ WARDYN v. VILNIAUS MIESTO SAVIVALDYBĖS ADMINISTRACIJA AND OTHERS (CJEU 12/05/2011, C-391/09).

Arts Rights Justice Working Group: cultureactioneurope.org (accessed 4/2016).

Culture-related action of the EU: ec.europa.eu/culture (accessed 4/2016).

Exiting the EU: Impact in Key UK Policy Areas: http://www.parliament.uk/eu-referendum (accessed 6/2016).

Andrzej Jakubowski

European Union Agency for Fundamental Rights (FRA)

DEF: The FRA, based in Vienna, was established by *Council Regulation (EC) No 168/2007* of 15 February 2007 as one of the EU permanent agencies, succeeding the European Monitoring Centre on Racism and Xenophobia (EUMC). Implementing EU law, it carries out tasks with regard to EU institutions and EU member states. The Agency's mandate is specified by a Multiannual Framework and consists of ten thematic areas related to fundamental rights. Gathering data on the fundamental rights situation in the EU is the core FRA task. A horizontal task of the Agency, even if not mentioned directly in its legal foundations, is also to help to fully implement the EU →Charter of Fundamental Rights. As a hybrid institution, the FRA is best defined by its activities, since characterising it as a research institute, an administrative EU institution, or a human rights monitoring body would not fully explain how it actually works.

INSTR: The FRA offers socio-legal research covering all EU member states, thus providing comparable information and analysis across the EU28, published in its reports (all of them accessible via webpage). The Agency focuses on rights holders (individuals) as opposed to duty bearers (states and their entities), thus providing information also on the situation on the ground (rather than the law in the books). It ensures outreach to civil society, including through its Fundamental Rights Platform that brings together over 450 NGOs through annual meetings and online consultations. The Agency plays an important role as an independent expert body within the EU, inter alia through its legal opinions on draft EU legislation or as a provider of practical handbooks (e.g. on data protection, children's rights). The FRA also offers a 'joined-up governance approach' to the protection of fundamental rights in the EU, taking full account of the contribution of local and regional actors as well as the United Nations and the Council of Europe, and developing networks with national equality bodies, National Human Rights Institutions or Ombudsman offices. The Agency is also tasked to raise awareness of fundamental rights and promote dialogue with civil society organisations.

The FRA helps to enforce a fundamental rights culture with regard to the implementation of public policies in the EU and its member states. It conducts quantitative and qualitative field research and gathers primary data. This type of research helps to address the lack of comparable and reliable information in the EU needed to shape evidence-based policies. The Agency uses its data to formulate comprehensive advice for both the EU and national institutions. In practice, the promotion of fundamental rights by the FRA contributes to improving the European legal culture, which can increasingly be verified in legislative proposals and measures of the EU institutions.

One of the Agency's tasks is specifically directed at enforcing respect for the cultural, religious and linguistic identity, as well as diversity of the Union. Opinions, research and surveys concerning different grounds of →discrimination, prepared, published and disseminated by the Agency, are visible in the whole EU.

CONCL: Some rightly suggest that the FRA represents a new way of speaking about rights in the European Union, using 'governance' language. On the other hand, the Agency does not act like a traditional human rights monitoring body, since its goals are not led by the headlines of the day. It aims at safeguarding systematically the rights of the most vulnerable groups in European society. That is why its reports, e.g. on the situation of →LGBT, →Roma people or →refugees, usually have a real impact on shaping European 'governance' and human rights protection systems, especially as regards EU policies. In order to fully live up to its potential, the visibility and effectiveness of the FRA at the national level could still be further improved to cover all areas of the EU fundamental rights culture that is in constant need of being enforced.

REFERENCES:

"Bringing rights to life: The fundamental rights landscape of the European Union", The European Union Agency for Fundamental Rights 2012.

Hinarejos, Alicia: "A Missed Opportunity: The Fundamental Rights Agency and Euro Area Crisis", 22(1) *European Law Journal* (January 2016).

Sokhi-Bulley, Bal: "The Fundamental Rights Agency of the European Union: A New Panopticims", 11(4) *Human Rights Law Review* (2011).

"The Fundamental Rights Agency – views from the new Member States and Germany", Centre for International Relations, Warsaw 2006.

Toggenburg, Gabriel: "Fundamental Rights and the European Union: How Does and How Should EU Agency for Fundamental Rights relate to the EU Charter of Fundamental Rights", *EUI Working Papers*, LAW 2013/13.

http://fra.europa.eu (accessed 05/2016).

Mirosław Wróblewski

Female Genital Mutilation

DEF: Female Genital Mutilation (FGM), also known as female circumcision, is a traditional practice involving the partial or total removal of the external female genitalia, or other injury to the female genital organs for non-medical reasons. An estimated 200 million girls and women worldwide have undergone this practice (UNICEF, 2016). FGM is classified as a form of Violence Against Women (VAW) and recognised as a human rights violation (Rahman and Toubia, 2000). Asylum seekers with a well-founded fear of persecution on FGM related grounds may qualify for refugee status under the 1951 Refugee Convention. In the EU, asylum systems receive several thousand applications relating directly to FGM every year (UNHCR, 2013).

INSTR/CASES: In the past decades, both the CoE and the EU have established a comprehensive legal and policy framework applicable to asylum claims on FGM related grounds. The Common European Asylum System (CEAS) plays a principal role and the new *Recast Directives* provide the framework for FGM and the right to asylum. In addition, the *Convention on Preventing and Combating VAW and Domestic Violence* (Istanbul Convention) is the first European legally binding instrument that includes a provision on FGM. Member States are obliged to respect the principle of *non-refoulement*, ensuring that victims of VAW who are in need of protection are not returned to any country where their life would be at risk or where they may be subjected to torture or inhuman or degrading treatment or punishment. Despite these efforts, there is a discrepancy between legal requirements and actual practice, in terms of the implementation of European asylum instruments. At the national level, cases where asylum is granted on FGM related grounds are rare. The same trend is observable at the European level. Although the ECtHR has repeatedly underlined in its decisions that subjecting a woman or a child to FGM would amount to ill-treatment contrary to Article 3 of the ECHR, none of the 13 cases by an asylum claimant on FGM related grounds were admitted. However, in some cases national authorities granted asylum to applicants after the claim was brought before the ECtHR.

CONCL: At the European level, the protection offered to asylum seekers who have a fear of persecution on FGM related grounds seems to be inadequate. A comprehensive analysis of the legal and policy asylum framework applicable to asylum claims on FGM related grounds identified several challenges that potentially hamper the achievement of better protection (Middelburg and Balta, 2016): First of all, there is a need for a harmonised approach to granting protection on FGM related grounds throughout Europe, because EU Member States offer different levels of protection (EIGE, 2013). Secondly, gender equality and cultural dimensions should be incorporated more often in the assessment of asylum claims in order to avoid that asylum decisions are biased by assumptions and beliefs, rather than rooted in reality. Lastly, special attention to the vulnerability of potential or actual victims of FGM is required. If these three challenges are taken into account, the level of protection afforded to asylum seekers could be enhanced.

REFERENCES:

European Institute for Gender Equality (EIGE): *Female Genital Mutilation in the European Union and Croatia* (2013).

Gruenbaum, Ellen: *The Female Circumcision Controversy: An Anthropological Perspective*, Pennsylvania: University of Pennsylvania Press (2001).

Middelburg, Annemarie and Balta, Alina: Female Genital Mutilation/Cutting as a Ground for Asylum in Europe, *International Journal of Refugee Law* (2016).

Rahman, Anika and Toubia, Nahid: *Female Genital Mutilation: A Guide to Laws and Policies Worldwide*, London: Zed Books (2000).

Shell-Duncan, Bettina and Hernlund, Ylva: *Female "Circumcision" in Africa: Culture, Controversy and Change*, London: Lynne Rienner Publishers (2000).

UNHCR: *Too much pain: Female Genital Mutilation and Asylum in the European Union: A Statistical Overview* (2013).

UNICEF: *Female Genital Mutilation/Cutting: A Global Concern* (2016).

Annemarie Middelburg

Food

(Right to, and Cultural Dimensions of, F.)

DEF: Following the 1996 World Food Summit, the draft of an *International Code of Conduct on the Human Right to Adequate Food* had been developed in 1997 by three NGOs, FIAN (Foodfirst Information and Action Network), WANAHR (the World Alliance for Food and Nutrition) and the Instituto Jacques Maritain. Article 4 of this Code defines the right to food as follows: 'The right to adequate food means that every man, woman and child alone and in community with others must have physical and economic access at all times to adequate food using a resource base appropriate for its procurement in ways consistent with human dignity.' Frequently, the right to food is connected with issues of rural water supply as a basis for agriculture (e.g. in parts of Africa, Palestine and Cyprus).

From a cultural perspective, we need to be aware of the fact that 'adequate food is not simply a matter of ingesting sufficient nutrients. Food has cultural, social, economic and political dimensions, as well as the very important dimension of the pleasure of eating. People in statistical or abstract and idealised economic systems need only ingest sufficient calories, proteins, vitamins, etc. ... But for real human beings the quality of the access to food is what always counts. The means and manner of access to food deeply affect one's quality of life and cultural expression' (Künnemann and Epal-Ratjen, 2004).

INSTR/CASES: The right to food is protected by international HR instruments, such as the ICESCR which recognises in Article 11(1) that the 'right to an adequate standard of living includes food, housing, clothing', thus following the UDHR of 1948, which had also mentioned in Article 25 food on top of a list of basic provisions for all of mankind. In 1999, the CESCR issued *General Comment No. 12 on the Right to Adequate Food*. Its definition of 'adequacy' includes 'cultural or consumer acceptability', which implies the need to take into account 'non-nutrient-based values attached to food and food consumption.' In a case concerning the Ogoni people in the Niger delta whose existence was threatened by oil companies [THE SOCIAL AND ECONOMIC RIGHTS ACTION CENTER, 2001], the African Commission on Human and Peoples' Rights asserted that the right to food is implicitly enshrined in provisions of the *African Charter*, such as the right to life (Article 4), the right to health (Article 16) and the right to economic, social and cultural development (Article 22).

In Europe, neither the ECHR (Council of Europe) nor the CFR (EU) mention food or nutrition explicitly whereas the OSCE Parliamentary Assembly *Helsinki Declaration* of 2015, recognises 'food as a fundamental right'. Traditional forms of *cuisine* can be found frequently on UNESCO's *Representative List of the Intangible Cultural Heritage of Humanity*. In addition, there exists a great variety of national – in some countries also constitutional – regulations governing food and agriculture. Among those with distinct cultural or religious traits, the taboo of cattle slaughter in most states of India ('Beef Ban') is often considered a striking example. In a – highly controversial – case involving a Jewish ultra-orthodox association [CHAÂRE SHALOM VE TSEDEK v. FRANCE, 2000], the ECtHR upheld the French ban of a special form of ritual slaughtering used to prepare kosher meat *(glatt)*. The majority of the judges argued that, while rites as such can be covered by the ECHR, Article 9 had not been interfered with since the association could obtain meat prepared in accordance with their religious prescriptions from various butchers in Belgium.

Outside of the scope of HR, food items and crops are among the most heavily regulated products, including but not limited to controlled designation of origin labels or *appellation d'origine contrôlée* (in France, the Roquefort cheese was, in 1411, the first officially protected food product).

VIEWS: The OHCHR 'Human Rights Indicators' (2012) particularly emphasise the right to food and Article 6(1) of the above draft *Code of Conduct on the Human Right to Adequate Food* calls for states to respect the access to adequate food and, in this context, not to take 'political or other measures destroying existing access by vulnerable populations', including the respect of 'ancestral lands and rights particularly of indigenous peoples.' However, states are not the only actors to consider, as land grabbing by international food companies, landlords and mining or forestry industries; 'dumping food' exported from the EU; huge fish trawlers etc. increasingly threaten the existence of small-scale farmers, landless peasants, nomads and peasants practising shifting cultivation or other rural people especially from ethnic and cultural communities practising traditional forms of agriculture, hunting or fishing. The need to safeguard their food resources is underlined in many studies and documents, for example in the 2006 Report of the UN Special Rapporteur on the Right to Food, Jean Ziegler, on his mission to India (E/CN.4/2006/44/Add.2), where he states, inter alia: 'Tribal peoples, particularly those living in forest and hill areas, are extremely marginalized, many having lost access to traditional forest livelihoods and food resources through the creation of Forest Reserves, and... also suffer disproportionately from displacement because of development projects such as dams, power plants, coal mines and mineral industries.'

CONCL: Land and water grabbing is a common phenomenon in both the global north and south and – despite the successful establishment of a parallel 'green agriculture' in the last decade – a growing number of small and medium-sized farms have been forced to close down. This affects also the diversity of food resources and related cultural meanings or practices.

The plan of a HRC working group to establish a *Declaration on the Rights of Peasants and Other People Living in Rural Areas* which includes not only the right to freedoms of association, opinion and expression (Article 12), but also the right to seeds and traditional agricultural knowledge and practice (Article 5) the right to the protection of local agricultural values (Article 9) and the right to biological diversity (Article 10), has not yet materialised. According to an old proverb, 'paper is tolerant' and a non-binding declaration can hardly be expected, in practice, to overrule economic interests. However, it could help to shed more light on important cultural dimensions of food and agriculture, as proposed by international NGO's and explorative studies such as 'The European Food Project', initiated by the European Institute for Comparative Cultural Research, whose *Rethymnon Declaration* (ERICarts, 1998) pointed out: 'Food is a cultural resource which brings people together at the same time reflecting their heritage, manners and way of life.' And: 'The defence of local and regional cultures requires the full and imaginative use by public authorities in partnership with civil society of the cultural resources and traditions available, including those relating to food and cuisine. In addition to food safety and nutritional value, emphasis should be placed on ensuring the authenticity of processes of production, the origin and quality of the product as well as the local customs and traditions surrounding their use.'

REFERENCES:

ERICarts: *The Rethymnon Declaration on Cuisine as a Cultural Resource.* Adopted in Rethymnon (Greece), 30 October 1998 at the EU sponsored Expert Conference "ELEA: Producing and Consuming Olive Oil: A contribution to European Culinary Heritage" (accessed 03/2016 via www.ericarts.org/web/projects.php).

Künnemann, Rolf and Epal-Ratjen, Sandra: *The Right to Food: A Resource Manual for NGOs*, Washington D.C.: AAAS Science and Human Rights Program / HURIDOCS (2004).

Office of the United Nations High Commissioner for Human Rights: *HUMAN RIGHTS INDICATORS. A Guide to Measurement and Implementation.* Geneva: UN/ OHCHR (2012).

JAKOBSKI v. POLAND (ECtHR, 07/12/2010, 18429/06).

THE SOCIAL AND ECONOMIC RIGHTS ACTION CENTER AND THE CENTER FOR ECONOMIC AND SOCIAL RIGHTS v. NIGERIA (African Commission on Human & Peoples' Rights 27/10/2001, 155/96).

Andreas Joh. Wiesand

Free trade
(and Cultural Diversity)

DEF: The notion of 'cultural diversity' addressed in a context of 'free trade' generally refers to the question of the relationship between trade and culture or, more specifically, to the recognition of the dual nature, economic and cultural, of cultural goods and services. As stated in Article 8 of the UNESCO *Universal Declaration on Cultural Diversity* (2001), '(i)n the face of present-day economic and technological change, opening up vast prospects for creation and innovation, particular attention must be paid to the diversity of the supply of creative work, to due recognition of the rights of authors and artists and to the specificity of cultural goods and services which, as vectors of identity, values and meaning, must not be treated as mere commodities or consumer goods'. This recognition can lead to the development of specific rules to govern trade in this sector, or to 'cultural exception' or 'cultural exemption' clauses leading to an exclusion of such goods and services from the scope of a free trade agreement. Over the last fifteen years, the concept of 'cultural diversity' gradually replaced, or has been added to, those of the exception or exemption. This represents a paradigm shift from a defensive to a more positive approach to promoting culture in trade between states, an approach now reflected in UNESCO's *Convention on the Protection and Promotion of the Diversity of cultural expressions* (hereafter the 2005 Convention).

INSTR: No cultural good or service is formally excluded from the scope of the WTO agreements, such as the *General Agreement on Tariffs and Trade* (GATT) and the *General Agreement on Trade in Services* (GATS). In addition, the WTO agreements and its dispute settlement body do not yet recognise the specificity of cultural goods and services. Thus, any →cultural policies related to those goods or services must comply with the principles of non-discrimination. There is no definition or list of the 'cultural goods' covered by the GATT, but it certainly includes books, magazines, periodicals, CDs, music and film (UNESCO/Guèvremont, 2015). As for 'cultural services', according to the majority of authors, it includes audio-visual services (like motion picture and video tape production and distribution services, motion picture projection services, radio and television transmission services, sound recording), in addition to the other cultural services (like entertainment services, news agency services, →libraries, archives, museums, etc.). The GATS classifies audio-visual services as 'Communication services', while the other cultural services are included in the 'Recreational, cultural and sporting services'.

The 2005 Convention, in contrast, recognises the 'distinctive nature of cultural activities, goods and services as vehicles of identity, values and meaning' (Article 1(g) and, therefore, reaffirms 'the sovereign right of states to maintain, adopt and implement policies and measures that they deem appropriate' to protect and promote the diversity of →cultural expressions (Articles 1(h), 5, 6, 7 and 8), 'irrespective of the commercial value' of such goods and services (Article 4(4)). In addition, the parties are asked 'to promote the objectives and principles of this Convention in other international forums' (Article 21). These and other principles of the Convention landed on fertile soil: In the past decade, states concluded numerous regional and bilateral free trade agreements, in which they used various techniques in order to recognise the specific nature of cultural goods and services. Several agreements exclude them from their scope, while others cover the cultural sector but enable reservations in order to protect some cultural goods and/or services, or some cultural policies, from the free trade rules. It is worth noting that seven trade agreements concluded by the European Union over the last decade go further, incorporating one or more explicit references to the 2005 Convention and annexing a 'Cultural Cooperation Protocol' to promote the objectives and principles of this instrument (e.g. in the *EU-CARIFORUM Economic Partnership Agreement*).

CASES: Since the creation of the WTO in 1995, two complaints have been brought by the USA before the Dispute Settlement Body of the WTO concerning measures related to cultural goods and services. The first case [CANADA, 1997] arose well before the adoption of the 2005 Convention. At the time, the WTO panel did not recognise the specificity of the cultural goods involved and stated that it was not judging Canada's right to protect its culture, but rather the instruments it used to achieve that goal (Shi, 2013). Canada's loss in this case raised the awareness of many states about the vulnerability of their cultural policies in the face of the WTO agreements. In the second case [CHINA, 2009], the panel proved to be a bit more open towards the acknowledgment of intangible dimensions of cultural goods and services in dealing with a complaint concerning several Chinese measures related to various cultural goods and services. It recognised a link between the intangible content of a number of cultural goods falling within the scope of the GATT and the objective of protecting public morality mentioned in Article XX a., dealing with general exceptions. The recognition of this link, as advocated by China, was influenced by the text of the *UNESCO Universal Declaration on Cultural Diversity* of 2001 (UNESCO/Guèvremont, 2015).

VIEWS: From the beginning of its elaboration until today, the USA opposed the 2005 UNESCO Convention as well as any kind of recognition of the dual nature of cultural goods and services. In line with neoliberal ideology and economic interests, free trade is seen as stimulating the dynamic process of cultural diversity instead of preventing it, whereby outdated cultural manifestations are continuously crowded out by new ones (Cowen, 2002). According to this view, the 2005 Convention is vague, ambiguous, anti-commercial and anti-American in nature, and probably contrary to UNESCO's Constitutional obligation to promote 'the free flow of ideas by word and image', since it allows protectionism without any constraints (Oliver, 2005). Other disagreements concern the main goal of the 2005 Convention, which 'has nothing to do with promoting cultural diversity. Everything is window dressing – it's an amendment to trade agreements' (Miller, 2003). In order to guarantee an uninhibited circulation of goods and services, the USA negotiates bilateral and regional free trade agreements, including the currently debated TTIP. While present agreements generally limit the right of states to adopt any kind of discriminatory policies, including cultural policies, their main objective in the field of culture is to prevent regulations that could affect the delivery of digital content (Bernier, 2004). Such contents are 'computer programs, text, video, images, sound recordings, and other products that are digitally encoded, regardless of whether they are fixed on a carrier medium or transmitted electronically' (see e.g. Article 14(4) of the *United States–Morocco Free Trade Agreement*, 2004).

CONCL: A decade after its adoption, the 2005 UNESCO Convention with its over 140 contracting parties can be considered a legal instrument of universal value, particularly because it managed to make a great number of states and the EU aware of the dual nature of cultural goods and services, including the importance of protecting and promoting the diversity of cultural expressions in the context of free trade agreements they conclude (UNESCO/Guèvremont, 2015). A new, productive mechanism for international cultural cooperation between its parties contributed to this success. The next big challenge facing the parties in the future will be to implement the Convention in the digital environment, considering the fact that digital technologies have fundamentally altered the way in which cultural goods and services are produced, distributed and accessed (UNESCO/Kulesz, 2015).

REFERENCES:

Bernier, Ivan: "The Recent Free Trade Agreements of the United States as Illustrations of Their New Strategy Regarding The Audiovisual Sector" (2004) (available at www.coalitionsuisse.ch accessed 06/2016).

Cowen, Tyler: "The Fate of Culture", in *The Wilson Quarterly* (2002).

Intergovernmental Committee for the Protection and Promotion of the Diversity of Cultural Expressions: *Strategic and action-oriented analytical summary of the quadrennial periodic reports*, CE/12/6.IGC/4, 10–14 December 2012.

Miller, Richard Terrell: *US Delegation to the UNESCO General Conference*. US Department of State (2003) (available at www.state.gov accessed 6/2016).

Obuljen, Nina and Smiers, Joost (ed.): *UNESCO's Convention on the Protection and Promotion of the Diversity of Cultural Expressions: Making it work*, Zagreb: Institute for International Relations (2006).

Shi, Jingxia: *Free trade and cultural diversity in international law*, Oxford: Hart Publishing (2013).

UNESCO: *Reshaping Cultural Policies*, 2005 Convention Global Report, UNESCO (2015).

Voon, Tania: *Cultural products and the World Trade Organization*, Cambridge: Cambridge University Press (2007).

CANADA – CERTAIN MEASURES CONCERNING PERIODICALS (1997, WT/DS31/R, Panel Report).

CHINA – MEASURES AFFECTING TRADING RIGHTS AND DISTRIBUTION SERVICES FOR CERTAIN PUBLICATIONS AND AUDIOVISUAL ENTERTAINMENT PRODUCTS (2009, WT/DS363/R, Panel Report).

Véronique Guèvremont

Fundamentalism

(Religious F.)

DEF: Fundamentalism refers to religious movement or point of view characterised by a return to *fundamental* principles or sacred religious texts. It indicates unwavering attachment to a set of irreducible beliefs and often implies intolerance toward other interpretations. The expression was first used to describe an organised Evangelical movement in the United States in the early 1900s that opposed Protestant liberalism. The term has been generalised to similar movements within Judaism, Islam and Hinduism (Armstrong, 2000). Fundamentalism can apply to any religious group stressing strict observance of religious principles and a literal interpretation of sacred texts. In its non-academic usage fundamentalism is often employed as a synonym for violent extremism.

INSTR: In the interpretation of religious dogmas, fundamentalism is covered by the freedom of thought, conscience and religion (Article 9 ECHR), which protects individuals and religious groups. Religious organisations in the exercise of their autonomy have the right to set limits to the exercise of religious freedom by their members within religious institutions (Doe, 2011).

In the West, the discussion around fundamentalism is focused not on the legitimacy of fundamentalist religious stances, but on its intention to impose a given religious view in the political and civil sphere and the resulting questioning of the principle of secularism intrinsic to the democratic state. It can become a threat to the democratic state in the guise of religious totalitarianism.

The secular nature of the state should not imply an anti-religious attitude. Secular ideals and the separation between church and state are meant to preserve religions against political interference as much as they are intended to safeguard the political sphere from religious intrusion. Secularism and secular values are understood as being protective of fundamental values, including religion, not opposed to them (Bauman & Weingarten, 2006).

CASES: In Europe and in particular in Turkey, the only signatory of the ECHR with a Muslim majority, the religious fundamentalism that has been questioned is primarily Islamic. In its rulings on cases involving Article 9, the ECtHR has largely been faithful to the principles of liberal secularism. The Court has frequently emphasised the state's role as the neutral and impartial organiser of the exercise of various religions, faiths and beliefs, and stated that this role is conducive to public order, religious harmony and tolerance in a democratic society.

Therefore, the practice and argumentation in more recent cases [REFAH PARTISI, 2003 and LEYLA SAHIN, 2005], conflict not only with the liberal tradition regarding individual displays of religious identity in the public sphere, but also with the liberal tradition of respecting a certain legal autonomy for religious groups, a principle that has otherwise been supported by the Court. These rulings follow political criteria more than legal ones, given the risk that fundamentalism may impose religious norms to regulate certain areas of civil life (Martínez-Torrón, 2009).

VIEWS: Fundamentalism is generally seen as a reaction to secularisation and modernisation (Bruce, 2008). In policy debates or in the media, the term is often employed as a synonym for violent extremism. Some academic definitions include the willingness to use violence as a defining characteristic of fundamentalism (Heitmeyer, Müller & Schröder, 1997). This usage, however, does not reflect the most common academic conceptions, which define fundamentalism as a set of religious attitudes, norms and ideals (Emerson and Hartman, 2006). Fundamentalism is generally distinguished from orthodoxy, which reflects the content of what is believed rather than (as is the case with fundamentalism) the way the beliefs are held (Laythe et al. 2002).

There is also a fundamentalist – as opposed to liberal – secularism, which seeks to impose a secular (non-religious) lifestyle on all individuals entering the public sphere and advocates a limit to religious expression in public. Fundamentalist secularism denies religious conviction or belief any place for expression in the public realm (Westerfield, 2006). The 'fundamentalist' aspect of this approach lies in the fact that it imposes a secularist way of life on all individuals when they enter the public domain (Thorson Plesner, 2005).

CONCL: Acceptance of diversity is an important principle, which implies that secularism, and any principles and policies based on secularism, ought to be subject to adjustment to accommodate a wide range of cultural, ethnic and religious diversity. Secularism should give way to multiculturalism and accommodation, at least to some extent. Theorists differ widely as to the preferable degree of accommodation (Bauman & Weingarten, 2006). Recognition of difference should be limited insofar as it undermines core political values. In other words, while accommodation to cultural difference is desirable, elements of cultures or religions that are oppressive or dangerous ought not to be accepted in the name of multicultural accommodation. Europe's legislators and policymakers, faced with serious challenges in integrating new minorities, must interpret both their own constitutional duties and the constitutional limitations on their powers.

Recent incidents and cases, e.g. [LEYLA SAHIN, 2005], as well as the passage of France's law on religious symbols in 2004, seem to indicate that current understandings of secularism are increasingly relegating religious expression exclusively to the private sphere (Westerfield, 2006). From this standpoint, the range of approaches to secularism developed by European courts appears to be questionable (Bauman & Weingarten, 2006).

REFERENCES:

Armstrong, Karen: *The Battle for God. Fundamentalism in Judaism, Christianity and Islam*. New York: Alfred Knopf (2000).

Bauman, Richard W. & Weingarten, Sarah L. M.: "Keeping Religious Fundamentalism under Wraps: The Clothing Controversy in Selected European Countries", 15(1) *Forum Constitutionnel* (2006).

Bruce, Steve: *Fundamentalism*. 2nd edn. Cambridge: Polity (2008).

Doe, Norman: *Law and Religion in Europe: A Comparative Introduction*. Oxford: Oxford University Press (2011).

Emerson, Michael O. & Hartman, David: "The Rise of Religious Fundamentalism", 32(1) *Annual Review of Sociology* (2006).

Heitmeyer, Wilhelm; Müller, Joachim & Schröder, Helmut: *Verlockender Fundamentalismus* [Seductive Fundamentalism]. Frankfurt: Suhrkamp (1997).

Koopmans, Ruud: "Religious Fundamentalism and Hostility against Out-groups", 41 *Journal of Ethnic and Migration Studies*, (2015).

Martínez-Torrón, Javier: "La cuestión del velo islámico en la jurispridencia de Estrasburgo", 4 *Derecho y religión* (2009).

Westerfield, Jennifer M.: "Behind the Veil: An American Legal Perspective on the European Headscarf Debate", 54(3) *The American Journal of Comparative Law* (2006).

LEYLA SAHIN v. TURKEY (ECtHR 10/1/2005, 44774/98).

REFAH PARTISI AND OTHERS v. TURKEY (ECtHR GC 13/02/2003, 41340/98, 41342/98, 41343/98, and 41344/98).

Montserrat Gas-Aixendri

Gender Stereotypes

DEF: Gender relates to the specific characteristics of women and men in a society. Although gender is neutral to human sex, identity and individual experience, it is heavily determined by cultural and social norms. Gender roles and relationships of and between women and men are also influenced by law. Gender is relevant to law and law is not neutral with regard to gender. Law also defines rights and obligations of spouses, parents, children or other family members. Law determines who is eligible to enter marital relationships, who is recognised as a mother or a father of a child or who is entitled to maternity leave, etc. When law draws distinctions based on biological differences between men and women, certain individual choices such as the choice of one's life companion may be either prohibited or remain outside the protection of law. However, law may also establish procedures enabling recognition of the preferred gender in case of individuals who experience gender incongruence. Moreover, law may be used to influence gender roles and change social practices. Under current human rights standards, law should be used to eradicate harmful gender stereotypes which generally mean preconceptions about the attributes, characteristics, and roles of men and women. Gender stereotypes are considered harmful when they are based on the idea of inferiority of either gender.

INSTR: Unlike other human characteristics, gender is defined under international law. Article 7(3) of the *Rome Statute* specifies that gender 'refers to the two sexes, male and female, within the context of society. The term 'gender' does not indicate any meaning different from the above.' Likewise, the *Istanbul Convention on Preventing and Combating Violence against Women and Domestic Violence* stipulates that gender 'shall mean the socially constructed roles, behaviours, activities and attributes that a given society considers appropriate for women and men' (Article 3(c)).

In the light of these definitions, it is clear that different societies attribute different roles to men and women and sanction different attitudes and activities as socially acceptable or desirable. International law interferes only with such preconceptions and practices which deny equal value of men and women and their capacity to make individual life choices concerning their appearance and body, sexuality and reproduction, parenting and child care, as well as education, training, profession, employment and public functions. International human rights law acknowledges that harmful gender stereotypes are an obstacle to equal enjoyment of right by women and men.

According to Article 5 of the *Convention on the Elimination of all Forms of Discrimination Against Women* (CEDAW) states shall take all appropriate measures '(a) to modify the social and cultural patterns of conduct of men and women, with a view to achieving the elimination of prejudices and customary and all other practices which are based on the idea of the inferiority or the superiority of either of the sexes or on stereotyped roles for men and women;' and '(b) to ensure that family education includes a proper understanding of maternity as a social function and the recognition of the common responsibility of men and women in the upbringing and development of their children, it being understood that the interest of the children is the primordial consideration in all cases.' It implies that harmful practices, even if recognised by tradition, custom or religion, need to be changed via law and policy. Similar provisions are found in Article 12(1) of the Istanbul Convention.

International law specifically prohibits manifestations of harmful gender stereotypes which lead to violations of human rights (Gender Stereotyping as a Human Rights Violation, 2013). In addition, some forms of gender-based violence inspired by gender stereotypes amount to unlawful →discrimination against women. They include →female genital mutilation, 'honour' crimes, forced marriages and child marriages, sexual assaults linked to date-rape drugs, feminicides, rape and marital rape. In order to address these violations, states need to tackle gender stereotypes. In this regard states have to eliminate wrongful gender stereotyping from the practice of public authorities (i.e. the judiciary, prosecution, law enforcement or health care) and non-state actors, and to adopt special measures promoting gender equality, in particular, in the media and educational programs (Cook/Cusack, 2010).

CASES: In the human rights case law, gender stereotypes are usually mentioned with regard to attitudes and decisions of domestic authorities which are influenced by gender stereotypes (sexual stereotypes, etc.) regarding the expected behaviour of women as victims of rape or domestic violence, as well as their realisation of reproductive functions. In [OPUZ, 2009] the ECtHR found that the judicial passivity in cases regarding domestic violence affected mainly women. Hence, the response of domestic authorities to domestic violence was insufficient and led to impunity of aggressors, despite legal reforms against the discrimination of women.

Similarly, gender stereotyping at work could be regarded as a case of (sexual) discrimination. The US Supreme Court held that sex discrimination entails not only stereotype-based discrimination against men and women but also discrimination based on individual failure to conform to the stereotypes associated with these groups [HOPKINS, 1989]. Although typically gender-based recruitment is not permitted under anti-discrimination law standards, in very exceptional cases the fact of being a woman could constitute essential characteristics for a job (e.g. the 'Hooters girls' as a business brand).

VIEWS: In recent years, the term 'gender' became a theatre of an ideological war. In many countries, conservative parties and groups took the offensive against so-called 'gender ideology' and specifically against the view that gender roles may be individually determined regardless of biological differences between women and men. In some countries the war with gender ideology has led to constitutional amendments defining marriage as a union between a man and a woman and legislation prohibiting the promotion of homosexuality (Gliszczyńska-Grabias, Śledzińska-Simon, 2016). These developments demonstrate that gender ideology is perceived as a risk to the natural order, in which men and women have equal but different (complementary) roles defined by their biological functions. In particular, some religious organisations argue that denying sexual differences would overturn the existing social relations (Scott, 2013). In this way, gender has become a 'site' of the cultural and ideological struggle over the meaning of natural differences, gender and sexual identity, as well as sexual orientation (McCrudden, 2015).

Gender stereotypes are also at the centre of human rights debates concerning redistribution and representation which is essential for labour and social laws and policies and the concept of →citizenship. In this regard, gender stereotypes appear not only as roots for gender-based violence, but also other forms of oppression and marginalisation through exclusion from certain professions or relegation to low-paid jobs and industries or unpaid care work. They are often perpetuated by protective laws and policies which take 'natural' differences into account, but contribute to gender injustice. In the perspective of critical theory, gender injustice was reinforced by the 'original' social contract that sanctioned the public/private divide and labour division between men and women (Pateman, 1988).

According to Nancy Fraser, gender justice in post-industrial society should move from the model of 'universal breadwinner' and 'caregiver parity' to the model of 'universal caregiver' (Fraser, 1994). A similar approach is promoted in the scholarship on institutionalisation of gender neutral family roles (Rubio Marin, 2015). It follows the view that gender justice presupposes gender →equality implying that there is an individual right not to be subjected to gender stereotypes, even the benevolent ones. In this context, Rikki Holmaat speaks of a fundamental right of women and men 'not to be confined to culturally defined constructions of femininity or masculinity, or to pre-fixed (and fixed) female and male parental roles' (Holtmaat, 2012:145).

In the arts and media domains, gender stereotypes and subsequent discrimination – including the marginalisation of women by 'gatekeepers' in certain professions, based on the traditional belief of a feminine 'lack of creativity' – have long been an issue in public debates and research (see e.g. Cliche/Wiesand, 2003). This has led to manifold artistic initiatives and, in some cases, also to successful public measures (such as increasing the share of women in panels awarding scholarships and prizes). For example, from 1996 to 2016, the *Fondazione Adkins Chiti Donne in Musica* (Italy) identified and collected sheet music and other material from over 18,000 female composers – one of the artistic professions where women are still widely neglected today.

CONCL: Gender, gender roles, and family models are constructed by law and society which remain in a mutual relationship. While law often reflects society, both law and society are dynamic and subject to change. Therefore, the crucial question concerns the scale of changes introduced by law which a given society deems necessary, and conversely, the scale of legal changes (or lack of such) which is perceived as unjust and illegitimate. As noted by CEDAW Committee, '(t)raditional attitudes by which women are regarded as subordinate to men or as having stereotyped roles perpetuate widespread practices involving violence or coercion (...)' (CEDAW, 1992), regardless of whether such prejudices and practices are justified as a form of protection or control of women.

REFERENCES:

CEDAW: General Recommendation No. 19 (11th session, 1992).

Cliche, Danielle; Wiesand, Andreas: "Exposing and Opening Gates… Introduction and Recommendations", in ERICarts (ed.): *Culture-Gates. Exposing Professional 'Gate-keeping' Processes in Music and New Media Arts*, Bonn: ARCult Media (2003).

Cook, Rebecca J. and Cusack, Simone: *Gender Stereotyping: Transnational Legal Perspectives*, Philadelphia: University of Pennsylvania Press (2010).

Fraser, Nancy: "After the Family Wage: Gender Equity and the Welfare State", 22(4) *Political Theory* (1994).

Gliszczyńska-Grabias, Aleksandra and Śledzińska-Simon, "Value Pluralism without the Value of Pluralism? 'Homosexual Propaganda' Bans as a Litmus Test for the Acceptance of Liberal and International Human Rights Norms in the Post-Communist States", 15 *Baltic Yearbook of International Law* (2015).

Holtmaat, Rikki: "Article 5" in: Freedman, Marsha, Chinkin, Christine, Beate, Rudolf (eds.), *The UN Convention on the Elimination of All Forms of Discrimination Against Women. A Commentary*, Oxford: Oxford University Press (2012).

McCrudden, Christopher: "Transnational culture wars", 13(2) *International Journal of Constitutional Law* (2015).

OHCHR: Gender Stereotyping as a Human Rights Violation, Report (2013).

Pateman, Carole: *Sexual Contract*, Stanford University Press (1988).

Rubio Marin, Ruth: "The (dis)establishment of gender: Care and gender roles in the family as a constitutional matter", 13(4) *International Journal of Constitutional Law* (2015).

Scott, Joan W.: "The Uses and Abuses of Gender", 1 *Tijdschirft voor Genderstudies* (2013).

OPUZ v. TURKEY (ECtHR 9/06/2009, 33401/02).

PRICE WATERHOUSE v. HOPKINS, 490 US 228 (1989).

Anna Śledzińska-Simon

Golden Rule

INTRO: Different worldviews, cultural practices or national legacies sometimes collide with basic values. However, such tensions can lead to productive outcomes. Consequently, the European Union forged its motto of 'Unity in Diversity' (2000). Today, some actors seem to interpret this concept merely as a call to defend strong national identities within the diverse European space, while neglecting →common values, shared ethics and dialogue – as demonstrated in the 2016 'Brexit' decision of the UK. A general idea of justice could remind us of common ground: Based on the principle of reciprocity, the *Golden Rule* is known in many cultures or world religions, but has also sources in European philosophy (e.g. Kant's 'Categorical Imperative').

DEF/VIEWS: According to Jürgen Neyer (2007), this standard holds 'that only those rules can claim to be just which do not impose on any other person more serious restrictions of freedom than one would be willing to accept for one's self.' While cultural and social interpretations of the reciprocity norm may differ when applied to specific situations, Neyer recognises a 'common normative intuition which is shared across many cultures and times.'

CONCL: The *Golden Rule* should not be equated with cultural relativism in its negative connotations. Rather, the 'sharing diversity' approach – explored 2008 in a study of the ERICarts Institute for the European Commission – could serve as a starting point when addressing cultural differences or interpretations, including in legal and policy contexts, thus paving the way to meaningful intercultural exchanges and solutions.

REFERENCES:

Neyer, Jürgen: *Supranationality and Transnational Justice*. Conference paper, Frankfurt/Oder: European University Viadrina (2007).

http://www.interculturaldialogue.eu (accessed 11/2015).

Andreas Joh. Wiesand

Governments
(and Cultural Rights)

DEF: Governments have at their disposal three main functions that need to be in place to achieve their cultural development goals: (1) regulations to give proposed or adopted rules, measures and means a legal character; (2) public services provision by organising and funding cultural institutions and infrastructures they find indispensable; and (3) promotion of cultural activities in the third and business sectors via public funding and other supportive measures to intervene in the cultural market when it performs insufficiently. For example, a Ministry or state →administration is part of the executive branch of power and can act as a protector, facilitator, promoter and advocate for arts and culture. However, such actions should observe human rights principles enshrined in treaties and other legal instruments ratified by the state. In this context, the contracting states 'assume obligations and duties under international law to respect, to protect and to fulfil human rights' (OHCHR, 2016), including those with cultural dimensions. Related measures could be negative: to refrain from intervening in (artistic) freedom of expression; and positive: to facilitate the enjoyment of culture-related human rights. On the one hand, governments are obliged to refrain from interfering with human rights and to protect individuals or groups of individuals against human rights abuses. On the other hand, they should strive to create the necessary climate and conditions within which arts and culture can be accessed and develop. While both components are important, the promotion and protection of the diversity of →cultural expressions is now placed so high on global agendas that, in 2005, →UNESCO adopted its Convention devoted particularly to contemporary expressions in the arts and media.

INSTR: Human rights' standards are more than empty promises. With regard to cultural rights such as the right to equitable →participation in cultural life (Article 15(1)(a) ICESCR), this is particularly significant. More and more governments execute their 'sovereign right to adopt measures and policies to protect and promote the diversity of cultural expressions within their territory' (Article 5(1), *2005 UNESCO Convention*). Their activity and the growing involvement of civil society stakeholders led to the development of, and on-going demands for, a wide range of policies, laws, measures and public bodies aiming to support, serve or regulate the arts, heritage, broadcasting and other media, languages or socio-cultural needs. This was especially the case in Europe, where access to culture for the general public is not protected in the ECHR but rather in a number of national constitutions and not all of these activities may be officially linked with the implementation or 'enjoyment' of culture-related human rights. However, national ministries in charge of culture as well as regional or local governments usually take care to underline positive implications of their planning and policies for the realisation of principles such as freedom of expression; cultural diversity (and the opposite, e.g. the exclusive protection of a national language); or equality/non-discrimination – the latter potentially leading to →affirmative action measures on behalf of special or disadvantaged groups in society (such as reduced admissions to cultural services for →children, →older people or the unemployed).

VIEWS: A closer look into e.g. the Council of Europe/ERICarts 'Compendium of Cultural Policies and Trends in Europe' reveals that solutions for cultural challenges and related policy approaches differ from one country to the next, depending on such factors as the individual country's history, the nature of its government as well as on its political, economic and social context. These approaches cannot be classified exclusively on the basis of who administers or finances them, since this may be done by a ministry (like in France), through 'arm's-length' or quasi-autonomous organisations (such as Arts Councils in the UK and other countries), in public-private partnerships or by other institutions, foundations and organisations with differing legal status. As well, due to the lack of a generally accepted definition of 'culture' as a governmental domain, areas of state or local action may be smaller or larger (but reach, especially in Europe, now often beyond the arts in a narrow understanding and include e.g. socio-cultural programmes, heritage protection or the development of private-sector 'creative industries'). Finally, also the basis and instruments for interventions speak against simple classifications since these may amount to direct public support in the form of subsidies or public institutions – as frequently found in Europe – or to indirect governmental incentives such as tax concessions like in the USA (Gournay, 1988).

CONCL: Despite such differences, an important shift 'from governing to governance' in →cultural policies can be recognised in the last decade, which has been described as 'joint and uneven terms of engagement with the complex field of economic, social, political and cultural power relations in which we are all *stakeholders*' (Mercer, 2012). The arm's length concept, which is based on the professional independence of the main cultural actors or beneficiaries, is facing the challenge of how to include other stakeholders and thus create productive 'multi- or inter-actor's dynamics' in the cultural domain – of course, without endangering freedom of expression or discouraging artistic passion.

REFERENCES:

Council of Europe/ERICarts (eds.): *Compendium of Cultural Policies and Trends in Europe*, Strasbourg/Bonn (accessed 06/2016 via www.culturalpolicies.net).

Gournay, Bernard: "Rapport National", in: *La politique culturelle de la France*, Paris: La Documentation Française (1988).

Klaić, Dragan: Resetting the Stage: Public Theatre between the Market and Democracy, Intellect Ltd. (2013).

Madden, Christopher: "The independence of government arts funding: A review", *D'Art Topics in Arts Policy*, No. 9, 2009. (available at www.ifacca.org/en/ accessed 06/2016).

McGuigan, Jim: *Rethinking cultural policy*. Berkshire: McGraw-Hill (2004).

Mercer, Colin: *Towards Cultural Citizenship: Tools for Cultural Policy and Development*, Stockholm: The Bank of Sweden Tercentenary Foundation & Gidlunds Förlag (2012).

Vesna Čopič

Hate Crimes

DEF: Hate crimes are crimes committed against persons from racial, religious, sexual or other minorities, because they are belonging to, or thought to be belonging to such a group. International human rights law imposes obligations on states to effectively investigate, prosecute and punish not only the underlying crimes, but also their discriminatory background, both when committed by state agents *and/or* private individuals or groups.

INSTR: In the past, when a person's right to life, right to family life, or right to be free from inhuman and degrading treatment were violated because that individual or group belonged to a racial, religious, sexual or other minority, states only had a duty to protect from, and sanction violations by its own agents (negative obligation). Today, their human rights duties go much further, in that they need to effectively investigate and prosecute such violations and their discriminatory motives (procedural obligations) not only when committed by state agents but also by private individuals (positive obligations).

CASES: The ECtHR and the IACHR have developed such standards on hate crimes mainly in cases involving race-based hate crimes [e.g. NACHOVA, 2005; STOICA, 2008; WALLACE DE ALMEIDA, 2009]. Similar protective standards emerge with regard to gender based violence before the IACtHR [e.g. GONZALES, 2009] and domestic violence before the ECtHR [e.g. OPUZ, 2009].

CONCL: The case law on hate crimes has mainly dealt with fact patterns arising out of racially motivated violence The standards on negative and positive obligations have also been applied to violence against religious [BEGHELURI, 2014] and LGBT minorities [IDENTOBA, 2015]. It will be interesting to see whether human rights bodies will draw on gender-based and domestic violence against women case law to develop uniform protection standards for all types of discriminatory hate crimes.

REFERENCES:

BEGHELURI v. GEORGIA (ECtHR 07/10/2014, 28490/02).

GONZALES v. MEXICO (IACtHR 16/11/2009, ser. C, no. 205).

IDENTOBA v. GEORGIA (ECtHR 12/05/2015, 73235/12).

NACHOVA v. BULGARIA (ECtHR 06/07/2005, 43577/98 and 43579/98).

OPUZ v. TURKEY (ECtHR 09/06/2009, 33401/02).

STOICA v. ROMANIA (ECtHR 04/03/2008, 42722/02).

WALLACE DE ALMEIDA v. BRAZIL (IACHR 20/03/2009, 12.440).

Mathias Möschel

Hijab

DEF: Generally, the H. can refer to any head, face, or body covering worn by Muslim women or girls beyond the age of puberty outside of their family home. In different countries (e.g. Turkey), the Hijab and similar types of clothing are seen as a symbol for standards of modesty. In a wider religious or philosophical perspective, *Al-hijab* is to signify 'the veil which separates man or the world from God' (Glassé, 2001); this would actually suggest that both men and women should avail themselves of such a symbol. Noteworthy are recent efforts of designers to harmonise the Hijab with contemporary fashion design.

VIEWS/CASES: However, some observers consider the Hijab as an instrument of social pressure with the intention of separating women from men in the public sphere, which may collide with human rights interpretations. It is banned in public/educational institutions e.g. in France, Belgium and in a few German *Länder*. As regards Germany, this practice was ruled unconstitutional as a general measure in 2015 [1 BvR 471/10], which questions earlier views of the ECtHR [DAHLAB, 2001 and LEYLA ŞAHIN, 2005]. The Human Rights Committee has found that a restriction on the wearing of the Hijab is an interference of the right to freedom of religion (Article 18 ICCPR) and that the freedom to manifest one's religion includes the right to wear religious clothing in public [HUDOYBERGANOVA, 2004].

CONCL: While wearing (or not wearing) a Hijab could be considered a matter of personal choice, this issue seems to become increasingly overshadowed by questions of principle such as, on the one hand, unreflected traditions or religious →fundamentalism and, on the other hand, a specific (and likewise 'fundamentalist') interpretation of secularism. This ambiguity could suggest further European and international efforts to reach a common approach to Hijab issues, taking into account what is appropriate or 'necessary in a democratic society' (Article 9.2 ECHR).

REFERENCES:

Glassé, Cyril: *The New Encyclopedia of Islam*, Lanham (2001).

Thomassen, Lasse: "The Politics of the Hijab at the European Court of Human Rights", in APSA 2012 Annual Meeting Paper.

DAHLAB v. SWITZERLAND (ECtHR 15/02/2001, 42393/98).

HUDOYBERGANOVA v. UZBEKISTAN (Human Rights Committee 08/12/2004, 931/2000).

LEYLA SAHIN v. FRANCE (ECtHR 10/11/2005, 44774/98).

Andreas Joh. Wiesand

Historical Truth

DEF: Memory laws are defined as legal regulations concerning the interpretation of historical events. They are also supposed to attach a specific legal qualification to these events. Negationism is a denial of historical facts, especially the crimes of genocide. In many states the law forbids the negation, belittling or trivialisation of the crime of genocide (also war crimes and crimes against humanity).

INSTR/CASES: The passing of memory laws leads to a number of controversies, both of a legal character (violation of freedom of expression and scientific research), and of an historical and sociological character (interference in historians' findings, manipulating the collective memory). Despite these controversies, such laws have been passed all over the world and basically take two forms: (1) of legal establishment of a certain official orthodoxy concerning historical facts, not connected with any sanctions or (2) a legal ban on interpreting historical facts in a certain way under threat of sanctions. The most frequently debated kind of memory laws are bans on negating the crime of genocide, especially the laws penalising Holocaust denial. Legal obligation for the EU states to introduce such legal bans was included in the *Council Framework Decision 2008/913/JHA*. The ECtHR has had to consider whether such laws are in compliance with the principle of freedom of expression. In the case of Holocaust denial, the Court has consistently ruled that limitations of freedom of expression are in compliance with the ECHR [GARAUDY, 2003, among others], but its attitude towards penalisation has been different in the case of denial of the Armenian genocide [PERINCEK, 2015].

CONCL: The judgment of the Grand Chamber of the ECtHR in [PERINCEK, 2015] indicates that the debate on acceptability of penalising certain historical statements is still open. It seems that the UN Human Rights Committee holds a similar opinion: In its *General Comment no. 34*, the Committee states that bans on expression of certain opinions of historical events, which are not accompanied by, e.g. incitement to hatred, excessively violate freedom of expression. This tendency may lead to more frequent questioning of the legitimacy of memory laws.

REFERENCES:

Douzinas, Costas: "History Trials: Can Law Decide History?", *Annual Review of Law and Social Science*, 8 (2012).
Hennebel, Ludovic, and Hochman, Thomas (eds.): *Genocide Denial and the Law*, Oxford: Oxford University Press (2011).
Lipstadt, Deborah: *History on Trial: My Day in Court with David Irving*, New York: Ecco (2005).
Osiel, Mark J.: *Mass Atrocity, Collective Memory, and the Law*, Edison (1997).
FAURISSON v. FRANCE, (HRCee 8/08/1996, 550/1993).
GARAUDY v. FRANCE (ECtHR 24/06/2003, 65831/01).
PERİNÇEK v. SWITZERLAND (ECtHR 15/10/2015, 27510/08).
SÕRO v. ESTONIA (ECtHR 3/09/2015, 22588/08).
counciloreuropeanstudies.org/research/research-networks/transnational-memory (accessed 10/2015).
humanrightscolumbia.org/ahda (accessed 10/2015).
www.lph-asso.fr (accessed 10/2015).

Aleksandra Gliszczyńska-Grabias

Housing

DEF: The right to adequate housing is universally recognised as a socio-economic right. It has two main components: (1) the socio-economic aspect which underlies positive obligations of the state to provide adequate accommodation, and (2) the privacy-related aspect which emphasises protection of the home against forced evictions, harassment and other types of intrusion. In essence, both the right to adequate housing and the right to protection of the home correspond to the basic human need of a safe shelter, which should be ensured without →discrimination. The culture-related aspect of housing signifies respect for the choice of the way of living and adequate consideration of a vulnerable status of certain groups, including cultural or ethnic minorities.

INSTR: State obligations following from international law (i.e. Article 25 UDHR, Article 11(1) ICESCR, Article 31 of the Revised ECSR) include the positive duty to take 'all appropriate means' to promote adequate housing and a negative duty to refrain from forced evictions (Article 7 ICCPR, Article 8 ECHR). According to the CESCR General Comment No. 4, the right to housing should not be interpreted restrictively and mean only the right to 'a roof over one's head'. Still, the realisation of the right to adequate housing depends on availability of resources, while the concept of adequacy referring to (a) legal security of tenure; (b) availability of services, materials, facilities and infrastructure; (c) affordability; (d) habitability; (e) accessibility; (f) location; (h) respect for cultural identity and diversity needs to be read in the light of local conditions. In the view of the CESCR adequate housing implies cultural adequacy which concerns the way of constructing houses and the use of building materials, as well as policies supporting this process. Both housing development and modernisation should enable the expression of cultural identity and diversity of housing, while ensuring that the cultural dimensions of housing are not sacrificed (CESCR, 1991).

In contrast, the protection against forced eviction is unqualified. According to the CESCR General Comment No. 7 forced eviction is a permanent or temporary removal against the will of individuals, families or communities from the homes and/or land which they occupy, without the provision of, and access to, appropriate legal protection. The African Commission on Human and People's Rights inferred that the minimal protection following from the right to shelter obliges states not to destroy the housing of citizens and not to obstruct efforts by individuals or communities to rebuild their lost homes [SERAC, 2001, 60–61]. Importantly, the state obligation to make legal protection against forced eviction or demolition effective also against third parties contributes to prevention of homelessness.

CASES: Beside the prohibition of discrimination in access to accommodation on any grounds (i.e. CRPD, CRC, CEDAW, CERD, *EU Directive 2000/43/EC*), international law recognises special needs of vulnerable minorities whose way of life shall be given adequate consideration in public policies concerning housing. Although no right to be provided with a 'home' can be derived from Article 8 of the ECHR, and the Strasbourg Court was unwilling to accept that states have positive obligation to secure adequate number of suitably equipped official sites for gypsy caravans [CHAPMAN, 2001], the recent case-law demonstrates that national authorities need to provide special protection of →Roma, Sinti and Travellers [D.H. and OTHERS, 2007] and in case of evictions provide them with adequate alternative housing [WINTERSTEIN, 2013]. In particular, according to the Court, 'the underprivileged status of a community must be a weighty factor in considering approaches to dealing with their unlawful settlement and if their removal is necessary, in deciding on its time, modalities, and, if possible arrangements for alternative shelter' [YORDANOVA, 2012, para. 133]. Whereas in the context of land use and →urban planning national authorities enjoy a wide →margin of appreciation, the ECHR offers protection against arbitrary expulsions from land traditionally occupied by Roma communities, albeit without legal permission. According to the →European Commission on Social Rights, states need to ensure that the housing conditions in Roma camps meet minimum standards and offer access to social housing for Roma and Travellers wishing to live in mobile homes [ERTF, 2012].

VIEWS: The dilemma usually related to socio-economic rights concerns the question whether the right to adequate housing is justiciable. The Indian Supreme Court confirmed in a precedential decision [OLGA TELLIS, 1985] that adequate housing is not only a matter of social policy, but also a fundamental right derivative from the protection of life. In consequence, the eviction of pavement and slum dwellers from the city of Bombay infringed their right to livelihood because their life depended on jobs in the city.

Yet, not all evictions violate international human rights standards. What distinguishes fair from unfair eviction is the form (manner, timing, etc.) of its enforcement, as well as the availability of alternative accommodation (relocation, resettlement, etc.) and effective legal remedies to those concerned.

In practice, evictions against vulnerable groups such as Roma, Sinti and Travellers do often violate human rights standards, including the right to protection of private and family life and the enjoyment of possession, notwithstanding illegal construction of dwellings, unlawful occupation of land or low value of their possessions, and/or lead to forced expulsion of →migrants.

CONCL: The right to adequate housing is a component of the right to an adequate standard of living, which is essential for the enjoyment of any human rights. It appears that the determination of standards of living in the course of drafting social policies or land use and urban planning should be made with respect to minority cultures and ensure their active participation. Often minority or vulnerable groups lack political representation and their engagement in decision making processes could compensate for this deficiency. In particular, policy-makers should be sensitive to different ways of life and cultures of those living in a community, which include nomadism and traditions regarding common use of land.

REFERENCES:

Hohmann, Jessie: *The Right to Housing: Law, Concepts, Possibilities*, Oxford: Hart Publishing (2013).

Nolan, Aoife: "'Aggravated Violations', Roma Housing Rights and Forced Expulsions in Italy: Recent Developments under the European Charter Collective Complaints System", 11(2) *Human Rights Law Review* (2011), 343.

Terminski, Bogumil: The Right to Adequate Housing in International Human Rights Law – Selected Bibliography, Geneva, (2013) (available at www.ssoar.info accessed 04/2016).

UN Committee on Economic, Social and Cultural Rights (CESCR), *General Comment No. 4: The Right to Adequate Housing (Art. 11(1) of the Covenant)*, 13 December 1991, E/1992/23.

UN Committee on Economic, Social and Cultural Rights (CESCR), *General Comment No. 7: The right to adequate housing (Art. 11(1)): forced evictions*, 20 May 1997, E/1998/22.

UN Special Rapporteur on the Right to Adequate Housing – Official website: www.ohchr.org (accessed 04/2016).

CHAPMAN v. UK (ECtHR 18/01/2001, 27238/95).

COHRE v. FRANCE (ECSR 28/06/2011, 58/2010).

COHRE v. ITALY (ECSR 25/06/2010, 58/2009).

D.H. AND OTHERS v. CZECH REPUBLIC (ECtHR 13/11/2007, 57325/00).

ERTF v. FRANCE (ECSR 24/01/2012, 64/2011).

OLGA TELLIS and ORS v. BOMBAY MUNICIPAL COUNCIL (Supreme Court of India 10/07/1985, 2 Supp SCR 51).

SERAC AND ANOTHER v. NIGERIA (ACHPR 15/10/2001,155/96).

WINTERSTEIN v. FRANCE (ECtHR 17/10/2013, 27013/07).

YORDANOVA v. BULGARIA (ECtHR 24/04/2012, 25446/06).

Anna Śledzińska-Simon

Human Dignity

DEF: The original Latin word *dignitas* has a twofold meaning of dignity as an ethical concept on the one hand and high status, superiority on the other. Theological views and philosophies are influenced by this twofold meaning throughout the development of the concept of human dignity from Roman times until today. Some believe that all human beings are born equal and remain so throughout their entire lives, while others differentiate between people as to the degree of worthiness they achieved. The former ontological concept is widely accepted by international and domestic norms – heavily influenced by the teachings of Immanuel Kant, who claimed that '(e)very rational being exists as an end in himself, not merely as means for arbitrary use' (Kant, 1972, p. 95).

INSTR: Human dignity in post-World-War-II legal documents serves a twofold purpose: it guarantees that the traumatic historic experiences of humanity never return, and lays down the foundations of a democratic order based on the rule of law (Hoffmann, 1993).

Many international human rights documents start the enumeration of rights with human dignity and there are a number of constitutions that chose dignity as their highest constitutional value (*Charter of the United Nations*, UDHR, ICCPR, ICESC, CRDP, CERD, CEDAW, the *Declaration of the Rights of the Child*, 1924/1959).

The ECHR does not expressly mention the notion, but its Preamble reaffirms the UDHR's values and principles including dignity. The case-law of the ECtHR acknowledges that certain treatments of humans – such a torture, violations of due process, violations of privacy and discrimination – are incompatible with the idea of inherent dignity. Dignity has a central role also in the EU context: according to the *Lisbon Treaty* it is one of the core values that the Union is based on, and it is also enshrined in the EU's bill of rights, the CFREU. The American Convention on Human Rights and the African Charter on Human and Peoples' Rights also contain references to dignity, heavily relied on by the attached case law (MEJÍA, 1996; KRISHNA, 1992).

Human dignity is elevated to the central value in some national constitutions. It is a framework right providing a 'common roof' for a wide variety of situations, and an all-encompassing right from which constitutional rights of lower level of generality can be derived. In this sense human dignity is called a mother right implying that it can give birth to other, so-called daughter rights (Barak, 2015, p. 156–169).

The German case is unique: Human dignity, *Menschenwürde*, according to the Basic Law, is an absolute right, not subject to limitation and is protected by the constitution's eternity clause, i.e. it cannot be changed by any future constitutional amendments. There is an explicit textual reference to human dignity in the title of the Israeli Basic Law, and the text also provides for its preservation and protection. In the South-African Constitution and the jurisprudence of the Constitutional Court dignity also has an eminent role [MAKWANYANE, 1995].

CASES: Human dignity in legal texts can either be a basic value to be achieved through the enforcement of human rights, or alternatively, it can be a human right in itself. There are many legal systems – like in Canada or the United States –, where human dignity has exclusively a constitutional *value* as opposed to being formulated in the rights language. In these jurisdictions human dignity has a twofold value: it may be invoked by courts as a tool of interpretation when determining the content of constitutional rights, or alternatively, it may help to assess the constitutionality of limitations imposed on constitutional rights through sub-constitutional norms.

There are also legal systems where human dignity is viewed as a constitutional *right*. A purposive interpretation of human dignity by apex courts allows them to recognise rights not expressly mentioned in the constitutional text instead of interpreting the lack of textual reference as a denial of constitutional embeddedness. This is often the case with regard to social rights or new areas, such as bioethics (Barak, 2015).

Whereas the ECHR does not directly refer to dignity, the ECtHR has relied heavily on the concept. It has accepted that respect for dignity is core to the ECHR and its protection is a matter of civilisation (SW, 1995). The relation between dignity and torture, inhuman, degrading treatment and punishment was established in the early case law [TYRER, 1978], and it was invoked with respect to the right to a fair hearing, [BOCK, 1989] the right to life [PRETTY, 2002] or the right to private life [GOODWIN, 2002]. By now the ECtHR sees human dignity as the very essence of the ECHR [PRETTY, 2002].

Human dignity was also incorporated into EU law, originally through judicial interpretation as a general principle of Community law, based on the constitutional traditions common to member states [OMEGA, 2004] and later by way of black letter law in the treaties and the CFR (McCrudden, 2008).

VIEWS: There are great differences in the regulation, interpretation and enforcement of human dignity. The concept has natural law connotations; its content is filled primarily with extra-legal values. Although dignity is often perceived as a universal standard, it is largely culture-dependent. Originally the constitutional definition of human dignity was based on individualism, and the 1789 French *Declaration of the Rights of Man and the Citizen* emphasised the rights of individuals versus the state. This approach was taken over by post-1945 constitutional texts.

In contrast to Western traditions, African and Asian ones emphasise both rights and duties concerning human rights in general, and more specifically human dignity. These cultures do not consider human rights from an individualistic worldview, but their concern is the individual's role and place in the community. The indigenous South African values include *ubuntu*, which can be translated into 'group solidarity, compassion, respect, human dignity, conformity to basic norms and collective unity (…) marking a shift from confrontation to conciliation' [MAKWANYANE, 1995]. *Ubuntu* stresses mutual interdependence, where group solidarity is central to the survival of communities.

Certain common points can be found between various cultures and jurisdictions, like the responsibilities derived from the German *Menschenwürde* and the notion of African *ubuntu*. In German theory and case-law, dignity involves both rights and obligations, and there is an emphasis on the individual 'existing in the social world' – a solution that is rather unique in Western cultures [MEPHISTO, 1971].

CONCL: Human dignity is a fluid concept, and its value lies in its vagueness, which enabled its universal acceptance in a post-1945 pluralistic world, with cultural, ideological, political and religious differences. Giving up on a concrete concept of human dignity had a functional advantage: it provided a foundation for human rights to be incorporated into legal documents, without the need for asking whether these rights pertain to all human beings (Carozza, 2013, p. 348). Human dignity became a normative and meta-legal principle, a theoretical source offering a foundational premise for all human rights, irrespectively of the nature of rights, 'thus promoting a holistic protection of humanity' (Dupré, 2016, p. 71). As a consequence human dignity was used to fulfil the promise of ensuring civilisation, democracy and the rule of law – in particular in the wake of inhuman and undemocratic regimes. Specifying what human dignity entails beyond its minimum core was not necessary and would even have been dysfunctional at the time of the acceptance of the UDHR or the ECHR. Therefore the determination of its exact content is left to international, regional and domestic apex courts, leading to significant differences in interpretation beyond the common core.

REFERENCES:

Arendt, Hannah: *The Origins of Totalitarianism*, San Diego/New York/London: Harcourt (1968).

Barak, Aharon: *Human Dignity: The Constitutional Value and the Constitutional Right*, Cambridge: Cambridge University Press (2015).

Carozza, Paolo G.: "Human Dignity". In: Dinah Shelton (ed.): *The Oxford Handbook of International Human Rights Law*, Oxford: Oxford University Press, (2013).

Dupré, Catherine: *The Age of Dignity: Human Rights and Constitutionalism in Europe*, Oxford: Hart (2015).

Feldman, David: "Human Dignity as a Legal Value – Part I", 4 *Public Law* 682 (1999).

Folkers, Horst: "Menschenwürde: Hintergründe und Grenzen eines Begriffs", 87 *Archiv für Rechts- und Sozialphilosophie* 328 (2001).

Hoffmann, Hasso: "Die versprochene Menschenwürde", 118 *Archiv des öffentlichen Rechts*, 353 (1993).

Kant, Immanuel: *The moral law: Kant's groundwork of the metaphysic of morals*, translated and analyzed by H.J. Paton, London: Hutchinson (1972).

McCrudden, Christopher: "Human Dignity and Judicial Interpretation of Human Rights", 19(4) *European Journal of International Law* 655 (2008).

Miguel, Carloz Ruiz: "Human Dignity: History of an Idea", 50 *Jahrbuch des Öffentlichen Rechts der Gegenwart* 281 (2002).

BOCK v. GERMANY (ECtHR 29/03/1989, 11118/84).

KRISHNA ACHUTAN v. MALAWI (ACHPR, Comm. No. 64/92 (October 10,1991), 68/92 (March 2, 1992), 78/92, (October 6, 1992)).

MEIJA v. PERU (Inter-Am.C.H.R., Case 10.970, Report No. 5/96, OEA/Ser.L/V/II.91 Doc. 7 (1996))

MEPHISTO (30 Bundesverfassungsgericht 173 (1971)).

OMEGA SPIELHALLEN UND AUTOMATENAUFSTELLUNG GMBH v. OBERBURGERMEISTERIN DER BUNDESSTADT BONN (ECJ Case C–36/02, [2004] ECR I–9609.

PRETTY v. THE UK (ECtHR 29/04/2002, 2346/02).

S v. MAKWANYANE AND ANOTHER (Constitutional Court of South Africa(CCT3/94) 1995 (6) BCLR 665; 1995 (3) SA 391; [1995] ZACC 3, (6 June 1995)).

TYRER v. THE UK (ECtHR 25/04/1978, 5856/72).

Petra Bárd

Human Rights Council

INSTR: The Human Rights Council was established on 15 March 2006 by UN General Assembly Resolution 60/251. It replaced the Commission on Human Rights as the primary human rights body. The Council is composed of 47 members. All UN member states are eligible for membership, seats are divided according to regional groupings: 13 seats for both Africa and Asia, eight for Latin America and the Caribbean, seven for Western Europe and six for Eastern Europe. The Council convenes at least three times per year and can convene for special sessions in response to serious human rights situations.

The principal duties of the Council include the promotion of universal respect for all human rights and fundamental freedoms for all, address and make recommendations on situations of violations of human rights and promote human rights education and learning. One of the primary tools of the Council is the Universal Periodic Review (UPR) which is a mechanism that oversees states' fulfilment of their human rights obligations. Under the UPR each of the UN member states is reviewed once every four and a half years. Reviews are based on three documents: (1) national report prepared by the state under review, (2) compilation of UN information, and (3) summary of relevant stakeholders such as NHRIs and NGOs. At the end of proceedings, a final outcome report is adopted that serves as the basis for the next review the state undergoes. The UPR mechanism has shown to be complementary to the procedures of the →UN treaty bodies, with the final outcome documents of UPR often containing encouragements to adopt treaty body recommendations.

The Council also has a complaint procedure, where a complaint can be brought by a person or group, claiming to be victims of violations of human rights, or a person or group (including NGOs) who have direct and reliable knowledge of alleged violations. The complaint must be substantiated, domestic remedies must have been exhausted, and the situation cannot be being dealt with by another international body. The Council complaint system is only concerned with more gross and systematic violations of human rights.

In 2009, the Council, through resolution 10/23, decided to establish, for a period of three years, a new special procedure entitled 'independent expert in the field of cultural rights'. The mandate was extended in 2012, and the mandate holder was conferred with the status Special Rapporteur in the field of cultural rights (resolution 19/6). The Special Rapporteur will report to the Council on a yearly basis.

REFERENCES:

Lintel, Ida and Ryngaert, Cedric: "The Interface between Non-governmental Organisations and the Human Rights Committee", *International Community Law Review*, Vol. 15 (2013).

McMahon, Edward and Ascherio, Marta: "A Step Ahead in Promoting Human Rights? The Universal Periodic Review of the UN Human Rights Council", *Global Governance*, Vol. 18 (2012).

Spohr, Maximilian: "United Nations Human Rights Council – Between Institution-Building Phase and Review of Status", *Max-Planck-Yearbook of United Nations Law*, Vol. 14 Munich (2010).

www.ohchr.org/EN/Issues/CulturalRights (accessed 03/2016).

Yvonne Donders

Human Security

INTRO: Traditional security models have focused on the security of the state under the tacit assumption that the security of its citizens in every societal aspect would follow from it. Numerous precedents have proved that assumption to be wishful thinking. Human security, in contrast, focuses on the subjective security of the individual. It is the focus on persons, families and communities that imbues human security with a strong cultural significance.

DEF/VIEWS: Human security was originally conceptualised to span seven dimensions of equal significance (UNDP, 1994): economic, food, health, environmental, personal, community, and political security – related to the principle of the triple bottom line. More recent models recognise the dominance of environmental security, providing support for the three pillars of socio-political, economic and health security (Lautensach & Lautensach, 2013). This raises numerous challenges for good governance and expands the discourse of security to arbitrate among conflicting cultural norms.

CONCL: The cultural dimension of human security manifests as values and key narratives that inform a country's policies, priorities and lifestyles, that affect its legal and socio-political frameworks, its economic systems, its public health, and the underlying integrity of environmental support systems.

REFERENCES:

Lautensach, Sabina W., and Lautensach, Alexander K.: "Introduction", in *Human Security in World Affairs: Problems and Opportunities*. Vienna, Austria: Caesarpress (2013). pp. XIX–XXXVIII.

UNDP (United Nations Development Programme): *Human Development Report: New Dimensions of Human Security*. New York: UNDP (1994).

Sabina Lautensach

Hybridity

DEF: In a cultural context, hybridity can be understood as an amalgamation or blending of different cultures and traditions via 'cross-cultural negotiation' or learning processes (Duxbury / Simons / Warfield, 2006). Learning from the experiences of both traditional and new minorities about 'shared spaces' and individual biographies demonstrating 'multiple identities' can lead to productive insights, in that respect.

INSTR: While the term 'hybridity' as such is not yet found in legal instruments, the *2005 UNESCO Convention* calls for related policies and measures that help to 'develop cultural interaction in the spirit of building bridges among peoples' (Article 1(d)) and to generate 'shared cultural expressions through dialogue and mutual respect' (Article 4(8)). The Council of Europe *Framework Convention on the Value of Cultural Heritage for Society* sees a need to 'establish processes for conciliation to deal equitably with situations where contradictory values are placed on the same cultural heritage by different communities' (Article 7(b)) and to 'reinforce social cohesion by fostering a sense of shared responsibility towards the places in which people live' (Article 8(c)). Clearly, answering to such demands is less an issue for national and international courts and much more one for cultural policies with an intercultural perspective.

VIEWS: During the last decades, hybridity became a central topic in cultural studies. Some authors see cultural hybridisation as part of globalisation or 'glocalisation' processes leading to 'crossover cultures' or 'translocal mélange' (Nederveen Pieterse, 2003), others speak of a 'World in Creolisation' (U. Hannerz, 1987), 'Bricolage' (J. Okely, 1994), 'blended worlds' (H. Bhabha, 1994) or 'Cultural Syncretism' (M. Canevacci, 1992). However, hybridity should not be mistaken as merely an academic playground, as demonstrated in a self-reflection of football hero Zinedine Zidane: 'Every day I think about where I come from and I am still proud to be who I am: first, a Kabyle from La Castellane (a neighbourhood in Marseille), then an Algerian from Marseille, and then a Frenchman' (The Observer, 3/4/2004).

CONCL: A hybrid identity means that a human being integrates different experiences, sensitivities, and competences in his/her life. And hybrid cultures or communities are those making use of different experiences, sensitivities, and competences in everyday life, thus shaping the structures and dynamic processes of societies. 'Inclusion of otherness' as the core principle of hybridity should not be understood as leading to one-way assimilation or 'melting pot' societies and rather as an attempt to capture difference as well as similarity, otherness as well as commonality. Related learning processes have the power to overcome segregation, 'dualism' or mono-cultural worldviews while recognising the complex allegiances of individuals and groups. Given the current reality of global migration flows and connected issues or fears, an observation of writer Salman Rushdie over 30 years ago could almost be seen as a prophecy: 'I don't think that migration, the process of being uprooted, necessarily leads to rootlessness. What it can lead to is a kind of multiple routings. It's not a traditional identity crisis of not knowing where you come from. The problem is that you come from too many places ... it's not that there are pulls in too many directions so much as too many voices speaking at the same time' (New York Times Book Review, 13/11/1983). In a positive connotation, hybridity can be understood as claiming the right to be equal – and different.

REFERENCES:

Duxbury, Nancy; Simons, Derek and Warfield, Katie: "Local policies and expressions of cultural diversity: Canada and the United States", Paper commissioned by Institut de Cultura, Barcelona in the framework of the study *Local Policies for Cultural Diversity*. Paris: UNESCO (2006).

ERICarts Institute: *Sharing Diversity*, Study for the European Commission, Bonn/Brussels (2008), cf. www.interculturaldialogue.eu (accessed 04/2016).

Nederveen Pieterse, Jan: *Globalization and culture: Global mélange*. Lanham, MD: Rowman and Littlefield (2003).

Tschernokoshewa, Elka: "Hybrid Worlds of Europe: Theoretical and Practical Aspects", in Kockel, Ullrich; Nic Craith, Máiréad; Frykman,

Jonas (eds.): *A Companion to the Anthropology of Europe*, Chichester: Wiley–Blackwell (2012).

Elka Tschernokoshewa/Andreas Joh. Wiesand

Illicit Trafficking of Cultural Objects

DEF: The Illicit Trafficking of Cultural Objects refers to the movement of stolen and illegally exported art and antiquities. Nearly every nation recognises the need to protect and preserve beautiful and historic objects. As a result, international and domestic laws have been created to protect and preserve cultural objects and archaeological context. The international market in art and antiquities works against many of these restrictions.

INSTR: There has been a concerted international effort to restrict the illicit trafficking in cultural objects. At the international level the UNESCO *Convention on the Means of Prohibiting and Preventing the Illicit Import, Export and Transfer of Ownership of Cultural Property* defines cultural property as 'property which, on religious or secular grounds, is specifically designated by each State as being of importance for archaeology, prehistory, history, literature, art or science'. Within Europe there are measures to provide the return of objects which have been wrongfully removed. *Council Directive 93/7/EEC* creates a framework for the return of cultural property within the European Union for cultural goods belonging to the national artistic, historical, or archaeological heritage which have been illicitly exported from a member state.

CASES: The →European Court of Human Rights (ECtHR) has had the opportunity to review some cases involving the individual right to property and the public interest in preserving art and culture. However, the Court has demonstrated a reluctance to go beyond a rigid application of the individual right of property under *Protocol I*, →European Convention of Human Rights (ECHR), to weigh the balance between individual rights and the communal interest in cultural objects. Recent legal decisions in the United States and the United Kingdom successfully allowed the application of foreign cultural patrimony laws in domestic courts. There remains though a great deal more work to be done to harmonise and develop the body of law which focuses on the illicit trafficking of cultural objects.

VIEWS: Much of the international movement of art can be considered illicit trafficking. A helpful distinction has often been made between nations of origin, and market nations. Origin nations often have a wealth of art or archaeological heritage which is valued by the art market. In contrast, market nations import works of art and antiquities. The distinction has proven useful, primarily due to the thoughtful scholarly contributions of the late legal writer John Henry Merryman. However, the distinction reveals its limits when we consider that every work of art or antiquity has a nation of origin. Even the United Kingdom, typically thought of as an important art market, has large quantities of cultural objects. Opponents of strong regulation at the level of nations of origin argue the restrictions merely drive legitimate trade in cultural objects towards the black market, further increasing the criminal and illicit aspects of the art and antiquities trade. On the other hand, advocates of these regulations argue archaeological sites are a limited resource which cannot be commercially exploited. They also point out how the restraints on the sale of cultural objects can limit the theft of cultural objects and looting of cultural patrimony.

CONCL: There are three components to effective regulation of cultural objects: First, an effective legal framework. Secondly, the necessary resources to implement that framework. And lastly, a desire on the part of a nation's citizens to protect and preserve their heritage. Few legal regimes have been able to effectively implement all three. Progress may be slow, yet the fight against the illicit trafficking of cultural objects moves steadily forward. Cultural patrimony's key role in human flourishing continues to gain deeper respect in international legal instruments, judicial decisions, and commentary.

REFERENCES:

Bator, Paul: "An Essay on the International Trade in Art" 34 *Stanford Law Review* 275 (1982).

Francioni, Francesco & Scheinin, Martin (eds.)

Culture, Heritage and Human Rights: An Introduction, Leiden: Nijhoff (2008).
Gerstenblith, Patty: "The Public Interest in the Restitution of Cultural Objects" 16 *Connecticut Journal of International Law* 197 (2000).
Greenfield, Jeanette: *The Return of Cultural Treasures*, Cambridge: Cambridge University Press (2007).
Manacorda, Stefano & Chappell, Duncan (eds.) *Crime in the Art and Antiquities World: Illegal Trafficking in Cultural Property*, Springer (2011).
Merryman, John Henry: "Two Ways of Thinking About Cultural Property" 80 *American Journal of International Law* 831 (1986).
O'Keefe, Patrick J.: *Commentary on the 1970 UNESCO Convention, Powys*: Institute of Art and Law (2007).
Vrdoljak, Ana Filipa: *International Law, Museums and the Return of Cultural Objects*, Cambridge: Cambridge University Press (2006).

Derek Fincham

Impact Assessment

DEF: According to a definition by the International Association for Impact Assessment, assessing impacts 'is the process of identifying the future consequences of a current or proposed action. The 'impact' is the difference between what would happen with the action and what would happen without it'. Since the 1990s Impact Assessment (IA) has been promoted particularly by the EU and the OECD, and has developed into a key governance technique.

INSTR/VIEWS: IA is a generalisation of Environmental Impact Assessment (EIA), which came into law with the US National Environmental Policy Act of 1969 (NEPA) in order to assure, amongst other things, 'aesthetically and culturally pleasing surroundings' and to 'preserve important historic, cultural, and natural aspects' of national heritage (Sec. 101 [42 USC § 4331]). Meanwhile, EIA has become an international legal and moral standard instrument focusing on physical impacts (UN Rio Declaration on Environment and Development, Principle 17, 1992; Francis, Laudato Si', sec. 182 et seqq.). Nowadays, the terms 'social impact assessment', 'human rights impact assessment' (see e.g. General Assembly, A/68/262, sec. 43; A/HRC/RES/15/9 sec. 8 et seq.; A/HRC/4/74, A/HRC/19/59/Add.5) and "cultural impact assessment" can also be found in several official UN texts. The term 'cultural impact assessment' is strongly linked with the consideration of Indigenous Peoples' Rights in the context of large infrastructure projects. Farida Shaheed, the UN Human Rights Council independent expert in the field of cultural rights, mentions in her 2011 report that states 'should utilise cultural impact assessments in the planning and implementation of development projects, in full cooperation with concerned communities' (General Assembly, A/HRC/17/38). In the EU administration, IA has been developing a promising tool for participatory and evidence-based policy making since 2002 (COM/2002/0276), with the intention to integrate all relevant interests. Legally, IA can be seen as an increasingly important instrument to prove the proportionality of policies and measures. However, cultural issues have not played a significant role in this context yet.

CONCL: Understanding IA as 'gathering and analysing evidence to support policy making' (EU Better Regulation Guidelines 2015) implies two disadvantages for 'culture': its necessities very often lack evidence due to resource reasons and many of its aspects are not evident in the sense of measurability. Therefore, it is still most desirable to develop and establish a standard methodology for cultural impact assessments similar to already available guidelines for e.g. social, gender and fundamental rights IA. Such a work could start from few existing guidelines on cultural heritage impact assessment as well as preparatory reflections (Partal, 2013; Schindler, 2011).

REFERENCES:

Partal, Adriana: *Impact Assessment: A Tool to Assist Cultural Sustainable Development*, Melbourne: Global Cities Research Institute, RMIT University (2013).
Schindler, Jörg Michael: *Kulturpolitik und Recht 3.0 – Von der Kulturverträglichkeitsprüfung zur kulturbezogenen Folgenabschätzung*, Köln/Cologne: ARCult Media (2011).

Jörg Michael Schindler

Indigenous Peoples
(Cultural rights of I. P.)

DEF: A single universal definition of indigeneity seems neither necessary nor appropriate, given that it will be either over- or under-inclusive, depending on which society it is applied to. Commonly accepted is the general description by Martinez-Cobo (1986/7) which includes the following criteria:

- historical continuity with pre-colonial societies contiguous with their territory;
- distinct from, and non-dominant over, other sectors of societies now prevailing on those territories;
- determined to preserve for future generations their ancestral territories and identity, in accordance with their own cultural patterns, social institutions and legal systems.

Occasional synonyms are aboriginals, tribal peoples, first peoples, native peoples.

INSTR: Underlying principles include the collective occupation of residual ancestral lands, common genetic ancestry and cultural heritage, language, the self-identification of individuals and their acceptance by the collective. The general description, as well as its principles, have been accepted in international law (especially Article 27 ICCPR, the provisions of the UN *Declaration on the Rights of Indigenous Peoples* (2007) (UNDRIP) and of *ILO Convention no. 169*). Article 33 of UNDRIP underlines the right to self-identification.

Article 27 of the ICCPR provides the key treaty provision supporting the rights to culture for indigenous peoples as a human right, irrespective of their status as ethnic minorities. In contrast to economic and social rights, cultural rights, both positive and negative, ensure participation in cultural life; sharing and benefiting from scientific advancement; and protection of intellectual property (UNHCHR, 2008).

Early post-contact contractual reconciliation of the disparate interests of indigenous peoples and their colonisers has benefited their subsequent relationship and the socioeconomic situation of the colonised. An example is the 1840 *Treaty of Waitangi*, which regulated land ownership, sovereignty and political rights of Maori in the new state of New Zealand. Maori have since enjoyed a relatively secure status in comparison to many other colonised peoples.

CASES: The 2006 European Consensus on Development commits the European Commission, Parliament and Council to policies towards building a more stable and equitable world, implicitly recognising indigenous peoples' interests to those ends, and established August 9 as the International Day of the World's Indigenous Peoples. The EU actively supports projects to 'integrate indigenous issues into all aspects of its external policies' through the *European Instrument for Democracy and Human Rights* (EIDHR) (EUEA, 2015).

Worldwide, the UNDRIP enshrines the cultural rights of indigenous peoples, as do numerous judicial decisions by the UN Human Rights Committee, the UN Committee on Economic, Social and Cultural Rights, the UN Committee on the Elimination of Racial Discrimination, the UN Committee on the Rights of the Child, the Inter-American Court of Human Rights, and the African Commission on Human and People's Rights. The Special Rapporteur of the OHCHR advises which human rights may be considered cultural, and how to further define their content (UNHRC, 2010).

In 2016 the UNGA appointed four advisors to the UN Permanent Forum on Indigenous Issues, to facilitate indigenous peoples' full participation in relevant UN bodies and to secure their free, prior and informed consent for activities that impact them, based on Resolution 70/232.

VIEWS: A common critique of indigenous claims (e.g. Fjordman, 2008) asserts that all peoples, including all Europeans, are equally indigenous, precluding any special claims. Such assertions are generally rejected as they contradict the Martinez-Cobo description.

Other critics question how it is possible that despite well-intentioned legal instruments, indigenous peoples worldwide are still economically and socio-politically disenfranchised (they make up 5% of the world's population and 15% of the world's poorest). Multinational corporations often ignore indigenous interests and claims, and at times employ assassination and intimidation tactics, as in the cases of Canadian mining corporations in Latin America. A just reconciliation, including full exercise of cultural rights, may have to await the moral transition to a sustainable environmental ethic and a reform of global capitalism (Burger, 1990).

Others point out that enshrining indigenous rights and entitlements in legal documents still reflects the patriarchal relationship of 'givers' and 'receivers'. In order to achieve effective decolonisation and cultural safety for indigenous peoples (Ramsden, 2005), the two sides must aim towards a more equitable cooperation. Six major indigenous non-governmental organisations work to circumvent the power differential between states and their indigenous minorities, promoting the legal protection of indigenous rights and self determination worldwide.

CONCL: The cultural rights of indigenous peoples have been affirmed by numerous legal judgments and declarations. As an example for the progress that countries can achieve, Bolivia became a 'plurinational state' in 2009, following the 1989 *ILO Convention 169 concerning Indigenous and Tribal Peoples*. Fully two thirds of Bolivians claim indigenous origins. Similar initiatives have been implemented in Cuba and Venezuela.

However, three major limitations apply to the exercise of cultural rights: Some elements of pre-contact indigenous cultures, such as their religions, were irretrievably extinguished by colonising powers; while the right to practice their own religion is included among their cultural rights, it can no longer be exercised. The lower socioeconomic status and poor state of public health in most indigenous communities, as well as their political disenfranchisement, constitute particular threats to their →human security, especially in light of globalising trends (OHCHR, 2013); occasionally, as in the case of Alberta oil sands mined on the land of the Cree, environmental destruction and loss of land rights hampers the exercise of cultural rights. Some cultural practices have been found to contravene human rights and are thus excluded from cultural rights (Deer, 2010).

To address those limitations and to increase the cultural freedom of indigenous peoples in the multicultural context, concrete measures towards their cultural safety have to be met with some success.

REFERENCES:

Burger, Julian: *The Gaia Atlas of First Peoples: A Future for the Indigenous World*, New York: Anchor Books (1990).

Deer, M. Kenneth: *The Complexities in Practical Terms: Cultural practices contrary to human rights, possible limitations to cultural rights, tensions around who defines culture and rights*, presented at an OHCHR Seminar, sct.2. Geneva (2010): www.ohchr.org (accessed 04/2016).

European Union External Action (EUEA): *EU's Policy on Indigenous Peoples* (2015): www.eeas.europa.eu (accessed 04/2016).

Fjordman: "Creating a European Indigenous Peoples' Movement", *The Brussels Journal* (04/06/2008): www.brusselsjournal.com (accessed 04/2016).

Office of the High Commissioner for Human Rights (OHCHR): "Poverty and economic, social and cultural rights", *OHCHR Report* (2013) 48: www.ohchr.org (accessed 04/2016).

Ramsden, Irihapeti: "Toward Cultural Safety", in Dianne Wepa (ed.): *Cultural Safety in Aetearoa New Zealand*, Auckland: Pearson Education (2005).

Martinez-Cobo, Jose: *Study of the Problem of Discrimination Against Indigenous Populations*, UN Doc. E/CN.4/Sub.2/1986/7Add. 4.

UN General Assembly: *Declaration on the Rights of Indigenous Peoples*, A/RES/61/L.67, New York: UN (2007).

UNHCHR: *Frequently Asked Questions on Economic, Social and Cultural Rights*, Fact Sheet no. 33 (2007).

UN Human Rights Council: *Report of the Independent Expert in the Field of Cultural Rights*, A/HRC/14/36 (2010): www.refworld.org (accessed 04/2016).

Wiessner, Siegfried: "The Cultural Rights of Indigenous Peoples: Achievements and Continuing Challenges", 22(1) *European Journal of International Law* (2011) 121.

Sabina Lautensach

Information
(Access to I.)

DEF: A right of access to governmental information can be seen as the main element of a broader right of free access to media/information (or 'Freedom of Information', as it is often referred to). As such, it includes access to cultural information (e.g. statistics, decisions on regulations and permissions, funding and state aid, as well as budget plans).

INSTR/CASES: In its developing case-law, the ECtHR has found in a highly controversial ruling, that Article 10 para. 1, ECHR constitutes a principle right of access to governmental information for journalists, as well as researchers, and for non-governmental organisations insofar as they play a 'role as a public watchdog of similar importance to that of the press' [GUSEVA, 2015]. Covering all EU institutions, Article 15 TFEU secures a right of access to official documents for everyone in the framework of a general 'concept of openness', which is substantiated in *Regulation (EC) No 1049/2001*. At present, the United Nations Economic Commission for Europe (UNECE) *Convention on Access to Information, Public Participation in Decision-making and Access to Justice in Environmental Matters* (Aarhus Convention) can be seen as the most powerful international legal regime concerning access to governmental information for everyone. It covers notably governmental information on 'cultural sites', which are defined in Article 1 of the UNESCO *World Heritage Convention*, 1972, and could serve as a model for legal instruments covering freedom of information in other domains, such as culture and media. Often less elaborate 'freedom of information' legislation exists on all administrative levels in many democratic countries; it marks a cultural turn from governmental secrecy to the principle of 'open government'.

CONCL: Claiming a right of access to governmental information, with or without any explicit personal interest in the information, can help people to enforce their (human) rights or to meaningfully participate in public debate. For example, this could mean putting pressure on an administration, by spreading, or merely threatening to spread, some information out of its control, or by using the material to pursue a judicial remedy. Future discourses on 'open government' will increasingly have to address private institutions which perform public functions and are, at present, widely uncovered in national freedom of information legislation.

REFERENCES:

GUSEVA v. BULGARIA (ECtHR 17/02/2015, 6987/07).
gijn.org/resources/freedom-of-information-laws/ (accessed 2/2016).
www.humanrightsinitiative.org (accessed 2/2016).

Jörg Michael Schindler

Intangible Cultural Heritage

DEF: Intangible cultural heritage (ICH) is defined by the 2003 UNESCO *Convention for the Safeguarding of the Intangible Cultural Heritage* (ICH Convention) as 'the practices, representations, expressions, knowledge, skills – as well as the instruments, objects, artefacts and cultural spaces associated therewith – that communities, groups and, in some cases, individuals recognize as part of their cultural heritage. This intangible cultural heritage, transmitted from generation to generation, is constantly recreated by communities and groups in response to their environment, their interaction with nature and their history, and provides them with a sense of identity and continuity, thus promoting respect for cultural diversity and human creativity' (Article 2.1). It is also popularly known as 'folklore' (even if this terminology is much criticized by anthropologists), or sometimes referred to as 'traditional cultural expressions' (for the purposes of →intellectual property protection).

INSTR: The purposes of the ICH Convention are primarily to safeguard ICH, to ensure respect for it, to raise awareness, and to promote international cooperation (Article 1). Raising awareness is probably the main medium through which those objectives can be reached, and is an objective in itself, according to the ICH Convention.

The main mechanisms through which these objectives are accomplished are the lists created by the ICH Convention. Two of those lists are modelled after the *World Heritage Convention*, and they are the Representative List of the Intangible Cultural Heritage of Humanity, and the List of Intangible Cultural Heritage in Need of Urgent Safeguarding. The ICH Convention also innovates in creating an Inventory of Best Practices for the Safeguarding of the Intangible Cultural Heritage.

Another important innovation of the ICH Convention is the inclusion of communities in cultural heritage management, as opposed to only States (which had been the case with other conventions under UNESCO).

Finally, the Convention only allows for the listing of ICH that complies with universal human rights standards, thus creating a human rights exception that is seen as a victory for the universality of human rights.

The Council of Europe *Framework Convention on the Value of Cultural Heritage for Society* ('Faro Convention', 2005) includes ICH and proposes, similar to the UNESCO instrument, a modern, people-centred approach to cultural heritage based on human rights. However, it also differs from the latter, e.g. with regard to its focus on ascribed values and wider socio-economic 'functions' of heritage.

CASES: There are very few cases that deal directly with ICH. The Inter-American Court has referred to ICH and the ICH Convention in three separate opinions by Judge Cançado Trindade (now at the International Court of Justice). In those three cases [MOIWANA v. SURINAME; YAKYE AXA v. PARAGUAY; SAWHOYAMAXA v. PARAGUAY, 2006], all involving indigenous or traditional communities, Judge Cançado Trindade used the ICH Convention to build an argument for a 'universal juridical conscience' around the protection of traditional cultures.

At the ECtHR and its, until 1998 operating, European Commission of Human Rights, there are no cases dealing directly with the term, but related issues came up under the ordinary term 'folklore'. The two most relevant of these cases at the Court [UNITED MACEDONIAN ORGANISATION ILINDEN-PIRIN AND OTHERS v. BULGARIA, 2011] and [SIDIROPULOS AND OTHERS v. GREECE, 1997] before the Commission have to do with the right to freedom of association (Article 11 of the ECHR) of groups seeking to obtain special minority status to 'Macedonian' minorities in those countries, and the parties have invoked traditional folklore as one of the reasons why the association exists and its goals are justified. In both cases, there was a violation of Article 11 ECHR.

VIEWS: The prevailing opinion in the literature is that ICH is an important concept to enshrine a move towards protecting the cultures of peoples, beyond the nation-state. Because the ICH Convention includes in its provisions the need to have communities participate in the safeguarding process, the majority of the literature sees that as a victory for the international protection of cultural heritage and cultural rights more generally. Similarly, the fast pace of ratification of the ICH Convention (which has been ratified by 163 States at the time of writing, which is just shy of 12 years since the approval of the text).

However, more critical opinions challenge whether the ICH Convention can actually change the dynamics of state-centric protection of cultural heritage in international law. These authors argue that the ICH Convention only pays lip service to community involvement, and that ultimately it is still the state that serves as the ultimate arbiter of what ICH is, whether it should be protected, and in what terms. As a result, communities can have the meanings of their ICH controlled by the state, potentially to their detriment.

CONCL: ICH is a powerful concept, and the immediate and widespread acceptance of the ICH Convention means those structures are here to stay. Awareness can and should be raised to ICH using the mechanisms under the ICH Convention, and particularly the Inventory of Best Practices for the Safeguarding of the Intangible Cultural Heritage. Community involvement is a welcome development in heritage management in international law, but one must be wary of the limits of this possibility in the implementation of the ICH Convention.

In terms of judicial use of ICH and the ICH Convention, it is still limited, but it may be widely used as a means to protect the right to cultural identity in international human rights cases. But the human rights exception in the ICH Convention needs to be taken into account, and one must be mindful that cultural identity will only be protected with the help of the ICH Convention in terms that comply with universally recognized standards.

Similarly, ICH and the ICH Convention should be considered in the design of other policies on cultural diversity, including intellectual property rights, and the protection of cultural industries. Because the ICH Convention has come largely to symbolise cultural diversity, law-makers must be mindful of making the ICH Convention work harmoniously with other programs designed in the future.

REFERENCES:

Blake, Janet: *Commentary on the UNESCO 2003 Convention on the Safeguarding of the Intangible Cultural Heritage*, London: Institute for Art and Law (2006).

Bortolotto, Chiara (ed.): *Le patrimoine culturel immaterial: Enjeux d'une nouvelle catégorie*, Paris: Éditions de la Maison des sciences de l'homme (2011).

Brown, Michael F: "Heritage Trouble: Recent Work on the Protection of Intangible Cultural Property", *Intl J of Cultural Property* 12 (2005), 40.

Deacon, Harriet; Dondolo, Luvuyo; Mrubata, Mbulelo; and Prosalendis, Sandra: *The Subtle Power of Intangible Heritage: Legal and Financial Instruments for Safeguarding Intangible Heritage*, Cape Town: Human Sciences Research Council (2004).

Kono, Toshiyuki (ed.): *Intangible Cultural Heritage and Intellectual Property: Communities, Cultural Diversity and Sustainable Development*, Mortsel: Intersentia (2009).

Lenzerini, Federico: "Intangible Cultural Heritage: The Living Culture of Peoples", *EJIL* 22(1) (2011), 101.

Lixinski, Lucas, "Selecting Heritage: The Interplay of Art, Politics and Identity", *EJIL* 22(1) (2011), 81.

Lixinski, Lucas: *Intangible Cultural Heritage in International Law*, Oxford: Oxford University Press (2013).

Seitel, Peter (ed.), *Safeguarding Traditional Culture: A Global Assessment*, Washington, D.C.: Smithsonian Institution (2001).

Smith, Laurajane; and Akagawa, Natsuko (eds.): *Intangible Heritage*, London: Routledge (2009).

Lucas Lixinski

Intellectual Property and Human Rights

DEF: On the face of it, intellectual property (IP) rights and human rights pursue two different rationales: IP rights as recognised in Part II, Section 1–7 of the *TRIPS Agreement* – a total of 8 IP types, including plant breeders' rights – specify rights of right-holders to determine conditions for how new products are to be commercially available to the public. In addition, most national legislations enable research that attempts to 'invent around' a patented technology. In contrast, human rights tend towards increasing the availability and physical and economic accessibility of new products. Moreover, the proprietary logic of IP legislation contrasts with cultural dimensions of human rights treaties: Since most IP legislations only recognise written descriptions to determine and protect novelty, the principle that IP rights cannot be extended to the usage of traditional knowledge or intangible heritage may be circumvented – which could work either to the detriment or to the benefit of traditional communities.

INSTR: The balance that human rights treaties provide is found particularly in the ICESCR, Article 15(1). It does recognise the moral and material interests of those contributing with literary, artistic and scientific works (15(1)(c)), as well as the right of everyone to enjoy the benefits of scientific progress and its applications (15(1)(b)), and the right of everyone to participate in cultural life (15(1)(a)).

While Article 15(1)(a) and 15(1)(c) have been clarified by General Comment 21 and General Comment 17 of the UN Committee on Economic, Social and Cultural Rights, Article 15(1)(b) has been subject to clarification by the *Venice Statement on the Right to Enjoy the Benefits of Scientific Progress and its Applications* (UNESCO 2009). General Comment 17 clarifies that the rights recognised by

ICESCR Article 15(1)(c) do not equal intellectual property rights, as human rights are inalienable and belonging only to the person or collective from where the invention originated, while IP can be granted, revoked and traded. A resolution (UN Sub-Commission on Human Rights 2000) and statement (UN Committee on Economic, Social and Cultural Rights 2001) were instrumental in highlighting the IP-HR-tensions.

The issue of who should be considered an 'author' of scientific production has been discussed by the former UN Special Rapporteur on the right to culture, clarifying that the protection of the moral and material interest can also include inventors, for inventions with which they have a strong personal link (UN Special rapporteur 2015, para. 34).

CASES: IP has been found by the ECtHR to fall under the right to property as recognised by Additional Protocol 1 (AP1) to the ECHR. The most controversial decision is [ANHEUSER-BUSCH INC, 2007], where human rights protection was extended to mere *applications* for a registration of trademarks.

Hence, the human right to property becomes justification for a stronger IP protection, and the two specifications for the right to property as only subject to the 'public interest' (AP1 Article 1(1)) or 'general interest' (AP1 Article 1(2)) have not been able to challenge this human rights justification of stronger IP protection.

However, Article 10 ECHR on freedom of expression has also been invoked: In [NEJI AND SUNDE KOLMISOPPI, 2013] and [ASHBY DONALD AND OTHERS, 2013] the ECtHR found the use of a copyrighted work to be an exercise of freedom of expression, even if this use resulted in a copyright infringement.

In the Court of Justice of the European Union (CJEU), the moral interests have been found to be encompassed by the *IP Enforcement Directive* (2004/48/EC) Article 13(1) – as the term 'actual prejudice suffered' encompasses moral interests: [CHRISTIAN LIFFERS, 2016].

VIEWS: There are several controversial cases of so-called bio-piracy, most of which are dealt with in appeal bodies within the patent offices. Within WIPO, the negotiations for international legal instruments on traditional knowledge (TK) and genetic resources – whose outcome is still not possible to assess – only resulted in higher awareness, the development of new tools to disclose prior art information, and an exchange of tools and experiences. While human rights provisions were found in the first drafts of proposed international legal instruments on TK and genetic resources, they have subsequently been removed.

There are two main approaches to IP and TK: a defensive approach, where the main purpose is to avoid bio-piracy, and a positive approach, where legislative provisions allow for inventions by farmers of indigenous peoples to be recognised and granted time-limited protection. Examples of the latter include the India Protection of Plant Varieties and Farmers' Rights Act of 2001 (Act 53), Section 39(1)(i), the Malaysian New Plant Varieties Act of 2004 (Act 634), Section 13(1)(d), and the Thailand Plant Varieties Protection Act of 1999 (Act 2542), with a separate chapter entitled 'Protection of Local Domestic Plant Varieties'. None of these states have been subject to criticism by any WTO bodies for these legislations (Haugen 2014). Hence, the TRIPS Agreement, unlike the UPOV Convention that regulates plant breeders' rights, give states much leeway in formulating legislation.

CONCL: There are a diverse range of encounters between human rights and IP (Haugen 2007). An obvious encounter where IP and human rights can be mutually enriching is in the realm of copyright, as these rights have a stronger link to the person than patents or trademarks – which used to be termed 'industrial property rights'. The encounter between IP and human rights in the realm of patents is more controversial and complex. Patents provide for time-limited exclusive rights over the commercial utilisation of a protected invention, and such IP protection is primarily enjoyed by corporations, not persons. As seen above, inventors fall under the protection scope of the ICESCR Article 15(1)(c), but only for inventions with which they have a strong personal link.

The WIPO runs two processes where human rights could have been included: First in the context of the Intergovernmental Committee on Intellectual Property and Genetic Resources, TK and Folklore, launched in 2000. Second, in the context of the Development Agenda, launched in 2005. As the ICESCR does recognise the balance between rewarding inventors and promoting access to new inventions, and also recognises the need to make 'full use of technical and scientific knowledge' in the context of → food (Article 11(2)(a)), and measures for the prevention, treatment and control of diseases in the context of health (Article 12(2)(c)), this failure to reflect issues through a human rights lens can be seen as a missed opportunity.

REFERENCES:

Haugen, Hans Morten: "The Right to Food, Farmers' Rights and Intellectual Property Rights: Can Competing Law Be Reconciled?", in Lea Brilmayer, Priscilla Claeys, Nadia Lombek and Adrienna Wong (eds.), *Rethinking Food Systems: Structural Challenges, New Strategies and the Law*, Springer, Heidelberg (2014).

Haugen, Hans Morten: "Patent rights and human rights: exploring their relationships", *Journal of World Intellectual Property* 10(2), 97–124 (2007).

UN Committee on Economic, Social and Cultural Rights: *E/C.12/2001/15, Human rights and intellectual property* (2001).

UN Committee on Economic, Social and Cultural Rights: *E/C.12/GC/17. General Comment No. 17 (2005). The right of everyone to benefit from the protection of the moral and material interests resulting from any scientific, literary or artistic production of which he or she is the author (article 15, paragraph 1 (c), of the Covenant)* (2006).

UN Committee on Economic, Social and Cultural Rights: *E/C.12/GC/21 General comment No. 21. Right of everyone to take part in cultural life (art. 15, para. 1 (a), of the International Covenant on Economic, Social and Cultural Rights)* (2009).

UN Special rapporteur: *Report of the Special Rapporteur in the field of cultural rights, A/70/279* (2015).

UN Sub-Commission on Human Rights: *E/CN.4/Sub.2/RES/2000/7, Intellectual property rights and human rights* (2000).

UNESCO: *The Right to Enjoy the Benefits of Scientific Progress and its Applications*, Paris, UNESCO (2009).

ANHEUSER-BUSCH INC. v. PORTUGAL (ECtHR 11/01/2007, 73049/01).

ASHBY DONALD AND OTHERS v. FRANCE (ECtHR 10/01/2013, 36769/08).

CHRISTIAN LIFFERS v. PRODUCCIONES MANDARINA SL AND MEDIASET ESPANA COMUNICACION (CJEU, SA [2016], Case C-99/15).

NEJI AND SUNDE KOLMISOPPI v. SWEDEN (ECtHR 19/02/2013, 40397/12).

Hans Morten Haugen

Inter-American Human Rights System

The Organization of American States (OAS), an international organisation comprised of 35 independent countries, created the Inter-American human rights system. This system is responsible for ensuring and monitoring implementation of human rights guarantees in the states that are members of the OAS. The OAS has drafted and promulgated multiple human rights documents and treaties. In 1948, the member states adopted the *American Declaration of the Rights and Duties of Man* (the American Declaration) and later promulgated a multilateral treaty: the *American Convention on Human Rights* (the Convention). These are the leading international instruments of the Inter-American system for the protection of human rights. All member states of the OAS are bound to respect the American Declaration; on the other hand, the compliance with the Convention is only obligatory to states that are a party to the Convention. The system contains two bodies: the Inter-American Commission on Human Rights (the Commission) and the Inter-American Court of Human Rights (the Court). Both entities can decide individual complaints concerning alleged human rights abuses (the recommendations of the Commission are not legally binding; the judgments of the Court are binding) and may request that a state adopt emergency protective measures to prevent irreparable harm. In addition, the Commission engages in a range of human rights monitoring and promotion activities, such as country or thematic studies. Moreover, the Court can issue advisory opinions on issues pertaining to the interpretation of the human rights documents and treaties, thereby assisting the member states in complying with their international human rights obligations.

The American Declaration on Human Rights contains several cultural rights, such as the right to education (Article XII) and the right to taken part in cultural life (Article XIII). The American Convention on Human Rights, however, hardly pays attention to cultural rights. In 1988, the OAS General Assembly adopted the *San Salvador Protocol on Economic, Social and Cultural Rights*, which contains provisions similar to the → ICESCR, including the right to take part in the cultural life of the community (Article 14). No specific rights concerning indigenous peoples or minorities were included. However, the Inter-American Commission and Court have dealt with many cases concerning indigenous peoples and their cultural rights, especially in relation to land issues. Landmark cases are [AWAS TINGI,, 2001], [MOIWANA COMMUNITY, 2005], [YAKYE AXA INDIGENOUS COMMUNITY, 2005] and [SAWHOYAMAXA INDIGENOUS COMMUNITY, 2006].

REFERENCES:

Buergenthal, Thomas and Shelton, Dinah: *Protecting Human Rights in the Americas: Cases and Materials*, Kehl: NP Engel (1995).

Goldman, Robert K.: "History in Action: The Inter-American Human Rights System and the Role of the Inter-American Commission on Human Rights" (2009) 31 HRQ 856.

Harris, David and Livingstone, Stephen (eds.): *The Inter-American System of Human Rights*, Oxford: Oxford University Press (1998).

Pasqualucci, Jo: *The Practice and Procedure of the Inter-American Court of Human Rights*. Cambridge: Cambridge University Press (2013).

Pasqualucci, Jo: "The Americas", in D. Moeckli, S. Shah and S. Sivakumaran (eds.). *International Human Rights Law*, Oxford: Oxford University Press (2014).

MAYAGNA (SUMO) INDIGENOUS COMMUNITY OF AWAS TINGI v. REPUBLIC OF NICARAGUA (Inter-American Court of Human Rights 31/08/2001, Ser. C, Case No. 79).

MOIWANA COMMUNITY v. SURINAME (Inter-American Court of Human Rights 15/06/2005, Series C No. 124).

SAWHOYAMAXA INDIGENOUS COMMUNITY v. PARAGUAY (Inter-American Court of Human Rights 29/03/2006, Series C No. 146).

YAKYE AXA INDIGENOUS COMMUNITY v. PARAGUAY (Inter-American Court of Human Rights 17/06/2005, Series C No. 125).

www.cidh.org (accessed 3/2016).

www.corteidh.or.cr (accessed 3/2016).

Yvonne Donders

Intercultural Competence

DEF: Intercultural competence can be divided into cultural sensitivity, awareness and skills. Acquiring and applying these competences is a normative demand on decision-makers in order to enhance satisfaction and compliance with the outcome of proceedings and, thereby, to strengthen the legitimacy and accountability of political and legal institutions in culturally diverse societies. As a subcategory, intercultural judicial competence requires judges to constantly strike a fair balance between establishing a universally valid (human rights) order while, at the same time, recognizing legitimate cultural diversity.

INSTR: Recent policy recommendations of global and regional international organisations consider acquiring intercultural competence(s) as the normative demand of a 'global culture of human rights' and as one of the crucial preconditions for stepping into meaningful interactions and successful intercultural dialogues between and among members of culturally diverse societies (CoE 2008, UNESCO 2013). During the 'International Decade for the Rapprochement of Cultures, 2013–2022', proclaimed by the General Assembly of the UN (GA, Res. 67/104), the UN-member states are particularly called upon to enhance their activities relating to interreligious and intercultural dialogue.

Generally, competent intercultural interaction is associated with promoting social cohesion, development, as well as peaceful and harmonious interaction within and among societies (GA, Res. 68/126). From the specific perspective of the Arabic world, applying 'methods and ethics' for cultural exchange are deemed crucial for addressing prevailing challenges such as the Arab–Israeli conflict or the fabrication of a clash between Islam and the West (ALESCO 2006). Due to the effects of globalisation, migration and the afflux of asylum seekers, intercultural competence is, also from the European viewpoint, considered indispensable to avoid a climate of stereotypical perception, intolerance, discrimination and exploitation of minorities (CoE 2008). The CoE defines normative framework conditions facilitating the acquisition and practice of intercultural competence, namely the common values of democracy, human rights and fundamental freedoms, the rule of law, pluralism, tolerance and non-discrimination towards minorities, equal dignity and mutual respect (CoE 2008 at 18 et seq.).

It is commonly acknowledged that public authorities carry a particular responsibility for providing these legal and political preconditions for the democratic governance of cultural diversity. Particular emphasis is placed on 'teaching and learning' of intercultural competences (Coe 2008 at 28 et seq.) and on the crucial role education-providers play for the democratic citizenship and human rights education of individuals (UNESCO 2013 at 22, CoE 2010). The significance attached to human rights reveals that the expectation of exercising intercultural competence has a twofold effect on the judiciary: courts are both providers and addressees of intercultural competence. As providers domestic and international adjudicative bodies can authoritatively set the legal and political framework conditions for successful intercultural exchange. As addressees, universal and regional human rights bodies are required to respect and recognize the diversity of humans when deciding a particular case and when establishing an international legal order universally valid for ethnic, religious, linguistic minorities as well as majorities. In this regard, they are expected to practice intercultural judicial skills in managing cultural diversity (Wiater, 2010) – that is in integrating cultural concerns (Ringelheim, 2008) into the interpretation and application of human rights.

CASES: Considering these political expectations in evaluating facets of, and framework conditions for intercultural competence in current legal practice, different *theoretical principles* and *legal methods* can be identified in the case-law of the ECtHR and other human rights bodies.

In assessing culturally motivated claims of applicants as well as submissions of contracting states, the ECtHR refers to several *theoretical principles* as superior normative reference points. By means of its jurisprudence, the ECtHR aims at fostering democracy as a 'fundamental feature of the European public order' and as 'the only political model' contemplated by and compatible with the ECHR [UNITED COMMUNIST PARTY OF TURKEY AND OTHERS v. TURKEY, para. 45]. Hallmarks of the European democratic society envisioned are the criteria of 'pluralism, tolerance and broadmindedness' [LEYLA ŞAHIN, para. 108]. In the ECtHR's view these demands of democracy dictate that – although individual interests must on occasion be subordinated to those of a group – democracy does not simply mean that the views of a majority must always prevail. Rather, it is important to strike a balance, which ensures the fair and proper treatment of people from minorities and avoids any abuse of a dominant position [YOUNG, JAMES AND WEBSTER v. THE UNITED KINGDOM, para. 63]. Religious pluralism is a main sub-principle constituting the pluralistic nature of European societies [KOKKINAKIS v. GREECE, para. 31].

The ECtHR defines further 'fundamental values' of democracy binding on state authorities in solving cultural conflicts on the domestic level: The rule of law, especially the protection of every individual from arbitrary exercise of state power in decision-making processes as well as the absolute prohibition of torture and of inhuman or degrading treatment or punishment [SOERING v. THE UNITED KINGDOM, para. 88] are of core importance in this regard. Also, the principles of equal dignity and equal enjoyment of rights form part of the unquestionable values of democracy [ÜNDÜZ v. TURKEY, para. 40]. Ethnic equality and gender equality are sub-principles of this democratic concept and express 'key principles underlying the Convention and a goal to be achieved by member States of the Council of Europe' [ABDULAZIZ, CABALES AND BALKANDALI v. THE UNITED KINGDOM, para. 78]. In pursuing this aim state authorities generally have to act as 'neutral and impartial organiser' of pluralist and often divergent societal interests [LEYLA ŞAHIN, para. 107]. In case of the particular vulnerability of a societal group, the ECtHR can impose the obligation on state authorities to positively protect group members from racist-induced violence [NACHOVA AND OTHERS v. BULGARIA, 2005, Nos. 43577/98 and 43579/98, para. 164] and to affirmatively promote substantive equality. As a possible effect, cultural claims of the applicant can require the introduction of appropriate exceptions from otherwise applicable legal obligations [THLIMMENOS, para. 48]. Without explicitly recognizing a 'right to culture', the ECtHR acknowledges that cultural concerns (e.g. the claim for particular linguistic rights, protection of cultural and natural heritage) can be protected under core civil rights, such as the right to respect for private and family life, the right to freedom of expression and the right to education (ECtHR, Research Division, 2011).

The ECtHR applies these normative precepts to particular cases by means of different *methodical tools*: On the level of interpretation the 'principle of effectiveness' [KLASS AND OTHERS v. GERMANY, para. 34] and the conviction that the ECHR is 'a living instrument' call for an understanding of the rights guaranteed which corresponds to the social reality and the 'present-day conditions' in European societies [TYRER v. THE UNITED KINGDOM, para. 31]. This view of the Convention has two effects: It allows integrating cultural changes and social developments into the interpretation of the ECHR and, at the same time, enables the Court to demand changes in cultural values and practices. For instance, the ECtHR set an end to the criminal punishment of certain homosexual acts in a contracting state – despite the religious reasoning of the state concerned [DUDGEON v. THE UNITED KINGDOM]. The method of comparative law – i.e. evaluating if domestic legal orders of the contracting states or other European and international law instruments form a 'European consensus' on the subject-matter – is another key-method of the ECtHR in assessing the legitimacy of cultural claims of applicants or contracting states. The Court considers the (non-)existence of common ground between the laws of the contracting states as relevant in defining the breadth of the margin of appreciation attributed to national authorities in deciding issues of social, religious, ethical or ethnical relevance [LAUTSI AND OTHERS v. ITALY para. 70; DUDGEON, para.60].

The practice of other human rights bodies reveals that the methodical approaches of the ECtHR are not limited to European human rights adjudication but exemplify facets of the global status quo of intercultural judicial skills: Establishing normative guidelines, more concretely, a core of fundamental untouchable rights and principles which no culture is permitted to exceed, is also adopted by other regional human rights bodies, e.g. by the IACtHR on the fundamental nature of the right to life in the case of the 'Street Children' [VILLAGRAN-MORALES ET AL. v. GUATEMALA]. The rule of rendering treaty interpretation effective – particularly by taking cultural traditions into account in determining the scope of human rights protection – is also applied by the HRCee [FRANCIS HOPU AND TEPOAITU BESSERT v. FRANCE], the IACtHR [THE XÁKMOK KÁSEK INDIGENOUS COMMUNITY v. PARAGUAY], as well as the ACHPR [ENDOROIS WELFARE COUNCIL v. KENYA].

VIEWS: Scientific definitions of intercultural competence differ like the notion itself – mainly depending on disciplinary focal points. As an alternative to intercultural competence (for an overview see Deardoff, 2009) some refer to 'cross cultural competence' (Chiu et al. 2013). The various definitions correspond to an understanding of intercultural competence as a combination of knowledge, empathy, motivation and attitude as well as a set of linguistic, cognitive, affective and behavioral skills. Following Chen and Starosta (1997, 1998, 2000), intercultural competence incorporates the three dimensions of sensitivity, awareness and skills. While sensitivity concerns the individual capacity to comprehend and appreciate cultural differences, awareness refers to the ability of understanding how culture affects thinking, behaviour, and interactions.

Translating these findings into the logic of human rights protection and adding insights of legal anthropology, the following framework emerges: On the level of sensitivity and awareness, socio-legal studies point to the interrelatedness of (human rights) law and culture, and particularly to the dichotomy of this relationship. On the one hand, every individual is subject to the process of 'enculturation' and unconsciously marked by the normative categories and standards of his/her culture. In this regard, exercising the 'right to culture' can be crucial for establishing one's identity and for the belonging to a social group. On the other hand, one's culture cannot be perceived as a static, homogenous and unified entity of values and practices 'capturing' the individual's free choice (Hoekema, 2005 at 11). Rather, both, the definition of cultural values and practices as well as precepts of state legality are social constructs, embedded in the field of power within and among social groups, produced through and questioned by hybridisation and, accordingly, open for change (Merry, 2001 at 46). This finding influences the level of skills: Just as cultural input can and must affect international and domestic legal systems, (human rights) law can evoke changes in culture. Although intercultural competences include the skills of respect and cultural humility, cultural concerns and claims are open for critical reconstruction.

The need to continuously construct and reconstruct the corpus of universally valid human rights by means of a critical attitude towards the culturally founded 'self' and the 'other' is approved by philosophical findings on 'transcultural' approaches to the claim of universality of human rights with respect to regional particularities of human rights concepts (for differentiation to 'neutral' and 'intercultural' approaches see Dhouib, 2014).

CONCL: From a legal standpoint, addressing the normative demand of intercultural competences to public authorities (especially the judiciary) has to be approved. It is an essential requirement for enhancing satisfaction and compliance with the outcome of proceedings and, thereby, for strengthening the legitimacy and accountability of political and legal institutions in culturally diverse societies. In particular, the general legal principles of justice and equality require the judicial branch to act in an intercultural competent manner when interpreting and applying (human rights) law.

However, exercising intercultural competence in adjudicating does not mean that every cultural value or practice, every claim founded in the religious, ethnical or social background of the individual(s) concerned has to be legally acknowledged and translated into the scope of human rights protection (harmful cultural practices). Rather, findings of socio-legal studies support the legal practice that human rights norms and judicial decisions can legitimately set limits to claims founded in the cultural diversity of the person concerned. Superior normative principles such as a core of untouchable and culturally unquestionable rights or the claims of pluralism and democracy can call for cultural changes and serve as guidelines in elaborating a demarcation between achieving human rights harmonisation and recognising diversity.

Yet, intercultural judicial skills are underdeveloped as long as human rights bodies do not realise the major challenges of transparency, changing perspectives and critical reconstruction. Both in defining superior theoretical principles and in applying legal methods to the particular case, the decisive factors influencing the Court's findings have to be revealed in order to guarantee that minority positions are sufficiently considered. This is a demand of the principle of procedural justice as part of intercultural judicial competences. By contrast to actively and independently reconstructing the cultural (religious, social, ethnical) claim at hand, the prerogative of assessing the legitimacy of 'cultural concerns' is extensively left to state authorities in the current practice of the ECtHR: In concretising the 'European consensus', the Court mainly refers to legal commitments of the ECHR contracting states. The 'margin of appreciation' doctrine is founded on the Court's conviction that – in religious, social or ethnical matters of particular controversy (e.g. religious symbols in public sphere) – national authorities, 'who by reason of their direct and continuous contact with the vital forces of their countries are in principle better placed than an international court to evaluate local needs and conditions' and to assess the necessity of the human rights interference [CHAPMAN, para. 91]. This approach is problematic. The demands of social justice attribute an active role to European human rights supervision in solving legal pluralistic conflicts (on legal pluralism see Benda-Beckmann, 2006), i.e. conflicts between precepts of the cultural normativity of applicants and state legality. A more progressive approach – and, in this regard, a higher level of intercultural judicial competence – is adopted by the CC of Colombia (exemplified by Isa 2014 at 739 et sqq.): In determining whether intercultural consensus on the core of culturally untouchable rights exists, the CC not only refers to human rights treaties, but also to testimonies of members of the minority (indigenous people) and to studies from anthropology and legal sociology dealing with the minority practices and values. This methodological openness should serve as a role model for other human rights bodies.

REFERENCES:

Arab League Educational, Cultural and Scientific Organization (ALECSO): "The Abu Dhabi Declaration on the Arab Position on Dialogue and Cultural Diversity", January 2006.

Benda-Beckmann, Franz von/ Benda-Beckmann, Keebet von: "The Dynamics of Change and Continuity in Plural Legal Orders", Journal of Legal Pluralism and Unofficial Law 53/54 (2006), 1.

Chen, Guo-Ming; Starosta, William J.: "A review of the concept of intercultural sensitivity", Human Communication 1 (1997), 1.

Chen, Guo-Ming; Starosta, William J.: "A review of the concept of intercultural awareness", Human Communication 2 (1998–9), 27.

Chen, Guo-Ming; Starosta, William J.: "The development and validation of the Intercultural Sensitivity Scale", Human Communication 3 (2000), 1.

Chiu, Chi-Yue; Lonner, Walter J., Matsumoto, David; Ward, Colleen: "Cross-Cultural Competence: Theory, Research, and Application", Journal of Cross-Cultural Psychology 44(6) 2013, 843.

Council of Europe: "White Paper on Intercultural Dialogue. Living together as equals in dignity", Strasbourg: Council of Europe Publishing (2008).

Council of Europe: "Council of Europe Charter on Education for Democratic Citizenship and Human Rights Education. Recommendation CM/Rec(2010)7 and explanatory memorandum 2010", Strasbourg: Council of Europe Publishing (2010).

Deardoff, Darla K.: "Synthesizing Conceptualizations of Intercultural Competence", in Darla K. Deardoff (ed.) *The SAGE Handbook of Intercultural Competence*, Los Angeles: SAGE (2009), 264.

Dhouib, Sarhan: "Unrechtserfahrung und die Universalisierung der Menschenrechte", in Johannes Ebert/Ronald Grätz (eds.) *Menschenrechte und Kultur*, Göttingen: Steidl (2014), 53.

European Court of Human Rights, Research Division: *Cultural rights in the case-law of the European Court of Human Rights*, Strasbourg: Council of Europe/European Court of Human Rights (2011).

General Assembly of the United Nations: "Promotion of interreligious and intercultural dialogue, understanding and cooperation for peace", Res. 67/104 adopted on 17 December 2012.

General Assembly of the United Nations: "Promotion of interreligious and intercultural dialogue, understanding and cooperation for peace", Res. 68/126 adopted on 18 December 2013.

Hoekema, André: "European Legal Encounters between Minority and Majority Culture: Cases of Interlegality", Journal of Legal Pluralism and Unofficial Law 51 (2005), 1.

Isa, Felipe Gómez: "Cultural Diversity, Legal Pluralism, and Human Rights from an Indigenous Perspective: The Approach by the Colombian Constitutional Court and the Inter-American Court of Human Rights", Human Rights Quarterly 36 (2014), 722.

Merry, Sally E.: "Changing rights, changing culture", in Jane K. Cowen/Marie-B. Dembour/ Richard A. Wilson (eds.) *Culture and Rights – Anthropological Perspectives*, Cambridge: (Cambridge University Press) 2001, 31.

Ringelheim, Julie: *Integrating Cultural Concerns in the Interpretation of General Individual Rights – Lessons from the International Human Rights Case Law*, Background paper to the fortieth session of the Committee on Economic, Social and cultural rights (2008).

United Nations Educational, Scientific and Cultural Organization (UNESCO): "Intercultural Competences. Conceptual and Operational Framework", Paris: UNESCO (2013).

Wiater, Patricia: *Intercultural Dialogue in the Framework of European Human Rights Protection* (White Paper Series – Volume 1), Strasbourg: Council of Europe Publishing (2010).

ABDULAZIZ, CABALES AND BALKANDALI v. THE UNITED KINGDOM (ECtHR 25/5/1985, No. 9214/80; 9473/81; 9474/81).

CHAPMAN v. THE UNITED KINGDOM (ECtHR 18/1/2001, 27238/95).

KOKKINAKIS v. GREECE (ECtHR 25/5/1993, 14307/88).

LEYLA ŞAHIN v. TURKEY (ECtHR 10/12/2005, 44774/98).

THLIMMENOS v. GREECE (ECtHR 6/4/2000, 34369/97.

YOUNG, JAMES AND WEBSTER v. THE UNITED KINGDOM (ECtHR 18/10/1982, 7601/76; 7806/77.

Patricia Wiater

International Covenant on Economic, Social and Cultural Rights (ICESCR)

DEF: The ICESCR is the first international instrument to deal extensively with economic, social and cultural (ESC) rights, the so-called second-generation human rights. ICESCR was adopted at the same time as the ICCPR and entered into force on 3 January 1976. Both ICESCR and ICCPR cover almost entirely all the rights enshrined in the → UDHR. As of today, there are 153 state parties to the ICESCR.

The ICESCR provides *inter alia* for the progressive realisation of the right to: self-determination; social security; an adequate standard of living, including adequate food, clothing and housing; protection of the family; the highest attainable standard of physical and mental health; education; participate in cultural life; benefit from scientific progress; and protection of an author's moral and material interests resulting from scientific, literary or artistic production. While some of the rights enshrined in the ICESCR are clearly categorised as cultural rights, all other ICESCR rights have been recognised as having a cultural dimension and their effective application and implementation is required to be culturally mediated. The implementation of the ICESCR rights is monitored by the Committee on Economic, Social, and Cultural Rights ('the Committee').

While at universal level the ICESCR deals with the ESC rights, the regional counterpart in Europe is the →*Charter of Fundamental Rights and Freedoms* of the →European Union and the *European Social Charter* of the →Council of Europe.

INSTR: Of all international human rights instruments, the ICESCR is the only treaty that refers to cultural rights in its title. Cultural rights under ICESCR encompass the right to education (Articles 13 and 14) and the rights guaranteed in Article 15 (echoing the wording of Article 27 UDHR): the right to take part in cultural life (Article 15 (1)(a)), the right to enjoy the benefits of scientific progress (Article 15 (1)(b)) and the right of authors/writers/artists to the protection of their moral and material interests (Article 15 (1)(c)).

The Committee has repeatedly confirmed that states parties have a core obligation to ensure the satisfaction of minimum essential levels of each of the rights enunciated in the Covenant; however, it accepts that a 'full realization of all economic, social and cultural rights will generally not be able to be achieved in a short period of time" and that their progressive realisation will take place 'under the prevailing circumstances' (CESCR General Comment No. 3, paras. 9–10). As of 2016, the Committee has adopted 23 General Comments; their normative value has been indispensable in affirming that ESC rights retain the same binding effect as civil and political rights. With regard to education, the Committee has defined the general and specific states' obligations and has set the minimum core obligations (which apply irrespective of the availability of resources) whereby states are to 'ensure the right of access to public educational institutions and programmes on a non-discriminatory basis; to ensure that education conforms to the objectives set out in Article 13 (1) ICESCR; to provide primary education for all in accordance with Article 13 (2)(a); to adopt and implement a national educational strategy which includes provision for secondary higher and fundamental education; and to ensure free choice of education without interference from the state or third parties, subject to the conformity with 'minimum educational standards' (CESCR Comment No. 13, para. 57). With respect to Article 15, the Committee has endorsed a broader understanding of 'culture' that includes its individual and collective dimensions and has affirmed the states' obligation to protect people against harmful practices attributed to customs and traditions and to take special measures for groups requiring special attention (migrants, minorities, indigenous peoples, women, children, older persons and persons with disabilities) in order to protect their cultural identity and to enable them to exercise the right to take part in, gain access and contribute to, on equal terms, all spheres of cultural life, i.e. access to one's own cultural and linguistic heritage, access to cultural materials, television programmes, films, theatre and other cultural activities, in accessible forms, etc. The Committee has taken a firm stand by stating that intellectual property rights, which are of temporary nature, are not to be equated with the human right in Article 15 (1) (c) (CESCR General Comment No. 17, para. 3).

The concept of 'cultural rights' is evolving as the concept of 'culture' and the identity of the right-holder is redefined on a normative level (see HRCee jurisprudence; *Maastricht Guidelines on Violations of Economic, Social and Cultural Rights*; *Limburg principles on the Implementation of the ICESCR Rights*, etc). The role of the Human Rights Committee, the Human Rights Council and the UN Special Rapporteurs cannot be ignored in this respect as they have affirmed the holistic nature of 'culture', the overlap with civil and political rights, and the cultural dimension of all human rights, i.e. freedom of religion, freedom of assembly/association, freedom of information. This trend to reinterpret cultural or culture-oriented rights in international law instruments and realign the scope of human rights through the prism of cultural connotations effectively enhanced the status of cultural rights and affirms the interlinkages between cultural rights and the universality of human rights.

CASES: Unlike the ICCPR's interstate or individual's complaint procedure, the ICESCR's implementation mechanism has been considered significantly weaker. The lack of a ICESCR complaints procedure for many decades enforced the belief that only civil and political rights are effectively justiciable. The vaguely worded ICESCR provisions and the nature of the rights therein *vis-a-vis* the ICCPR rights have also reinforced objections as to their justiciability in the international and domestic sphere.

The failure of the international community to adopt an international complaints mechanism under ICESCR for many decades has been pointed as the main reason for the side-stepping of ESC rights. However, domestic courts' decisions have demonstrated that ESC rights benefit from judicial protection and are subject to judicial enforcement in a number of domestic jurisdictions. Following lengthy and protracted negotiations, the Optional Protocol to the ICESCR was finally adopted on 10 December 2008. The Protocol provides a complaints mechanism similar to the one offered by the Optional Protocol to the ICCPR. Individual complaints, called 'communications', can be submitted by or on behalf of individuals or groups of individuals claiming to be victims of a violation of any of the economic, social or cultural rights enshrined in the Covenant. Additionally, the Committee may initiate inquiries if it has received reliable information containing well-founded indications of serious or systematic violations of the Covenant's rights in a state party. Since 2013, the Committee has received a handful of complaints out of which only two were admissible but they do not concern violations of cultural rights [I.D.G., 2014 and LÓPEZ RODRÍGUEZ, 2013].

The collective complaints procedure under ICESCR may stumble upon the Human Rights Committee jurisprudence in terms of the right holders, i.e. members of minorities or minorities themselves. The HRCee, through its interpretation of Article 27 ICCPR, has held that 'culture' manifests itself in many forms as are related rights, which include a way of life that is closely associated with the use of land resources and the activities conducted therein as well as the rights of persons belonging to minorities to enjoy their own culture as a group. While Article 27 does not refer to minorities per se, the HRCee has consistently affirmed that the right to culture can only be realised when exercised 'in a community' (see HRCee case-law). Thus the HRCee has allowed for individual communications which can have impact on the group while communications submitted by groups are not allowed. This link between the individual right to culture and its exercise in the collective context as recognised by the ICCPR is likely to take a new direction by the Committee in future case law. While the line between the individual and the collective right to culture under Article 27 ICCPR is thin, given that their protection depends on whether the 'ability of the minority group to maintain its culture, language or religion' is affected, the Committee may see itself deviating from the HRCee practice.

Furthermore, the extraterritorial scope of the ICESCR has been confirmed in the ICJ jurisprudence [DEMOCRATIC REPUBLIC OF CONGO, 2005, para. 216]. The ICJ held in [ADVISORY OPINION ON THE LEGAL CONSEQUENCES OF THE CONSTRUCTION OF A WALL IN THE OCCUPIED PALESTINIAN TERRITORY, 2004] that states have duties under the ICESCR to 'territories over which a State Party has sovereignty and to those over which that State exercises territorial jurisdiction' and found that Israel had effectively hindered access to educational facilities, water resources, etc. (paras. 111–113).

VIEWS: Since the adoption of the ICESCR concerns have been expressed over the status and justiciability of ESC rights and the lack of certainty about their boundaries and when and how they might be enforced. In the literature of 1970s and 1980s there has been a strong line of argumentation regarding the superiority of civil and political rights *vis-a-vis* the ESC rights alongside a misperceived belief that human rights formulate in a hierarchy of different generations of rights. To a certain extent this assumption explained the neglect and violation of ESC and the delay in establishing an individual or interstate complaint procedure. Cultural rights under the ICESCR and other international instruments have long been viewed as 'luxury'; a narrow understanding of their scope and content has associated cultural rights with the special rights recognised to minorities and indigenous peoples in order to enable them to preserve their cultural identity. While cultural rights are indeed granted to this category of groups, a number of states' have been reluctant to recognise collective cultural rights in fear of state fragmentation and separatism.

Despite the indivisibility and interdependence of all human rights, the fact that the content of cultural rights is less well-defined than civil and political rights, is rather indicative of their exclusion from or underrepresentation in processes of national and international adjudication. At national level there has been a persistent reluctance to afford courts any role in providing judicial remedies to address cultural rights' violations. The fact that the realisation of ESC rights is highly dependent on the budgetary constraints of different state parties has further tested their enforceability (see Article 2 of the Covenant, each state party to the Covenant agrees to 'take steps… to the maximum of its available resources, with a view to achieving progressively the full realization of the rights recognized' in the Covenant). Associated with this is the fact that only 21 states so far have ratified the Optional Protocol and accepted the Committee's competence on receiving complaints. The limited number of states (mainly from Europe and Latin America) indicates which geographical areas have shown an appetite for supranational supervision of the implementation of the ICESCR rights. However, this is only related to the nature of the ICESCR rights, the realisation of which depends on the resources and technical capacity of the states (i.e. technical co-operation, international assistance, etc.). Today, the categorisation of human rights is considered outdated and rather reflecting their chronological development.

CONCL: The considerable delay in adopting a complaint's mechanism and the slow ratification of the Optional Protocol to ICESCR illustrate states' reluctance to affirm ESC rights as legal entitlements and tools for empowerment and justice. Substantive concerns over the justiciability of ESC rights – often linked to sovereignty or procedural issues from a national legal order point of view – have hindered the progressive realisation of these rights. Despite the expectations for numerous cases to be submitted before the Committee once the Optional Protocol entered into force, as of 2016, only few complaints have been submitted. Should the Optional Protocol not receive ratifications from a substantial number of states, this would send a gloomy message over the future of cultural rights. By looking at other successful human rights instruments and complaints procedures, i.e. ICCPR and the Human Rights Committee, for ICESCR to gain flesh and blood and to be turned into a living instrument, more complaints need to be submitted before the Committee in order for it to accumulate a sturdy body of case-law and gain a proper understanding of the ICESCR provisions and their interpretation.

REFERENCES:

International Commission of Jurists: *Courts and the Legal Enforcement of Economic, Social and Cultural Rights–Comparative Experiences of Justiciability*, Geneva: International Commission of Jurists (2008).

Ringelheim, Julie: "Cultural Rights", in Daniel Moeckli, Saengeeta Shah and Sadness Sivakumaran (eds.): *International Human Rights Law*, Oxford: Oxford University Press (2014).

Scheinin, Martin, and Langford, Malcolm: "Evolution or Revolution? Extrapolating from the experience of the Human Rights Committee"

27 *Nordisktidsskrift For Menneskerettigheter* (2009).

Tomuschat, Christian: "An Optional Protocol for the International Covenant on Economic, Social and Cultural Rights", in Klaus Dicke, Stephan Hobe, Karl-Ulrich Meyn, Anne Peters, Eibe Riedel,Hans-Joachim Schütz and Christian Tietje (eds.): *Weltinnenrecht: Liber amicorum Jost Delbrück* , Berlin: Duncker and Humblot, (2005).

Human Rights Council Resolution 27/30, 26 September 2014, A/HRC/RES/27/30.

ICCPR. General Comment No. 23: Article 27 (Rights of Minorities).

ICESCR, General Comment No. 3: The nature of States parties obligations (Art. 2, par. 1).

ICESCR, General Comment No. 5: Persons with disabilities.

ICESCR, General comment No. 6: The economic, social and cultural rights of older persons.

ICESCR, General Comment No. 11: Plans of action for primary education (art.14).

ICESCR, General Comment No. 13, The right to education (article 13 of the Covenant).

ICESCR, General comment No. 16: The equal right of men and women to the enjoyment of all economic, social and cultural rights (art. 3 of the International Covenant on Economic, Social and Cultural Rights).

ICESCR, General Comment No. 17: The right of everyone to benefit from the protection of the moral and material interests resulting from any scientific, literary or artistic production of which he or she is the author.

ICESCR, General Comment No. 20: Non-discrimination in economic, social and cultural rights.

ICESCR, General comment No. 21: Right of everyone to take part in cultural life.

INTERNATIONAL COURT OF JUSTICE:

ADVISORY OPINION ON THE LEGAL CONSEQUENCES OF THE CONSTRUCTION OF A WALL IN THE OCCUPIED PALESTINIAN TERRITORY [2004] ICJ Rep 136.

DEMOCRATIC REPUBLIC OF CONGO v. UGANDA, (ICJ merits) [2005] ICJ Rep 168.

COMMITTEE ON ECONOMIC, SOCIAL AND CULTURAL RIGHTS:

I.D.G. v. SPAIN Communication No. 2/2014.

LÓPEZ RODRIGUEZ v. SPAIN, Communication No. 1/2013.

HUMAN RIGHTS COMMITTEE:

BEARD OMINAYAK OF LUBICON LAKE BAND v. CANADA, Communication No. 167/1984, CCPR/C/38/D/167/1984.

HOWARD v. CANADA, Communication No 879/1999, UN Doc CCPR/C/84/D/879/1999,, (2005).

IVAN KITOK v. SWEDEN, Communication No 197/1985, UN Doc CCPR/C/33/D/197/1985.

LANSMAN ET AL v. FINLAND, Communication No. 511/1992, UN Doc. CCPR / C / 52D / 511 / 1992.

LANSMAN ET AL v. FINLAND, Communication no. 671/1995, U.N. Doc. CCPR/C/58/D/671/1995.

LOVELACE v. CANADA, Communication No. 24/1977, UN Doc. CCPR/C/13/D/24/1977.

Kalliopi Chainoglou

Internet Access
(Right to I. A.)

DEF: The right to Internet access refers to state duties of ensuring connectivity with the global network of TCP/IP operated devices for all individuals within a state's jurisdiction, allowing them to access and impart data and opinions. While the human rights status of the right to Internet access remains unsettled, it is undoubtedly perceived as an implication of the freedom of expression and its composite rights: to access and to share information and ideas. As such the right to Internet access is a recognised civil right in national laws of a number of countries, including Finland, Estonia and Greece, with the latter stipulating 'the right to participate in the Information Society' and viewing the 'facilitation of access to electronically transmitted information, as well as of the production, exchange and diffusion thereof' as an 'obligation of the State' (Greek Constitution, Article 5(a)). The right to Internet access is postulated as a necessary condition for the exercise of other human rights in the time of the global information society, such as freedom of expression, freedom of conscience or the right to assembly. This perception is shared by civil society and international organisations, including the United Nations, Council of Europe and the European Union.

INSTR: The right to Internet access has been subject to considerations of many international forums and organisations. At the UN level it was the 2011 report of the UN Special Rapporteur on the freedom of expression, Frank La Rue, which took up the question of recognising the right to Internet access as a human right. In his report La Rue observed that 'the Internet has become an indispensable tool for realising a range of human rights, combating inequality, and accelerating development and human progress, ensuring universal access to the Internet should be a priority for all States.' (La Rue 2011). He went on to detail the role of states in ensuring this right, by stating that each state needs to 'develop a concrete and effective policy, (...) accessible and affordable to all segments of population.' In addition, the La Rue report reflects a broader perspective of the right to Internet access, observing that 'by acting as a catalyst for individuals to exercise their right to freedom of opinion and expression, the Internet also enables the realization of a range of other human rights'. This statement reflects the current international status of the right to Internet access: on the one hand, it may be viewed as an autonomous value to be protected by law, it may, on the other hand, be perceived solely as a precondition for the enjoyment of other human rights, without a separate reference to it included in their catalogue.

The Council of Europe takes a middle approach, and views the right to Internet access in the context of the 'public service value of the Internet' – a reference to necessary measures taken by states to ensure that everyone in their jurisdiction has online connectivity. The Council notes 'people's significant reliance on the Internet as an essential tool for their everyday activities (communication, information, knowledge, commercial transactions) and the resulting legitimate expectation that Internet services be accessible and affordable, secure, reliable and ongoing.' (Council of Europe, 2007) Ensuring Internet access is perceived as a means of combating discrimination, as per Article 14 ECHR.

CASES: The French Constitutional Council's reference to the right to Internet access as a fundamental right in its 2009 decision regarding a controversial French copyright law amendment (France, 2009) initiated a debate both in Europe and worldwide. The law proposed a ban on Internet access for those violating others' rights, with the relevant decision to be made by an administrative body. Provisions of the law that were to enable an Internet disconnection were revoked, because the Constitutional Council considered it as a too far-reaching sanction, since it would have disproportionately affected the individual right to access information.

The ECtHR [YILDIRIM, 2012] sets the limits of the right to Internet access. Although the ECtHR refrained from recognising explicitly the right to Internet access as a human right, it made important observations on the significance of the online environment for the exercise of the freedom of expression in the contemporary global society. The applicant in this case maintained a website within the Google Sites domain. The access to the domain, and effectively to Yildirim's site, was blocked following an order from a local court on the ground that one of the websites within the Google Sites domain, maintained by a user abroad, contained information violating Turkish law. As the Court was unable to prosecute the editor of the infringing content, it ordered the blocking of the entire domain, including the one of the applicant, although it was not being investigated or prosecuted. Yildirim claimed he was disabled from disseminating his academic work and views, which amounted to prior restraint, imposed without any court decision. Supporting his claim, the ECtHR observed that Article 10 applies not only to the content of information but also to the means of dissemination, 'since any restriction imposed on the latter necessarily interferes with the right to receive and impart information'. The court found the imposed restrictions unforeseeable, with Turkey failing to 'afford the applicant the degree of protection to which he was entitled by the rule of law in a democratic society'. Moreover, it held that the 'measure in question produced arbitrary effects and could not be said to have been aimed solely at blocking access to the offending website', which made the applied measure overbroad. The ECtHR also provided recommendations as to the means applicable to Internet blocking applied by states as a legal measure, observing that those states need to ensure judicial review of procedures concerning the blocking that guarantee avoiding abuse, in particular by 'blocking access in general' [YILDIRIM, 2012]. In this context, the Court confirmed that the right to access online information is not an absolute one, yet any restriction laid upon it must meet the criteria present in the rich case law on Article 10 of the ECHR, including measures of foreseeability and proportionality. This line of adjudication was further developed in later cases decided by the ECtHR.

VIEWS: There seems to be little debate on the fact that the Internet conditions the exercise of human rights in the 21st century. There is agreement in the literature that the global network altered the scope of the right to free expression as well as to sharing information and ideas. Therefore, many scholars opt for recognising the right to Internet access as a new, autonomous human right. Referring to the classical notions of human rights generations, they identify the right to Internet access as a fourth generation right, conditioned by the freedom of expression and the right to access and impart information. They observe, however, that the practical transposition of this dogmatic approach into legal instruments presents important challenges that are yet to be overcome. Freedom of expression, fundamental to the right of Internet access, is not an absolute right. The limitative clause, present in Article 10 ECHR, covers a vast array of cases where states may impose relevant restrictions. Since the global character of the network resulted in a new paradigm of state jurisdiction and law enforcement, identifying the limits of free online expression has proven more difficult than in the pre-Internet era. To ensure the right to Internet access to everyone, without discrimination and with respect of due process, a universal set of criteria would need to be identified. Such a task has so far proven impossible for international human rights law and seems unlikely to be achieved for the purpose of setting online standards. With regard to the multi-stakeholder environment of the Internet (governments, civil society and business), some authors refer to soft law and good practice as the tools to facilitate finding the right balance between protecting the right to Internet access and securing rights of third parties. In this context, business self-regulation is discussed as a contemporary solution for ensuring all human rights, including Internet access, to all actors in the global information society. Bottom-up endeavours such as the – primarily business-funded and managed – Global Network Initiative try to identify a contemporary human rights consensus, which should then be reflected in the terms of service offered by participating companies. Consequently, the right to Internet access is an issue in the UN Protect, Respect and Remedy Framework, which attempts to identify the human and civil rights obligations of transnational corporations and other business actors (Human Rights Council, 2008).

There are however scholars who opt for perceiving the right to Internet access as a new, yet coherent element of the human rights regime, one rooted in the right to free expression and assembly, with little need for identifying it as a separate legal category. One of Internet's original architects, Vinton Cerf, views technology as 'an enabler of rights, not a right itself' (Cerf, 2012) There are also some academics who opt for using other, well recognised legal constructs, such as the right to identity, as measures for ensuring human rights protection in online environments (De Hert, 2012).

CONCL: Considering that some European states explicitly recognise the right to Internet access in their national laws as well as the Council of Europe approach, case law and the relevant literature, Internet access can be viewed as an enabler of human rights in the information society, with its status as a specific human right remaining unconfirmed.

REFERENCES:

Cerf, Vinton G.: "Internet Access Is Not a Human Right" New York Times, (4 January 2012).

Council of Europe: Recommendation CM/Rec(2007)16 of the Committee of Ministers to member states on measures to promote the public service value of the Internet (2007).

De Hert, Paul: "A right to identity to face the information society" in W. Bruggeman, R. van Eert and A. van Veldhoven (eds.): *What's in a name? Identiteitsfraude en diefstal*, Antwerpen: Maklu (2012).

France, Loi n° 2009-669 du 12 juin 2009 favorisant la diffusion et la protection de la création sur internet, 2009, (loi HADOPI).

Human Rights Council: *Protect, Respect and Remedy: a Framework for Business and Human Rights*. Report of the Special Representative of the Secretary-General on the issue of human rights and transnational corporations and other business enterprises, John Ruggie. A/HRC/8/5 (2008).
AHMET YILDRIM v. TURKEY (ECtHR 18/12/2012, 3111/10).

Joanna Kulesza

Internet Content Suppression

DEF: Internet content suppression (ICS) practices impede the possibility to access, receive or impart information and thus impose restrictions on individual's right to freedom of expression as outlined in Article 19 of the ICCPR and Article 10 of the ECHR.

ICS (or internet censorship) results from legislative and technical measures. Technical measures (e.g., filtering and blocking) on information communication network or a part of it are used to cause temporary, permanent, *ex-ante* (e.g., blocking an Internet Protocol) or *ex-post* (e.g., removing comments) ICS.

INSTR/CASES: For ICS practices to be compatible with the human rights framework, ICS measures have to meet the criteria foreseen in Article 19(3) ICCPR or in Article 10(2) ECHR. Recently, more guidance on states' obligations on freedom of expression in the ICT has been provided in jurisprudence, international and regional declarations.

When faced with issues of ICS, the ECtHR on several occasions has applied a framework established in its case law interpreting Article 10(2) ECHR. In a case of [AHMET YILDIRIM, 2013], concerning the court order (in the third party case) blocking access to an online service, the ECtHR, when considering the formal and material criteria for ICS, stated that having a measure 'prescribed by law' does not suffice to limit freedom of expression. The measure should be precise, accessible to the public, result in predictable outcomes and be compatible with the rule of law. The ECtHR has been criticised for not developing minimum criteria for ICS and not invoking proportionality or necessity tests, which go beyond the requirement of the rule of law. The ECtHR decision in [DELFI, 2015] remained reluctant to such criticism and did not consider technical aspects of ICT. Instead, it invoked the margin of appreciation doctrine and concluded that a measure limiting freedom of expression of a news portal had been proportional with its aims and thus compatible with the ECHR.

CONCL: National laws provide legal ground for ICS. While many states fight illegal and harmful content (e.g., hate speech or child sexual abuse images), the scope of ICS laws varies among states and is shaped by social, legal and historical factors. Similar to the offline context, states' measures providing for restrictions on freedom of expression in the online context have to comply with the cumulative criteria outlined in Article 19(3) of the ICCPR. According to these criteria, limitations on the freedom of expression can be imposed if they 'are provided by law and are necessary (a) to protect the rights or reputations of others; (b) to protect national security or public order, or public health or morals'.

REFERENCES:

Joint Declaration on Freedom of Expression and responses to conflict situations, 4 May 2015 (available at www.ohchr.org accessed 06/2016).
UN Human Rights Committee: General Comment No. 34, Article 19 Freedoms of opinion and expression (CCPR/C/GC/34), 12 September 2011.
UN Human Rights Council: Report of the Special Rapporteur on the promotion and protection of the right to freedom of opinion and expression (A/HRC/17/27), 16 May 2011.
AHMET YILDIRIM v. TURKEY (ECtHR18/03/2013, 3111/10).
DELFI v. ESTONIA (ECtHR16/06/2015, 64569/09).

Paul de Hert/Lina Jasmontaite

Investigative Journalism (and Protection of Sources)

DEF: Investigative journalism (I.J.) is practised by journalists (reporters, editors) or Internet bloggers, sometimes assisted by documentalists, whistleblowers and other concerned citizens, who profoundly research, describe and publish issues of public interest. Protection of sources is often a requirement for I.J., since the practices or documents in question – e.g. political affairs, crimes or negative corporate practices – have usually been kept secret or confidential before their disclosure. One of the most prominent cases revealed by I.J. has been the 'Watergate Scandal' of 1972 (break-in at the headquarters of the Democratic Party in Washington), which later led to the resignation of US President Richard Nixon.

INSTR/CASES: In principle, the diverse forms of I.J. and the related protection of journalistic sources fall under the provisions of Article 19 UDHR and Article 10 ECHR (Freedom of Expression and Information). In this context, the ECtHR observed that 'the vital public watchdog role of the press could be undermined' if journalistic sources are not protected [GOODWIN, 1996] and that the use of surveillance systems by the Dutch secret service against two investigative journalists violated human rights [TELEGRAAF MEDIA…, 2012]. The court also found that even the interference in the private life of a witness by using a hidden camera in an interview could be justified due to 'the public interest in information on malpractice' of insurance brokers [HALDIMANN AND OTHERS, 2015]. On the other hand, the Grand Chamber of the ECtHR came to a different conclusion in a case [BÉDAT, 2016] involving 'sensationalist' reports based on unlawful investigations – such as quoting in a newspaper secret judicial records of interviews and letters sent by a defendant to a Swiss judge – as they were considered to endanger 'the right to protection of reputation' (Article 8 ECHR) and did not 'contribute[d] to any public debate on the ongoing investigation'.

CONCL: The soaring 'information overload' – due to millions of actors in the new digital media world and including deliberate disinformation, hidden campaigning or →'trolling' practices – could let the call of the ECtHR for 'accurate and reliable information in accordance with the ethics of journalism' [BLADET TROMSØ AND STENSAAS v. NORWAY, 1999] appear like a plea in a lost cause. However, the skills of investigative journalists with searching, evaluating, prioritising and verifying experience in both traditional and digital fields of communication have never been more important than they are today, not the least because they can also enhance 'information literacy' in the broader public. While the current case law favours – at least on the European level – independent journalistic investigation without interference of the state, NGOs such as the Global Investigative Journalism Network (http://gijn.org/) or Article 19 (www.article19.org) still see the need to provide advice or even legal and financial support for journalists, since governments and private companies do not always respect this standard.

REFERENCES:

BÉDAT v. SWITZERLAND (ECtHR 29/03/2016, 56925/08).
GOODWIN v.UNITED KINGDOM (ECtHR 27/03/1996, 17488/90).
HALDIMANN AND OTHERS v. SWITZERLAND (ECtHR 24/02/2015, 21830/09).
TELEGRAAF MEDIA NEDERLAND LANDELIJKE MEDIA B.V. v. THE NETHERLANDS (ECtHR 22/11/2012, 39315/06).

Andreas Joh. Wiesand

Journalists

DEF: Journalists and the media play a crucial role in democratic societies. They disseminate information and ideas (widely), thus influencing opinion-forming, and they perform the role of 'public watchdog' by monitoring governmental authorities and exposing corruption and wrongdoing. They therefore enjoy a high level of freedom of expression, but are also expected to adhere to journalistic codes of ethics. The nature of journalism has recently been undergoing major changes. Facilitated by Internet-based communications technologies, a growing range of actors now participate in public debate alongside journalists and the media. All too often, journalists reporting on controversial matters of public interest are killed, attacked, threatened, unlawfully detained or imprisoned as a result of their work. Impunity for the perpetrators of crimes against journalists is a grave problem in a number of European countries.

INSTR: Article 10 of the ECHR is the key European legal provision guaranteeing the right to freedom of expression. Article 10 ECHR and Article 19 of the ICCPR provide comparable levels of protection for the right to freedom of expression. Article 11 of the Charter of Fundamental Rights of the European Union also focuses on freedom of expression and the media; it should be read in the light of relevant case-law of the ECtHR. Other rights enshrined in the ECHR and ICCPR are also very important for securing the safety of journalists, e.g. the right to life, the right to freedom from torture, inhuman or degrading treatment or punishment, the right to liberty and security, right to a fair trial, etc. (McGonagle 2013, Parmar 2014). Article 10 ECHR guarantees everyone the right to freedom of expression, which includes the freedom to hold opinions and the right to receive and impart information and ideas without interference by public authority and regardless of frontiers. Although Article 10 does not specifically mention journalists, the Court recognises that freedom of expression is extremely important for them (McGonagle & Voorhoof, 2015). Within the Council of Europe, the Committee of Ministers, Parliamentary Assembly and Commissioner for Human Rights have all adopted standard-setting texts or issued reports and taken stances aimed at strengthening journalistic and media freedom. The Council of Europe, in partnership with leading journalism organisations, has launched an online platform to promote the protection of journalism and the safety of journalists. The OSCE Representative on Freedom of the Media (RFOM) is a very active and influential player in this field.

CASES: The ECtHR sees it as the 'task' of journalists and the media to impart information and ideas on matters of public interest and considers that the public has a 'right' to receive such information and ideas [THE SUNDAY TIMES (No. 1), 2009]. Thus, the Court examines the necessity of any restriction on the right to freedom of expression of journalists and the media very strictly. In order for journalists and the media to be able to act as public watchdogs, the Court accepts that they are entitled to enjoy a range of freedoms, including: protection of confidential sources [GOODWIN, 1996]; protection against searches of professional workplaces and private domiciles and against seizure of materials [DE HAES AND GIJSELS, 1997], and editorial and presentational autonomy [JERSILD, 1994], even including recourse to exaggeration and provocation. But journalistic freedoms are neither unlimited nor unconditional. Article 10(2) ECHR states that the exercise of the right to freedom of expression 'carries with it duties and responsibilities'. There is an expectation that journalists contributing to public debate act 'in good faith in order to provide accurate and reliable information in accordance with the ethics of journalism' [BLADET TROMSO AND STENSAAS, 1999].

VIEWS: In case-law and academic literature alike, the importance of journalism for democratic societies is undisputed (McQuail 2013). The expansion of journalism is also largely accepted, although the boundaries between professional and amateur ('citizen') journalists are sometimes contested (Schudson 2013) and their relationship is one of both competition and complementarity (McGonagle 2013). This prompts questions about whether and to what extent the freedoms, duties and responsibilities recognised by the ECtHR in respect of journalists also govern the activities of bloggers, whistle-blowers, academics, Internet intermediaries and other contributors to public debate (McGonagle, 2013; OSCE RFOM Open Journalism Project, Commissioner for Human Rights 2011). As in the case-law of the ECtHR and the work of intergovernmental organisations and civil society organisations, literature highlights common sources of chilling effect on journalism, public debate and freedom of expression generally: overbroad (criminal) →defamation and other laws, the arbitrary application of such laws, violence and threats against journalists, including online and in particular targeting female journalists, impunity for crimes against journalists, etc. (Council of Europe 2014, Horsley 2014). Dissenting opinions in the Court's case-law, echoed in academic literature, draw attention to the potential chilling effect of onerous duties and responsibilities (sometimes referred to by the Court as 'responsible journalism') on freedom of expression of journalists and other (media or Internet) actors in public debate (e.g. [DELFI A.S., 2015]).

CONCL: Besides the issues flagged above, other emerging issues include data journalism, algorithmic journalism and drone journalism (Andreotti 2015). All of these issues will continue to feature in the ECtHR's evolving case-law and in other standard-setting, monitoring and awareness-raising work by various Council of Europe bodies, the OSCE RFOM and relevant UN bodies. The challenges facing this work are threefold. First, there must be due appreciation of the important interplay between the range of rights and freedoms that enable journalists to carry out the tasks ascribed to them in democratic societies. Second, in light of the reconfigured media ecosystem, fresh thinking is required in order to achieve the appropriate calibration of the rights, duties and responsibilities that govern journalistic activities, including when carried out by actors who are not professional journalists. Third, redoubled efforts are required by the international community and national political leaders to ensure the effective implementation of existing legal frameworks for the protection of journalism and the safety of journalists and others who contribute to public debate. Very often this is a question of political will and determination.

REFERENCES:

Andreotti, Onur (ed.): *Journalism at risk: Threats, challenges and perspectives*, Strasbourg: Council of Europe Publishing (2015).

Commissioner for Human Rights (ed.): *Human rights and a changing media landscape*, Strasbourg: Council of Europe Publishing (2011).

Committee of Ministers of the Council of Europe: *Declaration on the protection of journalism and the safety of journalists and other media actors*, 30 April 2014.

Conference of Ministers responsible for Media and Information Society, "Freedom of Expression and Democracy in the Digital Age: Opportunities, Rights, Responsibilities", Belgrade, 7–8 November 2013.

Council of Europe: *Platform to promote the protection of journalism and safety of journalists*.

Horsley, William: *Safety of journalists Guidebook* (2nd edn.), Vienna: OSCE Representative on Freedom of the Media (2014).

McGonagle, Tarlach: "How to address current threats to journalism? The role of the Council of Europe in protecting journalists and other media actors", Expert paper, Doc. No. MCM 2013(009), Strasbourg: Council of Europe.

McGonagle, Tarlach (ed.), Voorhoof, Dirk et al.: *Freedom of Expression, the Media and Journalists: Case-law of the European Court of Human Rights*, IRIS Themes, Vol. III, new, updated edition, Strasbourg: European Audiovisual Observatory (2015).

McQuail, Denis: *Journalism and Society*, London: SAGE Publications Ltd. (2013).

Parmar, Sejal: "The Protection and Safety of Journalists: A Review of International and Regional Human Rights Law", Background paper, Seminar and Inter-regional Dialogue on the Protection of Journalists: Towards an effective framework of protection for the work of journalists and an end to impunity, Strasbourg, 3 November 2014.

Schudson, Michael: "Reluctant Stewards: Journalism in a Democratic Society", 142(2) *Daedalus* (2013) 159.

BLADET TROMSO AND STENSAAS v. NORWAY (ECtHR 20/05/1999, 21980/93).

DE HAES AND GIJSELS v. BELGIUM (ECtHR 24/02/1997, 19983/92).

DELFI AS v. ESTONIA (ECtHR 16/06/2015, 64569/09).

GOODWIN v. THE UNITED KINGDOM (ECtHR 27/03/1996, 28957/95).

JERSILD v. DENMARK (ECtHR 23/09/1994, 15890/89).

THE SUNDAY TIMES v. THE UNITED KINGDOM (NO.1) (ECtHR 26/04/1979, 6538/74).

Tarlach McGonagle

Landscapes
(Cultural L.)

DEF: Cultural landscapes represent the 'combined works of nature and of man' (Article 1 of the 1972 *World Heritage Convention*) reflecting thus the spiritual relationship of people with nature. Pursuant to the World Heritage Committee Guidelines (2012, Annex 3), cultural landscapes are 'illustrative of the evolution of human society and settlement over time, under the influence of the physical constraints and/or opportunities presented by their natural environment and of successive social, economic and cultural forces, both external and internal' and can be classified into three categories:

(1) landscape designed and created intentionally by man (garden and parkland landscapes which may be linked to religious or other buildings/ensembles);
(2) organically evolved landscape resulting from human interaction with the natural environment, subcategorised into relict/fossil landscape and continuing landscape; and
(3) associative cultural landscape 'justifiable by virtue of the powerful religious, artistic or cultural associations of the natural element rather than material cultural evidence, which may be insignificant or even absent'.

INSTR: In addition to the World Heritage Convention, UNESCO has set up a unique web of standard-setting conventions in the field of cultural heritage which may also apply to the protection of cultural landscapes depending on the issues in question, particularly as regards the →Protection of Cultural Property in the Event of Armed Conflict, the →Illicit Import, Export and Transfer of Cultural Property, the protection of the →Underwater Cultural Heritage and of the →Intangible Cultural Heritage. Complementary to these instruments a number of Recommendations have dealt with issues relevant to cultural landscapes such as conservation policies and practices in recognition of inherited →values and traditions of different cultural contexts: 1962 *Recommendation concerning the Safeguarding of Beauty and Character of Landscapes and Sites*; 1972 *Recommendation concerning the Protection, at National Level, of the Cultural and Natural Heritage*; 1976 *Recommendation concerning the Safeguarding and Contemporary Role of Historic Areas*; 2011 *Recommendation on the Historic Urban Landscape*.

A number of non-binding instruments have been adopted by various international bodies: 1964 the *Venice Charter* (International Charter for the Conservation and Restoration of Monuments and Sites); 1982 the *Florence Charter* (Historic gardens and landscapes); 1990 the Charter on →Archaeological Heritage; 2013 the *Burra Charter* (Conservation of Places of Cultural Significance); the 2004 *Nachitoches Declaration* (Heritage Sites) or the 2005 *Xi'an Declaration* (Conservation of the Setting of Heritage Structures, Sites and Areas).

Even though cultural landscapes are perceived as 'cultural heritage' in the framework of the World Heritage Convention, they still present a diverse formation of tangible and intangible expressions of human interaction with the natural environment. This overlap between nature and culture expands the legal framework within which cultural landscapes are protected on the international level. Key conventions in the field of biodiversity and natural heritage allow for linkages to be fostered between their protection and implementation frameworks and the management of cultural landscapes (1971 *Ramsar Convention on Wetlands*; 1973 *Convention on International Trade in Endangered Species of Wild Fauna and Flora*; 1979 *Convention on the Conservation of Migratory Species of Wild Animals*; 1992 *Convention on Biological Diversity*; 2001 *Treaty on Plant Genetic Resources for Food and Agriculture*). Increasingly, cultural landscape protection and management is based on the sustainable use of natural and cultural resources incorporating thus an environmental approach whereby 'decisions have to be made about which elements of the cultural landscape are: (1) to be conserved at all costs, (2) subject to limited change provided that the overall character and significance of the resource is maintained, and (3) suitable for exchange in return for other benefits' (World Heritage Cultural Landscapes, p. 27).

The Council of Europe *European Landscape Convention* (2000) is committed to the protection, management and planning of all landscapes (including ordinary landscapes and degraded areas, whether on land, water or sea), based on a balanced relationship between social needs, economic activity and the environment. Member states are to 'recognise landscapes in law as an essential component of people's surroundings, an expression of the diversity of their shared cultural and natural heritage, and a foundation of their identity' (Article 5). The implementation of the Convention is monitored by a Committee of Experts and further backed up by Guidelines of the Committee of Ministers, setting out principles for the promotion of awareness and public participation and integration of landscape dimension into territorial and sectoral policies. The extensive work of the Council of Europe to this direction is further reflected in a number of Resolutions and Recommendations, e.g. regarding Landscape Award (2008), an information system (2013) as well as the promotion of 'Landscape Awareness through Education' (2014) and pedagogical material for landscape education in primary school (2015).

At EU level, legislation has been predominately environment and agriculture-oriented; hence cultural landscapes could in principle fall under the protection scheme of the 1992 *Habitats Directive*, the 1979 *Birds Directive*, and the Natura 2000 sites network. However, these instruments lack a cultural heritage or people-centred dimension which is prevalent in the normative texts of other international organisations.

CASES: There is not yet substantial case-law on the protection of cultural landscapes either at international or European level. Limited cases from the ECtHR concerned striking a balance between the individual right to private property and the public interest in the conservation of national landscape [SUD FONDI SRL, 2009]. Yet, the American Court of Human Rights has taken a bold approach in affirming the right to use or enjoyment of property in light of the collective interest of cultural communities and local groups that live on that land [MAYAGNA (SUMO) AWAS TINGNI COMMUNITY, 2001 and MOIWANA COMMUNITY, 2005]. In March 2016, the Pre-Trial Chamber I of the International Criminal Court confirmed against Ahmad Al Faqi Al Mahdi the war crime charge regarding the destruction of historical and religious monuments in Timbuktu (Mali); this is the first international criminal court case where a person is solely charged for war crimes against an historic and cultural monument.

VIEWS: Concerns have been expressed at international, regional and local level with regard to the sustainability and management of cultural landscapes. Heritage professional communities are particularly eager to ensure the stability and integrity of cultural landscape components and the detectability or measurability (i.e. through data collection and identification of relevant indicators) of any changes in the cultural landscapes and its values that may occur due to natural processes, human use or over-use of the landscape. Even though cultural landscapes are predominately viewed as part of cultural heritage, there is significant conceptual connection between the World Heritage cultural landscapes and the international or regional protected areas (i.e. under the IUCN or the EU Natura 2000 sites framework). There is also actual spatial overlap between some World Heritage cultural landscapes and international or regional protected areas (i.e. IUCN-UNESCO Sacred Sites) which outline the need for synergies between IUCN, EU, ICOMOS, UNESCO and other relevant international bodies aiming at the substantial management and governance relations between the World Heritage cultural landscapes and such protected areas. Nowadays, there is a growing dialogue between intergovernmental and governmental bodies, non-governmental organisations and the civil society with regard to cultural landscape management issues ranging from coordination and monitoring of the management strategy, governance capacity (i.e. participatory governance, intergenerational commitment, active citizenship), tourism management to funding strategies and capacity building in terms of professional development, education and engagement of cultural associations and the communities in cultural landscapes.

Studies and initiatives organised by ICCROM, ICOM, IUCN and other relevant bodies have been particularly instrumental in enhancing the links between different actors and international heritage protection frameworks concerning cultural landscapes, protected areas and intangible heritage. Along these lines, in 2014 the ICOM *Siena Charter on Museums and Cultural Landscapes* recognised museums (including archives, libraries and cultural institutions) as duty-bearers with regard to the protection and preservation of cultural landscapes: 'a museum which is responsible for the landscape undertakes at the same time the interpretation centre of heritage and territory, promoting its knowledge and its symbols making inhabitants and visitors conscious of their constitute values and encouraging them to preserve, promote and enrich it'.

CONCL: Currently, there are 88 cultural landscapes on the World Heritage List, but also more than 25 landscapes enlisted in the List of World Heritage in Danger, including sites in conflict-affected countries such as Syria and Iraq. The destruction of such cultural landscapes directly affects the identity, dignity and future of local community and humanity as a whole. Although cultural landscapes sites are heavily affected during conflicts, mostly through collateral damage, their increasingly intentional destruction by terrorist groups and other non-state actors only highlights the institutional and enforcement lacunae in the existing international legal framework on the protection of cultural heritage, including cultural landscapes.

REFERENCES:

Blake, Janet: International Cultural Heritage Law. Oxford: Oxford University Press (2015).

Communication from the Commission to the European Parliament, the Council, the European Economic and Social Committee and the Committee of the Regions: Towards an integrated approach to cultural heritage for Europe, COM/2014/0477.

Finke, Gunnar: IUCN Linking Landscapes: Exploring the relationships between World Heritage Cultural Landscapes and IUCN protected areas, IUCN World Heritage Study No. 11, Gland: International Union for Conservation of Nature and Natural Resources (2013).

International Law Association, Johannesburg Conference 2016: *Committee on Cultural Heritage Law Report on the Law Pertaining to Cultural Landscapes Significant to Indigenous Peoples*, (accessed 06/2016 via www.ila-hq.org/).

Mitchell, Nora; Rössler, Mechthild; and Pierre-Marie Tricaud (eds.): *World Heritage Cultural Landscapes. A Handbook for Conservation and Management*. World Heritage Papers No. 26, Paris: UNESCO (2009).

Francioni Francesco. and James Gordley: *Enforcing International Cultural Heritage Law*, Oxford: Oxford University Press (2013).

MAYAGNA (SUMO) AWAS TINGNI COMMUNITY v. NICARAGUA (IACrtHR 31/08/2001, Ser. C No. 79).

MOIWANA COMMUNITY v. SURINAME (IACrtHR 15/06/2005, Ser. C No. 124).

SUD FONDI SRL v. ITALIA (ECtHR 20/01/2009; 75909/01).

Kalliopi Chainoglou

Language Rights in Europe

DEF: Traditional languages of autochthonous minorities have in the past often been repressed by nation states in the process of nation-building, in order to form a homogeneous nation with unitary language and culture. Despite all these efforts, a number of regional and minority languages have survived – and their speakers have for some time, called for respect of the cultural diversity inherited from the past. More and more states in Europe tend to acknowledge that there are good moral arguments, as well as grounds of political prudence (Kymlicka 2015, 11–17; Patten & Kymlicka, 2003, 1–51) to concede some positive language rights in favour of speakers of regional and minority languages in their national legislation – or to open (by means of devolution or regionalisation) an avenue for the regions concerned to pass their own legislation granting such rights (Pupavac, 2012, 24–50; Rautz, 1999, 23–38). The move towards the codification of such rights has been consolidated by the conclusion of some international conventions in the framework of the Council of Europe that define a certain minimum standard for the language rights of minority language speakers (Thornberry & Martín Estébanez, 2004, 89–168). The rights granted in these conventions concern, in particular, the granting of education in minority languages, or at least the teaching of these languages as a second or third language (Nogueira López et al., 2012, 247–288). They also cover the provision of media services in minority languages and some basic linguistic rights in the context of official settings, such as judicial courts, administration and public services, as well as a minimum level of support for cultural activities in these languages (Oeter, 2015, 66–73). As a starting-point, a number of international institutions, in particular the Council of Europe, the OSCE and the UN, acknowledge the reproduction of culture and of language as a human right; in addition, there are strong educational arguments in favour of the teaching of minority languages and states show a certain willingness to grant a minimum level of social and cultural rights envisaging the provision of some services in minority languages (Skutnabb-Kangas & Phillipson, 1995, 71–110). The scope of these rights is quite limited, however, since states accept only very broad formulations leaving a lot of leeway in fixing the operational details, or they insist on a 'menu approach' where choices in the rights provided for may be made with ratification (the case of the *Language Charter*).

INSTR: Languages of traditional minorities have gained some legal recognition in most European states and are covered by a minimum set of language rights, although even in the Council of Europe a number of states still oppose the trend towards granting formal language rights for speakers of regional or minority languages. In a growing number of national legal orders, language legislation of states provides for an extended set of language rights in favour of minorities (Hofmann, 1997, 356–382). This is true for nearly all states in central and Eastern Europe, the Balkans and the Scandinavian states, but also important states of Southern Europe such as Spain and Italy. The UK has also opened space for language rights in the context of devolution. The rights often are not granted to all regional or minority languages on an equal footing, but rely on asymmetrical regimes favouring some important languages and linguistic groups. There are also several legal documents at the international level that provide for language rights of linguistic minorities. These international legal documents often leave unspecified who is considered a minority, and thus leave it to the discretion of member states; sometimes they explicitly exclude migrants and their languages (Article 1(a) Language Charter).

In the framework of the OSCE, a minimum standard of minority protection has been elaborated at an early stage, with the famous *Copenhagen Document* of 1990; the substantial standards of Copenhagen were supplemented by the institutional innovation of the OSCE High Commissioner for National Minorities (Drzewicki, 2014, 59–94). The most important standard-setting, however, has happened in the context of the Council of Europe, where a certain activism developed during the early 1990s (Hofmann, 2009, 31–78). The political dynamics after the fall of the iron curtain resulted in the adoption of two Council of Europe conventions, the *European Charter for Regional or Minority Languages* of 1992 (Language Charter), and the *Framework Convention for the Protection of National Minorities* of 1995 (FCNM). Both instruments entered into force in 1998, with different numbers of contracting parties – in 2016 the Framework Convention had been ratified by 39 states, the Language Charter by 25 states.

Both treaties show a certain overlap, but differ in their main focus. The FCCM is drafted as a special human rights treaty operationalising human rights of members of ethnic minorities (Thornberry & Martín Estébanez, 2004, 92). When going into detail, it proved to be difficult to cover the broad range of problems with abstract formulations in the language of universal 'rights'. In order not to overburden member states with a too far-reaching rights language, the concrete formulations had to be watered down by a large number of softening formulations, limitation clauses and in-built reservations (Hofmann et al., 2015, 73). The ambition of the drafters of the Language Charter went into a completely different direction. The various drafting groups knew from the beginning that you cannot do justice to the needs and purposes of language protection by using a mere human rights language. Educational offers are needed, radio and television programmes in these languages must be provided, cultural and social activities must be supported by the state, options of usage in communication with state authorities should be created, the use of these languages in social life needs to be encouraged. It is difficult, if not impossible, to formulate these needs of 'positive action' in the language of absolute rights (Woehrling, 2005, 27). Accordingly, the Language Charter takes a clearly complementary approach to the human rights perspective of the FCNM, opting for an 'à-la-carte' approach according to the model of the *European Social Charter* (Boysen et al., 2011, 34). States may choose different levels of protection for each regional or minority language protected under part III of the Charter.

The source of inspiration for a significant number of the principles and undertakings in the FCNM has been the ECHR. A number of provisions of the FCNM simply spell out the minority-related contents and meanings of traditional human rights enshrined in the ECHR. A number of other provisions codify principles and undertakings known from traditional instruments of minority protection, such as the right to education in the minority language. One may group the undertakings in different clusters of rights and obligations (Thornberry & Martín Estébanez, 2004, 100). One such group are clearly the non-discrimination guarantees and the obligations to take positive measures in order to end discrimination and to achieve more substantial equality in diverse societies. A second group consists of the guarantee of cultural institutions and of cultural rights. In addition, Section II contains a series of language rights, and in particular educational guarantees and educational rights. These undertakings range from the general right of persons belonging to a national minority 'to use freely and without interference his or her minority language, in private and in public, orally and in writing', as it is enshrined in Article 10(1), to relatively specific educational rights. The general right to 'freely use the language' is extended in paragraphs 2 and 3 of Article 10 to some contextual guarantees to use minority languages in relation with administrative authorities and as an accused before a judicial court, although these formulations are full of caveats and reservations (Hofmann et al., 2015, 321). Another aspect of language rights are the use of the surname and first name in the minority language, as well as the display of minority language signs and inscriptions (Hofmann et al., 2015, 342). The undertaking to display traditional local names and topographical indications in minority languages is again very carefully worded and fraught with limiting formulations (Thornberry & Martín Estébanez, 2004, 106). The same is true for the undertaking to provide, under very limited conditions, 'adequate opportunities for being taught the minority language or for receiving instruction in this language' in the framework of public education systems (Hofmann et al., 2015, 414). The right for minorities to set up and manage their own private educational and training establishments is much less reserved, although it is clear that this, in principle, does not entail any financial obligations of support to such establishments. In addition, states commit themselves to take measures in the fields of education and research to foster knowledge of the culture, history, language and religion of their national minorities (Thornberry & Martín Estébanez, 2004, 106–107) and to provide adequate opportunities for teacher training and access to textbooks. In its institutional provisions on the monitoring mechanism, the FCNM follows the common approach of Council of Europe Conventions in the human rights field and sets out a standard reporting procedure (Phillips, 2004, 112–114). Member states have to submit reports on their policies pursued in accordance with the Convention to the Secretary-General, who will then transmit them to the Committee of Ministers. The Committee of Ministers is assisted in its task of monitoring by an Advisory Committee. The Advisory Committee shall consider the periodical reports of states and shall transmit ´opinions´ to the Committee of Ministers. On the basis of these opinions, the Committee of Ministers subsequently adopts conclusions and recommendations.

As far as the Language Charter is concerned, the decision to follow the model of the European Social Charter, with the resulting path decision for an 'à la carte' approach, meant that states kept a lot of leeway in determining the scope of obligations when ratifying the convention. The Charter is clearly not conceived as a human rights treaty, but as a treaty designed to set standards for the formulation and implementation of language policies. The primary object of protection thus are not minorities as groups or individual members of such minorities, but 'languages' as a cultural phenomenon (Boyen et al., 2011, 31; Nogueira López et al.„ 2012, 16–18). There are two operative parts that make up the Language Charter, Part II and Part III (Woehrling, 2005, 29). Part II provides for a 'minimum code' of elementary standards meant to create obligations for states vis-à-vis all minority and regional languages which exist upon the territory of a member state. The (programmatic) standards laid down in this part are binding in all its aspects and apply to each minority language covered. The standards as such, however, are rather vague and are more formulated as policy objectives than as concrete legal standards that could be applied directly by administrative authorities and courts (Boysen et al., 2011, 80). Part III constitutes the technical core of the Language Charter. It contains the specific 'menu' of protection for recognised minority languages with options of a much more concrete nature than the abstract principles and objectives of Part II. The Charter contains a list of nearly 100 options of specific measures in favour of minority languages, under which a state must select at least 35 options per protected language. The essence of such a 'menu' approach is about forcing states to make a choice on the level they are willing to take positive action (Woehrling, 2005, 27). This positive action includes in particular providing certain types of education in minority languages at state schools, offering programmes in minority languages in public service radio and television, and enabling speakers to use their language before administrative authorities and courts. Article 8 provides for a wide range of educational options (see in detail Nogueira López, 2012, 247–288), with models of education in the minority language (as a medium of instruction), bilingual types of education and models of education in the official state language with a certain level of teaching of the minority language (as an additional language taught in school). Article 9 envisages a differing degree of possibilities of using minority languages in the judicial system (as to the need for some flexibility in this regard see Dunbar, 2010, 178–180). Rather similar options exist with regard to language use in the administration provided for in Article 10, where usually only regional and local administrations open up to various degrees of minority language use (see Engbers, in Boysen et al., 2011, 265–270). There are obvious reasons behind the limited amount states make use of these options. Official use before courts and administrations requires a specific organisation of the court system and the administration and personnel with specific linguistic capabilities. More or less the same observation is true as far as media are concerned, the field regulated in Article 11. Options range here from entire TV and radio stations operating in minority languages to programmes broadcast in these languages, support for the production of audiovisual works in minority languages, the training of journalists and media staff in these languages and support given to minority language newspapers (see in detail Dunbar & Moring in Nogueira López et al., 2012, 373–424). Article 12 envisages various measures of support for cultural activities in minority languages, whereas Article 13 offers a range of measures encouraging the use of minority languages in economic and social life, with a practical priority in the operation of health systems (in particular hospitals) and homes for the elderly with service offers in minority languages (see Richter in Boysen et al., 2011, 341–346). Article 13 finally covers transfrontier exchanges, either in the framework of bilateral agreements with other states where the same languages are used, or via cooperation across borders of regional and local authorities. The implementation of these substantial obligations is again monitored, like with the FCNM, by an expert committee within the framework of a state reporting procedure (see in detail Oeter, 2004, 132–140).

VIEWS: Academic specialists, as well as the organisations representing minorities, have welcomed the introduction of the two Council of Europe conventions setting out basic language rights (Palermo, 2014, 181–192). The treaties are far from perfect, but they have brought a clear improvement and have contributed significantly to the development of a uniform normative standard (Hofmann, 2009, 64–73). The transparency of the institutional monitoring procedures also has helped in identifying the deficiencies and loopholes in the practical implementation of minority protection instruments. We now know, after more than fifteen years of monitoring, much more on what is needed for the protection and promotion of minority languages – and at the same time the concrete meaning of the standards set out in the conventions has gained very much concrete contours. The experience in both treaty settings also has set into motion a fruitful dialogue between, not only lawyers and sociolinguists, but also between academics and practitioners, identifying best practices as well as dead ends and traps of any normative endeavour to codify language rights (Palermo, 2014, 192–198). It is still a long way for these insights to find its way into majority discourse in societies, however. European public discourse hardly ever regards minority languages as a resource to be valued positively, and the overwhelmingly dominant topic in discourses on language policy (in particular in educational matters) still is the strengthening of 'national' languages, not paying sufficient attention to the potentials and advantages of societal multilingualism. There is – despite all the progress in research and standard-setting – a continuing legacy of outdated concepts of 'one language, one nation'.

CONCL: The last decades have brought significant progress in standard-setting as far as language rights of traditional minorities and their members are concerned. The two relevant Council of Europe conventions have achieved a far-reaching consensus on the adequate level of protection and promotion of minority languages and the corresponding catalogue of language rights (although not all states in Europe participate in such consensus). The state of implementation of these standards is patchy, however, as is visible in the evaluation reports of the relevant monitoring bodies. The most pressing issues so far may be found within the realm of education. Without adequate educational rights, the intergenerational transmission of minority languages is more and more endangered. The number of minority languages in peril is growing, and countering that trend needs adequate arrangements in education, in the media sector and in the promotion of culture. In particular, there is a need for legal schemes to support multilingualism in education in order to overcome a monolingual bias of schooling.

REFERENCES:

Boysen, Sigrid et al.: *Europäische Charta der Regional- oder Minderheitensprachen. Handkommentar*. Zürich/St. Gallen: Dike (2011).

Drzewicki, Krzysztof: "Minority Policies of the OSCE", in Daniel Thürer (ed.): *International Protection of Minorities – Challenges in Practice and Doctrine*, Zürich: Schulthess (2014).

Dunbar, Robert: "The Charter as a Living Instrument: Legal Challenges and Perspectives" in *Minority Language Protection in Europe: Into a New Decade*. Strasbourg: Council of Europe Publ. (2010).

Hofmann, Rainer: "Minority Rights: Individual or Group Rights? A Comparative View on European Legal Systems", 40 *German Yearbook of International Law* (1997) 356.

Hofmann, Rainer: "Minority Protection in Europe: Standard-Setting by the Council of Europe and the OSCE" in Daniel Thürer (ed.): *Managing Diversity: Protection of Minorities in International Law.* Zürich: Schulthess (2009).

Hofmann, Rainer et al.: *Rahmenübereinkommen zum Schutz nationaler Minderheiten. Handkommentar*. Baden-Baden: Nomos (2015).

Kymlicka, Will: "Multiculturalism and Minority Rights: West and East?", Journal on Ethnopolitics and Minority Rights in Europe – JEMIE 14/4 (2015) 4.

Nogueira López, Alba et al.: *Shaping Language Rights: Commentary on the European Charter for Regional or Minority Languages in Light of the Committee of Experts´ Evaluation*. Strasbourg: Council of Europe Publ. (2012).

Oeter, Stefan: "The European Charter for Regional or Minority Languages", in *Mechanisms for the Implementation of Minority Rights*. Strasbourg: Council of Europe Publ. (2004).

Oeter, Stefan: "Council of Europe – The European Charter for Regional or Minority Languages" in Daniel Thürer (ed.): *International Protection of Minorities – Challenges in Practice and Doctrine.* Zürich: Schulthess (2014).

Palermo, Francesco: "International Standards and New Challenges for the Protection of Minority Rights – A Few Proposals on the Example of Language Rights" in Daniel Thürer (ed.) *International Protection of Minorities – Challenges in Practice and Doctrine.* Zürich: Schulthess (2014).

Patten, Alan and Will Kymlicka: "Introduction: Language Rights and Political Theory" in Will Kymlicka and Alan Patten (eds.) *Language Rights and Political Theory*. Oxford: Oxford University Press. (2003).

Phillips, Alan: "The Framework Convention for the Protection of National Minorities" in *Mechanisms for the Implementation of Minority Rights*. Strasbourg: Council of Europe Publ. 109–129 (2004).

Pupavac, Vanessa: *Language Rights: From Free Speech to Linguistic Governance*, Basingstoke: Palgrave Macmillan (2012).

Rautz, Günther: *Die Sprachenrechte der Minderheiten: ein Rechtsvergleich zwischen Österreich und Italien*, Baden-Baden: Nomos (1999).

Skutnabb-Kangas, Tove and Phillipson, Robert: "Linguistic Human Rights, Past and Present" in Tove Skutnabb-Kangas and Robert Phillipson (eds.) *Linguistic Human Rights – Overcoming Linguistic Discrimination*. Berlin: de Gruyter (1995).

Thornberry, Patrick and Martín Estébanez, Maria Amor: *Minority Rights in Europe*. Strasbourg: Council of Europe Publ. (2004).

Woehrling, Jean-Marie: *The European Charter for Regional or Minority Languages. A Critical Commentary*. Strasbourg: Council of Europe Publ. (2005).

Stefan Oeter

Languages of Migrants

DEF: Languages of migrants, in contrast to languages of autochthonous minorities, are often regarded as a threat to social cohesion and not as a cultural resource. Yet, firstly, a number of supranational institutions, among them the EU, the OSCE and the UN acknowledge the reproduction of culture and of language as a human right; secondly, there are strong educational arguments in favour of the teaching of migrant languages (Cummins, 2003) and thirdly, it is increasingly problematic to distinguish migrant and indigenous minorities. Linguists, educators and politicians therefore demand language rights also for migrants. Languages of migrants can also play a role in granting asylum or citizenship (Language and National Origin Group, 2004).

INSTR: Generally, languages of migrants face much less protection than languages of traditional minorities as their speakers are regarded as 'foreigners' who are supposed to 'integrate', a discourse in which language use is central (Extra & Yagmur 2002:14). There are several legal documents that mention the rights of linguistic minorities (see de Varennes 1997 for an overview of existing policy documents), however these often leave unspecified who is considered a minority, or explicitly exclude migrants.

Concerning migrants' language rights in education, UNESCO (1953) maintains that 'it is axiomatic that the best medium for teaching a child is the child's mother tongue'. On the EU level, the major document on migrant language education is still a 1977 *Directive of the Council of the European Communities on the schooling of children of migrant workers* (77/486/EEC). Although it promotes migrant language instruction, it was limited, based on legitimating remigration in case of unemployment and has become outdated (Extra & Yagmur 2002, 44). The *International Convention on the Protection of the Rights of All Migrant Workers and Members of Their Families* (UN, 1990) proposes in Article 45,3: 'States of employment shall endeavour to facilitate for the children of migrant workers the teaching of their mother tongue and culture and, in this regard, States of origin shall collaborate whenever appropriate'. These – relatively soft – provisions are not yet relevant in the EU, because none of its member states has ratified this Convention.

Despite a growing tendency of international bodies to promote linguistic diversity and a large number of local initiatives, states have done little to create legal rights for migrants' languages and to overcome monolingual institutional structures.

CASES: There are few specific documents on migrant languages and language rights in Europe. The ECtHR addresses language in relation to the right to an interpreter in case of arrest or court rulings (ECHR Article 5 & 6) and demands the right to education (Protocol to the Convention, 1952, Article 2). In contrast to the USA, where legal debates on language issues in education are prominent [e.g. LAU v. NICHOLS, 414 U.S. 563 (1974)], there are no public or legal debates on whether or not this implies access to education in a language the pupil understands as the ECtHR has interpreted the article as 'only meaning that subjects have the right to avail themselves of the means of instruction [...], not to have any particular type of education established.' (Skutnabb-Kangas & Phillipson, 1995, 86).

Concerning the legal rights of migrants to immigrate or naturalise, there has been a court ruling of the CJEU that overturned a German law on language skills [NAIME DOGAN v. FEDERAL REPUBLIC OF GERMANY, 2014]. It had required German language skills before granting a visa to future spouses from certain non-EU countries. The law had affected primarily the Turkish minority in Germany. Non-EU illiterate individuals had been, in effect, banned from the right to take a German husband or wife (EurActiv, 2014).

VIEWS: In line with international bodies, academic, as well as educational sources, generally agree on the relevance of language rights for migrants, particularly in educational contexts. Research has confirmed the significantly better achievements of pupils who have access to literacy in their native language (e.g. Cummins, 2003). There has been disagreement on whether or not to differentiate between 'voluntary' and 'involuntary' minorities and their respective rights for cultural reproduction. Due to demographic developments, where in the EU an estimated third of the urban population has a migration history, this debate has become less relevant. However, European public discourse hardly ever regards migrant languages as a resource, and the overwhelmingly dominant topic is the acquisition of majority languages as prerequisite to immigration and naturalisation.

A linked issue is the role of languages in asylum seeking procedures, where linguists have been very critical of unfounded decisions to deport migrants on grounds of their language use, apparently demonstrating the illegitimacy of their claims (Language and National Origin Group, 2004). This is related to a vibrant linguistic debate on outdated concepts on language that rely on a simple mapping of 'one language, one nation' (Blommaert, 2009).

CONCL: The most pressing questions with regard to migrant languages are certainly within the realm of education. Access to meaningful education for migrants is important for social cohesion and is not necessarily the same as education for majority speakers. There is a need for legal schemes to support language education and literacy in more than one language to overcome a monolingual bias of schooling that often reproduces ethnic discrimination indirectly. Demographic developments and economic and cultural globalisation require that the linguistic resources of the multilingual population are utilised more effectively. The most difficult aspect in this is how to grant rights to individuals in an increasingly diverse setting in which diversity does not necessarily come in the form of established ethnic groups with clearly definable languages. The legal right to learn (and not merely to be exposed to) the majority language in public schooling has to become an obvious matter.

Another important issue is the role of language in asylum seeking procedures and the degree of (socio-) linguistic expertise necessary to take decisions. The future role of national and official languages in granting access to naturalisation requires a transparent debate as well as transparent legal and administrative processes.

REFERENCES:

Blommaert, Jan: "Language, Asylum, and the National Order", *Current Anthropology* 50 (2009).

Cummins, Jim: "BICS and CALP: Origins and Rationale for the Distinction", in Christina Bratt Paulston & G. Richard Tucker (eds.) *Sociolinguistics. The Essential Readings*. Oxford: Blackwell. 322–28 (2003).

De Varennes, Fernand: "To Speak or not to Speak. The Rights of Persons Belonging to Linguistic Minorities. Working Paper prepared for the UN Sub-Committee on the Rights of Minorities" Working Paper prepared for the UN Sub-Committee on the rights of minorities (1997).

EurActiv: "European Court of Justice Bans German Language Requirement for Turkish Spouse Visas" (2014) (www.euractiv.com, accessed 09/2015).

Extra, Guus and Kutlay Yagmur: *Language Diversity in Multicultural Europe. Comparative Perspectives on Immigrant Minority Languages at Home and at School*, Paris: UNESCO (2014).

Language and National Origin Group: *Guidelines for the Use of Language Analysis in Relation to Questions of National Origin in Refugee Cases*, (2004) (www.essex.ac.uk, accessed 2/2016).

Skutnabb-Kangas, Tove and Robert Phillipson: "Linguistic Human Rights, Past and Present" in Tove Skutnabb-Kangas and Robert Phillipson (eds.) *Linguistic Human Rights – Overcoming Linguistic Discrimination*. Berlin: de Gruyter. 71–110 (1995).

UNESCO: *The Use of Vernacular Languages in Education*, Paris: UNESCO (1953).

Britta Schneider

LGBT

DEF: LGBT is an acronym that stands for lesbian, gay, bisexual, and transgender. It may be used to refer to an yone who is non-heterosexual or non-cisgender. A variant of this acronym adds the letter Q for those who identify as queer and I for those who identify as intersex.

INSTR/CASES: In many countries, the LGBT culture questions traditional cultural or family models and faces different problems. For example, homosexual partnerships or marriages, LGBT adoption or parenting, protection against hate crimes are not recognised everywhere. LGBT rights are protected by the UN, Council of Europe (see e.g. Rec CM/Rec (2010) 5) as well as EU instruments. The UN bodies in their work use *the Yogyakarta Principles on the Application of International Human Rights Law in relation to Sexual Orientation and Gender Identity* (a document adopted in 2006 by a distinguished group of experts) that bring together and clarify existing international human rights law standards. The ECtHR issued several judgments concerning LGBT, among others in the context of discrimination in adoption procedures [e.g. E.B., 2008; X AND OTHERS, 2013], in exercising parental authority [SALGUEIRO DA SILVA MOUTA, 1999] or concerning civil partnerships [VALLIANATOS AND OTHERS, 2013; OLIARI AND OTHERS, 2015]. In the context of cultural rights, a case concerning the right to organise cultural events, such as gay prides, is of special interest [BACZKOWSKI AND OTHERS, 2007]. The right of transgender persons to legal recognition as members of the sex appropriate to their gender was confirmed by the ECtHR [CHRISTINE GOODWIN, 2002]. At EU level, the *Employment Equality Directive (*2000/78) requires all EU member states to provide for protection against discrimination based on sexual orientation in employment and occupation. According to the CJEU, unfavourable treatment because a transsexual person has undergone, or plans to undergo, gender reassignment amounts to discrimination on the grounds of sex [P, 1996].

CONCL: Protection of LGBT is progressively emerging as a new standard in international human rights law, especially at the European level, but less so in Africa and parts of Asia. However, the scope of this protection is still a subject of debate. In the European Union, one of the main problems is unequal protection against discrimination based on sexual orientation in comparison to more generous protection against discrimination based on race, ethnic origin or sex. The proposal of the European Commission to equalise the standard of protection (to combat discrimination outside the field of employment) within the EU in the form of a new – so called 'horizontal' – Directive is under discussion since 2008 (Pudzianowska, Śmiszek 2015).

REFERENCES:

Godzisz, Piotr and Pudzianowska, Dorota: "The case of anti-LGB hate crime laws in Poland", in Schweppe Jennifer and Walters Mark Austin: *The Globalisation of Hate Internationalising Hate Crime?*, Oxford: Oxford University Press (2016).

Johnson, Paul: *Homosexuality and the European Court of Human Rights*, Abingdon: Routledge (2013).

O'Flaherty, Michael and Fisher, John: "Sexual Orientation, Gender Identity and International Human Rights Law: Contextualizing the Yogyakarta Principles", 8(2) *Human Rights Law Review* (2008) 207.

Pudzianowska, Dorota and Śmiszek, Krzysztof: *Combating sexual orientation discrimination in the European Union*, Luxembourg: Publications Office of the European Union (2015).

BĄCZKOWSKI AND OTHERS v. POLAND (ECtHR 01/05/2007, 1543/06).

CHRISTINE GOODWIN v. UK (ECtHR 11/07/2002, 28957/95).

E.B. v. FRANCE (ECtHR, 22/01/2008, 43546/02).

OLIARI AND OTHERS v. ITALY (ECtHR 21/10/2015, 18766/11 and 36030/11).

P v. S AND CORNWALL COUNTY COUNCIL (CJEU 30/04/1996, C-13/94).

SALGUEIRO DA SILVA MOUTA v. PORTUGAL (ECtHR 21/12/1999, 33290/96).

VALLIANATOS AND OTHERS v. GREECE (ECtHR 07/11/2013, 29381/09 and 32684/09).

X AND OTHERS v. AUSTRIA (ECtHR 19/02/2013, 19010/07).

Dorota Pudzianowska

Libraries

(Access to L. Resources)

DEF: For centuries, libraries have served as a provider of literary inspiration and scientific or factual information, in many cities and towns also as cultural, educational and civic centres for all parts of the population. Access to culture and knowledge via libraries and, increasingly, to digitised or born digital content, is a key element of global and European policies of free access to →information.

The current digital revolution in the cultural sector changes the modes of access to information. Sometimes, these changes are seen as mainly technology-led. However, there is also legal uncertainty, specifically with regards to e-books (digital born content) and digitised collections (back catalogues; archives; letters; out of commerce works) which remain a major hindrance to enabling access to e-content.

INSTR: Libraries worldwide contribute towards turning everyone's human right of free →participation in cultural life (ICESCR, Article 15, 1a) into a reality. Their work is also protected by the ECHR, since Article 10(1) on freedom of expression includes also 'freedom to hold opinions and to receive and impart information and ideas without interference by public authority and regardless of frontiers', even if this clause has, until now, mostly been employed to secure access to administrative information or official documents. Within the European Union, a patchwork of legal exceptions and limitations as well as diverse national modes of implementing the *'InfoSoc Directive'* (2001/29/EC) did not fully clarify citizens' rights to access information via libraries.

According to a recent report (Crews, 2014), 153 out of the 186 WIPO member countries included statutory 'library exceptions' into their →authors' rights/copyright laws (covering e.g. the reproduction of copyrighted works for private research and study; preservation and replacement of works; document supply and interlibrary lending) – which also shows that 33 countries do not yet recognise such exceptions.

CASES: Until now, the ECtHR did not deal directly with issues concerning access to content via libraries. However, in its case-law the court made some important clarifications, including that the freedom to receive information protected in Article 10 ECHR is not limited only to political news and other reports of public concern, 'but covers in principle also cultural expressions as well as pure entertainment' [KHURSHID MUSTAFA, 2008, § 44] and that the public of any country should not be prevented from having access to a work that can be considered part of the 'European literary heritage' [AKDAŞ, 2010, § 30]. The CJEU addressed the issue of digital content in libraries more specifically, confirming that EU member states are entitled to grant public libraries the ancillary right to digitise individual books from their collection without the right holder's consent in order to make them accessible for the purpose of research or private study via dedicated terminals, based on a 'fair balance' between the interests of right holders and users of protected works [TECHNISCHE UNIVERSITÄT, 2014].

VIEWS: The present system of copyright protection and its role in either enabling or preventing creativity is now frequently under scrutiny (see e.g. Porsdam, 2016). A study has shown that most of the library stakeholders 'are strongly supportive of a EU copyright reform, arguing that democratic values as well as the EU Single Market would benefit', many of them proposing 'either a general *fair use* exception in EU copyright law, or adding several specific exceptions, e.g. for text and data mining; e-lending; publicly funded research openly available; and that contract terms and technical protection measures cannot override limitations and exceptions' (Andersdotter, 2015). While such demands are, as expected, questioned by many publishers (e.g. Börsenverein, 2015) and a few scholars, library organisations are focusing more on the concrete issue of how to uphold or further improve their service in the digital age. In 2013 and 2014, the European Bureau of Library, Information and Documentation Associations (EBLIDA) started a campaign for the 'right to e-read', maintaining that 'libraries guarantee free access to content, information, and culture for all European citizens' but facing a legal framework that 'prevents libraries from fulfilling these essential services to our society, especially regarding the provision of e-books'.

CONCL: Given that information is a key driver for an educated society in which libraries both physically and digitally play a key role, it is not acceptable that rights in a digital environment should fall below those in the traditional physical environment. The 'library everywhere' concept of the 1950s, designed to meet the needs of underprivileged citizens by ensuring their access to reading, could now become a reality thanks to technological developments. To that effect, legal barriers impeding the further improvement of access to both digital and digitised e-content need to be removed.

REFERENCES:

Andersdotter, Karolina: *Cross-border Copyfight. European libraries re-thinking the InfoSoc Directive*, Masteruppsats, Uppsala Universitet (2015).

Börsenverein des Deutschen Buchhandels: *Schwarzer Tag für Forschung und Lehre an deutschen Hochschulen*, Presseerklärung vom 17. April 2015 (A black day for German university research and teaching, Press statement of the German Publishers Association).

Crews, Kenneth: *Study on Copyright Limitations and Exceptions for Libraries and Archives*, Geneva: WIPO Standing Committee on Copyright and Related Rights, SCCR/29/3 (2014).

Porsdam, Helle: *Copyrighting Creativity: Creative Values, Cultural Heritage Institutions and Systems of Intellectual Property*, Oxford: Routledge (2016).

AKDAŞ v. TURKEY (ECtHR 16/02/2010, 41056/04).

KHURSHID MUSTAFA AND TARZIBACHI v. SWEDEN (ECtHR 16/12/2008, 23883/06).

TECHNISCHE UNIVERSITÄT DARMSTADT v. EUGEN ULMER KG (CJEU 11/09/2014, C-117/13).

www.eblida.org/e-read/home-campaign/ (accessed 04/2016).

Vincent Bonnet

Literary Expressions
(Freedom of L. E.)

DEF: Freedom of literary and artistic expression and access to culture for national, ethnic and linguistic minorities are protected in different legal instruments, including in the UDHR, whose Article 19 stipulates that 'everyone has the right to freedom of opinion and expression; this right includes freedom to hold opinions without interference and to seek, receive and impart information and ideas through any media and regardless of frontiers'. The ECHR takes up these issues in Articles 9 'Freedom of thought, conscience and religion' and Article 10 'Freedom of expression'. These articles were written in close relation with the idea of democracy which guarantees a free debate on every topic. Therefore, freedom of thought and expression can be considered the foundation of European democracies. An act of literary creation expressed in words in a given language (and possibly translated into other languages) is an inherent part of this concept.

INSTR: A writer as the author of thoughts has the right to express them according to Article 10 ECHR. Yet this article has a limitation clause in paragraph 2, which assumes that exercising freedom of expression may be subject to restrictions and penalties if these are 'in the interests of national security', if the 'territorial integrity or public safety' is being threatened or 'for the prevention of disorder or crime, for the protection of health or morals, for the protection of the reputation or rights of others, for preventing the disclosure of information received in confidence, or for maintaining the authority and impartiality of the judiciary'. Only as long as there is no conflict between free thoughts expressed by a writer in his/her literary work and these threats, he or she can enjoy freedom of expression to the full extent.

CASES: In democratic states there should be no censoring of speech or ideas expressed in public. The right to freedom of thought and expression results from the belief in a spiritual identity of an individual, in principles of pluralism and in the right to maintain contacts with a native culture. Constitutions of most European states share these assumptions and the system of conventions is supplemented by national measures. Yet there are examples of restricting the freedom of expression by state authorities, including bans on statements of a writer or on the circulation of his or her books, including confiscations of an edition, fines or a prohibition to print. As could be seen before, exercising literary freedom may entail 'duties' and 'responsibilities', which may be detrimental to literary expressions that belong to the world of literary fiction, even if they use a language of realism or are based on factual material. Famous cases of restrictions of freedom of literary expression resulted from accusations against:

shocking or obscene content, e.g. in a textbook on sex education [HANDYSIDE, 1976]; promoting immoral behaviour, e.g. through publishing Appolinaire's works [AKTAŞ, 2010]; offending religious feelings; defaming particular people, e.g. the leader of the Austrian Freedom Party, Jörg Haider [OBERSCHLICK, 1997] as well as institutions and organisations.

VIEWS: Literary →censorship, be it for political or 'moral' reasons, has been commonplace over centuries and still raised concerns throughout Europe in the not so distant past (Zimmer, 1966). Today, there is general agreement that freedom of expression may not pertain only to statements which are favourably received in a society. A human being has a need of individual expression, in literature it may even be overexpression. Among a wide range of various literary forms, the latter can take the form of iconoclasm, sarcasm, satire, irony, mockery, caricature, etc. They may be interpreted too literally, e.g. as a mockery of religion (*Charlie Hebdo*), as offensive towards public figures (political lampoons) or offending religious sensitivities (*Pussy Riot*). The ECHR protects freedom of expression in the name of pluralism of opinions, including the ability to communicate your opinions to other members of a society and the right of the society to learn about the opinion voiced by the author. Another important issue is the right to cultural expression of authors belonging to a national and ethnic minority and its culture. Such a collective dimension of freedom of expression lies at the heart of Article 10 of the ECHR. The issues that remain controversial are: 'the right to shock' and the right to present content close to pornography. Whether or not these phenomena are accepted is influenced by the concepts of 'individual good' and 'common good'. The right to shock may be respected in connection with the right to individual development and fulfilment of the author's potential as well as openness of people to other views. Yet invoking the 'common good' can suggest that it is acceptable for domestic authorities to interfere in literary and artistic manifestations that intend to shock [MÜLLER, 1988].

CONCL: Freedom of thought and different forms of expressing it in literature must remain guaranteed in democratic systems. It results from both individual and collective rights to personal freedom and collective freedom as well as from cultural diversity of contemporary societies; and the diversity entails the right to express different views. If we assume that a literary utterance includes an idea or value, the need to disseminate it could invoke the American concept of 'a marketplace of ideas' (with 'producers' of the idea and its 'consumers'), but also the willingness to share values. Allowing the largest possible array of literary utterances is tantamount with acceptance of development of human imagination, the need to disseminate information and access the axiological space. The marketplace of ideas guarantees progress and protects against dangers. It results from the belief that it is better to articulate even the most controversial literary concepts than to keep them in hiding. Hiding thoughts creates a greater danger than revealing them. Contents that raise concerns, outrage or offend the general public are part of a democratic reality, which is why they should remain part of the free circulation of information. A ban on circulating the information may result only from the need to protect the society against danger, e.g. with regard to children and teenagers. It is important to remember that a certain age must be reached to be ready for a reception of certain literary works. Maturity, the right level of education, (intellectual preparation for a reception of literary content) constitute the protection against shock or harmful emotional impact among young readers.

REFERENCES:

Alexander, Larry: *Is There a Right to Freedom of Expression?*, Cambridge: Cambridge Studies in Philosophy and Law (2005).

Barendt, Eric: *Freedom of Speech*, 2nd edn., Oxford: Clarendon Press (2005).

Bollinger, Lee: *The Tolerant Society*, Oxford: Oxford Universty Press (1988).

International Mechanisms for Promoting Freedom of Expression: Tenth Anniversary Joint Declaration: Ten Key Challenges to Freedom of Expression in the Next Decade (www.osce.org 2010).

Kamiński, Ireneusz C.: *Ograniczenie swobody wypowiedzi dopuszczalne w Europejskiej Kon-*

wencji Praw Człowieka. Analiza krytyczna, OF, Warszawa (2010).
Łętowska, Ewa: *Wolność wypowiedzi*, "Law through Experience" / 116881-CP-1-2004-SK-GRUNDTVIG-G11.
O'Rourke, Kevin C.: *John Stuart Mill and Freedom of Expression: The Genesis of a Theory*, London: Routledge (2001).
Van Mill, David: *Freedom of Speech*, Stanford Encyclopedia of Philosophy (available at plato.stanford.edu, accessed 04/2016).
Zimmer, Dieter E. (ed.): *Die Grenzen literarischer Freiheit*, Hamburg: Nannen 1966.
AKTAŞ v. TURKEY (ECtHR 08/04/2004, 26307/95).
HANDYSIDE v. THE UNITED KINGDOM (ECtHR 07/12/1976, 5493/72).
MÜLLER v. SWITZERLAND (ECtHR 24/05/1988, 10737/84).
OBERSCHLICK v. AUSTRIA (ECtHR 23/05/1991, 11662/85).

Bożena Gierat-Bieroń

Margin of Appreciation

DEF: The term 'margin of appreciation' refers to the room for manoeuvre that the ECtHR is prepared to accord domestic authorities in fulfilling their obligations under the ECHR (Greer, 2000). The margin of appreciation is used in determining whether state action which limits the application of a right is necessary in a democratic society. The doctrine is closely linked to the idea that the protection of human rights of the ECHR is subsidiary to the protection of domestic systems. It is essentially a judge-made doctrine as no reference to the margin of appreciation is found in the ECHR (as long as the new Protocol 15 has not entered into force).

CASES: The margin of appreciation has been applied in a wide range of cases and its application is often difficult to predict. Factors which influence the application and the width of the margin in a case include: the provision invoked, aims pursued by the interference, the context of the interference and any European consensus on the issue (Spielmann, 2012). The margin of appreciation is most frequently applied in cases of relevance for 'culture', involving the provisions in Articles 8–11 and 14 (private and family life; freedom of thought, conscience and religion; freedom of expression; freedom of association and prohibition of discrimination), but also regarding Article 15 (derogation) and Article 1 of Protocol 1 (protection of property).

Examples of cases where the margin has been applied include [HANDYSIDE, 1976] where the Court said that states are 'in principle in a better position than the international judge to give an opinion on the exact content' of ECHR requirements. In [LEYLA SAHIN, 2005], the Court granted Turkey a wide margin of appreciation in relation to restriction on the wearing of headscarves due to the significance of secularism in Turkey at the time. In a subsequent case also involving the wearing of a full face coverage [S.A.S, 2014], the Court found that as there was no European consensus on the banning of full-face coverage, France had a wide margin of appreciation and was therefore justified in banning such clothing. In the case of [A, B AND C, 2010], despite European consensus on the issue of abortion, the Court found there was a margin of appreciation for Ireland in balancing the rights of the foetus and the rights of the mother.

VIEWS: There is a vast amount of academic literature on the margin of appreciation doctrine containing a wide range of divergent opinions. A part of the debate revolves around the question of the →universalism/relativity of human rights. On the one hand there is the opinion that the ECtHR has not taken the doctrine far enough in its application (Lord Hoffman, 2009), on the other hand there are those like Judge De Mayer in a dissenting opinion [Z, 1997] who say that it should be abolished, and it should not be for states to decide what is acceptable and what is not. For Greer the doctrine is integral to the ECHR's interpretation, and the rights contained in the ECHR are both 'universal and capable of being interpreted and applied differently in varying national contexts' (Greer, 2010). It has also been argued that the doctrine should never be applied in the case of minorities as it is often the role of international human rights courts to provide protection for such groups (Benvenisiti, 1999).

CONCL: Protocol 15, when it enters into force, will add reference to the margin of appreciation doctrine to the end of the preamble to the ECHR. The margin of appreciation has moved from a doctrine developed by the court to almost a 'right' of states and it has been said that it brings the ECtHR into the 'age of subsidiarity' (Spano, 2014). The margin of appreciation doctrine will certainly continue to be used by the ECtHR as a method of interpreting the ECHR.

REFERENCES:

Benvenisti, Eyal: '"Margin of Appreciation, Consensus and Universal Standards", 31 *NYU Journal of International Law and Politics* (1998) 843.

Council of Europe, *Human Rights in Culturally Diverse Societies*, Strasbourg: Council of Europe Publishing (2016).

Gerards, Janneke: "Pluralism, Deference and the Margin of Appreciation Doctrine", 17(1) *European Law Journal* (2011) 80.

Greer, Steven: "The Margin of Appreciation: Interpretation and Discretion under the European Convention on Human Rights", Council of Europe, Human rights files, No. 17, (2000).

Greer, Steven: "The Interpretation of the European Convention of Human Rights: Universal Principle or Margin of Appreciation?", *UCL Human Rights Review* (2010) 1.

Hoffmann, Lord: "The Universality of Human Rights", Judicial Studies Board Annual Lecture, 19 March 2009.

Shany, Yuval: "Toward a General Margin of Appreciation Doctrine in International Law?", 16(5) *EJIL* (2005) 907.

Spano, Robert: "Universality or Diversity of Human Rights?", 14 *Human Rights Law Review* (2014) 487.

Spielmann, Dean: "Allowing the Right Margin the European Court of Human Rights and the National Margin of Appreciation Doctrine: Waiver or Subsidiarity of European Review", in *CELS Working Paper* (2012).

A, B AND C v. IRELAND (ECtHR 16/12/2010, 25579/05).

HANDYSIDE v. THE UNITED KINGDOM (ECtHR 07/12/1976, 5493/72).

LEYLA SAHIN v. TURKEY (ECtHR 10/11/2005, 44774/98).

S.A.S v. FRANCE (ECtHR 01/07/2014, 43835/11).

Z v. FINLAND (ECtHR 25/04/1997 22009/93).

Hans Fischer-Kerrane

Media Content

(Diversity of, and Access to, M. C.)

DEF: Media pluralism and media diversity are closely-related concepts. Media pluralism concerns the availability of a range of different types of media whereas media diversity mainly concerns variety in media content/output. It is widely accepted that media pluralism can contribute to media diversity, without necessarily guaranteeing it. Freedom of expression and freedom of the media are pre-conditions for media pluralism and diversity. The ability of individuals to express themselves freely via the media leads to the wide dissemination of information and opinions, which is very important for democratic societies. Different types of media help to foster diversity in different ways. For example, public service media must, in accordance with their mission, cater for the informational needs and interests of all groups in society by providing a diverse range of programming and services.

INSTR: The ECHR does not explicitly mention diversity of media content, but the ECtHR has explored the importance of media diversity in its case-law. The relationship between the right to freedom of expression and media diversity is circular: freedom to express ideas and opinions and disseminate information is a pre-requisite for media diversity, but media diversity is also very important for the freedom to receive information and ideas of all kinds. Media diversity has many facets, of which cultural and linguistic diversity are among the most salient. Besides the ECHR, various other Council of Europe treaties contain provisions that seek to promote (or have the effect of promoting) cultural and/or linguistic diversity via the media. Examples include the 1995 *Framework Convention for the Protection of National Minorities* (especially Article 9) and the 1992 *European Charter for Regional or Minority Languages* (especially Article 11). The same can be said of the 2005 UNESCO *Convention on the*

Protection and Promotion of the Diversity of Cultural Expressions. The Convention provides, for instance, that states parties 'may adopt measures aimed at protecting and promoting the diversity of cultural expressions within its territory', including 'measures aimed at enhancing diversity of the media, including through public service broadcasting' (Article 6(1) *juncto* 6(2)(h)). The *Charter of Fundamental Rights* of the European Union (2000, in force since 2009) contains provisions on freedom and pluralism of the media (Article 11(2)) and on cultural, religious and linguistic diversity (Article 22). The 1989 UN *Convention on the Rights of the Child*, recognising the role of the media, requires states parties to ensure that children have access to information and material from a diversity of sources (Article 17).

CASES: The ECtHR has consistently held that the state is the 'ultimate guarantor' of the principle of pluralism, especially 'in relation to audio-visual media, whose programmes are often broadcast very widely' [INFORMATIONSVEREIN LENTIA, 1993]. This means that the state has a positive obligation to uphold pluralism in the (audiovisual) media sector. The state must therefore ensure, amongst other things, that 'the public has access through television and radio to impartial and accurate information and a range of opinion and comment, reflecting inter alia the diversity of political outlook within the country' [MANOLE, 2009]. The Court has also held that it is important for all sections of the public to be able to receive a wide range of information, thus not only political and social news, but also 'cultural expressions and pure entertainment' [KHURSHID MUSTAFA, 2008]. The ECtHR has identified a particular role for public service media in the realisation of these objectives. The nature of that role has been developed in considerable detail by various standard-setting/policy-making activities, most notably by the Committee of Ministers of the Council of Europe. *Recommendation CM/Rec(2007)2* of the Committee to member states on media pluralism and diversity of media content is particularly pertinent in this connection.

VIEWS: In academic literature, the terms media pluralism and media diversity, are sometimes distinguished and sometimes (seemingly) used interchangeably. Media pluralism is generally taken to refer to issues of media ownership; of choices available to the public between providers of services. Diversity, for its part, is most often taken to refer to the range of programmes and services available to the public (McGonagle, 2011). Distinctions have been made between different levels of media pluralism: content, source and outlet (Gibbons, 1999 and the *Joint Declaration on Diversity in Broadcasting*, 2007). In discussions about media content, it is important to take account of the actual content and how it is produced. It can be useful to distinguish between content produced *by* certain groups and content produced *for* certain groups. The former is more likely to speak to the target groups owing to the involvement of members of the groups in its design and creation. It is also important to take account of the practical value of diversity in media content. It has been suggested that it is not enough to ensure the availability of diverse media content, but that the public must also be exposed to that diverse content, if it is to have societal impact. This is sometimes referred to as 'exposure diversity', which goes beyond 'supply diversity'. Recent literature explores the role of public service media in relation to exposure diversity, looking at modalities of 'active pluralism' (Gibbons, 2015), a 'public service navigator' role (Burri, 2015) and the use of 'algorithmic profiling and targeting to guide audiences and stimulate more diverse choices' (Helberger, 2015).

CONCL: As a media policy goal, the promotion of diverse media content remains a challenge. There is a risk of subjectivity in assessments of what level of media diversity is 'sufficient' in a democratic society and consequently, the usefulness of indicators as measurement tools is currently being explored in various quarters (e.g., the Media Pluralism Monitor Project). After affirming that the state is the ultimate guarantor of pluralism in the audiovisual media sector in 1993, the ECtHR was slow to spell out the implications of this positive obligation (see above). While a particular role for promoting diverse media content has been identified by the Court and others for public service media, the important contributions of other types of media (e.g., community media) are increasingly being recognised as well. There is also a growing awareness that the goal of promoting media diversity involves different challenges at different geographical levels (Barnett and Townend, eds., 2015). New, technology-driven, challenges have also emerged in recent years: so-called echo chambers (Sunstein, 2007) and filter bubbles (Pariser, 2011). This has prompted wide-ranging reflection among scholars (e.g. Karppinen, 2012, Valcke *et al.*, eds., 2016) and policy-makers alike about how to achieve the goal of media diversity in the new media ecosystem.

REFERENCES:

Barnett, Steven and Townend, Judith (eds.): *Media Power and Plurality: From Hyperlocal to High-Level Policy*, Hampshire: Palgrave Macmillan (2015).

Burri, Mira: "Contemplating a 'Public Service Navigator': In Search of New- (and Better-) Functioning Public Service Media", *International Journal of Communication* 9(2015), 1341.

Gibbons, Thomas: "Concentrations of Ownership and Control in a Converging Media Industry", in Marsden, Chris and Verhulst, Stefaan (eds.): *Convergence in European Digital TV Regulation*, London: Blackstone Press Ltd. (1999).

Gibbons, Thomas, "Active Pluralism: Dialogue and Engagement as Basic Media Policy Principles", *International Journal of Communication* 9 (2015), 1382.

Helberger, Natali: "Merely Facilitating or Actively Stimulating Diverse Media Choices? Public Service Media at the Crossroad", *International Journal of Communication* 9 (2015), 1324.

Joint Declaration on Diversity in Broadcasting, adopted by the UN Special Rapporteur on Freedom of Opinion and Expression, the OSCE RFOM, the OAS Special Rapporteur on Freedom of Expression and the ACHPR Special Rapporteur on Freedom of Expression and Access to Information, 12 December 2007.

Karppinen, Kari: *Rethinking Media Pluralism*, New York: Fordham University Press (2012).

McGonagle, Tarlach: *Minority Rights, Freedom of Expression and of the Media: Dynamics and Dilemmas*, Antwerp: Intersentia (2011).

Pariser, Eli: *The Filter Bubble: What the Internet is Hiding from You*, New York: Penguin Books (2011).

Sunstein, Cass R.: *Republic.com 2.0*, Princeton NJ: Princeton University Press (2007).

Valcke, Peggy, Sükösd, Miklós and Picard, Robert G. (eds.): *Media Pluralism and Diversity: Concepts, Risks and Global Trends*, Hampshire: Palgrave Macmillan (2016).

INFORMATIONSVEREIN LENTIA v. AUSTRIA (ECtHR 24/11/1993, 13914/88).

KHURSHID MUSTAFA & TARZIBACHI v. SWEDEN (ECtHR 16/12/2008, 23883/06).

MANOLE & OTHERS v. MOLDOVA (ECtHR 17/09/2009, 13936/02).

www.monitor.cmpf.eui.eu (accessed 04/2016).

Tarlach McGonagle

Migrants

(Cultural Rights of M.)

DEF: A 'migrant' is defined by the International Organization for Migration (IOM) as a 'person who is moving or has moved across an international border or within a State away from his/her habitual place of residence, regardless of (1) the person's legal status; (2) whether the movement is voluntary or involuntary; (3) what the causes for the movement are; or (4) what the length of the stay is' ('Key Migration Terms'). While IOM places emphasis on the aspect of movement, UNESCO opts for a residence-based perspective, qualifying a migrant as a 'person who lives temporarily or permanently in a country where he or she was not born, and has acquired some significant social ties to this country' ('International Migration and Multicultural Policies').

INSTR: The term 'migrant' encompasses a notable number of different realities, determined by both the reasons convincing a person to migrate, and his or her legal status in the country of migration. According to the UN Special Rapporteur on the human rights of migrants, the latter include persons who are outside the territory of the state of which they are nationals or citizens, and of which they do not enjoy its legal protection (UN Doc. A/57/292, 9 August 2002, 25). It follows that migrants, broadly speaking, include those who are in the territory of the host country both legally and illegally. To a similar extent, both voluntary and involuntary immigrants are included in the concept. In international law the most important categories of migrants are diplomats, →refugees, migrant workers, and, among illegal migrants, victims of human trafficking. The 1990 *International Convention on the Protection of the Rights of All Migrant Workers and Members of Their Families* provides for a number a cultural rights in favour of migrant workers, particularly the right to religion (Article 12), right to respect of their cultural identity (Articles 17 and 31), right to maintain their cultural links with their state of origin (Article 31), right to access to and participation in cultural life (Articles 43 and 45(1)), as well as right of the →children of migrant workers to be taught in their mother tongue and culture (Article 45.3). In March 2016, the Convention had been ratified by 48 countries, only four of which are European: Albania, Azerbaijan, Bosnia and Herzegovina and Turkey. To a similar extent, the 1977 *European Convention on the Legal Status of Migrant Workers* obliges states parties to take action to arrange special courses for the teaching of the migrant worker's mother tongue for migrant workers' children (Article 15). This Convention has so far been ratified by eleven countries. Article 10 of the 1975 ILO *Migrant Workers (Supplementary Provisions) Convention* (No. 143) requires States parties to develop national policies designed to guarantee equality of opportunities and treatment in respect of cultural rights for migrant workers or members of their families who are lawfully within its territory; Article 12(f) of the same Convention prescribes the right of the said persons to 'preserve their national and ethnic identity and their cultural ties with their country of origin, including the possibility for children to be given some knowledge of their mother tongue'. Last but not least, Article 29(1)(c) of the 1989 *Convention on the Rights of the Child* establishes that the education of children shall be directed to, *inter alia*, the development of respect for the child's own cultural identity, language and values, as well as for the national values of the country from which the child originates (which is of particular significance for migrant children).

CASES: At the UN level, the Committee on Economic, Social and Cultural Rights has affirmed that all cultural rights – just like any other right contemplated by the ICESCR – 'apply to everyone including non-nationals, such as refugees, asylum-seekers, stateless persons, migrant workers and victims of international trafficking, regardless of legal status and documentation' (General Comment No. 20).

Also the ECtHR has recognised the significance of migrants' cultural rights, although in some cases only implicitly. For instance, the Court has found that the wish of Greek Cypriots living in northern Cyprus 'to have their children educated in accordance with their cultural and ethnic tradition' is a legitimate one [CYPRUS v. TURKEY, 2001] and that, consequently, the lack of appropriate school facilities for those people translated into a violation of Article 2 of Protocol I, concerning the right to education. Similarly, in the event of administration of forcible medical treatment which is contrary to a person's cultural beliefs, a violation of Article 8 ECHR – relating to the right to respect for private and family life – occurs [MATTER v. SLOVAKIA, 1999; V.C. v. SLOVAKIA, 2011].

Finally, the Inter-American Court of Human Rights has noted, among other things, that '[b]asic labor rights are guaranteed to all workers, (including migrants), regardless of whether or not they are legally resident in the country' ('Juridical Condition and Rights of the Undocumented Migrants', Advisory Opinion OC-18/03, 17 September 2003, para. 44).

VIEWS: Once it has been established that migrants are entitled to cultural rights, the key issue concerns the identification of the exact meaning of the term 'migrant'. This operation is necessary to establish who is entitled to migrants' cultural rights. There are different views concerning the meaning of the term 'migrant' under international law. For instance, according to UNESCO a narrow definition should prevail, on the basis of which the term in discussion should only include 'people who make choices about when to leave and where to go, even though these choices are sometimes extremely constrained' ('International Migration and Multicultural Policies'). This position implies that refugees and other persons forced to leave their home country would be excluded. Differently, IOM and the UN Special Rapporteur on the human rights of migrants opt for a more comprehensive concept (see Key Migration Terms). The broader view is shared by the UN, which define the term 'international migrant' as 'any person who changes his or her country of usual residence' (Recommendations on Statistics of International Migration). The fact that a distinction is operated between 'long-term immigrants' (meaning persons who move to a country other than that of their usual residence for a period of at least a year) and 'short-term immigrants' (i.e. those who move to a country different than that of their usual residence for a period of at least three months but less than a year) is not significant in terms of entitlement to enjoy internationally recognised human rights (including cultural rights). In fact, relevant instruments refer to 'migrants' generally speaking, without operating any distinction based on the length of their stay in a country different than that of their usual residence.

CONCL: International law generally extends to migrants internationally recognised human rights. Among them, cultural rights attain a special significance, as their actual enjoyment allows migrants to preserve their own cultural identity in geographical and 'environmental' backgrounds where different cultural models are predominant. Preservation of migrants' cultural identity may translate into different positive obligations for host states, depending on the specific circumstances of each case. Among the most significant cultural rights of migrants, that of having their children educated in accordance with their culture and ethnic traditions, as well as to be taught their mother tongue, emerges. The right to maintain their cultural links with their state of origin, or with the ethnic group to which they belong, is also of particular importance. In addition to refugees the category of migrants with regard to which international law is particularly concerned is that of migrant workers and their families, whose condition is regulated by several conventions at both the universal and regional levels. However, in order to ensure effectiveness of the measures of protection established by such conventions, it would be necessary to increase the number of ratifying states, which is at present quite poor, especially as far as European countries are concerned. Furthermore, it is obvious that the provision of cultural rights on paper, although indispensable, may not be enough to ensure their full enjoyment by migrants if it is not accompanied by the promotion in national societies of a social environment characterised by tolerance, mutual understanding and appreciation for cultural diversities.

REFERENCES:

Appleyard, Reginald (ed.): *The Human Rights of Migrants*, New York: International Organization for Migration and the United Nations (2001).

Bauböck, Rainer: "Cultural Minority Rights for Immigrants", 30 *International Migration Review* (1996) 203.

Cholewinski, Ryszard, de Guchteneire, Paul and Pecoud, Antoine: *Migration and Human Rights: The United Nations Convention on Migrant Workers' Rights*, Cambridge: Cambridge University Press (2009).

Dembour, Marie-Benedicte and Kelly, Tobias (eds.): *Are Human Rights for Migrants? Critical Reflections on the Status of Irregular Migrants in Europe and the United States*, London,New York: Routledge (2011).

International Organization for Migration: "Key Migration Terms" (available at www.iom.int, accessed 3/2016).

O'Nions, Helen: "Minority and Cultural Rights of Migrants", in Chetail, Vincent and Bauloz, Céline (eds.): *Research Handbook on International Law and Migration*, Cheltenham: Edward Elgar Publishing (2014).

UNESCO: "International Migration and Multicultural Policies" (accessed 06/2016 via https://epthinktank.eu/2013/07/09/migration-in-the-eu/).

United Nations, Department of Economic and Social Affairs, *Recommendations on Statistics of International Migration. Revision 1*, New York: United Nations (1998).

United Nations, Office of the High Commissioner on Human Rights, *The Economic, Social and Cultural Rights of Migrants in an Irregular Situation*, New York and Geneva: United Nations (2014).

Federico Lenzerini

Movement of Cultural Objects

DEF: The legal provisions concerning the movement of cultural objects are expressed by international, European and domestic law, such as the 1954 *Hague Convention for the protection of cultural property in the event of armed conflict*, the 1970 *UNESCO Convention on the means of prohibiting and preventing the illicit import, export and transfer of ownership of cultural property*, the UNIDROIT 1995 *Convention on stolen or illegally exported cultural objects*, the 2001 *UNESCO Convention the protection of underwater cultural heritage*, as well as the EU *Regulation 116/2009* on the export of cultural goods and the *European Directive 2014/60* (recast) on the return of cultural objects unlawfully removed from the territory of a member state. During the last decades, there has been evidence of a 'conflict of values' between the reasons behind cultural nationalism – which see states as jealous guardians and supervisors of the circulation of cultural property and of their repatriation – and, conversely, the reasoning of the art market, which aims to grant the widest conditions for the circulation of goods, often characterised by a mannered universalism. While 'all cultural heritage represents a human rights value' (→Cultural Heritage in the Human Rights System), the difficult balance between the quest for safeguarding the integrity of a cultural heritage on the one side and for the free circulation of goods on the other, as well as the search for a compromise between the two is certainly one of the typical and recurring problems arising in this field.

INSTR: Each state retains control over the protection of its national heritage and import and export conditions concerning cultural objects differ substantially. The core provisions of the main relevant international conventions aim at both preventing the →illicit trafficking and urging states parties to take measures to facilitate the →restitution of stolen objects and the return of those illicitly exported from the country of origin. In particular, the 1995 UNIDROIT Convention – as a complement to the 1970 UNESCO Convention – establishes a principle providing for the restitution and return of stolen or illegally exported cultural objects at the request of a state or an individual, including the good faith possessor, who shall be entitled to the payment of fair and reasonable compensation provided that he can prove it exercised due diligence when acquiring the object. The failure to integrate the provisions of the 1970 UNESCO Convention in national legislations and the reluctance expressed by many states to the UNIDROIT Convention represent the main obstacles to applicate the machinery designed to facilitate the restitution and return of cultural objects. Whenever the international customary rules on the jurisdictional immunities of states and their property are not applicable, the protection of cultural objects on loan and the guarantee of their free and licit circulation mainly rely on the applicability of national legislations that provide for immunity from seizure. The problems of restitution and return have been more frequently and directly faced at a bilateral level, particularly over the last decades. This approach has been favoured by the unilateral adoption of domestic legislations by some importing countries (notably in relation to archaeological items), which refer to successive bilateral conventions aiming at a more effective struggle against the illicit trafficking of objects in provenance from certain specific states. This is the case of the *Cultural Property Implementation Act* adopted in the US in 1983, or of the Swiss Federal Law of 2005 on the *International Transfer of Cultural Objects* (LTBC).

CASES: Resort to the judicial settlement of disputes represents the first option for the parties to a dispute, as a rule after having exhausted without success any preliminary possibility of amicable resolution without success. Furthermore, according to the situation and under specific circumstances, judicial settlement may represent a fixed course that the parties must apply for, to their regret, in the absence of an alternative choice, or it may represent an instrumental tool used by the claimant to put the defendant under pressure, hoping to reach an agreement after a negotiation impossible to start at present. The application of the provisions contained in international conventions require that they be integrated by state parties in their domestic legislation. This is particularly true for the 1970 UNESCO Convention as the failure to implement its provisions constitutes an obstacle to its application. In fact, in 2006 the French *Cour de Cassation* – based on the same reasoning as the Italian *Corte di Cassazione* in 1996 – confirmed the rejection of a claim by the state of Nigeria, based on the provision of Article 13 of the 1970 UNESCO Convention, for the return of some *Nok* statues illicitly exported from its territory by a French antique dealer, arguing that the provisions of the Convention were not directly applicable in the domestic legal system, even though France had ratified the Convention without incorporating its main provision in domestic law. On the other hand, the Court of Appeal of England and Wales in [BARAKAT, 2007] recognised the application of Iranian public law on protection of the cultural heritage. The Court justified the recognition of such public law of a third state by referring to the principles of the 1970 UNESCO Convention, of the 1995 UNIDROIT Convention and of the EU Directive; it argued that even if some of the above instruments had no direct effect in domestic law, they nevertheless express the core of the principles shared by the international society and indicate the willingness of the UK to collaborate in the case of theft or illicit export.

VIEWS: According to one point of view, the practice of states should be investigated by looking for evidence of an attitude in favour of retention by the art rich (or art exporting) countries. According to an opposing point of view, any transfer of cultural objects is seen as a progressive impoverishment of the cultural heritage of countries with an important cultural tradition but with less economic power, in favour of countries less rich in art and cultural tradition but with a more competitive economic power. At the crossroads between the need to ensure both the protection of national heritages and the free movement of cultural objects, the search for the fair balance is crucial, even if it may not always fully satisfy all stakeholders (as demonstrated 2015/16 by the fierce opposition of art dealers and collectors against a German law project that tries to implement international rules against the illicit trafficking of protected objects). Furthermore, the outcome of the judicial claims for restitution and return of cultural objects is often uncertain and unpredictable due to reasons depending on factors such as the domestic applicable law, the rules of private international law, or the international conventions. In particular, the choice of the *lex rei sitae* – namely, the law of the place where the object is placed – is most frequently applied as the material law in order to decide on the request of the claimant, and this has often been criticised. With the aim of reducing these shortcomings, some commentators have suggested a departure from the above rule and the introduction of a rule of private international law making it possible to choose between the law of origin of the displaced item (*lex originis*) and the law of the *situs* in an action for recovery of a stolen item. Another suggestion aims at the introduction of a uniform law provision at the domestic level, based on the pattern of the 1995 UNIDROIT Convention. It should provide for the restitution of the stolen cultural object and the reversal of the burden of proof regarding the existence of good faith and/or the due diligence entitling the possessor to payment of fair compensation provided that the possessor neither knew, nor ought reasonably to have known, that the object was stolen and can prove that due diligence had been exercised when the object was acquired. In the absence of any clearly prevailing view, it is also to be noted that the judicial settlement of disputes may not always represent the best choice and not even a suitable solution in all cases concerning the circulation of cultural property. Such disputes are as well quite frequently settled by way of extra-judicial negotiations and agreements. Different kinds of disputes fall within this category, including those between states or public legal entities, where the settlement often relies on the so called diplomatic channels. In such cases a twofold outcome of the negotiation is theoretically possible: either the opposing parties may settle their dispute by way of a classic instrument of international law – namely the execution of an intergovernmental agreement – or they decide to resort to other tools of a contractual nature. Recent and contemporary international practice is marked by a variety of possible combinations: be they either an agreement on a long term loan or a deposit of the requested object, or on its donation, or on a restitution accompanied by scientific and artistic cooperation between the parties, or of the establishment of a trust in view of a future restitution, alternative solutions may be found. These have actually been found, notably in cases of disputes between states and individuals or public or private foreign entities.

CONCL: Unlike the *Belgian code of private international law* of 2004 which provides for the option between the application of the *lex situs* or of the *lex originis* (Article 90), the choice of the law applicable to claims for restitution or return of cultural objects is generally coincident with the *lex situs*. But even the choice of the *lex originis* – whenever this is possible – would not always assure the claimant as to the success of the relevant claim. At the European level, an approach method is being introduced that allows for a special jurisdiction, as it is the case with the EU *Regulation 1215/2012* providing that a civil claim for recovery of cultural objects may be initiated in the courts for the place where the object is situated at the time when the court is seized (Article 7(4)). A similar solution was adopted under the *Swiss law on private international law* of 2003 (Article 98(a)), whereby a special jurisdiction was provided. Possibly and also with a view to overcoming the problems connected with the recognition of foreign public laws, the best solution would be for domestic legislations to be inspired by a uniform pattern, such as that provided for by the 1995 UNIDROIT Convention. These would concern to the duty to restitute or return, the above mentioned effects of possession in good faith and the relevant due diligence standards. In this respect it would be useful to follow the example of the German BGB (sec. 932, para. 2) defining the good faith *a contrario* and considering that the judge should determine the requirement of due diligence, taking into account both objective and subjective elements.

As a more general strategic policy, one should take into account the need for a combination of actions, including the adoption of multilateral and bilateral international conventions, as well as the implementation of these conventions at the domestic level, namely in the states where they are not directly applicable. At the European level, a number of measures to check the growth of illicit trafficking and of illicit sales of cultural objects on the Internet, as has been suggested by →UNESCO, Interpol and ICOM, could be taken up in the form of an EU rule; all online sales websites could, for instance, publish a warning with a prescribed form of words.

REFERENCES:

Carducci, Guido: *La restitution internationale des biens culturels et des objets d'art*, LGDJ (1997).

Cornu M., Fromageau J., Wallaert C., (eds.): *Dictionnaire compare du droit du patrimoine culturel*, CNRS Editions, (2012).

Cornu M., Renold M.A.: *Le renouveau des restitutions de biens culturels: les modes alternatifs de règlement des litiges, Clunet*, 2009, 504.

Fellrath Grazzini, Isabelle: *The Role of Arbitration in Resolving Non-Contractual Disputes*, New York: Transnational Publishers, Inc. (2004).

Frigo, Manlio: *Circulation des biens culturels, dtermination de la loi applicable et methods de règlement des litiges, Recueil des Cours*, The Hague: Martinus Nijhoff (2015), 89.

Jayme, Erik: *Identité culturelle et integration: le droit international privé postmoderne, Recueil des Cours*, The Hague: Martinus Nijhoff (1996).

Nafziger James A.R. Paterson, Robert K (Eds): *Handbook on the Law of Cultural Heritage and International Trade*, Cheltenham: Edward Elgar (2014).

Prott Lyndel: « The Unidroit Convention on Stolen or Illegally Exported Cultural Objects. Ten Years On" *Uniform Law Review* (2009) 230.

Sanchez Cordero J.A. (ed.): *The 1970 Unesco Convention New Challenges*, C. Mexico, 2013.

Siehr Kurt: *International Art Trade and the Law, Recueil des Cours*, The Hague: Martinus Nijhoff (1994).

Van Woudenberg, Nout: *State Immunity and Cultural Objects on Loan*, The Hague: Martinus Nijhoff (2012).

Vrdoljak, AF: *International Law, Museums and the Return of Cultural Objects*, Cambridge: CUP (2006).

FRENCH MINISTRY OF CULTURE v. ITALIAN MINISTRY OF CULTURE AND DE CONTESSINI *Foro italiano*, 1996, I, 907 (1996).

IRAN v. BARAKAT (EWCA 21/12/2007, Civ 1374).

NIGERIA v. MONTBRISON, *JCP*, 2006, IV, 1917 (2006).

www.art-law.org/centre/liens_en.html (accessed 12/2015).

www.ial.uk.com/index.php (accessed 12/2015).

Manlio Frigo

Names
(Choice and Transcription of N.)

DEF: European countries have different norms governing names. A common tradition is for women to change their name when marrying, or rules securing linguistic cohesion of names. In Turkey, for example, a woman takes her husband's surname in marriage [ÜNAL TEKELI, 2004], and Kurdish naming, after a long ban, is still hindered by transcription rules [KEMAL TAŞKIN AND OTHERS, 2010].

INSTR/CASES: A name, be it first or last, carries a cultural meaning of belonging. Traditionally considered a symbol of connection to a male ancestor, a community, or a nation state, a name is a matter of *patrimony*. The state's interest of public order through cultural cohesion is expressed in rules governing names. With the rise of individual rights, the role of self-identification in determination of names becomes a legal and cultural issue.

The Courts in Strasbourg and Luxembourg seem to have developed different approaches. Before the ECtHR, rules governing personal names have primarily been evaluated as a matter of privacy and family life. Doing so, the Court has given a wide margin of appreciation to the state in determining the public interest of cultural cohesion [see e.g. STJERNA, 1994; REFAH PARTISI AND OTHERS v. TURKEY, 2003; GMB AND KM v. SWITZERLAND, 2001; MENTZEN ALIAS MENCENA v. LATVIA, 2004; BULGAKOV v. UKRAINE, 2007]. The CJEU, on the other hand, adhering to a regime of freedom of movement rather than privacy, has taken a more individual-oriented approach, focusing on the consequences of a name in everyday life for the individual at hand [see GARCIA AVELLO, 2003; GRUNKIN AND PAUL, 2008; SAYN-WITTGENSTEIN, 2010; RUNEVIČ-VARDYN, 2011]. Here, the individual is seen as a moving legal subject, with (some) right to choose her or his own cultural belonging.

CONCL: Looking at the European legal scene, we are left with a fragmented picture. The place for cultural agency in an internationalising context, where diverging national rules of patrimony and choice clash, leads to a series of questions for the future: Are harmonised legal regulations of names possible, or even desirable? Whose interests shall determine the transcription of a name? What ought to be the place for choice and cultural agency?

REFERENCES:

GRUNKIN AND PAUL (CJEU 14/10/2008, C-353/06).
KEMAL TAŞKIN AND OTHERS v. TURKEY (ECtHR 02/02/2010, 30206/04, 37038/04, 43681/04, 45376/04, 12881/05, 28697/05, 32797/05, 45609/05).
STJERNA v. FINLAND (ECtHR 25/11/1994, 18131/91).
ÜNAL TEKELI v. TURKEY (ECtHR 16/11/2004, 29865/96).

Daniela Alaattinoğlu

National Minorities

DEF: The explosion of minority rights in the early 1990s brought renewed attention to the cultural rights of national minorities. The right of members belonging to national minorities to practice their culture is recognised as an individual right in collective capacity (Article 27 ICCPR; Article 1 *UN Declaration on Persons Belonging to National or Ethnic, Religious and Linguistic Minorities* (UN DeclonMin)). It has a negative aspect and a positive aspect, the latter pointing towards the obligation of states to take positive measures to protect minority cultures (Article 4 UN DeclonMin, Articles 4(2) and 5 *Framework Convention on National Minorities* (FCNM)). The scope of the right is very wide, including tangible, intangible and natural heritage, and the minority ways of life.

INSTR: Members belonging to national minorities have the right to participate in the national culture without any discrimination (ICERD) as well as the right to practice their own culture (Article 27 ICCPR, Article 15 ICESCR, Article 5 FCNM). Assimilation is clearly prohibited (Articles 5 and 12 FCNM). The participation of members of minorities to their culture must be effective (Article 2(2) UN DeclonMin, Article 15 FCNM); hence it may include cultural autonomy. Unfortunately, it is up to the state to decide on the implementation of the right. Members of minorities must be acknowledged as the owners of their cultural heritage and participate in the exhibition of their artefacts. →UNESCO provisions that viewed cultures as ownership either of the states or the individual are being re-interpreted in light of cultural rights of national minorities; yet, more needs to be done. Minority artefacts must especially be protected in times of ethnic conflict and war. Minority ways of life are protected unless cultural practices contravene international human rights standards. Education and media must promote mutual knowledge and understanding of minority and majority cultures (Article 6 FCNM), whereas cultural links with kin states must be respected (Article 2(5) UN DeclonMin). In 2011, the Faro *Framework Convention on the Value of Cultural Heritage for Society* came into force which refers to 'heritage communities' and recognises collective rights.

CASES: Although neither cultural rights, nor minority rights are included in the →ECHR, the →ECtHR has discussed such rights using a dynamic interpretation of the Convention. Often, the Court has used the right to private life: in [CHAPMAN, 2001], the Court accepted the positive obligation of states to facilitate the minority (Roma) way of life, including consideration of their needs and their different lifestyle. In [KHURSHID MUSTAFA AND TARZIBACHI, 2008], the Court held that the eviction of tenants on account of their refusal to remove a satellite dish that enabled them access to television programmes in Arabic and Farsi of their country of origin was contrary to the right of members of minorities. In [MUNOZ DIAZ, 2009], the Court also held that refusal to recognise a marriage according to the special rites of the minority community (Roma) for hereditary matters amounted to a violation of prohibition of discrimination and protection of property. The ECtHR has recognised a significant link between linguistic rights and the maintaining of the cultural identity of national minorities. The Court has also discussed issues related to minority religious manifestations, widely seen as part of minority intangible culture: Recently, the principle of 'living together' set out in [S.A.S, 2014] as a requirement for minorities has been widely criticised.

VIEWS: It is important not to essentialise minority cultures and not to protect past manifestations; rather states must allow national minorities to decide on which elements should be protected. Recognition of cultural rights of national minorities often raises questions on potential violations of individual rights by illiberal practices. International law has tools to deal with such possible conflicts. The [LOVELACE, 1981] case and the *Siracusa Principles on the Limitation and Derogation Provisions in the International Covenant on Civil and Political Rights* guide the international community in applying restrictions to human rights. Any affected individuals need to have their voices respected, while minority communities must be the main interpreters of their own cultural practices. Cultural practices may be curbed, only if they are contrary to international standards, and limitations to minority cultural rights have to be interpreted restrictively. It is important that the restriction to minority cultural rights responds to a pressing public or social need and is proportionate.

Integration has been widely viewed as a positive vehicle for inclusion of national minorities to the society. However, the current implementation of the concept by European states weakens the right of national minorities to their culture. The Europeanisation of human rights values lead to unnecessary suspicion towards minority cultures. Furthermore, the idea of 'living together' as discussed in [SAS, 2014] introduces further criteria for restricting minority cultures which go beyond the existing standards.

CONCL: The protection of indigenous cultural rights is a fairly recent discussion in international human rights law, which has been intensified by similar – albeit more detailed- new provisions on indigenous cultural rights. Even though viewing culture as a way of life is not new, tangible and intangible heritage has traditionally been granted to states, rather than non-state actors. Policies and practices allowing the true input of minorities in the exhibition, design and protection of their artefacts are still in an embryonic state in many states and more attention has to be given to this issue by international organisations. The UNESCO, the World Intellectual Property Organization (WIPO) and the World Bank are slowly opening their outlooks to accommodate minority cultural heritage and to make their documents and policies more consistent to minority rights standards. Redress of violations of minority cultural rights is still scarce. Easier are the discussions on intangible cultural rights, such as cultural practices, language and names. The standards are clearer and judicial and quasi-judicial international bodies have often been discussing them. The balance between minority cultural rights and other interests is ongoing but should not be tipped over by voices that use such debates to restrict minority cultural rights. In general, there is a gradual realisation that the right of national minorities to culture acts also as a prerequisite for the enjoyment of other rights related to land, education, food and natural resources.

REFERENCES:

Stamatopoulou, Elsa: "Monitoring Cultural Human Rights: the Claims of Culture on Human Rights and the Response of Cultural Rights" 34 *Human Rights Quarterly* (2012) 1170.

Ringelheim, Julie (ed.): *Le droit and la diversite culturelle*, Paris: Bruylant (2011).

Holt, Sally: "Family, Private Life and Cultural Rights" in Marc Weller (ed.): *Universal Minority Rights, A Commentary on the Jurisprudence of International Courts and Treaty Bodies*, Oxford University Press (2007).

Borelli, Silvia: "Of Veils, Crosses and Turbans: The European Court of Human Rights and Religious Practices as Manifestations of Cultural Diversity" in Silvia Borelli and Federico Lenzerini (eds.): *Cultural Heritage, Cultural Rights, Cultural Diversity: New Developments in International Law*, Boston–Leiden: Brill–Nijhoff (2012) 55.

Makkonen, Timo: "Minorities' Right to Maintain and Develop Their Cultures: Legal Implications of Social Science Research" in Francesco Francioni and Martin Scheinin (eds.): *Cultural Human Rights*, Boston–Leiden: Brill–Nijhoff (2008).

Kymlicka, Will: *Minority rights to culture*, Oxford: Oxford University Press (1995).

Xanthaki, Alexandra: "Against Integration, In Favour of Human Rights" 20 *International Journal of Human Rights* (2016) 815.

Xanthaki, Alexandra: "Multiculturalism and International Law: Discussing Universal Standards" 32 *Human Rights Quarterly* (2010) 21.

CHAPMAN v. THE UNITED KINGDOM (ECtHR 18/01/2001, 27238/95).

KHURSHID MUSTAFA AND TARZIBACHI v. SWEDEN (ECtHR 16/12/2008, 23883/06).

MUNOZ DIAZ v. SPAIN (ECtHR 08/12/2009, 49151/07).

S.A.S v. FRANCE (ECtHR 01/07/2014, 43835/11).

SANDRA LOVELACE v. CANADA (HR Committee (1981), CCPR/C/13/D/24/1977).

Alexandra Xanthaki

Older Persons

(Participation in Cultural Life of O. P.)

DEF: There is no universally accepted definition of 'older persons', as virtually all provisions included in human rights treaties concerning older persons do not specify when old age begins. However, according to the CESCR (General Comment No. 6, 1995), the expression in point covers 'persons aged 60 and above'.

INSTR: Article 25 of the UDHR attributes old aged persons the right to a standard of living adequate for their health and well-being as well as the right to security. At the European level, Article 23 of the 1996 *Revised European Social Charter* establishes the right of elderly persons to social protection, which is aimed at enabling them to remain full members of society for as long as possible through leading a decent life and playing an active part in public, social and cultural life, as well as through freely choosing their life-style. Article 25 of the 2000 *Charter of Fundamental Rights of the European Union* recognizes and respects the rights of the elderly to lead a life of dignity and independence and to participate in social and cultural life. Last but not least, on 15 June 2015 the Organization of American States (OAS) adopted the *Inter-American Convention on Protecting the Human Rights of Older Persons*, which affirms 'the right (of such persons) to their cultural identity, to participate in the cultural and artistic life of the community, to enjoy the benefits of scientific and technological progress and those resulting from cultural diversity, and to share their knowledge and experience with other generations in any of the contexts in which they participate' (Article 21). According to the General Comments No. 6 (1995) and 21 (2009) of the CESCR, states must pay particular attention to the promotion and protection of the cultural rights of older persons, including through ensuring them appropriate access to education and to cultural institutions.

VIEWS/CONCL: As emphasised by the Population Division of the UN Secretariat, '(p)opulation ageing is one of humanity's greatest triumphs. It is also one of our greatest challenges and places increasing economic and social demands on all countries. Worldwide, the proportion of people aged 60 years and over is growing and will continue to grow faster than any other age group (...) The number of older people over 60 years is expected to increase from about 600 million in 2000 to over 2 billion in 2050' (World Population Prospects: the 2008 Revision). It is therefore essential that international law on elders' human rights – including cultural rights – is appropriately improved. In this respect, *Resolution 65/182* of 21 December 2010 – in which the UN General Assembly decided to establish a working group with the purpose of strengthening the protection of the human rights of older persons, including by considering the adoption of a new comprehensive and integral legal instrument – as well as parallel efforts of NGOs (see e.g. GAROP, 2015) are to be welcomed.

REFERENCES:

Dabbs Sciubba, Jennifer: "Explaining campaign timing and support for a UN Convention on the Rights of Older People", 18 *International Journal of Human Rights* (2014) 462.

Global Alliance for the Rights of Older People (GAROP): *Towards a Binding Convention on the Rights of Older Persons*, 2015.

Martin, Claudia, Diego Rodríguez-Pinzón and Bethany Brown: *Human Rights of Older People: Universal and Regional Legal Perspectives*, Springer: Dordrecht, Heidelberg, New York, London (2015).

OAS: *The Region's Commitment to the Rights of Older Persons* (available at www.oas.org accessed 3/2016).

Rodriguez-Pinzón, Diego, and Claudia Martin: "The International Human Rights Status of Elderly Persons", 18 *American University International Law Review* (2003) 915.

UN Committee on Economic, Social and Cultural Rights: *General Comment No. 6 – The economic, social and cultural rights of older persons* (1995).

Federico Lenzerini

Organisation for Security and Cooperation in Europe (OSCE)

INTRO: The OSCE is an intergovernmental organisation with 57 member states. Inspired by the *CSCE Helsinki Final Act* (1975) and the *Charter of Paris for a New Europe* (1990), it deals comprehensively with a wide range of issues relating to three dimensions of international and regional security: (1) politico-military, (2) economic and environmental, and (3) human aspects. All decisions are taken by consensus but are not legally binding. In 2010, the OSCE member states adopted the *Astana Commemorative Declaration* which was considered a significant step towards the commitment of the partners for a 'comprehensive, co-operative, equal and indivisible security, which relates the maintenance of peace to the respect for human rights and fundamental freedoms, and links economic and environmental co-operation with peaceful inter-State relations'.

Across the OSCE region, the organisation through its institutions and field operations is engaged in projects on the rights of minorities, rights of Roma and Sinti; rights of displaced persons; freedom of media and media pluralism; political participation; education; →housing; civil registration; and elimination of racism, →discrimination, xenophobia, anti-Semitism and intolerance against Christians and Muslims. Respect for human rights and democracy is a key part of the OSCE's agenda.

INSTR: The OSCE has established institutions and instruments that contribute to the monitoring of the human rights situation in all 57 participating countries:

(1) The OSCE's Office for Democratic Institutions and Human Rights (ODIHR) is mandated to ensure 'full respect for human rights and fundamental freedoms, to abide by the rule of law, to promote principles of democracy and ... to build, strengthen and protect democratic institutions, as well as promote tolerance throughout society' (Helsinki Final Act). The ODIHR *inter alia* observes elections, facilitates democracy assistance projects in the OSCE region, monitors judicial independence, promotes freedom of religion or belief through legal reviews and other activities of ODIHR's Panel of Experts on Freedom of Peaceful Assembly; assists in the capacity-building of human rights defenders; provides human rights education and training; promotes the rights of → Roma and Sinti through the ODIHR's Contact Point for Roma and Sinti Issues, and organises the annual OSCE Human Dimension Implementation Meeting which reviews states' policies and practices with regard to human rights.

(2) The OSCE's High Commissioner on National Minorities (HCNM) is an 'instrument of conflict prevention at the earliest possible stage'. The HCNM issues recommendations and offers context-specific advice in order to avoid or reduce tensions related to → national minority issues which could develop into conflict, i.e. respect for minority languages, the responsibility of states to offer opportunities to minorities to learn the official languages, minority representation at national, regional and local levels as a matter of good governance and good practices on integration, social cohesion and intercultural awareness.

(3) The Special Representative and Co-ordinator for Combating Trafficking in Human Beings assists the OSCE member states in developing and implementing effective policies on corruption and crime control; discrimination and inequality issues; and migration.

(4) The Representative on Freedom of the Media monitors media developments and violations of freedom expression across the OSCE region (i.e. → journalists prosecuted for their professional activities); reviews media regulation and legislation and promotes Internet → freedom of expression.

REFERENCES:

www.osce.org (accessed 06/2016).

Kalliopi Chainoglou

Parody

DEF: Parody is generally defined as an artistic composition in which the main characteristics of a particular work are exaggerated or applied to an inappropriate subject, especially for the purposes of ridicule. The essential elements of parody are thus its imitative character and the satirical or comical effect. In the European legal framework, these elements were confirmed by the CJEU judgment in the [DECKMYN, 2014] case, which also defined parody as an autonomous concept of EU law. The ECtHR noted that parody is a form of artistic expression that, by its features of exaggeration and distortion of reality, naturally aims to provoke and agitate [SOUSA GOUCHA, 2016].

INSTR: Parody, as exercise of the fundamental right to freedom of expression (Article 10 ECHR and Article 11 EU Charter of Fundamental Rights), is particularly relevant in connection to copyright (Article 1 of Protocol 1 ECHR and Article 17 of the Charter) and respect for personal and private life (Article 8 ECHR and Article 7 of the Charter). None of these being absolute, a fair balance has to be struck by the national authorities between the conflicting rights. For example, in EU legislation, parody is one of the optional exceptions on copyright, contained in Article 5(3)(k) of the *InfoSoc Directive*, but its application has to strike the fair balance between the author's rights and freedom of speech. As far as the right to respect for personal and private life is concerned, the ECtHR has stated that, when balancing it against the right to freedom of expression, one has to bear in mind that there is no hierarchical relationship between the two rights, and, for example, an obligation to protect one's reputation may arise where the statements go beyond the limits of what is considered acceptable under Article 10 [SOUSA GOUCHA, 2016]. It also introduced the criterion of the reasonable reader relating to issues of satirical material [NIKOWITZ AND VERLAGSGRUPPE, 2007].

CASES: ECtHR stated that freedom of expression constitutes one of the essential foundations of a democratic society and one of the basic conditions for its progress and for each individual's self-fulfilment. Subject to paragraph 2, it is applicable not only to 'information' or 'ideas' that are favourably received or regarded as inoffensive or as a matter of indifference, but also to those that offend, shock or disturb. Such are the demands of that pluralism, tolerance and broadmindedness without which there is no 'democratic society' [NILSEN AND JOHNSEN, 1999]. Any interference with the right to freedom of expression has to be in accordance with the three conditions enshrined in the second paragraph of Article 10 of the ECHR: legal, necessary and pursuing a legitimate aim. However, not being an absolute right, freedom of expression has to be always weighed against protection of general and particular interests and rights. This balancing exercise has to be done by the national authorities on a case-by-case basis, taking into consideration all the circumstances. For example, the ECtHR found that it is not sufficient to justify a restriction to one's artistic freedom of expression solely on the basis that a copyright law provision was infringed [ASHBY DONALD, 2013] and that a certain degree of exaggeration or even provocation is permissible for the press, especially when it concerns a question of public interest [KULIS AND RÓZYCKI, 2009].

VIEWS: Most authors argue that the legitimacy of parody is based on the principle of freedom of artistic expression. Some view copyright as a restriction on this freedom, in the sense that it can restrict the use and distribution of cultural goods and information products (Vorhoof, 1997). In this respect, some authors tend to see in a recent CJEU judgment [JOHAN DECKMYN AND VRIJHEIDSFONDS, 2014] a first attempt of the European jurisdiction towards a *de facto* harmonisation of moral rights across Europe (Rosati, 2015).

CONCL: The satirical genre being by definition excessive, it may seem difficult to fix limits between freedom of the press and abuses of the rights of third parties. However, excessive satirical actions cannot avoid civil responsibility (e.g. for defamation). The border between satirical genre and third parties' rights remains at the discretion of courts who will decide in favor of any of the conflicting rights involved, without ruling on the good or poor taste of the contentious artwork. Both the CJEU and the ECtHR judgments provide some guidance for courts to operate this balancing test, by introducing criteria for examining the proportionality of the different measures taken at national level to protect one or the other of the conflicting rights. If, for example, CJEU judgments on matters of copyright are read in conjunction with ECtHR judgments on freedom of expression and respect for private life, national authorities have enough guidance for correctly applying the proportionality test. When deciding on the conflicting rights, national authorities enjoy a fairly large margin of appreciation (depending on the content), the only condition in order to avoid arbitrariness being to bear in mind that there is no hierarchy between the different rights at stake. Fairness of such a test implies, for example, a certain predictability of the outcome, by establishing at national level a clear set of criteria like the ECtHR did in [AXEL SPRINGER, 2012], in balancing Articles 8 and 10 of the ECHR. It remains to be seen if and how national authorities will set such criteria, including through case law.

REFERENCES:

Directive No. 2001/29/EC on the harmonization of certain aspects of copyright and related rights in the information society.

Michaux, Benoît: La bande dessinée et le droit des tiers. Mais quelles sont les limites à la liberté de création?, in *Droit d'auteur et bande dessinée*, Bruxelles: Bruylant (1997).

Rosati, Eleonora: "Just a laughing matter? Why the decision in *Deckmyn* is broader than parody", 52 *Common Market Law Review* (2015) 511.

Voorhoof, Dirk: "La parodie et les droits moraux. Le droit au respect de l'auteur d'une bande dessinée: un obstacle insurmontable pour la parodie?", in *Droit d'auteur et Bande dessinée*, Bruxelles: Bruylant, (1997).

AHMET YILDIRIM v. TURKEY (ECtHR 18/12/2012, 3111/10).
ALVES DA SILVA v. PORTUGAL (ECtHR 20/10/2009, 41665/07).
ASHBY DONALD AND OTHERS v. FRANCE (ECtHR 10/01/2013, 36769/08).
AXEL SPRINGER AG v. GERMANY (ECtHR 07/02/2012, 39954/08).
JOHAN DECKMYN AND VRIJHEIDSFONDS VZW v. HELENA VANDERSTEEN AND OTHERS (CJEU 03/09/2014, C-201/13).
KULIS AND RÓZYCKI v. POLAND (ECtHR 06/10/2009, 27209/03).
NIKOWITZ AND VERLAGSGRUPPE NEWS GMBH v. AUSTRIA (ECtHR 22/02/2007, 5266/03).
NILSEN AND JOHNSEN v. NORWAY (ECtHR 25/11/1999, 23118/93).
SCARLET EXTENDED SA v. SOCIÉTÉ BELGE DES AUTEURS, COMPOSITEURS ET ÉDITEURS SCRL (SABAM) (CJEU 24/11/2011, C-70/10).
SOUSA GOUCHA v. PORTUGAL (ECtHR 22/03/2016, 70434/12).

Geanina Munteanu

Participation in Cultural Life

DEF: The right to participate in cultural life is double-faceted, similar to a great number of other human rights. There is, on the one hand, the negative right to participate in cultural life which entails the freedom to participate without interference from the state. On the other hand, there is the positive side of this right, which entails positive obligations for the state such as the obligation to develop →cultural policies aiming at broadening access and participation in cultural life.

INSTR: At the international level, the most specific formulation of the right to participate in cultural life can be found in Article 27 of the UDHR and Article 15, 1, a), of the UN *International Covenant on Economic, Social and Cultural Rights*. This last provision reads as follow: 'The States Parties to the present Covenant recognise the right of everyone [...] to take part in cultural life'. Originally, the right to participate in cultural life, at the international level, had been conceived essentially as a freedom to participate in cultural life and as a right to access the set of major artworks of a given community. The legal sources of this human right are also rooted in international and regional legal instruments on cultural policies. The 2005 UNESCO *Convention on the Protection and Promotion of the Diversity of Cultural Expressions*, for instance, embodies explicit references to fundamental rights such as the right to participate in cultural life as requirements, but also as limits to cultural diversity.

The ECHR does not clearly recognise a right to participate in cultural life. The *Charter of Fundamental Rights* (EU) limits the benefit of the right to participate in cultural life to the elderly (Article 25). Within the European legal space, a short review of national Constitutions shows that only those in Belgium and Portugal fully recognise a right to participate in cultural life. Other Constitutions either limit themselves to the recognition of a right to access to culture (e.g. in Poland, the Czech Republic, Romania or Slovakia), to the recognition of artistic freedom (almost all European Constitutions) or to the protection of minority cultural rights (e.g. in Austria, Estonia or the FYR of Macedonia).

CASES: The interpretation of the right to participate in cultural life has evolved significantly in the last decades under the actions of the UN Committee on Economic, Social and Cultural Rights (CESCR) and regional jurisdictions. Article 15 of the ICESCR was firstly constructed as a right to participate in the diversity of cultural life, before being interpreted, in some statements of expert bodies and commentators, as a right to cultural identity (notably the *General Comment no. 21* of the CESCR). This interpretation of Article 15 as a right to cultural identity remains uncertain: in its Concluding Observations, the Committee recommends that states parties take appropriate measures to protect the general capacity of minorities and indigenous groups to maintain and practice their way of life by referring itself to a *combination* of different provisions, rather than on the sole basis of Article 15 ICESCR. Still at the international level, it is striking to note that, despite the multiple elaborations on this human right, the invocation of the right to participate in cultural life never played a decisive role in international case law.

At the regional level, this right was at the centre of a case decided by the African Commission on Human Rights [ENDOROIS, 2010]. As regards the ECtHR, it took up some of the dimensions of the right to participate in cultural life by recognising the freedom not to suffer from any interference in accessing, or participating in, cultural life [ADKAS v. TURKEY, 2010], artistic freedom [since MÜLLER v. SWITZERLAND, 1988] and the freedom of association in the cultural sector [GORZELIK AND OTHERS v. POLAND, 2004]. The Court also protects cultural interests by integrating cultural considerations in the interpretation of restrictions to the right to property [e.g. BEYELER v. ITALY, 2000].

VIEWS: Firstly, a converging opinion in the literature is that the interpretation of the right to participate in cultural life has moved towards a right protecting cultural identities at the international, national and regional levels. Clearly, a change in the interpretation of the word 'culture' in the international cultural rights discourse is now widely recognised. Some authors note that states regularly report to the CESCR information concerning the protection of minorities' cultural identities (beyond their cultural practices) and ways of life.

Secondly, some authors actively participated in the drafting of General Comment no. 21 and/or promote a broad, anthropological conception of cultural life which constitutes the object of Article 15 (1) (a) of the ICESCR. These authors form part of a group known as '*Groupe de Fribourg*', an academic association which aims at promoting the advancement of cultural rights. They adopt a normative point of view on this right, promoting a certain vision of it, which is mainly in line with communitarian theories.

Thirdly, other studies examine the evolution of the interpretation of Article 15 (1) (a) of the ICESCR and try to identify the normative content of that right. They discuss what could be a legal definition and legal regime of that right. In this context, some authors focus on a potential interaction between the right to participate in cultural life and copyright or with ICT and attempt to identify ethical foundations of the right. As well, some authors try to unravel economic and social issues that certain soothing discourses on this human right might obscure (e.g. inequalities, cultural homogenisation).

Finally, some authors analyse the influence of EU law or of other legal orders (like that of the WTO) on the recognition, protection and promotion of the right to participate in cultural life. They try to explain the following paradox: While the right to participate in cultural life has been the subject of much attention and elaboration in discourses (law in books), it had almost no effect in legal practice (law in action). They try to adopt an analytical insight and to explain the link between the broadness of the current definition of the right and its qualification as a 'soft law' instrument by the vast majority of the legal doctrine.

CONCL: It can be said that there are two different rights to participate in cultural life: The first one is a right to 'ways of life', a right to 'cultural identity', whose broad object has not yet been fully defined, and whose scope remains uncertain – as are its legal and political effects. This 'right' appears sometimes in the form of a principle of interpretation: the idea would be to interpret every human right 'culturally'. It draws attention to the situation of minorities of autochthonous peoples but also to all distinct 'ways of life'.

The second right is a distinct human right to participate in a diverse cultural life. This implies multiple, precise prerogatives: freedom of artistic and creative expression; the right to conservation, development and diffusion of the diversity of cultural heritages and expressions; the right to access to cultural life and cultural information; the right to actively contribute to the diversity of cultural life; freedom of choice (the possibility to choose to participate or not to participate in cultural life, and also the choice to determine which forms of cultural life to be involved in); the right to participate in decision-making in cultural matters (this is the procedural facet of the right to participate in cultural life) and non-discrimination in participation in cultural life. This second right to participate in cultural life is intimately bound with cultural democratisation / democracy policies and cultural diversity. It is more linked with the fight against inequalities and with questions raised by cultural policies.

REFERENCES:

Bidault, Mylène: *La protection internationale des droits culturels*, Brussels: Bruylant (2010).

Donders, Yvonne: *Towards a Right to Cultural Identity?*, Antwerpen: Intersentia (2002).

Romainville, Céline: *Le droit à la culture, une réalité juridique. Le régime juridique du droit de participer à la vie culturelle en droit constitutionnel et en droit international*, Brussels: Bruylant (2014).

Romainville, Céline: 'The right to participate in cultural life under EU law' 2 *European Journal of Human Rights/Journal Européen des droits humains* (2015) 145.

Saul, Ben, Kinley, David, et Mowbray, Jaqueline: "Article 15: Cultural Rights" in Ben Saul, David Kinley, and Jaqueline Mowbray (eds.), *The International Covenant on Economic, Social and Cultural Rights: Commentary, Cases and Materials*, Oxford, Oxford University Press (2014) 1175.

Stamatopoulou, Elissavet: "Monitoring Cultural Human Rights: The Claims of Culture on Human Rights and the Response of Cultural Rights" 34 *Human Rights Quarterly* (2012) 1170.

AKDAS v. TURKEY (ECtHR 16/07/2010, 41056/04).

ENDOROIS case: Centre for Minority Rights Development (Kenya) and Minority Rights Group International On Behalf of ENDOROIS WELFARE COUNCIL v. KENYA, 276/2003 AHRLR 75, 04/02/2010.

http://www.ohchr.org/EN/HRBodies/CESCR/Pages/ContributionsDGD2008.aspx (Background papers of experts for the General Discussion Day on the Right to participate in cultural life at the UN CESCR) (accessed 10/2015).

Celine Romainville

Peoples' Rights

DEF: The term 'peoples' rights' refers to certain rights recognised by international law to pluralities of individuals considered as collectivities, due to their common characteristics and/or collective self-identification. Peoples' rights are intended to be enjoyed collectively and refer *inter alia* to the following rights to: exist, self-determination, peace, security, development, land, natural resources, health, environment and culture. Such rights are inherent and complementary to individual human rights. Yet, they are also often perceived as undermining or colliding with other human rights.

INSTR/CASES/VIEWS: Although international law does not define 'peoples', it has recognised various rights in favour of pluralities of individuals, considered and/or self-identified as wholes. The equal right to self-determination is primordial to peoples' rights. Incorporated into the UN Charter (Articles 1 and 55), enshrined in the ICCPR (Article 1) and ICESCR (Article 1), and developed during the era of decolonisation, entails the right of every people to freely decide on its sovereignty and choose its international status. Self-determination, mostly seen in political terms, has gradually extended to other dimensions of peoples' existence, including the right to peace and free pursuit of economic, social and cultural development. Such rights, labelled as 'third-generation human rights' (Vasak, 1984), are enumerated, *inter alia* in the *Algiers Declaration of the Rights of Peoples* (1976), *UNGA Declarations on Right of Peoples to* Peace (1984) and on the *Right to Development* (1986). On the level of treaty law, peoples' rights are enshrined in the ACHPR (1981), to a degree not matched by other binding international human rights law instruments. Alongside the right to self-determination, the ACHPR recognises peoples' rights to: equality, existence, free disposal of their wealth and natural resources, economic, social and cultural development, peace and security and 'a generally satisfactory environment'. Thus, the ACHPR positions peoples' rights as inherent and complementary to individual human rights, representing distinct, but inter-linked human aspirations and objectives (Viljoen, 2012). The notion of peoples' rights is sometimes perceived as losing importance in the current post-colonial and post-Cold War reality, due to their conceptual vagueness and non-justiciability (Alston, 2001). The right to self-determination of peoples is generally treated as an unenforceable right under international human rights monitoring regimes. In particular, the HR Committee does not deal with collective claims to the right to self-determination, under Article 1 ICCPR, brought pursuant to individual communications procedure (LUBICON LAKE BAND, 1990). The neutralisation of peoples' rights is also attributed to other factors: the end of most socialist regimes, that championed collective rights at the expense of individuals' rights, phenomenon of globalisation, development of specific groups-oriented legal regimes (national minorities and indigenous peoples). Indeed, the notion of peoples' rights seems today to float towards the expanding realm of collective rights, encompassing community and minority rights. Among collective rights, cultural rights are seen as fundamental for determining the 'self' of a given group or community. In fact, the CESCR, while dealing with collective aspects of the right of everyone to take part in cultural life (Article 15 ICESCR), has referred to certain well-defined communities: indigenous peoples and minorities (CESCR, 2009), rather than to 'peoples' in general. Importantly, the collective cultural dimension may affect the understanding and realisation of particular individual human rights within a given societal and legal context, as evidenced the jurisprudence of the IACHR and AfComHPR. Thus, the recognition and enforcement of collective cultural rights may contribute to maximising the effectiveness of human rights standards (Lenzerini, 2014). Collective rights and individual rights are usually mutually supportive, although in certain circumstances some antagonism between them may arise, especially between individual and collective cultural rights.

CONCL: The notion of peoples' rights is inherently tied to self-determination. Yet, both terms pose serious questions as to the catalogue of entities, other than states, who can be considered 'peoples' and as to exact content and form in which the right to self-determination can be exercised. The concept of peoples' rights may also refer to other distinct rights, linked to self-determination, and enjoyed by a plurality of persons as a whole. Today the collective dimension of the right to culture is increasingly recognised as necessary for human well-being, and thus important in interpreting and realising other human rights. Arguably, the notion of peoples' rights in relation to culture seems to be associated with collective cultural rights and their role in preserving, enjoying and transmitting cultural identity and cultural heritage of a given community to future generations.

REFERENCES:

Alston, Philip (ed.): *People's Rights*, Oxford: Oxford University Press (2001).

CESCR: "General Comment No. 21", UN Doc. E/C.12/GC/21 (2009).

Crawford, James R. (ed.): *Rights of Peoples*, Oxford: Clarendon Press (1988).

Lenzerini, Federico: *The Culturalization of Human Rights Law*, Oxford: Oxford University Press (2014).

Paupp, Terrence E.: *Redefining Human Rights in the Struggle for Peace and Development*, New York: Cambridge University Press (2014).

Vasak, Karel: "Pour une troisième génération des droits de l'homme", in Christophe Swinarski (ed.) *Essays on International Humanitarian Law and Red Cross Principles in Honour of Jean Pictet*, Leiden–Boston: Nijhoff, (1984).

Viljoen, Frans: *International Human Rights Law in Africa*, 2nd edn., Oxford: Oxford University Press (2012).

LUBICON LAKE BAND v. CANADA (HR Committee (1990), CCPR/C/38/D/167/1984).

Andrzej Jakubowski

Pornography / Obscenity

DEF: Pornography is a concept largely found in practically all contemporary legal traditions, often addressed as 'obscenity' in common law systems. The first usage of the word pornography (from Greek πόρνη, a prostitute, and γράφειν, to write or to record) dates back to a French novel of the 18th century about prostitution (Rétif, 1769). Yet gradually the meaning of this term evolved towards the portrayal of various sexual subject matters meant to incite sexual arousal. The judicial legacy of anti-erotic → censorship in Europe is a genetic offspring of the Judeo–Christian ethics within legal reasoning, with its fear of images embedded in various religious interpretations of the Second Commandment (Belavusau, 2010). This partially explains why most forms of contemporary censorship of pornographic expression are focused more on imaginary expression (pictures, movies, illustrations, etc.) rather than on written forms of sexual expression, e.g. in books (Adler, 2012–13).

Historically there have been two major modes of dealing with the sexual: *ars erotica* and *scientia sexualis* (Foucault, 1976). In the Greco–Roman world and in pre-modern societies of China, Japan and India, for example, sexuality was conceived as an 'ars erotica' (erotic art) where sex is apprehended as a special creative experience, i.e. not something dirty and shameful. Western society, to the contrary, constructed what Foucault called 'scientia sexualis' (the science of sexuality). Its original 17th century conception is based on a confession. A fixation with finding out the 'truth' about sexuality arises, a truth that is to be confessed and kept censored. This mode of censoring historical artefacts has influenced the 19th century's rise of museums and special secrete sections in those museums displaying erotic art (Walter, 1996).

HIST/INSTR: Initially, pornography was a distinctly European concept shaped by two major traditions: continental (in France) and common law (where it has been referred to under the tag of obscenity, in the British Empire). Roman law supplied a notion of *boni mores* ('good morals') that played its special role in contractual obligations and was substantially different from contemporary moralistic connotations. The French Civil Code of 1804 has initially incorporated that contractual terminology of *bonnes mœurs*. In 1810, France adopted its Criminal Code where the notion of *bonnes mœurs* was borrowed from private law into public law and underwent a significant semantic mutation, meant to limit the proliferation of pornographic literature. Likewise, the first restriction on the law of the freedom of press in France became an offence of '*outrage aux bonnes mœurs*' (1882), a notion which migrated afterwards into criminal legislation or doctrine in most continental legal traditions, including German: *gute Sitten*, Dutch: *goede zeden*, Italian: *buon costume*, etc. In 1857, Britain adopted its first *Obscene Publication Act* that survived two modifications (1959 and 1964), and is still in force in England and Wales. The Act became the first piece of legislation enabling police constables to seize obscene material and seek its destruction before magistrates, thus affecting the trade in pornography. This 'English' concept of 'obscenity' afterwards entered all common law traditions (USA, Canada, Australia, India, etc). Thus, the notion of pornography (or obscenity) was spread to the rest of the world's legal systems through European colonial law in the 19th century, affecting non-Western legal traditions in Asia and Africa.

On the international level, two major instruments have been adopted in the 20th century: The *Agreement for the Suppression of Obscene Publications* (1910) and the *International Convention for the Suppression of the Circulation of and Traffic in Obscene Publications* (1923). The 'gravament' of the offence under the 1923 Convention on the trade of pornography is the distribution across national boundaries. This offence is generally considered to be in desuetude and only a few states have remained bound by the Convention on the subject. Article 19 ICCPR (1966) contains a restriction on freedom of speech for the protection of 'public morals'. European law has also largely incorporated the continental legal clause on 'public morality', which penetrated the language of international treaties as an exception to commercial and artistic freedoms. In particular, Article 10 ECHR mentions 'protection of morals' as a plausible ground for restrictions on free speech. Likewise, Article 36 TFEU permits restrictions on free movement of goods justified on the grounds of 'public morality'.

CASES: The ECtHR has a relatively rich body of case-law on pornography, in particular in the context of artistic expression. Most of these cases have been dealt as a matter of potential violation of freedom of expression and have been adjudicated, respectively, on the basis of Article 10 (2) ECHR. The Court has had a tendency to largely leave the decision on qualification of morality and public outrage to the →margin of appreciation of Member States [HANDYSIDE, 1976; MÜLLER, 1988; VEREINIGUNG BILDENDER KÜNSTLER, 2007]. The position of the Court seems to differ with regard to situations when a piece of art enjoys a longstanding recognised acceptation, like for example, in a case concerning publication of an erotic novel by G. Apollinaire in Turkey [AKDAŞ, 2010]. The Court noted that there is no unanimity in the legal and social order of various European states on the issue of obscenity. Yet it also established that a hundred years had passed since Apollinaire's book's first publication in France. Nowadays, therefore, the book had acquired a wide recognition in many countries and undoubtedly constitutes part of the European literary heritage (para. 30 in AKDAŞ, 2010). In contrast, the CJEU has fostered an entirely moral-neutral legal position on the trade of pornographic goods in the EU [HENN & DARBY, 1979; CONEGATE, 1986; EROTIC CENTER, 2010]. It has advanced a flexible internal market with free movement of sexual goods following liberalisation of sexuality in EU states, with an emphasis on the principle of mutual recognition (Belavusau, 2015).

VIEWS: There is a long-standing debate on the permissibility of pornography in the public space. Censorship of pornography unavoidably raises problems of incompatibility with freedom of – in particular, artistic and scientific – expression, as well as with an emancipated pursuit of individual sexuality. Liberal scholars generally challenge the wide ban on obscene expression, advocating a possibility of moral choices, life styles and, ultimately, opposing the arguments restricting the pursuit of happiness, pleasure and individualistic conceptions of self (Schroeder, 1938; R. Dworkin, 1986; Sadurski, 1996; Koppelman, 2008). The adversaries of pornography refer to a number of alternative arguments. Conservative opponents invoke family values, protection of public morality and minors, along with their freedom of religion, as a defence for restrictions (Guyenot, 2000; Shytov, 2005). Radical feminist scholars often portray pornography as a visualized form of patriarchy and implicit rape of the female subject for the pleasure of men (A. Dworkin, 1991; Mackinnon, 1993). In contrast, the so-called 'pro-sex' feminists, see a liberating force in pornography as a way for a general sexual emancipation (Willis, 1981; Benjamin, 1983, Carol, 1994). These two camps have been distinctly represented in American feminist jurisprudence, leading to the so-called 'feminist sex war' in the 1990s when several US states tried to establish anti-pornography ordinances.

CONCL: Pornography is a distinctly Western concept, with its roots in Judeo–Christian censorship of images, culture of 'secrete museums' and 19th-century codifications in France and the British Empire. Through colonial systems, this Western concept has spread to the rest of the world. Likewise, it has entered the language of both international and European law. Regulation of pornography remains a hotly contested area, with various cultural artefacts (from Ancient Greece, Rome, India, China, etc.) to be easily classified as pornographic according to the prudish perceptions of nudity and sexual intercourse. Although equally problematic and contested for a number of reasons, a more general consensus appears to exist with regard to the censorship of paedophile pornography, extreme violence and cruelty towards animals. Various countries continue to abuse the restriction on pornography as a pretext for political censorship; restriction of art; protection of a dominant religion; suppression of women and sexual minorities.

REFERENCES:

Adler, Amy M.: "The First Amendment and the Second Commandment", 57 *NYU Law Review* 41 (2012–13).

Belavusau, Uladzislau: "Art, Pornography and Foucauldian Reconstruction of Comparative Law", 17 *Maastricht Journal of European Law* 252 (2010).

Belavusau, Uladzislau: "EU Sexual Citizenship: Sex Beyond the Internal Market", 6 *EUI Law Working Paper* (2015) [also forthcoming in Kochenov, D.: (ed.), *EU Citizenship and Federalism: The Role of Rights*, Cambridge: CUP (2016).

Benjamin, Jessica: "Master and Slave: the Fantasy of Erotic Domination", in Snitow, Ann (ed.): *Powers of Desire: The Politics of Sexuality*, Monthly Review Press (1983).

Carol, Avedon, Nudes: *Prudes and Attitudes: Pornography and Censorship*, New Clarion Press (1994).

Dworkin, Andrea: *Pornography – Men Possessing Women*, Plume (1991).

Dworkin, Ronald: "Do We Have a Right to Pornography", in *A Mater of Principle*, Oxford: Oxford University Press (1986).

Foucault, Michel: *Histoire de la Sexualité: La volonté de savoir*, Editions Gallimard (1976).

Guyenot, Laurent: *Le livre noire de l'industrie rose. De la pornographie à la criminalité sexuelle*, Imago (2000).

Koppelman, Andrew: "Is Pornography 'Speech'?", 14 *Legal Theory* 71 (2008).

MacKinnon, Catharine A.: *Only Words*, Harvard University Press (1993).
Rétif, Nicolas-Edme: *Le Pornographe* (1769).
Sadurski, Wojciech: "On 'Seeing Speech Through an Equality Lens': A Critique of Egalitarian Arguments for Suppression of Hate Speech and Pornography", 16 *Oxford Journal of Legal Studies* 713 (1996).
Schroeder, Theodore: *A Challenge of Sex Censors* (privately printed to promote the aims of the Free Speech League), New York (1938).
Shytov, Alexander: "Indecency on the Internet and International Law", 13 *International Journal of Law and Information Technology* 260 (2005).
Walter, Kendrick: *The Secret Museum: Pornography in Modern Culture*, University of California Press (1996).
Willis, Ellen: "Lust Horizons: Is the Women's Movement Pro-Sex?", 1981.
AKDAŞ v. TURKEY (ECtHR 16/02/2010, 41056/04).
CONEGATE v. HM CUSTOMS & EXCISE (CJEU 11/03/1986, C-121/85).
EROTIC CENTER BVBA v. BELGISCHE STAAT (CJEU 18/03/2010, C-3/09).
HANDYSIDE v. UK (ECtHR 07/12/1976, 5493/72).
MÜLLER AND OTHERS v. SWITZERLAND (ECtHR 24/05/1988, 10737/84).
REGINA v. HENN & DARBY (CJEU, 14/12/1979, C-34/79).
VEREINIGUNG BILDENDER KÜNSTLER v. AUSTRIA (ECtHR 25/01/2007, 68354/01).

Uladzislau Belavusau

Poverty
(and Access to Culture)

DEF: In terms of human rights, poverty may be defined as a human condition characterised by sustained or chronic deprivation of the resources, capabilities, choices, security and power necessary for the enjoyment of an adequate standard of living and other civil, cultural, economic, political and social rights (CESCR, 2001). This definition reflects a common trend in international discourses as well as in human rights law to understand poverty more broadly than merely in terms of income poverty, thus improving chances of addressing different aspects of life affected by poverty, including its impact on access to culture by impoverished people and their ability to enjoy their own culture.

INSTR: One of the developments in international human rights law is a new approach to poverty eradication. At the UN level, the Human Rights Council adopted, in September 2012, a soft law instrument, the *Guiding Principles on Extreme Poverty and Human Rights*. Inter alia, these global policy guidelines provided recommendations with regard to specific rights, including the rights to take part in cultural life and to enjoy the benefits of scientific progress and its applications, whose enjoyment by persons living in poverty is particularly limited and obstructed, and in relation to which state policies are often inadequate or counterproductive. The Guiding Principles were preceded by the establishment of a Special Rapporteur on extreme poverty and human rights in 1998 by the UN Commission on Human Rights.

The relation between poverty and the right of everyone to take part in cultural life has also been elaborated 2009 in the CESCR General Comment No. 21, which underlines that 'in practice, poverty seriously restricts the ability of a person or a group of persons to exercise the right to take part in, gain access and contribute to, on equal terms, all spheres of cultural life, and more importantly, seriously affects their hopes for the future and their ability to enjoy effectively their own culture.' As a consequence, and based on Article 15 ICESCR, states would be obliged to adopt, without delay, concrete measures to ensure adequate protection and the full exercise of the right of persons living in poverty and their communities to enjoy, and take part in, cultural life.

On the European level, the main reference point for a human rights approach to poverty is the *Revised European Social Charter* of 1996 (CETS No. 163). In order to ensure an effective exercise of 'the right to protection against poverty and social exclusion', Article 30(2a) of the Charter obliges states to 'take measures within the framework of an overall and co-ordinated approach to promote the effective access of persons who live or risk living in a situation of social exclusion or poverty, as well as their families, to, in particular, employment, housing, training, education, culture and social and medical assistance'.

CASES: The question of the relation between poverty and culture does not yet appear in the jurisprudence of the main human right bodies, especially the ECtHR. A possible explanation for this lack of case-law can be seen in the fact that the ECHR is not an instrument specifically dedicated to the protection of economic social and cultural rights. However, the ECtHR in its jurisprudence ruled that an interpretation of the Convention may extend into the sphere of social and economic rights because there is no watertight division separating that sphere from the field covered by the Convention [AIREY, 1979]. Poverty-related issues were also raised in another judgment [M.S.S., 2011], in which the Court did not exclude the possibility of state responsibility in the context of poverty under Article 3, which prohibits inhuman treatment. According to the court, such possibility exists where an applicant, in circumstances wholly dependent on state support, found herself faced with official indifference while experiencing a situation of serious deprivation or need incompatible with human dignity (para. 235).

The European Committee of Social Rights, in its practice, also does not directly tackle the issue of the relation between poverty and culture. However, the ECSCR (Conclusions 2003, France, p. 214) has declared that living in a situation of poverty and social exclusion violates the dignity of human beings. Concerning requirements derived from article 30 of the *Revised European Social Charter*, the Committee declared that states are required to adopt an overall and coordinated approach, which should consist of an analytical framework, a set of priorities and measures to prevent and remove obstacles to access fundamental social rights. Monitoring mechanisms should also exist involving all relevant actors, including civil society and persons affected by poverty and exclusion. This approach must link and integrate policies in a consistent way, moving beyond a purely sectorial or target group approach.

VIEWS: The relationship between poverty and the right to culture is not yet properly covered in literature. However, poverty influences culture in at least two dimensions. First, poverty seriously restricts the ability of individuals or groups to exercise their right to take part in cultural life. Second, poverty has an impact on the ability of people experiencing it to enjoy their own culture. This is exactly the case of indigenous peoples and other minorities which live in poverty, such as →Roma people.

On the other hand, culture can influence poverty eradication. A study for the European Commission (Woods et al, 2004) finds that cultural activities can be instrumental in helping people to overcome poverty and social exclusion, through e.g. 'building skills and self-confidence' and 'enhancing self-esteem and identity'.

CONCL: People experiencing poverty, or even worse, extreme poverty, are clearly suffering from a denial of human rights. Consequently, a human rights based approach can assist efforts to eradicate poverty. Emerging human rights law and jurisprudence provide some guidance on how human rights of poor people should be respected in policies designated to the eradication of poverty. The essence of such an approach to poverty is comprehensiveness, which means that, despite attention on access of impoverished persons to basic necessities like the right to food, water and shelter, attention is also to be paid on other rights and freedoms, including those to take part in cultural life and to enjoy their own culture. While this approach is relatively new, it will probably be further developed in the years to come.

REFERENCES:

CESCR: *Substantive Issues Arising in the Implementation of the International Covenant on Economic, Social and Cultural Rights: Poverty and the International Covenant on Economic, Social and Cultural Rights*, (2001).

European Committee of Social Rights: Conclusions 2003, France, 214, (ECSCR).

Eversole, Robyn; McNeishand, John-Andrew; d. Cimadamore, Alberto (ed.): *Indigenous peoples and poverty: an international perspective*, London: Zed Books (2005).

Khan, Irene: *The Unheard truth Poverty and human rights*, Amnesty International, New York–London (2009).

OHCR, *Human Rights and Poverty Reduction: A Conceptual Framework*, New York, Geneva (2004).

Pogge, Thomas (ed.): *Freedom from Poverty as a*

Human Right: Who Owes What to the Very Poor?, Oxford: Oxford University Press (2007).

Redefining and combating poverty Human rights, democracy and common goods in today's Europe; Paris: Council of Europe Publishing (2012).

Spicker, Paul; Alvarez-Leguizamón, Sonia; Gordon, David: *Poverty An International Glossary*, (Second Edition) London: Zed Books (2007).

Woods, Roberta; Dobbs, Lynn; Gordon, Christopher; Moore, Craig; Simpson, Glen: *The role of culture in preventing and reducing poverty and social exclusion*. Study for the European Commission, Brussels (2004).

AIREY v. IRELAND (ECtHR 09/10/1979, 6289/73).

M.S.S. v. BELGIUM AND GREECE (ECtHR 21/01/2011, 30696/09).

Adam Ploszka

Press Freedom

DEF: Some key elements mark the democratic archetype: fairness of elections, citizens' participation, protection of human rights and the rule of law (Diamond, 2004). Alongside these basic requirements, another value typifies modern democracies: the freedom of the press. Despite being generally recognised as a cornerstone in the advancement of the 'rule of the people' doctrine, this freedom is currently under threat in many parts of Europe and the world: from Turkey, where the press is being forcibly converted into a mere state tool, to EU members like Greece or the Netherlands, where journalists are discouraged from reporting on national migration policies, or to China, where the government is harassing family members of journalists to silence dissident voices.

INSTR: Although not explicitly mentioned in the ECHR, freedom of the press is broadly covered by Article 10 ECHR (Freedom of Expression and Information (FoE)), as underlined by relevant jurisprudence of the ECtHR. In addition, it is protected by Article 11 of the EU *Charter of Fundamental Rights*. However, the provisions set for by the EU Charter would have left a legislative vacuum if not supported by the ECtHR's case-law: the Court's extensive interpretation of Article 10, its strict scrutiny of national authorities' interferences in FoE regarding issues of public interest covered by critical media in their role of public watchdog (Voorhoof, 2014), has provided a higher protection to journalistic activities, stressing the state's positive obligation descending from Article 10 ECHR to promote, guarantee and safeguard the enjoyment of this right. Press freedom, interpreted as an indicator of a functioning democratic society, has thus transformed into a fundamental constitutional standard. Once envisaged as a free, independent and objective 'Fourth Estate' (Carlyle, 1837), it is now considered a core value for the implementation of the rule of law and citizens' effective participation in democratic dialogue (Muižnieks, 2014).

CASES: [SUNDAY TIMES, 1979] was the first effective contribution to a broad interpretation of Article 10. The ECtHR recognised the importance of press reporting on issues of public interest and found the UK guilty of violating the mandate of this provision. In the decision, the Court stressed that mass media, while respecting the bounds imposed for a proper administration, are entitled to impart information in areas of public interest and the public has the right to receive them. Following this judgment, extensive case-law has further extended the scope of Article 10, especially by improving the protection of journalistic activities in a broader sense, including contributions from activists, opinion leaders or NGOs and underlining the importance of such activities for public debate and the democratic process [YOUTH INITIATIVE FOR HUMAN RIGHTS, 2013]. The positive obligation binding states to ensure press freedom has assumed greater significance in cases where the actors involved are, or could be, subjected to personal life threats [OZGŰR GŰNDEM, 2000].

VIEWS: The 'World Press Freedom Index 2015', published by the NGO Reporters Sans Frontières (RSF/RWB), registered a worldwide deterioration in freedom of information and investigative journalism. According to the Index, severe threats to media freedom are found in smaller countries such as Azerbaijan, 'Macedonia' or Turkmenistan as much as in large ones like China, Egypt, Russia or Turkey. Indeed, Turkey recently became an obvious example for countries where the rights of the media are exposed to constant non-observance and constriction. The escalation dates back to the Gezi Park events of summer 2013: Media coverage of the protests was harshly censored and resulted, according to the Turkish Journalists' Union (TGS), in the dismissal of 22 journalists and the forced resignations of another 37 professionals. The raid of December 2014, in which prominent journalists were arrested, led to reactions from the EU, the Council of Europe and the OSCE. Since then, further attacks on media pluralism and freedom rights have followed, particularly 2016 as regards the antagonist or independent press.

For the tenth consecutive year, global press freedom declined to its lowest point, according to the annual mapping report 'Freedom of the Press 2015' published by Freedom House: Out of 199 countries assessed, the press is only partly free in 71 countries, and not free at all in 65 countries. The role of the press and of journalists to raise awareness among citizens on issues of public relevance is curbed by legislation grounded on Article 19(3) of the ICCPR, or on Article 10(2) of the ECHR, granting states the right to limit press freedom for national security reasons (*ordre public*). However, as stressed by the *Johannesburg Principles* (U.N. Doc. E/CN.4/1996/39), any restriction based on national security claims must have a 'genuine purpose and demonstrable effect of protecting a legitimate national security interest' (Article 1(2)). In addition, as stipulated by the ECtHR's jurisprudence, states have a positive obligation to create a favourable environment for everyone to participate in public debates and to express opinions and ideas freely, avoiding any kind of self-censorship or fear. Accepting or supporting criticism, listening to counterparts' demands and needs contribute to modern democratic societies. In order to prevent the risk of state censorship via an exploitation of the *ordre public* provisions, the European Parliament has developed a strategy aiming to monitor and implement the status of press freedom within and outside regional borders: the methodology (European Parliament resolution, 2013) focuses on the effectiveness of press freedom as a basic, undeniable right, entrusting the monitoring of national policies to EU's Fundamental Rights Agency.

CONCL: With regard to press freedom, three main functions of the media should be kept in mind: (1) enabling, and participating in, the debate over the public sphere; (2) providing information to citizens on recent administrative decisions; (3) safeguarding governments' transparency. Since the subsidiary protection that is currently granted to the press by Article 10 ECHR and Article 11 of the EU CFR remains insufficient, important steps must still be taken to adopt and implement measures to protect the crucial role of media for a stable, democratic order.

Although generally safeguarded by international covenants, national constitutions and the ECtHR's jurisprudence, the central role of the press as a tool for enhancing democracy and fundamental rights is currently under pressure: the function of the media as a public 'watchdog' is often restricted, sometimes prevented, especially when reporting on sensitive topics. Political actors and supra-national institutions should not refrain from fulfilling their human rights obligations whenever freedom of expression in its individual or collective forms – and especially press freedom as one of the pillars of democracy – are threatened. Avoiding protests against national encroachments on media or against acts of censorship and authoritarianism could indeed lead to an illiberal reinterpretation of the concept of fundamental freedoms, dismissing their inner value and the progressive development of mankind. Press freedom and other civil liberties – as 'essentially contested concepts' (Gallie, 1956) – should not suffer from further discrimination and misunderstandings that may slowly erode the foundations of modern democratic governance.

REFERENCES:

Carlyle, Thomas: "The French Revolution: A History", 1837, in *Thomas Carlyle*, Dumfries and Galloways (2008).

Diamond, Larry: "What is Democracy", Lecture at Hilla University for Humanistic Studies (2004).

European Parliament Resolution: *EU Charter: standard settings for media freedom across Europe*, adopted on March 2013.

Gallie, Walter Bryce: *Essentially contested concept*, paper presented at the Aristotelian Society, London, (1956).

Muižnieks, Nils: "The Alarming Situation of Press Freedom in Europe", in *Transatlantic Relations:*

a European Perspective, The Regent's Report, London: Regent's University London (2014).
Voorhoof, Dirk: "The Right to Freedom of Expression and Information under the European Human Rights System: Towards a more Transparent Democratic Society", Robert Schuman Centre for Advanced Studies Centre for Media Pluralism and Media Freedom, European University Institute, Florence, EUI Working Paper RSCAS 2014/12 (2014).
OZGÜR GÜNDEM v. TURKEY (ECtHR 16/03/2000, 23144/93).
SUNDAY TIMES v. UK (ECtHR 26/04/1979, 6538/74).
YOUTH INITIATIVE FOR HUMAN RIGHTS v. SERBIA (ECtHR 25/06/2013, 48315/06).
Freedom House: freedomhouse.org (accessed 04/2016).
Reporters Without Borders/Sans Frontières: rsf.org/en (accessed 04/2016).

Roberto Frifrini

Privacy

DEF: Privacy can be understood either as a sphere of private or professional life which is normally kept 'private', i.e. not accessible by other persons, organisations, state agencies etc., or as limiting the access others have to one's personal information based on individual choices. While securing the latter, e.g. by using encryption technology, could be seen as falling mainly into one's own responsibility, the protection of a person's private sphere is a fundamental human right, recognised by the main international legal instruments that place obligations on states. It is closely related to →human dignity, democracy and core HR such as freedom of association and belief, but may collide with freedom of expression, economic efficiency or national security policies.

New digital technologies have changed our lives, and offer new possibilities for personal development and communication. On the other hand, areas of retreat become rare in digitally networked societies, where on consistent basis, information about human behaviour is collected, connected and valorised. Large and interconnected data sets or 'Big Data' under commercial or state control are increasingly seen as a danger to democratic processes because of their potential to manipulate and restrain citizens in the exercise of their rights. In the media and in artistic practice, threats to privacy can also lead to self-censorship or conformity.

INSTR: Specific references to the protection of privacy can be found in many international as well as European and other regional instruments. For example, the UDHR reads, in Article 12: 'No one shall be subjected to arbitrary interference with his privacy, family, home or correspondence, nor to attacks upon his honour and reputation. Everyone has the right to the protection of the law against such interference or attacks.' Similar wording can be found in Article 17 of the ICCPR, except that the word 'unlawful' has been added before 'attacks'. While Article 8 ECHR guarantees privacy in a similar manner, this right can be subject to restrictions or interference by public authorities that are 'in accordance with law' and 'necessary in a democratic society in the interests of national security, public safety or the economic well-being of the country, for the prevention of disorder or crime, for the protection of health or morals, or for the protection of the rights and freedoms of others'. Because of states' wide →margin of appreciation of such restrictions, this article is considered to be 'one of the most open-ended provisions of the Convention' (Wicks et al. 2014, p. 334).

The CoE *Convention for the Protection of Individuals with regard to Automatic Processing of Personal Data* of 1981 aims to secure respect for everyone's rights and fundamental freedoms 'and in particular his/her right to privacy' (Article 1) and, more specifically, provides that 'personal data revealing racial origin, political opinions or religious or other beliefs, as well as personal data concerning health or sexual life, may not be processed automatically unless domestic law provides appropriate safeguards' (Article 6). However, Article 9 also provides for a derogation of such guarantees e.g. on grounds of state security or even the 'monetary interests of the State'.

Despite provisions in the →*Charter of Fundamental Rights* (Articles 7 and 8) that can also be relevant for state surveillance, privacy regulations of EU bodies today specifically focus on the use of data by technology companies. For example, the *E-Privacy Directive 2002/58/EC*, amended by

Directive 2009/136/EC, referring explicitly to Article 8 of the ECHR and ECtHR case-law, prohibits listening, tapping, storage or other kinds of interception or surveillance of communications and the related traffic data without the consent of the users concerned, thus forcing companies to obtain consent for cookies and similar technologies. A new Directive is under preparation (2016), that would enable Internet users to request companies to apply the 'right to be forgotten' and delete personal information that is no longer relevant.

CASES: While in the past, case-law of the ECtHR frequently dealt with a breach of privacy on account of a specific sexual orientation [e.g. MODINOS, 1993], more recent cases address, inter alia, state surveillance. In [ROTARU, 2000], the Court reiterated its position that storing 'information relating to an individual's private life in a secret register and the release of such information come within the scope of Article 8(1)'. As well, 'public information can fall within the scope of private life where it is systematically collected and stored in files held by the authorities. This is all the truer where such information concerns a person's distant past'. Where personal information is stored for national security reasons, adequate and effective guarantees against an abuse by the state should exist, 'since a system of secret surveillance designed to protect national security entails the risk of undermining or even destroying democracy on the ground of defending it' [KLASS AND OTHERS, 1978]. Measures guaranteeing transparency and an eventual deletion of unfounded information could also concern the storage of investigation reports in a police database [BRUNET, 2014].

National courts contributed to limiting states' surveillance practice. For example, the German Constitutional Court developed, in a landmark ruling of February 2008, a new 'basic right to the confidentiality and integrity of information-technological systems' (1 BvR 370/07), limiting secret online searches of computers by government agencies – called 'Federal Trojan' by privacy activists (Chaos Computer Club) – to individual cases where 'factual indications for a concrete danger' for the life, body and freedom of persons or for the foundations of the state or humanity could, after approval by a judge, justify such measures. This decision, as well as a more recent one in April 2016 declaring parts of a law granting anti-terror surveillance power to the Federal Criminal Police (BKA) unconstitutional, complemented earlier privacy rulings of the Court, including the 'right to informational self-determination' (1983) and the right to an 'absolute protection of the core area of the private conduct of life' (2004).

While the main objective of Article 8 ECHR is to protect individuals against arbitrary interference by public authorities and may require positive obligations of states [AIREY, 1979, § 32], these obligations now cover also professional or commercial activities [NIEMIETZ, 1992] and the sphere of relations between individuals, including on the Internet, where an 'effective deterrence' against grave violations of fundamental values and privacy by users or access providers calls for 'efficient criminal-law provisions' [K.U., 2008]. This view could gain additional weight with regard to spying capacities of contemporary technological devices such as smartphones or 'Google Glass'.

Google has also been involved in a recent case of the CJEU [GOOGLE SPAIN SL, 2014] that dealt with the question whether citizens could demand to be excluded from the results produced by the search engine of the company. Referring to provisions of the EU →*Charter of Fundamental Rights* protecting personal data and privacy, the Court held that individuals without an important role in public life may, in the light of their 'fundamental rights under Articles 7 and 8 of the Charter, request that the information in question no longer be made available to the general public' and that 'those rights override, as a rule, not only the economic interest of the operator of the search engine but also the interest of the general public in having access to that information upon a search relating to the data subject's name'. In another case [MAXIMILLIAN SCHREMS, 2015], the CJEU also found the 'safe harbour' decision of the EU Commission, under which surveillance data are transmitted to the USA, to be invalid.

VIEWS: While privacy is often considered to be a precondition for liberal democracy and freedom, surveillance and state control of all citizens as well as certain forms of networked, data-rich marketing can, at best, result in 'modulated societies' (Cohen, 2013). Following the rapid development of information technologies and 'social' (actually: commercial) networks or platforms based on continuous, pervasively distributed, and persistent data mining, 'Big Data' issues moved on top of the news and also led to intense research efforts (see e.g. Fuchs et al, 2012). In addition, the revelations of →whistleblowers and NGOs (e.g. Privacy International) about state surveillance programmes in the USA and other countries helped shape international debates on privacy issues and prompted legal and political action.

Despite the progress that has been made in recent years, mostly via case-law, many citizens and particularly Internet bloggers remain sceptical and fear that governments or state agencies will 'stretch' exception clauses in their future practice. A recent empirical study in the USA (Stoycheff, 2016) confirmed a 'silencing effect' or self-censorship among a majority of citizens with dissenting opinions once they are aware of government surveillance, most of them reacting by suppressing opinions that they perceived to be in the minority. In an interview (Washington Post, 28 March 2016), lead researcher Elizabeth Stoycheff found that the 'fundamental human right to have control over one's self-presentation and image, in private, and now, in search histories and metadata' is endangered and that 'the adoption of surveillance techniques, by both the government and private sectors, undermines the Internet's ability to serve as a neutral platform for honest and open deliberation'.

Policy makers, for their part, seem to be torn between security concerns and defence of HR: Overshadowed by extremist activities, both on the Internet and on the ground, the 2015 *Helsinki Declaration of the OSCE* summed up a widespread understanding of issues at stake by calling on states 'to take all necessary measures to prevent the use of information and communication technologies for terrorist purposes, while promoting a multidimensional approach to cyber security that takes into account the interests of various stakeholders and ensures respect for freedom of expression'.

CONCL: Data protection, and thus the respect for individual privacy as an expression of human dignity, is of the highest importance for safeguarding the achievements of liberal democracy. It demands both more awareness of connected issues on the part of 'net citizens' as well as self-restraints on the part of state authorities and commercial actors. Since state agencies and private companies permanently and causelessly collect personal data of citizens, treaties where privacy as a HR is either absent or only vaguely defined, such as the ICCPR, may need to be supplemented by a protocol to adapt to technological innovations. Negotiations that have been taking place for some time between the European Commission and US authorities with a view to introducing a new, more privacy protective arrangement to replace the existing 'Safe Harbor' agreement led, in 2016, to a new framework. However, experts seriously doubt that this so-called 'Privacy Shield' can actually bring the practice of copious and causeless mass surveillance to an end, a practice that proved to be of no value in the necessary fight against crime or terrorism.

REFERENCES:

Baum, Gerhart R.: *Rettet die Grundrechte! Bürgerfreiheit contra Sicherheitswahn – Eine Streitschrift.* Cologne: Kiepenheuer & Witsch (2009).

Cohen, Julie E.: "What Privacy is For", 126 *Harvard Law Review* (2013), 1912.

De Schutter, Olivier: *International Human Rights Law: Cases, Materials, Commentary*, Cambridge: Cambridge University Press (2014).

Fuchs, Christian; Boersma, Kees; Albrechtslund, Anders; Sandoval, Marisol (eds.): *Internet and Surveillance. The Challenges of Web 2.0 and Social Media*, Oxford: Routledge (2012).

Stoycheff, Elizabeth: "Under Surveillance: Examining Facebook's Spiral of Silence Effects in the Wake of NSA Internet Monitoring", *Journalism & Mass Communication Quarterly* (2016), 1.

Wicks, Elizabeth; Rainey, Bernadette; Ovey, Clare (eds.): *Jacobs, White and Ovey: the European Convention on Human Rights.* Oxford: OUP (2014).

European Court of Human Rights/Research Division: *Case-law Research Reports* (National security/Internet), www.echr.coe.int (accessed 04/2016).

European Union Agency for Fundamental Rights/Council of Europe: *Handbook on European data protection law*, Luxembourg: Publications Office of the European Union, 2014.

AIREY v. IRELAND (ECtHR 09/10/1979, 6289/73).
BRUNET v. FRANCE (ECtHR 05/02/2009, 42117/04).
GOOGLE SPAIN SL, GOOGLE INC. v. AGENCIA ESPAÑOLA DE PROTECCIÓN DE DATOS, MARIO COSTEJA GONZÁLEZ (CJEU/GC, 13/05/2014, C-131/12).
K.U. v. FINLAND (ECtHR 02/12/2008, 2872/02).
KLASS AND OTHERS v. GERMANY (ECtHR 06/09/1978, 5029/71).
MAXIMILLIAN SCHREMS v. DATA PROTECTION COMMISSIONER (CJEU/GC, 06/10/2015, C-362/14).
MODINOS v. CYPRUS (ECtHR 22/04/1993, 15070/1989).
NIEMIETZ v. GERMANY (ECtHR 16/12/1992, 13710/88).
ROTARU v. ROMANIA (ECtHR 04/05/2000, 28341/95).
www.privacyinternational.org/legal-actions (accessed 03/2016).

Gerhart Rudolf Baum

Producers

DEF: Producers' activity in the arts and media domains can be manifold; it is rarely a subject of human rights' debates and is rather guided by professional or contractual law. However, there are instances where producers have had to face controversial issues in the context of conflicting rights.

CASES: A fair balance has to be struck between every person's right to protection of privacy, including one's own or family's reputation, as covered by Article 8 ECHR and the right of media and producers to freedom of expression guaranteed under Article 10 ECHR. This balancing exercise may be subject to ECtHR scrutiny. For example, in [PUTISTIN, 2014], the Court examined a press article that reproduced statements made by a film director and a film producer about a possible film production based on historical events during WW II. Studying the circumstances of that case, the Court concluded that the applicant's Article 8 rights were marginally, and only in an indirect manner, affected by an article reproducing statements of the makers of the proposed film and considered that the domestic courts in Ukraine had not failed to strike an appropriate balance between the applicant's rights and those responsible for the newspaper report. In another case [SALIYEV, 2010], the ECtHR pointed out 'that the relationship between a journalist and an editor-in-chief (or publisher, producer, director of programmes, and so on) is not only or always a business relationship', thus all interests at stake must be thoroughly examined. Particularly interesting cases were brought before the Court concerning broadcasting licencing [MELTEX, 2008], the obligation of news producers to disclose information [NAGLA, 2013] or divulgation of confidential information [RICCI, 2014].

CONCL: Directly or indirectly, producers' interests and rights may be caught in a balancing exercise of conflicting rights and thus their position has to be duly examined by the national authorities called upon to rule on different interests at stake.

REFERENCES:

PUTISTIN v. UKRAINE (ECtHR, 21/02/2014, 16882/03).
SALIYEV v. RUSSIA (ECtHR, 21/10/2010, 35016/03).
MELTEX LTD. AND MESROP MOVSESYAN v. ARMENIA (ECtHR 17/06/2008, 32283/04).
NAGLA v. LATVIA (ECtHR 16/07/2013, 73469/10).
RICCI v. ITALY (ECtHR, 08/01/2014, 30210/06).

Geanina Munteanu

Public Broadcasting

(Access to / Diversity of Public Service Media)

DEF: Public service media (PSM) are crucial to enable high-quality cultural content: Media with editorial independence, where they exist, can drive the diversity of cultural expressions of → producers, commissioners, distributors, disseminators and cultural mediators, whatever the means and technologies used. Elements of such aims are also part of the self-definition of PSM as expressed by the European Broadcasting Union (EBU, 2016), which declares that its member organisations are 'promoting public values by informing, educating and entertaining' and that 'trust is at the centre of the relationship with the audiences to ensure their place as the most credible, diverse and creative national media broadcaster'. In a majority of the European countries, public broadcasting organisations are funded by license fees paid by all households (with advertising revenues only as a minor source of income).

Today's quantum leap in access to media outlets and greater choices does not mean that the →media content available via those channels is necessarily 'freer' or a guarantee of diversity of content and expressions. Therefore, freedom of information laws and their effective implementation, together with transparent licensing obligations, are essential, as there can be no media diversity without media freedom. The multiplicity of languages used is a vital dimension of diversity and often subject to positive regulation and public policies.

INSTR: The right to freedom of expression is guaranteed in Article 10 ECHR and includes the 'freedom to hold opinions and to receive and impart information and ideas without interference by public authority and regardless of frontiers'. However, this provision does not prevent states from requiring the licensing of broadcasting, television or cinema enterprises. In the EU, the latter is actually a condition for the derogation from the general ban on state aid (Article 106(2) TFEU), based on the *Amsterdam Protocol* (1997) to the *Treaty of the European Community*, which ties funding of PSM in the EU member states with the 'fulfilment of the public service remit' in order to cover 'the democratic, social and cultural needs of each society' and to 'preserve media pluralism'. In most European countries, this is reflected in specific broadcasting or media laws and regulations, which often include cultural obligations or quota for specific types of programmes (Council of Europe/ERICarts, 2016).

Similar principles regarding public broadcasting and other PSM as well as independent media producers are found among the core messages of the *2005 UNESCO Convention*, comprising

- the enhancement of media diversity for achieving the Convention's objectives across the cultural value chain, including through public service media;
- the need to ensure freedom of thought, expression and information, the free exchange and circulation of ideas as well as diversity of the media for cultural expressions to flourish within societies;
- the principle of technological neutrality, hence the prevalence of cultural content over technological channels of transmission; and
- the articulation of binding policy standards regarding the *dual* nature of cultural goods and services that should achieve a balanced and specific treatment of cultural and audiovisual goods and services in international trade policies.

CASES: In the field of audio-visual broadcasting, the ECtHR considered that a public monopoly 'imposes the greatest restrictions on the freedom of expression'. Therefore and because such restrictions are not any more state of the art due to 'the number of frequencies and channels available', they 'can only be justified where they correspond to a pressing need' [INFORMATIONSVEREIN LENTIA AND OTHERS v. AUSTRIA, 1993]. However, 'where a State... decide[s] to create a public broadcasting system,... domestic law and practice must guarantee that the system provides a pluralistic service' that provides citizens with access to 'a range of opinion and comment, reflecting inter alia the diversity of political outlook within the country' [MANOLE AND OTHERS, 2010]; in this case, the Court reflected both the plurality of views of journalists, editors and producers working in the state-owned broadcasting company of Moldova and the (insufficient) composition of supervisory bodies. Similar views were held in the case of a local public journal whose copies were withdrawn because of the viewpoints expressed in an article [SALIYEV v. RUSSIA, 2010]. The Court concluded that this withdrawal violated Article 10 ECHR and pointed out 'that the relationship between a →journalist and an editor-in-chief (or publisher, producer, director of programmes, and so on) is not only or always a business relationship'. Therefore, in carrying out its mission to inform the population about the social, political and cultural life, a public utility institution normally has to follow stricter rules regarding the diversity of expressions than would be the case with private media.

However, as regards audio-visual regulations promoting cultural content and diversity, the CJEU confirmed the legality of related measures also for private television companies, referring inter alia to the 2005 UNESCO-Convention [UTECA, 2009]. A Royal Decree requiring television operators to allocate 5% of their operating revenue to the funding of cinematographic films and European films made for television as well as 60% of that funding to the production of films in one of the official languages of Spain has been found to be compatible with *Council Directive 89/552/EEC* (1989) that coordinates regulations of television broadcasting activities in member states of the EU.

VIEWS: High levels of sustained investment in original (local) cultural content through PSM, in general, and public broadcasters, in particular, remain a key policy priority in a converging media environment in order to promote the diversity of cultural expressions. Due to the tension between cultural objectives and the marketplace, enhancing the diversity of the media is a difficult but necessary task, in particular with regard to commercial broadcasting and private newspaper publishers, which can only promote public communication and the diversity of cultural expressions if also economically viable as enterprises. If successful, the partly contradictory demands made on the media sector and media culture might be reconciled.

A vibrant array of high-quality →media content will contribute substantially to achieving the 2005 UNESCO-Convention's objectives, while at the same time becoming a driver of diversity in the media sector and the cultural economy as a whole. This clearly indicates the need to use the knowledge exchange through the 2005 UNESCO-Convention as well as the technical assistance in cultural governance to go for integrated policies concerning media, culture and networks, adapting their regulatory frameworks to the new digital conditions.

CONCL: Given the current dominance of vertically-integrated media conglomerates and of the internet's oligopoly, policies for the diversity of media 3.0 will need to give priority to high-quality content, most likely through the means of production investment/subsidies across the cultural value chain and through investing in the next generation 4.0 of public service media. More specifically, existing national broadcasting and media laws are required to take the 2005 UNESCO Convention fully into account through heeding various HR principles such as freedom of information and securing access for users and providers, in addition to safeguarding technological neutrality and promoting cultural diversity via competition policies and consumer protection. →Gender equality as a top priority of the UN needs to be reflected, also as regards the diversity of cultural expressions, with a 'gender lens' in the reporting of PSM, in order to enhance the visibility of women as creators, producers, innovators and decision makers in the cultural economy. Media diversity needs media freedom: Implementing the 2005 UNESCO-Convention means taking up pro-actively freedom of expression and connected basic rights as well as still existing problems, including gender issues, self-censorship or the safety and impunity of journalists and other media professionals. Therefore, the announcement of German broadcaster ZDF that it will provide – despite the debatable content of a satirical poem insulting Turkish President Recep Tayyip Erdoğan (telecasted end of March 2016) – legal assistance to comedian Jan Böhmermann in his upcoming court proceedings could be considered a justified, pro-active behaviour.

REFERENCES:

Bernier, Ivan: "Article 6, Rights of Parties at the National Level. Drafting History, Wording, Conclusion", in Sabine von Schorlemer, Peter-Tobias Stoll (eds.): *The UNESCO Convention on the Protection and Promotion of the Diversity of Cultural Expressions. Explanatory Notes*. Heidelberg: Springer (2012).

Council of Europe: *The role of independent productions in promoting cultural diversity*. CoE Doc.H/Inf, Strasbourg (2009).

Council of Europe/ERICarts: *Compendium of Cultural Policies and Trends in Europe*. County Profiles, Chapters 4.2.6 and 5.3.7 (accessed 04/2016 via www.culturalpolicies.net).

European Commission: *Green paper, Preparing for*

a Fully Converged Audiovisual World: Growth, Creation and Values, Brussels (2013).
Merkel, Christine M.: "New voices: Encouraging media diversity", in UNESCO: *Re/Shaping Cultural Policies. 2005 Convention Global Report*, Paris (2015).
UNESCO: *World Trends in Freedom of Expression and Media Development*. Paris (2014).
UNESCO: *Global Survey on Gender and Media*, Paris (2015).
UNESCO, IGC Information document: *Assessment of policies and measures aimed at enhancing diversity of the media, including through Public Service Broadcasting*, prepared by Christine M. Merkel, CE/14/8.IGC/INF.6, Paris (2014).
MANOLE AND OTHERS v. MOLDOVA (ECtHR 13/07/2010, 13936/02).
UTECA v. ADMINISTRACIÓN GENERAL DEL ESTADO (CJEU 05/03/2009, C-222/07).
EBU – European Broadcasting Union: http://www3.ebu.ch/about/public-service-media (accessed 04/2016).

Christine M. Merkel

Public Space

DEF: According to the definition of the '*Charter of Public Space*', adopted during the II Biennial of Public Space in Rome (2013), public spaces are 'all places publicly owned or of public use, accessible and enjoyable by all for free and without a profit motive'. Concretised by UN-HABITAT resolutions, this includes streets, open spaces and public facilities.

INSTR/VIEWS: Although public space is occasionally claimed to be a human right (e.g. in 2014 by the UN Secretary-General's Envoy on Youth, Ahmad Alhendawi), this opinion so far is not reflected in official UN texts (cf. *UN-HABITAT Resolution 23/4*, 2011). Clearly, public space is not an end in itself. However, it fulfills very important functions for the exercise of freedoms of expression, information, assembly and association. This is why, for example, the UN Special Rapporteur in the field of cultural rights, Farida Shaheed, recognised the regulation over the use of public space as a central topic to cultural (human) rights. In her 2013 report, she identifies the main difficulties for people engaged in creative activities in public spaces, and encourages states, private institutions and donors 'to find creative solutions so as to enable artists to display or perform in public space' (General Assembly, A/HRC/23/34). The above-mentioned trends indicate that a subsidiary (human) right to public space is developing, which requires an adequate minimum amount of effective public space in every municipality, and access to it for unlimited political, cultural and social purposes. Remarkably, the contemporary discourse on public space in a human rights context is strongly linked to the notion of an 'increasing encroachment of public space by private properties' (loc. cit.) and commercial interests (cf. *World Charter on the Right to the City*, 2004/2005, Preamble), exemplified also by the 2013 Gezi Park protests in Istanbul/Turkey.

CONCL: The United Nations Conference on Housing and Sustainable Urban Development (Habitat III), held 2016 in Quito, already benefited from the '*Charter of Public Space*'. On that basis, further legal clarifications and policies relating to public space issues are to be expected.

REFERENCES:

Smithsimon, Gregory and Zukin, Sharon: "The City's Commons: Privatization vs. Human Rights", in: van Lindert, Thijs and Lettinga, Doutje (eds.), *The Future of Human Rights in an Urban World*, Amnesty International Netherlands (2014), 41.
APPLEBY AND OTHERS v. THE UNITED KINGDOM (ECtHR 06/05/2003, 44306/98).
FRAPORT decision (German Federal Constitutional Court 22/02/2011, 1 BvR 699/06).

Jörg Michael Schindler

Refugees

(Cultural Rights of R.)

DEF: According to the *Convention Relating to the Status of Refugees* (Geneva Convention, 1951), a 'refugee' is a person who, 'owing to well-founded fear of being persecuted for reasons of race, religion, nationality, membership of a particular social group or political opinion, is outside the country of his nationality and is unable or, owing to such fear, is unwilling to avail himself of the protection of that country; or who, not having a nationality and being outside the country of his former habitual residence (...) is unable or, owing to such fear, is unwilling to return to it' (Article 1(A)(2)). In Africa the meaning of the term extends to 'every person who, owing to external aggression, occupation, foreign domination or events seriously disturbing public order in either part or the whole of his country of origin or nationality, is compelled to leave his place of habitual residence in order to seek refuge in another place outside his country of origin or nationality' (1969 AU Convention, Article I(2)).

INSTR: Just like all other human beings, refugees are entitled to the enjoyment of the full measure of internationally recognised human rights, including cultural rights. As emphasised by the ESCR Committee, the rights established by the ICESCR 'apply to everyone including non-nationals, such as refugees, asylum-seekers, stateless persons, migrant workers and victims of international trafficking, regardless of legal status and documentation' (General comment No. 20, 2009, para. 30). Moreover, to a large extent the situation of refugees overlaps with that of other →Migrants, implying that many specific rules applicable to the latter also extend to the former. In some cases, violations of cultural rights can be the cause triggering refugee flows, when encroachment of such rights can be qualified as persecution. *At least* three of the grounds of persecution included in the definition of 'refugee' (i.e. religion, membership of a particular social group and political opinion) are – or may be – directly linked with culture.

As for cultural rights explicitly recognised to refugees, Article 4 of the 1951 Geneva Convention requests states parties to 'accord to refugees within their territories treatment at least as favourable as that accorded to their nationals with respect to freedom to practise their religion and freedom as regards the religious education of their children'. Article 14 of the same Convention establishes that, with respect to artistic rights and industrial property, 'a refugee shall be accorded in the country in which he has his habitual residence the same protection as is accorded to nationals of that country', while in the territory of any other state party 'he shall be accorded the same protection as is accorded in that territory to nationals of the country in which he has his habitual residence'.

VIEWS: The 1984 *Cartagena Declaration*, in Part III, para. 11, emphasises the need to 'make a study, in countries in the area which have a large number of refugees, of the possibilities of integrating them into the productive life of the country (...) thus making it possible for refugees to enjoy their economic, social and cultural rights'. Furthermore, per effect of Article 27 ICCPR – stating the right of members of ethnic, religious or linguistic minorities, in community with the other members of their group, to enjoy their own culture, to profess and practise their own religion, or to use their own language – states parties have an obligation to provide refugees with 'schooling (...) in their own language (...) or (...) a venue for cultural and religious practice' (Persaud, 2006, 24); the Human Rights Committee has confirmed that refugees may well belong to ethnic, religious or linguistic minorities, as members of such minorities 'need not be nationals or citizens, they need not be permanent residents' (General Comment No. 23, 1994, para. 5.2).

The UNHCR (2002) has underlined that integration of refugees in the host state should not lead them 'to forego their own cultural identity', that 'host governments and relevant institutions should (...) promote the principles of mutual respect, cultural diversity and tolerance for differences, and support opportunities for cultural exchange and education' (da Costa, 2006, 32), as well as that host states must 'ensure that all refugee children benefit from primary education of a satisfactory quality, that respects their cultural identity' (ExCom Conclusion, 1987, para. (o)).

CONCL: International law, traditionally, has not been particularly concerned with refugees under the perspective of cultural rights, mainly concentrating on their most urgent and primary need, i.e. protection from persecution. This reality is confirmed by the main international instruments applicable in the field – particularly the 1951 Geneva Convention and the 1969 AU Convention. In recent times, however, international monitoring bodies and other institutions are increasingly emphasising the need that integration of refugees within host states is carried out through modalities adequate to ensure that the →Cultural Identity of the persons concerned is appropriately safeguarded, including as regards the education of refugee →Children. As emphasised by UNHCR in 2002, refugee integration must be 'the end product of a multi-faceted and on-going process (...) which requires a preparedness on the part of the refugees to adapt to the host society, *without having to forego their own cultural identity*. From the host society, it requires communities that are welcoming and responsive to refugees, and public institutions that are able to meet the needs of a diverse population' (emphasis added), including in particular cultural needs.

REFERENCES:

Cartagena Declaration on Refugees, 1984, (1984 Cartagena Declaration).

Committee on Economic, Social and Cultural Rights: General comment No. 20, UN Doc. E/C.12/GC/20 (2009).

da Costa, Rosa: "Rights of Refugees in the Context of Integration: Legal Standards and Recommendations", UNHCR, Legal and Protection Policy Research Series, June 2006, (available at www.unhcr.org accessed 06/2016).

Goodwin-Gill, Guy S. and McAdams, Jane J.: *The Refugee in International Law*, 3rd edn., Oxford: OUP (2007).

Human Rights Committee: General Comment No. 23, UN Doc. CCPR/C/21/Rev.1/Add.5, 1994.

OAU (now AU) *Convention Governing the Specific Aspects of Refugee Problems in Africa* (1969 AU Convention), (www.achpr.org/instruments accessed 06/2016).

Persaud, Santhosh: "Protecting refugees and asylum seekers under the International Covenant on Civil and Political Rights", New Issues in Refugee Research, Research Paper No. 132, Nov. 2006, (available at www.unhcr.org accessed 06/2016).

UNHCR: "Refugee Children" ExCom Conclusion No. 47 (XXXVIII), (1987).

UNHCR: *Refugee Resettlement: An International Handbook to Guide Reception and Integration*, (2002).

Federico Lenzerini

Regional and Minority Languages

DEF: The most comprehensive definition of regional and minority languages (RML) is provided in the *European Charter for Regional or Minority Languages* (ECRML), which points to the following features of such languages: (1) having traditional presence in a particular state, (2) being used by nationals of that state who form a minority, (3) being different from the official language. It covers both languages with a defined historical territory as well as those that are non-territorial (ECRML: Article 1(a)(i-ii)). The inclusion of the terms 'regional' and 'minority' languages does not render any difference in their status despite their potential distinctive features (ECRML Explanatory report: para. 18) usually embedded in the legal terminology of a particular state (e.g. Kashub in Poland).

RMLs differ in terms of their language vitality, i.e. demographic situation, their active use in public life and the level of the speakers' linguistic competence. Due to these differences between RMLs, it is clear that ECRML instruments of ratification, which provide a uniform set of undertakings for all RMLs covered in a particular state (Bosnia & Herzegovina, Poland, Serbia), pose significant challenges in their implementation and evaluation.

INSTR: The ECRML obliges the ratifying party to recognise RMLs as 'an expression of cultural wealth' (ECRML Article 7(1)(a)). The importance of culture is manifested in the structure of the ECRML with a separate Article devoted to cultural activities (Article 12), one of the obligatory fields to be selected by the ratifying state (→Language Rights). Its significance is also obvious in other fields such as education (Article 8), media (Article 10), transfrontier exchanges (Article 14). Hence culture is interpreted by the ECRML as 'the community's way of life and thought' (Donders 2008, 5) and not elitist or purely folkloristic activity.

Article 12 on culture obliges the state to encourage various types of cultural expression (Article 12(1)(a)), translation and dubbing both into and from RML (Article 12(1)(b-c)), incorporation of the use of RMLs by bodies responsible for organising cultural activities also through staff competent in the RML (Article 12(1)(d-e)), direct participation of RML speakers in planning cultural activities (Article 12(1)(f)), creation and maintenance of bodies collecting works in RML (Article 12(1)(g)), financing the creation of appropriate terminology in the RML to enable its use in public life (Article 12(1)(h)), promoting cultural activities outside the traditional area (Article 12(2)) and finally, cultural policy abroad (Article 12(3)). The scope of Article 12 comprises preservation measures but more importantly actions that foster the development of RML culture as a living experience of the community (Oszmiańska-Pagett, 2015, 14–16). The state is obliged to choose at least three of the undertakings contained in this Article.

The ECRML is a Council of Europe convention and thus not obligatory within the EU. Some of its important member states have not ratified it, e.g. France, Italy, Portugal, while several non-EU states are parties to the convention, e.g. Ukraine, Norway, Armenia.

CASES: Since the ECRML grants neither individual nor group rights (ECRML. Explanatory Report, para. 17), this section will focus on the Committee of Experts (COMEX) evaluation reports and CM recommendations.

Despite this legal reservation, the monitoring mechanism emphasises the *speakers' needs* in policy development (UK 1(2004)). Therefore, the conclusions on the fulfilment of the undertakings are always determined by the unique situation of a particular RML and concerns raised by its speakers (Poland 1(2011), para. 108).

Articles on culture and media require the *involvement of RML speakers* in planning and organising cultural activities and decisions made by programming boards. In both cases, COMEX insists on the speakers' participation in the process (Croatia 1(2001)).

Culture as representing the community's life and thought is manifested in the evaluation of *media* coverage in the RML. The focus is on the quality of programmes and broadcast time to reach a wide audience, including the younger generation (Hungary 4(2010) paras. 163–164).

In *education*, the teaching of history and culture related to the RML is covered by a separate undertaking (Article 8(1)(g)). However, the COMEX has always seen RML teaching not only as facilitating →children's proficiency in the language but also their cultural competence (Sweden 4(2011) paras. 115, 166).

The teaching of *history and culture* is also seen as contributing to awareness raising required in the curricula for both minority schools and mainstream education, especially in the RML's traditional area (Croatia 5(2015) paras. 113–114).

VIEWS: RMLs are treated as an essential aspect of European linguistic and cultural diversity, whose importance is perceived as a value in itself (White Paper on Linguistic Diversity, 2016, 17). Reasons for promoting RMLs are also interpreted in terms of environmental sustainability and adaptation (Skutnabb-Kangas, 2002). Criticism of RML promotion points to the roots of their minority status in historical inevitability, in turn rendering the promotion of RMLs a futile task, which hampers the social mobility of RML speakers (cf. May 2003 for discussion). On the other hand, the right to use the RML is interpreted as an inalienable human right, especially in the field of education (Skutnabb-Kangas, 2008). Despite its merits as a convention for setting standards for promoting RMLs, the ECRML has been criticised for lacking the power to punish non-complying states (Romaine, 2002).

CONCL: Analysing the case of RMLs in the context of cultural rights makes it clear how inseparable culture and language are. Access to culture is provided not only through cultural events or cultural heritage, but also through education and media. In this way RMLs play an essential role in fostering culture understood as developing the 'everyday life and thought' of their respective communities. For some RML communities, which have lost competence in their language, traditional heritage (e.g. literary works or songs) provides the only access to their culture. Both the right to culture as heritage and as a 'way of life' are included in the obligations of the ECRML and in its monitoring practice.

However, granting non-discrimination and the right to use the language is a hollow phrase if the authorities do not facilitate the conditions that enable RML speakers to use it.

REFERENCES:

Donders, Yvonne: *Cultural Life in the context of Human Rights*, Geneva: UN (2008) (available at www.ohchr.org accessed 06/2016).

ECRML: "Explanatory Report to the European Charter for Regional or Minority Languages" (Strasbourg, 5.XI.1992) (available at www.coe.int accessed 06/2016).

ECRML Evaluation Reports (available at www.coe.int): *Croatia 1*, ECRML (2001) 2 (20/09/2001); *Croatia 5*, ECRML (2015) 2 (15/04/2015); *Hungary 4*, ECRML (2010) 2 (10/03/2010); *Poland 1*, ECRML (2011) 5 (07/12/2011); *Sweden 4*, ECRML (2011) 4 (12/10/2011). *UK 1*, ECRML (2004) 1 (24/03/2004).

Lainio, Jarmo: "White Paper on Linguistic Diversity" (2016) (available at www.mercatornetwork.eu accessed 06/2016).

May, Stephen: "Rearticulating the case for minority language rights", 4(2) *Current Issues In Language Planning* (2003).

Oszmiańska-Pagett, Aleksandra: *The protection of children's rights under the European Charter for Regional or Minority Languages*, Strasbourg: Council of Europe (2015).

Romaine, Suzanne: "The impact of language policy on endangered languages", 4(2) *International Journal on Multicultural Societies* (2002) 194.

Skutnabb-Kangas, Tove: *Why should linguistic diversity be maintained and supported in Europe?* Strasbourg: Council of Europe (2002).

Skutnabb-Kangas, Tove: "Human rights and language policy in education", in Stephen May and Nancy Hornberger (eds.): *Encyclopedia of Language and Education*, New York: Springer (2008) 107.

Aleksandra Oszmiańska-Pagett

Religious Education

DEF: Religious education (RE) differs in its goals, actors and scope from 'catechesis' or 'religious instruction', since the latter denotes the instruction conducted by churches or religious groups, with a view to the inculcation of adherence to their faith. In almost all European countries (with the exception of France and Albania), RE is part of the curriculum in primary and secondary state schools. RE may adopt two main models: (1) 'non-denominational' teaching about religions (as in Sweden), which may comprise learning about religions and /or learning from religions; (2) denominational teaching of religion (as in Spain, Finland or Romania).

INSTR: In both of the two main models of RE, three fundamental/human rights are implicated: (1) the right to education (Article 26.1 UDHR; Article 14.1 CFREU; Article 13 ICESCR; Article 2 1st Protocol ECHR): RE guarantees a more comprehensive knowledge for a full and informed participation in religiously diverse societies; (2) the right of parents to choose the kind of education that shall be given to their children (Article 26.3 UDHR; Article 18 ICESCR) in conformity with their religious, philosophical and pedagogical convictions (Article 14.3 CFREU; *see* also Article 2, 1st Protocol ECHR and Article 5, 1981 UN Declaration): given the responsibilities attached to parents concerning their children, the law guarantees the accomplishment of this task according to their convictions, harmonising that right with child's age and evolving maturity. (3) freedom of religion or belief (Article 18 UDHR; Article 18 ICCPR; Article 10 CFREU; Article 9 ECHR) both of parents and of children, in the positive and negative dimension of this fundamental right. The Parliamentary Assembly of the Council of Europe has invited member states to promote education about religions (Recommendation 1396 (1999) "Religion and democracy").

CASES: The ECtHR has addressed several issues concerning RE:

- As long as a non-denominational subject gives preponderant weight to Christianity, the opt-out system must be workable and consistent with the rights enshrined in the ECHR [FOLGERØ AND OTHERS, 2007];
- Denominational teaching of religion should not generate any sort of discrimination in pupils' marks [GRZELAK, 2010];
- Religious culture and ethics lessons must respect the religious and philosophical convictions of religious groups (like in this case the

followers of Alevism, a branch of Islam) and provide a possibility of exemption (which Christians and Jews actually have in Turkey) [HASAN AND EYLEM ZENGİN, 2007; see also MANSUR YALÇIN AND OTHERS v. TURKEY, 2014].

In a recent case, the Supreme Court of Canada found: The Ministry of Education should not impose to private denominational institutions the RE neutrality standards of the curriculum of Ethics and Religious Culture (ERC), as long as an alternative equivalent course is guaranteed [LOYOLA HIGH SCHOOL v. QUEBEC, 2015]. In general, RE is consistent with international instruments. However, specific national practices may encroach fundamental rights recognised for parents, students or professors.

VIEWS: The two main models of RE have been criticised by scholars and religious actors: (1) 'Non-denominational' teaching about religions: Religion, as multi-faceted reality, cannot be understood in all its implications but from within (Jamal and Panjwani, 2011). Besides, 'if religious education is limited to a presentation of the different religions, in a comparative and 'neutral' way, it creates confusion or generates religious relativism or indifferentism' (Congregation for Catholic Education, 2009); (2) Denominational teaching of religion: international legal instruments and the principle of state neutrality leave no room for providing denominational teaching in state schools. 'However, teaching about religion in a neutral and objective way in public schools is ultimately compatible with international human rights law' (Temperman, 2010).

The ECtHR affirms that RE is not contrary to the Convention: 'The Convention safeguarded against indoctrination, not against acquiring knowledge: all information imparted through the school system would – irrespective of subject matter or class level – to some degree contribute to the development of the child and assist the child in making individual decisions' [FOLGERØ AND OTHERS, 2007].

CONCL: Due to its sensitive nature, RE may involve contentious issues (syllabus content, opt-out system, non-discrimination, teachers' training, appointment and removal, etc.). Preventing, avoiding or solving these issues requires a nuanced and balanced approach and comprises several minimum standards, which depend on the model of RE, among others:

1. Teaching about religions may be mandatory. However, educational authorities should implement an opt-out system to avoid any illegitimate conflict with parents' and/or pupils' consciences (especially when RE isn't taught in an objective, critical and pluralistic manner, or when it promotes relativism).
2. Where RE is offered, it should be always optional for students (according to parents' and/or pupils' preferences). Depending on various factors (like religious demography, agreements with religious denominations, teachers' training, educational budget, etc.), denominational teaching of religion should be extended to as many relevant religious groups as possible. The system should avoid discrimination, both to those pupils who do not attend classes and to those who attend them. Educational authorities should respect religious autonomy (especially concerning RE content).

REFERENCES:

Congregation for Catholic Education: "Circular Letter to the Presidents of Bishops' Conferences on Religious Education in Schools", (5/5/2009).

Davis, Derek; Miroshnikova, Elena (eds.): *The Routledge International Handbook of Religious Education*, Milton Park, Abingdon, Oxon: New York: Routledge (2012).

Jamal, Arif; Panjwani, Farid: "Having Faith in Our Schools: Struggling with Defintions of Religion", in Myriam Hunter-Hénin (ed.) *Law, religious freedoms and education in Europe*, Farnham; Burlington: Ashgate (2011).

Martínez López-Muñiz, José Luis; De Groof, Jan; Lauwers, Gracienne (eds.): *Religious education in public schools: study of comparative law*, Dordrecht: Springer (2006).

Office for Democratic Institutions and Human Rights (ed.): *Toledo guiding principles on teaching about religions and beliefs in public schools*, OSCE. Office for Democratic Institutions and Human Rights, Warsaw (2007).

FOLGERØ AND OTHERS v. NORWAY (ECtHR 29/06/2007, 15472/02).
GRZELAK v. POLAND (ECtHR 15/06/201, 7710/02).
HASAN AND EYLEM ZENGIN v. TURKEY (ECtHR 09/10/2007, 1448/04).
LOYOLA HIGH SCHOOL v. QUEBEC (2015 SCC 12).

Rafael Palomino

Religious Minorities

DEF: International human rights law does not define (religious) 'minorities' and the concept has not been internationally agreed upon. The most influential interpretation has been provided by Francesco Capotorti, defining a minority as:

- a group *numerically inferior* to the rest of the population of a state;
- in a *non-dominant position*;
- whose members – being nationals of the state – possess ethnic, religious or linguistic *characteristics differing* from those of the rest of the population;
- and show, if only implicitly, a *sense of solidarity*, directed towards preserving their culture, traditions, religion or language.

INSTR: International human rights law stipulates that in those states in which religious minorities exist, persons belonging to such minorities shall not be denied the right, in community with the other members of their group, to profess and practice their own religion (Article 27 UN *International Covenant on Civil and Political Rights*).

While the right to freedom of religion or belief is formulated as an individual right, international human rights law firmly underscores that persons must be able to enjoy this freedom 'in community with others' (Article 18 ICCPR and Article 9 ECHR).

The right to freedom of religion or belief, moreover, contains an internal dimension (*forum internum*) and an external dimension (*forum externum*). The former part includes the right to have or to adopt a religion or belief of one's choice. The *forum internum* includes the freedom to change one's religion (Article 18 UDHR; Article 9 ECHR). The *forum externum* covers manifestations of one's religion, including worship, observance, practice and teaching. The freedom to manifest one's religion has been further proclaimed by the UN *Declaration on the Elimination of All Forms of Intolerance and of Discrimination Based on Religion or Belief* (1981).

CASES: In [KOKKINAKIS, 1993] the ECtHR makes a distinction between proper and 'improper proselytism' and found that Greece had breached Article 9 ECHR since Greece's ban on proselytism was not sufficiently specific.

The ECtHR has held that state parties must eradicate, in addition to direct discrimination of members of religious minorities, also *indirect* discrimination. The applicant, a Jehovah's Witness, in [THLIMMENOS, 2000] was refused an appointment as chartered accountant on account of a previous criminal conviction which had resulted from his refusing military service. The ECtHR held that 'unlike other convictions for serious criminal offences, a conviction for refusing on religious or philosophical grounds to wear the military uniform cannot imply any dishonesty or moral turpitude likely to undermine the offender's ability to exercise this profession'.

In [DAHLAB, 2001], [LEYLA ŞAHIN, 2004], and [S.A.S., 2014] the ECtHR respectively held that a ban on a teacher's headscarf, restrictions on university students' religious dress, and the French generic law on prohibiting face-covering dress (including the *burqa* and *niqab*) all did *not* violate Article 9 of the ECHR.

VIEWS: Judge Tulkens' dissent in [LEYLA ŞAHIN, 2004] is among the most influential minority opinions in the area of religious dress. In particular, she vehemently attacked the notion, used by the ECtHR, of a headscarf as a 'powerful external symbol' and also questioned the Court's paternalistic assumptions premised on gender equality. She stated that it 'is not the Court's role to make an appraisal of this type – in this instance a unilateral and negative one – of a religion or religious practice, just as it is not its role to determine in a general and abstract way the signification of wearing the headscarf or to impose its viewpoint on the applicant. The applicant, a young adult university student, said – and there is nothing to suggest that she was not telling the truth – that she wore the headscarf of her own free will. In this connection, I fail to see how the principle of sexual equality can justify prohibiting a woman from following a practice which, in the absence of proof to the contrary, she must be taken to have freely adopted. Equality and non-discrimination are subjective rights which must remain under the control of those who are entitled to benefit from them.'

Furthermore, UN experts, including the UN Special Rapporteur on freedom of religion or belief, and the UN Human Rights Committee, notably in [RANJIT SINGH, 2011], concerning a Sikh turban, are far more critical of restrictions on religious dress than the ECtHR.

CONCL: The ECtHR's recognition in [THLIMMENOS, 2000] of the need for the state to eradicate *indirect* discrimination is useful. However, the exact ramifications for religious minorities remain unclear since additional findings by this Court of violations premised on this notion are scarce.

The ECtHR's approach to religious dress deviates from the one adopted by UN experts. The ECtHR could and arguably should realign itself by applying the necessity test more rigorously. The argument that 'it cannot be denied outright that the wearing of a headscarf might have some kind of proselytising effect' [DAHLAB, 2001] or that headscarves necessarily foster gender inequality [SAHIN, 2004] are not convincing. Where limits on religious freedom are concerned both state parties and the ECtHR may be expected to concretely show the need to sacrifice fundamental rights in favour of another important good.

REFERENCES:

Evans, Carolyn: *Freedom of Religion under the European Convention on Human Rights*, Oxford: Oxford University Press, 2001.

Evans, Malcolm: *Religious Liberty and International Law in Europe*, Cambridge: Cambridge University Press, 1997.

Kirkham, David (ed.): *State Responses to Religious Minorities*, Aldershot: Ashgate (2013).

Temperman, Jeroen: *State–Religion Relationships and Human Rights Law*, Leiden/Boston: Martinus Nijhoff Publishers (2010).

Temperman, Jeroen (ed.): *The Lautsi Papers: Multidisciplinary Reflections on Religious Symbols in the Public School Classroom*, Leiden/Boston: Brill (2012).

Temperman, Jeroen: *Religious Hatred and International Law*, Cambridge: Cambridge University Press (2016).

DAHLAB v. SWITZERLAND (ECtHR 15/02/2001, 42393/98).

LEYLA ŞAHIN v. TURKEY (ECtHR 10/11/2005, 44774/98).

KOKKINAKIS v. GREECE (ECtHR 25/03/1993, 14307/88).

RANJIT SINGH v. FRANCE (Human Rights Committee 22/07/2011, 1876/2009).

S.A.S. v. FRANCE (ECtHR 01/07/2014, 43835/11).

THLIMMENOS v. GREECE (ECtHR 06/04/2000, 34369/97).

www.strasbourgconsortium.org (accessed 2/2016).

Jeroen Temperman

Religious Symbols

DEF: Religious symbols are symbols or clothing worn or displayed based on a religion or belief, including not only those symbols worn or displayed by people because they see it as an obligation of their religion or belief, but also those linked to, or inspired by religion or belief, even if there is no obligation. Skull caps, headscarves, face covering veils, burqas, crosses or crucifixes, turbans, Kara bangles and dreadlocks are all seen as religious symbols.

The terms 'religion' and 'belief' have been given a wide interpretation by the ECtHR and include all traditional religions and beliefs as well as non-religious beliefs (e.g. pacifism, veganism and atheism). Religious or philosophical convictions or beliefs are also protected if they attain a certain level of cogency, seriousness, cohesion and importance; are worthy of respect in a democratic society; are not incompatible with human dignity; do not conflict with fundamental rights; and, relate to a weighty and substantial aspect of human life and behaviour [CAMPBELL AND COSANS, 1982].

The display or wearing of religious symbols is considered a manifestation of religion or belief. Manifestations can be restricted when this is prescribed by law and necessary in a democratic society for the protection of public safety, public health or morals or for the protection of the rights and freedoms of others (Article 9(2)). Restrictions can thus be justified under certain circumstances.

INSTR: [LAUTSI AND OTHERS, 2011] concerned the display of a crucifix on classroom walls in schools. The Italian Government argued that the cross was not only a religious symbol, but also a cultural one. Moreover, it was a passive symbol that did not influence teaching. The Grand Chamber of the ECtHR held that it was not for the Court to take a position as to the meaning of the crucifix but that it was, above all, a religious symbol. The ECtHR stated that there was no evidence that the display of a religious symbol on a class room wall has any influence on pupils and is not in itself sufficient to denote a process of indoctrination on the part of the state. It was a matter falling within the state's margin of appreciation to decide whether crucifixes should be present in class rooms.

On the other hand, the ECtHR has held [DAHLAB, 2001], that it was difficult to assess the impact of a powerful external symbol such as the Muslim headscarf on the freedom of conscience or religion of very young children, but that this might have some proselytizing effect. The ECtHR came to this conclusion even though there was no evidence of the teacher trying to influence the children in her class. In fact, the teacher had worn the headscarf for five years without any complaints from the head of the school, parents or pupils. The ECtHR did not mention anything about whether the headscarf was a religious symbol but it seemed to readily accept that it was, and that the applicant was manifesting her religion through wearing it. The ECtHR then considered whether the interference was justified.

In Germany, several courts have held that exemptions for Christian and occidental symbols in laws prohibiting the wearing of religious clothing or symbols by teachers did not breach the constitutional prohibition of discrimination, because these symbols were traditional, cultural and historical, and were divorced from their religious meaning (Howard, 2012, 92–93).

In [DAHLAB, 2001], and many subsequent cases, the ECtHR has quite readily accepted that the wearing of a headscarf, face veil, cross, turban and other forms of dress is a manifestation of the individual claimant's religion or belief, and has moved swiftly on to examine the justification of alleged interferences with these manifestations. The term 'necessary in a democratic society' in Article 9(2) means that the interference must fulfil a pressing social need and must be proportionate to the legitimate aim pursued. The justification test is thus a proportionality test and this means that a balancing of all rights involved needs to take place.

CASES: There has been a shift in the way the ECtHR deals with cases about bans on the display or wearing of religious symbols. Not only does the ECtHR now readily accept that the applicant is manifesting their religion or belief, the application of the proportionality test has also changed. In earlier cases [e.g. DAHLAB, 2001 and SAHIN, 2004/2005] the ECtHR did not seem to give much attention to the importance of the manifestation for the religious applicant themselves when balancing the interests of applicants with the interests of the State Party. But, in later cases, the ECtHR considered this in some more detail. In [ARSLAN AND OTHERS, 2010], members of a religious group were convicted for touring the streets of Ankara while wearing turbans and distinctive trousers and tunic, a dress code based on their religious beliefs. The ECtHR found a violation of Article 9 because the Government had not convincingly established the necessity of the restriction. The ECtHR also considered that there was no evidence that the applicants had represented a threat to public order or had been involved in proselytizing by exerting inappropriate pressure on passers-by.

In [EWEIDA AND OTHERS, 2013], two applicants, Eweida, an airline check-in person, and Chaplin, a nurse, were refused permission to wear a small cross with their uniform. The ECtHR gave greater weight to the importance of the manifestation for the applicants themselves, considering that 'on one side of the scales was Eweida's desire to manifest her religious belief' and that 'the importance for the second applicant (Chaplin) of being permitted to manifest her religion by wearing her cross visibly must weigh heavily in the balance'. The ECtHR held that the refusal in Eweida's case was not justified, but in Chaplin's case it was justified for health and safety reasons.

In [S.A.S., 2014], a challenge to the French ban on the wearing of face covering clothing in all public spaces, the ECtHR referred to the face covering veil as being 'a full expression of a cultural identity' but also accepted it as a religious manifestation. In assessing the justification of the ban, the ECtHR considered the impact on women who wear the face covering veil for religious reasons, especially because they were forced to choose to go against their religious belief and not wear the veil when going out or, to go out while wearing the veil and thus laying themselves open to criminal sanctions. The ECtHR concluded that the ban was justified as it pursued the legitimate aim of 'living together' which fell under the 'protection of the rights and freedoms of others'.

VIEWS: There are some contradictions in the different decisions of the ECtHR (for example, between [DAHLAB], 2001 and [LAUTSI, 2009]). A Muslim headscarf is seen as a 'powerful external symbol' which could have a proselytizing effect on schoolchildren, but a crucifix on a class room wall is seen as a passive symbol which does not, of itself, influence them.

In [ARSLAN AND OTHERS, 2010], the ECtHR stressed that there was a distinction between wearing religious dress in public areas open to all and wearing it in schools or other public establishments where religious neutrality might take precedence over the right to manifest one's religion or belief. This would suggest that the French general ban in all public space (at issue in [S.A.S., 2014]), would also be held to be an unjustified interference with Article 9 (Vickers, 2014). But the ECtHR distinguished the two cases because the full-face Islamic veil entirely concealed the face, while in [ARSLAN AND OTHERS, 2014] the face remained visible. The ECtHR has been praised for rejecting the arguments that the ban was necessary for public safety in the absence of concrete evidence of a safety threat; that bans were necessary to guarantee gender equality; and, that bans were necessary to protect human dignity. But, the ECtHR has been criticised for stretching the legitimate aims in Article 9(2) too far in accepting 'living together' as a legitimate aim (Berry, 2014; Brems, 2014; Howard, 2014; Vickers, 2014). The ECtHR said that 'living together' was a flexible notion which needed careful examination, but then it did not appear to do so in this case and concluded that it was a legitimate aim. The dissenting judges called the aim far-fetched and vague and concluded that the ban was disproportionate. They also stated that there is no right not to be shocked or provoked by different models of cultural and religious identity and there is no right to enter into contact with other people in public places against their will.

There is also divergence between the ECtHR and the UN Human Rights Committee (HRCee) under Article 18 of the International Covenant on Civil and Political Rights (ICCPR), which guarantees freedom of religion in similar terms to Article 9 ECHR. The question was whether the French requirement to appear bareheaded in identity photographs (without a turban), was a breach of Article 9 ECHR / 18 ICCPR. In [MANN SINGH, 2008 – identity photograph on a driving licence], the ECtHR found that this requirement did not breach Article 9 as it was justified by the legitimate aim of public safety. The HRCee came to the opposite conclusion regarding the same applicant, but this time concerning a passport: that it was a violation of his right to manifest his religion in Article 18 ICCPR [MANN SINGH, HRCee, 2013]. See also: [RANJIT SINGH, HRCee, 2011 – identity photograph for a residence permit].

CONCL: Mixed messages are sent out by the ECtHR in relation to the display and wearing of religious symbols and whether bans on doing so are a breach of Article 9 ECHR. The case law does not always seem consistent, and debates on restrictions on the manifestation of religion or belief will continue both in the ECtHR and beyond.

But there have been some positive developments in more recent case law. First of all, the ECtHR does accept a broad range of manifestations as qualifying for the protection of Article 9. In [EWEIDA AND OTHERS, 2013], the ECtHR accepted that, in order to establish that an act is a manifestation of religion or belief for the purposes of Article 9, the applicant does not have to establish that he/she acted in fulfilment of a duty mandated by the religion in question. It is sufficient to establish the existence of a sufficiently close and direct nexus between the act and the underlying belief. In fact, the ECtHR does now appear to accept reasonably easily that a manifestation is at stake and moves quickly on to the question whether the interference is justified. This is a positive development, because the justification test includes a proportionality test, a balancing test where all interests can be taken into account, the interests of the applicant as well as the interests of the state and the rights of others.

A second positive development is that the ECtHR appears to apply a more rigorous proportionality test when assessing whether a restriction or limitation is justified under Article 9(2). The proportionality test requires, as mentioned, a balancing of all interests involved and, recently, the Court has given more attention to the importance of the manifestation for the individual applicant and how the restriction on this right affects them.

A third positive development is the abandoning of the view that, if an individual cannot manifest his/her religion at work by the wearing of religious symbols, there is no interference because he/she can solve this problem by getting another job. In [EWEIDA AND OTHERS, 2013], the ECtHR considered that, where an individual complains of a restriction on his or her freedom of religion in the workplace, rather than holding that the possibility of changing jobs would negate any interference with the right, the better approach would be to weigh this possibility in the overall balance when considering whether or not the restriction is proportionate. This moves the decision under Article 9(2) and the justification and proportionality test, where a balancing of all interests can take place, rather than rejecting a claim under Article 9(1). It also recognises that choosing between your religious principles and your job, is not as simple as it was previously made out to be, and that resigning is often not a realistic option for many people.

REFERENCES:

Berry, Stephanie: "SAS v. France: Does anything remain of the right to manifest religion?", (Blogpost 2/7/2014) (available at www.ejiltalk.org accessed 3/2016).

Brems, Eva: "S.A.S. v. France as a problematic precedent, Strasbourg Observers", (Blogpost 9/7/2014) (available at www. Strasbourgobservers.com accessed 3/2016).

Evans, Malcolm: *Manual on the wearing of religious symbols in public areas*, Strasbourg: Council of Europe Publishing (2009).

Howard, Erica: *Law and the wearing of religious symbols. European bans on the wearing of religious symbols in education*, London/New York: Routledge, (2012).

Howard, Erica: "S.A.S. v. France: Living Together or Increased Social Division?", (Blogpost 7/7/2014) (available at www.ejiltalk.org accessed 3/2016).

Vickers, Lucy: "S.A.S. v. France: The French burqa ban and religious freedom", (Blogpost 10/9/2014) (available at www.e-ir.info accessed 3/2016):.

ARSLAN AND OTHERS v. TURKEY (ECtHR 23/02/2010, 41135/98).

CAMPBELL AND COSANS v. THE UK (ECtHR 22/03/1983, 7511/76).

DAHLAB v. SWITZERLAND (ECtHR 15/02/2001, 42393/98).

EWEIDA AND OTHERS v. THE UK (ECtHR 15/01/2013, 48420/10, 59842/10, 51671/10 and 36516/10).

LAUTSI AND OTHERS v. ITALY ECtHR 18/03/2011 (GC), 30814/06.

MANN SINGH v. FRANCE (ECtHR 13/11/2008, 24479/07).

MANN SINGH v. FRANCE (HRCee 26/09/2013, CCPR/C/108/D/1928/2010).

RANJIT SINGH v. FRANCE (HRCee 27/09/2011, CCPR/C/102/D/1876/2009).

S.A.S. v. FRANCE (ECtHR 01/07/2014, 43835/11).

SAHIN v. TURKEY (ECtHR 29/06/2004 (Chamber), 10/11/2005 (Grand Chamber) 44774/98).

Erica Howard

Restitution and Return of Cultural Objects

DEF: Restitution is the restoration of freedom, legal rights, social status, citizenship or goods. Restitution aims at reversing the effect of a former breach of the law. Within the context of cultural heritage disputes, this applies both to looting during war, and theft or illegal export during times of peace. It may also apply to colonial removal of cultural objects. Although restitution and return are often used inconsistently, restitution regards primarily stolen objects (theft), whereas return regards illegally exported cultural objects.

INSTR/VIEWS: Although restitution and return have both clear legal connotations (see 1995 *UNIDROIT Convention*), the notions are frequently used interchangeably. The inconsistent use of terminology, however, leaves the door open to further negotiations, as claims are often made on ethical and historical rather than legal grounds, thereby deliberately avoiding legal terminology. In particular, the term restitution often raises concerns among the parties involved, as it is implicitly connected to other legal questions of compensation and non-retroactivity, and might conflict with third party (ownership) rights. Thus, either 'return' or the rather neutral and unencumbered notion of 'transfer' is frequently utilised in bilateral agreements between states and/or museums. Whereas the 1970 UNESCO *Convention on the Means of Prohibiting and Preventing the Illicit Import, Export and Transfer of Ownership of Cultural Property* uses both 'repatriation' (Article 2) and 'return' (Article 7), more recent legal texts use 'return' (*Directive 2014/60/EU*). In case of theft or illegal export / removal, a cultural object can be restituted / returned / transferred to a state (UNIDROIT and UNESCO Convention and EU Directive), the private (former) owner or its heirs (e.g. Nazi looted art), a people (indigenous people; e.g. U.S. 1990 *Native–American Repatriation Act*, NAGPRA) or (religious) community.

CONCL: Return and restitution are often used interchangeably. The use of the term 'return' – or sometimes simply 'transfer' – by negotiating parties in disputes has become frequent in settings that ought to use legal terminology to designate legal rights. Whereas the term 'restitution' is generally associated with claims or disputes and theft, it almost never appears in the wording that attests the actual legal and/or moral settlement of cultural heritage disputes. Claims in national/international courts are rare, voluntary returns more frequent.

REFERENCES:

Principles for Cooperation in the Mutual Protection and Transfer of Cultural Material, adopted by the International Law Association (2006).

Prott, Lyndel: "The History and Development of Processes for the Recovery of Cultural Heritage", in *Art, Antiquity and Law* XIII (2008) 175.

The International Bureau of the Permanent Court of Arbitration (ed.): *Resolution of Cultural Property Disputes*, The Hague: Kluwer (2004).

Vrdoljak, Ana Filipa: *International Law, Museums and the Return of Cultural Objects*, Cambridge: Cambridge Press (2006).

BEYELER v. ITALY (ECtHR 05/01/2000, 33202/96).

IRAN v. BARAKAT GALLERIES Ltd. (UK Court of Appeal, 21/12/07, EWCA Civ. 1374).

Robert Peters

Right to Science and Culture

DEF: 'Science' is 'the enterprise whereby mankind, acting individually or in small or large groups, makes an organised attempt, by means of the objective study of observed phenomena, to discover and master the chain of causalities; (and) bring together in a coordinated form the resultant sub-systems of knowledge by means of systematic reflection and conceptualisation' (UNESCO, 1974). It encompasses the life, physical, social and behavioural sciences (Shaheed, 2012). It is an iterative, logical and empirically based process (AAAS, 2013) as well as a body of knowledge (Shaheed, 2012). Peer review and adherence to ethical standards are essential elements of science (AAAS, 2013). Science and culture are considered by some as being linked, both relating to the 'pursuit of knowledge and understanding and to human creativity' (Shaheed, 2012). Except in commentary concerning →intellectual property, the rights are almost never treated together.

INSTR: The rights to participate in cultural life and to enjoy the benefits of scientific progress and its applications are recognised in the UDHR, the ICESCR, the *Additional Protocol to the American Convention on Human Rights in the area of Economic, Social and Cultural Rights*, and the *Arab Charter of Human Rights*, but not in the ECHR. They are both closely tied to other civil, political, economic and social rights. Specific aspects of the right to science are also recognised in international and regional instruments related to biomedicine. Interpretation of the right to enjoy the benefits of scientific progress should avoid the limited view that reduces the right to a necessary prerequisite for other rights (e.g. the rights to food and health). It is also a right unto itself. The benefits of science for society include the knowledge generated by science and the material benefits that result from that knowledge (e.g. medicines and technology) but also conceptual, methodological, and cultural benefits. The right to access those benefits exists along a bi-directional continuum. A person's position on this continuum can change over time, depending on their interests, ability and training (AAAS, 2013). Realisation of the right requires international cooperation (Shaheed, 2012), including open availability of data and publications, and the free circulation of scientists (Chapman, 2009, Claude, 2002). The obligations of states to implement the right include a responsibility to build an appropriate enabling environment (UNESCO, 2007), including funding for research and development, quality science education, and information and communication technologies (AAAS 2013). Though the right is not explicit on this topic, it is important to recognise that scientific freedom is not absolute. Scientists bear internal responsibilities to their profession and research subjects, and external responsibilities to society (UNESCO, 2009).

The increased commercialisation of both the scientific endeavour and cultural expressions needs to be counter-balanced by government initiatives that promote and protect science and culture in a manner that ensures equality and non-discrimination and emphasises their social benefit rather than their economic values.

CASES: Due to a lack of a conceptual understanding about the meaning of the right to benefit from scientific progress, it has seldom been used as the basis for litigation. One known exception arose in Venezuela. In that instance, a national administrative law court found a violation of the right in the case of 37 patients who were denied access to HIV/AIDS treatment by the Venezuelan Social Security Institute [CITIZEN'S ACTION AGAINST AIDS vs. MINSTRY OF HEALTH, 1999].

The right has the potential to inform cases concerned with protection of the welfare of scientists, dissemination of accurate scientific information on key issues (e.g. HIV/AIDS transmission), and the non-discriminatory provision of quality science education.

Despite the absence of the right to participate in cultural life in the ECHR, the ECtHR has been willing to address issues of cultural concern (e.g. artistic expression, linguistic rights, cultural heritage, historical truth) as they relate to rights recognised in the Convention, including the rights to freedom of expression, respect for private and family life and freedom of thought, conscience and religion (ECtHR, 2011).

VIEWS:

(1) Several commentators are exploring how/whether the right to enjoy the benefits of scientific progress could become the basis for a new conceptual framework for addressing intellectual property protections in the context of human rights. One potentially promising argument emerging from the literature starts from the premise that science and culture are public goods (e.g. Shaver 2010, Haugen 2012).

(2) Chapman argues that, although the right to benefit from scientific progress is recognised in human rights treaties, perhaps it should not be considered legally binding because of the challenges associated with requiring states *at all levels of development* to implement the right, given the significant human and financial resources needed to ensure full implementation (Chapman 2009).

(3) Ensuring broad dissemination of scientific literature and scientific information, generally, is consistent with the right. Scholarly publishers argue that any model for open access should take into account the costs and value associated with ensuring peer review of scientific articles. Professional societies that are also publishers add that funding from publications helps support programs that strengthen the scientific enterprise for the benefit of society (AAAS 2013).

CONCL: The meaning of the right to benefit from scientific progress is still being debated and is yet to be definitively addressed by the Committee on Economic, Social and Cultural Rights, the UN body responsible for monitoring implementation of the right at the international level. Nonetheless, existing literature on the right suggests several key potential consequences of this right for contemporary social challenges and the legal and policy options for addressing them, including the responsibility of governments to:

- regulate and/or incentivise industry to ensure adequate funding and appropriate pricing for neglected fields of medicine affecting marginalised and vulnerable populations;
- disseminate to the public and/or support the sharing of accurate and actionable health, environmental and other important scientific information;
- provide or ensure the provision of quality science education at the primary and secondary levels;
- appropriately regulate dual-use technologies.

In addition to the obligations of governments are the obligations of the scientific community with regard to ensuring the responsible conduct of research, and defining the social responsibilities of scientists, including with regard to the broad dissemination of scientific information.

When this right has been better understood and an authoritative interpretation adopted, the opportunity and challenge will then exist to define the relationship among the rights in Article 27 of the UDHR and Article 15 of the ICESCR. For the moment, principally that discussion is occurring in the context of efforts to redefine intellectual property protection to ensure greater access to the benefits of scientific progress as well as of cultural expressions in their various forms.

REFERENCES:

AAAS Science and Human Rights Coalition: "Defining the Right to Enjoy the Benefits of Scientific Progress and Its Applications: American Scientists' Perspectives" (Report prepared by Margaret Weigers Vitullo and Jessica Wyndham), Washington, DC (October 2013).

Chapman, Audrey: "Towards an Understanding of the Right to Enjoy the Benefits of Scientific Progress and Its Applications", *Journal of Human Rights* (2009).

Claude, Richard P.: "Scientists' Rights and the Human Rights to the Benefits of Science", in Chapman, A and Russell, S (eds.): *Core Obligations: Building a Framework for Economic, Social and Cultural Rights*, Cambridge: Intersentia (2002).

European Court of Human Rights: *Cultural Rights in the Case-Law of the European Court of Human Rights*, Research Division Report, Strasbourg: Council of Europe (2011).

Haugen, H.M.: "Technology and Human Rights – Friends or Foes? Highlighting Innovations Applying to Natural Resources and Medicine", *Human Rights Series* 2 (2012).

Shaheed, Farida: *The Right to Enjoy the Benefits of Scientific Progress and its Applications*, A/HRC/20/26, HRC, Geneva (2012).

Shaver, Lea: "The Right to Science and Culture", *Wisconsin Law Review*, (2010).

UNESCO: *Recommendation on the Status of Scientific Researchers*, 18C/Res.40, adopted on 20 November 1974.

UNESCO: *Venice Statement on the Right to Enjoy the Benefits of Scientific Progress and Its Applications* (2009).

Jessica M. Wyndham

Roma Culture

DEF: The term 'Roma' includes all groups that self-identify as such, including those who self-identify as Sinti, Kale, Travellers or Gypsies (UN Special Rapporteur for Minority Issues 2015). The Council of Europe uses the term 'Roma and Travellers' in an operational sense, covering a) Roma, Sinti/Manush, Calé, Kaale, Romanichals, Boyash/Rudari; b) Balkan Egyptians (Egyptians and Ashkali); c) Eastern groups (Dom, Lom and Abdal); and groups such as Travellers, Yenish and the populations designated under the administrative term '*Gens du voyage*', as well as persons who identify themselves as Gypsies.

INSTR: The cultural rights of Roma are protected by the ICPPR (Article 27) and other international human rights instruments. In Europe, they are in many countries covered by international conventions under the aspects of the rights of →national minorities (FCNM) and/or linguistic rights (ECRML).

The FCNM, ratified by 39 European states including most countries with important Roma populations (except Turkey and Greece), demands adequate measures to promote full equality also in cultural life, in order to enable persons belonging to minorities to 'maintain and develop their culture, and to preserve the essential elements of their identity, namely their religion, language, traditions and cultural heritage' (Article 5).

Under the ECRML (ratified by 25 European states, excluding several countries with large Roma populations), the Romani language is protected in 16 states; 14 of these have included Romani in their respective instrument of ratification. Only a limited number of Charter provisions can be applied to Romani as a traditionally present non-territorial language, including Articles 7(3) and 7(5). The far-reaching protection under Part III ECRML (concerning education, interaction with judicial and other public authorities, media, cultural activities, economic and social life, transfrontier exchanges) is currently offered only in Bosnia & Herzegovina, Germany, Hungary, Montenegro, Serbia and the Slovak Republic.

CASES: The → ECtHR has not often decided on the cultural rights of Roma. In several cases the Court proscribed discriminatory segregation of Roma in the education system of various member states [e.g. D.H. AND OTHERS, 2007]. In 2002, an attempt to overturn the local injunction against holding a traditional Gypsy Horse Fair through the ECtHR failed [GYPSY COUNCIL, 2002].

The opinions of the FCNM monitoring mechanism (Advisory Committee) concentrate on education (other priority themes being housing, health and the labour market), and only occasionally on other Roma-related cultural issues such as the insufficient participation in the cultural life of the community; the scope and modalities of state support for cultural activities; or the role of regular TV and radio programmes in Romani language.

The ECRML monitoring mechanism (Committee of Experts) has published critical comments and recommends improvements e.g. on the often inadequate teaching of Romani in school, the absence of dual-language street signs, and the situation of Romani-language media content.

VIEWS: Roma culture is complex and multilayered, marked by internal diversity as well as by similarities (Matras 2016). Its protection through international human rights instruments must therefore be sufficiently flexible in order to strike a balance between a dynamic understanding of culture, (local and regional) traditions, human rights standards, assimilatory pressures and withdrawal tendencies. So far, the cultural, economic and social situation of Roma—often described as Europe's most discriminated minority—is generally understood as highly vulnerable, so that European institutions and member states are giving priority to an improved access of Roma to education, health provision, housing and employment. The protection and promotion of Roma culture is hence frequently seen as secondary, not least also because policy makers often have a distorted and biased understanding of what Roma culture actually is. A greater attention to cultural aspects would however also strengthen the self-confidence of Roma, facilitating their social inclusion in other areas.

CONCL: Millions of European Roma live at the extreme margins of society and lack access to essential infrastructures and services. The current basic-needs strategy for Roma inclusion can however only succeed if the widespread anti-Roma sentiment ('anti-Gypsyism') in mainstream society is tackled and Roma culture and Roma identity are adequately supported and protected. The new 'European Roma Institute for Arts and Culture' (set up in Berlin in 2016 by the Council of Europe, the Open Society Foundations and a group of Roma artists) is expected to fill this gap at least partly; its mission is to strengthen the public awareness that Roma possess a rich culture worthy of appreciation and support, and are making important contributions to European culture.

REFERENCES:

Advisory Committee on the FCNM: (www.coe.int/en/web/minorities/country-specific-monitoring-2016 accessed 06/2016).

Committee of Experts on the ECRML: *Reports and Recommendations* (available at www.coe.int accessed 06/2016).

Matras, Yaron: *Roma Culture: An Introduction*, in: University of Graz/Council of Europe, *Education of Roma children in Europe* (available at romafacts.uni-graz.at accessed 06/2016).

UN Special Rapporteur on Minority Issues: *Comprehensive study of the human rights situation of Roma worldwide, with a particular focus on the phenomenon of anti-Gypsyism*, (A/HRC/29/24) Geneva: Human Rights Council (2015).

D.H. AND OTHERS v. THE CZECH REPUBLIC (ECtHR 13/11/2007, 57325/00).

THE GYPSY COUNCIL AND OTHERS v. THE UNITED KINGDOM (ECtHR 14/05/2002, 66336/01).

Ulrich Bunjes

Secularism and Islamic Law

DEF: A general stance that modern democracy is based on 'secularism', i.e. the separation of religion from the state, opens extremely complex theological, philosophical and legal questions in the relationship between state and religion. Clearly, the idea of popular sovereignty as the main source of law contrasts with the Islamic belief that sovereignty belongs exclusively to God. The Qur'an (central religious text of Islam) and Sunnah (portion of Islamic law based on the words and acts of the Prophet Muhammad) define the standards of Islamic divine law, while Shari'ah (religious legal system of Islam) is the foundation of Islamic law. The relationship between the Shari'ah and political power is burdened with the problem of limiting the power of the ruler who has an obligation to support the divine law. The concept of consultatative deliberation (ahl al-shura) includes resistance towards autocratic governance (al-hukm bi'li hawa wa al-tasallut) and despotism (al-istibdad).

VIEWS: Secular democracies were developed on the basis of three distinct categories: liberty, equality and fraternity. There are many overlaps between these secular categories and social and moral principles of Islamic divine law: pursuing justice through social cooperation and mutual assistance; establishing a non-autocratic / consultative method of governance; and institutionalising mercy and compassion and social interactions. The principles of liberty, equality and fraternity are addressed in the Qur'an where it says that 'God created people different and grouped them into nations and tribes so that they would come to know one another.' This provision of the Qur'an indicates the need for harmony and equality among people, groups, tribes and nations in order to achieve justice as the divine imperative and represents the sovereignty of the divine (49:13). Such signs of compatibility between Islamic divine law and secularism largely disappear in interpretations of the divine law by human agents that raise the question of the appointment, removal and power of the ruler (Caliph), who implements the will of God on earth and determines the role of law in Islam. Hence, the main problem is not the Islamic law as such and rather the human interpretation of Islamic divine law and its application.

CONCL: Shari'ah law and Fiqh (Islamic Law) are not the divine law. While Shari'ah proposes a human ideal of interpretation of divine sovereignty, Fiqh is a human interpretation of understanding how Shari'ah law can be applied. The obligation to live in accordance with God's law, specified through interpretations by human agents (Shari'ah and Fiqh), leaves much room for human errors in the interpretation of the divine law. Law applied by the state is only potentially God's law (school themukhatti'ah), 'unless the person to whom the law applies believes it to be God's will and command' (school musawwibah). Solving the legal conflict between the Qur'an and Sunnah (Islamic Divine Law), from one side, and the Shari'ah and Fiqh, on the other hand, could open a much broader space for determining responsibilities in Islamic law and thus the possibility to address the problem of a 'closed cycle of violence in Islam', which contributes to the growth of global terrorism.

REFERENCES:

Hamidullah, Muhammad: *The Prophet's Establishing a State and His Succession*, Islamabad: Pakistan Hijra Council (1988).

Khaled Abou El Fadl: "Islam and the Challenge of Democracy", 1(1) *Journal of Scholarly Perspectives* (2005) 3.

Rosenthal, Erwin IJ: *Political Thought in Medieval Islam*, Cambridge: Cambridge University Press (1988).

Nedzad Basic

Social Media
(and Freedom of Expression)

DEF/INTRO: The emergence of social media had already been predicted before the invention of web and mobile apps that are now being used by these information and exchange platforms: Such 'new practices of subjectification of a post media' would be 'facilitated by a concerted re-appropriation of information and communication technologies', leading to 'innovative forms of consultation and collective interaction, and, a reinvention of democracy' (Guattari, 1989).

However, it was also observed that cyber freedom as 'the post-mediatic promise of singularity was easily corrupted by the intrusion of corporate mediocrity into the medium at every level' (Genosko, 2009). We look at such intrusions and challenges faced by social media users and groups mostly from a European perspective.

INSTR: Despite the existence of more general conventions like the ICCPR or the ECHR, the lack of a globally adopted, specific set of social media regulations or firmly binding and deterrent common legal instruments of regional institutions such as the EU or the Council of Europe endangers rights and freedoms of the users in individual countries. For example, some national authorities tend to focus on punitive measures for existing and potential misuses of social media, which can seriously impact on the safeguarding of rights and freedoms of social media communities, sometimes resulting in the banning of the entire platform in question. For example, Turkey's comprehensive Law No 5651, *Regulation of Publications on the Internet and Suppression of Crimes Committed by Means of Such Publications*, has been systematically used since 2007. Following the mass protests around *Gezi Park* in Istanbul in June 2013, this has raised the number of blocked websites to 40,000.

Social media companies have their own *Terms of Service* which allows them to monitor and filter content, and suspend or remove user accounts under defined criteria or through system filters such as: content with spam; incitement of violence; hate speech; threats; pornography; or copyright violation.

In principle, social media presence enables users to generate or share content for publicising charitable causes, defending human rights and social justice, promoting diversity and cultural heritage, and highlighting the importance of a culture of peace, tolerance and solidarity. However, according to a recent workshop at the European Dialogue on Internet Governance (EuroDIG 2016), it is not always possible to maintain a balance between freedom of expression and compliance with the rules when acting on social media.

CASES: National authorities' interpretation of a misuse of social media varies greatly, ranging from inciting riots in the case of the British Facebook users Jordan Blackshaw and Perry Sutcliffe-Keenan (2011), to criticising the Turkish President Recep Tayyip Erdogan via Twitter in the case of Dutch–Turkish journalist Ebru Umar (2016), or to insulting the dog of the King of Thailand via Facebook in the case of Thanakorn Siripaiboon (2015).

A number of cases on banned social media sites reached the ECtHR, among them many applications against Turkey (one of the member states of the Council of Europe with the highest number of cases brought against them). Regarding Turkey's outright ban of *YouTube* between May 2008 and October 2010, the ECtHR ruled in favour of the applicants [CENGIZ AND OTHERS, 2016].

VIEWS: With regard to the unclear legal status of social media, the prevailing opinion holds that further guidelines and a set of recommendations could motivate the national authorities into taking constructive steps towards legislative reforms and improved practices. There is also a general belief that such standards would make it easier for social media companies to deal with queries of state authorities about social media user accounts or contents.

The UN Human Rights Council has recently adopted a resolution on human rights on the Internet (2016) which follows earlier ones, but reaffirms that the same rights that people have offline must also be protected online. It also condemns measures to prevent or disrupt access, and calls on all states to refrain from and cease such measures. It further recognises the importance of access to

→information and →privacy online for the realisation of the right to freedom of expression and to hold opinions without interference.

Based *inter alia* on a recent report on laws and practices of 47 →Council of Europe member states on blocking, filtering and removal of Internet content (Institut suisse de droit comparé, 2015), which found many of the national regulatory practices not to be in compliance with Article 10 of the ECHR, the CoE Committee of Ministers urged governments to ensure that their legal frameworks and procedures are clear, transparent and to provide safeguards for freedom of expression and access to information; this *Recommendation on Internet Freedom* (2016) also contains 'Internet Freedom Indicators' on the basis of which states are urged to 'periodically evaluate the level of respect for and implementation of human rights and fundamental freedom standards with regard to the Internet'.

Critical opinions question the implementation and sustainability of judgments delivered by the ECtHR in this domain, seeing that national authorities continue with their banning practices after a while. They also question whether social media companies would genuinely be combining their skills and energies with other non-state actors in developing long term constructive campaigns for greater tolerance by the national authorities.

CONCL: Social media platforms will indeed continue to be an essential part of the contemporary way of life due to their accessibility, instantaneity, sociability and the sentiments of achievement and appreciation offered to the user. However, the freedom of expression on these platforms is often challenged, when users provide content regarding their own cultural heritage, ethnic background, political views and gender or faith orientation.

Since they do not have to disclose their true name and identity and thus can avoid direct physical confrontations, some users will continue to operate as voluntary or recruited online →trolls that show abusive behaviour. Social media companies will possibly continue to invest their research and development resources on containing the users within the online sphere rather than venturing into the offline world with physical human communication and interaction.

Judgments by the ECtHR against repressive practices in some states send powerful messages; however, they are currently not perceived as sustainable deterrents. Legal action should be supported with other forms of preventive and dissuasive alternatives. One such initiative is, since 2012, the Council of Europe's youth-led campaign *No Hate Speech Movement* (NHSM); it aims to tackle online →hate crimes and develop counter narratives through social media and other online techniques against stereotypes, intolerance, →discrimination, racism, and sexism.

REFERENCES:

Council of Europe: Recommendation of the Committee of Ministers to member States on Internet freedom, CM/Rec(2016)5.

Fuller, Thomas: "Thai Man May Go to Prison for Insulting King's Dog", New York Times, (14/12/2015) (accessed 06/2016 via www.nytimes.com/).

Genosko, Gary: *Felix Guattari – A Critical Introduction*, London: Pluto (2009).

Guattari, Felix: "From Postmodernism to the Postmedia Era" (1989), in *Schizoanalytical Cartographies*, London: Bloomsbury (2013).

Institut Suisse de droit comparé: *Comparative Study on Blocking, Filtering and Take-Down of Illegal Internet Content*, Lausanne (2015) (accessed 06/2016 via www.coe.int).

Schenkkan, Nate: "May 2013 – July 2014: Turkey's Long Year of Content Restrictions Online", Freedom House Reports (accessed 06/2016 via freedomhouse.org).

UN Human Rights Council Resolution on The promotion, protection and enjoyment of human rights on the Internet (27/06/2016, A/HRC/32/L.20, accessed 07/2016 via documents-dds-ny.un.org).

CENGIZ AND OTHERS v. TURKEY (ECtHR 01/03/2016, 48226/10 and 14027/11).

www.eurodig.org/eurodig-2016 (accessed 06/2016).

nohatespeechmovement.org (accessed 06/2016).

Umit Ozturk

Status of Artists

DEF: An 'artists' statute' is generally understood to mean legal and administrative measures taken by the authorities to adapt the general legal system to artists' specific working conditions and way of life. Artists generate →intellectual property rights but, despite the expansion of the cultural and creative sectors, artistic activities take place in conditions which are clearly less secure than those of other professions. Small businesses, unremunerated research/development, irregular and uncertain income, short-term project-based contracts, accelerated physical and mental strain, high levels of mobility and multi-tasking are elements which the ordinary framework of laws too often ignores in tax and social-security legislation.

INSTR: The UNESCO *Recommendation concerning the Status of the Artist* (1980) asserted – for the first time – the need to devise a status for artists as *cultural workers*. Based on the fundamental social rights recognised by the 1948 *Universal Declaration of Human Rights* (especially articles 22 to 25, 27 and 28) and the 1966 *International Covenant on Economic, Social and Cultural Rights* (articles 6 and 15), this status should improve the legal, social and fiscal conditions for creative and performance-related artistic activities, whilst respecting creative freedoms, to allow artists to live with dignity. More recently, the 2005 UNESCO *Convention on the Protection and Promotion of the Diversity of Cultural Expressions* recognises the dual *economic and cultural* nature of artistic activity. As stipulated especially in articles 7, 13 and 16, this activity should therefore enjoy a specific and targeted legal, social and fiscal environment which encourages artistic activity (status) and facilitates the movement of artists (visas, taxation). The European Parliament adopted two resolutions: in 1999 on the role of artists in the European Union, and in 2007 on the social status of artists, focusing particularly on their unusual contractual situation, on access to social security and on fairer tax arrangements.

Several states have adopted partial measures which take certain aspects of the artist's condition into account: for example, special social insurance for self-employed artists (Germany, France), supplementary or guaranteed income for artists (Luxembourg, the Netherlands), the artist's choice between employee or self-employed status (Belgium), access to unemployment insurance for all artists (Belgium), special unemployment insurance rules (Belgium, France), reduced social-security contributions (Belgium), special social-security contributions for certain businesses (Austria, Germany, France), collective employment agreements in the sector (Belgium, Canada, Germany, France), taxation of staggered income, flat-rate costs, and partial or total tax exemptions. But these steps do not generally constitute a set of measures that is sufficiently integrated and consistent to result in a more satisfactory status.

CASES: The European Court of Justice has removed major restrictions on the movement of artists within the EU, for example by recognising the self-secondment of self-employed opera singers in their member state of origin [BANKS v. THEATRE ROYAL DE LA MONNAIE, 2000] and by regarding as a block to the free provision of services the French definition of wage-earner applicable to performance artists established as self-employed workers in the member state of origin where they regularly provide analogous services [EUROPEAN COMMISSION v. FRANCE, 2006].

VIEWS: Some questions remain unanswered: *Who is an artist?* Current discussions focus on the personal application of measures favourable to artists, particularly in terms of social security (e.g. AT: opinion of the *Künstlerkommission*; BE: *Visa Artiste* granted by the Commission Artistes). *Who is a professional artist?* The Slovak Coalition for Cultural Diversity operates by defining the *professional* artist compared with the *amateur* artist (2013).

What measures should be taken in the 21st century? Some professional bodies, such as the FIM and FIA, consider that the 1980 Recommendation should be brought into line with the aims of the 2005 UNESCO Convention, for example by providing new legal frameworks that offer all artist-performers, whatever their legal status, a package of professional rights, ongoing training, special social protection, accident insurance, fair taxation and the advantages of collective agreements. The Convention Européenne des artistes des arts visuels et plastiques (2008) also demands the assurance of fair pay, that peripheral activities be taken into account in the extension of creative work, social protection extending to occupational illnesses, and a policy for diffusing artistic knowhow. These associations wish to be included in processes of decision-making.

CONCL: Even if the 1980 Recommendation remains relevant, it seems necessary to revise it in light of the 2005 UNESCO Convention by taking account of the place of artists in a globalised world, together with three aspects – social, economic and cultural – of creative and performance-related activities. A new *Charter for the Status of the Artist and Artistic Activities* could be an instrument that is more specific, relevant and restrictive. This Charter could be accompanied by an Orientation Guide containing a set of clear, simple and integrated proposals for the use of decision-makers in the various areas of activity. The definitions of artist and artistic activity should be more specific and take account of developments in artistic expressions and techniques. They should incorporate both peripheral activities and those involving the diffusion of artistic knowhow. New legal structures (for example, the shared project contract) which transcend the notion of subordination should be devised. New resources could be earmarked to provide financing for adjustments to social security, ongoing training and other necessary measures.

If the status of the artist is not properly defined, can freedom of creation really exist?

REFERENCES:

Capiau, Suzanne: *La création d'un environnement juridique et économique approprié pour les activités artistiques – Nécessité et urgence d'une intervention publique*, Council of Europe, DGIV/CULT/MOSAIC(2000) 22.

Capiau, Suzanne and Wiesand, Andreas Johannes: *The Status of artists in Europe*, ERICarts Study for the European Parliament, CULTURE AND EDUCATION IP/B/CULT/ST/2005-89, PE 375.321 (2006).

Convention Européenne des artistes des arts visuels et plastiques: *Livre Blanc*, Paris: Maison des Artistes (2009).

Eurostat: *Cultural statistics*, Luxembourg (2011).

FIM-FIA: *Manifesto on the Status of the Artist / Manifeste sur la Condition de l'Artiste*, Brussels (2014).

Jones, Susan: "Artists low income and status are international issues", The Guardian, 1. 12. 2015.

Slovak Coalition for Cultural Diversity: *Status of the Artist. Working Document for a General International Debate*, Bratislava (2013).

UNESCO: *World Observatory on the Status of the Artist* (available through en.unesco.org).

Suzanne Capiau

Trolling and Shitstorms

DEF: A 'troll' is a person who posts inflammatory material on the Internet with the intention of upsetting other users, usually on forums and blogs. A troll may single out victims such as in the case of the two twitter trolls who threatened to kill and rape the feminist campaigner Caroline Criado-Perez. A 'shitstorm' is a public outcry, primarily on the Internet, which can reach epic proportions. The slang term seems to be particularly popular in Germany and Finland.

INSTR: Several treaties provide against →hate speech, without actually referring to it as such. For example, the CoE Additional Protocol to the *Cybercrime Convention* requires Parties to adopt measures to criminalise racist or xenophobic material, while Articles 6 and 9 of the *Framework Convention for the Protection of National Minorities* (FCPNM), read together, pre-empt hate speech of an intercultural nature. Drafted in a pre-smartphone, pre-social media era, the online dimension of hate speech is nonetheless seen as increasingly important for the monitoring activities of the FCPNM under its Article 9 on Freedom of Expression (FoE). The ECtHR examines hate speech cases under Article 10 (FoE), and under Article 17 (prohibition of abuse of a right) ECHR, in cases of racism, anti-semitism or Islamophobia. Anonymity, a key ally of online hate speech, is recognised as important for FoE by principle 7 of the *CoE Declaration of Freedom of Communication on the Internet*, but it also encourages Member states to take measures to prevent criminal acts. Section 127 of the UK *Communications Act* 2003 prohibits the sending of electronic communications that are grossly offensive, indecent, obscene or menacing. Also drawn up in a pre-social media era, it has been used to prosecute content normally protected by FoE, such as jokes on Twitter. Guidelines have now been issued to aid its application.

CASES: Expression becomes hate speech at the point it crosses the threshold of 'offend, shock and disturb' [HANDYSIDE, 1976]. Trolling and shitstorm episodes that reach this point are helped by online anonymity. Recognising anonymity's importance for FoE, in [DELFI, 2015], the ECtHR said a person can be anonymous publicly on the Internet, but identifiable to a service provider, as long as there are effective remedies for violations of personal rights. In [KU, 2008] the release of private information was made subject to restrictions. In a seminal trolling case (BROOKES, 2012) in the UK, the High Court compelled Facebook to reveal identities and in doing so extended its jurisdiction to the US. The responsibility of portals for third-party hate speech was examined in [DELFI, 2015]; the ECtHR held that a portal must remove hate speech 'without delay' on constructive knowledge of its unacceptability. In an earlier case, [KRONE VERLAG, 2006], it held that shifting liability for defamation to a media company, usually better off financially, from the defamer was not a disproportionate interference with the company's FoE. However, the ECJ in [SCARLET, 2011], a case on copyright infringement, said intermediaries had no obligation to monitor and filter social media posts, since this could undermine citizens' FoE. The ECJ has also said that information can only be removed on request if it is inaccurate, inadequate or no longer relevant [GOOGLE SPAIN, 2014].

VIEWS: A comprehensive overview of the dissenting opinions on hate speech is given in [DELFI, 2015]. In this case, a minority of judges cautioned against extending liability of portal operators for third party hate speech since it may provide a strong incentive to discontinue offering comments sections. It might also lead to self-censorship of operators and private-party → censorship, as posts are removed prior to publication, affecting speech ordinarily protected by FoE. They disapproved of the court's endorsement of a constructive knowledge approach for potential violations, requiring operators to remove hate speech comments 'without delay', which they said, was not the prevailing standard of genuine democracies. The comments may have been excessive or impermissible, but the matter, they said, was of public interest and the comments were part of the debate. They questioned whether a call for violence or a wish to see someone killed on the Internet would have the same effect as a similar statement made in a face-to-face encounter, since it was not a call to arms by an extremist group. They acknowledged that racist comments could not be protected by freedom of expression, but the judgment nonetheless lacked proper analysis as to what extent the comments constituted a real threat.

CONCL: Internet and public platforms have inadvertently built an effective delivery mechanism for hate speech. A European HR framework to counter this is emerging: increasingly, more Internet cases are treated by the ECtHR, the CoE Cybercrime Convention and FCPNM that address hate speech, although they do not refer to hate speech per se. Some argue against the regulation of the Internet because it obstructs the flow of ideas, and democracy depends on a plurality of voices. Anonymity and the Internet's global reach, however, have made it an ideal tool for hatemongers, leading to a stark rise in online hate groups and activities. Domestic regulation has not always been easy, e.g. the UK *Communications Act* (s127) led to people being convicted for jokes on Twitter. Critics say [DELFI, 2015] has given private companies a free rein to censor, leaving free expression unprotected by the courts which then have lesser opportunity to develop this grey area further. The problem of jurisdiction, once a major online obstacle, is slowly being resolved in cases such as [PERRIN v. UK, 2005] and in [BROOKES v. FACEBOOK, 2012] in which the UK High Court agreed to extend its jurisdiction to the USA, issuing a disclosure order on Facebook.

In resolving these issues, encouraging responsible Internet behaviour may be a better alternative to regulation. Legal and policy decisions require IT expertise to ensure they don't give rise to extra rights' problems and the international community may need to come to an agreement on jurisdiction issues to avoid incoherency.

REFERENCES:

Council of Europe: Declaration on freedom of communication on the Internet (Adopted by the Committee of Ministers on 28 May 2003 at the 840th meeting of the Ministers' Deputies).

Cruz-Cunha, Maria Manuela, Portela Irene Maria (ed.): *Handbook of Research on Digital Crime, Cyberspace Security, and Information Assurance*, Pennsylvania: ICI Global (2015).

Halliday, Josh, "Facebook forced into revealing identities of cyberbullies", (The Guardian 8 June 2012).

DELFI v. ESTONIA (ECtHR 16/06/2015 64569/09).

GOOGLE SPAIN SL, GOOGLE INC. v. AGENCIA ESPAÑOLA DE PROTECCIÓN DE DATOS, MARIO COSTEJA GONZÁLEZ (ECJ 13/05/2014 C-131/12).

HANDYSIDE v. UK 1976, (ECtHR 07/12/1976 5493/72).

KRONE VERLAG v. AUSTRIA (no. 4) (ECtHR 09/11/2006 72331/01).

KU v. FINLAND (ECtHR 02/12/2008 2872/02).

SCARLET EXTENDED SA v. SOCIETE BELGE DES AUTEURS, COMPOSITEURS ET EDITEURS SCRL (SABAM) (ECJ 24/11/2011 C-70/10).

blogs.lse.ac.uk (accessed 31/01/2016).

blogs.spectator.ac.uk (accessed 31/01/2016).

shura.shu.ac.uk/6901/ (accessed 31/01/2016).

spiked-online.com (accessed 31/01/2016).

ukhumanrightsblog.com (accessed 31/01/2016).

Siobhan Montgomery

UN Treaty Bodies

All of the core human rights treaties have a body of independent experts that monitors the implementation of the relevant treaty. The treaty bodies are composed of between 10 and 23 elected persons of high moral character and with recognised competence in the field of human rights. Members serve in their personal capacity and may be re-elected if nominated.

All states parties to the relevant treaty are required to submit regular reports to the treaty body on the implementation of the norms of the relevant treaty. All treaty bodies have emphasised the importance of the contribution of NGOs, who often submit 'shadow' reports to treaty bodies. Consideration of reports takes place in public session and once the hearings are done the treaty body adopts 'concluding observations' which identify progress, along with highlighting remaining problems and concerns, and recommendations on improving implementation. Where a state fails to submit a report the states performance is examined on the basis of existing information from relevant stakeholders.

All treaty bodies issue 'General Comments' or 'General Recommendations', which provide authoritative guidance on general treaty obligations or interpretations on the provisions of the treaty. Although not legally binding, General Comments are often invoked by states and complainants in complaints procedures, and increasingly, by international, regional, and national courts.

An important part of the UN human rights system is the complaints procedures of the treaty bodies. There is an inter-state complaints procedure available but to date there have been no inter-state complaints. Seven treaty bodies, the Human Rights Committee, the Committee against Torture, the Committee for the Elimination of Discrimination against Women, the Committee on the Rights of Persons with Disabilities, the Committee on Enforced Disappearances, and the Committee on Economic, Social and Cultural Rights, have optional individual complaints procedures. In order for an individual complaint to be brought against a state, the state must have accepted the competence of the committee to hear the complaint. Admissibility criteria are that the complainant must be personally affected by the state action, the complaint must relate to events which occurred after the entry into force of the complaint mechanism, the matter must not be under review by another international procedure, and the complainant must have all domestic remedies. The decisions made by treaty bodies are not legally binding.

Since several treaties monitored by the treaty bodies contain cultural rights, the treaty bodies regularly deal with these rights. They have also adopted several General Comments on specific human rights provisions or cultural rights issues. Examples are General Comment 21 on the right to take part in cultural life by the Committee on Economic, Social and Cultural Rights, General Comment 24 on the right of members of minorities to enjoy their culture and the joint General Recommendation/General Comment 31 of the Committee on the Elimination of Discrimination against Women and 18 of the Committee on the Rights of the Child on harmful practices.

REFERENCES:

Alston, Philip: "The General Comments of the UN Committee on Ecomomic, Socialand Cultural Rights" *American Society of International Law Proceedings* (2010) 3.

Connors, Jane and Schmidt, Markus: "United Nations" in Moeckli, Daniel; Shah, Sangeeta and Sivakumaran, Sandesh (eds.): *International Human Rights Law*, 2nd edn., Oxford: Oxford University Press (2013).

Lintel, Ida and Ryngaert, Cedric: "The Interface between Non-governmental Organisations and the Human Rights Committee" 15 *International Community Law Review* (2013) 359.

McMahon, Edward and Ascherio, Marta: "A Step Ahead in Promoting Human Rights? The Universal Periodic Review of the UN Human Rights Council" 18 *Global Governance* (2012) 231.

Spohr, Maximilian: "United Nations Human Rights Council" 14 *Max Planck Yearbook of United Nations Law* (2010) 169.

Yvonne Donders

Underwater Cultural Heritage

1. The UNCLOS

Today the capacity of a few states and private entities to use advanced technological means to explore the seabed at increasing depths not only allows access to a huge amount of cultural heritage, but also entails the risk of such heritage being looted. In this regard, rules of international law are far from being satisfactory.

The regime provided by the 1982 *United Nations Convention on the Law of the Sea* (UNCLOS) for underwater cultural heritage is composed of only two provisions, namely Article 149 and Article 303. They are in a conceptual contradiction with one another and the latter can be interpreted as a covert invitation to loot underwater cultural heritage. The fact that the subject of underwater cultural heritage was taken into consideration only in the last period of a negotiation that lasted for about ten years cannot be a justification for such a regime.

Article 303(1), of the UNCLOS sets forth a general obligation of protection and cooperation which applies to all archaeological and historical objects, wherever they are found at sea. Despite its broad content, some legal consequences can be drawn from this provision. A state which knowingly destroys or allows the destruction of objects belonging to underwater cultural heritage can be held responsible for breach of an international obligation. A state which persistently disregards any request by other states to negotiate on forms of cooperation aimed at protecting underwater cultural heritage can also be held responsible for an internationally wrongful act.

It is implied in the UNCLOS that the full sovereignty which the coastal state enjoys within the internal maritime waters and the territorial sea also covers underwater cultural heritage. Beyond the territorial sea, Article 303(2), UNCLOS allows the coastal state to prevent the removal of archaeological and historical objects in the waters between the 12 and the 24 nautical mile (so-called archaeological contiguous zone).

The UNCLOS does not establish any regime relating to underwater cultural heritage found in the space located between the 24-mile contiguous zone and the 200-mile exclusive economic zone. The rights of the coastal state within such a zone are limited to the exploration and exploitation of the natural resources and cannot be extended to man-made objects, such as those belonging to underwater cultural heritage. This legal vacuum greatly threatens the protection of cultural heritage, as it brings into the picture the principle of freedom of the seas that could easily lead to a first-come-first-served approach. Availing himself of this principle, any person on board a ship could explore the exclusive economic zone adjacent to any coastal state, bring any archaeological and historical objects to the surface, become their owner under domestic legislation (in most cases, the flag state legislation), take the objects away and sell them on the private market. If this were the case, there would be no guarantee that the objects are disposed of for public benefit rather than for private commercial purposes and personal gain. Nor could a state which has a direct cultural link with the objects prevent the continuous pillage of its historical heritage.

The danger of freedom of fishing for underwater cultural heritage under the UNCLOS regime is increased by Article 303(3), which subjects the whole of Article 303 to 'the law of salvage and other rules of admiralty'. If there is a conflict between the general objective to protect underwater cultural heritage (Article 303(1)), on the one hand, and the provisions of salvage law and other rules of admiralty, on the other, the latter prevails. In many countries, the notion of salvage is only related to the attempts to save a ship or its cargo from imminent marine peril on behalf of its owner, but is never intended to apply to ancient sunken ships which, far from being in peril, have been definitively lost since hundreds, or even thousands of years. On the contrary, in a minority of common law countries, and in particular in the United States, the notion of salvage law has been enlarged by some court decisions to cover also activities which have very little to do with ships in peril, but are aimed at underwater cultural heritage. In particular, the law of finds seems to mean that a person who discovers a shipwreck in navigable waters that has been long lost and abandoned and who reduces the property to actual or constructive possession becomes the property's owner. In its turn, the law of salvage gives the salvor a lien (or right *in rem*) over the object.

Yet the expression 'the law of salvage and other rules of admiralty' simply means the application of a first-come-first-served or freedom-of-fishing approach, which can only serve the interest of private commercial gain. If this is the case, a state which has a cultural link with the underwater archaeological or historical objects is deprived of any means to prevent the pillage of its historical heritage. In fact, the body of 'the law of salvage and other rules of admiralty' is today typical of a few common law systems, but remains a complete stranger to the legislation of many other countries. Because of the lack of corresponding concepts, the very words 'salvage' and 'admiralty' cannot be properly translated into languages other than English. In the French and Spanish official text of the UNCLOS they are rendered with expressions – 'droit de récupérer des épaves et (...) autres règles du droit maritime'; 'las normas sobre salvamento u otras normas del derecho marítimo' – which give the provision a broader and quite different meaning. This worsens the picture of Article 303, at least if read in the English version of the UNCLOS. Does this provision, while apparently protecting underwater cultural heritage, strengthen a regime which results in the use of much of this heritage for commercial purposes, regardless of its importance from the cultural point of view? Does Article 303 give an overarching status to a body of rules that cannot provide any effective means for the protection of the heritage in question? This doubt is far from being trivial, especially for those countries (for example Italy) where national legislation is based on priority given to the duty of the state to preserve cultural heritage for the purposes of public interest, in particular research and exhibition.

The second UNCLOS provision on underwater cultural heritage (Article 149) deals only with heritage found in the so-called Area, that is, the seabed and ocean floor beyond the 200-mile limit of national jurisdiction. It provides that 'all objects of an archaeological and historical nature found in the Area shall be preserved or disposed of for the benefit of mankind as a whole, particular regard being paid to the preferential rights of the State or country of origin, or the State of cultural origin, or the State of historical and archaeological origin'. The provision appears complicated in its wording and devoid of details that could ensure its practical application. However, it embodies two excellent ideas. First, Article 149 shows a preference for uses of archaeological and historical objects that promote the 'benefit of mankind as a whole'. Private interests, such as the search for and the disposal of the objects for trade and personal gain, are given little weight, if any. Second, some categories of states which have a link with the objects, namely, the state of cultural origin, the state of historical and archaeological origin, the state or country of origin *tout court*, are given preferential rights, although Article 149 does not specify either the content of these rights or the manner in which they should be harmonised with the concept of 'benefit of mankind as a whole'. Despite its vague wording, Article 149 is in total contradiction with the freedom of fishing regime implied by Article 303(3).

2. The CPUCH

The 2001 *Convention on the Protection of the Underwater Cultural Heritage* (CPUCH) was adopted within the framework of the UNESCO. It defines underwater cultural heritage as 'all traces of human existence having a cultural, historical or archaeological character which have been partially or totally under water, periodically or continuously, for at least 100 years'. Notable, as far as human rights are concerned, is Article 2(9) CPUCH, according to which 'States Parties shall ensure that proper respect is given to all human remains located in maritime waters'.

The CPUCH builds on the excellent ideas contained in Article 149 UNCLOS, in particular the preservation and use of cultural heritage for the benefit of mankind and the preferential rights granted to certain states, and essentially aims to prevent the risks posed by a freedom of fishing regime. It provides in general that states parties are bound to 'preserve underwater cultural heritage for the benefit of humanity' and that 'underwater cultural heritage shall not be commercially exploited'.

While most states participating in the negotiations for the CPUCH concurred in rejecting the application of the law of salvage and the law of finds to underwater cultural heritage, a minority of states were not prepared to accept an absolute ban. To achieve a reasonable compromise, Article 4 CPUCH provides that any activity relating to underwater cultural heritage is not to be subject to the law of salvage or law of finds, unless it is authorised by the competent authorities, is in full conformity with the CPUCH and ensures that any recovery of the underwater cultural heritage achieves its maximum protection. Although it does not totally exclude the law of salvage and law of finds, the CPUCH regime has the practical effect of preventing all the undesirable effects that would result from the application of these rules. Freedom of fishing for archaeological and historical objects is definitely banned.

The majority of the states participating in the negotiations for the CPUCH were ready to extend the jurisdiction of the coastal state to the underwater cultural heritage found within the 200-mile exclusive economic zone. However, a minority of states assumed, as they did during the negotiations for the UNCLOS, that the extension of the jurisdiction of coastal states beyond the limit of the territorial sea would have altered the delicate balance embodied in the UNCLOS between the rights and obligations of the coastal state and those of other states. Finally, as an attempt to reach a compromise, a procedural mechanism was envisaged which involves the participation of all the states linked to the heritage. It is based on a three-step procedure (reporting, consultations, urgent measures).

As regards the first step (reporting), the CPUCH bans secret activities or discoveries. states parties must require their nationals or vessels flying their flag to report activities directed at underwater cultural heritage or discoveries to them.

As regards the second step (consultations), the coastal state is bound to consult all states parties which have declared their interest in being consulted on how to ensure the effective protection of the underwater cultural heritage in question. This declaration is based on a verifiable link, especially a cultural, historical or archaeological link, to the underwater cultural heritage concerned. No attempt was made to define the rather vague concept of 'verifiable link'. The coastal state is entitled to coordinate the consultations, unless it expressly declares that it does not wish to do so, in which case the states parties which have declared an interest in being consulted are called to appoint another coordinating state.

As regards the third step (urgent measures), the coordinating state may take all practicable measures and issue any necessary authorisations to prevent any immediate danger to the underwater cultural heritage, whether arising from human activities or any other cause, including looting. It would have been illusory to subordinate the right to adopt urgent measures to the final outcome of consultations that are normally expected to last for some time. It would also have been illusory to grant this right to the flag state, considering the risk of activities carried out by vessels flying the flag of non-parties or a flag of convenience. By definition, in case of urgency a state must be entitled to take immediate measures without losing time with procedural requirements. The CPUCH clearly sets forth that in coordinating consultations, taking measures, conducting preliminary research and issuing authorisations, the coordinating state acts 'on behalf of the States Parties as a whole and not in its own interest'.

Regrettably, the text of the CPUCH, which was the outcome of a difficult negotiation, could not be adopted by consensus. It was put to vote (87 States in favour, 4 against and 15 abstentions). Some states cast a negative vote or abstained because they could not accept the coastal state's right to adopt provisional measures and considered it as a sign of 'creeping jurisdiction'. Today the CPUCH, which entered into force in 2009, is binding for only 55 states.

In fact, the CPUCH may be seen as a reasonable defence of the underwater cultural heritage against the results of the counterproductive regime of the UNCLOS. If the looting of the heritage is the result of the UNCLOS regime, it is the UNCLOS that is wrong on this specific matter, irrespective of all the balances that it might wish to preserve.

Tullio Scovazzi

UNESCO

DEF: The United Nations Organization for Education, Science and Culture (UNESCO) was founded on 16 November 1945. It has 195 Members and 8 Associate Members (states) and is governed by the General Conference and the Executive Board. The Secretariat, headed by the Director-General, implements the decisions of these two bodies. The Organisation has over 50 field offices globally.

For UNESCO, culture encompasses 'art and literature, lifestyles, ways of living together, value systems, traditions and beliefs'. Recognising the transformative power of culture, the organisation protects heritage as the embodiment of identity and fosters creativity as a cornerstone for open, inclusive and pluralistic societies.

INSTR: The unique constellation of eight cultural conventions constitutes the bedrock on which UNESCO's action is founded, including the *Convention on the Protection and Promotion of the Diversity of Cultural Expressions* (2005); the *Convention for the Safeguarding of the Intangible Cultural Heritage* (2003); the *Universal Declaration on Cultural Diversity* (2001); the *Convention on the Protection of the Underwater Cultural Heritage* (2001); the *Convention for the Protection of the World Cultural and Natural Heritage* (1972); the *Convention on the Protection of Copyright and Neighbouring Rights* (1952, 1971) the *Convention on the Means of Prohibiting and Preventing the Illicit Traffic of Cultural Property* (1970); the *Hague Convention for the Protection of Cultural Property in the Event of Armed Conflict* (1954).

To ensure culture is a constant reference in development strategies and processes, UNESCO pursues a three-pronged action:

(a) Leading worldwide advocacy in relation to the implementation of the 2030 Agenda for Sustainable Development;
(b) Engaging with other actors to set up clear policies and legal frameworks; and
(c) Supporting governments and local stakeholders to safeguard heritage, strengthen creative industries and encourage cultural pluralism.

CONCL: Issues of attention are: the elaboration of tools and approaches tailored to the specific needs within the 2030 Agenda; special provisions within humanitarian and peace-building frameworks to protect against attacks on cultural heritage; and the further entrenchment in human rights principles and standards in the context of implementing cultural conventions.

REFERENCES:

UNESCO (ed.): *Re|Shaping Cultural Policies – A Decade of promoting the diversity of cultural expressions for development*. 2005 Convention Global Report, Paris (2015).

UNESCO World Report – *Investing in Cultural Diversity and Intercultural Dialogue*. Paris (2009).

en.unesco.org/themes/protecting-our-heritage-and-fostering-creativity (accessed 5/2016).

Konstantinos Tararas

Universal Declaration of Human Rights (UDHR)

DEF: The Preamble to the Charter of United Nations (1945) reaffirms 'faith in fundamental human rights' and in 'the dignity of the human person.' The *Universal Declaration of Human Rights* (1948) results from the mandate established in the Charter, which states that the 'General Assembly shall initiate studies and make recommendations for the purpose of ... assisting in the realization of human rights and fundamental freedoms for all without distinction as to race, sex, language, or religion'. Thus, one of the main traits of the rights contained in the UDHR is their universal character. This is why, as proposed by one of the drafters of the UDHR, R. Cassin, the title of the document uses the word 'Universal' instead of 'International' (Gross Spiell, 1998).

INSTR: Being a declaration, the UDHR has not the same legal value as a treaty. However, many of its dispositions are currently part of international customary law – that is, international law generated through states' practice (von Bernstorff, 2008). Some of them are even norms of *ius cogens* from which no derogation is permitted, e.g. in the case of the prohibition of torture.

The Cold War ideological division prevented the transformation of the UDHR into a whole and unitary treaty and, as a declaration, the UDHR does not provide for the monitoring of states' compliance. However, several United Nations HR treaties further developed its dispositions and Committees have been established for the monitoring of such treaties. This is the case, among others, of the →Human Rights Committee which monitors states' compliance with the *International Covenant on Civil and Political Rights* and the Committee on Economic, Social and Cultural Rights which does so with the →*International Covenant on Economic, Social and Cultural Rights*, both signed in 1966.

HIST: It has been claimed that the UDHR uses a Eurocentric understanding of HR. Sometimes, such critiques confuse the principles of the UDHR with justifications of 'imperialist' actions, which sadly have been not infrequent. In fact, concerning the text of the UDHR itself, it must be noted that it was achieved through a process dominated by acute awareness of the need for an intercultural basis for HR, following their neglect during WW II. Moreover, the text is silent concerning the identification of the cultural / philosophical / ideological 'foundations' of such rights. The UDHR establishes in its Preamble that 'a common understanding of these rights and freedoms is of the greatest importance for the full realization [of their respect and observance]'. The drafters were thus aware that finding common grounds of HR is essential to achieve their effectiveness. Only on the basis of these common grounds can its universal application be legitimated. But, as mentioned above, the UDHR did not identify this 'common understanding' of the HR that it recognises. The text does not even refer to human dignity as the source of HR, as would be done later by other HR instruments (Gross Spiell, 1998). Such a lack of identification of the 'common understanding' of human rights was intentional: the impression that a specific understanding might have priority over others was to be avoided. Such silence can rightly be seen as a refreshing opportunity for the intercultural embodiment of HR and also as a convincing argument against those claiming the absolute Eurocentric approach of the UDHR.

Indeed, it can legitimately be said that Western ideas were overrepresented in the genesis of the UDHR. Supporting this interpretation is the Western education of Charles Habib Malik (from Lebanon) and P. C. Chang (China), members of the Commission charged with the formulation of the UDHR. Other members of the Commission were Alexandre Bogomolov (Soviet Union), René Cassin (France), Eleanor Roosevelt (USA), Charles Dukes (United Kingdom), William Hodgson (Australia), Hernan Santa Cruz (Chile), John P. Humphrey (Canada).

However, the diversity of the origins of the members of the Commission is not the sole indicator for the intention of creating a culturally universal text. The importance of the Report on 'The grounds of an international declaration of human rights' of the Committee on the Philosophic Principles of the Rights of Man to the Commission on Human Rights of the United Nations (UNESCO, 1947) must be emphasised, in that context. The General Director of →UNESCO at that time, Julian Huxley, sent a questionnaire concerning the principles that might sustain a future declaration to several philosophers as well as to governments. Based on the answers received, this Report was elaborated and sent to the United Nations. Among the philosophers asked were Mahatma Gandhi,

Jacques Maritain, Aldous Huxley and Pierre Teilhard de Chardin. The final report of the Committee set down 'a schematic formulation of basic rights which in its opinion can and should be vindicated by all men' (ibid). The open character of the common grounds of HR and the implicit inappropriateness of identifying precise and definitive grounds of HR were both noted in the final report of the Committee which called for a deeper re-examination of the bases of HR. In fact, enriching HR or their interpretation, based on new developments and insights, should be seen as a never-ending process.

In his answer to Julian Huxley's question of where he would place the basis of HR, Gandhi wrote: 'I learned from my illiterate but wise mother that all rights to be deserved and preserved come from duty well done.' (UNESCO, 1969). This view proves the intercultural embodiment possibilities of such rights and is far from Western concepts, in which human duties have a role for the guarantee of HR, as derived from them, but not in their foundation, which is only of a 'individualistic' nature. The differences between the Western and the Indian conception of HR are evident. There is not, in fact, a translation in Sanskrit for the word 'Rights': following Pandeya, there exists only the word 'Adhikara' (just claim) that is used 'in the context where one has performed some act, or performed a duty' (Patel, 2005). 'Adhikara' must be understood in the light of a central doctrine of Hindu thought: 'Dharma', where Human Rights lawyers and philosophers place the grounds of HR in Indian culture. This word 'means to uphold, sustain and nourish. It is a comprehensive term, which includes duty, morality, ritual, law, order and justice... It is a mode of life or a code of conduct, which regulates a man's work and activities as a member of society and as an individual.' (ibid).

Therefore, it is clear that philosophical ideas other than the European were taken into account in the elaboration of the UDHR. Concerning the Indian ideas and Gandhi's aforementioned contribution it must be emphasised that the UDHR in its Article 29 specifically establishes that 'everyone has duties to the community in which alone the free and full development of his personality is possible.' It is not by coincidence that the very first article of the UDHR establishes that 'all human beings are born free and equal in dignity and rights. They are endowed with reason and conscience and should act towards one another in a spirit of brotherhood'. Other cultural regions like Latin America were also important in giving philosophical foundation to the UDHR (Sikkink, 2015). If the European ideas were important, they were not the only ones. Nevertheless, the UDHR was finally approved with the abstention of the communist countries, as well as South Africa and Saudi Arabia.

CASES: Consistent with the erroneous failure to take into account the diversity of foundations of the UDHR is the trend to place the controversies regarding the universal nature of human rights only in 'cultures' other than the European. The truth is that, fortunately, there is not a wholly homogenous 'culture' where perfect agreements regarding all social issues exist. Europe is not exempt from such controversies, as can be seen in the ECtHR case-law [JOHNSTON, 1986].

VIEWS: As already mentioned, there are many criticisms of the UDHR, and specifically of the universal character of the rights it contains. Such criticisms are more broadly criticisms of the intended →universalism of HR and sometimes, for that reason, also of the very notion of human rights itself.

Two of the most important criticisms were, firstly, that formulated by the American Association of Anthropology (AAA) in 1947 and, secondly, that stated by some Asian countries in the context of the Vienna World Conference on Human Rights in 1993. Both are linked to the often manipulated and misunderstood debate between universalists and cultural relativists. In opposition to universalism, which maintains that common HR standards can apply to all human beings, →cultural relativism has been generally understood by international HR lawyers to mean the rejection of the possibility of making moral judgements – and thus, of establishing common human rights – for all human beings regardless of the culture to which they belong. However, the debate between universalists and cultural relativists seems to have arrived at an impasse. B. de Sousa Santos rightly describes this blocked situation: 'The debate... is an inherently false debate, whose polar concepts are both and equally detrimental to an emancipatory conception of human rights. All cultures are relative, but cultural relativism, as a philosophical posture, is wrong. All cultures aspire to ultimate concerns and values, but cultural universalism, as a philosophical posture, is wrong ...' (de Sousa Santos, 2004). Ultimately, the misconception of what culture truly is, is at the bottom of such an impasse.

The criticism of the UDHR formulated by the AAA in 1947 was wrongly understood by international HR lawyers as 'a denial of the ability to make moral judgements' instead of as an assertion 'of moral values that includes tolerance for cultural difference as one of those values' (Merry, 2003). Besides, criticisms of the AAA statement tend to forget the context in which it was issue which was the pressures experienced by minority societies to 'change under influence of euro-american expansion and colonialism' (ibid; see also Goodale, 2003).

The criticisms of the notion of human rights (including those contained in the UDHR) during the Vienna World Conference on Human Rights (1993) were made by some Asia states through the 'Bangkok Declaration' in the name of the preservation of their own culture. The final Declaration of the Vienna Conference recognised that 'while ... cultural particularities ... must be borne in mind, it is the duty of states, regardless of their ... cultural systems, to promote and protect all human rights.' Such a recognition was not meaningful in practical terms. The actors involved have assumed a wrong concept of culture.

It is only very recently that international HR law can be said to definitively abandon such and attitude and start to put into question the wrong conceptions of culture that have been used. During several years, international HR law has been using an essentialist conception of culture, which understood it as 'a coherent, static, and unchanging set of values' (Merry, 2003). Like current anthropology, which considers culture as something 'fluid, contested, and connected to relations of power' (ibid.), current international HR law recognises that 'actual (cultural) practices on the ground are usually more varied than suggested by formalised versions projected in discourse as well as under the law' (Special Rapporteur in the field of cultural rights, 2012). This shift in the concept of culture within international HR law is neatly represented by the approach to culture of the United Nations Special Rapporteur in the field of Cultural Rights, who was appointed in 2009.

CONCL: Actions to overcome the problems and misunderstandings concerning HR and 'culture' need to be taken by different players, beyond those belonging to the cultural sphere:

There is a need to emphasise the extra-European elements present at the genesis of the UDHR. This action, together with that of critical reflection of the real enforcement of 'our' European cultural values would contribute to a more accurate and fair description of the reality of how people truly live their cultures. It might be useful to stress the internal diversity of each culture which is also present in 'European culture', and to avoid the use of the old-fashioned essentialist concepts of culture which tend to contribute to the creation 'imagined communities' (Roy, 2006).

Emphasising the dynamic role of culture in 'the questioning by human beings of (their) own achievements, and in their seeking untiringly for new meanings' (*Mexico City Declaration on Cultural Policies*, 1982) can be helpful to recognise the relevance and the need of including the diversity of cultures in the foundation and the creation of common human rights standards.

The inclusion of cultural diversity issues of the UDHR in its teaching need to be promoted. It would be interesting to teach it together with the *Universal Declaration of Cultural Diversity* (UNESCO, 2001). The design of adequate educational policies in cultural diversity is essential (Carbó, 2015). It would contribute to avoiding the creation of stereotypes which also concerns the relation of the diverse communities with human rights. Stressing the fact that the right to equitable →participation in cultural life is a human right recognised in the UDHR is also important, as well as insisting on the firm impossibility of invoking culture as an excuse for the violation of human rights. When addressing violations to human rights occurring in the context of minority cultures, power, economic and social issues need to be addressed together with the cultural ones (Cismas, 2014).

All this calls for a serious engagement in the study of such a complex relation between cultural diversity and HR (Donders, 2010) as well as the decided will of different actors: designers of cultural policies, social activists, anthropologists, human rights lawyers and defenders, education professionals and politicians.

REFERENCES:

Bernstorff, Jochen von: "The Changing Fortunes of the Universal Declaration of Human Rights: Genesis and Symbolic Dimensions of the Turn to Rights in International Law", in *EJIL*, Vol. 19 nº 5 (2008).
Carbó, Gemma: "From intercultural education to critical education in cultural diversity: the UNESCO Diversity Kit for Youth", in *Revista de Educación*, Year 6, nº 8 (2015).
Cismas, Ioana: *Religious Actors in International Law*, Oxford: Oxford University Press (2014).
De Sousa Santos, Boaventura: "Toward a multicultural conception of Human Rights" in Felipe Gómez Isa and Koen de Feyter (eds.): *International Protection of Human Rights: Achievements and Challenges*, Bilbao: Universidad de Deusto (2004).
Donders, Yvonne: "Do Cultural Diversity and Human Rights Make a Good Match?" *ISSJ* (November 25, 2010).
Goodale, Mark: "Anthropology and the Grounds of Human Rights" in Dinah Shelton (ed.): *The Oxford Handbook on International Human Rights Law*, Oxford: Oxford University Press (2013).
Gross Spiell, Héctor: "Universality of *Human Rights* and *Cultural Diversity*", in *ISSJ, 158 Paris: UNESCO* (1998).
Merry, Sally: "Human Rights Law and the Demonization of Culture (And Anthropology Along the Way)", in *PolAR*, Vol. 26, nº 1 (2003).
Patel, D.: "The Religious Foundations of Human Rights: A perspective from the Judeo-Christian Tradition and Hinduism", in *Human Rights Law Commentary*, Vol. 1 (2005).
Roy, Oliver: *Globalized Islam: The search of a New Umah*, Columbia University Press (2006).
Special Rapporteur in the Field of Cultural Rights: *Report on the Enjoyment of Cultural Rights by Women on an Equal Basis with Men* (2012).
Sikkink, Kathryn: "Latin America's Protagonist Role in Human Rights" in *Sur*, 22 (2015).
UNESCO: *The grounds of an International Declaration of Human Rights* (31/07/1947), Doc. Phil/10.
UNESCO: "Ghandhi's views on education" in *The UNESCO Courier* (October 1969).
JOHNSTON v. IRELAND (ECtHR 18/12/1986, 9697/82).

Gemma Carbó/Beatriz Barreiro

Universalism and Cultural Relativism

DEF: The term 'cultural relativism' originally denotes a school in anthropology, in the first half of the 20th Century. Famous relativists include F. Boas, M. Herskovits, R. Benedict and W. Sumner. Relativists state that the principles used for judging behaviour are only valid inside a particular culture. Hence they reject the idea of universal human rights. Later, the same term was used to indicate culture-based critiques of human rights, expressed mainly by government representatives and scholars from East and Southeast Asia, Sub-Sahara Africa and the Islamic World. These critiques claim that human rights are overly Western, and should be allowed to take different shapes in other contexts. Relativism is generally opposed to universalism, i.e. the belief that universal norms are desirable.

INSTR: The 'universalism vs. cultural relativism' debate on human rights focused at its origins around the →UDHR. When the UN Commission on Human Rights was drafting the UDHR, the American Anthropological Association published a 'Statement on Human Rights' in 1947, advising to drop the whole idea of universal rights. In that sense, the adoption of the UDHR of 1948 can be read as a setting aside of cultural relativist objections.

More recently, the debate took centre stage in the course of the preparations for the UN World Conference on Human Rights in Vienna in 1993. In particular, the Asian regional conference issued a *Bangkok Declaration* that was largely perceived as relativist. Also, the Organisation of the Islamic Conference submitted the *Cairo Declaration on Human Rights in Islam*, a document that was widely seen to state the priority of Islam over human rights. The final document of the World Conference, the *Vienna Declaration*, explicitly confirmed the universality of all human rights, adding that 'while the significance of national and regional particularities and various historical, cultural and religious backgrounds must be borne in mind, it is the duty of States, regardless of their political, economic and cultural systems, to promote and protect all human rights and fundamental freedoms'.

CASES: Today, it is widely accepted that universality does not imply uniformity, i.e. that the same human rights can be formulated in different manners in different contexts, and that similarly formulated HR can be interpreted differently in different countries. When supranational courts deal with this issue of 'universality and diversity', it is generally either by discussing the room that national authorities have to devise 'culturally specific' human rights interpretations, or by engaging themselves in such 'cultural' interpretation.

An example of the former is the ECtHR use of the doctrine of the → 'margin of appreciation' of the member states, to accommodate national cultural context. A famous early example is the [HANDYSIDE v. UNITED KINGDOM, 1976] case, in which the Court held that a UK ban on grounds of obscenity of a publication that freely circulated in other European states, did not violate the freedom of expression. The Court held that 'by reason of their direct and continuous contact with the vital forces of their countries', domestic authorities are 'in principle in a better position than the international judge' to give an opinion on the exact content of the requirements of the protection of morals.

An example of the latter is the Inter-American Court of Human Right's interpretation of the HR to property of indigenous peoples in such a way as to include both a collective dimension and a spiritual dimension, e.g. [AWAS TINGNI v. NICARAGUA, 2001].

VIEWS: Today it is largely accepted that the idea of a 'trench war' between 'cultural relativists' and 'universalists' is more mythology than reality. It is now widely recognised that cultural critiques have a point, as Western dominance in international relations has indeed led to a degree of Western bias in HR. Some developments, such as the upgrading of economic, social and cultural rights, the recognition of a human right to development, and the recognition of group rights for indigenous communities, can be read as attempts to correct that bias.

In literature, consensus has emerged that universal HR can accommodate cultural differences. Universality does not require uniformity. Across academic disciplines, similar conclusions are reached through different methodologies. Roughly, a distinction can be made between authors who have examined the issue in a top-down manner and others who have used a bottom-up approach. The former, mainly lawyers and political scientists, have taken international HR standards, and the international HR protection system, as a starting point, and have argued that it is both desirable and feasible to integrate contextual diversity within these domains. At the same time, those examining human rights in action in the field – mainly anthropologists – have described how local communities instrumentalise and adapt HR discourses, norms and procedures in their quest for justice and fairness, and have argued the value and legitimacy of such 'vernacularisation' of human rights.

CONCL: The remaining challenges in this field are huge, as the consensus in scholarly literature about the principle of diversity within universality is not necessarily shared by political actors. Moreover, the agreement about the principle goes hand in hand with disagreement about the degree of diversity that can be accepted within universal HR, the criteria for determining this, and especially the application to concrete cases. It is widely recognised that this matter can only advance through constructive inter-cultural dialogue on human rights.

REFERENCES:

An-Na'im, Abdullahi Ahmed (ed.): *Human Rights in Cross-Cultural Perspectives: a Quest for Consensus*, Philadelphia: University of Pennsylvania Press, 1991.

Brems, Eva: *Human Rights: Universality and Diversity*, Leiden, Nijhoff (2001).

Cowan, Jane K., Marie-Bénédicte Dembour and Richard A. Wilson (eds.): *Culture and Rights: Anthropological Perspectives*, Cambridge: Cambridge University Press (2001).

Donnelly, Jack: *Universal Human Rights in Theory and Practice*, Cornell University Press (2013).
Goodale, Mark and Sally Engle Merry (eds.): *The Practice of Human Rights; Tracking Law Between the Global and the Local*, Cambridge: Cambridge University Press, (2007).
Mutua, Makau: *Human Rights: A Political and Cultural Critique*, Pennsylvania: University of Pennsylvania Press (2002).
Wilson, Richard (ed.): *Human Rights, Culture & Contest; Anthropological Perspectives*, London: Pluto Press (1997).

Eva Brems

Urban Planning

DEF: 'Urban planning' (the most important subset of 'spatial planning') is the anticipatory arrangement of future living conditions from an architectural and engineering perspective. Under the rule of law, its concept implies the juridification of urban plans (legal urban plans). Legal urban plans serve as a main basis of building regulation.

INSTR: On the one hand, urban planning usually aims at intensifying the use of land for various purposes of individuals and communities ('development plans'); in this case it serves as a political instrument to create: 1. *more* space for housing (Article 25 UDHR and Article 34(3) CFR) and working (Article 6 ICESCR and Article 15 CFR) or 2. *Better conditions*, especially for safe and healthy housing (Article 25 UDHR) and working (Article 7 ICESCR and Article 31(1) CFR). On the other hand, legal urban plans define the freedom of property (Article 17 UDHR, Article 17(1) CFR and Article 1 protocol 1 ECHR) and limit the general right to liberty (Article 6 CFR), e.g. the freedom to settle (Article 12(1) ICCPR) or to stay settled 'at home'. It has various (including external) effects on the establishment, the persistence and the removal of, amongst others, →public space, cultural infrastructure (e.g. studios, religious buildings) and cultural property (e.g. →architectural heritage). The Council of Europe's 'European regional/spatial planning Charter' (*Recommendation No. R (84) 2* of the Committee of Ministers) stresses the need to take into account (especially regional) cultural aspects.

CONCL: The two most important topics concerning urban planning from a cultural human rights-based approach currently are:

1. a human right to home(-land), which could help people living in old parts of towns or cultural landscapes that are endangered by 'development' projects; it could be deduced in a synopsis of a) the freedom of residence (e.g. Article 13(2) UDHR and Article 12(1) ICCPR) and b) the right to respect for private life (e.g. Article 17(1) ICCPR and Article 7 CFR).
2. the question, whether the right to a sociocultural minimum existence (GFCC, 2012) and Article 15(1)(a) ICESCR or Article 25 CFR could lead to a commitment of urban planning to a minimum of (especially public) space open for cultural action.

REFERENCES:

Bishwapriya, Sanyal (ed.): *Comparative Planning Cultures*, New York/London, Routledge (2005).
United Nations: *Habitat III Issue Papers, 4 – Urban Culture and Heritage*, New York (31/05/2015).
van Lindert, Thijs and Lettinga, Doutje (ed.): *The Future of Human Rights in an Urban World*, Amsterdam: Amnesty International Netherlands (2014).
GFCC – ASYLUM SEEKERS BENEFITS ACT (Judgment of the First Senate 18/07/2012, 1 BvL 10/10, available at www.bverfg.de accessed 04/2016).

Jörg Michael Schindler

Values
(Cultural /Traditional V.)

DEF: Values are powerful convictions about right and wrong, worth, truth and beauty, that inform the behaviour of individuals and groups. Value is imparted on objects, sentiments and actions on the basis of intrinsic considerations (e.g. respecting life forms) or extrinsic/utilitarian considerations (i.e. means to ulterior ends). Reconciling between those two ways of valuing is a key aim of moral reasoning (Singer, 1989). Values arise from *and* inform dogma, jurisprudence, cultural norms and traditions. At the individual level, values develop according to personal experiences, socialisation and enculturation. Thus, values are cultural when they are shared, and individual when they are constructed from experience.

INSTR: Values manifest in legal codes, cultural rules and taboos, discourse, political programs (e.g. multiculturalism) and organisational agenda. They determine attitudes and decision-making through which they inform behaviour. They are mainly perpetuated as memes by ideologies, the collective conceptual constructs through which cultures make sense of and conduct themselves within their world. Thus, legislation implicitly reflects dominant ideologies. Values frequently clash and contradict. Sometimes an action that is arguably just, nevertheless contravenes legal norms, as in cases of →whistleblowing. Although jurisprudence addresses the relationships between utilitarianism, deontology and virtue ethics it often does not readily help reconcile them.

Provisions of human rights treaties established that certain fundamental rights cannot be the object of derogation or suspension even in time of public emergency threatening the security of the state (in particular, Article 4 ICCPR, Article 15 ECHR, Article 27 ACHR). Those rights are considered as reflecting fundamental values shared by the whole community (international or regional) to which the treaty relates. The UDHR provided the globally acknowledged cornerstone for national legislation and jurisprudence. Basic underlying values include autonomy, dignity, inviolability and welfare at the levels of the individual, groups and cultures.

CASES: Recognising the primacy of human rights led, on the one hand, to multiculturalism as a strategic goal to address the need for the *cultural safety* of minorities. On the other hand, universal human rights define the limits of cultural relativism in multicultural policies through principles like the common good and the →Golden Rule (e.g. supporting intolerance toward culturally sanctioned patriarchy). The European Union was founded on the →Common Values of freedom, equality and democracy.

The ECtHR tends to uphold universalist interpretations, as in a decision to uphold a French ban on wearing the hijab at the workplace [EBRAHIMIAN, 2015]. The ECtHR also has affirmed the prohibition of torture and inhuman or degrading treatment or punishment as those practices violate human dignity as 'a fundamental value of a democratic society'. It thus prohibits the exercise of culture-specific punitive traditions.

The primacy of such universal values necessitates and facilitates that conflicting values be meta-ethically assessed for their universal benefits. This assessment can eventually lead to legislative change against the objections of some cultural groups, as with environmental strictures, disestablishing child labour, conscientious objection to military service, and women's reproductive autonomy.

VIEWS: Socially acceptable limits to moral absolutism and universalism are constantly contended and amended. Some cultural groups dissociate themselves from this negotiation process, often invoking religious exceptionalism. Occasionally they are compelled by the courts to comply with legal norms such as providing standard medical care for children (including immunisation), desegregation of ethno-cultural groups and genders, and women's freedom to make reproductive decisions.

In contrast to moral exceptionalism, moral nihilism negates the validity of any values as grounds to enforce certain behavioural norms. This view is sometimes extended to such basic values as the rule of law and the →Golden Rule, which renders it incapable of supporting any social order beyond anarchy. More moderate nihilists tend to associate with cultural relativism.

Sometimes the behaviour of individuals contradicts the values and norms they explicitly advocate: Religious canons often do not lead to individual compliance (Decety, 2015); legal norms are collectively set but individually transgressed when impunity beckons. Underlying value conflicts are often left unexamined. Values change over time as cultures transmute and intermingle (as in 'globalisation'); as ideologies compete (e.g. in the Cold War); and as environments change (e.g. scarcities, technological innovation) (Finnemore & Sikki nk, 1998). Legislative examples of value transitions are environmentalism in the 20th century and the abolition of slavery in the 19th.

CONCL: The European →refugee crisis has brought the significance of values and cultural norms to public attention. It signifies the prospect of a global crisis, as homelands worldwide become increasingly uninhabitable in the course of global change. Economic de-growth and the worsening socioeconomic inequity worldwide are pushing more people towards poverty. This elevates non-violence to the primary guiding value for conflict resolution. Resource depletion, pollution and climate change are straining humanity's life support systems. Inappropriate value priorities are hampering decision makers' efforts at coordination, prevention, and prediction.

The need for cultural safety and human security renders humanitarian values an indispensable focus for discussion. First and foremost, it is values that inform people's behaviour. In order to ensure a safe operating space for humanity (Rockström et al, 2009), a Great Transition (Raskin et al, 2002) will be required, for which attention to value priorities under the ideal of global →citizenship and precaution (Sandin, 2004) will be indispensable. The 2015 UN Climate Conference of the Parties to the 1992 UN *Framework Convention on Climate Change* negotiated the *Paris Agreement*, representing the consensus of the 196 parties and will become legally binding if ratified by at least 55 countries representing at least 55% of the world's greenhouse gas emissions – confirming sustainability as a universal value.

REFERENCES:

Decety, Jean and Jason Cowell: "Our brains are wired for morality: evolution, development and neuroscience", 4(3) *Neuroscience* (2016) 1.

Finnemore, Martha and Sikkink, Kathryn: "International Norm Dynamics and Political Change", 52(4) *International Organization* (1998) 887.

Raskin, Paul, Tariq Banuri, Gilberto Gallopín, Pablo Gutman, Al Hammond, Robert Kates and Rob Swart: *Great Transition: The Promise and Lure of the Times Ahead*, Stockholm Environment Institute Polestar Report no. 10, Boston: SEI (2002).

Rockström, J., Steffen, W., Noone, K., Persson, A., Chapin, F. S. III, Lambin, E., Lenton, T. M., Scheffer, M., Folke, C., Schellnhuber, H. J., Nykvist, B., de Wit, C. A., Hughes, T., van der Leeuw, S., Rodhe, H., Sörlin, S., Snyder, P. K., Costanza, R., Svedin, U., Falkenmark, M., Karlberg, L., Corell, R. W., Fabry, V. J., Hansen, J., Walker, B., Liverman, D., Richardson, K., Crutzen, P. and Foley, J.: "A Safe Operating Space for Humanity", 461 *Nature* (September 24, 2009) 472.

Sandin, Per: "The precautionary principle and the concept of precaution", 13 *Environmental Values* (2004) 461.

Singer, Peter: *Practical Ethics*, Cambridge: Cambridge University Press (1989).

United Nations Framework Convention on Climate Change (UNFCCC): *The Paris Agreement*, New York: United Nations (2015) (unfccc.int, accessed 03/2016).

EBRAHIMIAN v. FRANCE (ECtHR 26/11/2015, 64846/11).

Alex Lautensach

Whistleblowing

DEF: Whistleblowing is the raising of a concern by a worker (regardless of employment status) about illegal, illegitimate, or unethical workplace practices, to somebody who might be able to effect action. Whistleblower protection extends the right to freedom of expression into the workplace.

INSTR/CASES: Whistleblowing mechanisms ensure society will be warned when organisational wrongdoing cannot be stopped internally. Political activist Ralph Nader was the first in 1971 to use the term 'whistleblowing' in this sense, taking the position that public interests override organisational secrecy. By 2016, more than 30 countries, as well as some intergovernmental organisations have whistleblower legislation.

In an ECtHR landmark case [GUJA, 2008] the Court held that a Moldova government official's disclosure to the →press was protected by Article 10 of the ECHR. The Committee of Ministers of the CoE adopted Recommendation (2014/7) on the protection of whistleblowers. These 29 principles grasp the current consensus of good practice. A crucial element is that protection is offered when a whistleblower raises a concern successively inside the organisation, to a regulator, and then to the press. In practice, very little legislation at national level protects whistleblowing to the media.

CONCL: Whistleblowing can be a counterweight to organisational secrecy. As such it is an activity that is crucial for maintaining democracy. In order to strengthen democracy a necessary condition for new legislation is that whistleblowers are protected when they disclose to the press. However, this remains a point of concern.

REFERENCES:

Brown, AJ, Lewis, David, Moberly, Richard & Vandekerckhove, Wim (eds.): *International Handbook of Whistleblowing Research*, Cheltenham: Edward Elgar (2014).

GUJA v. MOLDOVA (ECtHR 12/02/2008, 14277/04).

www.whistleblowingnetwork.org (accessed 3/2016).

Wim Vandekerckhove

Youth

DEF: Youth is the transitional phase between childhood and adulthood. The UN *Convention on the Rights of the Child (CRC)* defines youth as persons between the ages of 15 and 24, while the African Union's *African Youth Charter (AYC)* defines youth as any individual between 15 and 35 years old. Other bodies, including the EU, do not have a standard definition of youth. Moreover, it is defined differently in the various EU member states. The AYC can be considered a particularly interesting case as regards cultural perspectives of the younger generation and the nexus between youth and culture.

INSTR: There is no legally binding European treaty specifically on youth, but various instruments on youth policy exist. The ECHR (generally), the EU *Lisbon Treaty* (Article 165) and the *Charter of Fundamental Rights of the European Union* (Article 24) partially cover issues relating to young persons, other than children. Furthermore, in 2011 the Parliamentary Assembly of the CoE adopted Recommendation 1978: 'Towards a European framework convention on youth rights'.

In the context of the United Nations, the CRC provides for the recognition and protection of the rights of some young people (those between the ages of 15 and 18 years). Youth, as a group, enjoy the human rights protected under the various international human instruments generally. However, only the *Ibero-American Convention on the Rights of Youth of 2005* (in Article 22–34) and the AYC specifically address the rights of youth as such as well as issues of youth and culture. In particular, Article 20 of the AYC addresses some key cultural issues, including: harmful and positive traditional practices (20(1)(a) and (b)); dissemination of culture (20(1)(c)); African culture, values and indigenous knowledge (20(1)(d)); intercultural awareness (20(1)(g)); communication technology and youth cultures (20(2)(b)); and the nexus between contemporary youth culture and traditional African culture (20(2)(c)).

CONCL: The AYC aims to strengthen, reinforce and consolidate efforts to empower young people through their participation and equal partnership in driving Africa's development agenda. The overall objective of the AYC is to encourage and support programmes and actions for youth in Africa. It also provides a basis for states to formulate informed individual national youth policies. Most significantly, the AYC is the only binding international legal instrument on youth that also articulates some cultural issues which are specifically relevant to the youth as a category of human rights-holders. It has established a template that future instruments can only improve upon.

REFERENCES:

Angel, William (ed.): *The international Law of Youth Rights*, (2nd rev. edn.), Leiden: Brill/Martinus Nijhoff Publishers (2015).

Council of Europe/PACE: Recommendation 1978 (2011): *Towards a Framework Convention on the Rights of Young Peoples.*

European Youth Forum: *Policy Paper on Youth Rights*, (Adopted by European Youth Forum General Assembly, Maribor, Slovenia 22–25 November, 2012).

African Youth Charter, (available at www.africa-youth.org – accessed 2/2016).

Ibero-American Convention on Rights of Youth, (available at www.refworld.org – accessed 2/2016).

Tiyanjana Maluwa

Part III: **Subject index**

Subject Index

Notes: Terms and page numbers in **bold** relate to the titles of respective overview articles or keyword entries, terms in regular text to the content of other contributions. Terms with →arrows indicate related terms in the Index or point towards another keyword or overview article that deals more precisely with the matter. INTR refers to the Editor's Introduction, PREF1 or PREF2 to the two prefaces.
For the sake of clarity, this Index does not list court cases or names of authors – which can be found on the project website www.culture-rights.net – and only exceptionally other personalities. As well, research projects, institutions, companies or products are only registered if they are highlighted in an article. Similarly, human rights treaties or other legal instruments and respective courts or treaty bodies are listed only where they are first introduced or specified in the text with regard to important consequences for an issue at stake. The latter limitation is particularly relevant for the ECHR and the ECtHR (as they are referenced in most of the articles), similarly for instruments such as the UDHR, the ICESCR or the CFR and related treaty bodies.

B

Part IV: **Biographical notes of contributors**

Editors and Scientific Committee

Heiner Bielefeldt: Professor of human rights and human rights politics at University of Erlangen–Nuremberg. From 2003 until 2009 he was Director of the German Institute for Human Rights, i.e. Germany's accredited National Human Rights Institute. Between 2010 and 2016 he served as UN Special Rapporteur on freedom of religion or belief. Recent publications include *Auslaufmodell Menschenwürde?* (Freiburg, 2009) and *Freedom of Religion or Belief* (Bonn, 2014).

Janet Blake: Associate Professor of Law at Shahid Beheshti University (Tehran), where she is a member of the UNESCO Chair for Human Rights and the Centre for Excellence in Education for Sustainable Development. She is also a member of the Cultural Heritage Law Committee of the International Law Association and has acted as an International Consultant to UNESCO since 1999, mostly in the field of intangible cultural heritage. Her research monograph on *International Cultural Heritage Law* was published by Oxford University Press in June 2015.

Kalliopi Chainoglou: Lecturer in International and European Institutions at the University of Macedonia, Thessaloniki (Greece) and Research Fellow at the Centre on Human Rights in Conflict, University of East London. She completed her PhD in International Law at King's College London and is an Associate Fellow of the British Higher Education Academy. Her main fields of research are human rights law, cultural rights and policies, and international peace and security. She is an expert of the Council of Europe/ERICarts *Compendium of Cultural Policies & Trends in Europe* and has published extensively on human rights and international law; her most recent publication: *Injustice, Memory and Faith in Human Rights* (Routledge, 2017).

Yvonne Donders: Professor of International Law and Cultural Diversity and Head of the Department of International and European Law at the University of Amsterdam; PhD at Maastricht University on cultural human rights and the right to cultural identity. Her research interests include public international law, international human rights law, in particular economic, social and cultural rights, and human rights and cultural diversity. She teaches courses on public international law and human rights law and gives lectures on cultural rights and cultural diversity. She has previously worked as a Programme Specialist at UNESCO's Human Rights Department. She is currently member of the Dutch National Commission for UNESCO; Member of the Human Rights Committee of the Advisory Council on International Affairs; Member of the Advisory Council to the Netherlands National Institute for Human Rights; Member of Editorial Board of the Netherlands Quarterly of Human Rights; and Member of the European Expert Network on Culture.

Paul De Hert: Human rights and law & technology scholar working in the area of constitutionalism, criminal law and surveillance law. He is interested both in legal practice and more fundamental reflections about law. At the Vrije Universiteit Brussel (VUB), he holds the chair of European Criminal Law. In the past he has taught Historical Constitutionalism, Human Rights, Legal Theory and Constitutional Criminal Law. He is Director of the Research Group on Fundamental Rights and Constitutionalism (FRC), Director of the Department of Interdisciplinary Studies of Law (Metajuridics) and a co-director of the Research Group Law Science Technology & Society (LSTS). He is an associated-professor at Tilburg University where he teaches Privacy and Data Protection at Master level at the Tilburg Institute of Law, Technology, and Society (TILT).

Andrzej Jakubowski: Assistant Professor at the Institute of Law Studies of the Polish Academy of Sciences (Warsaw). He has published primarily in the area of international cultural heritage law, including *State Succession in Cultural Property* (OUP, 2015). He currently chairs an international collaborative research project entitled 'HEURIGHT – The Right to Cultural Heritage – Its Protection and Enforcement through Cooperation in the European Union' within the programme HERITAGE PLUS, co-financed by the European Union (Horizon 2020).

Annamari Laaksonen: Research Manager at the International Federation of Arts Councils and Culture Agencies (IFACCA) in charge of the knowledge and analysis programme of the Federation. Prior to IFACCA, she worked for more than a decade at Interarts Foundation in the field of culture, development, human rights and international cooperation. Her publications include *Making culture accessible: Access, participation and cultural provision in the context of cultural rights in Europe* (Council of Europe, 2010).

Federico Lenzerini: Professor of International Law, University of Siena (Italy). He is also Professor at the LL.M. Program in Intercultural Human Rights at the St. Thomas University School of Law, Miami, USA, Consultant to UNESCO (Paris), and Rapporteur of the ILA Committee on 'Implementation of the Rights of Indigenous Peoples'. His main fields of research are human rights law, rights of indigenous peoples, asylum and refugee law, law of cultural heritage.

Anna Śledzińska-Simon: Assistant Professor in the Chair of Constitutional Law at the Faculty of Law, Administration and Economics of the University in Wroclaw. She received her S.J.D. and LL.M. degree in comparative constitutional law from the Central European University (Budapest) and has worked as a national legal expert for the Agency of Fundamental Rights, the Polish Helsinki Foundation of Human Rights and the Israel Democracy Institute. She specialises in comparative constitutional law, human rights and anti-discrimination law. She is also a regular speaker at the Academy of European Law in Trier. Her current research concerns the application of the principle of proportionality in courts and the role of women in constitution-making.

Andreas Joh. Wiesand: Executive Director, European Institute for Comparative Cultural Research (ERICarts) and Publisher, ARCult Media (Cologne). Professor emeritus, State Academy for Music and Theatre, Hamburg and Lecturer at different European universities. He wrote his PhD on the mobility of journalists. He is an expert for the EU; Council of Europe; UNESCO; etc. and (co-)author or main editor of ca. 50 books on the status of artists; political, economic and legal questions in the arts and media; European cooperation; gender equality; etc. Numerous honorary positions, e.g. former SG, German Arts Council (Dt. Kulturrat), former Chair Board of Governors, VG Bild-Kunst (copyright licensing society) and current SG, European Association of Cultural Researchers (ECURES).

Authors of Keyword Entries

Daniela Alaattinoğlu: PhD researcher in law at the European University Institute in Florence, Italy. Her research and publications focus on gender (violence) and law, intersectionality and human rights. She studied at the University of Helsinki and Istanbul Bilgi University and worked at the Police College of Finland, academia, the Finnish State and an Istanbul-based human rights NGO.

Jessica Almqvist: Senior Researcher and Lecturer in public international law and international relations at the Autónoma University of Madrid. Ph.D. in law, EUI. She has published books, articles and policy-papers in the field of international human rights, with a focus on the role of courts in protecting these rights in times of cultural diversity, in the global fight against terrorism, and in transitions to democracy.

Katya Andrusz: Journalistic Editor, European Union Agency for Fundamental Rights (FRA), author / editor of articles on migrant integration, racism and xenophobia, violence against women and other key human rights topics. A correspondent for many years, writing for Bloomberg News, the Economist, The Guardian, Reuters and others. Fellow of the Royal Society for the encouragement of Arts, Manufactures and Commerce.

Jordi Baltà Portolés: Consultant and trainer in cultural policy and international relations. An expert of the Agenda 21 for culture (UCLG) and a member of the Group of Experts of the UNESCO Convention on the Diversity of Cultural Expressions, he teaches at the Open University of Catalonia (UOC), University of Girona (UdG) and Ramon Llull University (URL).

Petra Bárd: Senior researcher at the National Institute of Criminology, Hungary and Head of the Division of Criminal Law Sciences. She is visiting Professor at the Central European University's (CEU) Legal Studies Department, she teaches *inter alia* EU constitutional law, EU criminal law and human rights in the EU. She is also Associate Professor at ELTE School of Law and Visiting Lecturer at other universities across Europe from Belgrade to Frankfurt and participates at several international research projects. She has worked for the EU Network of Experts of Fundamental Rights and is a member of different scientific associations or civil society organisations. Her current research focuses on extremist speech and hate crimes.

Beatriz Barreiro: Lecturer of Public International Law at the Rey Juan Carlos University (Madrid). She previously worked as a researcher in the Department of Law & Anthropology of the Max Planck Institute for Social Anthropology (Halle) and at the Institute of Public International and European Law, University of Gottingen. She has delivered papers at International Conferences, including "Living with World Heritage in Africa"

(2012, South Africa) and "UNESCO and the Cold War" (2010, University of Heidelberg). She holds a PhD in Human Rights (Carlos III University of Madrid) and a Master in European Law (Free University of Brussels).

Nedzad Basic: Professor of International Law and International Relations at the University in Bihac, Bosnia & Herzegovina. Once PhD and former Fulbright scholar, he now leads the Human Rights Conflict Prevention Centre at this university. His present lectures, research and publications focus, *inter alia*, on the political and legal system of the EU and global structural changes, Islamic identity, human rights conflicts and security issues.

Gerhart Rudolf Baum: Liberal politician and human rights lawyer in Cologne, Germany; former Federal Minister of the Interior (in charge of culture). He has worked for the UN (e.g. as Human Rights Commissioner for Sudan, 2001–03). Numerous honorary positions in culture-related organisations and initiatives (e.g. since 2005 Chair of the arts advocacy council *Kulturrat NRW*).

Uladzislau Belavusau: Assistant Professor of European Law at the University of Amsterdam. He conducts research in the fields of EU law, human rights, comparative constitutional law, law and society, extensively publishing, in particular, on freedom of speech and anti-discrimination law.

Mark Bell: Regius Professor of Laws at Trinity College Dublin. He conducts research in the areas of Equality Law and Employment Law. He works regularly with European NGOs dealing with equality issues, as well as with the European Commission and the International Labour Organisation.

Vincent Bonnet: Director of the European Bureau of Library, Information and Documentation Associations (EBLIDA) since 2010. He combines his passion for libraries with his interest in European affairs, copyright and access to information. Before the EBLIDA he worked in France, both as a trainer for a private company that serves libraries and as a civil servant in public libraries.

Johanne Bouchard: Anthropologist, since 2007 Scientific Collaborator at the Interdisciplinary Institute for Ethics and Human Rights, University of Fribourg (Switzerland), and at the Observatory of Diversity and Cultural Rights. She contributed to numerous projects of applied and policy research mainly on cultural rights. In January 2015, she joined the United Nations Office of the High Commissioner for Human Rights, supporting the mandate of Special Procedure in the field of cultural rights.

Eva Brems: Professor of Human Rights Law at Ghent University, where she founded the Human Rights Centre in 2002. Her research interests cover most areas of European and international human rights law, with emphasis on the protection of the rights of non-dominant groups and individuals. She has a keen interest in multi- and interdisciplinary research and served on the board of several Belgian human rights NGOs, including as the Chair of Amnesty International (Flemish section).

Wojciech Brzozowski: Assistant professor at the Department of Law on Religious Denominations, Faculty of Law and Administration, University of Warsaw, Poland. Legislation expert at the Chancellery of the Sejm (lower house of the Polish parliament). Doctor of Law (2009). Author of publications in the field of constitutional law.

Ulrich Bunjes: Sociologist who worked between 2014–2016 as the Special Representative of the Secretary General of the Council of Europe for Roma Issues. For the Council of Europe, he previously coordinated the preparation of the *White Paper on Intercultural Dialogue* and held various positions in the fields of youth and education. He also has extensive NGO experience.

Dominika Bychawska-Siniarska: Lawyer in Warsaw and PhD candidate at the Polish Academy of Sciences. As a Graduate of the College of Europe, she has worked at the European Court of Human Rights and at the European Integration Office of the Polish Government. She coordinated a number of projects at the Helsinki Foundation for Human Rights, where she is a member of the Board since 2016. She received the award of Polish Journalistic Association "Article 54" for her work on freedom of expression in Poland.

Suzanne Capiau: Lawyer in Brussels, Lecturer at the Free University of Brussels (Audio-visual and performing arts law) and Assistant Lecturer at the University of Lorraine in Metz (Digital communication law). Author of reference works on the social, fiscal and intellectual status of artists, she assisted in the development of an artists' statute in Belgium, certain aspects of which have already been adopted. She regularly advises and defends artists, activity centres and professional organisations, as well as producers and distributors in the creative and cultural sectors.

Gemma Carbó: Director of the UNESCO Chair in Cultural Policies and Cooperation at the University of Girona. PhD in Education, she gained an Advanced Studies Diploma in Culture and Law, a Master in Cultural Management and a Bachelor of Arts (History). She is also lecturer at the University of Girona and coordinator of the Virtual Master in Cultural Management (UOC-UdG-UIB) and the postgraduate program: Education and culture, management programs and projects. Her professional development and current research explores the relationship between cultural policy and education; education and cultural diversity; and education and creativity.

Maria Adele Carrai: Max Weber Post-Doctoral Fellow at the European University Institute, Florence. She conducts research in the areas of Chinese legal history and international law, focusing on the current Chinese attitudes toward international law and on future developments of the global legal order.

María Soledad Cisternas Reyes: Legal expert, political scientist and consultant, and Director of the Legal Programme on Disability, Faculty of Law, Diego Portales University (Santiago de Chile). In addition, she is Chair of the Committee on the Rights of Persons with Disabilities, and works for UN Human Rights Office of the High Commissioner for Human Rights (OHCHR), Chile.

Vesna Čopič: Legal expert, Lecturer at the University of Ljubljana and independent consultant, following a career in the Slovenian Ministry of Education. Her research and expertise focuses on legal issues in culture and European cooperation; the status of artists; human and cultural rights; cultural administration and management; cultural policies in South East Europe; *desétatisation* and privatisation issues. She currently acts as President, European Association of Cultural Researchers (ECURES).

Milena Dragićević Šešić: Professor of Cultural Policy & Art Management, and a UNESCO expert. She is former President of University of Arts, Belgrade. She has published 100 essays, 16 books (Culture: management, animation, marketing; Neo-folk culture; Art and alternative; Horizons of reading, Art management in turbulent times, Intercultural mediation in the Balkans. Translated in 17 languages.)

Irene Drakou: Associate Expert to the UNESCO 1954 Hague Convention for the Protection of Cultural Property in the Event of Armed Conflict and its (1954 and 1999) Protocols. She has an MA in International Politics and Human Rights, International LL.M./LPC.

Khalid Ermilate: Associate Programme Specialist at UNESCO. He holds an LL.M. in Public International Law from Université Libre de Bruxelles.

Derek Fincham: Associate professor of law at South Texas College of Law in Houston. He writes about the intersection of law and cultural heritage and serves on the Editorial Board of the International Journal of Cultural Property.

Hans Fischer-Kerrane: Masters student at the University of Amsterdam where he studies European and International Law. His primary area of interest is international human rights law. He has previous experience working for an NGO in Ireland.

Roberto Frifrini: Legal researcher at the Human Rights Agenda Association *Insan Hakları Gűndemi Derneği*, Ankara, Turkey, with a focus on minority rights, migrants, civil and constitutional rights. He is a member of: Pro-Bono service within the Rights in Exile Progamme – International Refugees Rights Initiative; GALE – European Strategy Group; Institut des Hautes Études sur la Justice, Paris, France. He is also an Op-ed contributor at *Today's Zaman* (up to March 2016), and *L'Humanité*.

Manilo Frigo: Full professor of International and European Law and of International Contracts and Arbitration Law at the Milan State University (*Università degli Studi di Milano*), Department of International, Juridical, Political and Historical Studies. He is a member of both the Steering Committee of the PhD in International Economic Law of the Bocconi University, Milan, and the Committee on Cultural Heritage Law of the ILA (*International Law Association*). He has been a member of the Milan Bar since 1980.

Montserrat Gas-Aixendri: Associate Professor of Law at the Universitat Internacional de Catalunya (Barcelona, Spain), where she teaches Law and Religion. She holds a PhD from the Universidad Complutense de Madrid. Author of more than forty articles and three books, and editor of three books. Her research interests are religious freedom, migrations, cultural rights and the governance of religious diversity in European societies.

Bożena Gierat-Bieroń: Lecturer at the Institute of European Studies at the Jagiellonian University, and a visiting scholar at Trinity College (Dublin), Glasgow University (UK), Sassari University (Italy), Osaka University (Japan) and the Summer School of Polish Culture in Rome, as well as former co-ordinator of *Euroculture* Programme. She has a Ph.D in Humanities (Polish Literature and Drama Studies). Her main academic interests are: European models of cultural policy; EU cultural policy; history of European culture; theory of arts. She authored 3 books and 28 articles and has been the editor or co-editor of six other books. She worked at the National Centre of Culture (Warsaw) as well as the Collegium Civitas in Warsaw and participated in various international projects and conferences.

Aleksandra Gliszczyńska-Grabias: Policy and legal expert in the fields of anti-discrimination law, freedom of speech vs. hate speech, "memory laws" and transitional justice. She holds a PhD from the Polish Academy of Sciences. She is currently a Senior Researcher at the Poznan Human Rights Centre, Institute of Legal Studies of the Polish Academy of Sciences.

Dorota Anna Gozdecka: Senior Lecturer at College of Law, Australia National University. She holds a PhD and is a Senior Fellow of the Higher Education Academy (SFHEA, UK) as well as Adjunct Professor (Docent) at the University of Helsinki. Her research interests include critical legal theory; law and humanities; international and European human rights; and feminist legal theory.

Ulrike Guerin: Responsible for the Underwater Cultural Heritage Programme and the 2001 Convention at UNESCO in Paris. As such she organises the Meetings of States Parties, intergovernmental meetings and UNESCO operational projects, from trainings and exhibitions to emergency assistance missions. She is a lawyer by training.

Véronique Guèvremont: Professor at Université Laval, Québec (Canada), where she teaches international law with a focus on culture, cultural diversity and sustainable development, and international economic law. She was actively involved in the negotiation of the 2005 UNESCO Convention on the Protection and Promotion of the Diversity of Cultural Expressions. She is also the co-founder of the International Network of Lawyers for the Diversity of Cultural Expressions (RIJDEC).

Hans Morten Haugen: Professor at VID Specialized University in Oslo. His publications include *The Right to Food and the TRIPS Agreement* (M. Nijhoff 2007), *Technology and Human Rights: Friends or Foes?* (Republic of Letters, 2012), and over 10 articles and over 5 book chapters on IP issues; the last two appearing in Elsevier's online *Food Science Reference Module*.

Jan Hladík: Chief, Cultural Heritage Protection Treaties Section, UNESCO. He is responsible for the implementation of programmes related to the 1954 Hague Convention for the Protection of Cultural Property in the Event of Armed Conflict and its two (1954 and 1999) Protocols and the 2001 Convention on the Protection of the Underwater Cultural Heritage. He holds an MA International Law, and *iuris doctor* (Charles University, Prague, Czech Republic)

Erica Howard: Associate Professor of Law, Middlesex University, London. She holds a PhD in European discrimination law. She has conducted extensive research in the area of freedom of religion and religious discrimination, publishing a book – *Law and the Wearing of Religious Symbols: European Bans on the Wearing of Religious Symbols in Education* (London and New York: Routledge) – and a number of articles on these subjects.

Yudhishthir Raj Isar: Professor of Cultural Policy Studies at The American University of Paris; Adjunct Professor at the Institute for Culture and Society, Western Sydney University. He is co-editor of the *Cultures and Globalization Series* (SAGE). His work straddles different worlds of cultural theory and practice. Previously, at UNESCO, he was notably Executive Secretary of the World Commission on Culture and Development.

Lina Jasmontaite: Certified Information Privacy Professional (CIPP/E, IAPP). She joined the Centre for IT & IP Law, a research center at the Faculty of Law of the University of Leuven (KU Leuven), in June 2014. Her research interests include human rights, regulation of new technologies, and the protection of personal data.

Susanne Keuchel: Director of the Akademie der Kulturellen Bildung, Remscheid (Academy for Arts Education, Remscheid) and Chairperson of the Institut für Bildung und Kultur (IBK). Honorary Professor at the Institut für Kulturpolitik, University of Hildesheim and Lecturer, Hochschule für Musik und Darstellende Kunst in Hamburg. She is also a graduated musicologist.

Tomasz Tadeusz Koncewicz: Professor of law and the Director of the Department of the European and Comparative Law at the University of Gdansk. In 2015–2016 he was Fulbright Visiting Professor at the Berkeley Law School, University of California; where he taught comparative constitutional law. He is an attorney and Member of the Polish Bar, specialising in the strategic litigation before European supranational courts. In the past he served as the Referendaire at the Court of the European Union in Luxembourg and acted as a legal adviser at the Office of the Polish Constitutional Court.

Joanna Kulesza: Professor of international law and Internet governance at the University of Lodz, Poland and an expert on human rights online for the Council of Europe. She has also been an expert for the Sino-European Cybersecurity Dialogue (SECD) and serves as Membership Committee Chair for the Global Internet Governance Academic Network (GigaNet).

Lorenz Langer: Lecturer at the Law Faculty of the University of Zurich (Switzerland) and Senior Researcher at the University's Centre for Democracy Studies as well as Managing Editor of the Swiss Review of International & European Law. His research focuses on human rights and on democratic participation. Currently, he is writing a monograph on judicial elections.

Alexander Lautensach: Associate Professor in the School of Education at the University of Northern British Columbia. He is also deputy director of the Human Security Institute, and associate editor of the *Journal of Human Security*. His research interests span environmental science, bioethics, and education.

Sabina Lautensach: Lecturer in anthropology, human security and development studies. She is the founding editor-in-chief of the *Journal of Human Security*. As director of the Human Security Institute she coordinates collaborations worldwide. In 2013 she co-edited the first university graduate level textbook in human security, *Human Security in World Affairs: Problems and Opportunities* (Caesarpress).

Lucas Lixinski: Senior Lecturer at Faculty of Law, UNSW Australia. He holds a PhD in Law from the European University Institute, and an LL.M in Human Rights from Central European University. He is the author of *Intangible Cultural Heritage in International Law* (Oxford University Press, 2013) and many other publications.

Tiyanjana Maluwa: H. Laddie Montague Chair in Law at Pennsylvania State University School of Law. His most recent book is *Law, Politics and Rights: Essays in Memory of Kader Asmal* (Brill, 2013). He is co-editing a book titled: *The Pursuit of a Brave New World in International Law.*

Tarlach McGonagle: Senior researcher/lecturer at the Institute for Information Law (IViR), Faculty of Law, University of Amsterdam. He holds a PhD from the University of Amsterdam. He regularly writes expert studies on freedom of expression, media law and policy, and journalism for various branches of the Council of Europe and the OSCE. He has been a member of the Council of Europe's Committees of Experts on protection of journalism and safety of journalists (2014–2015) and media pluralism and transparency of media ownership (2016–)

Christine M. Merkel: Historian, Psychologist in Cologne, Germany. One of 45 UNESCO experts to advise governments on cultural and media policies aligned with the 2005 UNESCO-Convention on the Diversity of cultural expressions. Regional Focus North Africa (CONNEXXIONS program). She participated in expert missions for IDEA International, European Union, Council of Europe, the Euro-Mediterranean Human Rights Foundation and UNESCO to over 20 countries.

Patrice Meyer-Bisch: Philosopher, coordinator of the Interdisciplinary Institute for Ethics and Human Rights and of the UNESCO Chair on Human Rights and Democracy, University of Fribourg (Switzerland). He teaches in political ethics on human rights, democratic governance and economic ethics and coordinated the work on cultural rights of the "Groupe de Fribourg". In 2004, he created the Observatory of Diversity and Cultural Rights.

Aleksandra Mężykowska: Co-Agent of the Government of Poland since 2004 in cases and proceedings before the European Court of Human Rights. She holds a Ph.D. and has lectured, from 2007 to 2013, in public international law and human rights at Łazarski University in Warsaw. Since 2013 she is co-author of the Blog *Review of the Public International Law* (http://przegladpm.blogspot.com). She specialises in international law, particularly international mechanisms of protection of human rights, discrimination and corporate social responsibility.

Annemarie Middelburg: Human rights law consultant with an LL.M degree in Public International Law and Human Rights. She completed her PhD at the International Victimology Institute Tilburg (INTERVICT) at Tilburg University in the Netherlands in March 2016. Her PhD research focuses on compliance with the human rights framework in relation to Female Genital Mutilation (FGM) in Senegal.

Siobhan Montgomery: Senior Project Advisor on Culture and Democracy, Council of Europe. Her work on human rights includes: overseeing the CoE project on strengthening awareness-raising of the human rights dimension of local and regional level; panellist at the Wroclaw Public Forum on the Cultural Dimension of Human Rights, 2015. She holds an LLB and LLM (specialisation Human Rights, University of London)

Mathias Möschel: Associate Professor at Central European University. His research, teaching and publications fall broadly in the field of comparative (constitutional) law, international human rights law and non-discrimination law, mainly from a critical race theory and gender perspective.

Geanina Munteanu: Human rights lawyer and former diplomat, with international academic background and relevant professional experience both in the public sector (having served as a lawyer at the European Court of Human Rights, the Council of Europe and the European Commission) and in the NGO sector (having participated in several projects for the implementation of human rights across Europe). She holds an LL.B.(Romania); M.A.(Romania); LL.M.(Belgium).

Stefan Oeter: Professor for German and Comparative Public Law and Public International Law, University of Hamburg Law School, Germany (since 1999). He holds a Dr. jur and is a member (and Vice-Chairperson) of the Independent Committee of Experts of the European Charter for Regional or Minority Languages (Council of Europe) as well as a member of the Permanent Court of Arbitration and of the Academy of Science in Hamburg.

Aleksandra Oszmiańska-Pagett: Lecturer at Samuel B. Linde College of Modern Languages, Poznań. She is a Member of the Committee of Experts of the European Charter for Regional or Minority Languages (ECRML) at the Council of Europe on behalf of Poland.

Umit Ozturk: Linguist and journalist from Turkey who lives in the UK since 1992. He has worked as a human rights reporter, editor, broadcaster, media analyst and trainer with expertise on freedom of press, social media and cyber rights and liberties. He is the founder and current coordinator of the strategic research charity Euro-Mediterranean Resources Network.

Rafael Palomino: Professor of Law at Universidad Complutense de Madrid and Researcher at the Human Rights Institute of that university. He is an associate member of the Royal Academy of Law (Spain). He is also Vice-Director of *Anuario de Derecho Eclesiástico del Estado* [Church–State Law Spanish Yearbook] and a Member of the Editorial Board of the *Revista General de Derecho Canónico y Derecho Eclesiástico del Estado* [Church–State & Canon Law Review].

András L. Pap: Professor of Constitutional Law and a SASRO-Marie Skłodowska-Curie Fellow at the Institute of Sociology of the Slovak Academy of Sciences in Bratislava; Research Chair and Head of Department for the Study of Constitutionalism and the Rule of Law at the Hungarian Academy of Sciences Institute Centre for Social Sciences Institute for Legal Studies; as well as Adjunct Professor at Central European University's Nationalism Studies Programme and Professor at the National University of Public Service in Budapest. His research interests include constitutional law, human rights, minority rights and law enforcement issues.

Vagelis Papakonstantinou: Co-founder of MPlegal Law Firm in Athens, Greece, as well as a researcher at the Research Group on Law Science Technology & Society (LSTS) at the Vrije Universiteit Brussel.

Sejal Parmar: Assistant Professor at the Department of Legal Studies and a core faculty member of the Center for Media, Data and Society at the Central European University, Budapest. Her main field of expertise and research is international and European human rights law, particularly on freedom of expression. She previously served as Senior Legal Officer at ARTICLE 19.

Robert Peters: Legal Officer for the Federal Government Commissioner for Culture and the Media, Germany. Previously, he worked in the Office of Legal Affairs at UNESCO. He obtained his Ph.D. in the field of International Cultural Heritage Law with a specific focus on restitution disputes.

Adam Ploszka: PhD student at the Centre for Human Rights, Faculty of Law and Administration, University of Warsaw, and a lawyer for the Polish NGO Helsinki Foundation for Human Rights.

Dorota Pudzianowska: Assistant Professor at the Faculty of Law, Warsaw University. She specialises in public law with particular interest in human rights, migration law, nationality law and anti-discrimination law. She also works as a lawyer at the Helsinki Foundation for Human Rights in Warsaw where she is responsible for strategic litigation of discrimination cases. She has been an alternate member of the Board of the European Union Agency for Fundamental Rights.

Jacek Purchla: Art historian, economist. Chair of Economic and Social History and the UNESCO Chair of Cultural Heritage and Urban Studies at the Krakow University of Economics and head of the Centre of European Heritage, Institute of European Studies at the Jagiellonian University. His areas of research are urban development, social history, and art history of the 19th and 20th centuries, as well as the theory and protection of cultural heritage. His scientific output includes numerous books and over 300 articles published in many languages. Since 1991 he is the organiser and director of the International Cultural Centre in Krakow.

Arturo Rey da Silva: Works since 2011 within UNESCO's Secretariat of the 2001 Convention on the Protection of the Underwater Cultural Heritage, in Paris (France). In 2007 he specialised in Maritime and Underwater Archaeology at Southampton University (England), then worked at the Spanish National Underwater Archaeology Museum ARQUA (2009–2010) and has taken part in different international research projects, publishing numerous specialised articles.

Céline Romainville: Professor at Université catholique de Louvain (Belgium), where she teaches constitutional law. Her research deals with issues of national and comparative constitutional law, with a special focus on cultural policies. Recent book publications include *European law and cultural policies* (2015) and *Le droit à la culture, une réalité juridique* (2014).

Jörg Michael Schindler: Administration manager and lawyer in the Department of Urban Planning and Building Regulation of the Bavarian Capital City of Munich. He is also lecturer for public law at Dresden International University. He holds a Dr. iur and an M.A.

Britta Schneider: Sociolinguist, working as a Primary Researcher at Freie Universität Berlin. Her bi-national PhD Dissertation dealt with *Language and Transnationalism* (2012). Her research interests focus on how language is affected by ethnic diversity and transnational discourse. In addition, she has worked on language policies and language rights in educational contexts and on language ideologies in transnational communities of practice constituted by music and dance.

Tullio Scovazzi: Professor of international law at the University of Milano-Bicocca, Milan, Italy. He occasionally participates, as a legal expert, in negotiations and meetings relating to law of the sea, human rights, and cultural properties.

Izabela Skomerska-Muchowska: Assistant Professor at the Chair of European Constitutional Law at the Faculty of Law & Administration, University of Łódź (Poland). She teaches and writes primarily in the area of the law and policy of the European Union. Her main research interests focus on EU citizenship and EU system of judicial protection.

Krzysztof Śmiszek: President of the Polish Society of Antidiscrimination Law. From 2008 to 2010 he worked as a Policy Officer and Policy Coordinator for EQUINET-European Network of Equality Bodies. Expert in sexual orientation and gender discrimination. Since 2011 he has been working at the University of Warsaw, Human Rights Centre, Faculty of Law and Administration.

Kristina Stoeckl: Assistant professor of sociology at the University of Innsbruck, Austria, and principle investigator of the ERC Starting Grant project (2015-676804) *Postsecular Conflicts*. She works on public religions and transnational religious traditionalism with a special focus on Russian Orthodox Christianity.

Peter Stone OBE: UNESCO Chair in Cultural Property Protection and Peace, Newcastle University. A specialist in protecting cultural property during armed conflict, Professor Stone has advised the UK government regarding the identification and protection of the cultural heritage in Iraq. He is also Chair of the UK Committee for the Blue Shield; the cultural heritage equivalent of the Red Cross.

Konstantinos Tararas: Programme Specialist, Sector for Social and Human Sciences, UNESCO Headquarters, Paris. He is a legal Expert with a focus on human rights and democracy. Publications include: *Human Rights: Questions and Answers*, 2013 (with Leah Levin).

Jeroen Temperman: Associate Professor of public international law at Erasmus University Rotterdam. He is also the editor-in-chief of *Religion & Human Rights*. His most recent book is entitled *Religious Hatred and International Law* and is published by Cambridge University Press. In 2014 he was awarded a Fulbright Scholarship, facilitating a visiting professorship at American University Washington College of Law.

Elka Tschernokoshewa: Associate Professor, cultural anthropologist and philosopher. She holds a PhD and is a former head of the Department of cultural studies at the Sorbian Institute Bautzen/Cottbus. She is an expert for trans-cultural issues (new and old minorities; intercultural dialogue; hybridity) and editor of the book series *Hybride Welten* ("Hybrid Worlds") as well as a Board member of the European Association of Cultural Researchers (ECURES). Her main research interest is challenging dualistic thinking and acting.

Wim Vandekerckhove: Teaches Business Ethics at the University of Greenwich and has been researching whistleblowing for more than 10 years. He has provided expertise for NGOs, professional bodies, regulators, and the Council of Europe. He holds a PhD in Applied Ethics from Ghent University.

Charlotte Waelde: Professor of Intellectual Property Law at Coventry University, Centre for Dance Research. She recently co-led the AHRC funded project *InVisible Difference: Disability, Dance and Law*, during which she worked with a number of dancers with disabilities, investigating their daily lives and work, developing and illuminating their place within the copyright framework and the importance of this body of law to their daily practice.

Patricia Wiater: Senior Research Fellow at the University of Munich. She holds a French–German doctorate in Law with a thesis on European Human Rights Law and Cultural Pluralism from the University of Strasbourg, France, and the University of Leipzig, Germany, as well as a doctorate in Political Sciences from the University of Freiburg, Germany. She is currently working on her Habilitation thesis on international procedural rights of individuals.

Mirosław Wróblewski: Lawyer and political scientist. Since 2007 he acts as Head of the Constitutional, International and European Law Department in the Office of the

Ombudsman of Poland. Since 2012 he is a member of the FRA Management Board and from 2015 a member of FRA Executive Committee.

Jessica Wyndham: Associate Director of the Scientific Responsibility, Human Rights and Law Program of the American Association for the Advancement of Science (AAAS). She is responsible for overseeing the organisation's human rights activities and coordinates the AAAS Science and Human Rights Coalition, a network of scientific, engineering, and health associations that recognise the role of science and technology in human rights.

Alexandra Xanthaki: Reader at Brunel University, UK, where she teaches human rights and minority rights. She has published widely on minority and indigenous rights. Her work on cultural rights has been cited widely in scholarship and UN documents.

Athanasios Yupsanis: Currently working as an independent researcher on a comparative analysis of the existing cultural autonomy regimes in Central, Eastern and South – East Europe. He holds a Law Degree, a M.A. degree and a Ph.D. diploma in international law from the Law Faculty of the Aristotle University of Thessaloniki and has taught as an adjunct Lecturer at the postgraduate classes of the Law Faculty of Democritus University. His publications include different articles on indigenous and minority rights.

www.ingramcontent.com/pod-product-compliance
Lightning Source LLC
Chambersburg PA
CBHW080932240926
51849CB00003BA/436
9783110440508